# Promises of the Quran

# Compiled by Gregory Heary

This book is a compilation of Quranic promises. The Quran being the literal speech of Allah, the Universe's Creator and only entity deserving of worship, such promises are weighty and a guaranteed forecast of events. The title is meant to be specific and limiting, as I have not included Allah's other promises that have been made known to mankind in hadith or via the tongues of prophets or the Toraut, Zabur, Injeel, Suhuf etc. but have restricted this compilation to the Quran's promises. This is because the Quranic promise holds a higher merit than other promises of Allah due to the miraculous nature of the Quran, its preserved status and the lofty rank of being Allah's uncreated Speech AND for the fact that we lack authentic copies of the Toraut, Zabur, Injeel and Suhuf as well as authentic reports from prophets other than Muhammad; peace be upon them. Such promises should cultivate our character, motivating us to do good and frightening us from doing evil. These promises should change one's life. There is no guide better than the Creator and for the one allowed to stray by the Creator there is no guide for them other than Satan though they may think and claim they are guided to the right prophetic way.

# Promises of the Quran

## Quran 2:2

ذَٰلِكَ ٱلۡكِتَٰبُ لَا رَيۡبَ فِيهِ هُدٗى لِّلۡمُتَّقِينَ

*This is the Book (the Qur'ân), whereof there is no doubt, a guidance to those who are Al-Muttaqûn [the pious and righteous persons who fear Allâh much (abstain from all kinds of sins and evil deeds which He has forbidden) and love Allâh much (perform all kinds of good deeds which He has ordained)]. (2)*

## Quran 2:23-28

وَإِن كُنتُمۡ فِى رَيۡبٖ مِّمَّا نَزَّلۡنَا عَلَىٰ عَبۡدِنَا فَأۡتُواْ بِسُورَةٖ مِّن مِّثۡلِهِۦ وَٱدۡعُواْ شُهَدَآءَكُم مِّن دُونِ ٱللَّهِ إِن كُنتُمۡ صَٰدِقِينَ فَإِن لَّمۡ تَفۡعَلُواْ وَلَن تَفۡعَلُواْ فَٱتَّقُواْ ٱلنَّارَ ٱلَّتِى وَقُودُهَا ٱلنَّاسُ وَٱلۡحِجَارَةُ أُعِدَّتۡ لِلۡكَٰفِرِينَ وَبَشِّرِ ٱلَّذِينَ ءَامَنُواْ وَعَمِلُواْ ٱلصَّٰلِحَٰتِ أَنَّ لَهُمۡ جَنَّٰتٖ تَجۡرِى مِن تَحۡتِهَا ٱلۡأَنۡهَٰرُ كُلَّمَا رُزِقُواْ مِنۡهَا مِن ثَمَرَةٖ رِّزۡقٗا قَالُواْ هَٰذَا ٱلَّذِى رُزِقۡنَا مِن قَبۡلُ وَأُتُواْ بِهِۦ مُتَشَٰبِهٗا وَلَهُمۡ فِيهَآ أَزۡوَٰجٞ مُّطَهَّرَةٞ وَهُمۡ فِيهَا خَٰلِدُونَ ۝ إِنَّ ٱللَّهَ لَا يَسۡتَحۡىِۦٓ أَن يَضۡرِبَ مَثَلٗا مَّا بَعُوضَةٗ فَمَا فَوۡقَهَا فَأَمَّا ٱلَّذِينَ ءَامَنُواْ فَيَعۡلَمُونَ أَنَّهُ ٱلۡحَقُّ مِن رَّبِّهِمۡ وَأَمَّا ٱلَّذِينَ كَفَرُواْ فَيَقُولُونَ مَاذَآ أَرَادَ ٱللَّهُ بِهَٰذَا مَثَلٗا يُضِلُّ بِهِۦ كَثِيرٗا وَيَهۡدِى بِهِۦ كَثِيرٗا وَمَا يُضِلُّ بِهِۦٓ إِلَّا ٱلۡفَٰسِقِينَ ٱلَّذِينَ يَنقُضُونَ عَهۡدَ ٱللَّهِ مِنۢ بَعۡدِ مِيثَٰقِهِۦ وَيَقۡطَعُونَ مَآ أَمَرَ ٱللَّهُ بِهِۦٓ أَن يُوصَلَ وَيُفۡسِدُونَ فِى

ٱلْأَرْضِ أُوْلَٰٓئِكَ هُمُ ٱلْخَٰسِرُونَ ۝ كَيْفَ تَكْفُرُونَ بِٱللَّهِ وَكُنتُمْ
أَمْوَٰتًا فَأَحْيَٰكُمْ ۖ ثُمَّ يُمِيتُكُمْ ثُمَّ يُحْيِيكُمْ ثُمَّ إِلَيْهِ تُرْجَعُونَ ۝

*And if you (Arab pagans, Jews, and Christians) are in doubt concerning that which We have sent down (i.e. the Qur'ân) to Our slave (Muhammad), then produce a Sûrah (chapter) of the like thereof and call your witnesses (supporters and helpers) besides Allâh, if you are truthful. (23) But if you do it not, and you can never do it, then fear the Fire (Hell) whose fuel is men and stones, prepared for the disbelievers. (24) And give glad tidings to those who believe and do righteous good deeds, that for them will be Gardens under which rivers flow (Paradise). Every time they will be provided with a fruit therefrom, they will say: "This is what we were provided with before," and they will be given things in resemblance (i.e. in the same form but different in taste) and they shall have therein Azwâjun Mutahharatun (purified mates or wives), and they will abide therein forever. (25) Verily, Allâh is not ashamed to set forth a parable even of a mosquito or so much more when it is bigger (or less when it is smaller) than it. And as for those who believe, they know that it is the Truth from their Lord, but as for those who disbelieve, they say: "What did Allâh intend by this parable?" By it He misleads many, and many He guides thereby. And He misleads thereby only those who are Al-Fâsiqûn (the rebellious, disobedient to Allâh). (26) Those who break Allâh's Covenant after ratifying it, and sever* what Allâh has ordered to be joined (as regards Allâh's religion of Islâmic Monotheism, and to practise its legal laws on the earth and also as regards keeping good relations with kith and kin), and do mischief on earth, it is they who are the losers. (27) How can you disbelieve in Allâh? Seeing that you were dead and He gave you life. Then He will give you death, then again will bring you to life (on the Day of Resurrection) and then unto Him you will return. (28)

## Quran 2:38-39

قُلْنَا ٱهْبِطُواْ مِنْهَا جَمِيعًا فَإِمَّا يَأْتِيَنَّكُم مِّنِّى هُدًى فَمَن تَبِعَ هُدَايَ فَلَا خَوْفٌ عَلَيْهِمْ وَلَا هُمْ يَحْزَنُونَ وَٱلَّذِينَ كَفَرُواْ وَكَذَّبُواْ بِـَٔايَٰتِنَآ أُوْلَٰٓئِكَ أَصْحَٰبُ ٱلنَّارِ هُمْ فِيهَا خَٰلِدُونَ

We said: "Get down all of you from this place (the Paradise), then whenever there comes to you Guidance from Me, and whoever follows My Guidance, there shall be no fear on them, nor shall they grieve (38) But those who disbelieve and belie Our Ayât (proofs, evidences, verses, lessons, signs, revelations, etc.)- such are the dwellers of the Fire, They shall abide therein forever. (39)

## Quran 2:110-114

وَأَقِيمُواْ ٱلصَّلَوٰةَ وَءَاتُواْ ٱلزَّكَوٰةَ وَمَا تُقَدِّمُواْ لِأَنفُسِكُم مِّنْ خَيْرٍ تَجِدُوهُ عِندَ ٱللَّهِ إِنَّ ٱللَّهَ بِمَا تَعْمَلُونَ بَصِيرٌ وَقَالُواْ لَن يَدْخُلَ ٱلْجَنَّةَ إِلَّا مَن كَانَ هُودًا أَوْ نَصَٰرَىٰ تِلْكَ أَمَانِيُّهُمْ قُلْ هَاتُواْ بُرْهَٰنَكُمْ إِن كُنتُمْ صَٰدِقِينَ بَلَىٰ مَنْ أَسْلَمَ وَجْهَهُ لِلَّهِ وَهُوَ مُحْسِنٌ فَلَهُ أَجْرُهُ عِندَ رَبِّهِ وَلَا خَوْفٌ عَلَيْهِمْ وَلَا هُمْ يَحْزَنُونَ

وَقَالَتِ ٱلۡيَهُودُ لَيۡسَتِ ٱلنَّصَٰرَىٰ عَلَىٰ شَيۡءٍ وَقَالَتِ ٱلنَّصَٰرَىٰ لَيۡسَتِ ٱلۡيَهُودُ عَلَىٰ شَيۡءٍ وَهُمۡ يَتۡلُونَ ٱلۡكِتَٰبَ كَذَٰلِكَ قَالَ ٱلَّذِينَ لَا يَعۡلَمُونَ مِثۡلَ قَوۡلِهِمۡ فَٱللَّهُ يَحۡكُمُ بَيۡنَهُمۡ يَوۡمَ ٱلۡقِيَٰمَةِ فِيمَا كَانُواْ فِيهِ يَخۡتَلِفُونَ وَمَنۡ أَظۡلَمُ مِمَّن مَّنَعَ مَسَٰجِدَ ٱللَّهِ أَن يُذۡكَرَ فِيهَا ٱسۡمُهُ وَسَعَىٰ فِى خَرَابِهَآ أُوْلَٰٓئِكَ مَا كَانَ لَهُمۡ أَن يَدۡخُلُوهَآ إِلَّا خَآئِفِينَ لَهُمۡ فِى ٱلدُّنۡيَا خِزۡىٌ وَلَهُمۡ فِى ٱلۡأَخِرَةِ عَذَابٌ عَظِيمٌ

And perform As-Salât and give Zakât, and whatever of good (deeds that Allâh loves) you send forth for yourselves before you, you shall find it with Allâh. Certainly, Allâh is All-Seer of what you do. (110) And they say, "None shall enter Paradise unless he be a Jew or a Christian." These are their own desires. Say, "Produce your proof if you are truthful." (111) Yes, but whoever submits his face (himself) to Allâh (i.e. follows Allâh's Religion of Islâmic Monotheism) and he is a Muhsin then his reward is with his Lord (Allâh), on such shall be no fear, nor shall they grieve. (112) The Jews said that the Christians follow nothing (i.e. are not on the right religion); and the Christians said that the Jews follow nothing (i.e. are not on the right religion); though they both recite the Scripture. Like unto their word, said (the pagans) who know not. Allâh will judge between them on the Day of Resurrection about that wherein they have been differing. (113) And who are more unjust than those who forbid that Allâh's Name be glorified and mentioned much (i.e. prayers and invocations, etc.) in Allâh's mosques and strive for their ruin? It was not fitting that such should themselves enter them (Allâh's Mosques) except in fear. For them there is disgrace in this world, and they will have a great torment in the Hereafter. (114)

## Quran 2:120-121

وَلَن تَرْضَىٰ عَنكَ ٱلْيَهُودُ وَلَا ٱلنَّصَٰرَىٰ حَتَّىٰ تَتَّبِعَ مِلَّتَهُمْۗ قُلْ إِنَّ هُدَى ٱللَّهِ هُوَ ٱلْهُدَىٰۗ وَلَئِنِ ٱتَّبَعْتَ أَهْوَآءَهُم بَعْدَ ٱلَّذِى جَآءَكَ مِنَ ٱلْعِلْمِۙ مَا لَكَ مِنَ ٱللَّهِ مِن وَلِيٍّ وَلَا نَصِيرٍ ٱلَّذِينَ ءَاتَيْنَٰهُمُ ٱلْكِتَٰبَ يَتْلُونَهُۥ حَقَّ تِلَاوَتِهِۦٓ أُو۟لَٰٓئِكَ يُؤْمِنُونَ بِهِۦۗ وَمَن يَكْفُرْ بِهِۦ فَأُو۟لَٰٓئِكَ هُمُ ٱلْخَٰسِرُونَ

Never will the Jews nor the Christians be pleased with you till you follow their religion. Say: "Verily, the Guidance of Allâh (i.e. Islâmic Monotheism) that is the (only) Guidance. And if you were to follow their (Jews and Christians) desires after what you have received of Knowledge (i.e. the Qur'ân), then you would have against Allâh neither any Walî (protector or guardian) nor any helper. (120) Those (who embraced Islâm from Banî Israel) to whom We gave the Book [the Taurât (Torah)] [or those (Muhammad's companions) to whom We have given the Book (the Qur'ân)] recite it (i.e. obey its orders and follow its teachings) as it should be recited (i.e. followed), they are the ones that believe therein. And whoso disbelieves in it (the Qur'ân), those are they who are the losers. (121)

## Quran 2:123

وَٱتَّقُواْ يَوْمًا لَّا تَجْزِى نَفْسٌ عَن نَّفْسٍ شَيْـًٔا وَلَا يُقْبَلُ مِنْهَا عَدْلٌ وَلَا تَنفَعُهَا شَفَٰعَةٌ وَلَا هُمْ يُنصَرُونَ

*And fear the Day (of Judgement) when no person shall avail another, nor shall compensation be accepted from him, nor shall intercession be of use to him, nor shall they be helped. (123)*

## Quran 2:126

وَإِذْ قَالَ إِبْرَٰهِـۧمُ رَبِّ ٱجْعَلْ هَٰذَا بَلَدًا ءَامِنًا وَٱرْزُقْ أَهْلَهُ مِنَ ٱلثَّمَرَٰتِ مَنْ ءَامَنَ مِنْهُم بِٱللَّهِ وَٱلْيَوْمِ ٱلْأَخِرِ قَالَ وَمَن كَفَرَ فَأُمَتِّعُهُ قَلِيلًا ثُمَّ أَضْطَرُّهُ إِلَىٰ عَذَابِ ٱلنَّارِ وَبِئْسَ ٱلْمَصِيرُ

*And (remember) when Ibrâhim (Abraham) said, "My Lord, make this city (Makkah) a place of security and provide its people with fruits, such of them as believe in Allâh and the Last Day." He (Allâh) answered: "As for him who disbelieves, I shall leave him in contentment for a while, then I shall compel him to the torment of the Fire, and worst indeed is that destination!" (126)*

## Quran 2:130

وَمَن يَرْغَبُ عَن مِّلَّةِ إِبْرَٰهِـۧمَ إِلَّا مَن سَفِهَ نَفْسَهُ وَلَقَدِ ٱصْطَفَيْنَٰهُ فِى ٱلدُّنْيَا وَإِنَّهُ فِى ٱلْأَخِرَةِ لَمِنَ ٱلصَّٰلِحِينَ

*And who turns away from the religion of Ibrâhim (Abraham) (i.e. Islâmic Monotheism) except him who befools himself? Truly, We chose him in this world and verily, in the Hereafter he will be among the righteous. (130)*

## Quran 2:137

فَإِنْ ءَامَنُواْ بِمِثْلِ مَآ ءَامَنتُم بِهِۦ فَقَدِ ٱهْتَدَواْ وَّإِن تَوَلَّواْ فَإِنَّمَا هُمْ فِى شِقَاقٍ فَسَيَكْفِيكَهُمُ ٱللَّهُ وَهُوَ ٱلسَّمِيعُ ٱلْعَلِيمُ

*So if they believe in the like of that which you believe,*
*then they are rightly guided, but if they turn away, then*
*they are only in opposition. So Allâh will suffice for you*
*against them. And He is the All-Hearer, the All-Knower.*
*(137)*

## Quran 2:148

وَلِكُلٍّ وِجْهَةٌ هُوَ مُوَلِّيهَا فَٱسْتَبِقُواْ ٱلْخَيْرَاتِ أَيْنَ مَا تَكُونُواْ يَأْتِ بِكُمُ ٱللَّهُ جَمِيعًا إِنَّ ٱللَّهَ عَلَىٰ كُلِّ شَىْءٍ قَدِيرٌ

*For every nation there is a direction to which they face*
*(in their prayers). So hasten towards all that is good.*
*Wheresoever you may be, Allâh will bring you together*
*(on the Day of Resurrection). Truly, Allâh is Able to do*
*all things. (148)*

## Quran 2:152-157

فَٱذْكُرُونِىٓ أَذْكُرْكُمْ وَٱشْكُرُواْ لِى وَلَا تَكْفُرُونِ يَـٰٓأَيُّهَا ٱلَّذِينَ ءَامَنُواْ ٱسْتَعِينُواْ بِٱلصَّبْرِ وَٱلصَّلَوٰةِ إِنَّ ٱللَّهَ مَعَ ٱلصَّـٰبِرِينَ وَلَا تَقُولُواْ لِمَن يُقْتَلُ فِى سَبِيلِ ٱللَّهِ أَمْوَٰتٌ بَلْ أَحْيَآءٌ وَلَـٰكِن لَّا تَشْعُرُونَ وَلَنَبْلُوَنَّكُم بِشَىْءٍ مِّنَ ٱلْخَوْفِ وَٱلْجُوعِ وَنَقْصٍ مِّنَ ٱلْأَمْوَٰلِ وَٱلْأَنفُسِ وَٱلثَّمَرَٰتِ وَبَشِّرِ ٱلصَّـٰبِرِينَ ٱلَّذِينَ إِذَآ

أَصَـٰبَتْهُم مُّصِيبَةٌ قَالُوٓاْ إِنَّا لِلَّهِ وَإِنَّآ إِلَيْهِ رَٰجِعُونَ ۞ أُوْلَـٰٓئِكَ عَلَيْهِمْ صَلَوَٰتٌ مِّن رَّبِّهِمْ وَرَحْمَةٌ ۖ وَأُوْلَـٰٓئِكَ هُمُ ٱلْمُهْتَدُونَ

*Therefore remember Me (by praying, glorifying,). I will remember you, and be grateful to Me (for My countless Favours on you) and never be ungrateful to Me. (152) O you who believe! Seek help in patience and As-Salât (the prayer). Truly! Allâh is with As-Sâbirun (the patient.) (153) And say not of those who are killed in the Way of Allâh, "They are dead." Nay, they are living, but you perceive (it) not. (154) And certainly, We shall test you with something of fear, hunger, loss of wealth, lives and fruits, but give glad tidings to As-Sâbirun (the patient) (155) Who, when afflicted with calamity, say: "Truly! To Allâh we belong and truly, to Him we shall return." (156) They are those on whom are the Salawât (i.e. who are blessed and will be forgiven) from their Lord, and (they are those who) receive His Mercy, and it is they who are the guided-ones. (157)*

## Quran 2:159-162

إِنَّ ٱلَّذِينَ يَكْتُمُونَ مَآ أَنزَلْنَا مِنَ ٱلْبَيِّنَـٰتِ وَٱلْهُدَىٰ مِنۢ بَعْدِ مَا بَيَّنَّـٰهُ لِلنَّاسِ فِى ٱلْكِتَـٰبِ ۙ أُوْلَـٰٓئِكَ يَلْعَنُهُمُ ٱللَّهُ وَيَلْعَنُهُمُ ٱللَّـٰعِنُونَ إِلَّا ٱلَّذِينَ تَابُواْ وَأَصْلَحُواْ وَبَيَّنُواْ فَأُوْلَـٰٓئِكَ أَتُوبُ عَلَيْهِمْ ۚ وَأَنَا ٱلتَّوَّابُ ٱلرَّحِيمُ إِنَّ ٱلَّذِينَ كَفَرُواْ وَمَاتُواْ وَهُمْ كُفَّارٌ أُوْلَـٰٓئِكَ عَلَيْهِمْ لَعْنَةُ ٱللَّهِ وَٱلْمَلَـٰٓئِكَةِ وَٱلنَّاسِ أَجْمَعِينَ خَـٰلِدِينَ فِيهَا ۖ لَا يُخَفَّفُ عَنْهُمُ ٱلْعَذَابُ وَلَا هُمْ يُنظَرُونَ

*Verily, those who conceal the clear proofs, evidences and the guidance, which We have sent down, after We have made it clear for the people in the Book, they are the ones cursed by Allâh and cursed by the cursers. (159) Except those who repent and do righteous deeds, and openly declare (the truth which they concealed). These, I will accept their repentance. And I am the One Who accepts repentance, the Most Merciful. (160) Verily, those who disbelieve, and die while they are disbelievers, it is they on whom is the Curse of Allâh and of the angels and of mankind, combined. (161) They will abide therein (under the curse in Hell), their punishment will neither be lightened, nor will they be reprieved. (162)*

## Quran 2:165-167

وَمِنَ ٱلنَّاسِ مَن يَتَّخِذُ مِن دُونِ ٱللَّهِ أَندَادًا يُحِبُّونَهُمْ كَحُبِّ ٱللَّهِ وَٱلَّذِينَ ءَامَنُوٓاْ أَشَدُّ حُبًّا لِّلَّهِ وَلَوْ يَرَى ٱلَّذِينَ ظَلَمُوٓاْ إِذْ يَرَوْنَ ٱلْعَذَابَ أَنَّ ٱلْقُوَّةَ لِلَّهِ جَمِيعًا وَأَنَّ ٱللَّهَ شَدِيدُ ٱلْعَذَابِ إِذْ تَبَرَّأَ ٱلَّذِينَ ٱتُّبِعُواْ مِنَ ٱلَّذِينَ ٱتَّبَعُواْ وَرَأَوُاْ ٱلْعَذَابَ وَتَقَطَّعَتْ بِهِمُ ٱلْأَسْبَابُ وَقَالَ ٱلَّذِينَ ٱتَّبَعُواْ لَوْ أَنَّ لَنَا كَرَّةً فَنَتَبَرَّأَ مِنْهُمْ كَمَا تَبَرَّءُواْ مِنَّا كَذَٰلِكَ يُرِيهِمُ ٱللَّهُ أَعْمَٰلَهُمْ حَسَرَٰتٍ عَلَيْهِمْ وَمَا هُم بِخَٰرِجِينَ مِنَ ٱلنَّارِ

*And of mankind are some who take (for worship) others besides Allâh as rivals (to Allâh). They love them as they love Allâh. But those who believe, love Allâh more (than anything else). If only, those who do wrong could see,*

when they will see the torment, that all power belongs to
Allâh and that Allâh is Severe in punishment. (165)
When those who were followed, disown (declare
themselves innocent of) those who followed (them), and
they see the torment, then all their relations will be cut
off from them. (166) And those who followed will say: "If
only we had one more chance to return (to the worldly
life), we would disown (declare ourselves as innocent
from) them as they have disowned (declared themselves
as innocent from) us." Thus Allâh will show them their
deeds as regrets for them. And they will never get out of
the Fire. (167)

## Quran 2:174

إِنَّ ٱلَّذِينَ يَكْتُمُونَ مَآ أَنزَلَ ٱللَّهُ مِنَ ٱلْكِتَٰبِ وَيَشْتَرُونَ بِهِۦ ثَمَنًا
قَلِيلًا أُو۟لَٰٓئِكَ مَا يَأْكُلُونَ فِى بُطُونِهِمْ إِلَّا ٱلنَّارَ وَلَا يُكَلِّمُهُمُ ٱللَّهُ
يَوْمَ ٱلْقِيَٰمَةِ وَلَا يُزَكِّيهِمْ وَلَهُمْ عَذَابٌ أَلِيمٌ

Verily, those who conceal what Allâh has sent down of
the Book, and purchase a small gain therewith (of worldly
things), they eat into their bellies nothing but fire. Allâh
will not speak to them on the Day of Resurrection, nor
purify them, and theirs will be a painful torment. (174)

## Quran 2:200-203

فَإِذَا قَضَيْتُم مَّنَٰسِكَكُمْ فَٱذْكُرُوا۟ ٱللَّهَ كَذِكْرِكُمْ ءَابَآءَكُمْ أَوْ
أَشَدَّ ذِكْرًا فَمِنَ ٱلنَّاسِ مَن يَقُولُ رَبَّنَآ ءَاتِنَا فِى ٱلدُّنْيَا وَمَا لَهُۥ
فِى ٱلْءَاخِرَةِ مِنْ خَلَٰقٍ وَمِنْهُم مَّن يَقُولُ رَبَّنَآ ءَاتِنَا فِى ٱلدُّنْيَا

حَسَنَةٌ وَفِى ٱلْأَخِرَةِ حَسَنَةٌ وَقِنَا عَذَابَ ٱلنَّارِ أُوْلَٰٓئِكَ لَهُمْ نَصِيبٌ مِّمَّا كَسَبُوا۟ وَٱللَّهُ سَرِيعُ ٱلْحِسَابِ ۝ وَٱذْكُرُوا۟ ٱللَّهَ فِىٓ أَيَّامٍ مَّعْدُودَاتٍ فَمَن تَعَجَّلَ فِى يَوْمَيْنِ فَلَآ إِثْمَ عَلَيْهِ وَمَن تَأَخَّرَ فَلَآ إِثْمَ عَلَيْهِ لِمَنِ ٱتَّقَىٰ وَٱتَّقُوا۟ ٱللَّهَ وَٱعْلَمُوٓا۟ أَنَّكُمْ إِلَيْهِ تُحْشَرُونَ

*So when you have accomplished your Manasik remember Allâh as you remember your forefathers or with a far more remembrance. But of mankind there are some who say: "Our Lord! Give us (Your Bounties) in this world!" and for such there will be no portion in the Hereafter. (200) And of them there are some who say: "Our Lord! Give us in this world that which is good and in the Hereafter that which is good, and save us from the torment of the Fire!" (201) For them there will be alloted a share for what they have earned. And Allâh is Swift at reckoning. (202) And remember Allâh during the appointed Days. But whosoever hastens to leave in two days, there is no sin on him and whosoever stays on, there is no sin on him, if his aim is to do good and obey Allâh (fear Him), and know that you will surely be gathered unto Him. (203)*

## Quran 2:212-214

زُيِّنَ لِلَّذِينَ كَفَرُوا۟ ٱلْحَيَوٰةُ ٱلدُّنْيَا وَيَسْخَرُونَ مِنَ ٱلَّذِينَ ءَامَنُوا۟ وَٱلَّذِينَ ٱتَّقَوْا۟ فَوْقَهُمْ يَوْمَ ٱلْقِيَٰمَةِ وَٱللَّهُ يَرْزُقُ مَن يَشَآءُ بِغَيْرِ حِسَابٍ كَانَ ٱلنَّاسُ أُمَّةً وَٰحِدَةً فَبَعَثَ ٱللَّهُ ٱلنَّبِيِّۦنَ مُبَشِّرِينَ

وَمُنذِرِينَ وَأَنزَلَ مَعَهُمُ ٱلْكِتَٰبَ بِٱلْحَقِّ لِيَحْكُمَ بَيْنَ ٱلنَّاسِ فِيمَا
ٱخْتَلَفُوا۟ فِيهِ وَمَا ٱخْتَلَفَ فِيهِ إِلَّا ٱلَّذِينَ أُوتُوهُ مِنۢ بَعْدِ مَا
جَآءَتْهُمُ ٱلْبَيِّنَٰتُ بَغْيًۢا بَيْنَهُمْ فَهَدَى ٱللَّهُ ٱلَّذِينَ ءَامَنُوا۟ لِمَا ٱخْتَلَفُوا۟
فِيهِ مِنَ ٱلْحَقِّ بِإِذْنِهِ وَٱللَّهُ يَهْدِى مَن يَشَآءُ إِلَىٰ صِرَٰطٍ مُّسْتَقِيمٍ
أَمْ حَسِبْتُمْ أَن تَدْخُلُوا۟ ٱلْجَنَّةَ وَلَمَّا يَأْتِكُم مَّثَلُ ٱلَّذِينَ خَلَوْا۟ مِن
قَبْلِكُم مَّسَّتْهُمُ ٱلْبَأْسَآءُ وَٱلضَّرَّآءُ وَزُلْزِلُوا۟ حَتَّىٰ يَقُولَ ٱلرَّسُولُ
وَٱلَّذِينَ ءَامَنُوا۟ مَعَهُ مَتَىٰ نَصْرُ ٱللَّهِ أَلَآ إِنَّ نَصْرَ ٱللَّهِ قَرِيبٌ

*Beautified is the life of this world for those who disbelieve, and they mock at those who believe. But those who obey Allâh's Orders and keep away from what He has forbidden, will be above them on the Day of Resurrection. And Allâh gives (of His Bounty, Blessings, Favours, Honours, on the Day of Resurrection) to whom He wills without limit. (212) Mankind were one community and Allâh sent Prophets with glad tidings and warnings, and with them He sent the Scripture in truth to judge between people in matters wherein they differed. And only those to whom (the Scripture) was given differed concerning it after clear proofs had come unto them through hatred, one to another. Then Allâh by His Leave guided those who believed to the truth of that wherein they differed. And Allâh guides whom He wills to a Straight Path. (213) Or think you that you will enter Paradise without such (trials) as came to those who passed away before you? They were afflicted with severe poverty and ailments and were so shaken that even the*

*Messenger and those who believed along with him said,*
*"When (will come) the Help of Allâh?" Yes! Certainly,*
*the Help of Allâh is near! (214)*

## Quran 2:217-218

يَسْـَٔلُونَكَ عَنِ ٱلشَّهْرِ ٱلْحَرَامِ قِتَالٍ فِيهِ قُلْ قِتَالٌ فِيهِ كَبِيرٌ وَصَدٌّ
عَن سَبِيلِ ٱللَّهِ وَكُفْرٌ بِهِ وَٱلْمَسْجِدِ ٱلْحَرَامِ وَإِخْرَاجُ أَهْلِهِ مِنْهُ
أَكْبَرُ عِندَ ٱللَّهِ وَٱلْفِتْنَةُ أَكْبَرُ مِنَ ٱلْقَتْلِ وَلَا يَزَالُونَ يُقَٰتِلُونَكُمْ
حَتَّىٰ يَرُدُّوكُمْ عَن دِينِكُمْ إِنِ ٱسْتَطَٰعُوا وَمَن يَرْتَدِدْ مِنكُمْ عَن
دِينِهِ فَيَمُتْ وَهُوَ كَافِرٌ فَأُولَٰئِكَ حَبِطَتْ أَعْمَٰلُهُمْ فِى ٱلدُّنْيَا
وَٱلْءَاخِرَةِ وَأُولَٰئِكَ أَصْحَٰبُ ٱلنَّارِ هُمْ فِيهَا خَٰلِدُونَ إِنَّ ٱلَّذِينَ
ءَامَنُوا وَٱلَّذِينَ هَاجَرُوا وَجَٰهَدُوا فِى سَبِيلِ ٱللَّهِ أُولَٰئِكَ
يَرْجُونَ رَحْمَتَ ٱللَّهِ وَٱللَّهُ غَفُورٌ رَّحِيمٌ

*They ask you concerning fighting in the Sacred Months*
*(i.e. 1st, 7th, 11th and 12th months of the Islâmic*
*calendar). Say, "Fighting therein is a great*
*(transgression) but a greater (transgression) with Allâh*
*is to prevent mankind from following the Way of Allâh,*
*to disbelieve in Him, to prevent access to Al-Masjid-Al-*
*Harâm (at Makkah), and to drive out its inhabitants, and*
*Al-Fitnah is worse than killing. And they will never*
*cease fighting you until they turn you back from your*
*religion (Islâmic Monotheism) if they can. And*
*whosoever of you turns back from his religion and dies as*
*a disbeliever, then his deeds will be lost in this life and in*
*the Hereafter, and they will be the dwellers of the Fire.*

They will abide therein forever." (217) Verily, those who have believed, and those who have emigrated (for Allâh's Religion) and have striven hard in the Way of Allâh, all these hope for Allâh's Mercy. And Allâh is Oft-Forgiving, Most-Merciful. (218)

## Quran 2:225

لَّا يُؤَاخِذُكُمُ ٱللَّهُ بِٱللَّغْوِ فِىٓ أَيْمَٰنِكُمْ وَلَٰكِن يُؤَاخِذُكُم بِمَا كَسَبَتْ قُلُوبُكُمْ وَٱللَّهُ غَفُورٌ حَلِيمٌ

Allâh will not call you to account for that which is unintentional in your oaths, but He will call you to account for that which your hearts have earned. And Allâh is Oft-Forgiving, Most-Forbearing. (225)

## Quran 2:245

مَّن ذَا ٱلَّذِى يُقْرِضُ ٱللَّهَ قَرْضًا حَسَنًا فَيُضَٰعِفَهُۥ لَهُۥٓ أَضْعَافًا كَثِيرَةً وَٱللَّهُ يَقْبِضُ وَيَبْصُطُ وَإِلَيْهِ تُرْجَعُونَ

Who is he that will lend to Allâh a goodly loan so that He may multiply it to him many times? And it is Allâh that decreases or increases (your provisions), and unto Him you shall return. (245)

## Quran 2:254

يَٰٓأَيُّهَا ٱلَّذِينَ ءَامَنُوٓا۟ أَنفِقُوا۟ مِمَّا رَزَقْنَٰكُم مِّن قَبْلِ أَن يَأْتِىَ يَوْمٌ لَّا بَيْعٌ فِيهِ وَلَا خُلَّةٌ وَلَا شَفَٰعَةٌ وَٱلْكَٰفِرُونَ هُمُ ٱلظَّٰلِمُونَ

O you who believe! Spend of that with which We have provided for you, before a Day comes when there will be no bargaining, nor friendship, nor intercession. And it is the disbelievers who are the Zâlimûn (wrong-doers). (254)

## Quran 2:256-258

لَآ إِكْرَاهَ فِى ٱلدِّينِ ۖ قَد تَّبَيَّنَ ٱلرُّشْدُ مِنَ ٱلْغَىِّ ۚ فَمَن يَكْفُرْ بِٱلطَّـٰغُوتِ وَيُؤْمِنۢ بِٱللَّهِ فَقَدِ ٱسْتَمْسَكَ بِٱلْعُرْوَةِ ٱلْوُثْقَىٰ لَا ٱنفِصَامَ لَهَا ۗ وَٱللَّهُ سَمِيعٌ عَلِيمٌ ٱللَّهُ وَلِىُّ ٱلَّذِينَ ءَامَنُوا۟ يُخْرِجُهُم مِّنَ ٱلظُّلُمَـٰتِ إِلَى ٱلنُّورِ ۖ وَٱلَّذِينَ كَفَرُوٓا۟ أَوْلِيَآؤُهُمُ ٱلطَّـٰغُوتُ يُخْرِجُونَهُم مِّنَ ٱلنُّورِ إِلَى ٱلظُّلُمَـٰتِ ۗ أُو۟لَـٰٓئِكَ أَصْحَـٰبُ ٱلنَّارِ ۖ هُمْ فِيهَا خَـٰلِدُونَ أَلَمْ تَرَ إِلَى ٱلَّذِى حَآجَّ إِبْرَٰهِـۧمَ فِى رَبِّهِۦٓ أَنْ ءَاتَىٰهُ ٱللَّهُ ٱلْمُلْكَ إِذْ قَالَ إِبْرَٰهِـۧمُ رَبِّىَ ٱلَّذِى يُحْىِۦ وَيُمِيتُ قَالَ أَنَا۠ أُحْىِۦ وَأُمِيتُ ۖ قَالَ إِبْرَٰهِـۧمُ فَإِنَّ ٱللَّهَ يَأْتِى بِٱلشَّمْسِ مِنَ ٱلْمَشْرِقِ فَأْتِ بِهَا مِنَ ٱلْمَغْرِبِ فَبُهِتَ ٱلَّذِى كَفَرَ ۗ وَٱللَّهُ لَا يَهْدِى ٱلْقَوْمَ ٱلظَّـٰلِمِينَ

*There is no compulsion in religion. Verily, the Right Path has become distinct from the wrong path. Whoever disbelieves in Tâghût and believes in Allâh, then he has grasped the most trustworthy handhold that will never break. And Allâh is All-Hearer, All-Knower. (256) Allâh is the Walî (Protector or Guardian) of those who believe. He brings them out from darkness into light. But as for those who disbelieve, their Auliyâ (supporters and helpers) are Tâghût [false deities and false leaders], they bring them out from light into darkness. Those are the dwellers of the Fire, and they will abide therein forever.*

(257) Have you not looked at him who disputed with Ibrâhim (Abraham) about his Lord (Allâh), because Allâh had given him the kingdom? When Ibrâhim (Abraham) said (to him): "My Lord (Allâh) is He Who gives life and causes death." He said, "I give life and cause death." Ibrâhim (Abraham) said, "Verily! Allâh causes the sun to rise from the east; then cause it you to rise from the west." So the disbeliever was utterly defeated. And Allâh guides not the people, who are Zâlimûn (wrong-doers). (258)

## Quran 2:261-262

مَّثَلُ ٱلَّذِينَ يُنفِقُونَ أَمْوَٰلَهُمْ فِى سَبِيلِ ٱللَّهِ كَمَثَلِ حَبَّةٍ أَنْبَتَتْ سَبْعَ سَنَابِلَ فِى كُلِّ سُنْبُلَةٍ مِّائَةُ حَبَّةٍ ۗ وَٱللَّهُ يُضَٰعِفُ لِمَن يَشَآءُ ۗ وَٱللَّهُ وَٰسِعٌ عَلِيمٌ ٱلَّذِينَ يُنفِقُونَ أَمْوَٰلَهُمْ فِى سَبِيلِ ٱللَّهِ ثُمَّ لَا يُتْبِعُونَ مَآ أَنفَقُواْ مَنًّا وَلَآ أَذًىٰ لَّهُمْ أَجْرُهُمْ عِندَ رَبِّهِمْ وَلَا خَوْفٌ عَلَيْهِمْ وَلَا هُمْ يَحْزَنُونَ

The likeness of those who spend their wealth in the Way of Allâh, is as the likeness of a grain (of corn); it grows seven ears, and each ear has a hundred grains. Allâh gives manifold increase to whom He wills. And Allâh is All-Sufficient for His creatures' needs, All-Knower (261) Those who spend their wealth in the Cause of Allâh, and do not follow up their gifts with reminders of their generosity or with injury, their reward is with their Lord. On them shall be no fear, nor shall they grieve (262)

وَمَآ أَنفَقْتُم مِّن نَّفَقَةٍ أَوْ نَذَرْتُم مِّن نَّذْرٍ فَإِنَّ ٱللَّهَ يَعْلَمُهُۥ ۗ وَمَا لِلظَّـٰلِمِينَ مِنْ أَنصَارٍ ۗ إِن تُبْدُوا۟ ٱلصَّدَقَـٰتِ فَنِعِمَّا هِىَ ۖ وَإِن تُخْفُوهَا وَتُؤْتُوهَا ٱلْفُقَرَآءَ فَهُوَ خَيْرٌ لَّكُمْ ۚ وَيُكَفِّرُ عَنكُم مِّن سَيِّـَٔاتِكُمْ ۗ وَٱللَّهُ بِمَا تَعْمَلُونَ خَبِيرٌ ۞ لَّيْسَ عَلَيْكَ هُدَىٰهُمْ وَلَـٰكِنَّ ٱللَّهَ يَهْدِى مَن يَشَآءُ ۗ وَمَا تُنفِقُوا۟ مِنْ خَيْرٍ فَلِأَنفُسِكُمْ ۚ وَمَا تُنفِقُونَ إِلَّا ٱبْتِغَآءَ وَجْهِ ٱللَّهِ ۚ وَمَا تُنفِقُوا۟ مِنْ خَيْرٍ يُوَفَّ إِلَيْكُمْ وَأَنتُمْ لَا تُظْلَمُونَ لِلْفُقَرَآءِ ٱلَّذِينَ أُحْصِرُوا۟ فِى سَبِيلِ ٱللَّهِ لَا يَسْتَطِيعُونَ ضَرْبًا فِى ٱلْأَرْضِ يَحْسَبُهُمُ ٱلْجَاهِلُ أَغْنِيَآءَ مِنَ ٱلتَّعَفُّفِ تَعْرِفُهُم بِسِيمَـٰهُمْ لَا يَسْـَٔلُونَ ٱلنَّاسَ إِلْحَافًا ۗ وَمَا تُنفِقُوا۟ مِنْ خَيْرٍ فَإِنَّ ٱللَّهَ بِهِۦ عَلِيمٌ ٱلَّذِينَ يُنفِقُونَ أَمْوَٰلَهُم بِٱلَّيْلِ وَٱلنَّهَارِ سِرًّا وَعَلَانِيَةً فَلَهُمْ أَجْرُهُمْ عِندَ رَبِّهِمْ وَلَا خَوْفٌ عَلَيْهِمْ وَلَا هُمْ يَحْزَنُونَ ٱلَّذِينَ يَأْكُلُونَ ٱلرِّبَوٰا۟ لَا يَقُومُونَ إِلَّا كَمَا يَقُومُ ٱلَّذِى يَتَخَبَّطُهُ ٱلشَّيْطَـٰنُ مِنَ ٱلْمَسِّ ۚ ذَٰلِكَ بِأَنَّهُمْ قَالُوٓا۟ إِنَّمَا ٱلْبَيْعُ مِثْلُ ٱلرِّبَوٰا۟ ۗ وَأَحَلَّ ٱللَّهُ ٱلْبَيْعَ وَحَرَّمَ ٱلرِّبَوٰا۟ ۚ فَمَن جَآءَهُۥ مَوْعِظَةٌ مِّن رَّبِّهِۦ فَٱنتَهَىٰ فَلَهُۥ مَا سَلَفَ وَأَمْرُهُۥٓ إِلَى ٱللَّهِ ۖ وَمَنْ عَادَ فَأُو۟لَـٰٓئِكَ أَصْحَـٰبُ ٱلنَّارِ ۖ هُمْ فِيهَا خَـٰلِدُونَ يَمْحَقُ ٱللَّهُ ٱلرِّبَوٰا۟ وَيُرْبِى ٱلصَّدَقَـٰتِ ۗ وَٱللَّهُ لَا يُحِبُّ كُلَّ كَفَّارٍ أَثِيمٍ إِنَّ ٱلَّذِينَ ءَامَنُوا۟ وَعَمِلُوا۟ ٱلصَّـٰلِحَـٰتِ وَأَقَامُوا۟ ٱلصَّلَوٰةَ وَءَاتَوُا۟ ٱلزَّكَوٰةَ لَهُمْ أَجْرُهُمْ عِندَ رَبِّهِمْ وَلَا خَوْفٌ عَلَيْهِمْ وَلَا هُمْ يَحْزَنُونَ

*And whatever you spend for spendings (e.g., in - charity,*
*for Allâh's Cause) or whatever vow you make, be sure*
*Allâh knows it all. And for the Zâlimûn (wrong-doers)*

*there are no helpers. (270) If you disclose your Sadaqât (alms-giving), it is well, but if you conceal them, and give them to the poor, that is better for you. (Allâh) will expiate you some of your sins. And Allâh is Well-Acquainted with what you do. (271) Not upon you is their guidance, but Allâh guides whom He wills. And whatever you spend in good, it is for yourselves, when you spend not except seeking Allâh's Countenance. And whatever you spend in good, it will be repaid to you in full, and you shall not be wronged. (272) (Charity is) for Fuqarâ (the poor), who in Allâh's Cause are restricted (from travel), and cannot move about in the land (for trade or work). The one who knows them not, thinks that they are rich because of their modesty. You may know them by their mark, they do not beg of people at all. And whatever you spend in good, surely Allâh knows it well. (273) Those who spend their wealth (in Allâh's Cause) by night and day, in secret and in public, they shall have their reward with their Lord. On them shall be no fear, nor shall they grieve. (274) Those who eat Ribâ (usury) will not stand (on the Day of Resurrection) except like the standing of a person beaten by Shaitân (Satan) leading him to insanity. That is because they say: "Trading is only like Ribâ (usury)," whereas Allâh has permitted trading and forbidden Ribâ (usury). So whosoever receives an admonition from his Lord and stops eating Ribâ (usury) shall not be punished for the* past; his case is for Allâh (to judge); but whoever returns [to Ribâ (usury)], such are the dwellers of the Fire - they will abide therein (275) Allâh will destroy Ribâ (usury) and will give increase for Sadaqât (deeds of charity, alms, etc.) And Allâh likes not the disbelievers, sinners. (276) Truly those who believe, and do deeds of righteousness, and perform As-Salât (Iqâmat-as-Salât), and give Zakât, they will have their reward with their Lord. On them shall be no fear, nor shall they grieve. (277)

## Quran 2:278-281

يَـٰٓأَيُّهَا ٱلَّذِينَ ءَامَنُوا۟ ٱتَّقُوا۟ ٱللَّهَ وَذَرُوا۟ مَا بَقِىَ مِنَ ٱلرِّبَوٰٓا۟ إِن كُنتُم مُّؤْمِنِينَ فَإِن لَّمْ تَفْعَلُوا۟ فَأْذَنُوا۟ بِحَرْبٍ مِّنَ ٱللَّهِ وَرَسُولِهِۦ وَإِن تُبْتُمْ فَلَكُمْ رُءُوسُ أَمْوَٰلِكُمْ لَا تَظْلِمُونَ وَلَا تُظْلَمُونَ وَإِن كَانَ ذُو عُسْرَةٍ فَنَظِرَةٌ إِلَىٰ مَيْسَرَةٍ وَأَن تَصَدَّقُوا۟ خَيْرٌ لَّكُمْ إِن كُنتُمْ تَعْلَمُونَ وَٱتَّقُوا۟ يَوْمًا تُرْجَعُونَ فِيهِ إِلَى ٱللَّهِ ثُمَّ تُوَفَّىٰ كُلُّ نَفْسٍ مَّا كَسَبَتْ وَهُمْ لَا يُظْلَمُونَ

O you who believe! Be afraid of Allâh and give up what remains (due to you) from Ribâ (usury) (from now onward), if you are (really) believers. (278) And if you do not do it, then take a notice of war from Allâh and His Messenger but if you repent, you shall have your capital sums. Deal not unjustly (by asking more than your capital sums), and you shall not be dealt with unjustly (by receiving less than your capital sums). (279) And if the debtor is in a hard time (has no money), then grant him time till it is easy for him to repay, but if you remit it by way of charity, that is better for you if you did but know. (280) And be afraid of the Day when you shall be brought back to Allâh. Then every person shall be paid what he earned, and they shall not be dealt with unjustly. (281)

## Quran 2:284

لِّلَّهِ مَا فِى ٱلسَّمَٰوَٰتِ وَمَا فِى ٱلۡأَرۡضِۗ وَإِن تُبۡدُواْ مَا فِىٓ أَنفُسِكُمۡ أَوۡ تُخۡفُوهُ يُحَاسِبۡكُم بِهِ ٱللَّهُۖ فَيَغۡفِرُ لِمَن يَشَآءُ وَيُعَذِّبُ مَن يَشَآءُۗ وَٱللَّهُ عَلَىٰ كُلِّ شَىۡءٍ قَدِيرٌ

To Allâh belongs all that is in the heavens and all that is on the earth, and whether you disclose what is in your ownselves or conceal it, Allâh will call you to account for it. Then He forgives whom He wills and punishes whom He wills. And Allâh is Able to do all things. (284)

## Quran 2:286

لَا يُكَلِّفُ ٱللَّهُ نَفۡسًا إِلَّا وُسۡعَهَاۚ لَهَا مَا كَسَبَتۡ وَعَلَيۡهَا مَا ٱكۡتَسَبَتۡۗ رَبَّنَا لَا تُؤَاخِذۡنَآ إِن نَّسِينَآ أَوۡ أَخۡطَأۡنَاۚ رَبَّنَا وَلَا تَحۡمِلۡ عَلَيۡنَآ إِصۡرًا كَمَا حَمَلۡتَهُ عَلَى ٱلَّذِينَ مِن قَبۡلِنَاۚ رَبَّنَا وَلَا تُحَمِّلۡنَا مَا لَا طَاقَةَ لَنَا بِهِۦۖ وَٱعۡفُ عَنَّا وَٱغۡفِرۡ لَنَا وَٱرۡحَمۡنَآۚ أَنتَ مَوۡلَىٰنَا فَٱنصُرۡنَا عَلَى ٱلۡقَوۡمِ ٱلۡكَٰفِرِينَ

Allâh burdens not a person beyond his scope. He gets reward for that (good) which he has earned, and he is punished for that (evil) which he has earned. "Our Lord! Punish us not if we forget or fall into error, our Lord!

*Lay not on us a burden like that which You did lay on those before us (Jews and Christians); our Lord! Put not on us a burden greater than we have strength to bear. Pardon us and grant us Forgiveness. Have mercy on us. You are our Maulâ (Patron, Supporter and Protector, etc.) and give us victory over the disbelieving people."*
*(286)*

## Quran 3:4

نَزَّلَ عَلَيْكَ ٱلْكِتَـٰبَ بِٱلْحَقِّ مُصَدِّقًا لِّمَا بَيْنَ يَدَيْهِ وَأَنزَلَ ٱلتَّوْرَىٰةَ وَٱلْإِنجِيلَ (٣) مِن قَبْلُ هُدًى لِّلنَّاسِ وَأَنزَلَ ٱلْفُرْقَانَّ إِنَّ ٱلَّذِينَ كَفَرُوا۟ بِـَٔايَـٰتِ ٱللَّهِ لَهُمْ عَذَابٌ شَدِيدٌ وَٱللَّهُ عَزِيزٌ ذُو ٱنتِقَامٍ (٤)

*It is He Who has sent down the Book (the Qur'ân) to you (Muhammad) with truth, confirming what came before it. And he sent down the Taurât and the Injeel (3) Aforetime, as a guidance to mankind, And He sent down the criterion [of judgement between right and wrong (this Qur'ân)]. Truly, those who disbelieve in the Ayât (proofs, evidences, verses, lessons, signs, revelations, etc.) of Allâh, for them there is a severe torment; and Allâh is All-Mighty, All-Able of Retribution. (4)*

## Quran 3:7-12

هُوَ ٱلَّذِىٓ أَنزَلَ عَلَيْكَ ٱلْكِتَـٰبَ مِنْهُ ءَايَـٰتٌ مُّحْكَمَـٰتٌ هُنَّ أُمُّ ٱلْكِتَـٰبِ وَأُخَرُ مُتَشَـٰبِهَـٰتٌ فَأَمَّا ٱلَّذِينَ فِى قُلُوبِهِمْ زَيْغٌ فَيَتَّبِعُونَ

مَا تَشَٰبَهَ مِنْهُ ٱبْتِغَآءَ ٱلْفِتْنَةِ وَٱبْتِغَآءَ تَأْوِيلِهِۦۗ وَمَا يَعْلَمُ تَأْوِيلَهُۥٓ إِلَّا ٱللَّهُۗ وَٱلرَّٰسِخُونَ فِى ٱلْعِلْمِ يَقُولُونَ ءَامَنَّا بِهِۦ كُلٌّ مِّنْ عِندِ رَبِّنَاۗ وَمَا يَذَّكَّرُ إِلَّآ أُوْلُواْ ٱلْأَلْبَٰبِ (٧) رَبَّنَا لَا تُزِغْ قُلُوبَنَا بَعْدَ إِذْ هَدَيْتَنَا وَهَبْ لَنَا مِن لَّدُنكَ رَحْمَةًۚ إِنَّكَ أَنتَ ٱلْوَهَّابُ (٨) رَبَّنَا إِنَّكَ جَامِعُ ٱلنَّاسِ لِيَوْمٍ لَّا رَيْبَ فِيهِۚ إِنَّ ٱللَّهَ لَا يُخْلِفُ ٱلْمِيعَادَ (٩) إِنَّ ٱلَّذِينَ كَفَرُواْ لَن تُغْنِىَ عَنْهُمْ أَمْوَٰلُهُمْ وَلَآ أَوْلَٰدُهُم مِّنَ ٱللَّهِ شَيْـًٔاۖ وَأُوْلَٰئِكَ هُمْ وَقُودُ ٱلنَّارِ (١٠) كَدَأْبِ ءَالِ فِرْعَوْنَ وَٱلَّذِينَ مِن قَبْلِهِمْۚ كَذَّبُواْ بِـَٔايَٰتِنَا فَأَخَذَهُمُ ٱللَّهُ بِذُنُوبِهِمْۗ وَٱللَّهُ شَدِيدُ ٱلْعِقَابِ (١١) قُل لِّلَّذِينَ كَفَرُواْ سَتُغْلَبُونَ وَتُحْشَرُونَ إِلَىٰ جَهَنَّمَۚ وَبِئْسَ ٱلْمِهَادُ (١٢)

*It is He Who has sent down to you (Muhammad) the Book (this Qur'ân). In it are Verses that are entirely clear, they are the foundations of the Book [and those are the Verses of Al-Ahkâm (commandments), Al-Farâ'id (obligatory duties) and Al-Hudud (legal laws for the punishment of thieves, adulterers)]; and others not entirely clear. So as for those in whose hearts there is a deviation (from the truth) they follow that which is not entirely clear thereof, seeking Al-Fitnah (polytheism and trials), and seeking for its hidden meanings, but none knows its hidden meanings save Allâh. And those who are firmly grounded in knowledge say: "We believe in it; the whole of it (clear and unclear Verses) are from our Lord." And none receive admonition except men of understanding. (7) (They say): "Our Lord! Let not our hearts deviate (from the truth) after You have guided us,* and grant us mercy from You. Truly, You are the Bestower," (8) Our Lord! Verily, it is You Who will gather mankind together on the Day about which there is no doubt. Verily, Allâh never breaks His Promise," (9) Verily, those who disbelieve, neither their properties nor their offspring will avail them whatsoever against Allâh; and it is they who will be fuel of the Fire. (10) Like the behaviour of the people of Fir'aun (Pharaoh) and those before them; they belied Our Ayât (proofs, evidences, verses, lessons, signs, revelations, etc.), so Allâh seized (destroyed) them for their sins. And Allâh is Severe in punishment. (11) Say (O Muhammad) to those who disbelieve: "You will be defeated and gathered together to Hell, and worst indeed is that place to rest." (12)

## Quran 3:15-19

قُلْ أَؤُنَبِّئُكُم بِخَيْرٍ مِّن ذَٰلِكُمْ لِلَّذِينَ ٱتَّقَوْاْ عِندَ رَبِّهِمْ جَنَّٰتٌ تَجْرِى مِن تَحْتِهَا ٱلْأَنْهَٰرُ خَٰلِدِينَ فِيهَا وَأَزْوَٰجٌ مُّطَهَّرَةٌ وَرِضْوَٰنٌ مِّنَ ٱللَّهِ وَٱللَّهُ بَصِيرٌ بِٱلْعِبَادِ (١٥) ٱلَّذِينَ يَقُولُونَ رَبَّنَآ إِنَّنَآ ءَامَنَّا فَٱغْفِرْ لَنَا ذُنُوبَنَا وَقِنَا عَذَابَ ٱلنَّارِ (١٦) ٱلصَّٰبِرِينَ وَٱلصَّٰدِقِينَ وَٱلْقَٰنِتِينَ وَٱلْمُنفِقِينَ وَٱلْمُسْتَغْفِرِينَ بِٱلْأَسْحَارِ (١٧) شَهِدَ ٱللَّهُ أَنَّهُ لَا إِلَٰهَ إِلَّا هُوَ وَٱلْمَلَٰئِكَةُ وَأُوْلُواْ ٱلْعِلْمِ قَآئِمًا بِٱلْقِسْطِ لَا إِلَٰهَ إِلَّا هُوَ ٱلْعَزِيزُ ٱلْحَكِيمُ (١٨) إِنَّ ٱلدِّينَ عِندَ ٱللَّهِ ٱلْإِسْلَٰمُ وَمَا ٱخْتَلَفَ ٱلَّذِينَ أُوتُواْ ٱلْكِتَٰبَ إِلَّا مِنۢ بَعْدِ مَا جَآءَهُمُ ٱلْعِلْمُ بَغْيًا بَيْنَهُمْ وَمَن يَكْفُرْ بِـَٔايَٰتِ ٱللَّهِ فَإِنَّ ٱللَّهَ سَرِيعُ ٱلْحِسَابِ (١٩)

*Say: "Shall I inform you of things far better than those? For Al-Muttaqûn (the pious) there are Gardens (Paradise) with their Lord, underneath which rivers flow. Therein (is their) eternal (home) and Azwâjun Mutahharatun (purified mates or wives), And Allâh will be pleased with them. And Allâh is All-Seer of the (His) slaves" (15) Those who say: "Our Lord! We have indeed believed, so forgive us our sins and save us from the punishment of the Fire." (16) (They are) those who are patient, those who are true (in Faith, words, and deeds), and obedient with sincere devotion in worship to Allâh. Those who spend [give the Zakât and alms in the Way of Allâh] and those who pray and beg Allâh's Pardon in the last hours of the night. (17) Allâh bears witness that Lâ ilâha illa Huwa (none has the right to be worshipped but He), and the angels, and those having knowledge (also give this witness); (He always) maintains His creation in Justice. Lâ ilâh illa Huwa (none has the right to be worshipped but He), the All-Mighty, the All-Wise. (18) Truly, the religion with Allâh is Islâm. Those who were given the Scripture (Jews and Christians) did not differ except, out of mutual jealousy, after knowledge had come to them. And whoever disbelieves in the Ayât (proofs, evidences, verses, signs, revelations, etc.) of Allâh, then surely, Allâh is Swift in calling to account. (19)*

**Quran 3:25-32**

فَكَيْفَ إِذَا جَمَعْنَـٰهُمْ لِيَوْمٍ لَّا رَيْبَ فِيهِ وَوُفِّيَتْ كُلُّ نَفْسٍ مَّا كَسَبَتْ وَهُمْ لَا يُظْلَمُونَ (٢٥) قُلِ اللَّهُمَّ مَـٰلِكَ الْمُلْكِ تُؤْتِى الْمُلْكَ مَن تَشَاءُ وَتَنزِعُ الْمُلْكَ مِمَّن تَشَاءُ وَتُعِزُّ مَن تَشَاءُ وَتُذِلُّ مَن تَشَاءُ بِيَدِكَ الْخَيْرُ إِنَّكَ عَلَىٰ كُلِّ شَىْءٍ قَدِيرٌ (٢٦) تُولِجُ الَّيْلَ فِى النَّهَارِ وَتُولِجُ النَّهَارَ فِى الَّيْلِ وَتُخْرِجُ الْحَىَّ مِنَ الْمَيِّتِ وَتُخْرِجُ الْمَيِّتَ مِنَ الْحَىِّ وَتَرْزُقُ مَن تَشَاءُ بِغَيْرِ حِسَابٍ (٢٧) لَّا يَتَّخِذِ الْمُؤْمِنُونَ الْكَـٰفِرِينَ أَوْلِيَاءَ مِن دُونِ الْمُؤْمِنِينَ وَمَن يَفْعَلْ ذَٰلِكَ فَلَيْسَ مِنَ اللَّهِ فِى شَىْءٍ إِلَّا أَن تَتَّقُوا مِنْهُمْ تُقَاةً وَيُحَذِّرُكُمُ اللَّهُ نَفْسَهُ وَإِلَى اللَّهِ الْمَصِيرُ (٢٨) قُلْ إِن تُخْفُوا مَا فِى صُدُورِكُمْ أَوْ تُبْدُوهُ يَعْلَمْهُ اللَّهُ وَيَعْلَمُ مَا فِى السَّمَـٰوَٰتِ وَمَا فِى الْأَرْضِ وَاللَّهُ عَلَىٰ كُلِّ شَىْءٍ قَدِيرٌ (٢٩) يَوْمَ تَجِدُ كُلُّ نَفْسٍ مَّا عَمِلَتْ مِنْ خَيْرٍ مُّحْضَرًا وَمَا عَمِلَتْ مِن سُوءٍ تَوَدُّ لَوْ أَنَّ بَيْنَهَا وَبَيْنَهُ أَمَدًا بَعِيدًا وَيُحَذِّرُكُمُ اللَّهُ نَفْسَهُ وَاللَّهُ رَءُوفٌ بِالْعِبَادِ (٣٠) قُلْ إِن كُنتُمْ تُحِبُّونَ اللَّهَ فَاتَّبِعُونِى يُحْبِبْكُمُ اللَّهُ وَيَغْفِرْ لَكُمْ ذُنُوبَكُمْ وَاللَّهُ غَفُورٌ رَّحِيمٌ (٣١) قُلْ أَطِيعُوا اللَّهَ وَالرَّسُولَ فَإِن تَوَلَّوْا فَإِنَّ اللَّهَ لَا يُحِبُّ الْكَـٰفِرِينَ (٣٢)

*How (will it be) when We gather them together on the Day about which there is no doubt (i.e. the Day of Resurrection). And each person will be paid in full what he has earned? And they will not be dealt with unjustly. (25) Say (O Muhammad): "O Allâh! Possessor of the kingdom, You give the kingdom to whom You will, and You take the kingdom from whom You will, and You endue with honor whom You will, and You humiliate*

*whom You will. In Your Hand is the good. Verily, You
are Able to do all things. (26) You make the night to
enter into the day, and You make the day to enter into the
night (i.e. increase and decrease in the hours of the night
and the day during winter and summer), You bring the
living out of the dead, and You bring the dead out of the
living. And You give wealth and sustenance to whom
You will, without limit (measure or account). (27) Let
not the believers take the disbelievers as Auliyâ
(supporters, helpers) instead of the believers, and
whoever does that will never be helped by Allâh in any
way, except if you indeed fear a danger from them. And
Allâh warns you against Himself (His Punishment), and
to Allâh is the final return. (28) Say (O Muhammad):
"Whether you hide what is in your breasts or reveal it,
Allâh knows it, and He knows what is in the heavens and
what is in the earth. And Allâh is Able to do all things."
(29) On the Day when every person will be confronted
with all the good he has done, and all the evil he has done,
he will wish that there were a great distance between him
and his evil. And Allâh warns you against Himself (His
Punishment) and Allâh is full of Kindness to the (His)
slaves. (30) Say (O Muhammad to mankind): "If you
(really) love Allâh then follow me (i.e. accept Islâmic
Monotheism, follow the Qur'ân and the Sunnah), Allâh
will love you and forgive you your sins. And Allâh is
Oft-Forgiving, Most Merciful." (31) Say: "Obey Allâh*

and the Messenger (Muhammad)." But if they turn away, then Allâh does not like the disbelievers (32)

## Quran 3:54-57

وَمَكَرُواْ وَمَكَرَ ٱللَّهُ وَٱللَّهُ خَيْرُ ٱلْمَـٰكِرِينَ (٥٤) إِذْ قَالَ ٱللَّهُ يَـٰعِيسَىٰٓ إِنِّى مُتَوَفِّيكَ وَرَافِعُكَ إِلَىَّ وَمُطَهِّرُكَ مِنَ ٱلَّذِينَ كَفَرُواْ وَجَاعِلُ ٱلَّذِينَ ٱتَّبَعُوكَ فَوْقَ ٱلَّذِينَ كَفَرُواْ إِلَىٰ يَوْمِ ٱلْقِيَـٰمَةِۖ ثُمَّ إِلَىَّ مَرْجِعُكُمْ فَأَحْكُمُ بَيْنَكُمْ فِيمَا كُنتُمْ فِيهِ تَخْتَلِفُونَ (٥٥) فَأَمَّا ٱلَّذِينَ كَفَرُواْ فَأُعَذِّبُهُمْ عَذَابًا شَدِيدًا فِى ٱلدُّنْيَا وَٱلْأَخِرَةِ وَمَا لَهُم مِّن نَّـٰصِرِينَ (٥٦) وَأَمَّا ٱلَّذِينَ ءَامَنُواْ وَعَمِلُواْ ٱلصَّـٰلِحَـٰتِ فَيُوَفِّيهِمْ أُجُورَهُمْۗ وَٱللَّهُ لَا يُحِبُّ ٱلظَّـٰلِمِينَ (٥٧)

And they (disbelievers) plotted [to kill 'Īsā (Jesus)], and Allâh plotted too. And Allâh is the Best of those who plot. (54) And (remember) when Allâh said: "O 'Īsā (Jesus)! I will take you and raise you to Myself and clear you [of the forged statement that 'Īsā (Jesus) is Allâh's son] of those who disbelieve, and I will make those who follow you (Monotheists, who worship none but Allâh) superior to those who disbelieve [in the Oneness of Allâh, or disbelieve in some of His Messengers, e.g. Muhammad, 'Īsā (Jesus), Mûsâ (Moses), etc., or in His Books, e.g. the Taurât (Torah), the Injeel, the Qur'ân] till the Day of Resurrection. Then you will return to Me and I will judge between you in the matters in which you used to dispute." (55) "As to those who disbelieve, I will punish

them with a severe torment in this world and in the
Hereafter, and they will have no helpers." (56) And as for
those who believe (in the Oneness of Allâh) and do
righteous good deeds, Allâh will pay them their reward in
full. And Allâh does not like the Zâlimûn (polytheists
and wrong-doers). (57)

## Quran 3:69

وَدَّت طَّآئِفَةٌ مِّنْ أَهْلِ ٱلْكِتَـٰبِ لَوْ يُضِلُّونَكُمْ وَمَا يُضِلُّونَ إِلَّا
أَنفُسَهُمْ وَمَا يَشْعُرُونَ (٦٩)

A party of the people of the Scripture (Jews and
Christians) wish to lead you astray. But they shall not
lead astray anyone except themselves, and they perceive
not. (69)

## Quran 3:76-77

بَلَىٰ مَنْ أَوْفَىٰ بِعَهْدِهِۦ وَٱتَّقَىٰ فَإِنَّ ٱللَّهَ يُحِبُّ ٱلْمُتَّقِينَ (٧٦) إِنَّ
ٱلَّذِينَ يَشْتَرُونَ بِعَهْدِ ٱللَّهِ وَأَيْمَـٰنِهِمْ ثَمَنًا قَلِيلاً أُوْلَـٰئِكَ لَا خَلَـٰقَ
لَهُمْ فِى ٱلْأَخِرَةِ وَلَا يُكَلِّمُهُمُ ٱللَّهُ وَلَا يَنظُرُ إِلَيْهِمْ يَوْمَ ٱلْقِيَـٰمَةِ
وَلَا يُزَكِّيهِمْ وَلَهُمْ عَذَابٌ أَلِيمٌ (٧٧)

Yes, whoever fulfils his pledge and fears Allâh much;
verily, then Allâh loves those who are Al-Muttaqûn (the
pious). (76) Verily, those who purchase a small gain at
the cost of Allâh's Covenant and their oaths, they shall
have no portion in the Hereafter (Paradise). Neither will
Allâh speak to them, nor look at them on the Day of

*Resurrection, nor will He purify them, and they shall*
*have a painful torment. (77)*

## Quran 3:83-92

أَفَغَيْرَ دِينِ ٱللَّهِ يَبْغُونَ وَلَهُۥ أَسْلَمَ مَن فِى ٱلسَّمَٰوَٰتِ وَٱلْأَرْضِ
طَوْعًا وَكَرْهًا وَإِلَيْهِ يُرْجَعُونَ (٨٣) قُلْ ءَامَنَّا بِٱللَّهِ وَمَآ
أُنزِلَ عَلَيْنَا وَمَآ أُنزِلَ عَلَىٰٓ إِبْرَٰهِيمَ وَإِسْمَٰعِيلَ وَإِسْحَٰقَ
وَيَعْقُوبَ وَٱلْأَسْبَاطِ وَمَآ أُوتِىَ مُوسَىٰ وَعِيسَىٰ وَٱلنَّبِيُّونَ مِن
رَّبِّهِمْ لَا نُفَرِّقُ بَيْنَ أَحَدٍ مِّنْهُمْ وَنَحْنُ لَهُۥ مُسْلِمُونَ (٨٤) وَمَن
يَبْتَغِ غَيْرَ ٱلْإِسْلَٰمِ دِينًا فَلَن يُقْبَلَ مِنْهُ وَهُوَ فِى ٱلْأَخِرَةِ مِنَ
ٱلْخَٰسِرِينَ (٨٥) كَيْفَ يَهْدِى ٱللَّهُ قَوْمًا كَفَرُواْ بَعْدَ إِيمَٰنِهِمْ
وَشَهِدُوٓاْ أَنَّ ٱلرَّسُولَ حَقٌّ وَجَآءَهُمُ ٱلْبَيِّنَٰتُ وَٱللَّهُ لَا يَهْدِى
ٱلْقَوْمَ ٱلظَّٰلِمِينَ (٨٦) أُوْلَٰٓئِكَ جَزَآؤُهُمْ أَنَّ عَلَيْهِمْ لَعْنَةَ ٱللَّهِ
وَٱلْمَلَٰٓئِكَةِ وَٱلنَّاسِ أَجْمَعِينَ (٨٧) خَٰلِدِينَ فِيهَا لَا يُخَفَّفُ عَنْهُمُ
ٱلْعَذَابُ وَلَا هُمْ يُنظَرُونَ (٨٨) إِلَّا ٱلَّذِينَ تَابُواْ مِنۢ بَعْدِ ذَٰلِكَ
وَأَصْلَحُواْ فَإِنَّ ٱللَّهَ غَفُورٌ رَّحِيمٌ (٨٩) إِنَّ ٱلَّذِينَ كَفَرُواْ بَعْدَ
إِيمَٰنِهِمْ ثُمَّ ٱزْدَادُواْ كُفْرًا لَّن تُقْبَلَ تَوْبَتُهُمْ وَأُوْلَٰٓئِكَ هُمُ
ٱلضَّآلُّونَ (٩٠) إِنَّ ٱلَّذِينَ كَفَرُواْ وَمَاتُواْ وَهُمْ كُفَّارٌ فَلَن يُقْبَلَ
مِنْ أَحَدِهِم مِّلْءُ ٱلْأَرْضِ ذَهَبًا وَلَوِ ٱفْتَدَىٰ بِهِۦٓ أُوْلَٰٓئِكَ لَهُمْ
عَذَابٌ أَلِيمٌ وَمَا لَهُم مِّن نَّٰصِرِينَ (٩١) لَن تَنَالُواْ ٱلْبِرَّ حَتَّىٰ
تُنفِقُواْ مِمَّا تُحِبُّونَ وَمَا تُنفِقُواْ مِن شَىْءٍ فَإِنَّ ٱللَّهَ بِهِۦ عَلِيمٌ
(٩٢)

*Do they seek other than the religion of Allâh (the true*
*Islâmic Monotheism worshipping none but Allâh Alone),*
*while to Him submitted all creatures in the heavens and*

*the earth, willingly or unwillingly. And to Him shall they all be returned. (83) Say (O Muhammad): "We believe in Allâh and in what has been sent down to us, and what was sent down to Ibrâhim (Abraham), Ismâ'il (Ishmael), Ishâq (Isaac), Ya'qûb (Jacob) and Al-Asbât [the offspring twelve sons of Ya'qûb (Jacob)] and what was given to Mûsa (Moses), 'Îsâ (Jesus) and the Prophets from their Lord. We make no distinction between one another among them and to Him (Allâh) we have submitted (in Islâm)." (84) And whoever seeks a religion other than Islâm, it will never be accepted of him, and in the Hereafter he will be one of the losers. (85) How shall Allâh guide a people who disbelieved after their belief and after they bore witness that the Messenger (Muhammad) is true and after clear proofs had come unto them? And Allâh guides not the people who are Zâlimûn (polytheists and wrong-doers). (86) They are those whose recompense is that on them (rests) the Curse of Allâh, of the angels, and of all mankind. (87) They will abide therein (Hell). Neither will their torment be lightened, nor will it be delayed or postponed (for a while). (88) Except for those who repent after that and do righteous deeds. Verily, Allâh is Oft-Forgiving, Most Merciful. (89) Verily, those who disbelieved after their Belief and then went on increasing in their disbelief (i.e. disbelief in the Qur'ân and in Prophet Muhammad) - never will their repentance be accepted [because they repent only by their tongues* and not from their hearts]. And they are those who are astray. (90) Verily, those who disbelieved, and died while they were disbelievers, the (whole) earth full of gold will not be accepted from anyone of them even if they offered it as a ransom. For them is a painful torment and they will have no helpers. (91) By no means shall you attain Al-Birr (piety, righteousness - here it means Allâh's Reward, i.e. Paradise), unless you spend (in Allâh's Cause) of that which you love; and whatever of good you spend, Allâh knows it well. (92)

## Quran 3:100

يَـٰٓأَيُّهَا ٱلَّذِينَ ءَامَنُوٓا إِن تُطِيعُوا فَرِيقًا مِّنَ ٱلَّذِينَ أُوتُوا ٱلْكِتَـٰبَ يَرُدُّوكُم بَعْدَ إِيمَـٰنِكُمْ كَـٰفِرِينَ

O you who believe! If you obey a group of those who were given the Scripture (Jews and Christians), they would (indeed) render you disbelievers after you have believed! (100)

## Quran 3:104-116

وَلْتَكُن مِّنكُمْ أُمَّةٌ يَدْعُونَ إِلَى ٱلْخَيْرِ وَيَأْمُرُونَ بِٱلْمَعْرُوفِ وَيَنْهَوْنَ عَنِ ٱلْمُنكَرِ وَأُوْلَـٰٓئِكَ هُمُ ٱلْمُفْلِحُونَ (١٠٤) وَلَا تَكُونُوا كَٱلَّذِينَ تَفَرَّقُوا وَٱخْتَلَفُوا مِنْ بَعْدِ مَا جَاءَهُمُ ٱلْبَيِّنَـٰتُ وَأُوْلَـٰٓئِكَ لَهُمْ عَذَابٌ عَظِيمٌ (١٠٥) يَوْمَ تَبْيَضُّ وُجُوهٌ وَتَسْوَدُّ وُجُوهٌ فَأَمَّا ٱلَّذِينَ ٱسْوَدَّتْ وُجُوهُهُمْ أَكَفَرْتُم بَعْدَ إِيمَـٰنِكُمْ فَذُوقُوا ٱلْعَذَابَ بِمَا كُنتُمْ تَكْفُرُونَ (١٠٦) وَأَمَّا ٱلَّذِينَ ٱبْيَضَّتْ

وُجُوهُهُمْ فَفِى رَحْمَةِ ٱللَّهِ هُمْ فِيهَا خَٰلِدُونَ (١٠٧) تِلْكَ ءَايَٰتُ
ٱللَّهِ نَتْلُوهَا عَلَيْكَ بِٱلْحَقِّ ۗ وَمَا ٱللَّهُ يُرِيدُ ظُلْمًا لِّلْعَٰلَمِينَ (١٠٨)
وَلِلَّهِ مَا فِى ٱلسَّمَٰوَٰتِ وَمَا فِى ٱلْأَرْضِ ۚ وَإِلَى ٱللَّهِ تُرْجَعُ
ٱلْأُمُورُ (١٠٩) كُنتُمْ خَيْرَ أُمَّةٍ أُخْرِجَتْ لِلنَّاسِ تَأْمُرُونَ
بِٱلْمَعْرُوفِ وَتَنْهَوْنَ عَنِ ٱلْمُنكَرِ وَتُؤْمِنُونَ بِٱللَّهِ ۗ وَلَوْ ءَامَنَ
أَهْلُ ٱلْكِتَٰبِ لَكَانَ خَيْرًا لَّهُم ۚ مِّنْهُمُ ٱلْمُؤْمِنُونَ وَأَكْثَرُهُمُ
ٱلْفَٰسِقُونَ (١١٠) لَن يَضُرُّوكُمْ إِلَّا أَذًى ۖ وَإِن يُقَٰتِلُوكُمْ
يُوَلُّوكُمُ ٱلْأَدْبَارَ ثُمَّ لَا يُنصَرُونَ (١١١) ضُرِبَتْ عَلَيْهِمُ ٱلذِّلَّةُ
أَيْنَ مَا ثُقِفُوٓا۟ إِلَّا بِحَبْلٍ مِّنَ ٱللَّهِ وَحَبْلٍ مِّنَ ٱلنَّاسِ وَبَآءُو
بِغَضَبٍ مِّنَ ٱللَّهِ وَضُرِبَتْ عَلَيْهِمُ ٱلْمَسْكَنَةُ ۚ ذَٰلِكَ بِأَنَّهُمْ كَانُوا۟
يَكْفُرُونَ بِـَٔايَٰتِ ٱللَّهِ وَيَقْتُلُونَ ٱلْأَنۢبِيَآءَ بِغَيْرِ حَقٍّ ۚ ذَٰلِكَ بِمَا
عَصَوا۟ وَّكَانُوا۟ يَعْتَدُونَ (١١٢) ۞ لَيْسُوا۟ سَوَآءً ۗ مِّنْ أَهْلِ
ٱلْكِتَٰبِ أُمَّةٌ قَآئِمَةٌ يَتْلُونَ ءَايَٰتِ ٱللَّهِ ءَانَآءَ ٱلَّيْلِ وَهُمْ يَسْجُدُونَ
(١١٣) يُؤْمِنُونَ بِٱللَّهِ وَٱلْيَوْمِ ٱلْأَخِرِ وَيَأْمُرُونَ بِٱلْمَعْرُوفِ
وَيَنْهَوْنَ عَنِ ٱلْمُنكَرِ وَيُسَٰرِعُونَ فِى ٱلْخَيْرَٰتِ وَأُو۟لَٰٓئِكَ مِنَ
ٱلصَّٰلِحِينَ (١١٤) وَمَا يَفْعَلُوا۟ مِنْ خَيْرٍ فَلَن يُكْفَرُوهُ ۗ وَٱللَّهُ
عَلِيمٌ بِٱلْمُتَّقِينَ (١١٥) إِنَّ ٱلَّذِينَ كَفَرُوا۟ لَن تُغْنِىَ عَنْهُمْ
أَمْوَٰلُهُمْ وَلَآ أَوْلَٰدُهُم مِّنَ ٱللَّهِ شَيْـًٔا ۖ وَأُو۟لَٰٓئِكَ أَصْحَٰبُ ٱلنَّارِ ۚ هُمْ
فِيهَا خَٰلِدُونَ (١١٦)

*Let there arise out of you a group of people inviting to all that is good (Islâm), enjoining Al-Ma'rûf (i.e. Islâmic Monotheism and all that Islâm orders one to do) and forbidding Al-Munkar (polytheism and disbelief and all that Islâm has forbidden). And it is they who are the successful. (104) And be not as those who divided and* differed among themselves after the clear proofs had come to them. It is they for whom there is an awful torment. (105) On the Day (i.e. the Day of Resurrection) when some faces will become white and some faces will become black; as for those whose faces will become black (to them will be said): "Did you reject Faith after accepting it? Then taste the torment (in Hell) for rejecting Faith." (106) And for those whose faces will become white, they will be in Allâh's Mercy (Paradise), therein they shall dwell forever. (107) These are the Verses of Allâh: We recite them to you (O Muhammad) in truth, and Allâh wills no injustice to the 'Alâmîn (mankind and jinn all that exist). (108) And to Allâh belongs all that is in the heavens and all that is in the earth. And all matters go back (for decision) to Allâh. (109) You [true believers in Islâmic Monotheism, and real followers of Prophet Muhammad and his Sunnah] are the best of peoples ever raised up for mankind; you enjoin Al-Ma'rûf (i.e. Islâmic Monotheism and all that Islâm has ordained) and forbid Al-Munkar (polytheism, disbelief and all that Islâm has forbidden), and you believe in Allâh. And had the people of the Scripture (Jews and Christians) believed, it would have been better for them; among them are some who have faith, but most of them are Al-Fâsiqûn (disobedient to Allâh - and rebellious against Allâh's Command). (110) They will do you no harm, barring a trifling annoyance; and if they fight against you, they will show *you their backs, and they will not be helped. (111) Indignity is put over them wherever they may be, except when under a covenant (of protection) from Allâh, and from men; they have drawn on themselves the Wrath of Allâh, and destruction is put over them. This is because they disbelieved in the Ayât (proofs, evidences, verses, lessons, signs, revelations, etc.) of Allâh and killed the Prophets without right. This is because they disobeyed (Allâh) and used to transgress beyond bounds (in Allâh's disobedience, crimes and sins). (112) Not all of them are alike; a party of the people of the Scripture stand for the right, they recite the Verses of Allâh during the hours of the night, prostrating themselves in prayer. (113) They believe in Allâh and the Last Day; they enjoin Al-Ma'rûf (Islâmic Monotheism, and following Prophet Muhammad) and forbid Al-Munkar (polytheism, disbelief and opposing Prophet Muhammad); and they hasten in (all) good works; and they are among the righteous. (114) And whatever good they do, nothing will be rejected of them; for Allâh knows well those who are Al-Muttaqûn (the pious ). (115) Surely, those who reject Faith (disbelieve Allah and in Muhammad as being Allâh's Messenger and in all that which he has brought from Allâh), neither their properties, nor their offspring will avail them aught against Allâh. They are the dwellers of the Fire, therein they will abide. (116)*

**Quran 3:118-120**

يَـٰٓأَيُّهَا ٱلَّذِينَ ءَامَنُواْ لَا تَتَّخِذُواْ بِطَانَةً مِّن دُونِكُمْ لَا يَأْلُونَكُمْ خَبَالاً وَدُّواْ مَا عَنِتُّمْ قَدْ بَدَتِ ٱلْبَغْضَآءُ مِنْ أَفْوَٰهِهِمْ وَمَا تُخْفِى صُدُورُهُمْ أَكْبَرُ قَدْ بَيَّنَّا لَكُمُ ٱلْأَيَـٰتِ إِن كُنتُمْ تَعْقِلُونَ (١١٨) هَـٰٓأَنتُمْ أُوْلَآءِ تُحِبُّونَهُمْ وَلَا يُحِبُّونَكُمْ وَتُؤْمِنُونَ بِٱلْكِتَـٰبِ كُلِّهِ وَإِذَا لَقُوكُمْ قَالُوٓاْ ءَامَنَّا وَإِذَا خَلَوْاْ عَضُّواْ عَلَيْكُمُ ٱلْأَنَامِلَ مِنَ ٱلْغَيْظِ قُلْ مُوتُواْ بِغَيْظِكُمْ إِنَّ ٱللَّهَ عَلِيمٌ بِذَاتِ ٱلصُّدُورِ (١١٩) إِن تَمْسَسْكُمْ حَسَنَةٌ تَسُؤْهُمْ وَإِن تُصِبْكُمْ سَيِّئَةٌ يَفْرَحُواْ بِهَا وَإِن تَصْبِرُواْ وَتَتَّقُواْ لَا يَضُرُّكُمْ كَيْدُهُمْ شَيْئًا إِنَّ ٱللَّهَ بِمَا يَعْمَلُونَ مُحِيطٌ (١٢٠)

*O you who believe! Take not as (your) Bitânah (advisors, consultants, protectors, helpers, friends) those outside your religion (pagans, Jews, Christians, and hypocrites) since they will not fail to do their best to corrupt you. They desire to harm you severely. Hatred has already appeared from their mouths, but what their breasts conceal is far worse. Indeed We have made plain to you the Ayât (proofs, evidences, verses) if you understand. (118) Lo! You are the ones who love them but they love you not, and you believe in all the Scriptures [i.e. you believe in the Taurât (Torah) and the Injeel, while they disbelieve in your Book, the Qur'ân]. And when they meet you, they say, "We believe". But when they are alone, they bite the tips of their fingers at you in rage. Say: "Perish in your rage. Certainly, Allâh knows what is in the breasts (all the secrets)." (119) If a good befalls you, it grieves them, but if some evil overtakes you, they* rejoice at it. But if you remain patient and become Al-Muttaqûn (the pious), not the least harm will their cunning do to you. Surely, Allâh surrounds all that they do. (120)

## Quran 3:124-127

إِذْ تَقُولُ لِلْمُؤْمِنِينَ أَلَن يَكْفِيَكُمْ أَن يُمِدَّكُمْ رَبُّكُم بِثَلَثَةِ ءَالَفٍ مِّنَ ٱلْمَلَٰئِكَةِ مُنزَلِينَ (١٢٤) بَلَىٰٓ إِن تَصْبِرُواْ وَتَتَّقُواْ وَيَأْتُوكُم مِّن فَوْرِهِمْ هَٰذَا يُمْدِدْكُمْ رَبُّكُم بِخَمْسَةِ ءَالَفٍ مِّنَ ٱلْمَلَٰئِكَةِ مُسَوِّمِينَ (١٢٥) وَمَا جَعَلَهُ ٱللَّهُ إِلَّا بُشْرَىٰ لَكُمْ وَلِتَطْمَئِنَّ قُلُوبُكُم بِهِۦ وَمَا ٱلنَّصْرُ إِلَّا مِنْ عِندِ ٱللَّهِ ٱلْعَزِيزِ ٱلْحَكِيمِ (١٢٦) لِيَقْطَعَ طَرَفًا مِّنَ ٱلَّذِينَ كَفَرُواْ أَوْ يَكْبِتَهُمْ فَيَنقَلِبُواْ خَآئِبِينَ (١٢٧)

(Remember) when you (Muhammad) said to the believers, "Is it not enough for you that your Lord (Allâh) should help you with three thousand angels; sent down?" (124) "Yes, if you hold on to patience and piety, and the enemy comes rushing at you; your Lord will help you with five thousand angels having marks (of distinction)." (125) Allâh made it not but as a message of good news for you and as an assurance to your hearts. And there is no victory except from Allâh, the All-Mighty, the All-Wise. (126) That He might cut off a part of those who disbelieve, or expose them to infamy, so that they retire frustrated. (127)

## Quran 3:130-136

يَـٰٓأَيُّهَا ٱلَّذِينَ ءَامَنُوا۟ لَا تَأْكُلُوا۟ ٱلرِّبَوٰٓا۟ أَضْعَـٰفًا مُّضَـٰعَفَةً ۖ وَٱتَّقُوا۟ ٱللَّهَ لَعَلَّكُمْ تُفْلِحُونَ (١٣٠) وَٱتَّقُوا۟ ٱلنَّارَ ٱلَّتِىٓ أُعِدَّتْ لِلْكَـٰفِرِينَ (١٣١) وَأَطِيعُوا۟ ٱللَّهَ وَٱلرَّسُولَ لَعَلَّكُمْ تُرْحَمُونَ (١٣٢) ۞ وَسَارِعُوٓا۟ إِلَىٰ مَغْفِرَةٍ مِّن رَّبِّكُمْ وَجَنَّةٍ عَرْضُهَا ٱلسَّمَـٰوَٰتُ وَٱلْأَرْضُ أُعِدَّتْ لِلْمُتَّقِينَ (١٣٣) ٱلَّذِينَ يُنفِقُونَ فِى ٱلسَّرَّآءِ وَٱلضَّرَّآءِ وَٱلْكَـٰظِمِينَ ٱلْغَيْظَ وَٱلْعَافِينَ عَنِ ٱلنَّاسِ ۗ وَٱللَّهُ يُحِبُّ ٱلْمُحْسِنِينَ (١٣٤) وَٱلَّذِينَ إِذَا فَعَلُوا۟ فَـٰحِشَةً أَوْ ظَلَمُوٓا۟ أَنفُسَهُمْ ذَكَرُوا۟ ٱللَّهَ فَٱسْتَغْفَرُوا۟ لِذُنُوبِهِمْ وَمَن يَغْفِرُ ٱلذُّنُوبَ إِلَّا ٱللَّهُ وَلَمْ يُصِرُّوا۟ عَلَىٰ مَا فَعَلُوا۟ وَهُمْ يَعْلَمُونَ (١٣٥) أُو۟لَـٰٓئِكَ جَزَآؤُهُم مَّغْفِرَةٌ مِّن رَّبِّهِمْ وَجَنَّـٰتٌ تَجْرِى مِن تَحْتِهَا ٱلْأَنْهَـٰرُ خَـٰلِدِينَ فِيهَا ۚ وَنِعْمَ أَجْرُ ٱلْعَـٰمِلِينَ (١٣٦)

O you who believe! Eat not Ribâ (usury) doubled and multiplied, but fear Allâh that you may be successful. (130) And fear the Fire, which is prepared for the disbelievers. (131) And obey Allâh and the Messenger (Muhammad) that you may obtain mercy. (132) And march forth in the way (which leads to) forgiveness from your Lord, and for Paradise as wide as are the heavens and the earth, prepared for Al-Muttaqûn (the pious). (133) Those who spend [in Allâh's Cause] in prosperity and in adversity, who repress anger, and who pardon men; verily, Allâh loves Al-Muhsinûn (the good - doers). (134) And those who, when they have committed Fahishah (illegal sexual intercourse) or wronged themselves with evil, remember Allâh and ask forgiveness for their sins; - and none can forgive sins but Allâh - And do not persist in what (wrong) they have done, while they know. (135) For such, the reward is Forgiveness from their Lord, and Gardens with rivers flowing underneath (Paradise), wherein they shall abide forever. How excellent is this reward for the doers (who do righteous deeds according to Allâh's Orders). (136)

## Quran 3:138-145

هَٰذَا بَيَانٌ لِّلنَّاسِ وَهُدًى وَمَوْعِظَةٌ لِّلْمُتَّقِينَ (١٣٨) وَلَا تَهِنُواْ وَلَا تَحْزَنُواْ وَأَنتُمُ ٱلْأَعْلَوْنَ إِن كُنتُم مُّؤْمِنِينَ (١٣٩) إِن يَمْسَسْكُمْ قَرْحٌ فَقَدْ مَسَّ ٱلْقَوْمَ قَرْحٌ مِّثْلُهُۥ وَتِلْكَ ٱلْأَيَّامُ نُدَاوِلُهَا بَيْنَ ٱلنَّاسِ وَلِيَعْلَمَ ٱللَّهُ ٱلَّذِينَ ءَامَنُواْ وَيَتَّخِذَ مِنكُمْ شُهَدَآءَ وَٱللَّهُ لَا يُحِبُّ ٱلظَّٰلِمِينَ (١٤٠) وَلِيُمَحِّصَ ٱللَّهُ ٱلَّذِينَ ءَامَنُواْ وَيَمْحَقَ ٱلْكَٰفِرِينَ (١٤١) أَمْ حَسِبْتُمْ أَن تَدْخُلُواْ ٱلْجَنَّةَ وَلَمَّا يَعْلَمِ ٱللَّهُ ٱلَّذِينَ جَٰهَدُواْ مِنكُمْ وَيَعْلَمَ ٱلصَّٰبِرِينَ (١٤٢) وَلَقَدْ كُنتُمْ تَمَنَّوْنَ ٱلْمَوْتَ مِن قَبْلِ أَن تَلْقَوْهُ فَقَدْ رَأَيْتُمُوهُ وَأَنتُمْ تَنظُرُونَ (١٤٣) وَمَا مُحَمَّدٌ إِلَّا رَسُولٌ قَدْ خَلَتْ مِن قَبْلِهِ ٱلرُّسُلُ أَفَإِيْن مَّاتَ أَوْ قُتِلَ ٱنقَلَبْتُمْ عَلَىٰٓ أَعْقَٰبِكُمْ وَمَن يَنقَلِبْ عَلَىٰ عَقِبَيْهِ فَلَن يَضُرَّ ٱللَّهَ شَيْئًا وَسَيَجْزِى ٱللَّهُ ٱلشَّٰكِرِينَ (١٤٤) وَمَا كَانَ لِنَفْسٍ أَن تَمُوتَ إِلَّا بِإِذْنِ ٱللَّهِ كِتَٰبًا مُّؤَجَّلًا وَمَن يُرِدْ ثَوَابَ ٱلدُّنْيَا نُؤْتِهِۦ مِنْهَا وَمَن يُرِدْ ثَوَابَ ٱلْأَخِرَةِ نُؤْتِهِۦ مِنْهَا وَسَنَجْزِى ٱلشَّٰكِرِينَ (١٤٥)

This (the Qur'ân) is a plain statement for mankind, a guidance and instruction to those who are Al-Muttaqûn (the pious). (138) So do not become weak (against your *enemy), nor be sad, and you will be superior (in victory) if you are indeed (true) believers. (139) If a wound (and killing) has touched you, be sure a similar wound (and killing) has touched the others. And so are the days (good and not so good), We give to men by turns, that Allâh may test those who believe, and that He may take martyrs from among you. And Allâh likes not the Zâlimûn (polytheists and wrong¬doers). (140) And that Allâh may test (or purify) the believers (from sins) and destroy the disbelievers (141) Do you think that you will enter Paradise before Allâh tests those of you who fought (in His Cause) and (also) tests those who are As-Sâbirun (the patient)? (142) You did indeed wish for death (Ash¬Shahâdah - martyrdom) before you met it. Now you have seen it openly with your own eyes. (143) Muhammad is no more than a Messenger, and indeed (many) Messengers have passed away before him. If he dies or is killed, will you then turn back on your heels (as disbelievers)? And he who turns back on his heels, not the least harm will he do to Allâh, and Allâh will give reward to those who are grateful. (144) And no person can ever die except by Allâh's Leave and at an appointed term. And whoever desires a reward in (this) world, We shall give him of it; and whoever desires a reward in the Hereafter, We shall give him thereof. And We shall reward the grateful. (145)*

**Quran 3:149-152**

يَـٰٓأَيُّهَا ٱلَّذِينَ ءَامَنُوٓاْ إِن تُطِيعُواْ ٱلَّذِينَ كَفَرُواْ يَرُدُّوكُمْ عَلَىٰٓ أَعْقَـٰبِكُمْ فَتَنقَلِبُواْ خَـٰسِرِينَ (١٤٩) بَلِ ٱللَّهُ مَوْلَـٰكُمْۖ وَهُوَ خَيْرُ ٱلنَّـٰصِرِينَ (١٥٠) سَنُلْقِى فِى قُلُوبِ ٱلَّذِينَ كَفَرُواْ ٱلرُّعْبَ بِمَآ أَشْرَكُواْ بِٱللَّهِ مَا لَمْ يُنَزِّلْ بِهِۦ سُلْطَـٰنًاۖ وَمَأْوَىٰهُمُ ٱلنَّارُۚ وَبِئْسَ مَثْوَى ٱلظَّـٰلِمِينَ (١٥١) وَلَقَدْ صَدَقَكُمُ ٱللَّهُ وَعْدَهُۥٓ إِذْ تَحُسُّونَهُم بِإِذْنِهِۦۖ حَتَّىٰٓ إِذَا فَشِلْتُمْ وَتَنَـٰزَعْتُمْ فِى ٱلْأَمْرِ وَعَصَيْتُم مِّنۢ بَعْدِ مَآ أَرَىٰكُم مَّا تُحِبُّونَۚ مِنكُم مَّن يُرِيدُ ٱلدُّنْيَا وَمِنكُم مَّن يُرِيدُ ٱلْأَخِرَةَۚ ثُمَّ صَرَفَكُمْ عَنْهُمْ لِيَبْتَلِيَكُمْۖ وَلَقَدْ عَفَا عَنكُمْۗ وَٱللَّهُ ذُو فَضْلٍ عَلَى ٱلْمُؤْمِنِينَ (١٥٢)

*O you who believe! If you obey those who disbelieve, they will send you back on your heels, and you will turn back (from Faith) as losers. (149) Nay, Allâh is your Maulâ (Patron, Lord, Helper and Protector), and He is the Best of helpers. (150) We shall cast terror into the hearts of those who disbelieve, because they joined others in worship with Allâh, for which He had sent no authority; their abode will be the Fire and how evil is the abode of the Zâlimûn (polytheists and wrong¬doers). (151) And Allâh did indeed fulfil His Promise to you when you were killing them (your enemy) with His Permission; until (the moment) you lost your courage and fell to disputing about the order, and disobeyed after He showed you (of the booty) which you love. Among you are some that desire this world and some that desire the Hereafter. Then He made you flee from them (your enemy), that He*

might test you. But surely, He forgave you, and Allâh is
Most Gracious to the believers. (152)

## Quran 3:157-158

وَلَئِن قُتِلْتُمْ فِى سَبِيلِ ٱللَّهِ أَوْ مُتُّمْ لَمَغْفِرَةٌ مِّنَ ٱللَّهِ وَرَحْمَةٌ خَيْرٌ
مِّمَّا يَجْمَعُونَ (١٥٧) وَلَئِن مُّتُّمْ أَوْ قُتِلْتُمْ لَإِلَى ٱللَّهِ تُحْشَرُونَ
(١٥٨)

And if you are killed or die in the Way of Allâh,
forgiveness and mercy from Allâh are far better than all
that they amass. (157) And whether you die, or are killed,
verily, unto Allâh you shall be gathered. (158)

## Quran 3:160-162

إِن يَنصُرْكُمُ ٱللَّهُ فَلَا غَالِبَ لَكُمْ وَإِن يَخْذُلْكُمْ فَمَن ذَا ٱلَّذِى
يَنصُرُكُم مِّنۢ بَعْدِهِۦ وَعَلَى ٱللَّهِ فَلْيَتَوَكَّلِ ٱلْمُؤْمِنُونَ (١٦٠) وَمَا
كَانَ لِنَبِىٍّ أَن يَغُلَّ وَمَن يَغْلُلْ يَأْتِ بِمَا غَلَّ يَوْمَ ٱلْقِيَٰمَةِ ثُمَّ
تُوَفَّىٰ كُلُّ نَفْسٍ مَّا كَسَبَتْ وَهُمْ لَا يُظْلَمُونَ (١٦١) أَفَمَنِ
ٱتَّبَعَ رِضْوَٰنَ ٱللَّهِ كَمَنۢ بَآءَ بِسَخَطٍ مِّنَ ٱللَّهِ وَمَأْوَىٰهُ جَهَنَّمُ
وَبِئْسَ ٱلْمَصِيرُ (١٦٢)

If Allâh helps you, none can overcome you; and if He
forsakes you, who is there after Him that can help you?
And in Allâh (Alone) let believers put their trust. (160)
It is not for any Prophet to take illegally a part of booty
(Ghulul), and whosoever deceives his companions as
regards the booty, he shall bring forth on the Day of
Resurrection that which he took (illegally). Then every

43

*person shall be paid in full what he has earned, - and they shall not be dealt with unjustly. (161) Is then one who follows (seeks) the good Pleasure of Allâh (by not taking illegally a part of the booty) like the one who draws on himself the Wrath of Allâh (by taking a part of the booty illegally - Ghulul)? - his abode is Hell, - and worst, indeed is that destination! (162)*

## Quran 3:169-172

وَلَا تَحْسَبَنَّ ٱلَّذِينَ قُتِلُوا۟ فِى سَبِيلِ ٱللَّهِ أَمْوَٰتًۢا بَلْ أَحْيَآءٌ عِندَ رَبِّهِمْ يُرْزَقُونَ (١٦٩) فَرِحِينَ بِمَآ ءَاتَىٰهُمُ ٱللَّهُ مِن فَضْلِهِۦ وَيَسْتَبْشِرُونَ بِٱلَّذِينَ لَمْ يَلْحَقُوا۟ بِهِم مِّنْ خَلْفِهِمْ أَلَّا خَوْفٌ عَلَيْهِمْ وَلَا هُمْ يَحْزَنُونَ (١٧٠) ۞ يَسْتَبْشِرُونَ بِنِعْمَةٍ مِّنَ ٱللَّهِ وَفَضْلٍ وَأَنَّ ٱللَّهَ لَا يُضِيعُ أَجْرَ ٱلْمُؤْمِنِينَ (١٧١) ٱلَّذِينَ ٱسْتَجَابُوا۟ لِلَّهِ وَٱلرَّسُولِ مِنۢ بَعْدِ مَآ أَصَابَهُمُ ٱلْقَرْحُ لِلَّذِينَ أَحْسَنُوا۟ مِنْهُمْ وَٱتَّقَوْا۟ أَجْرٌ عَظِيمٌ (١٧٢)

*Think not of those who are killed in the Way of Allâh as dead. Nay, they are alive, with their Lord, and they have provision- (169) They rejoice in what Allâh has bestowed upon them of His Bounty, rejoice for the sake of those who have not yet joined them, but are left behind (not yet martyred) that on them no fear shall come, nor shall they grieve. (170) They rejoice in a Grace and a Bounty from Allâh, and that Allâh will not waste the reward of the believers. (171) Those who answered (the Call of) Allâh and the Messenger (Muhammad) after being wounded;*

*for those of them who did good deeds and feared Allâh,*
*there is a great reward.* (172)

## Quran 3:175-182

إِنَّمَا ذَٰلِكُمُ ٱلشَّيْطَٰنُ يُخَوِّفُ أَوْلِيَآءَهُۥ فَلَا تَخَافُوهُمْ وَخَافُونِ إِن
كُنتُم مُّؤْمِنِينَ (١٧٥) وَلَا يَحْزُنكَ ٱلَّذِينَ يُسَٰرِعُونَ فِى ٱلْكُفْرِ
إِنَّهُمْ لَن يَضُرُّواْ ٱللَّهَ شَيْـًٔا يُرِيدُ ٱللَّهُ أَلَّا يَجْعَلَ لَهُمْ حَظًّا فِى
ٱلْءَاخِرَةِ وَلَهُمْ عَذَابٌ عَظِيمٌ (١٧٦) إِنَّ ٱلَّذِينَ ٱشْتَرَوُاْ ٱلْكُفْرَ
بِٱلْإِيمَٰنِ لَن يَضُرُّواْ ٱللَّهَ شَيْـًٔا وَلَهُمْ عَذَابٌ أَلِيمٌ (١٧٧) وَلَا
يَحْسَبَنَّ ٱلَّذِينَ كَفَرُوٓاْ أَنَّمَا نُمْلِى لَهُمْ خَيْرٌ لِّأَنفُسِهِمْ إِنَّمَا نُمْلِى
لَهُمْ لِيَزْدَادُوٓاْ إِثْمًا وَلَهُمْ عَذَابٌ مُّهِينٌ (١٧٨) مَّا كَانَ ٱللَّهُ لِيَذَرَ
ٱلْمُؤْمِنِينَ عَلَىٰ مَآ أَنتُمْ عَلَيْهِ حَتَّىٰ يَمِيزَ ٱلْخَبِيثَ مِنَ ٱلطَّيِّبِ
وَمَا كَانَ ٱللَّهُ لِيُطْلِعَكُمْ عَلَى ٱلْغَيْبِ وَلَٰكِنَّ ٱللَّهَ يَجْتَبِى مِن رُّسُلِهِۦ
مَن يَشَآءُ فَـَٔامِنُواْ بِٱللَّهِ وَرُسُلِهِۦ وَإِن تُؤْمِنُواْ وَتَتَّقُواْ فَلَكُمْ أَجْرٌ
عَظِيمٌ (١٧٩) وَلَا يَحْسَبَنَّ ٱلَّذِينَ يَبْخَلُونَ بِمَآ ءَاتَىٰهُمُ ٱللَّهُ مِن
فَضْلِهِۦ هُوَ خَيْرًا لَّهُم بَلْ هُوَ شَرٌّ لَّهُمْ سَيُطَوَّقُونَ مَا بَخِلُواْ بِهِۦ
يَوْمَ ٱلْقِيَٰمَةِ وَلِلَّهِ مِيرَٰثُ ٱلسَّمَٰوَٰتِ وَٱلْأَرْضِ وَٱللَّهُ بِمَا
تَعْمَلُونَ خَبِيرٌ (١٨٠) لَّقَدْ سَمِعَ ٱللَّهُ قَوْلَ ٱلَّذِينَ قَالُوٓاْ إِنَّ ٱللَّهَ
فَقِيرٌ وَنَحْنُ أَغْنِيَآءُ سَنَكْتُبُ مَا قَالُواْ وَقَتْلَهُمُ ٱلْأَنۢبِيَآءَ بِغَيْرِ حَقٍّ
وَنَقُولُ ذُوقُواْ عَذَابَ ٱلْحَرِيقِ (١٨١) ذَٰلِكَ بِمَا قَدَّمَتْ أَيْدِيكُمْ
وَأَنَّ ٱللَّهَ لَيْسَ بِظَلَّٰمٍ لِّلْعَبِيدِ (١٨٢)

*It is only Shaitân (Satan) that suggests to you the fear of*
*his Auliyâ' [supporters and friends (polytheists,*
*disbelievers in the Oneness of Allâh and in His*
*Messenger, Muhammad)], so fear them not, but fear Me,*

*if you are (true) believers. (175) And let not those grieve you who rush with haste to disbelieve; verily, not the least harm will they do to Allâh. It is Allâh's Will to give them no portion in the Hereafter. For them there is a great torment. (176) Verily, those who purchase disbelief at the price of Faith, not the least harm will they do to Allâh. For them, there is a painful torment. (177) And let not the disbelievers think that Our postponing of their punishment is good for them. We postpone the punishment only so that they may increase in sinfulness. And for them is a disgracing torment. (178) Allâh will not leave the believers in the state in which you are now, until He distinguishes the wicked from the good. Nor will Allâh disclose to you the secrets of the Ghaib (unseen), but Allâh chooses of His Messengers whom He wills. So believe in Allâh and His Messengers. And if you believe and fear Allâh, then for you there is a great reward. (179) And let not those who covetously withhold of that which Allâh has bestowed on them of His Bounty (Wealth) think that it is good for them (and so they do not pay the obligatory Zakât). Nay, it will be worse for them; the things which they covetously withheld shall be tied to their necks like a collar on the Day of Resurrection. And to Allâh belongs the heritage of the heavens and the earth; and Allâh is Well¬Acquainted with all that you do. (180) Indeed, Allâh has heard the statement of those (Jews) who say: "Truly, Allâh is poor and we are rich!" We shall* record what they have said and their killing of the Prophets unjustly, and We shall say: "Taste you the torment of the burning (Fire)." (181) This is because of that (evil) which your hands have sent before you. And certainly, Allâh is never unjust to (His) slaves. (182)

## Quran 3:185-188

كُلُّ نَفْسٍ ذَآئِقَةُ ٱلْمَوْتِ وَإِنَّمَا تُوَفَّوْنَ أُجُورَكُمْ يَوْمَ ٱلْقِيَـٰمَةِ فَمَن زُحْزِحَ عَنِ ٱلنَّارِ وَأُدْخِلَ ٱلْجَنَّةَ فَقَدْ فَازَ وَمَا ٱلْحَيَوٰةُ ٱلدُّنْيَا إِلَّا مَتَـٰعُ ٱلْغُرُورِ (١٨٥) ۞ لَتُبْلَوُنَّ فِىٓ أَمْوَٰلِكُمْ وَأَنفُسِكُمْ وَلَتَسْمَعُنَّ مِنَ ٱلَّذِينَ أُوتُواْ ٱلْكِتَـٰبَ مِن قَبْلِكُمْ وَمِنَ ٱلَّذِينَ أَشْرَكُواْ أَذًى كَثِيرًا وَإِن تَصْبِرُواْ وَتَتَّقُواْ فَإِنَّ ذَٰلِكَ مِنْ عَزْمِ ٱلْأُمُورِ (١٨٦) وَإِذْ أَخَذَ ٱللَّهُ مِيثَـٰقَ ٱلَّذِينَ أُوتُواْ ٱلْكِتَـٰبَ لَتُبَيِّنُنَّهُۥ لِلنَّاسِ وَلَا تَكْتُمُونَهُۥ فَنَبَذُوهُ وَرَآءَ ظُهُورِهِمْ وَٱشْتَرَوْاْ بِهِۦ ثَمَنًا قَلِيلًا فَبِئْسَ مَا يَشْتَرُونَ (١٨٧) لَا تَحْسَبَنَّ ٱلَّذِينَ يَفْرَحُونَ بِمَآ أَتَواْ وَّيُحِبُّونَ أَن يُحْمَدُواْ بِمَا لَمْ يَفْعَلُواْ فَلَا تَحْسَبَنَّهُم بِمَفَازَةٍ مِّنَ ٱلْعَذَابِ وَلَهُمْ عَذَابٌ أَلِيمٌ (١٨٨)

Everyone shall taste death. And only on the Day of Resurrection shall you be paid your wages in full. And whoever is removed away from the Fire and admitted to Paradise, he indeed is successful. The life of this world is only the enjoyment of deception (a deceiving thing). (185) You shall certainly be tried and tested in your wealth and properties and in your personal selves, and you shall certainly hear much that will grieve you from those who received the Scripture before you (Jews and

Christians) and from those who ascribe partners to Allâh; but if you persevere patiently, and become Al-Muttaqûn (the pious) then verily, that will be a determining factor in all affairs. (186) (And remember) when Allâh took a covenant from those who were given the Scripture (Jews and Christians) to make it (the news of the coming of Prophet Muhammad and the religious knowledge) known and clear to mankind, and not to hide it, but they threw it away behind their backs, and purchased with it some miserable gain! And indeed worst is that which they bought. (187) Think not that those who rejoice in what they have done, and love to be praised for what they have not done,- think not you that they are rescued from the torment, and for them is a painful torment. (188)

## Quran 3:191-200

ٱلَّذِينَ يَذْكُرُونَ ٱللَّهَ قِيَـٰمًا وَقُعُودًا وَعَلَىٰ جُنُوبِهِمْ وَيَتَفَكَّرُونَ
فِى خَلْقِ ٱلسَّمَـٰوَٰتِ وَٱلْأَرْضِ رَبَّنَا مَا خَلَقْتَ هَـٰذَا بَـٰطِلًا
سُبْحَـٰنَكَ فَقِنَا عَذَابَ ٱلنَّارِ (١٩١) رَبَّنَآ إِنَّكَ مَن تُدْخِلِ ٱلنَّارَ
فَقَدْ أَخْزَيْتَهُۥ ۖ وَمَا لِلظَّـٰلِمِينَ مِنْ أَنصَارٍ (١٩٢) رَبَّنَآ إِنَّنَا
سَمِعْنَا مُنَادِيًا يُنَادِى لِلْإِيمَـٰنِ أَنْ ءَامِنُوا۟ بِرَبِّكُمْ فَـَٔامَنَّا ۚ رَبَّنَا
فَٱغْفِرْ لَنَا ذُنُوبَنَا وَكَفِّرْ عَنَّا سَيِّـَٔاتِنَا وَتَوَفَّنَا مَعَ ٱلْأَبْرَارِ
(١٩٣) رَبَّنَا وَءَاتِنَا مَا وَعَدتَّنَا عَلَىٰ رُسُلِكَ وَلَا تُخْزِنَا يَوْمَ
ٱلْقِيَـٰمَةِ ۗ إِنَّكَ لَا تُخْلِفُ ٱلْمِيعَادَ (١٩٤) فَٱسْتَجَابَ لَهُمْ رَبُّهُمْ أَنِّى
لَا أُضِيعُ عَمَلَ عَـٰمِلٍ مِّنكُم مِّن ذَكَرٍ أَوْ أُنثَىٰ ۖ بَعْضُكُم مِّنۢ
بَعْضٍ ۖ فَٱلَّذِينَ هَاجَرُوا۟ وَأُخْرِجُوا۟ مِن دِيَـٰرِهِمْ وَأُوذُوا۟ فِى

سَبِيلِى وَقَـٰتَلُواْ وَقُتِلُواْ لَأُكَفِّرَنَّ عَنْهُمْ سَيِّئَاتِهِمْ وَلَأُدْخِلَنَّهُمْ جَنَّـٰتٍ تَجْرِى مِن تَحْتِهَا ٱلْأَنْهَٰرُ ثَوَابًا مِّنْ عِندِ ٱللَّهِ وَٱللَّهُ عِندَهُۥ حُسْنُ ٱلثَّوَابِ (١٩٥) لَا يَغُرَّنَّكَ تَقَلُّبُ ٱلَّذِينَ كَفَرُواْ فِى ٱلْبِلَٰدِ (١٩٦) مَتَٰعٌ قَلِيلٌ ثُمَّ مَأْوَىٰهُمْ جَهَنَّمُ وَبِئْسَ ٱلْمِهَادُ (١٩٧) لَـٰكِنِ ٱلَّذِينَ ٱتَّقَوْاْ رَبَّهُمْ لَهُمْ جَنَّـٰتٌ تَجْرِى مِن تَحْتِهَا ٱلْأَنْهَٰرُ خَٰلِدِينَ فِيهَا نُزُلًا مِّنْ عِندِ ٱللَّهِ وَمَا عِندَ ٱللَّهِ خَيْرٌ لِّلْأَبْرَارِ (١٩٨) وَإِنَّ مِنْ أَهْلِ ٱلْكِتَٰبِ لَمَن يُؤْمِنُ بِٱللَّهِ وَمَا أُنزِلَ إِلَيْكُمْ وَمَا أُنزِلَ إِلَيْهِمْ خَٰشِعِينَ لِلَّهِ لَا يَشْتَرُونَ بِـَٔايَٰتِ ٱللَّهِ ثَمَنًا قَلِيلًا أُوْلَـٰئِكَ لَهُمْ أَجْرُهُمْ عِندَ رَبِّهِمْ إِنَّ ٱللَّهَ سَرِيعُ ٱلْحِسَابِ (١٩٩) يَـٰٓأَيُّهَا ٱلَّذِينَ ءَامَنُواْ ٱصْبِرُواْ وَصَابِرُواْ وَرَابِطُواْ وَٱتَّقُواْ ٱللَّهَ لَعَلَّكُمْ تُفْلِحُونَ (٢٠٠)

*Those who remember Allâh (always, and in prayers)
standing, sitting, and lying down on their sides, and
think deeply about the creation of the heavens and the
earth, (saying): "Our Lord! You have not created (all)
this without purpose, glory to You! (Exalted are You
above all that they associate with You as partners). Give
us salvation from the torment of the Fire. (191) "Our
Lord! Verily, whom You admit to the Fire, indeed, You
have disgraced him, and never will the Zâlimûn
(polytheists and wrong-doers) find any helpers. (192)
"Our Lord! Verily, we have heard the call of one
(Muhammad) calling to Faith: 'Believe in your Lord,'
and we have believed. Our Lord! Forgive us our sins and
expiate from us our evil deeds, and make us die (in the
state of righteousness) along with Al-Abrâr (the pious*

*believers of Islamic Monotheism). (193) "Our Lord!*
*Grant us what You promised unto us through Your*
*Messengers and disgrace us not on the Day of*
*Resurrection, for You never break (Your) Promise."*
*(194) So their Lord accepted of them (their supplication*
*and answered them), "Never will I allow to be lost the*
*work of any of you, be he male or female. You are*
*(members) one of another, so those who emigrated and*
*were driven out from their homes, and suffered harm in*
*My Cause, and who fought, and were killed (in My*
*Cause), verily, I will expiate from them their evil deeds*
*and admit them into Gardens under which rivers flow (in*
*Paradise); a reward from Allâh, and with Allâh is the*
*best of rewards." (195) Let not the free disposal (and*
*affluence) of the disbelievers throughout the land deceive*
*you. (196) A brief enjoyment; then, their ultimate abode*
*is Hell; and worst indeed is that place for rest. (197) But,*
*for those who fear their Lord, are Gardens under which*
*rivers flow (in Paradise); therein are they to dwell (for*
*ever), an entertainment from Allâh; and that which is*
*with Allâh is the Best for Al-Abrâr (the pious believers of*
*Islamic Monotheism). (198) And there are, certainly,*
*among the people of the Scripture (Jews and Christians),*
*those who believe in Allâh and in that which has been*
*revealed to you, and in that which has been revealed to*
*them, humbling themselves before Allâh. They do not sell*
*the Verses of Allâh for a little price, for them is a reward*

with their Lord. Surely, Allâh is Swift in account. (199)
O you who believe! Endure and be more patient (than
your enemy), and guard your territory by stationing
army units permanently at the places from where the
enemy can attack you, and fear Allâh, so that you may be
successful. (200)

## Quran 4:10

إِنَّ ٱلَّذِينَ يَأْكُلُونَ أَمْوَالَ ٱلْيَتَـٰمَىٰ ظُلْمًا إِنَّمَا يَأْكُلُونَ فِى
بُطُونِهِمْ نَارًا ۖ وَسَيَصْلَوْنَ سَعِيرًا (١٠)

Verily, those who unjustly eat up the property of
orphans, they eat up only a fire into their bellies, and
they will be burnt in the blazing Fire! (10)

## Quran 4:13-14

تِلْكَ حُدُودُ ٱللَّهِ ۚ وَمَن يُطِعِ ٱللَّهَ وَرَسُولَهُ يُدْخِلْهُ جَنَّـٰتٍ تَجْرِى
مِن تَحْتِهَا ٱلْأَنْهَـٰرُ خَـٰلِدِينَ فِيهَا ۚ وَذَٰلِكَ ٱلْفَوْزُ ٱلْعَظِيمُ (١٣)
وَمَن يَعْصِ ٱللَّهَ وَرَسُولَهُ وَيَتَعَدَّ حُدُودَهُ يُدْخِلْهُ نَارًا خَـٰلِدًا
فِيهَا وَلَهُ عَذَابٌ مُّهِينٌ (١٤)

These are the limits (set by) Allâh (or ordainments as
regards laws of inheritance), and whosoever obeys Allâh
and His Messenger (Muhammad) will be admitted to
Gardens under which rivers flow (in Paradise), to abide
therein, and that will be the great success. (13) And
whosoever disobeys Allâh and His Messenger
(Muhammad), and transgresses His limits, He will cast

him into the Fire, to abide therein; and he shall have a
disgraceful torment. (14)

## Quran 4:17-18

إِنَّمَا ٱلتَّوْبَةُ عَلَى ٱللَّهِ لِلَّذِينَ يَعْمَلُونَ ٱلسُّوءَ بِجَهَٰلَةٍ ثُمَّ يَتُوبُونَ
مِن قَرِيبٍ فَأُوْلَٰٓئِكَ يَتُوبُ ٱللَّهُ عَلَيْهِمْۗ وَكَانَ ٱللَّهُ عَلِيمًا حَكِيمًا
(١٧) وَلَيْسَتِ ٱلتَّوْبَةُ لِلَّذِينَ يَعْمَلُونَ ٱلسَّيِّئَاتِ حَتَّىٰٓ إِذَا حَضَرَ
أَحَدَهُمُ ٱلْمَوْتُ قَالَ إِنِّى تُبْتُ ٱلْـَٰٔنَ وَلَا ٱلَّذِينَ يَمُوتُونَ وَهُمْ
كُفَّارٌۚ أُوْلَٰٓئِكَ أَعْتَدْنَا لَهُمْ عَذَابًا أَلِيمًا (١٨)

Allâh accepts only the repentance of those who do evil in
ignorance and foolishness and repent soon afterwards; it
is they whom Allâh will forgive and Allâh is Ever
All¬Knower, All¬Wise. (17) And of no effect is the
repentance of those who continue to do evil deeds until
death faces one of them and he says: "Now I repent;" nor
of those who die while they are disbelievers. For them We
have prepared a painful torment. (18)

## Quran 4:25-32

وَمَن لَّمْ يَسْتَطِعْ مِنكُمْ طَوْلاً أَن يَنكِحَ ٱلْمُحْصَنَٰتِ ٱلْمُؤْمِنَٰتِ
فَمِن مَّا مَلَكَتْ أَيْمَٰنُكُم مِّن فَتَيَٰتِكُمُ ٱلْمُؤْمِنَٰتِۚ وَٱللَّهُ أَعْلَمُ
بِإِيمَٰنِكُمْۚ بَعْضُكُم مِّن بَعْضٍۚ فَٱنكِحُوهُنَّ بِإِذْنِ أَهْلِهِنَّ وَءَاتُوهُنَّ
أُجُورَهُنَّ بِٱلْمَعْرُوفِ مُحْصَنَٰتٍ غَيْرَ مُسَٰفِحَٰتٍ وَلَا مُتَّخِذَٰتِ
أَخْدَانٍۚ فَإِذَآ أُحْصِنَّ فَإِنْ أَتَيْنَ بِفَٰحِشَةٍ فَعَلَيْهِنَّ نِصْفُ مَا عَلَى
ٱلْمُحْصَنَٰتِ مِنَ ٱلْعَذَابِۚ ذَٰلِكَ لِمَنْ خَشِىَ ٱلْعَنَتَ مِنكُمْۚ وَأَن
تَصْبِرُواْ خَيْرٌ لَّكُمْۗ وَٱللَّهُ غَفُورٌ رَّحِيمٌ (٢٥) يُرِيدُ ٱللَّهُ لِيُبَيِّنَ لَكُمْ

وَيَهْدِيَكُمْ سُنَنَ ٱلَّذِينَ مِن قَبْلِكُمْ وَيَتُوبَ عَلَيْكُمْ وَٱللَّهُ عَلِيمٌ حَكِيمٌ (٢٦) وَٱللَّهُ يُرِيدُ أَن يَتُوبَ عَلَيْكُمْ وَيُرِيدُ ٱلَّذِينَ يَتَّبِعُونَ ٱلشَّهَوَاتِ أَن تَمِيلُواْ مَيْلاً عَظِيمًا (٢٧) يُرِيدُ ٱللَّهُ أَن يُخَفِّفَ عَنكُمْ وَخُلِقَ ٱلْإِنسَانُ ضَعِيفًا (٢٨) يَٰٓأَيُّهَا ٱلَّذِينَ ءَامَنُواْ لَا تَأْكُلُوٓاْ أَمْوَٰلَكُم بَيْنَكُم بِٱلْبَٰطِلِ إِلَّآ أَن تَكُونَ تِجَٰرَةً عَن تَرَاضٍ مِّنكُمْ وَلَا تَقْتُلُوٓاْ أَنفُسَكُمْ إِنَّ ٱللَّهَ كَانَ بِكُمْ رَحِيمًا (٢٩) وَمَن يَفْعَلْ ذَٰلِكَ عُدْوَٰنًا وَظُلْمًا فَسَوْفَ نُصْلِيهِ نَارًا وَكَانَ ذَٰلِكَ عَلَى ٱللَّهِ يَسِيرًا (٣٠) إِن تَجْتَنِبُواْ كَبَآئِرَ مَا تُنْهَوْنَ عَنْهُ نُكَفِّرْ عَنكُمْ سَيِّـَٔاتِكُمْ وَنُدْخِلْكُم مُّدْخَلاً كَرِيمًا (٣١) وَلَا تَتَمَنَّوْاْ مَا فَضَّلَ ٱللَّهُ بِهِۦ بَعْضَكُمْ عَلَىٰ بَعْضٍ لِّلرِّجَالِ نَصِيبٌ مِّمَّا ٱكْتَسَبُواْ وَلِلنِّسَآءِ نَصِيبٌ مِّمَّا ٱكْتَسَبْنَ وَسْـَٔلُواْ ٱللَّهَ مِن فَضْلِهِۦ إِنَّ ٱللَّهَ كَانَ بِكُلِّ شَىْءٍ عَلِيمًا (٣٢)

And whoever of you have not the means wherewith to wed free, believing women, they may wed believing girls from among those (slaves) whom your right hands possess, and Allâh has full knowledge about your Faith, you are one from another. Wed them with the permission of their own folk (guardians, Auliyâ' or masters) and give them their Mahr according to what is reasonable; they (the above said captive and slave-girls) should be chaste, not adulterous, nor taking boy-friends. And after they have been taken in wedlock, if they commit illegal sexual intercourse, their punishment is half that for free (unmarried) women. This is for him among you who is afraid of being harmed in his religion or in his body; but it is better for you that you practise self-restraint, and

*Allâh is Oft¬Forgiving, Most Merciful (25) Allâh wishes to make clear (what is lawful and what is unlawful) to you, and to show you the ways of those before you, and accept your repentance, and Allâh is All¬Knower, All¬Wise. (26) Allâh wishes to accept your repentance, but those who follow their lusts, wish that you (believers) should deviate tremendously away (from the Right Path). (27) Allâh wishes to lighten (the burden) for you; and man was created weak (cannot be patient to leave sexual intercourse with woman). (28) O you who believe! Eat not up your property among yourselves unjustly except it be a trade amongst you, by mutual consent. And do not kill yourselves (nor kill one another). Surely, Allâh is Most Merciful to you. (29) And whoever commits that through aggression and injustice, We shall cast him into the Fire, and that is easy for Allâh. (30) If you avoid the great sins which you are forbidden to do, We shall expiate from you your (small) sins, and admit you to a Noble Entrance (i.e. Paradise). (31) And wish not for the things in which Allâh has made some of you to excel others. For men there is reward for what they have earned, (and likewise) for women there is reward for what they have earned, and ask Allâh of His Bounty. Surely, Allâh is Ever All¬Knower of everything. (32)*

**Quran 4:35**

وَإِنْ خِفْتُمْ شِقَاقَ بَيْنِهِمَا فَٱبْعَثُواْ حَكَمًا مِّنْ أَهْلِهِ وَحَكَمًا مِّنْ
أَهْلِهَآ إِن يُرِيدَآ إِصْلَـٰحًا يُوَفِّقِ ٱللَّهُ بَيْنَهُمَآ إِنَّ ٱللَّهَ كَانَ عَلِيمًا
خَبِيرًا (٣٥)

*If you fear a breach between them twain (the man and his
wife), appoint (two) arbitrators, one from his family and
the other from her's; if they both wish for peace, Allâh
will cause their reconciliation. Indeed Allâh is Ever
All¬Knower, Well¬Acquainted with all things. (35)*

## Quran 4:40-42

إِنَّ ٱللَّهَ لَا يَظْلِمُ مِثْقَالَ ذَرَّةٍ وَإِن تَكُ حَسَنَةً يُضَـٰعِفْهَا وَيُؤْتِ مِن
لَّدُنْهُ أَجْرًا عَظِيمًا (٤٠) فَكَيْفَ إِذَا جِئْنَا مِن كُلِّ أُمَّةٍ بِشَهِيدٍ
وَجِئْنَا بِكَ عَلَىٰ هَـٰٓؤُلَآءِ شَهِيدًا (٤١) يَوْمَئِذٍ يَوَدُّ ٱلَّذِينَ كَفَرُواْ
وَعَصَوُاْ ٱلرَّسُولَ لَوْ تُسَوَّىٰ بِهِمُ ٱلْأَرْضُ وَلَا يَكْتُمُونَ ٱللَّهَ
حَدِيثًا (٤٢)

*Surely! Allâh wrongs not even of the weight of an atom
(or a small ant), but if there is any good (done), He
doubles it, and gives from Him a great reward (40) How
(will it be) then, when We bring from each nation a
witness and We bring you (O Muhammad) as a witness
against these people? (41) On that day those who
disbelieved and disobeyed the Messenger (Muhammad)
will wish that they were buried in the earth, but they will
never be able to hide a single fact from Allâh. (42)*

## Quran 4:45

وَٱللَّهُ أَعْلَمُ بِأَعْدَآئِكُمْ وَكَفَىٰ بِٱللَّهِ وَلِيًّا وَكَفَىٰ بِٱللَّهِ نَصِيرًا (٤٥)

*Allâh has full knowledge of your enemies, and Allâh is*
*Sufficient as a Walî (Protector), and Allâh is Sufficient*
*as a Helper. (45)*

## Quran 4:48-52

إِنَّ ٱللَّهَ لَا يَغْفِرُ أَن يُشْرَكَ بِهِ وَيَغْفِرُ مَا دُونَ ذَٰلِكَ لِمَن يَشَآءُ
وَمَن يُشْرِكْ بِٱللَّهِ فَقَدِ ٱفْتَرَىٰ إِثْمًا عَظِيمًا (٤٨) أَلَمْ تَرَ إِلَى
ٱلَّذِينَ يُزَكُّونَ أَنفُسَهُمْ بَلِ ٱللَّهُ يُزَكِّى مَن يَشَآءُ وَلَا يُظْلَمُونَ
فَتِيلاً (٤٩) ٱنظُرْ كَيْفَ يَفْتَرُونَ عَلَى ٱللَّهِ ٱلْكَذِبَ وَكَفَىٰ بِهِ
إِثْمًا مُّبِينًا (٥٠) أَلَمْ تَرَ إِلَى ٱلَّذِينَ أُوتُواْ نَصِيبًا مِّنَ ٱلْكِتَٰبِ
يُؤْمِنُونَ بِٱلْجِبْتِ وَٱلطَّٰغُوتِ وَيَقُولُونَ لِلَّذِينَ كَفَرُواْ هَـٰٓؤُلَاءِ
أَهْدَىٰ مِنَ ٱلَّذِينَ ءَامَنُواْ سَبِيلاً (٥١) أُوْلَـٰئِكَ ٱلَّذِينَ لَعَنَهُمُ ٱللَّهُ
وَمَن يَلْعَنِ ٱللَّهُ فَلَن تَجِدَ لَهُ نَصِيرًا (٥٢)

*Verily, Allâh forgives not that partners should be set up*
*with Him (in worship), but He forgives except that*
*(anything else) to whom He wills; and whoever sets up*
*partners with Allâh in worship, he has indeed invented a*
*tremendous sin. (48) Have you not seen those (Jews and*
*Christians) who claim sanctity for themselves. Nay, but*
*Allâh sanctifies whom He wills, and they will not be*
*dealt with injustice even equal to the extent of a scalish*
*thread in the long slit of a date-stone. (49) Look, how they*
*invent a lie against Allâh, and enough is that as a*
*manifest sin. (50) Have you not seen those who were*
*given a portion of the Scripture? They believe in Jibt and*

Tâghût and say to the disbelievers that they are better guided as regards the way than the believers (Muslims). (51) They are those whom Allâh has cursed, and he whom Allâh curses, you will not find for him (any) helper, (52)

## Quran 4:56-57

إِنَّ ٱلَّذِينَ كَفَرُواْ بِـَٔايَٰتِنَا سَوْفَ نُصْلِيهِمْ نَارًا كُلَّمَا نَضِجَتْ جُلُودُهُم بَدَّلْنَٰهُمْ جُلُودًا غَيْرَهَا لِيَذُوقُواْ ٱلْعَذَابَۗ إِنَّ ٱللَّهَ كَانَ عَزِيزًا حَكِيمًا (٥٦) وَٱلَّذِينَ ءَامَنُواْ وَعَمِلُواْ ٱلصَّٰلِحَٰتِ سَنُدْخِلُهُمْ جَنَّٰتٍ تَجْرِى مِن تَحْتِهَا ٱلْأَنْهَٰرُ خَٰلِدِينَ فِيهَآ أَبَدًاۖ لَّهُمْ فِيهَآ أَزْوَٰجٌ مُّطَهَّرَةٌۖ وَنُدْخِلُهُمْ ظِلًّا ظَلِيلًا (٥٧)

Surely! Those who disbelieved in Our Ayât (proofs, evidences, verses, lessons, signs, revelations, etc.) We shall burn them in Fire. As often as their skins are roasted through, We shall change them for other skins that they may taste the punishment. Truly, Allâh is Ever Most Powerful, All¬Wise. (56) But those who believe (in the Oneness of Allâh - Islâmic Monotheism) and do deeds of righteousness, We shall admit them to Gardens under which rivers flow (Paradise), abiding therein forever. Therein they shall have Azwâjun Mutahharatun [purified mates or wives] and We shall admit them to shades wide and ever deepening (Paradise). (57)

## Quran 4:59-62

يَـٰٓأَيُّهَا ٱلَّذِينَ ءَامَنُوٓاْ أَطِيعُواْ ٱللَّهَ وَأَطِيعُواْ ٱلرَّسُولَ وَأُوْلِى
ٱلْأَمْرِ مِنكُمْ فَإِن تَنَـٰزَعْتُمْ فِى شَىْءٍ فَرُدُّوهُ إِلَى ٱللَّهِ وَٱلرَّسُولِ
إِن كُنتُمْ تُؤْمِنُونَ بِٱللَّهِ وَٱلْيَوْمِ ٱلْأَخِرِ ذَٰلِكَ خَيْرٌ وَأَحْسَنُ تَأْوِيلاً
(٥٩) أَلَمْ تَرَ إِلَى ٱلَّذِينَ يَزْعُمُونَ أَنَّهُمْ ءَامَنُواْ بِمَآ أُنزِلَ إِلَيْكَ
وَمَآ أُنزِلَ مِن قَبْلِكَ يُرِيدُونَ أَن يَتَحَاكَمُوٓاْ إِلَى ٱلطَّـٰغُوتِ وَقَدْ
أُمِرُوٓاْ أَن يَكْفُرُواْ بِهِ وَيُرِيدُ ٱلشَّيْطَـٰنُ أَن يُضِلَّهُمْ ضَلَـٰلاً بَعِيدًا
(٦٠) وَإِذَا قِيلَ لَهُمْ تَعَالَوْاْ إِلَىٰ مَآ أَنزَلَ ٱللَّهُ وَإِلَى ٱلرَّسُولِ
رَأَيْتَ ٱلْمُنَـٰفِقِينَ يَصُدُّونَ عَنكَ صُدُودًا (٦١) فَكَيْفَ إِذَآ
أَصَـٰبَتْهُم مُّصِيبَةٌ بِمَا قَدَّمَتْ أَيْدِيهِمْ ثُمَّ جَآءُوكَ يَحْلِفُونَ بِٱللَّهِ إِنْ
أَرَدْنَآ إِلَّآ إِحْسَـٰنًا وَتَوْفِيقًا (٦٢)

*O you who believe! Obey Allâh and obey the Messenger
(Muhammad), and those of you (Muslims) who are in
authority. (And) if you differ in anything amongst
yourselves, refer it to Allâh and His Messenger, if you
believe in Allâh and in the Last Day. That is better and
more suitable for final determination. (59) Have you seen
those (hyprocrites) who claim that they believe in that
which has been sent down to you, and that which was
sent down before you, and they wish to go for judgement
(in their disputes) to the Tâghût (false unislamic judges)
while they have been ordered to reject them. But Shaitân
(Satan) wishes to lead them far astray. (60) And when it
is said to them: "Come to what Allâh has sent down and
to the Messenger (Muhammad)," you (Muhammad) see
the hypocrites turn away from you (Muhammad) with
aversion (61) How then, when a catastrophe befalls them*

because of what their hands have sent forth, they come to you swearing by Allâh, "We meant no more than goodwill and conciliation!" (62)

## Quran 4:69

وَمَن يُطِعِ ٱللَّهَ وَٱلرَّسُولَ فَأُوْلَٰئِكَ مَعَ ٱلَّذِينَ أَنْعَمَ ٱللَّهُ عَلَيْهِم مِّنَ ٱلنَّبِيِّنَ وَٱلصِّدِّيقِينَ وَٱلشُّهَدَاءِ وَٱلصَّٰلِحِينَ ۚ وَحَسُنَ أُوْلَٰئِكَ رَفِيقًا (٦٩)

And whoso obeys Allâh and the Messenger (Muhammad), then they will be in the company of those on whom Allâh has bestowed His Grace, of the Prophets, the Siddiqûn (those followers of the Prophets who were first and foremost to believe in them), the martyrs, and the righteous. And how excellent these companions are! (69)

## Quran 4:74-76

﴾ فَلْيُقَٰتِلْ فِى سَبِيلِ ٱللَّهِ ٱلَّذِينَ يَشْرُونَ ٱلْحَيَوٰةَ ٱلدُّنْيَا بِٱلْأَخِرَةِ ۚ وَمَن يُقَٰتِلْ فِى سَبِيلِ ٱللَّهِ فَيُقْتَلْ أَوْ يَغْلِبْ فَسَوْفَ نُؤْتِيهِ أَجْرًا عَظِيمًا (٧٤) وَمَا لَكُمْ لَا تُقَٰتِلُونَ فِى سَبِيلِ ٱللَّهِ وَٱلْمُسْتَضْعَفِينَ مِنَ ٱلرِّجَالِ وَٱلنِّسَاءِ وَٱلْوِلْدَٰنِ ٱلَّذِينَ يَقُولُونَ رَبَّنَا أَخْرِجْنَا مِنْ هَٰذِهِ ٱلْقَرْيَةِ ٱلظَّالِمِ أَهْلُهَا وَٱجْعَل لَّنَا مِن لَّدُنكَ وَلِيًّا وَٱجْعَل لَّنَا مِن لَّدُنكَ نَصِيرًا (٧٥) ٱلَّذِينَ ءَامَنُوا۟ يُقَٰتِلُونَ فِى سَبِيلِ ٱللَّهِ ۖ وَٱلَّذِينَ كَفَرُوا۟ يُقَٰتِلُونَ فِى سَبِيلِ ٱلطَّٰغُوتِ فَقَٰتِلُوٓا۟ أَوْلِيَاءَ ٱلشَّيْطَٰنِ ۖ إِنَّ كَيْدَ ٱلشَّيْطَٰنِ كَانَ ضَعِيفًا (٧٦)

Let those (believers) who sell the life of this world for the
Hereafter fight in the Cause of Allâh, and whoso fights in
the Cause of Allâh, and is killed or gets victory, We shall
bestow on him a great reward. (74) And what is wrong
with you that you fight not in the Cause of Allâh, and for
those weak, ill¬treated and oppressed among men,
women, and children, whose cry is: "Our Lord! Rescue
us from this town whose people are oppressors; and raise
for us from You one who will protect, and raise for us
from You one who will help." (75) Those who believe,
fight in the Cause of Allâh, and those who disbelieve,
fight in the cause of Tâghût (Satan,). So fight you against
the friends of Shaitân (Satan); Ever feeble indeed is the
plot of Shaitân (Satan). (76)

## Quran 4:82

أَفَلَا يَتَدَبَّرُونَ ٱلْقُرْءَانَ وَلَوْ كَانَ مِنْ عِندِ غَيْرِ ٱللَّهِ لَوَجَدُواْ فِيهِ
ٱخْتِلَٰفًا كَثِيرًا (٨٢)

Do they not then consider the Qur'ân carefully? Had it
been from other than Allâh, they would surely have
found therein many contradictions. (82)

## Quran 4:85

مَّن يَشْفَعْ شَفَٰعَةً حَسَنَةً يَكُن لَّهُۥ نَصِيبٌ مِّنْهَا وَمَن يَشْفَعْ
شَفَٰعَةً سَيِّئَةً يَكُن لَّهُۥ كِفْلٌ مِّنْهَا وَكَانَ ٱللَّهُ عَلَىٰ كُلِّ شَىْءٍ مُّقِيتًا
(٨٥)

*Whosoever intercedes for a good cause will have the
reward thereof, and whosoever intercedes for an evil
cause will have a share in its burden. And Allâh is Ever
All-Able to do (and also an All-Witness to) everything.
(85)*

## Quran 4:87-88

اللَّهُ لَا إِلَٰهَ إِلَّا هُوَ لَيَجْمَعَنَّكُمْ إِلَىٰ يَوْمِ الْقِيَٰمَةِ لَا رَيْبَ فِيهِ وَمَنْ
أَصْدَقُ مِنَ اللَّهِ حَدِيثًا (٨٧) ۞ فَمَا لَكُمْ فِى الْمُنَٰفِقِينَ فِئَتَيْنِ
وَاللَّهُ أَرْكَسَهُم بِمَا كَسَبُوٓا۟ أَتُرِيدُونَ أَن تَهْدُوا۟ مَنْ أَضَلَّ اللَّهُ
وَمَن يُضْلِلِ اللَّهُ فَلَن تَجِدَ لَهُۥ سَبِيلًا (٨٨)

*Allâh! Lâ ilâha illa Huwa (none has the right to be
worshipped but He). Surely, He will gather you together
on the Day of Resurrection about which there is no
doubt. And who is truer in statement than Allâh? (87)
Then what is the matter with you that you are divided
into two parties about the hypocrites? Allâh has cast
them back (to disbelief) because of what they have earned.
Do you want to guide him whom Allâh has made to go
astray? And he whom Allâh has made to go astray, you
will never find for him any way (of guidance). (88)*

## Quran 4:97-100

إِنَّ الَّذِينَ تَوَفَّىٰهُمُ الْمَلَٰٓئِكَةُ ظَالِمِىٓ أَنفُسِهِمْ قَالُوا۟ فِيمَ كُنتُمْ قَالُوا۟
كُنَّا مُسْتَضْعَفِينَ فِى الْأَرْضِ قَالُوٓا۟ أَلَمْ تَكُنْ أَرْضُ اللَّهِ وَٰسِعَةً
فَتُهَاجِرُوا۟ فِيهَا فَأُو۟لَٰٓئِكَ مَأْوَىٰهُمْ جَهَنَّمُ وَسَآءَتْ مَصِيرًا (٩٧)

إِلَّا ٱلْمُسْتَضْعَفِينَ مِنَ ٱلرِّجَالِ وَٱلنِّسَاءِ وَٱلْوِلْدَانِ لَا
يَسْتَطِيعُونَ حِيلَةً وَلَا يَهْتَدُونَ سَبِيلاً (٩٨) فَأُوْلَـٰئِكَ عَسَى ٱللَّهُ
أَن يَعْفُوَ عَنْهُمْ وَكَانَ ٱللَّهُ عَفُوًّا غَفُورًا (٩٩) ۞ وَمَن يُهَاجِرْ
فِى سَبِيلِ ٱللَّهِ يَجِدْ فِى ٱلْأَرْضِ مُرَاغَمًا كَثِيرًا وَسَعَةً وَمَن
يَخْرُجْ مِنْ بَيْتِهِ مُهَاجِرًا إِلَى ٱللَّهِ وَرَسُولِهِ ثُمَّ يُدْرِكْهُ ٱلْمَوْتُ
فَقَدْ وَقَعَ أَجْرُهُ عَلَى ٱللَّهِ وَكَانَ ٱللَّهُ غَفُورًا رَّحِيمًا (١٠٠)

Verily! As for those whom the angels take (in death) while they are wronging themselves (as they stayed among the disbelievers even though emigration was obligatory for them), they (angels) say (to them): "In what (condition) were you?" They reply: "We were weak and oppressed on earth." They (angels) say: "Was not the earth of Allâh spacious enough for you to emigrate therein?" Such men will find their abode in Hell - What an evil destination! (97) Except the weak ones among men, women and children who cannot devise a plan, nor are they able to direct their way. (98) These are they whom Allâh is likely to forgive them, and Allâh is Ever Oft-Pardoning, Oft-Forgiving. (99) He who emigrates (from his home) in the Cause of Allâh, will find on earth many dwelling places and plenty to live by. And whosoever leaves his home as an emigrant unto Allâh and His Messenger, and death overtakes him, his reward is then surely incumbent upon Allâh. And Allâh is Ever Oft¬Forgiving, Most Merciful. (100)

**Quran 4:110-112**

وَمَن يَعْمَلْ سُوٓءًا أَوْ يَظْلِمْ نَفْسَهُۥ ثُمَّ يَسْتَغْفِرِ ٱللَّهَ يَجِدِ ٱللَّهَ
غَفُورًا رَّحِيمًا (١١٠) وَمَن يَكْسِبْ إِثْمًا فَإِنَّمَا يَكْسِبُهُۥ عَلَىٰ
نَفْسِهِۦ ۚ وَكَانَ ٱللَّهُ عَلِيمًا حَكِيمًا (١١١) وَمَن يَكْسِبْ خَطِيٓئَةً أَوْ
إِثْمًا ثُمَّ يَرْمِ بِهِۦ بَرِيٓئًا فَقَدِ ٱحْتَمَلَ بُهْتَٰنًا وَإِثْمًا مُّبِينًا (١١٢)

*And whoever does evil or wrongs himself but afterwards*
*seeks Allâh's Forgiveness, he will find Allâh*
*Oft¬Forgiving, Most Merciful. (110) And whoever earns*
*sin, he earns it only against himself. And Allâh is Ever*
*All-Knowing, All-Wise. (111) And whoever earns a fault*
*or a sin and then throws it on to someone innocent, he*
*has indeed burdened himself with falsehood and a*
*manifest sin. (112)*

## Quran 4:114-124

۞ لَّا خَيْرَ فِى كَثِيرٍ مِّن نَّجْوَىٰهُمْ إِلَّا مَنْ أَمَرَ بِصَدَقَةٍ أَوْ
مَعْرُوفٍ أَوْ إِصْلَٰحٍ بَيْنَ ٱلنَّاسِ ۚ وَمَن يَفْعَلْ ذَٰلِكَ ٱبْتِغَآءَ
مَرْضَاتِ ٱللَّهِ فَسَوْفَ نُؤْتِيهِ أَجْرًا عَظِيمًا (١١٤) وَمَن يُشَاقِقِ
ٱلرَّسُولَ مِنۢ بَعْدِ مَا تَبَيَّنَ لَهُ ٱلْهُدَىٰ وَيَتَّبِعْ غَيْرَ سَبِيلِ
ٱلْمُؤْمِنِينَ نُوَلِّهِۦ مَا تَوَلَّىٰ وَنُصْلِهِۦ جَهَنَّمَ ۖ وَسَآءَتْ مَصِيرًا
(١١٥) إِنَّ ٱللَّهَ لَا يَغْفِرُ أَن يُشْرَكَ بِهِۦ وَيَغْفِرُ مَا دُونَ ذَٰلِكَ
لِمَن يَشَآءُ ۚ وَمَن يُشْرِكْ بِٱللَّهِ فَقَدْ ضَلَّ ضَلَٰلًۢا بَعِيدًا (١١٦) إِن
يَدْعُونَ مِن دُونِهِۦٓ إِلَّآ إِنَٰثًا وَإِن يَدْعُونَ إِلَّا شَيْطَٰنًا مَّرِيدًا
(١١٧) لَّعَنَهُ ٱللَّهُ ۘ وَقَالَ لَأَتَّخِذَنَّ مِنْ عِبَادِكَ نَصِيبًا مَّفْرُوضًا
(١١٨) وَلَأُضِلَّنَّهُمْ وَلَأُمَنِّيَنَّهُمْ وَلَءَامُرَنَّهُمْ فَلَيُبَتِّكُنَّ ءَاذَانَ
ٱلْأَنْعَٰمِ وَلَءَامُرَنَّهُمْ فَلَيُغَيِّرُنَّ خَلْقَ ٱللَّهِ ۚ وَمَن يَتَّخِذِ ٱلشَّيْطَٰنَ وَلِيًّا

مِّن دُونِ ٱللَّهِ فَقَدْ خَسِرَ خُسْرَانًا مُّبِينًا (١١٩) يَعِدُهُمْ وَيُمَنِّيهِمْ ۖ وَمَا يَعِدُهُمُ ٱلشَّيْطَنُ إِلَّا غُرُورًا (١٢٠) أُوْلَٰٓئِكَ مَأْوَىٰهُمْ جَهَنَّمُ وَلَا يَجِدُونَ عَنْهَا مَحِيصًا (١٢١) وَٱلَّذِينَ ءَامَنُواْ وَعَمِلُواْ ٱلصَّٰلِحَٰتِ سَنُدْخِلُهُمْ جَنَّٰتٍ تَجْرِى مِن تَحْتِهَا ٱلْأَنْهَٰرُ خَٰلِدِينَ فِيهَآ أَبَدًا ۖ وَعْدَ ٱللَّهِ حَقًّا ۚ وَمَنْ أَصْدَقُ مِنَ ٱللَّهِ قِيلًا (١٢٢) لَّيْسَ بِأَمَانِيِّكُمْ وَلَآ أَمَانِيِّ أَهْلِ ٱلْكِتَٰبِ ۗ مَن يَعْمَلْ سُوٓءًا يُجْزَ بِهِ وَلَا يَجِدْ لَهُۥ مِن دُونِ ٱللَّهِ وَلِيًّا وَلَا نَصِيرًا (١٢٣) وَمَن يَعْمَلْ مِنَ ٱلصَّٰلِحَٰتِ مِن ذَكَرٍ أَوْ أُنثَىٰ وَهُوَ مُؤْمِنٌ فَأُوْلَٰٓئِكَ يَدْخُلُونَ ٱلْجَنَّةَ وَلَا يُظْلَمُونَ نَقِيرًا (١٢٤)

*There is no good in most of their secret talks save (in)*
*him who orders Sadaqah (charity in Allâh's Cause), or*
*Ma'rûf (Islâmic Monotheism and all the good and*
*righteous deeds which Allâh has ordained), or*
*conciliation between mankind, and he who does this,*
*seeking the good Pleasure of Allâh, We shall give him a*
*great reward (114) And whoever contradicts and opposes*
*the Messenger (Muhammad) after the right path has been*
*shown clearly to him, and follows other than the*
*believers' way. We shall keep him in the path he has*
*chosen, and burn him in Hell - what an evil destination.*
*(115) Verily! Allâh forgives not (the sin of) setting up*
*partners (in worship) with Him, but He forgives whom*
*He wills sins other than that, and whoever sets up*
*partners in worship with Allâh, has indeed strayed far*
*away. (116) They (all those who worship others than*
*Allâh) invoke nothing but female deities besides Him*

*(Allâh), and they invoke nothing but Shaitân (Satan), a persistent rebel! (117) Allâh cursed him. And he [Shaitân (Satan)] said: "I will take an appointed portion of your slaves; (118) Verily, I will mislead them, and surely, I will arouse in them false desires; and certainly, I will order them to slit the ears of cattle, and indeed I will order them to change the nature created by Allâh." And whoever takes Shaitân (Satan) as a Walî (protector or helper) instead of Allâh, has surely suffered a manifest loss. (119) He [Shaitan (Satan)] makes promises to them, and arouses in them false desires; and Shaitan's (Satan) promises are nothing but deceptions. (120) The dwelling of such (people) is Hell, and they will find no way of escape from it. (121) But those who believe (in the Oneness of Allâh - Islâmic Monotheism) and do deeds of righteousness, We shall admit them to the Gardens under which rivers flow (i.e. in Paradise) to dwell therein forever. Allâh's Promise is the Truth, and whose words can be truer than those of Allâh? (Of course, none). (122) It will not be in accordance with your desires (Muslims), nor those of the people of the Scripture (Jews and Christians), whosoever works evil, will have the recompense thereof, and he will not find any protector or helper besides Allâh. (123) And whoever does righteous good deeds, male or female, and is a (true) believer [in the Oneness of Allâh (Muslim)], such will enter Paradise*

and not the least injustice, even to the size of a speck on the back of a date-stone, will be done to them. (124)

## Quran 4:128-130

وَإِنِ ٱمْرَأَةٌ خَافَتْ مِنْ بَعْلِهَا نُشُوزًا أَوْ إِعْرَاضًا فَلَا جُنَاحَ عَلَيْهِمَا أَن يُصْلِحَا بَيْنَهُمَا صُلْحًا وَٱلصُّلْحُ خَيْرٌ وَأُحْضِرَتِ ٱلْأَنفُسُ ٱلشُّحَّ وَإِن تُحْسِنُوا۟ وَتَتَّقُوا۟ فَإِنَّ ٱللَّهَ كَانَ بِمَا تَعْمَلُونَ خَبِيرًا (١٢٨) وَلَن تَسْتَطِيعُوٓا۟ أَن تَعْدِلُوا۟ بَيْنَ ٱلنِّسَآءِ وَلَوْ حَرَصْتُمْ فَلَا تَمِيلُوا۟ كُلَّ ٱلْمَيْلِ فَتَذَرُوهَا كَٱلْمُعَلَّقَةِ وَإِن تُصْلِحُوا۟ وَتَتَّقُوا۟ فَإِنَّ ٱللَّهَ كَانَ غَفُورًا رَّحِيمًا (١٢٩) وَإِن يَتَفَرَّقَا يُغْنِ ٱللَّهُ كُلًّا مِّن سَعَتِهِۦ وَكَانَ ٱللَّهُ وَٰسِعًا حَكِيمًا (١٣٠)

And if a woman fears cruelty or desertion on her husband's part, there is no sin on them both if they make terms of peace between themselves; and making peace is better. And human inner-selves are swayed by greed. But if you do good and keep away from evil, verily, Allâh is Ever Well¬Acquainted with what you do. (128) You will never be able to do perfect justice between wives even if it is your ardent desire, so do not incline too much to one of them (by giving her more of your time and provision) so as to leave the other hanging (i.e. neither divorced nor married). And if you do justice, and do all that is right and fear Allâh by keeping away from all that is wrong, then Allâh is Ever Oft¬Forgiving, Most Merciful. (129) But if they separate (by divorce), Allâh will provide *abundance for everyone of them from His Bounty. And Allâh is Ever All¬Sufficient for His creatures' need, All¬Wise. (130)*

## Quran 4:134-146

مَّن كَانَ يُرِيدُ ثَوَابَ ٱلدُّنْيَا فَعِندَ ٱللَّهِ ثَوَابُ ٱلدُّنْيَا وَٱلْأَخِرَةِ وَكَانَ ٱللَّهُ سَمِيعًۢا بَصِيرًا (١٣٤) ۞ يَـٰٓأَيُّهَا ٱلَّذِينَ ءَامَنُوا۟ كُونُوا۟ قَوَّٰمِينَ بِٱلْقِسْطِ شُهَدَآءَ لِلَّهِ وَلَوْ عَلَىٰٓ أَنفُسِكُمْ أَوِ ٱلْوَٰلِدَيْنِ وَٱلْأَقْرَبِينَ إِن يَكُنْ غَنِيًّا أَوْ فَقِيرًا فَٱللَّهُ أَوْلَىٰ بِهِمَا فَلَا تَتَّبِعُوا۟ ٱلْهَوَىٰٓ أَن تَعْدِلُوا۟ وَإِن تَلْوُۥٓا۟ أَوْ تُعْرِضُوا۟ فَإِنَّ ٱللَّهَ كَانَ بِمَا تَعْمَلُونَ خَبِيرًا (١٣٥) يَـٰٓأَيُّهَا ٱلَّذِينَ ءَامَنُوٓا۟ ءَامِنُوا۟ بِٱللَّهِ وَرَسُولِهِۦ وَٱلْكِتَٰبِ ٱلَّذِى نَزَّلَ عَلَىٰ رَسُولِهِۦ وَٱلْكِتَٰبِ ٱلَّذِىٓ أَنزَلَ مِن قَبْلُ وَمَن يَكْفُرْ بِٱللَّهِ وَمَلَـٰٓئِكَتِهِۦ وَكُتُبِهِۦ وَرُسُلِهِۦ وَٱلْيَوْمِ ٱلْأَخِرِ فَقَدْ ضَلَّ ضَلَـٰلًۢا بَعِيدًا (١٣٦) إِنَّ ٱلَّذِينَ ءَامَنُوا۟ ثُمَّ كَفَرُوا۟ ثُمَّ ءَامَنُوا۟ ثُمَّ كَفَرُوا۟ ثُمَّ ٱزْدَادُوا۟ كُفْرًا لَّمْ يَكُنِ ٱللَّهُ لِيَغْفِرَ لَهُمْ وَلَا لِيَهْدِيَهُمْ سَبِيلًۢا (١٣٧) بَشِّرِ ٱلْمُنَٰفِقِينَ بِأَنَّ لَهُمْ عَذَابًا أَلِيمًا (١٣٨) ٱلَّذِينَ يَتَّخِذُونَ ٱلْكَٰفِرِينَ أَوْلِيَآءَ مِن دُونِ ٱلْمُؤْمِنِينَ أَيَبْتَغُونَ عِندَهُمُ ٱلْعِزَّةَ فَإِنَّ ٱلْعِزَّةَ لِلَّهِ جَمِيعًا (١٣٩) وَقَدْ نَزَّلَ عَلَيْكُمْ فِى ٱلْكِتَٰبِ أَنْ إِذَا سَمِعْتُمْ ءَايَٰتِ ٱللَّهِ يُكْفَرُ بِهَا وَيُسْتَهْزَأُ بِهَا فَلَا تَقْعُدُوا۟ مَعَهُمْ حَتَّىٰ يَخُوضُوا۟ فِى حَدِيثٍ غَيْرِهِۦٓ إِنَّكُمْ إِذًا مِّثْلُهُمْ إِنَّ ٱللَّهَ جَامِعُ ٱلْمُنَٰفِقِينَ وَٱلْكَٰفِرِينَ فِى جَهَنَّمَ جَمِيعًا (١٤٠) ٱلَّذِينَ يَتَرَبَّصُونَ بِكُمْ فَإِن كَانَ لَكُمْ فَتْحٌ مِّنَ ٱللَّهِ قَالُوٓا۟ أَلَمْ نَكُن مَّعَكُمْ وَإِن كَانَ لِلْكَٰفِرِينَ نَصِيبٌ قَالُوٓا۟ أَلَمْ نَسْتَحْوِذْ عَلَيْكُمْ وَنَمْنَعْكُم مِّنَ ٱلْمُؤْمِنِينَ فَٱللَّهُ يَحْكُمُ بَيْنَكُمْ يَوْمَ ٱلْقِيَٰمَةِ وَلَن يَجْعَلَ ٱللَّهُ لِلْكَٰفِرِينَ عَلَى ٱلْمُؤْمِنِينَ سَبِيلًا

(١٤١) إِنَّ ٱلْمُنَٰفِقِينَ يُخَٰدِعُونَ ٱللَّهَ وَهُوَ خَٰدِعُهُمْ وَإِذَا قَامُوٓاْ إِلَى ٱلصَّلَوٰةِ قَامُواْ كُسَالَىٰ يُرَآءُونَ ٱلنَّاسَ وَلَا يَذْكُرُونَ ٱللَّهَ إِلَّا قَلِيلًا (١٤٢) مُّذَبْذَبِينَ بَيْنَ ذَٰلِكَ لَآ إِلَىٰ هَٰٓؤُلَآءِ وَلَآ إِلَىٰ هَٰٓؤُلَآءِ وَمَن يُضْلِلِ ٱللَّهُ فَلَن تَجِدَ لَهُۥ سَبِيلًا (١٤٣) يَٰٓأَيُّهَا ٱلَّذِينَ ءَامَنُواْ لَا تَتَّخِذُواْ ٱلْكَٰفِرِينَ أَوْلِيَآءَ مِن دُونِ ٱلْمُؤْمِنِينَ أَتُرِيدُونَ أَن تَجْعَلُواْ لِلَّهِ عَلَيْكُمْ سُلْطَٰنًا مُّبِينًا (١٤٤) إِنَّ ٱلْمُنَٰفِقِينَ فِى ٱلدَّرْكِ ٱلْأَسْفَلِ مِنَ ٱلنَّارِ وَلَن تَجِدَ لَهُمْ نَصِيرًا (١٤٥) إِلَّا ٱلَّذِينَ تَابُواْ وَأَصْلَحُواْ وَٱعْتَصَمُواْ بِٱللَّهِ وَأَخْلَصُواْ دِينَهُمْ لِلَّهِ فَأُوْلَٰٓئِكَ مَعَ ٱلْمُؤْمِنِينَ وَسَوْفَ يُؤْتِ ٱللَّهُ ٱلْمُؤْمِنِينَ أَجْرًا عَظِيمًا (١٤٦)

*Whoever desires a reward in this life of the world, then with Allâh (Alone and none else) is the reward of this worldly life and of the Hereafter. And Allâh is Ever All¬Hearer, All¬Seer. (134) O you who believe! Stand out firmly for justice, as witnesses to Allâh, even though it be against yourselves, or your parents, or your kin, be he rich or poor, Allâh is a Better Protector to both (than you). So follow not the lusts (of your hearts), lest you avoid justice, and if you distort your witness or refuse to give it, verily, Allâh is Ever Well¬Acquainted with what you do. (135) O you who believe! Believe in Allâh, and His Messenger (Muhammad), and the Book (the Qur'ân) which He has sent down to His Messenger, and the Scripture which He sent down to those before (him), and whosoever disbelieves in Allâh, His Angels, His Books, His Messengers, and the Last Day, then indeed he has strayed far away (136) Verily, those who believe, then disbelieve, then believe (again), and (again) disbelieve, and go on increasing in disbelief; Allâh will not forgive them, nor guide them on the (Right) Way (137) Give to the hypocrites the tidings that there is for them a painful torment. (138) Those who take disbelievers for Auliyâ' (protectors or helpers or friends) instead of believers, do they seek honour, power and glory with them? Verily, then to Allâh belongs all honour, power and glory. (139) And it has already been revealed to you in the Book (this Qur'ân) that when you hear the Verses of Allâh being denied and mocked at, then sit not with them, until they engage in a talk other than that; (but if you stayed with them) certainly in that case you would be like them. Surely, Allâh will collect the hypocrites and disbelievers all together in Hell, (140) Those (hyprocrites) who wait and watch about you; if you gain a victory from Allâh, they say: "Were we not with you?" But if the disbelievers gain a success, they say (to them): "Did we not gain mastery over you and did we not protect you from the believers?" Allâh will judge between you (all) on the Day of Resurrection. And never will Allâh grant to the disbelievers a way (to triumph) over the believers. (141) Verily, the hypocrites seek to deceive Allâh, but it is He Who deceives them. And when they stand up for As-Salât (the prayer), they stand with laziness and to be seen of men, and they do not remember Allâh but little. (142)*

(They are) swaying between this and that, belonging neither to these nor to those, and he whom Allâh sends astray, you will not find for him a way (to the truth - Islâm). (143) O you who believe! Take not for Auliyâ' (protectors or helpers or friends) disbelievers instead of believers. Do you wish to offer Allâh a manifest proof against yourselves? (144) Verily, the hyprocrites will be in the lowest depths (grade) of the Fire; no helper will you find for them. (145) Except those who repent (from hypocrisy), do righteous good deeds, hold fast to Allâh, and purify their religion for Allâh (by worshipping none but Allâh, and do good for Allâh's sake only, not to show off), then they will be with the believers. And Allâh will grant the believers a great reward. (146)

**Quran 4:150-152**

إِنَّ ٱلَّذِينَ يَكْفُرُونَ بِٱللَّهِ وَرُسُلِهِ وَيُرِيدُونَ أَن يُفَرِّقُوا۟ بَيْنَ ٱللَّهِ وَرُسُلِهِ وَيَقُولُونَ نُؤْمِنُ بِبَعْضٍ وَنَكْفُرُ بِبَعْضٍ وَيُرِيدُونَ أَن يَتَّخِذُوا۟ بَيْنَ ذَٰلِكَ سَبِيلاً (١٥٠) أُو۟لَـٰئِكَ هُمُ ٱلْكَـٰفِرُونَ حَقًّا ۚ وَأَعْتَدْنَا لِلْكَـٰفِرِينَ عَذَابًا مُّهِينًا (١٥١) وَٱلَّذِينَ ءَامَنُوا۟ بِٱللَّهِ وَرُسُلِهِ وَلَمْ يُفَرِّقُوا۟ بَيْنَ أَحَدٍ مِّنْهُمْ أُو۟لَـٰئِكَ سَوْفَ يُؤْتِيهِمْ أُجُورَهُمْ ۚ وَكَانَ ٱللَّهُ غَفُورًا رَّحِيمًا (١٥٢)

Verily, those who disbelieve in Allâh and His Messengers and wish to make distinction between Allâh and His Messengers (by believing in Allâh and disbelieving in His Messengers) saying, "We believe in some but reject others," and wish to adopt a way in between. (150) They are in truth disbelievers. And We have prepared for the disbelievers a humiliating torment. (151) And those who believe in Allâh and His Messengers and make no distinction between any of them (Messengers), We shall give them their rewards, and Allâh is Ever Oft¬Forgiving, Most Merciful. (152)

## Quran 4:156-159

وَبِكُفْرِهِمْ وَقَوْلِهِمْ عَلَىٰ مَرْيَمَ بُهْتَـٰنًا عَظِيمًا (١٥٦) وَقَوْلِهِمْ إِنَّا قَتَلْنَا ٱلْمَسِيحَ عِيسَى ٱبْنَ مَرْيَمَ رَسُولَ ٱللَّهِ وَمَا قَتَلُوهُ وَمَا صَلَبُوهُ وَلَـٰكِن شُبِّهَ لَهُمْ وَإِنَّ ٱلَّذِينَ ٱخْتَلَفُواْ فِيهِ لَفِى شَكٍّ مِّنْهُ مَا لَهُم بِهِ مِنْ عِلْمٍ إِلَّا ٱتِّبَاعَ ٱلظَّنِّ وَمَا قَتَلُوهُ يَقِينًا (١٥٧) بَل رَّفَعَهُ ٱللَّهُ إِلَيْهِ وَكَانَ ٱللَّهُ عَزِيزًا حَكِيمًا (١٥٨) وَإِن مِّنْ أَهْلِ ٱلْكِتَـٰبِ إِلَّا لَيُؤْمِنَنَّ بِهِ قَبْلَ مَوْتِهِ وَيَوْمَ ٱلْقِيَـٰمَةِ يَكُونُ عَلَيْهِمْ شَهِيدًا (١٥٩)

And because of their (Jews) disbelief and uttering against Maryam (Mary ) a grave false charge (that she has committed illegal sexual intercourse); (156) And because of their saying (in boast), "We killed Messiah 'Īsā (Jesus), son of Maryam (Mary), the Messenger of Allâh," - but they killed him not, nor crucified him, but the resemblance of 'Īsā (Jesus) was put over another man (and they killed that man), and those who differ therein are full of doubts. They have no (certain) knowledge, they follow nothing but conjecture. For surely; they killed him not [i.e. 'Īsā (Jesus), son of Maryam (Mary)]: (157) But

Allâh raised him ['Īsā (Jesus)] up (with his body and soul) unto Himself (and he is in the heavens). And Allâh is Ever All-Powerful, All-Wise. (158) And there is none of the people of the Scripture (Jews and Christians), but must believe in him ['Īsā (Jesus), son of Maryam (Mary), as only a Messenger of Allâh and a human being], before his ['Īsā (Jesus) or a Jew's or a Christian's] death (at the time of the appearance of the angel of death). And on the Day of Resurrection, he ['Īsā (Jesus)] will be a witness against them (159)

## Quran 4:161-162

وَأَخْذِهِمُ ٱلرِّبَوٰاْ وَقَدْ نُهُواْ عَنْهُ وَأَكْلِهِمْ أَمْوَٰلَ ٱلنَّاسِ بِٱلْبَٰطِلِ وَأَعْتَدْنَا لِلْكَٰفِرِينَ مِنْهُمْ عَذَابًا أَلِيمًا (١٦١) لَّٰكِنِ ٱلرَّٰسِخُونَ فِى ٱلْعِلْمِ مِنْهُمْ وَٱلْمُؤْمِنُونَ يُؤْمِنُونَ بِمَآ أُنزِلَ إِلَيْكَ وَمَآ أُنزِلَ مِن قَبْلِكَ وَٱلْمُقِيمِينَ ٱلصَّلَوٰةَ وَٱلْمُؤْتُونَ ٱلزَّكَوٰةَ وَٱلْمُؤْمِنُونَ بِٱللَّهِ وَٱلْيَوْمِ ٱلْأَخِرِ أُوْلَٰئِكَ سَنُؤْتِيهِمْ أَجْرًا عَظِيمًا (١٦٢)

And their taking of Ribâ (usury) though they were forbidden from taking it and their devouring of men's substance wrongfully (bribery). And We have prepared for the disbelievers among them a painful torment. (161) But those among them who are well-grounded in knowledge, and the believers, believe in what has been sent down to you (Muhammad) and what was sent down before you, and those who perform As-Salât (Iqâmat-as-Salât), and give Zakât and believe in Allâh and in the

*Last Day, it is they to whom We shall give a great reward. (162)*

## Quran 4:168-175

إِنَّ ٱلَّذِينَ كَفَرُواْ وَظَلَمُواْ لَمْ يَكُنِ ٱللَّهُ لِيَغْفِرَ لَهُمْ وَلَا لِيَهْدِيَهُمْ طَرِيقًا (١٦٨) إِلَّا طَرِيقَ جَهَنَّمَ خَٰلِدِينَ فِيهَآ أَبَدًا وَكَانَ ذَٰلِكَ عَلَى ٱللَّهِ يَسِيرًا (١٦٩) يَٰٓأَيُّهَا ٱلنَّاسُ قَدْ جَآءَكُمُ ٱلرَّسُولُ بِٱلْحَقِّ مِن رَّبِّكُمْ فَـَٔامِنُواْ خَيْرًا لَّكُمْ وَإِن تَكْفُرُواْ فَإِنَّ لِلَّهِ مَا فِى ٱلسَّمَٰوَٰتِ وَٱلْأَرْضِ وَكَانَ ٱللَّهُ عَلِيمًا حَكِيمًا (١٧٠) يَٰٓأَهْلَ ٱلْكِتَٰبِ لَا تَغْلُواْ فِى دِينِكُمْ وَلَا تَقُولُواْ عَلَى ٱللَّهِ إِلَّا ٱلْحَقَّ إِنَّمَا ٱلْمَسِيحُ عِيسَى ٱبْنُ مَرْيَمَ رَسُولُ ٱللَّهِ وَكَلِمَتُهُۥٓ أَلْقَىٰهَآ إِلَىٰ مَرْيَمَ وَرُوحٌ مِّنْهُ فَـَٔامِنُواْ بِٱللَّهِ وَرُسُلِهِۦ وَلَا تَقُولُواْ ثَلَٰثَةٌ ٱنتَهُواْ خَيْرًا لَّكُمْ إِنَّمَا ٱللَّهُ إِلَٰهٌ وَٰحِدٌ سُبْحَٰنَهُۥٓ أَن يَكُونَ لَهُۥ وَلَدٌ لَّهُۥ مَا فِى ٱلسَّمَٰوَٰتِ وَمَا فِى ٱلْأَرْضِ وَكَفَىٰ بِٱللَّهِ وَكِيلًا (١٧١) لَّن يَسْتَنكِفَ ٱلْمَسِيحُ أَن يَكُونَ عَبْدًا لِّلَّهِ وَلَا ٱلْمَلَٰٓئِكَةُ ٱلْمُقَرَّبُونَ وَمَن يَسْتَنكِفْ عَنْ عِبَادَتِهِۦ وَيَسْتَكْبِرْ فَسَيَحْشُرُهُمْ إِلَيْهِ جَمِيعًا (١٧٢) فَأَمَّا ٱلَّذِينَ ءَامَنُواْ وَعَمِلُواْ ٱلصَّٰلِحَٰتِ فَيُوَفِّيهِمْ أُجُورَهُمْ وَيَزِيدُهُم مِّن فَضْلِهِۦ وَأَمَّا ٱلَّذِينَ ٱسْتَنكَفُواْ وَٱسْتَكْبَرُواْ فَيُعَذِّبُهُمْ عَذَابًا أَلِيمًا وَلَا يَجِدُونَ لَهُم مِّن دُونِ ٱللَّهِ وَلِيًّا وَلَا نَصِيرًا (١٧٣) يَٰٓأَيُّهَا ٱلنَّاسُ قَدْ جَآءَكُم بُرْهَٰنٌ مِّن رَّبِّكُمْ وَأَنزَلْنَآ إِلَيْكُمْ نُورًا مُّبِينًا (١٧٤) فَأَمَّا ٱلَّذِينَ ءَامَنُواْ بِٱللَّهِ وَٱعْتَصَمُواْ بِهِۦ فَسَيُدْخِلُهُمْ فِى رَحْمَةٍ مِّنْهُ وَفَضْلٍ وَيَهْدِيهِمْ إِلَيْهِ صِرَٰطًا مُّسْتَقِيمًا (١٧٥)

*Verily, those who disbelieve and did wrong [by concealing the truth about Prophet Muhammad and his message of true Islâmic Monotheism written in the Taurât (Torah) and the Injeel with them], Allâh will not forgive them, nor will He guide them to any way, - (168) Except the way of Hell, to dwell therein forever, and this is ever easy for Allâh. (169) O mankind! Verily, there has come to you the Messenger (Muhammad) with the truth from your Lord, so believe in him, it is better for you. But if you disbelieve, then certainly to Allâh belongs all that is in the heavens and the earth. And Allâh is Ever All-Knowing, All-Wise. (170) O people of the Scripture! Do not exceed the limits in your religion, nor say of Allâh aught but the truth. The Messiah Īsā(Jesus), son of Maryam (Mary), was (no more than) a Messenger of Allâh and His Word, ("Be!" - and he was) which He bestowed on Maryam (Mary) and a spirit (Rûh) created by Him; so believe in Allâh and His Messengers. Say not: "Three (trinity)!" Cease! (it is) better for you. For Allâh is (the only) One Ilâh (God), glory be to Him (Far Exalted is He) above having a son. To Him belongs all that is in the heavens and all that is in the earth. And Allâh is All¬Sufficient as a Disposer of affairs. (171) The Messiah will never be proud to reject to be a slave of Allâh, nor the angels who are near (to Allâh). And whosoever rejects His worship and is proud, then He will gather them all together unto Himself. (172) So, as for those who believed (in the Oneness of Allâh - Islâmic Monotheism) and did deeds of righteousness, He will*

give their (due) rewards, and more out of His Bounty.
But as for those who refused His worship and were
proud, He will punish them with a painful torment . And
they will not find for themselves besides Allâh any
protector or helper. (173) O mankind! Verily, there has
come to you a convincing proof (Prophet Muhammad)
from your Lord, and We sent down to you a manifest
light (this Qur'ân). (174) So, as for those who believed in
Allâh and held fast to Him, He will admit them to His
Mercy and Grace (i.e. Paradise), and guide them to
Himself by a Straight Path. (175)

## Quran 5:3

حُرِّمَتْ عَلَيْكُمُ ٱلْمَيْتَةُ وَٱلدَّمُ وَلَحْمُ ٱلْخِنزِيرِ وَمَآ أُهِلَّ لِغَيْرِ ٱللَّهِ
بِهِ وَٱلْمُنْخَنِقَةُ وَٱلْمَوْقُوذَةُ وَٱلْمُتَرَدِّيَةُ وَٱلنَّطِيحَةُ وَمَآ أَكَلَ ٱلسَّبُعُ
إِلَّا مَا ذَكَّيْتُمْ وَمَا ذُبِحَ عَلَى ٱلنُّصُبِ وَأَن تَسْتَقْسِمُوا۟ بِٱلْأَزْلَـٰمِ
ذَٰلِكُمْ فِسْقٌ ٱلْيَوْمَ يَئِسَ ٱلَّذِينَ كَفَرُوا۟ مِن دِينِكُمْ فَلَا تَخْشَوْهُمْ
وَٱخْشَوْنِ ٱلْيَوْمَ أَكْمَلْتُ لَكُمْ دِينَكُمْ وَأَتْمَمْتُ عَلَيْكُمْ نِعْمَتِى
وَرَضِيتُ لَكُمُ ٱلْإِسْلَـٰمَ دِينًا فَمَنِ ٱضْطُرَّ فِى مَخْمَصَةٍ غَيْرَ
مُتَجَانِفٍ لِّإِثْمٍ فَإِنَّ ٱللَّهَ غَفُورٌ رَّحِيمٌ (٣)

Forbidden to you (for food) are: Al-Maitah (the dead
animals - cattle - beast not slaughtered), blood, the flesh
of swine, and that on which Allâh's Name has not been
mentioned while slaughtering, (that which has been
slaughtered as a sacrifice for others than Allâh, or has
been slaughtered for idols) and that which has been killed

*by strangling, or by a violent blow, or by a headlong fall, or by the goring of horns - and that which has been (partly) eaten by a wild animal - unless you are able to slaughter it (before its death) - and that which is sacrificed (slaughtered) on An-Nusub (stone-altars). (Forbidden) also is to use arrows seeking luck or decision; (all) that is Fisqun (disobedience of Allâh and sin). This day, those who disbelieved have given up all hope of your religion; so fear them not, but fear Me. This day, I have perfected your religion for you, completed My Favour upon you, and have chosen for you Islâm as your religion. But as for him who is forced by severe hunger, with no inclination to sin (such can eat these above mentioned meats), then surely, Allâh is Oft-Forgiving, Most Merciful. (3)*

## Quran 5:9-10

وَعَدَ ٱللَّهُ ٱلَّذِينَ ءَامَنُواْ وَعَمِلُواْ ٱلصَّلِحَٰتِ لَهُم مَّغْفِرَةٌ وَأَجْرٌ عَظِيمٌ (٩) وَٱلَّذِينَ كَفَرُواْ وَكَذَّبُواْ بِـَٔايَٰتِنَآ أُوْلَٰٓئِكَ أَصْحَٰبُ ٱلْجَحِيمِ (١٠)

*Allâh has promised those who believe (in the Oneness of Allâh - Islâmic Monotheism) and do deeds of righteousness, that for them there is forgiveness and a great reward (i.e. Paradise) (9) And those who disbelieve and deny our Ayât (proofs, evidences, verses, lessons, signs, revelations, etc.) are those who will be the dwellers of the Hell-fire. (10)*

۞ وَلَقَدْ أَخَذَ ٱللَّهُ مِيثَـٰقَ بَنِىٓ إِسْرَٰٓءِيلَ وَبَعَثْنَا مِنْهُمُ ٱثْنَىْ
عَشَرَ نَقِيبًا ۖ وَقَالَ ٱللَّهُ إِنِّى مَعَكُمْ ۖ لَئِنْ أَقَمْتُمُ ٱلصَّلَوٰةَ وَءَاتَيْتُمُ
ٱلزَّكَوٰةَ وَءَامَنتُم بِرُسُلِى وَعَزَّرْتُمُوهُمْ وَأَقْرَضْتُمُ ٱللَّهَ قَرْضًا
حَسَنًا لَّأُكَفِّرَنَّ عَنكُمْ سَيِّـَٔاتِكُمْ وَلَأُدْخِلَنَّكُمْ جَنَّـٰتٍ تَجْرِى مِن
تَحْتِهَا ٱلْأَنْهَـٰرُ ۚ فَمَن كَفَرَ بَعْدَ ذَٰلِكَ مِنكُمْ فَقَدْ ضَلَّ سَوَآءَ
ٱلسَّبِيلِ (١٢) فَبِمَا نَقْضِهِم مِّيثَـٰقَهُمْ لَعَنَّـٰهُمْ وَجَعَلْنَا قُلُوبَهُمْ
قَـٰسِيَةً ۖ يُحَرِّفُونَ ٱلْكَلِمَ عَن مَّوَاضِعِهِ ۙ وَنَسُوا۟ حَظًّا مِّمَّا ذُكِّرُوا۟
بِهِ ۚ وَلَا تَزَالُ تَطَّلِعُ عَلَىٰ خَآئِنَةٍ مِّنْهُمْ إِلَّا قَلِيلًا مِّنْهُمْ ۖ فَٱعْفُ
عَنْهُمْ وَٱصْفَحْ ۚ إِنَّ ٱللَّهَ يُحِبُّ ٱلْمُحْسِنِينَ (١٣) وَمِنَ ٱلَّذِينَ قَالُوٓا۟
إِنَّا نَصَـٰرَىٰٓ أَخَذْنَا مِيثَـٰقَهُمْ فَنَسُوا۟ حَظًّا مِّمَّا ذُكِّرُوا۟ بِهِۦ
فَأَغْرَيْنَا بَيْنَهُمُ ٱلْعَدَاوَةَ وَٱلْبَغْضَآءَ إِلَىٰ يَوْمِ ٱلْقِيَـٰمَةِ ۚ وَسَوْفَ
يُنَبِّئُهُمُ ٱللَّهُ بِمَا كَانُوا۟ يَصْنَعُونَ (١٤)

*Indeed Allâh took the covenant from the Children of
Israel (Jews), and We appointed twelve leaders among
them. And Allâh said: "I am with you if you perform As-
Salât (Iqâmat-as-Salât) and give Zakât and believe in My
Messengers; honour and assist them, and lend a good
loan to Allâh. Verily, I will expiate your sins and admit
you to Gardens under which rivers flow (in Paradise).
But if any of you after this, disbelieved, he has indeed
gone astray from the Straight Path." (12) So because of
their breach of their covenant, We cursed them, and made
their hearts grow hard. They change the words from their
(right) places and have abandoned a good part of the*

Message that was sent to them. And you will not cease to discover deceit in them, except a few of them. But forgive them, and overlook (their misdeeds). Verily, Allâh loves Al¬Muhsinûn (good¬doers). (13) And from those who call themselves Christians, We took their covenant, but they have abandoned a good part of the Message that was sent to them. So We planted amongst them enmity and hatred till the Day of Resurrection (when they discarded Allâh's Book, disobeyed Allâh's Messengers and His Orders and transgressed beyond bounds in Allâh's disobedience), and Allâh will inform them of what they used to do. (14)

## Quran 5:18

وَقَالَتِ ٱلْيَهُودُ وَٱلنَّصَارَىٰ نَحْنُ أَبْنَٰٓؤُا۟ ٱللَّهِ وَأَحِبَّٰٓؤُهُۥ قُلْ فَلِمَ يُعَذِّبُكُم بِذُنُوبِكُم بَلْ أَنتُم بَشَرٌ مِّمَّنْ خَلَقَ يَغْفِرُ لِمَن يَشَآءُ وَيُعَذِّبُ مَن يَشَآءُ وَلِلَّهِ مُلْكُ ٱلسَّمَٰوَٰتِ وَٱلْأَرْضِ وَمَا بَيْنَهُمَا وَإِلَيْهِ ٱلْمَصِيرُ (١٨)

And (both) the Jews and the Christians say: "We are the children of Allâh and His loved ones." Say: "Why then does He punish you for your sins?" Nay, you are but human beings, of those He has created, He forgives whom He wills and He punishes whom He wills. And to Allâh belongs the dominion of the heavens and the earth and all that is between them, and to Him is the return (of all). (18)

## Quran 5:36-37

إِنَّ ٱلَّذِينَ كَفَرُوا لَوْ أَنَّ لَهُم مَّا فِى ٱلْأَرْضِ جَمِيعًا وَمِثْلَهُ مَعَهُ لِيَفْتَدُوا بِهِ مِنْ عَذَابِ يَوْمِ ٱلْقِيَـٰمَةِ مَا تُقُبِّلَ مِنْهُمْ وَلَهُمْ عَذَابٌ أَلِيمٌ (٣٦) يُرِيدُونَ أَن يَخْرُجُوا مِنَ ٱلنَّارِ وَمَا هُم بِخَـٰرِجِينَ مِنْهَا وَلَهُمْ عَذَابٌ مُّقِيمٌ (٣٧)

*Verily, those who disbelieve, if they had all that is in the earth, and as much again therewith to ransom themselves thereby from the torment on the Day of Resurrection, it would never be accepted of them, and theirs would be a painful torment. (36) They will long to get out of the Fire, but never will they get out therefrom, and theirs will be a lasting torment. (37)*

## Quran 5:41-42

۞ يَـٰٓأَيُّهَا ٱلرَّسُولُ لَا يَحْزُنكَ ٱلَّذِينَ يُسَـٰرِعُونَ فِى ٱلْكُفْرِ مِنَ ٱلَّذِينَ قَالُوٓا ءَامَنَّا بِأَفْوَٰهِهِمْ وَلَمْ تُؤْمِن قُلُوبُهُمْ وَمِنَ ٱلَّذِينَ هَادُوا سَمَّـٰعُونَ لِلْكَذِبِ سَمَّـٰعُونَ لِقَوْمٍ ءَاخَرِينَ لَمْ يَأْتُوكَ يُحَرِّفُونَ ٱلْكَلِمَ مِنۢ بَعْدِ مَوَاضِعِهِ يَقُولُونَ إِنْ أُوتِيتُمْ هَـٰذَا فَخُذُوهُ وَإِن لَّمْ تُؤْتَوْهُ فَٱحْذَرُوا وَمَن يُرِدِ ٱللَّهُ فِتْنَتَهُ فَلَن تَمْلِكَ لَهُ مِنَ ٱللَّهِ شَيْـًٔا أُوْلَـٰٓئِكَ ٱلَّذِينَ لَمْ يُرِدِ ٱللَّهُ أَن يُطَهِّرَ قُلُوبَهُمْ لَهُمْ فِى ٱلدُّنْيَا خِزْيٌ وَلَهُمْ فِى ٱلْأَخِرَةِ عَذَابٌ عَظِيمٌ (٤١) سَمَّـٰعُونَ لِلْكَذِبِ أَكَّـٰلُونَ لِلسُّحْتِ فَإِن جَآءُوكَ فَٱحْكُم بَيْنَهُمْ أَوْ أَعْرِضْ عَنْهُمْ وَإِن تُعْرِضْ عَنْهُمْ فَلَن يَضُرُّوكَ شَيْـًٔا وَإِنْ حَكَمْتَ فَٱحْكُم بَيْنَهُم بِٱلْقِسْطِ إِنَّ ٱللَّهَ يُحِبُّ ٱلْمُقْسِطِينَ (٤٢)

*O Messenger (Muhammad)! Let not those who hurry to fall into disbelief grieve you, of such who say: "We believe" with their mouths but their hearts have no faith. And of the Jews are men who listen much and eagerly to lies - listen to others who have not come to you. They change the words from their places; they say, "If you are given this, take it, but if you are not given this, then beware!" And whomsoever Allâh wants to put in Al¬Fitnah [error, because of his rejecting the Faith], you can do nothing for him against Allâh. Those are the ones whose hearts Allâh does not want to purify (from disbelief and hypocrisy); for them there is a disgrace in this world, and in the Hereafter a great torment. (41) (They like to) listen to falsehood, to devour anything forbidden. So if they come to you, either judge between them, or turn away from them. If you turn away from them, they cannot hurt you in the least. And if you judge, judge with justice between them. Verily, Allâh loves those who act justly. (42)*

## Quran 5:54-56

يَـٰٓأَيُّهَا ٱلَّذِينَ ءَامَنُوا۟ مَن يَرْتَدَّ مِنكُمْ عَن دِينِهِۦ فَسَوْفَ يَأْتِى ٱللَّهُ بِقَوْمٍ يُحِبُّهُمْ وَيُحِبُّونَهُۥٓ أَذِلَّةٍ عَلَى ٱلْمُؤْمِنِينَ أَعِزَّةٍ عَلَى ٱلْكَـٰفِرِينَ يُجَـٰهِدُونَ فِى سَبِيلِ ٱللَّهِ وَلَا يَخَافُونَ لَوْمَةَ لَآئِمٍ ذَٰلِكَ فَضْلُ ٱللَّهِ يُؤْتِيهِ مَن يَشَآءُ وَٱللَّهُ وَٰسِعٌ عَلِيمٌ (٥٤) إِنَّمَا وَلِيُّكُمُ ٱللَّهُ وَرَسُولُهُۥ وَٱلَّذِينَ ءَامَنُوا۟ ٱلَّذِينَ يُقِيمُونَ ٱلصَّلَوٰةَ وَيُؤْتُونَ

ٱلزَّكَوٰةَ وَهُمْ رَٰكِعُونَ (٥٥) وَمَن يَتَوَلَّ ٱللَّهَ وَرَسُولَهُۥ وَٱلَّذِينَ
ءَامَنُواْ فَإِنَّ حِزْبَ ٱللَّهِ هُمُ ٱلْغَٰلِبُونَ (٥٦)

*O you who believe! Whoever from among you turns back from his religion (Islâm), Allâh will bring a people whom He will love and they will love Him; humble towards the believers, stern towards the disbelievers, fighting in the Way of Allâh, and never fear of the blame of the blamers. That is the Grace of Allâh which He bestows on whom He wills. And Allâh is All-Sufficient for His creatures' needs, All-Knower. (54) Verily, your Walî (Protector or Helper) is none other than Allâh, His Messenger, and the believers, - those who perform As-Salât (Iqâmat-as-Salât), and give Zakât, and they are Rakiun (those who bow down or submit themselves with obedience to Allâh in prayer). (55) And whosoever takes Allâh, His Messenger, and those who have believed, as Protectors, then the party of Allâh will be the victorious. (56)*

## Quran 5:64-67

وَقَالَتِ ٱلْيَهُودُ يَدُ ٱللَّهِ مَغْلُولَةٌ غُلَّتْ أَيْدِيهِمْ وَلُعِنُواْ بِمَا قَالُواْ بَلْ
يَدَاهُ مَبْسُوطَتَانِ يُنفِقُ كَيْفَ يَشَاءُ وَلَيَزِيدَنَّ كَثِيرًا مِّنْهُم مَّآ
أُنزِلَ إِلَيْكَ مِن رَّبِّكَ طُغْيَٰنًا وَكُفْرًا وَأَلْقَيْنَا بَيْنَهُمُ ٱلْعَدَاوَةَ
وَٱلْبَغْضَاءَ إِلَىٰ يَوْمِ ٱلْقِيَٰمَةِ كُلَّمَآ أَوْقَدُواْ نَارًا لِّلْحَرْبِ أَطْفَأَهَا
ٱللَّهُ وَيَسْعَوْنَ فِي ٱلْأَرْضِ فَسَادًا وَٱللَّهُ لَا يُحِبُّ ٱلْمُفْسِدِينَ
(٦٤) وَلَوْ أَنَّ أَهْلَ ٱلْكِتَٰبِ ءَامَنُواْ وَٱتَّقَوْاْ لَكَفَّرْنَا عَنْهُمْ
سَيِّئَاتِهِمْ وَلَأَدْخَلْنَٰهُمْ جَنَّٰتِ ٱلنَّعِيمِ (٦٥) وَلَوْ أَنَّهُمْ أَقَامُواْ

ٱلتَّوۡرَىٰةَ وَٱلۡإِنجِيلَ وَمَآ أُنزِلَ إِلَيۡهِم مِّن رَّبِّهِمۡ لَأَكَلُواْ مِن
فَوۡقِهِمۡ وَمِن تَحۡتِ أَرۡجُلِهِمۚ مِّنۡهُمۡ أُمَّةٌ مُّقۡتَصِدَةٌۖ وَكَثِيرٌ مِّنۡهُمۡ سَآءَ
مَا يَعۡمَلُونَ (٦٦) ۞ يَـٰٓأَيُّهَا ٱلرَّسُولُ بَلِّغۡ مَآ أُنزِلَ إِلَيۡكَ مِن
رَّبِّكَۖ وَإِن لَّمۡ تَفۡعَلۡ فَمَا بَلَّغۡتَ رِسَالَتَهُۥۚ وَٱللَّهُ يَعۡصِمُكَ مِنَ
ٱلنَّاسِۗ إِنَّ ٱللَّهَ لَا يَهۡدِى ٱلۡقَوۡمَ ٱلۡكَـٰفِرِينَ (٦٧)

*The Jews say: "Allâh's Hand is tied up (i.e. He does not give and spend of His Bounty)." Be their hands tied up and be they accursed for what they uttered. Nay, both His Hands are widely outstretched. He spends (of His Bounty) as He wills. Verily, the Revelation that has come to you from your Lord (Allâh) increases in most of them (their) obstinate rebellion and disbelief. We have put enmity and hatred amongst them till the Day of Resurrection. Every time they kindled the fire of war, Allâh extinguished it; and they (ever) strive to make mischief on earth. And Allâh does not like the Mufsidûn (mischief-makers). (64) And if only the people of the Scripture (Jews and Christians) had believed (in Muhammad) and warded off evil (sin, ascribing partners to Allâh) and had become Al¬Muttaqûn (the pious) We would indeed have expiated from them their sins and admitted them to Gardens of pleasure (in Paradise). (65) And if only they had acted according to the Taurât (Torah), the Injeel, and what has (now) been sent down to them from their Lord (the Qur'ân), they would surely have gotten provision from above them and from underneath their feet. There are from among them people* who are on the right course (i.e. they act on the revelation and believe in Prophet Muhammad), but many of them do evil deeds. (66) O Messenger (Muhammad)! Proclaim (the Message) which has been sent down to you from your Lord. And if you do not, then you have not conveyed His Message. Allâh will protect you from mankind. Verily, Allâh guides not the people who disbelieve. (67)

## Quran 5:86

وَٱلَّذِينَ كَفَرُواْ وَكَذَّبُواْ بِـَٔايَٰتِنَآ أُوْلَٰٓئِكَ أَصۡحَٰبُ ٱلۡجَحِيمِ (٨٦)

But those who disbelieved and belied Our Ayât (proofs, evidences, verses, lessons, signs, revelations, etc.), they shall be the dwellers of the (Hell) Fire. (86)

## Quran 5:94-96

يَٰٓأَيُّهَا ٱلَّذِينَ ءَامَنُواْ لَيَبۡلُوَنَّكُمُ ٱللَّهُ بِشَىۡءٍ مِّنَ ٱلصَّيۡدِ تَنَالُهُۥٓ أَيۡدِيكُمۡ وَرِمَاحُكُمۡ لِيَعۡلَمَ ٱللَّهُ مَن يَخَافُهُۥ بِٱلۡغَيۡبِ فَمَنِ ٱعۡتَدَىٰ بَعۡدَ ذَٰلِكَ فَلَهُۥ عَذَابٌ أَلِيمٌ (٩٤) يَٰٓأَيُّهَا ٱلَّذِينَ ءَامَنُواْ لَا تَقۡتُلُواْ ٱلصَّيۡدَ وَأَنتُمۡ حُرُمٌ وَمَن قَتَلَهُۥ مِنكُم مُّتَعَمِّدًا فَجَزَآءٌ مِّثۡلُ مَا قَتَلَ مِنَ ٱلنَّعَمِ يَحۡكُمُ بِهِۦ ذَوَا عَدۡلٍ مِّنكُمۡ هَدۡيًۢا بَٰلِغَ ٱلۡكَعۡبَةِ أَوۡ كَفَّٰرَةٌ طَعَامُ مَسَٰكِينَ أَوۡ عَدۡلُ ذَٰلِكَ صِيَامًا لِّيَذُوقَ وَبَالَ أَمۡرِهِۦ عَفَا ٱللَّهُ عَمَّا سَلَفَ وَمَنۡ عَادَ فَيَنتَقِمُ ٱللَّهُ مِنۡهُ وَٱللَّهُ عَزِيزٌ ذُو ٱنتِقَامٍ (٩٥) أُحِلَّ لَكُمۡ صَيۡدُ ٱلۡبَحۡرِ وَطَعَامُهُۥ مَتَٰعًا لَّكُمۡ وَلِلسَّيَّارَةِ

وَحُرِّمَ عَلَيْكُمْ صَيْدُ ٱلْبَرِّ مَا دُمْتُمْ حُرُمًا ۗ وَٱتَّقُوا۟ ٱللَّهَ ٱلَّذِىٓ إِلَيْهِ تُحْشَرُونَ (٩٦)

*O you who believe! Allâh will certainly make a trial of you with something in (the matter of) the game that is well within reach of your hands and your lances, that Allâh may test who fears Him unseen. Then whoever transgresses thereafter, for him there is a painful torment (94) O you who believe! Kill not game while you are in a state of Ihrâm for Hajj or 'Umrah (pilgrimage), and whosoever of you kills it intentionally, the penalty is an offering, brought to the Ka'bah, of an eatable animal (i.e. sheep, goat, cow) equivalent to the one he killed, as adjudged by two just men among you; or, for expiation, he should feed Masâkin (poor persons), or its equivalent in Saum (fasting), that he may taste the heaviness (punishment) of his deed. Allâh has forgiven what is past, but whosoever commits it again, Allâh will take retribution from him. And Allâh is All¬Mighty, All-Able of Retribution (95) Lawful to you is (the pursuit of) water¬game and its use for food - for the benefit of yourselves and those who travel, but forbidden is (the pursuit of) land¬game as long as you are in a state of Ihrâm (for Hajj or 'Umrah). And fear Allâh to Whom you shall be gathered back. (96)*

**Quran 5:105**

يَـٰٓأَيُّهَا ٱلَّذِينَ ءَامَنُواْ عَلَيْكُمْ أَنفُسَكُمْ ۖ لَا يَضُرُّكُم مَّن ضَلَّ إِذَا
ٱهْتَدَيْتُمْ ۚ إِلَى ٱللَّهِ مَرْجِعُكُمْ جَمِيعًا فَيُنَبِّئُكُم بِمَا كُنتُمْ تَعْمَلُونَ
(١٠٥)

*O you who believe! Take care of your ownselves, If you*
*follow the (right) guidance (and enjoin what is right*
*Islâmic Monotheism and all that Islâm orders one to do)*
*and forbid what is wrong (polytheism, disbelief and all*
*Islâm has forbidden) no hurt can come to you from those*
*who are in error. The return of you all is to Allâh, then*
*He will inform you about (all) that which you used to do.*
*(105)*

## Quran 5:109-119

۞ يَوْمَ يَجْمَعُ ٱللَّهُ ٱلرُّسُلَ فَيَقُولُ مَاذَآ أُجِبْتُمْ ۖ قَالُواْ لَا عِلْمَ لَنَآ ۖ
إِنَّكَ أَنتَ عَلَّـٰمُ ٱلْغُيُوبِ (١٠٩) إِذْ قَالَ ٱللَّهُ يَـٰعِيسَى ٱبْنَ مَرْيَمَ
ٱذْكُرْ نِعْمَتِى عَلَيْكَ وَعَلَىٰ وَٰلِدَتِكَ إِذْ أَيَّدتُّكَ بِرُوحِ ٱلْقُدُسِ
تُكَلِّمُ ٱلنَّاسَ فِى ٱلْمَهْدِ وَكَهْلًا ۖ وَإِذْ عَلَّمْتُكَ ٱلْكِتَـٰبَ وَٱلْحِكْمَةَ
وَٱلتَّوْرَىٰةَ وَٱلْإِنجِيلَ ۖ وَإِذْ تَخْلُقُ مِنَ ٱلطِّينِ كَهَيْئَةِ ٱلطَّيْرِ بِإِذْنِى
فَتَنفُخُ فِيهَا فَتَكُونُ طَيْرًا بِإِذْنِى ۖ وَتُبْرِئُ ٱلْأَكْمَهَ وَٱلْأَبْرَصَ
بِإِذْنِى ۖ وَإِذْ تُخْرِجُ ٱلْمَوْتَىٰ بِإِذْنِى ۖ وَإِذْ كَفَفْتُ بَنِى إِسْرَٰٓئِيلَ
عَنكَ إِذْ جِئْتَهُم بِٱلْبَيِّنَـٰتِ فَقَالَ ٱلَّذِينَ كَفَرُواْ مِنْهُمْ إِنْ هَـٰذَآ إِلَّا
سِحْرٌ مُّبِينٌ (١١٠) وَإِذْ أَوْحَيْتُ إِلَى ٱلْحَوَارِيِّـۧنَ أَنْ ءَامِنُواْ
بِى وَبِرَسُولِى قَالُوٓاْ ءَامَنَّا وَٱشْهَدْ بِأَنَّنَا مُسْلِمُونَ (١١١) إِذْ
قَالَ ٱلْحَوَارِيُّونَ يَـٰعِيسَى ٱبْنَ مَرْيَمَ هَلْ يَسْتَطِيعُ رَبُّكَ أَن يُنَزِّلَ
عَلَيْنَا مَآئِدَةً مِّنَ ٱلسَّمَآءِ ۖ قَالَ ٱتَّقُواْ ٱللَّهَ إِن كُنتُم مُّؤْمِنِينَ

قَالُواْ نُرِيدُ أَن نَّأْكُلَ مِنْهَا وَتَطْمَئِنَّ قُلُوبُنَا وَنَعْلَمَ أَن (١١٢)
قَدْ صَدَقْتَنَا وَنَكُونَ عَلَيْهَا مِنَ ٱلشَّـٰهِدِينَ (١١٣) قَالَ عِيسَى
ٱبْنُ مَرْيَمَ ٱللَّهُمَّ رَبَّنَآ أَنزِلْ عَلَيْنَا مَآئِدَةً مِّنَ ٱلسَّمَآءِ تَكُونُ لَنَا
عِيدًا لِّأَوَّلِنَا وَءَاخِرِنَا وَءَايَةً مِّنكَ وَٱرْزُقْنَا وَأَنتَ خَيْرُ
ٱلرَّازِقِينَ (١١٤) قَالَ ٱللَّهُ إِنِّى مُنَزِّلُهَا عَلَيْكُمْ فَمَن يَكْفُرْ بَعْدُ
مِنكُمْ فَإِنِّىٓ أُعَذِّبُهُۥ عَذَابًا لَّآ أُعَذِّبُهُۥٓ أَحَدًا مِّنَ ٱلْعَـٰلَمِينَ (١١٥)
وَإِذْ قَالَ ٱللَّهُ يَـٰعِيسَى ٱبْنَ مَرْيَمَ ءَأَنتَ قُلْتَ لِلنَّاسِ ٱتَّخِذُونِى
وَأُمِّىَ إِلَـٰهَيْنِ مِن دُونِ ٱللَّهِ قَالَ سُبْحَـٰنَكَ مَا يَكُونُ لِىٓ أَنْ أَقُولَ
مَا لَيْسَ لِى بِحَقٍّ إِن كُنتُ قُلْتُهُۥ فَقَدْ عَلِمْتَهُۥ تَعْلَمُ مَا فِى نَفْسِى
وَلَآ أَعْلَمُ مَا فِى نَفْسِكَ إِنَّكَ أَنتَ عَلَّـٰمُ ٱلْغُيُوبِ (١١٦) مَا قُلْتُ
لَهُمْ إِلَّا مَآ أَمَرْتَنِى بِهِۦٓ أَنِ ٱعْبُدُواْ ٱللَّهَ رَبِّى وَرَبَّكُمْ وَكُنتُ
عَلَيْهِمْ شَهِيدًا مَّا دُمْتُ فِيهِمْ فَلَمَّا تَوَفَّيْتَنِى كُنتَ أَنتَ ٱلرَّقِيبَ
عَلَيْهِمْ وَأَنتَ عَلَىٰ كُلِّ شَىْءٍ شَهِيدٌ (١١٧) إِن تُعَذِّبْهُمْ فَإِنَّهُمْ
عِبَادُكَ وَإِن تَغْفِرْ لَهُمْ فَإِنَّكَ أَنتَ ٱلْعَزِيزُ ٱلْحَكِيمُ (١١٨) قَالَ
ٱللَّهُ هَـٰذَا يَوْمُ يَنفَعُ ٱلصَّـٰدِقِينَ صِدْقُهُمْ لَهُمْ جَنَّـٰتٌ تَجْرِى مِن
تَحْتِهَا ٱلْأَنْهَـٰرُ خَـٰلِدِينَ فِيهَآ أَبَدًا رَّضِىَ ٱللَّهُ عَنْهُمْ وَرَضُواْ عَنْهُ
ذَٰلِكَ ٱلْفَوْزُ ٱلْعَظِيمُ (١١٩)

*On the Day when Allâh will gather the Messengers*
*together and say to them: "What was the response you*
*received (to your teaching)? They will say: "We have no*
*knowledge, verily, only You are the All¬Knower of all*
*that is hidden (or unseen)." (109) (Remember) when*
*Allâh will say (on the Day of Resurrection). "O 'Īsā*
*(Jesus), son of Maryam (Mary)! Remember My Favour*
*to you and to your mother when I supported you with*

Rûh-ul-Qudus [Jibrail (Gabriel)] so that you spoke to the people in the cradle and in maturity; and when I taught you writing, Al¬Hikmah (the power of understanding), the Taurât (Torah) and the Injeel; and when you made out of the clay, a figure like that of a bird, by My Permission, and you breathed into it, and it became a bird by My Permission, and you healed those born blind, and the lepers by My Permission, and when you brought forth the dead by My Permission; and when I restrained the Children of Israel from you (when they resolved to kill you) as you came unto them with clear proofs, and the disbelievers among them said: 'This is nothing but evident magic.' " (110) And when I (Allâh) revealed Al-Hawârîyyun (the disciples) [of 'Īsā (Jesus)] to believe in Me and My Messenger, they said: "We believe. And bear witness that we are Muslims." (111) (Remember) when Al-Hawârîyyûn (the disciples) said: "O 'Īsā (Jesus), son of Maryam (Mary)! Can your Lord send down to us a table spread (with food) from heaven?" 'Īsā (Jesus) said: "Fear Allâh, if you are indeed believers." (112) They said: "We wish to eat thereof and to satisfy your heart (to be stronger in Faith), and to know that you have indeed told us the truth and that we ourselves be its witnesses." (113) 'Īsā (Jesus), son of Maryam (Mary), said: "O Allâh, our Lord! Send us from heaven a table spread (with food) that there may be for us - for the first and the last of us - a festival and a sign from You; and provide us

*sustenance, for You are the Best of sustainers." (114)*
*Allâh said: "I am going to send it down unto you, but if*
*any of you after that disbelieves, then I will punish him*
*with a torment such as I have not inflicted on anyone*
*among (all) the 'Alamîn (mankind and jinn)." (115) And*
*(remember) when Allâh will say (on the Day of*
*Resurrection): "O 'Īsā (Jesus), son of Maryam (Mary)!*
*Did you say unto men: 'Worship me and my mother as*
*two gods besides Allâh?' " He will say: "Glory be to*
*You! It was not for me to say what I had no right (to*
*say). Had I said such a thing, You would surely have*
*known it. You know what is in my inner-self though I do*
*not know what is in Yours, truly, You, only You, are the*
*All-Knower of all that is hidden (and unseen). (116)*
*"Never did I say to them aught except what You (Allâh)*
*did command me to say: 'Worship Allâh, my Lord and*
*your Lord.' And I was a witness over them while I dwelt*
*amongst them, but when You took me up, You were the*
*Watcher over them, and You are a Witness to all things.*
*(117) "If You punish them, they are Your slaves, and if*
*You forgive them, verily You, only You are the*
*All¬Mighty, the All¬Wise." (118) Allâh will say: "This*
*is a Day on which the truthful will profit from their*
*truth: theirs are Gardens under which rivers flow (in*
*Paradise) - they shall abide therein forever. Allâh is*
*pleased with them and they with Him. That is the great*
*success (Paradise). (119)*

## Quran 6:2

هُوَ ٱلَّذِى خَلَقَكُم مِّن طِينٍ ثُمَّ قَضَىٰٓ أَجَلًا ۖ وَأَجَلٌ مُّسَمًّى عِندَهُۥ ۖ ثُمَّ أَنتُمْ تَمْتَرُونَ (٢)

*He it is Who has created you from clay, and then has decreed a (stated) term (for you to die). And there is with Him another determined term (for you to be resurrected), yet you doubt (in the Resurrection). (2)*

## Quran 6:5

فَقَدْ كَذَّبُوا۟ بِٱلْحَقِّ لَمَّا جَآءَهُمْ ۖ فَسَوْفَ يَأْتِيهِمْ أَنۢبَـٰٓؤُا۟ مَا كَانُوا۟ بِهِۦ يَسْتَهْزِءُونَ (٥)

*Indeed, they rejected the truth (the Qur'ân and Muhammad) when it came to them, but there will come to them the news of that (the torment) which they used to mock at. (5)*

## Quran 6:12-17

قُل لِّمَن مَّا فِى ٱلسَّمَـٰوَٰتِ وَٱلْأَرْضِ ۖ قُل لِّلَّهِ ۚ كَتَبَ عَلَىٰ نَفْسِهِ ٱلرَّحْمَةَ ۚ لَيَجْمَعَنَّكُمْ إِلَىٰ يَوْمِ ٱلْقِيَـٰمَةِ لَا رَيْبَ فِيهِ ۚ ٱلَّذِينَ خَسِرُوٓا۟ أَنفُسَهُمْ فَهُمْ لَا يُؤْمِنُونَ (١٢) ۞ وَلَهُۥ مَا سَكَنَ فِى ٱلَّيْلِ وَٱلنَّهَارِ ۚ وَهُوَ ٱلسَّمِيعُ ٱلْعَلِيمُ (١٣) قُلْ أَغَيْرَ ٱللَّهِ أَتَّخِذُ وَلِيًّا فَاطِرِ ٱلسَّمَـٰوَٰتِ وَٱلْأَرْضِ وَهُوَ يُطْعِمُ وَلَا يُطْعَمُ ۗ قُلْ إِنِّىٓ أُمِرْتُ أَنْ أَكُونَ أَوَّلَ مَنْ أَسْلَمَ ۖ وَلَا تَكُونَنَّ مِنَ ٱلْمُشْرِكِينَ (١٤) قُلْ إِنِّىٓ أَخَافُ إِنْ عَصَيْتُ رَبِّى عَذَابَ يَوْمٍ عَظِيمٍ (١٥) مَّن يُصْرَفْ عَنْهُ يَوْمَئِذٍ فَقَدْ رَحِمَهُۥ ۚ وَذَٰلِكَ ٱلْفَوْزُ

ٱلۡمُبِينُ (١٦) وَإِن يَمۡسَسۡكَ ٱللَّهُ بِضُرٍّ فَلَا كَاشِفَ لَهُۥ إِلَّا هُوَ
وَإِن يَمۡسَسۡكَ بِخَيۡرٍ فَهُوَ عَلَىٰ كُلِّ شَيۡءٍ قَدِيرٌ (١٧)

Say: "To whom belongs all that is in the heavens and the earth?" Say: "To Allâh. He has prescribed Mercy for Himself. Indeed He will gather you together on the Day of Resurrection, about which there is no doubt. Those who have lost themselves will not believe [in Allâh as being the only Ilâh (God), and Muhammad as being one of His Messengers, and in Resurrection]. (12) And to Him belongs whatsoever exists in the night and the day, and He is the All¬Hearing, the All¬Knowing." (13) Say: "Shall I take as a Walî (helper, protector, Lord or God) any other than Allâh, the Creator of the heavens and the earth? And it is He Who feeds but is not fed." Say: "Verily, I am commanded to be the first of those who submit themselves to Allâh (as Muslims)." And be not you (O Muhammad) of the Mushrikûn (polytheists, pagans, idolaters and disbelievers in the Oneness of Allâh). (14) Say: "I fear, if I disobey my Lord, the torment of a Mighty Day." (15) He Who is averted from (such a torment) on that Day, (Allâh) has surely been Merciful to him. And that would be the obvious success (16) And if Allâh touches you with harm, none can remove it but He, and if He touches you with good, then He is Able to do all things (17)

**Quran 6:20-32**

ٱلَّذِينَ ءَاتَيْنَٰهُمُ ٱلْكِتَٰبَ يَعْرِفُونَهُۥ كَمَا يَعْرِفُونَ أَبْنَآءَهُمْ ٱلَّذِينَ خَسِرُوٓاْ أَنفُسَهُمْ فَهُمْ لَا يُؤْمِنُونَ (٢٠) وَمَنْ أَظْلَمُ مِمَّنِ ٱفْتَرَىٰ عَلَى ٱللَّهِ كَذِبًا أَوْ كَذَّبَ بِـَٔايَٰتِهِۦٓ إِنَّهُۥ لَا يُفْلِحُ ٱلظَّٰلِمُونَ (٢١) وَيَوْمَ نَحْشُرُهُمْ جَمِيعًا ثُمَّ نَقُولُ لِلَّذِينَ أَشْرَكُوٓاْ أَيْنَ شُرَكَآؤُكُمُ ٱلَّذِينَ كُنتُمْ تَزْعُمُونَ (٢٢) ثُمَّ لَمْ تَكُن فِتْنَتُهُمْ إِلَّآ أَن قَالُواْ وَٱللَّهِ رَبِّنَا مَا كُنَّا مُشْرِكِينَ (٢٣) ٱنظُرْ كَيْفَ كَذَبُواْ عَلَىٰٓ أَنفُسِهِمْ وَضَلَّ عَنْهُم مَّا كَانُواْ يَفْتَرُونَ (٢٤) وَمِنْهُم مَّن يَسْتَمِعُ إِلَيْكَ وَجَعَلْنَا عَلَىٰ قُلُوبِهِمْ أَكِنَّةً أَن يَفْقَهُوهُ وَفِىٓ ءَاذَانِهِمْ وَقْرًا وَإِن يَرَوْاْ كُلَّ ءَايَةٍ لَّا يُؤْمِنُواْ بِهَا حَتَّىٰٓ إِذَا جَآءُوكَ يُجَٰدِلُونَكَ يَقُولُ ٱلَّذِينَ كَفَرُوٓاْ إِنْ هَٰذَآ إِلَّآ أَسَٰطِيرُ ٱلْأَوَّلِينَ (٢٥) وَهُمْ يَنْهَوْنَ عَنْهُ وَيَنْـَٔوْنَ عَنْهُ وَإِن يُهْلِكُونَ إِلَّآ أَنفُسَهُمْ وَمَا يَشْعُرُونَ (٢٦) وَلَوْ تَرَىٰٓ إِذْ وُقِفُواْ عَلَى ٱلنَّارِ فَقَالُواْ يَٰلَيْتَنَا نُرَدُّ وَلَا نُكَذِّبَ بِـَٔايَٰتِ رَبِّنَا وَنَكُونَ مِنَ ٱلْمُؤْمِنِينَ (٢٧) بَلْ بَدَا لَهُم مَّا كَانُواْ يُخْفُونَ مِن قَبْلُ وَلَوْ رُدُّواْ لَعَادُواْ لِمَا نُهُواْ عَنْهُ وَإِنَّهُمْ لَكَٰذِبُونَ (٢٨) وَقَالُوٓاْ إِنْ هِىَ إِلَّا حَيَاتُنَا ٱلدُّنْيَا وَمَا نَحْنُ بِمَبْعُوثِينَ (٢٩) وَلَوْ تَرَىٰٓ إِذْ وُقِفُواْ عَلَىٰ رَبِّهِمْ قَالَ أَلَيْسَ هَٰذَا بِٱلْحَقِّ قَالُواْ بَلَىٰ وَرَبِّنَا قَالَ فَذُوقُواْ ٱلْعَذَابَ بِمَا كُنتُمْ تَكْفُرُونَ (٣٠) قَدْ خَسِرَ ٱلَّذِينَ كَذَّبُواْ بِلِقَآءِ ٱللَّهِ حَتَّىٰٓ إِذَا جَآءَتْهُمُ ٱلسَّاعَةُ بَغْتَةً قَالُواْ يَٰحَسْرَتَنَا عَلَىٰ مَا فَرَّطْنَا فِيهَا وَهُمْ يَحْمِلُونَ أَوْزَارَهُمْ عَلَىٰ ظُهُورِهِمْ أَلَا سَآءَ مَا يَزِرُونَ (٣١) وَمَا ٱلْحَيَوٰةُ ٱلدُّنْيَآ إِلَّا لَعِبٌ وَلَهْوٌ وَلَلدَّارُ ٱلْأَخِرَةُ خَيْرٌ لِّلَّذِينَ يَتَّقُونَ أَفَلَا تَعْقِلُونَ (٣٢)

*Those to whom We have given the Scripture (Jews and Christians) recognize him (i.e. Muhammad as a*

*Messenger of Allâh, and they also know that there is no Ilah (God) but Allâh and Islâm is Allâh's religion), as they recognize their own sons. Those who have lost (destroyed) themselves will not believe. (20) And who does more wrong aggression and than he who invents a lie against Allâh or rejects His Ayât (proofs, evidences, verses, lessons, or revelations)? Verily, the Zâlimûn (polytheists and wrong-doers,) shall never be successful. (21) And on the Day when We shall gather them all together, We shall say to those who joined partners (in worship with Us): "Where are your partners (false deities) whom you used to assert (as partners in worship with Allâh)?" (22) There will then be (left) no Fitnah (excuses or statements or arguments) for them but to say: "By Allâh, our Lord, we were not those who joined others in worship with Allâh." (23) Look! How they lie against themselves! But the (lie) which they invented will disappear from them. (24) And of them there are some who listen to you; but We have set veils on their hearts, so they understand it not, and deafness in their ears; and even if they see every one of the Ayât (proofs, evidences, verses, lessons, signs, revelations, etc.) they will not believe therein; to the point that when they come to you to argue with you, the disbelievers say: "These are nothing but tales of the men of old." (25) And they prevent others from him (from following Prophet Muhammad) and they themselves keep away from him, and (by doing so) they destroy not but their ownselves, yet they perceive (it) not. (26) If you could but see when they will be held over the (Hell) Fire! They will say: "Would that we were but sent back (to the world)! Then we would not deny the Ayât (proofs, evidences, verses, lessons, revelations, etc.) of our Lord, and we would be of the believers!" (27) Nay, it has become manifest to them what they had been concealing before. But if they were returned (to the world), they would certainly revert to that which they were forbidden. And indeed they are liars. (28) And they said: "There is no (other life) but our (present) life of this world, and never shall we be resurrected (on the Day of Resurrection)." (29) If you could but see when they will be held (brought and made to stand) in front of their Lord! He will say: "Is not this (Resurrection and the taking of the accounts) the truth?" They will say: "Yes, by our Lord!" He will then say: "So taste you the torment because you used not to believe." (30) They indeed are losers who denied their Meeting with Allâh, until all of a sudden, the Hour (signs of death) is on them, and they say: "Alas for us that we gave no thought to it," while they will bear their burdens on their backs; and evil indeed are the burdens that they will bear! (31) And the life of this world is nothing but play and amusement. But far better is the house in the Hereafter for those who are Al¬Muttaqûn (the pious ). Will you not then understand? (32)*

## Quran 6:36

۞ إِنَّمَا يَسْتَجِيبُ ٱلَّذِينَ يَسْمَعُونَ ۗ وَٱلْمَوْتَىٰ يَبْعَثُهُمُ ٱللَّهُ ثُمَّ إِلَيْهِ يُرْجَعُونَ (٣٦)

*It is only those who listen (to the Message of Prophet Muhammad), will respond (benefit from it), but as for the dead (disbelievers), Allâh will raise them up, then to Him they will be returned (for their recompense). (36)*

## Quran 6:38-45

وَمَا مِن دَآبَّةٍ فِى ٱلْأَرْضِ وَلَا طَٰئِرٍ يَطِيرُ بِجَنَاحَيْهِ إِلَّا أُمَمٌ أَمْثَالُكُم ۚ مَّا فَرَّطْنَا فِى ٱلْكِتَٰبِ مِن شَىْءٍ ۚ ثُمَّ إِلَىٰ رَبِّهِمْ يُحْشَرُونَ (٣٨) وَٱلَّذِينَ كَذَّبُوا۟ بِـَٔايَٰتِنَا صُمٌّ وَبُكْمٌ فِى ٱلظُّلُمَٰتِ ۗ مَن يَشَإِ ٱللَّهُ يُضْلِلْهُ وَمَن يَشَأْ يَجْعَلْهُ عَلَىٰ صِرَٰطٍ مُّسْتَقِيمٍ (٣٩) قُلْ أَرَءَيْتَكُمْ إِنْ أَتَىٰكُمْ عَذَابُ ٱللَّهِ أَوْ أَتَتْكُمُ ٱلسَّاعَةُ أَغَيْرَ ٱللَّهِ تَدْعُونَ إِن كُنتُمْ صَٰدِقِينَ (٤٠) بَلْ إِيَّاهُ تَدْعُونَ فَيَكْشِفُ مَا تَدْعُونَ إِلَيْهِ إِن شَآءَ وَتَنسَوْنَ مَا تُشْرِكُونَ (٤١) وَلَقَدْ أَرْسَلْنَآ إِلَىٰٓ أُمَمٍ مِّن قَبْلِكَ فَأَخَذْنَٰهُم بِٱلْبَأْسَآءِ وَٱلضَّرَّآءِ لَعَلَّهُمْ يَتَضَرَّعُونَ (٤٢) فَلَوْلَآ إِذْ جَآءَهُم بَأْسُنَا تَضَرَّعُوا۟ وَلَٰكِن قَسَتْ قُلُوبُهُمْ وَزَيَّنَ لَهُمُ ٱلشَّيْطَٰنُ مَا كَانُوا۟ يَعْمَلُونَ (٤٣) فَلَمَّا نَسُوا۟ مَا ذُكِّرُوا۟ بِهِۦ فَتَحْنَا عَلَيْهِمْ أَبْوَٰبَ كُلِّ شَىْءٍ حَتَّىٰٓ إِذَا فَرِحُوا۟ بِمَآ أُوتُوٓا۟ أَخَذْنَٰهُم بَغْتَةً فَإِذَا هُم مُّبْلِسُونَ (٤٤) فَقُطِعَ دَابِرُ ٱلْقَوْمِ ٱلَّذِينَ ظَلَمُوا۟ ۚ وَٱلْحَمْدُ لِلَّهِ رَبِّ ٱلْعَٰلَمِينَ (٤٥)

*There is not a moving (living) creature on earth, nor a bird that flies with its two wings, but are communities like you. We have neglected nothing in the Book, then*

unto their Lord they (all) shall be gathered. (38) Those
who reject Our Ayât (proofs, evidences, verses, lessons,
signs, revelations, etc.) are deaf and dumb in darkness.
Allâh sends astray whom He wills and He guides on the
Straight Path whom He wills. (39) Say (O Muhammad):
"Tell me if Allâh's Torment comes upon you, or the
Hour comes upon you, would you then call upon any one
other than Allâh? (Reply) if you are truthful!" (40) Nay!
To Him Alone you would call, and, if He wills, He would
remove that (distress) for which you call upon Him, and
you would forget at that time whatever partners you
joined (with Him in worship)! (41) Verily, We sent
(Messengers) to many nations before you (O
Muhammad). And We seized them with extreme poverty
(or loss in wealth) and loss in health with calamities so
that they might believe with humility. (42) When Our
Torment reached them, why then did they not humble
themselves (believe with humility)? But their hearts
became hardened, and Shaitân (Satan) made fair-seeming
to them that which they used to do. (43) So, when they
forgot (the warning) with which they had been reminded,
We opened for them the gates of every (pleasant) thing,
until in the midst of their enjoyment in that which they
were given, all of a sudden, We took them (in
punishment), and lo! They were plunged into destruction
with deep regrets and sorrows. (44) So the roots of the
people who did wrong was cut off. And all the praises

and thanks are to Allâh, the Lord of the 'Alamîn
(mankind, jinn, and all that exists). (45)

## Quran 6:48-49

وَمَا نُرْسِلُ ٱلْمُرْسَلِينَ إِلَّا مُبَشِّرِينَ وَمُنذِرِينَ فَمَنْ ءَامَنَ
وَأَصْلَحَ فَلَا خَوْفٌ عَلَيْهِمْ وَلَا هُمْ يَحْزَنُونَ (٤٨) وَٱلَّذِينَ
كَذَّبُواْ بِـَٔايَـٰتِنَا يَمَسُّهُمُ ٱلْعَذَابُ بِمَا كَانُواْ يَفْسُقُونَ (٤٩)

And We send not the Messengers but as givers of glad
tidings and as warners. So whosoever believes and does
righteous good deeds, upon such shall come no fear, nor
shall they grieve. (48) But those who reject Our Ayât
(proofs, evidences, verses, lessons, signs, revelations,
etc.), the torment will touch them for their disbelief (and
for their belying the Message of Muhammad). (49)

## Quran 6:60-62

وَهُوَ ٱلَّذِى يَتَوَفَّىٰكُم بِٱلَّيْلِ وَيَعْلَمُ مَا جَرَحْتُم بِٱلنَّهَارِ ثُمَّ
يَبْعَثُكُمْ فِيهِ لِيُقْضَىٰ أَجَلٌ مُّسَمًّى ثُمَّ إِلَيْهِ مَرْجِعُكُمْ ثُمَّ يُنَبِّئُكُم
بِمَا كُنتُمْ تَعْمَلُونَ (٦٠) وَهُوَ ٱلْقَاهِرُ فَوْقَ عِبَادِهِ وَيُرْسِلُ
عَلَيْكُمْ حَفَظَةً حَتَّىٰ إِذَا جَاءَ أَحَدَكُمُ ٱلْمَوْتُ تَوَفَّتْهُ رُسُلُنَا وَهُمْ
لَا يُفَرِّطُونَ (٦١) ثُمَّ رُدُّوٓاْ إِلَى ٱللَّهِ مَوْلَىٰهُمُ ٱلْحَقِّ أَلَا لَهُ ٱلْحُكْمُ
وَهُوَ أَسْرَعُ ٱلْحَـٰسِبِينَ (٦٢)

It is He Who takes your souls by night (when you are
asleep), and has knowledge of all that you have done by
day, then He raises (wakes) you up again that a term
appointed (your life period) be fulfilled, then (in the end)

unto Him will be your return. Then He will inform you of that which you used to do. (60) He is the Irresistible, Supreme over His slaves, and He sends guardians (angels guarding and writing all of one's good and bad deeds) over you, until when death approaches one of you, Our Messengers (angel of death and his assistants) take his soul, and they never neglect their duty (61) Then they are returned to Allâh, their Maulâ [True Master (God), the Just Lord (to reward them)]. Surely, for Him is the judgement and He is the Swiftest in taking account (62)

## Quran 6:70

وَذَرِ ٱلَّذِينَ ٱتَّخَذُواْ دِينَهُمْ لَعِبًا وَلَهْوًا وَغَرَّتْهُمُ ٱلْحَيَوٰةُ ٱلدُّنْيَا ۚ وَذَكِّرْ بِهِ أَن تُبْسَلَ نَفْسٌ بِمَا كَسَبَتْ لَيْسَ لَهَا مِن دُونِ ٱللَّهِ وَلِىٌّ وَلَا شَفِيعٌ وَإِن تَعْدِلْ كُلَّ عَدْلٍ لَّا يُؤْخَذْ مِنْهَا ۗ أُوْلَٰئِكَ ٱلَّذِينَ أُبْسِلُواْ بِمَا كَسَبُواْ ۖ لَهُمْ شَرَابٌ مِّنْ حَمِيمٍ وَعَذَابٌ أَلِيمٌ بِمَا كَانُواْ يَكْفُرُونَ (٧٠)

And leave alone those who take their religion as play and amusement, and whom the life of this world has deceived. But remind (them) with it (the Qur'ân) lest a person be given up to destruction for that which he has earned, when he will find for himself no protector or intercessor besides Allâh, and even if he offers every ransom, it will not be accepted from him. Such are they who are given up to destruction because of that which they have earned. For them will be a drink of boiling water and a painful torment because they used to disbelieve. (70)

## Quran 6:72-73

وَأَنْ أَقِيمُوا۟ ٱلصَّلَوٰةَ وَٱتَّقُوهُ وَهُوَ ٱلَّذِىٓ إِلَيْهِ تُحْشَرُونَ (٧٢)
وَهُوَ ٱلَّذِى خَلَقَ ٱلسَّمَوَٰتِ وَٱلْأَرْضَ بِٱلْحَقِّ وَيَوْمَ يَقُولُ كُن
فَيَكُونُ قَوْلُهُ ٱلْحَقُّ وَلَهُ ٱلْمُلْكُ يَوْمَ يُنفَخُ فِى ٱلصُّورِ عَـٰلِمُ
ٱلْغَيْبِ وَٱلشَّهَـٰدَةِ وَهُوَ ٱلْحَكِيمُ ٱلْخَبِيرُ (٧٣)

*And to perform As-Salât (Iqâmat-as-Salât)", and to be obedient to Allâh and fear Him, and it is He to Whom you shall be gathered. (72) It is He Who has created the heavens and the earth in truth, and on the Day (i.e. the Day of Resurrection) He will say: "Be!", - and it is! His Word is the truth. His will be the dominion on the Day when the trumpet will be blown. All-Knower of the unseen and the seen. He is the All-Wise, Well-Aware (of all things). (73)*

## Quran 6:93-95

وَمَنْ أَظْلَمُ مِمَّنِ ٱفْتَرَىٰ عَلَى ٱللَّهِ كَذِبًا أَوْ قَالَ أُوحِىَ إِلَىَّ وَلَمْ
يُوحَ إِلَيْهِ شَىْءٌ وَمَن قَالَ سَأُنزِلُ مِثْلَ مَآ أَنزَلَ ٱللَّهُ وَلَوْ تَرَىٰٓ
إِذِ ٱلظَّـٰلِمُونَ فِى غَمَرَٰتِ ٱلْمَوْتِ وَٱلْمَلَـٰٓئِكَةُ بَاسِطُوٓا۟ أَيْدِيهِمْ
أَخْرِجُوٓا۟ أَنفُسَكُمُ ٱلْيَوْمَ تُجْزَوْنَ عَذَابَ ٱلْهُونِ بِمَا كُنتُمْ
تَقُولُونَ عَلَى ٱللَّهِ غَيْرَ ٱلْحَقِّ وَكُنتُمْ عَنْ ءَايَـٰتِهِ تَسْتَكْبِرُونَ
(٩٣) وَلَقَدْ جِئْتُمُونَا فُرَٰدَىٰ كَمَا خَلَقْنَـٰكُمْ أَوَّلَ مَرَّةٍ وَتَرَكْتُم مَّا
خَوَّلْنَـٰكُمْ وَرَآءَ ظُهُورِكُمْ وَمَا نَرَىٰ مَعَكُمْ شُفَعَآءَكُمُ ٱلَّذِينَ
زَعَمْتُمْ أَنَّهُمْ فِيكُمْ شُرَكَـٰٓؤُا۟ لَقَد تَّقَطَّعَ بَيْنَكُمْ وَضَلَّ عَنكُم مَّا
كُنتُمْ تَزْعُمُونَ (٩٤) ۞ إِنَّ ٱللَّهَ فَالِقُ ٱلْحَبِّ وَٱلنَّوَىٰ يُخْرِجُ

الْحَيِّ مِنَ الْمَيِّتِ وَمُخْرِجُ الْمَيِّتِ مِنَ الْحَيِّ ذَٰلِكُمُ اللَّهُ فَأَنَّىٰ تُؤْفَكُونَ (٩٥)

*And who can be more unjust than he who invents a lie against Allâh, or says: "A revelation has come to me," whereas as no revelation has come to him in anything; and who says, "I will reveal the like of what Allâh has revealed." And if you could but see when the Zâlimûn (polytheists and wrong-doers) are in the agonies of death, while the angels are stretching forth their hands (saying): "Deliver your souls! This day you shall be recompensed with the torment of degradation because of what you used to utter against Allâh other than the truth. And you used to reject His Ayât (proofs, evidences, verses, lessons, signs, revelations etc.) with disrespect!" (93) And truly you have come unto Us alone (without wealth, companions or anything else) as We created you the first time. You have left behind you all that which We had bestowed on you. We see not with you your intercessors whom you claimed to be partners with Allâh. Now all relations between you and them have been cut off, and all that you used to claim has vanished from you. (94) Verily! It is Allâh Who causes the seed-grain and the fruit-stone (like date-stone) to split and sprout. He brings forth the living from the dead, and it is He Who brings forth the dead from the living. Such is Allâh, then how are you deluded away from the truth? (95)*

**Quran 6:108-110**

وَلَا تَسُبُّوا۟ ٱلَّذِينَ يَدْعُونَ مِن دُونِ ٱللَّهِ فَيَسُبُّوا۟ ٱللَّهَ عَدْوًۢا بِغَيْرِ عِلْمٍ ۗ كَذَٰلِكَ زَيَّنَّا لِكُلِّ أُمَّةٍ عَمَلَهُمْ ثُمَّ إِلَىٰ رَبِّهِم مَّرْجِعُهُمْ فَيُنَبِّئُهُم بِمَا كَانُوا۟ يَعْمَلُونَ (١٠٨) وَأَقْسَمُوا۟ بِٱللَّهِ جَهْدَ أَيْمَٰنِهِمْ لَئِن جَآءَتْهُمْ ءَايَةٌ لَّيُؤْمِنُنَّ بِهَا ۚ قُلْ إِنَّمَا ٱلْءَايَٰتُ عِندَ ٱللَّهِ ۖ وَمَا يُشْعِرُكُمْ أَنَّهَآ إِذَا جَآءَتْ لَا يُؤْمِنُونَ (١٠٩) وَنُقَلِّبُ أَفْـِٔدَتَهُمْ وَأَبْصَٰرَهُمْ كَمَا لَمْ يُؤْمِنُوا۟ بِهِۦٓ أَوَّلَ مَرَّةٍ وَنَذَرُهُمْ فِى طُغْيَٰنِهِمْ يَعْمَهُونَ (١١٠)

And insult not those whom they (disbelievers) worship besides Allâh, lest they insult Allâh wrongfully without knowledge. Thus We have made fair¬seeming to each people its own doings; then to their Lord is their return and He shall then inform them of all that they used to do. (108) And they swear their strongest oaths by Allâh, that if there came to them a sign, they would surely believe therein. Say: "Signs are but with Allâh and what will make you (Muslims) perceive that (even) if it (the sign) came, they will not believe?" (109) And We shall turn their hearts and their eyes away (from guidance), as they refused to believe therein for the first time, and We shall leave them in their trespass to wander blindly. (110)

## Quran 6:116-117

وَإِن تُطِعْ أَكْثَرَ مَن فِى ٱلْأَرْضِ يُضِلُّوكَ عَن سَبِيلِ ٱللَّهِ ۚ إِن يَتَّبِعُونَ إِلَّا ٱلظَّنَّ وَإِنْ هُمْ إِلَّا يَخْرُصُونَ (١١٦) إِنَّ رَبَّكَ هُوَ أَعْلَمُ مَن يَضِلُّ عَن سَبِيلِهِۦ ۖ وَهُوَ أَعْلَمُ بِٱلْمُهْتَدِينَ (١١٧)

*And if you obey most of those on the earth, they will
mislead you far away from Allâh's Path. They follow
nothing but conjectures, and they do nothing but lie.
(116) Verily, your Lord! It is He Who knows best who
strays from His Way, and He knows best the rightly
guided ones. (117)*

## Quran 6:120

وَذَرُواْ ظَـٰهِرَ ٱلْإِثْمِ وَبَاطِنَهُۥٓ إِنَّ ٱلَّذِينَ يَكْسِبُونَ ٱلْإِثْمَ سَيُجْزَوْنَ
بِمَا كَانُواْ يَقْتَرِفُونَ (١٢٠)

*Leave ( all kinds of) sin, open and secret. Verily, those
who commit sin will get due recompense for that which
they used to commit (120)*

## Quran 6:123-135

وَكَذَٰلِكَ جَعَلْنَا فِى كُلِّ قَرْيَةٍ أَكَـٰبِرَ مُجْرِمِيهَا لِيَمْكُرُواْ فِيهَا ۖ
وَمَا يَمْكُرُونَ إِلَّا بِأَنفُسِهِمْ وَمَا يَشْعُرُونَ (١٢٣) وَإِذَا
جَاءَتْهُمْ ءَايَةٌ قَالُواْ لَن نُّؤْمِنَ حَتَّىٰ نُؤْتَىٰ مِثْلَ مَا أُوتِىَ رُسُلُ
ٱللَّهِ ۚ ٱللَّهُ أَعْلَمُ حَيْثُ يَجْعَلُ رِسَالَتَهُۥ ۗ سَيُصِيبُ ٱلَّذِينَ أَجْرَمُواْ
صَغَارٌ عِندَ ٱللَّهِ وَعَذَابٌ شَدِيدٌۢ بِمَا كَانُواْ يَمْكُرُونَ (١٢٤)
فَمَن يُرِدِ ٱللَّهُ أَن يَهْدِيَهُۥ يَشْرَحْ صَدْرَهُۥ لِلْإِسْلَـٰمِ ۖ وَمَن يُرِدْ أَن
يُضِلَّهُۥ يَجْعَلْ صَدْرَهُۥ ضَيِّقًا حَرَجًا كَأَنَّمَا يَصَّعَّدُ فِى ٱلسَّمَاءِ ۚ
كَذَٰلِكَ يَجْعَلُ ٱللَّهُ ٱلرِّجْسَ عَلَى ٱلَّذِينَ لَا يُؤْمِنُونَ (١٢٥)
وَهَـٰذَا صِرَٰطُ رَبِّكَ مُسْتَقِيمًا ۗ قَدْ فَصَّلْنَا ٱلْءَايَـٰتِ لِقَوْمٍ يَذَّكَّرُونَ
(١٢٦) ۞ لَهُمْ دَارُ ٱلسَّلَـٰمِ عِندَ رَبِّهِمْ ۖ وَهُوَ وَلِيُّهُم بِمَا كَانُواْ
يَعْمَلُونَ (١٢٧) وَيَوْمَ يَحْشُرُهُمْ جَمِيعًا يَـٰمَعْشَرَ ٱلْجِنِّ قَدِ

أَسْتَكْثَرْتُم مِّنَ ٱلْإِنسِ ۖ وَقَالَ أَوْلِيَآؤُهُم مِّنَ ٱلْإِنسِ رَبَّنَا ٱسْتَمْتَعَ بَعْضُنَا بِبَعْضٍ وَبَلَغْنَآ أَجَلَنَا ٱلَّذِىٓ أَجَّلْتَ لَنَا ۚ قَالَ ٱلنَّارُ مَثْوَىٰكُمْ خَٰلِدِينَ فِيهَآ إِلَّا مَا شَآءَ ٱللَّهُ ۗ إِنَّ رَبَّكَ حَكِيمٌ عَلِيمٌ (١٢٨) وَكَذَٰلِكَ نُوَلِّى بَعْضَ ٱلظَّٰلِمِينَ بَعْضًۢا بِمَا كَانُوا۟ يَكْسِبُونَ (١٢٩) يَٰمَعْشَرَ ٱلْجِنِّ وَٱلْإِنسِ أَلَمْ يَأْتِكُمْ رُسُلٌ مِّنكُمْ يَقُصُّونَ عَلَيْكُمْ ءَايَٰتِى وَيُنذِرُونَكُمْ لِقَآءَ يَوْمِكُمْ هَٰذَا ۚ قَالُوا۟ شَهِدْنَا عَلَىٰٓ أَنفُسِنَا ۖ وَغَرَّتْهُمُ ٱلْحَيَوٰةُ ٱلدُّنْيَا وَشَهِدُوا۟ عَلَىٰٓ أَنفُسِهِمْ أَنَّهُمْ كَانُوا۟ كَٰفِرِينَ (١٣٠) ذَٰلِكَ أَن لَّمْ يَكُن رَّبُّكَ مُهْلِكَ ٱلْقُرَىٰ بِظُلْمٍ وَأَهْلُهَا غَٰفِلُونَ (١٣١) وَلِكُلٍّ دَرَجَٰتٌ مِّمَّا عَمِلُوا۟ ۚ وَمَا رَبُّكَ بِغَٰفِلٍ عَمَّا يَعْمَلُونَ (١٣٢) وَرَبُّكَ ٱلْغَنِىُّ ذُو ٱلرَّحْمَةِ ۚ إِن يَشَأْ يُذْهِبْكُمْ وَيَسْتَخْلِفْ مِنۢ بَعْدِكُم مَّا يَشَآءُ كَمَآ أَنشَأَكُم مِّن ذُرِّيَّةِ قَوْمٍ ءَاخَرِينَ (١٣٣) إِنَّ مَا تُوعَدُونَ لَءَاتٍ ۖ وَمَآ أَنتُم بِمُعْجِزِينَ (١٣٤) قُلْ يَٰقَوْمِ ٱعْمَلُوا۟ عَلَىٰ مَكَانَتِكُمْ إِنِّى عَامِلٌ ۖ فَسَوْفَ تَعْلَمُونَ مَن تَكُونُ لَهُۥ عَٰقِبَةُ ٱلدَّارِ ۗ إِنَّهُۥ لَا يُفْلِحُ ٱلظَّٰلِمُونَ (١٣٥)

And thus We have set up in every town great ones of its wicked people to plot therein. But they plot not except against their ownselves, and they perceive (it) not. (123) And when there comes to them a sign (from Allâh) they say: "We shall not believe until we receive the like of that which the Messengers of Allâh had received." Allâh knows best with whom to place His Message. Humiliation and disgrace from Allâh and a severe torment will overtake the criminals (polytheists, sinners) for that which they used to plot. (124) And whomsoever

*Allâh wills to guide, He opens his breast to Islâm, and whomsoever He wills to send astray, He makes his breast closed and constricted, as if he is climbing up to the sky. Thus Allâh puts the wrath on those who believe not. (125) And this is the Path of your Lord (the Qur'ân and Islâm) leading Straight. We have detailed Our Revelations for a people who take heed. (126) For them will be the home of peace (Paradise) with their Lord. And He will be their Walî (Helper and Protector) because of what they used to do. (127) And on the Day when He will gather them (all) together (and say): "O you assembly of jinn! Many did you mislead of men," and their Auliyâ' (friends and helpers) amongst men will say: "Our Lord! We benefited one from the other, but now we have reached our appointed term which You did appoint for us." He will say: "The Fire be your dwelling¬place, you will dwell therein forever, except as Allâh may will. Certainly your Lord is All¬Wise, All¬Knowing." (128) And thus We do make the Zâlimûn (polytheists and wrong-doers) Auliyâ' (supporters and helpers) of one another (in committing crimes), because of that which they used to earn. (129) O you assembly of jinn and mankind! "Did not there come to you Messengers from amongst you, reciting unto you My Verses and warning you of the meeting of this Day of yours?" They will say: "We bear witness against ourselves." It was the life of this world that deceived them. And they will bear witness* against themselves that they were disbelievers (130) This is because your Lord would not destroy the (populations of) towns for their wrong¬doing (i.e. associating others in worship along with Allâh) while their people were unaware (so the Messengers were sent). (131) For all there will be degrees (or ranks) according to what they did. And your Lord is not unaware of what they do. (132) And your Lord is Rich (Free of all wants), full of Mercy, if He wills, He can destroy you, and in your place make whom He wills as your successors, as He raised you from the seed of other people. (133) Surely, that which you are promised will verily come to pass, and you cannot escape (from the Punishment of Allâh). (134) Say (O Muhammad): "O my people! Work according to your way, surely, I too am working (in my way), and you will come to know for which of us will be the (happy) end in the Hereafter. Certainly the Zâlimûn (polytheists and wrong¬doers) will not be successful." (135)

## Quran 6:138-139

وَقَالُواْ هَٰذِهِۦ أَنْعَٰمٌ وَحَرْثٌ حِجْرٌ لَّا يَطْعَمُهَآ إِلَّا مَن نَّشَآءُ بِزَعْمِهِمْ وَأَنْعَٰمٌ حُرِّمَتْ ظُهُورُهَا وَأَنْعَٰمٌ لَّا يَذْكُرُونَ ٱسْمَ ٱللَّهِ عَلَيْهَا ٱفْتِرَآءً عَلَيْهِ سَيَجْزِيهِم بِمَا كَانُواْ يَفْتَرُونَ (١٣٨) وَقَالُواْ مَا فِى بُطُونِ هَٰذِهِ ٱلْأَنْعَٰمِ خَالِصَةٌ لِّذُكُورِنَا وَمُحَرَّمٌ عَلَىٰٓ أَزْوَٰجِنَا وَإِن يَكُن مَّيْتَةً فَهُمْ فِيهِ شُرَكَآءُ سَيَجْزِيهِمْ وَصْفَهُمْ إِنَّهُۥ حَكِيمٌ عَلِيمٌ (١٣٩)

And according to their claim, they say that such and such cattle and crops are forbidden, and none should eat of them except those whom we allow. And (they say) there are cattle forbidden to be used for burden (or any other work), and cattle on which (at slaughtering) the Name of Allâh is not pronounced; lying against Him (Allâh). He will recompense them for what they used to fabricate. (138) And they say: "What is in the bellies of such and such cattle (milk or foetus) is for our males alone, and forbidden to our females (girls and women), but if it is born dead, then all have shares therein." He will punish them for their attribution (of such false orders to Allâh). Verily, He is All¬Wise, All¬Knower. (139)

## Quran 6:144

وَمِنَ ٱلْإِبِلِ ٱثْنَيْنِ وَمِنَ ٱلْبَقَرِ ٱثْنَيْنِۗ قُلْ ءَآلذَّكَرَيْنِ حَرَّمَ أَمِ ٱلْأُنثَيَيْنِ أَمَّا ٱشْتَمَلَتْ عَلَيْهِ أَرْحَامُ ٱلْأُنثَيَيْنِۖ أَمْ كُنتُمْ شُهَدَآءَ إِذْ وَصَّىٰكُمُ ٱللَّهُ بِهَٰذَاۚ فَمَنْ أَظْلَمُ مِمَّنِ ٱفْتَرَىٰ عَلَى ٱللَّهِ كَذِبًا لِّيُضِلَّ ٱلنَّاسَ بِغَيْرِ عِلْمٍۗ إِنَّ ٱللَّهَ لَا يَهْدِى ٱلْقَوْمَ ٱلظَّٰلِمِينَ (١٤٤)

And of the camels two (male and female), and of oxen two (male and female). Say: "Has He forbidden the two males or the two females or (the young) which the wombs of the two females enclose? Or were you present when Allâh ordered you such a thing? Then who does more wrong than one who invents a lie against Allâh, to lead mankind astray without knowledge. Certainly Allâh guides not the people who are Zâlimûn (polytheists and wrong-doers)." (144)

## Quran 6:147

فَإِن كَذَّبُوكَ فَقُل رَّبُّكُمْ ذُو رَحْمَةٍ وَأسِعَةٍ وَلَا يُرَدُّ بَأْسُهُ عَنِ ٱلْقَوْمِ ٱلْمُجْرِمِينَ (١٤٧)

If they belie you (Muhammad) say: "Your Lord is the Owner of Vast Mercy, and never will His Wrath be turned back from the people who are Mujrimûn (criminals, polytheists, or sinners)." (147)

## Quran 6:152-153

وَلَا تَقْرَبُوا۟ مَالَ ٱلْيَتِيمِ إِلَّا بِٱلَّتِى هِىَ أَحْسَنُ حَتَّىٰ يَبْلُغَ أَشُدَّهُ وَأَوْفُوا۟ ٱلْكَيْلَ وَٱلْمِيزَانَ بِٱلْقِسْطِ لَا نُكَلِّفُ نَفْسًا إِلَّا وُسْعَهَا وَإِذَا قُلْتُمْ فَٱعْدِلُوا۟ وَلَوْ كَانَ ذَا قُرْبَىٰ وَبِعَهْدِ ٱللَّهِ أَوْفُوا۟ ذَٰلِكُمْ وَصَّىٰكُم بِهِۦ لَعَلَّكُمْ تَذَكَّرُونَ (١٥٢) وَأَنَّ هَٰذَا صِرَٰطِى مُسْتَقِيمًا فَٱتَّبِعُوهُ وَلَا تَتَّبِعُوا۟ ٱلسُّبُلَ فَتَفَرَّقَ بِكُمْ عَن سَبِيلِهِۦ ذَٰلِكُمْ وَصَّىٰكُم بِهِۦ لَعَلَّكُمْ تَتَّقُونَ (١٥٣)

"And come not near to the orphan's property, except to improve it, until he (or she) attains the age of full strength; and give full measure and full weight with justice. We burden not any person, but that which he can bear. And whenever you give your word (i.e. judge between men or give evidence), say the truth even if a near relative is concerned, and fulfill the Covenant of

Allâh, This He commands you, that you may remember. (152) "And verily, this (i.e. Allâh's Commandments) is my Straight Path, so follow it, and follow not (other) paths, for they will separate you away from His Path. This He has ordained for you that you may become Al-Muttaqûn (the pious)." (153)

## Quran 6:155-160

وَهَـٰذَا كِتَـٰبٌ أَنزَلْنَـٰهُ مُبَارَكٌ فَٱتَّبِعُوهُ وَٱتَّقُواْ لَعَلَّكُمْ تُرْحَمُونَ (١٥٥) أَن تَقُولُوٓاْ إِنَّمَآ أُنزِلَ ٱلْكِتَـٰبُ عَلَىٰ طَآئِفَتَيْنِ مِن قَبْلِنَا وَإِن كُنَّا عَن دِرَاسَتِهِمْ لَغَـٰفِلِينَ (١٥٦) أَوْ تَقُولُواْ لَوْ أَنَّآ أُنزِلَ عَلَيْنَا ٱلْكِتَـٰبُ لَكُنَّآ أَهْدَىٰ مِنْهُمْ فَقَدْ جَآءَكُم بَيِّنَةٌ مِّن رَّبِّكُمْ وَهُدًى وَرَحْمَةٌ فَمَنْ أَظْلَمُ مِمَّن كَذَّبَ بِـَٔايَـٰتِ ٱللَّهِ وَصَدَفَ عَنْهَا سَنَجْزِى ٱلَّذِينَ يَصْدِفُونَ عَنْ ءَايَـٰتِنَا سُوٓءَ ٱلْعَذَابِ بِمَا كَانُواْ يَصْدِفُونَ (١٥٧) هَلْ يَنظُرُونَ إِلَّآ أَن تَأْتِيَهُمُ ٱلْمَلَـٰٓئِكَةُ أَوْ يَأْتِيَ رَبُّكَ أَوْ يَأْتِيَ بَعْضُ ءَايَـٰتِ رَبِّكَ يَوْمَ يَأْتِى بَعْضُ ءَايَـٰتِ رَبِّكَ لَا يَنفَعُ نَفْسًا إِيمَـٰنُهَا لَمْ تَكُنْ ءَامَنَتْ مِن قَبْلُ أَوْ كَسَبَتْ فِىٓ إِيمَـٰنِهَا خَيْرًا قُلِ ٱنتَظِرُوٓاْ إِنَّا مُنتَظِرُونَ (١٥٨) إِنَّ ٱلَّذِينَ فَرَّقُواْ دِينَهُمْ وَكَانُواْ شِيَعًا لَّسْتَ مِنْهُمْ فِى شَىْءٍ إِنَّمَآ أَمْرُهُمْ إِلَى ٱللَّهِ ثُمَّ يُنَبِّئُهُم بِمَا كَانُواْ يَفْعَلُونَ (١٥٩) مَن جَآءَ بِٱلْحَسَنَةِ فَلَهُۥ عَشْرُ أَمْثَالِهَا وَمَن جَآءَ بِٱلسَّيِّئَةِ فَلَا يُجْزَىٰٓ إِلَّا مِثْلَهَا وَهُمْ لَا يُظْلَمُونَ (١٦٠)

And this is a blessed Book (the Qur'ân) which We have sent down, so follow it and fear Allâh (i.e. do not disobey His Orders), that you may receive mercy (i.e. be saved from the torment of Hell). (155) Lest you (pagan Arabs) should say: "The Book was sent down only to two sects before us (the Jews and the Christians), and for our part, we were in fact unaware of what they studied." (156) Or lest you (pagan Arabs) should say: "If only the Book had been sent down to us, we would surely have been better guided than they (Jews and Christians)." So now has come unto you a clear proof (the Qur'ân) from your Lord, and a guidance and a mercy. Who then does more wrong than one who rejects the Ayât (proofs, evidences, verses, lessons, signs, revelations, etc.) of Allâh and turns away therefrom? We shall requite those who turn away from Our Ayât with an evil torment, because of their turning away (from them). (157) Do they then wait for anything other than that the angels should come to them, or that your Lord (Allah) should come, or that some of the Signs of your Lord should come (i.e. portents of the Hour e.g., arising of the sun from the west)! The day that some of the Signs of your Lord do come, no good will it do to a person to believe then, if he believed not before, nor earned good (by performing deeds of righteousness) through his Faith. Say: "Wait you! we (too) are waiting." (158) Verily, those who divide their religion and break up into sects (all kinds of religious sects), you (O Muhammad) have no concern in them in the least. Their affair is only with Allâh, Who then will tell them what they used to do. (159) Whoever brings a

good deed (Islâmic Monotheism and deeds of obedience to
Allâh and His Messenger) shall have ten times the like
thereof to his credit, and whoever brings an evil deed
(polytheism, disbelief, hypocrisy, and deeds of
disobedience to Allâh and His Messenger) shall have only
the recompense of the like thereof, and they will not be
wronged.(160)

**Quran 6:164-165**

قُلْ أَغَيْرَ ٱللَّهِ أَبْغِى رَبًّا وَهُوَ رَبُّ كُلِّ شَىْءٍ وَلَا تَكْسِبُ كُلُّ
نَفْسٍ إِلَّا عَلَيْهَا وَلَا تَزِرُ وَازِرَةٌ وِزْرَ أُخْرَىٰ ثُمَّ إِلَىٰ رَبِّكُم
مَّرْجِعُكُمْ فَيُنَبِّئُكُم بِمَا كُنتُمْ فِيهِ تَخْتَلِفُونَ (١٦٤) وَهُوَ ٱلَّذِى
جَعَلَكُمْ خَلَٰئِفَ ٱلْأَرْضِ وَرَفَعَ بَعْضَكُمْ فَوْقَ بَعْضٍ دَرَجَٰتٍ
لِّيَبْلُوَكُمْ فِى مَا ءَاتَىٰكُمْ إِنَّ رَبَّكَ سَرِيعُ ٱلْعِقَابِ وَإِنَّهُۥ لَغَفُورٌ
رَّحِيمٌ (١٦٥)

Say: "Shall I seek a lord other than Allâh, while He is the
Lord of all things? No person earns any (sin) except
against himself (only), and no bearer of burdens shall
bear the burden of another. Then unto your Lord is your
return, so He will tell you that wherein you have been
differing." (164) And it is He Who has made you
generations coming after generations, replacing each
other on the earth. And He has raised you in ranks, some
above others that He may try you in that which He has
bestowed on you. Surely your Lord is Swift in
retribution, and certainly He is Oft-Forgiving, Most
Merciful. (165)

## Quran 7:6-9

فَلَنَسْـَٔلَنَّ ٱلَّذِينَ أُرْسِلَ إِلَيْهِمْ وَلَنَسْـَٔلَنَّ ٱلْمُرْسَلِينَ (٦) فَلَنَقُصَّنَّ عَلَيْهِم بِعِلْمٍ وَمَا كُنَّا غَآئِبِينَ (٧) وَٱلْوَزْنُ يَوْمَئِذٍ ٱلْحَقُّ فَمَن ثَقُلَتْ مَوَٰزِينُهُ فَأُو۟لَٰٓئِكَ هُمُ ٱلْمُفْلِحُونَ (٨) وَمَنْ خَفَّتْ مَوَٰزِينُهُ فَأُو۟لَٰٓئِكَ ٱلَّذِينَ خَسِرُوٓا۟ أَنفُسَهُم بِمَا كَانُوا۟ بِـَٔايَٰتِنَا يَظْلِمُونَ (٩)

*Then surely, We shall question those (people) to whom it (the Book) was sent and verily, We shall question the Messengers. (6) Then surely, We shall narrate unto them (their whole story) with knowledge, and indeed We were not been absent. (7) And the weighing on that day (Day of Resurrection) will be the true (weighing). So as for those whose scale (of good deeds) will be heavy, they will be the successful (by entering Paradise). (8) And as for those whose scale will be light, they are those who will lose their ownselves (by entering Hell) because they denied and rejected Our Ayât (proofs, evidences, verses, lessons, signs, revelations, etc.). (9)*

## Quran 7:14-15

قَالَ أَنظِرْنِىٓ إِلَىٰ يَوْمِ يُبْعَثُونَ (١٤) قَالَ إِنَّكَ مِنَ ٱلْمُنظَرِينَ (١٥)

*(Iblîs) said: "Allow me respite till the Day they are raised up (i.e. the Day of Resurrection)." (14) (Allâh) said: "You are of those respited." (15)*

## Quran 7:18

قَالَ ٱخْرُجْ مِنْهَا مَذْءُومًا مَّدْحُورًا ۖ لَّمَن تَبِعَكَ مِنْهُمْ لَأَمْلَأَنَّ جَهَنَّمَ مِنكُمْ أَجْمَعِينَ

(Allâh) said (to Iblîs) "Get out from this (Paradise) disgraced and expelled. Whoever of them (mankind) will follow you, then surely I will fill Hell with you all." (18)

## Quran 7:24-25

قَالَ ٱهْبِطُواْ بَعْضُكُمْ لِبَعْضٍ عَدُوٌّ ۖ وَلَكُمْ فِى ٱلْأَرْضِ مُسْتَقَرٌّ وَمَتَٰعٌ إِلَىٰ حِينٍ (٢٤) قَالَ فِيهَا تَحْيَوْنَ وَفِيهَا تَمُوتُونَ وَمِنْهَا تُخْرَجُونَ (٢٥)

(Allâh) said: "Get down, one of you is an enemy to the other [i.e. Adam, Hawwa (Eve), and Shaitân (Satan),]. On earth will be a dwelling-place for you and an enjoyment, - for a time." (24) He said: "Therein you shall live, and therein you shall die, and from it you shall be brought out (i.e. Resurrected)." (25)

## Quran 7:29-32

قُلْ أَمَرَ رَبِّى بِٱلْقِسْطِ ۖ وَأَقِيمُواْ وُجُوهَكُمْ عِندَ كُلِّ مَسْجِدٍ وَٱدْعُوهُ مُخْلِصِينَ لَهُ ٱلدِّينَ ۚ كَمَا بَدَأَكُمْ تَعُودُونَ (٢٩) فَرِيقًا هَدَىٰ وَفَرِيقًا حَقَّ عَلَيْهِمُ ٱلضَّلَٰلَةُ ۗ إِنَّهُمُ ٱتَّخَذُواْ ٱلشَّيَٰطِينَ أَوْلِيَآءَ مِن دُونِ ٱللَّهِ وَيَحْسَبُونَ أَنَّهُم مُّهْتَدُونَ (٣٠) ۞ يَٰبَنِىٓ ءَادَمَ خُذُواْ زِينَتَكُمْ عِندَ كُلِّ مَسْجِدٍ وَكُلُواْ وَٱشْرَبُواْ وَلَا تُسْرِفُوٓاْ

إِنَّهُ لَا يُحِبُّ ٱلْمُسْرِفِينَ ﴿٣١﴾ قُلْ مَنْ حَرَّمَ زِينَةَ ٱللَّهِ ٱلَّتِىٓ أَخْرَجَ لِعِبَادِهِۦ وَٱلطَّيِّبَـٰتِ مِنَ ٱلرِّزْقِ قُلْ هِىَ لِلَّذِينَ ءَامَنُواْ فِى ٱلْحَيَوٰةِ ٱلدُّنْيَا خَالِصَةً يَوْمَ ٱلْقِيَـٰمَةِ كَذَٰلِكَ نُفَصِّلُ ٱلْأَيَـٰتِ لِقَوْمٍ يَعْلَمُونَ ﴿٣٢﴾

*Say (O Muhammad): My Lord has commanded justice and (said) that you should face Him only (i.e. worship none but Allâh and face the Qiblah, i.e. the Ka'bah at Makkah during prayers) in every place of worship, in prayers (and not to face other false deities and idols), and invoke Him only making your religion sincere to Him (by not joining in worship any partner to Him and with the intention that you are doing your deeds for Allâh's sake only). As He brought you (into being) in the beginning, so shall you be brought into being [on the Day of Resurrection (in two groups, one as a blessed one (believers), and the other as a wretched one (disbelievers)]. (29) A group He has guided, and a group deserved to be in error; (because) surely they took the Shayâtin (devils) as Auliyâ' (protectors and helpers) instead of Allâh, and think that they are guided. (30) O Children of Adam! Take your adornment (by wearing your clean clothes), while praying and going round (the Tawâf of ) the Ka'bah, and eat and drink but waste not by extravagance, certainly He (Allâh) likes not Al-Musrifûn (those who waste by extravagance). (31) Say (O Muhammad): "Who has forbidden the adornment with* clothes given by Allâh, which He has produced for His slaves, and At-Taiyyibât [all kinds of Halâl (lawful) things] of food?" Say: "They are, in the life of this world, for those who believe, (and) exclusively for them (believers) on the Day of Resurrection (the disbelievers will not share them)." Thus We explain the Ayât (Islâmic laws) in detail for people who have knowledge. (32)

## Quran 7:34-53

وَلِكُلِّ أُمَّةٍ أَجَلٌ فَإِذَا جَآءَ أَجَلُهُمْ لَا يَسْتَأْخِرُونَ سَاعَةً وَلَا يَسْتَقْدِمُونَ (٣٤) يَٰبَنِىٓ ءَادَمَ إِمَّا يَأْتِيَنَّكُمْ رُسُلٌ مِّنكُمْ يَقُصُّونَ عَلَيْكُمْ ءَايَٰتِى فَمَنِ ٱتَّقَىٰ وَأَصْلَحَ فَلَا خَوْفٌ عَلَيْهِمْ وَلَا هُمْ يَحْزَنُونَ (٣٥) وَٱلَّذِينَ كَذَّبُواْ بِـَٔايَٰتِنَا وَٱسْتَكْبَرُواْ عَنْهَآ أُوْلَٰٓئِكَ أَصْحَٰبُ ٱلنَّارِ هُمْ فِيهَا خَٰلِدُونَ (٣٦) فَمَنْ أَظْلَمُ مِمَّنِ ٱفْتَرَىٰ عَلَى ٱللَّهِ كَذِبًا أَوْ كَذَّبَ بِـَٔايَٰتِهِۦٓ أُوْلَٰٓئِكَ يَنَالُهُمْ نَصِيبُهُم مِّنَ ٱلْكِتَٰبِ حَتَّىٰٓ إِذَا جَآءَتْهُمْ رُسُلُنَا يَتَوَفَّوْنَهُمْ قَالُوٓاْ أَيْنَ مَا كُنتُمْ تَدْعُونَ مِن دُونِ ٱللَّهِ قَالُواْ ضَلُّواْ عَنَّا وَشَهِدُواْ عَلَىٰٓ أَنفُسِهِمْ أَنَّهُمْ كَانُواْ كَٰفِرِينَ (٣٧) قَالَ ٱدْخُلُواْ فِىٓ أُمَمٍ قَدْ خَلَتْ مِن قَبْلِكُم مِّنَ ٱلْجِنِّ وَٱلْإِنسِ فِى ٱلنَّارِ كُلَّمَا دَخَلَتْ أُمَّةٌ لَّعَنَتْ أُخْتَهَا حَتَّىٰٓ إِذَا ٱدَّارَكُواْ فِيهَا جَمِيعًا قَالَتْ أُخْرَىٰهُمْ لِأُولَىٰهُمْ رَبَّنَا هَٰٓؤُلَآءِ أَضَلُّونَا فَـَٔاتِهِمْ عَذَابًا ضِعْفًا مِّنَ ٱلنَّارِ قَالَ لِكُلٍّ ضِعْفٌ وَلَٰكِن لَّا تَعْلَمُونَ (٣٨) وَقَالَتْ أُولَىٰهُمْ لِأُخْرَىٰهُمْ فَمَا كَانَ لَكُمْ عَلَيْنَا مِن فَضْلٍ فَذُوقُواْ ٱلْعَذَابَ بِمَا كُنتُمْ تَكْسِبُونَ (٣٩) إِنَّ ٱلَّذِينَ كَذَّبُواْ بِـَٔايَٰتِنَا وَٱسْتَكْبَرُواْ عَنْهَا لَا تُفَتَّحُ لَهُمْ

أَبْوَابُ ٱلسَّمَاءِ وَلَا يَدْخُلُونَ ٱلْجَنَّةَ حَتَّىٰ يَلِجَ ٱلْجَمَلُ فِى سَمِّ ٱلْخِيَاطِ وَكَذَٰلِكَ نَجْزِى ٱلْمُجْرِمِينَ (٤٠) لَهُم مِّن جَهَنَّمَ مِهَادٌ وَمِن فَوْقِهِمْ غَوَاشٍ وَكَذَٰلِكَ نَجْزِى ٱلظَّٰلِمِينَ (٤١) وَٱلَّذِينَ ءَامَنُوا۟ وَعَمِلُوا۟ ٱلصَّٰلِحَٰتِ لَا نُكَلِّفُ نَفْسًا إِلَّا وُسْعَهَآ أُو۟لَٰٓئِكَ أَصْحَٰبُ ٱلْجَنَّةِ هُمْ فِيهَا خَٰلِدُونَ (٤٢) وَنَزَعْنَا مَا فِى صُدُورِهِم مِّنْ غِلٍّ تَجْرِى مِن تَحْتِهِمُ ٱلْأَنْهَٰرُ وَقَالُوا۟ ٱلْحَمْدُ لِلَّهِ ٱلَّذِى هَدَىٰنَا لِهَٰذَا وَمَا كُنَّا لِنَهْتَدِىَ لَوْلَآ أَنْ هَدَىٰنَا ٱللَّهُ لَقَدْ جَآءَتْ رُسُلُ رَبِّنَا بِٱلْحَقِّ وَنُودُوٓا۟ أَن تِلْكُمُ ٱلْجَنَّةُ أُورِثْتُمُوهَا بِمَا كُنتُمْ تَعْمَلُونَ (٤٣) وَنَادَىٰٓ أَصْحَٰبُ ٱلْجَنَّةِ أَصْحَٰبَ ٱلنَّارِ أَن قَدْ وَجَدْنَا مَا وَعَدَنَا رَبُّنَا حَقًّا فَهَلْ وَجَدتُّم مَّا وَعَدَ رَبُّكُمْ حَقًّا قَالُوا۟ نَعَمْ فَأَذَّنَ مُؤَذِّنٌ بَيْنَهُمْ أَن لَّعْنَةُ ٱللَّهِ عَلَى ٱلظَّٰلِمِينَ (٤٤) ٱلَّذِينَ يَصُدُّونَ عَن سَبِيلِ ٱللَّهِ وَيَبْغُونَهَا عِوَجًا وَهُم بِٱلْأَخِرَةِ كَٰفِرُونَ (٤٥) وَبَيْنَهُمَا حِجَابٌ وَعَلَى ٱلْأَعْرَافِ رِجَالٌ يَعْرِفُونَ كُلًّا بِسِيمَٰهُمْ وَنَادَوْا۟ أَصْحَٰبَ ٱلْجَنَّةِ أَن سَلَٰمٌ عَلَيْكُمْ لَمْ يَدْخُلُوهَا وَهُمْ يَطْمَعُونَ (٤٦) ۞ وَإِذَا صُرِفَتْ أَبْصَٰرُهُمْ تِلْقَآءَ أَصْحَٰبِ ٱلنَّارِ قَالُوا۟ رَبَّنَا لَا تَجْعَلْنَا مَعَ ٱلْقَوْمِ ٱلظَّٰلِمِينَ (٤٧) وَنَادَىٰٓ أَصْحَٰبُ ٱلْأَعْرَافِ رِجَالًا يَعْرِفُونَهُم بِسِيمَٰهُمْ قَالُوا۟ مَآ أَغْنَىٰ عَنكُمْ جَمْعُكُمْ وَمَا كُنتُمْ تَسْتَكْبِرُونَ (٤٨) أَهَٰٓؤُلَآءِ ٱلَّذِينَ أَقْسَمْتُمْ لَا يَنَالُهُمُ ٱللَّهُ بِرَحْمَةٍ ٱدْخُلُوا۟ ٱلْجَنَّةَ لَا خَوْفٌ عَلَيْكُمْ وَلَآ أَنتُمْ تَحْزَنُونَ (٤٩) وَنَادَىٰٓ أَصْحَٰبُ ٱلنَّارِ أَصْحَٰبَ ٱلْجَنَّةِ أَنْ أَفِيضُوا۟ عَلَيْنَا مِنَ ٱلْمَآءِ أَوْ مِمَّا رَزَقَكُمُ ٱللَّهُ قَالُوٓا۟ إِنَّ ٱللَّهَ حَرَّمَهُمَا عَلَى ٱلْكَٰفِرِينَ

(٥٠) ٱلَّذِينَ ٱتَّخَذُوا۟ دِينَهُمْ لَهْوًا وَلَعِبًا وَغَرَّتْهُمُ ٱلْحَيَوٰةُ ٱلدُّنْيَا ۚ فَٱلْيَوْمَ نَنسَىٰهُمْ كَمَا نَسُوا۟ لِقَآءَ يَوْمِهِمْ هَٰذَا وَمَا كَانُوا۟ بِـَٔايَٰتِنَا يَجْحَدُونَ (٥١) وَلَقَدْ جِئْنَٰهُم بِكِتَٰبٍ فَصَّلْنَٰهُ عَلَىٰ عِلْمٍ هُدًى وَرَحْمَةً لِّقَوْمٍ يُؤْمِنُونَ (٥٢) هَلْ يَنظُرُونَ إِلَّا تَأْوِيلَهُۥ ۚ يَوْمَ يَأْتِى تَأْوِيلُهُۥ يَقُولُ ٱلَّذِينَ نَسُوهُ مِن قَبْلُ قَدْ جَآءَتْ رُسُلُ رَبِّنَا بِٱلْحَقِّ فَهَل لَّنَا مِن شُفَعَآءَ فَيَشْفَعُوا۟ لَنَآ أَوْ نُرَدُّ فَنَعْمَلَ غَيْرَ ٱلَّذِى كُنَّا نَعْمَلُ ۚ قَدْ خَسِرُوٓا۟ أَنفُسَهُمْ وَضَلَّ عَنْهُم مَّا كَانُوا۟ يَفْتَرُونَ (٥٣)

And every nation has its appointed term; when their term comes, neither can they delay it nor can they advance it an hour (or a moment). (34) O Children of Adam! If there come to you Messengers from amongst you, reciting to you, My Verses, then whosoever becomes pious and righteous, on them shall be no fear, nor shall they grieve (35) But those who reject Our Ayât (proofs, evidences, verses, lessons, signs, revelations,) and treat them with arrogance, they are the dwellers of the (Hell) Fire, they will abide therein forever (36) Who is more unjust than one who invents a lie against Allâh or rejects His Ayât (proofs, evidences, verses, lessons, signs, revelations)? For such their appointed portion (good things of this worldly life and their period of stay therein) will reach them from the Book (of Decrees) until, when Our Messengers (the angel of death and his assistants) come to them to take their souls, they (the angels) will *say: "Where are those whom you used to invoke and worship besides Allâh," they will reply, "They have vanished and deserted us." And they will bear witness against themselves, that they were disbelievers. (37) (Allâh) will say: "Enter you in the company of nations who passed away before you, of men and jinn, into the Fire." Every time a new nation enters, it curses its sister nation (that went before), until they will be gathered all together in the Fire. The last of them will say to the first of them: "Our Lord! These misled us, so give them a double torment of the Fire." He will say: "For each one there is double (torment), but you know not." (38) The first of them will say to the last of them: "You were not better than us, so taste the torment for what you used to earn." (39) Verily, those who belie Our Ayât (proofs, evidences, verses, lessons, signs, revelations) and treat them with arrogance, for them the gates of heaven will not be opened, and they will not enter Paradise until the camel goes through the eye of the needle (which is impossible). Thus do We recompense the Mujrimûn (criminals, polytheists, and sinners). (40) Theirs will be a bed of Hell (Fire), and over them coverings (of Hell-fire). Thus do We recompense the Zâlimûn (polytheists and wrong-doers). (41) But those who believed (in the Oneness of Allâh - Islâmic Monotheism), and worked righteousness - We tax not any person beyond his scope, — such are the dwellers of Paradise. They will abide therein. (42) And We shall remove from their breasts any (mutual) hatred or sense of injury (which they had, if at all, in the life of this world); rivers flowing under them, and they will say: "All the praises and thanks be to Allâh, Who has guided us to this, and never could we have found guidance, were it not that Allâh had guided us! Indeed, the Messengers of our Lord did come with the truth." And it will be cried out to them: "This is the Paradise which you have inherited for what you used to do." (43) And the dwellers of Paradise will call out to the dwellers of the Fire (saying): "We have indeed found true what our Lord had promised us; have you also found true, what your Lord promised (warnings)?" They shall say: "Yes." Then a crier will proclaim between them: "The Curse of Allâh is on the Zâlimûn (polytheists and wrong-doers)," (44) Those who hindered (men) from the Path of Allâh, and would seek to make it crooked, and they were disbelievers in the Hereafter. (45) And between them will be a (barrier) screen and on Al-A'râf (a wall with elevated places) will be men (whose good and evil deeds would be equal in scale), who would recognise all (of the Paradise and Hell people), by their marks (the dwellers of Paradise by their white faces and the dwellers of Hell by their black faces), they will call out to the dwellers of Paradise, "Salâmun 'Alaikûm" (peace be on you), and at that time they (men on Al-A'râf) will not yet have entered it (Paradise), but they will hope to enter (it) with certainty. (46) And when their eyes will be turned towards the dwellers of the Fire, they will say: "Our Lord! Place us not with the people who are Zâlimûn (polytheists and wrong-doers)." (47) And the men on Al-A'râf (the wall) will call unto the men whom they would recognize by their marks, saying: "Of what benefit to you were your great numbers (and hoards of wealth), and your arrogance (against Faith)?" (48) Are they those, of whom you swore that Allâh would never show them mercy. (Behold! It has been said to them): "Enter Paradise, no fear shall be on you, nor shall you grieve." (49) And the dwellers of the Fire will call to the dwellers of Paradise: "Pour on us some water or anything that Allâh has provided you with." They will say: "Both (water and provision) Allâh has forbidden to the disbelievers." (50) "Who took their religion as an amusement and play, and the life of the world deceived them." So this Day We shall forget them as they forgot their meeting of this Day, and as they used to reject Our Ayât (proofs, evidences, verses, lessons, signs, revelations). (51) Certainly, We have brought them a Book (the Qur'ân) which We have explained in detail with knowledge, - a guidance and a mercy to a people who believe. (52) Await they just for the final fulfillment of the event? On the Day the event is finally fulfilled (i.e. the Day of Resurrection), those who neglected it before will say: "Verily, the Messengers of our Lord did come*

with the truth, now are there any intercessors for us that they might intercede on our behalf? Or could we be sent back (to the first life of the world) so that we might do (good) deeds other than those (evil) deeds which we used to do?" Verily, they have lost their ownselves (i.e. destroyed themselves) and that which they used to fabricate (invoking and worshipping others besides Allâh) has gone away from them. (53)

## Quran 7:56-57

وَلَا تُفْسِدُواْ فِى ٱلْأَرْضِ بَعْدَ إِصْلَٰحِهَا وَٱدْعُوهُ خَوْفًا وَطَمَعًا ۚ إِنَّ رَحْمَتَ ٱللَّهِ قَرِيبٌ مِّنَ ٱلْمُحْسِنِينَ (٥٦) وَهُوَ ٱلَّذِى يُرْسِلُ ٱلرِّيَٰحَ بُشْرًۢا بَيْنَ يَدَىْ رَحْمَتِهِۦ ۖ حَتَّىٰٓ إِذَآ أَقَلَّتْ سَحَابًا ثِقَالًا سُقْنَٰهُ لِبَلَدٍ مَّيِّتٍ فَأَنزَلْنَا بِهِ ٱلْمَآءَ فَأَخْرَجْنَا بِهِۦ مِن كُلِّ ٱلثَّمَرَٰتِ ۚ كَذَٰلِكَ نُخْرِجُ ٱلْمَوْتَىٰ لَعَلَّكُمْ تَذَكَّرُونَ (٥٧)

And do not do mischief on the earth, after it has been set in order, and invoke Him with fear and hope; Surely, Allâh's Mercy is (ever) near unto the good-doers. (56)And it is He Who sends the winds as heralds of glad tidings, going before His Mercy (rain). Till when they have carried a heavy-laden cloud, We drive it to a land that is dead, then We cause water (rain) to descend thereon. Then We produce every kind of fruit therewith. Similarly, We shall raise up the dead, so that you may remember or take heed. (57)

## Quran 7:96

وَلَوْ أَنَّ أَهْلَ ٱلْقُرَىٰ ءَامَنُواْ وَٱتَّقَوْاْ لَفَتَحْنَا عَلَيْهِم بَرَكَٰتٍ مِّنَ ٱلسَّمَآءِ وَٱلْأَرْضِ وَلَٰكِن كَذَّبُواْ فَأَخَذْنَٰهُم بِمَا كَانُواْ يَكْسِبُونَ

*And if the people of the towns had believed and had the Taqwâ (piety), certainly, We should have opened for them blessings from the heaven and the earth, but they belied (the Messengers). So We took them (with punishment) for what they used to earn (polytheism and crimes). (96)*

## Quran 7:146-147

سَأَصْرِفُ عَنْ ءَايَٰتِىَ ٱلَّذِينَ يَتَكَبَّرُونَ فِى ٱلْأَرْضِ بِغَيْرِ ٱلْحَقِّ وَإِن يَرَوْاْ كُلَّ ءَايَةٍ لَّا يُؤْمِنُواْ بِهَا وَإِن يَرَوْاْ سَبِيلَ ٱلرُّشْدِ لَا يَتَّخِذُوهُ سَبِيلًا وَإِن يَرَوْاْ سَبِيلَ ٱلْغَىِّ يَتَّخِذُوهُ سَبِيلًا ذَٰلِكَ بِأَنَّهُمْ كَذَّبُواْ بِـَٔايَٰتِنَا وَكَانُواْ عَنْهَا غَٰفِلِينَ (١٤٦) وَٱلَّذِينَ كَذَّبُواْ بِـَٔايَٰتِنَا وَلِقَآءِ ٱلْأَخِرَةِ حَبِطَتْ أَعْمَٰلُهُمْ هَلْ يُجْزَوْنَ إِلَّا مَا كَانُواْ يَعْمَلُونَ (١٤٧)

*I shall turn away from My Ayât (verses of the Qur'ân) those who behave arrogantly on the earth, without a right, and (even) if they see all the Ayât (proofs, evidences, verses, lessons, signs, revelations, etc.), they will not believe in them. And if they see the way of righteousness (monotheism, piety, and good deeds), they* will not adopt it as the Way, but if they see the way of error (polytheism, crimes and evil deeds), they will adopt that way, that is because they have rejected Our Ayât (proofs, evidences, verses, lessons, signs, revelations, etc.) and were heedless (to learn a lesson) from them (146)Those who deny Our Ayât (proofs, evidences, verses, lessons, signs, revelations, etc.) and the Meeting in the Hereafter (Day of Resurrection,), vain are their deeds. Are they requited with anything except what they used to do? (147)

## Quran 7:152

إِنَّ ٱلَّذِينَ ٱتَّخَذُوا۟ ٱلْعِجْلَ سَيَنَالُهُمْ غَضَبٌ مِّن رَّبِّهِمْ وَذِلَّةٌ فِى ٱلْحَيَوٰةِ ٱلدُّنْيَا وَكَذَٰلِكَ نَجْزِى ٱلْمُفْتَرِينَ

Certainly, those who took the calf (for worship), wrath from their Lord and humiliation will come upon them in the life of this world. Thus do We recompense those who invent lies. (152)

## Quran 7:157

ٱلَّذِينَ يَتَّبِعُونَ ٱلرَّسُولَ ٱلنَّبِىَّ ٱلْأُمِّىَّ ٱلَّذِى يَجِدُونَهُ مَكْتُوبًا عِندَهُمْ فِى ٱلتَّوْرَىٰةِ وَٱلْإِنجِيلِ يَأْمُرُهُم بِٱلْمَعْرُوفِ وَيَنْهَىٰهُمْ عَنِ ٱلْمُنكَرِ وَيُحِلُّ لَهُمُ ٱلطَّيِّبَٰتِ وَيُحَرِّمُ عَلَيْهِمُ ٱلْخَبَٰٓئِثَ وَيَضَعُ عَنْهُمْ إِصْرَهُمْ وَٱلْأَغْلَٰلَ ٱلَّتِى كَانَتْ

عَلَيْهِمْ فَٱلَّذِينَ ءَامَنُواْ بِهِۦ وَعَزَّرُوهُ وَنَصَرُوهُ وَٱتَّبَعُواْ ٱلنُّورَ ٱلَّذِىٓ أُنزِلَ مَعَهُۥٓ أُوْلَٰٓئِكَ هُمُ ٱلْمُفْلِحُونَ

*Those who follow the Messenger, the Prophet who can neither read nor write (i.e. Muhammad) whom they find written with them in the Taurât (Torah), - he commands them for Al-Ma'rûf (i.e. Islâmic Monotheism and all that Islâm has ordained); and forbids them from Al-Munkar (i.e. disbelief, polytheism of all kinds, and all that Islâm has forbidden); he allows them as lawful At-Tayyibât (i.e. all good and lawful as regards things, deeds, beliefs, persons, foods), and prohibits them as unlawful Al-Khabâ'ith (i.e. all evil and unlawful as regards things, deeds, beliefs, persons and foods), he releases them from their heavy burdens (of Allâh's Covenant with the children of Israel), and from the fetters (bindings) that were upon them. So those who believe in him (Muhammad), honour him, help him, and follow the light (the Qur'ân) which has been sent down with him, it is they who will be successful. (157)*

## Quran 7:179-180

وَلَقَدْ ذَرَأْنَا لِجَهَنَّمَ كَثِيرًا مِّنَ ٱلْجِنِّ وَٱلْإِنسِ لَهُمْ قُلُوبٌ لَّا يَفْقَهُونَ بِهَا وَلَهُمْ أَعْيُنٌ لَّا يُبْصِرُونَ بِهَا وَلَهُمْ ءَاذَانٌ لَّا يَسْمَعُونَ بِهَآ أُوْلَٰٓئِكَ كَٱلْأَنْعَٰمِ بَلْ هُمْ أَضَلُّ أُوْلَٰٓئِكَ هُمْ

ٱلْغَفِلُونَ (١٧٩) وَلِلَّهِ ٱلْأَسْمَاءُ ٱلْحُسْنَىٰ فَٱدْعُوهُ بِهَا وَذَرُواْ
ٱلَّذِينَ يُلْحِدُونَ فِىٓ أَسْمَـٰٓئِهِۦ سَيُجْزَوْنَ مَا كَانُواْ يَعْمَلُونَ (١٨٠)

And surely, We have created many of the jinn and mankind for Hell. They have hearts wherewith they understand not, and they have eyes wherewith they see not, and they have ears wherewith they hear not (the truth). They are like cattle, nay even more astray; those! They are the heedless ones. (179)And (all) the Most Beautiful Names belong to Allâh, so call on Him by them, and leave the company of those who belie or deny (or utter impious speech against) His Names. They will be requited for what they used to do. (180)

## Quran 7:182-183

وَٱلَّذِينَ كَذَّبُواْ بِـَٔايَـٰتِنَا سَنَسْتَدْرِجُهُم مِّنْ حَيْثُ لَا يَعْلَمُونَ
(١٨٢) وَأُمْلِى لَهُمْ إِنَّ كَيْدِى مَتِينٌ (١٨٣)

Those who reject Our Ayât (proofs, evidences, verses, lessons, signs, revelations, etc.), We shall gradually seize them with punishment in ways they perceive not. (182)And I respite them; certainly My Plan is strong. (183)

## Quran 8:7-10

وَإِذْ يَعِدُكُمُ ٱللَّهُ إِحْدَى ٱلطَّآئِفَتَيْنِ أَنَّهَا لَكُمْ وَتَوَدُّونَ أَنَّ غَيْرَ
ذَاتِ ٱلشَّوْكَةِ تَكُونُ لَكُمْ وَيُرِيدُ ٱللَّهُ أَن يُحِقَّ ٱلْحَقَّ بِكَلِمَـٰتِهِۦ

وَيَقْطَعَ دَابِرَ ٱلْكَٰفِرِينَ (٧) لِيُحِقَّ ٱلْحَقَّ وَيُبْطِلَ ٱلْبَٰطِلَ وَلَوْ
كَرِهَ ٱلْمُجْرِمُونَ (٨) إِذْ تَسْتَغِيثُونَ رَبَّكُمْ فَٱسْتَجَابَ لَكُمْ أَنِّى
مُمِدُّكُم بِأَلْفٍ مِّنَ ٱلْمَلَٰٓئِكَةِ مُرْدِفِينَ (٩) وَمَا جَعَلَهُ ٱللَّهُ إِلَّا
بُشْرَىٰ وَلِتَطْمَئِنَّ بِهِ قُلُوبُكُمْ وَمَا ٱلنَّصْرُ إِلَّا مِنْ عِندِ ٱللَّهِ إِنَّ ٱللَّهَ
عَزِيزٌ حَكِيمٌ (١٠)

And (remember) when Allâh promised you (Muslims)
one of the two parties (of the enemy i.e. either the army or
the caravan) that it should be yours, you wished that the
one not armed (the caravan) should be yours, but Allâh
willed to justify the truth by His Words and to cut off the
roots of the disbelievers (i.e. in the battle of Badr).
(7)That He might cause the truth to triumph and bring
falsehood to nothing, even though the Mujrimûn
(disbelievers, polytheists, sinners, criminals,) hate it.
(8)(Remember) when you sought help of your Lord and
He answered you (saying): "I will help you with a
thousand of the angels each behind the other (following
one another) in succession." (9)Allâh made it only as
glad tidings, and that your hearts be at rest therewith.
And there is no victory except from Allâh. Verily, Allâh
is All-Mighty, All-Wise. (10)

**Quran 8:12-14**

إِذْ يُوحِى رَبُّكَ إِلَى ٱلْمَلَٰٓئِكَةِ أَنِّى مَعَكُمْ فَثَبِّتُواْ ٱلَّذِينَ ءَامَنُواْ
سَأُلْقِى فِى قُلُوبِ ٱلَّذِينَ كَفَرُواْ ٱلرُّعْبَ فَٱضْرِبُواْ فَوْقَ

الْأَعْنَاقِ وَاضْرِبُواْ مِنْهُمْ كُلَّ بَنَانٍ (١٢) ذَٰلِكَ بِأَنَّهُمْ شَآقُّواْ
اللَّهَ وَرَسُولَهُۥ وَمَن يُشَاقِقِ اللَّهَ وَرَسُولَهُۥ فَإِنَّ اللَّهَ شَدِيدُ الْعِقَابِ
(١٣) ذَٰلِكُمْ فَذُوقُوهُ وَأَنَّ لِلْكَافِرِينَ عَذَابَ النَّارِ (١٤)

(Remember) when your Lord revealed to the angels,
"Verily, I am with you, so keep firm those who have
believed. I will cast terror into the hearts of those who
have disbelieved, so strike them over the necks, and smite
over all their fingers and toes." (12)This is because they
defied and disobeyed Allâh and His Messenger. And
whoever defies and disobeys Allâh and His Messenger,
then verily, Allâh is Severe in punishment (13)This is
(the torment), so taste it, and surely for the disbelievers is
the torment of the Fire. (14)

## Quran 8:18

ذَٰلِكُمْ وَأَنَّ اللَّهَ مُوهِنُ كَيْدِ الْكَافِرِينَ

This (is the fact) and surely, Allâh weakens the deceitful
plots of the disbelievers. (18)

## Quran 8:29

يَـٰٓأَيُّهَا الَّذِينَ ءَامَنُوٓاْ إِن تَتَّقُواْ اللَّهَ يَجْعَل لَّكُمْ فُرْقَانًا وَيُكَفِّرْ
عَنكُمْ سَيِّـَٔاتِكُمْ وَيَغْفِرْ لَكُمْ وَاللَّهُ ذُو الْفَضْلِ الْعَظِيمِ

O you who believe! If you obey and fear Allâh, He will
grant you Furqân [(a criterion to judge between right
and wrong), or (Makhraj, i.e. a way for you to get out

from every difficulty)], and will expiate for you your sins, and forgive you; and Allâh is the Owner of the Great Bounty. (29)

## Quran 8:36-38

إِنَّ ٱلَّذِينَ كَفَرُواْ يُنفِقُونَ أَمۡوَٰلَهُمۡ لِيَصُدُّواْ عَن سَبِيلِ ٱللَّهِ فَسَيُنفِقُونَهَا ثُمَّ تَكُونُ عَلَيۡهِمۡ حَسۡرَةً ثُمَّ يُغۡلَبُونَ وَٱلَّذِينَ كَفَرُواْ إِلَىٰ جَهَنَّمَ يُحۡشَرُونَ (٣٦) لِيَمِيزَ ٱللَّهُ ٱلۡخَبِيثَ مِنَ ٱلطَّيِّبِ وَيَجۡعَلَ ٱلۡخَبِيثَ بَعۡضَهُۥ عَلَىٰ بَعۡضٍ فَيَرۡكُمَهُۥ جَمِيعًا فَيَجۡعَلَهُۥ فِى جَهَنَّمَ أُوْلَٰئِكَ هُمُ ٱلۡخَٰسِرُونَ (٣٧) قُل لِّلَّذِينَ كَفَرُواْ إِن يَنتَهُواْ يُغۡفَرۡ لَهُم مَّا قَدۡ سَلَفَ وَإِن يَعُودُواْ فَقَدۡ مَضَتۡ سُنَّتُ ٱلۡأَوَّلِينَ (٣٨)

Verily, those who disbelieve spend their wealth to hinder (men) from the Path of Allâh, and so will they continue to spend it; but in the end it will become an anguish for them. Then they will be overcomed. And those who disbelieve will be gathered unto Hell (36) In order that Allâh may distinguish the wicked (disbelievers, polytheists and doers of evil deeds) from the good (believers of Islâmic Monotheism and doers of righteous deeds), and put the wicked (disbelievers, polytheists and doers of evil deeds) one over another, heap them together and cast them into Hell. Those! it is they who are the losers. (37) Say to those who have disbelieved, if they cease (from disbelief) their past will be forgiven. But if they return (thereto), then the examples of those (punished) before them have already preceded (as a warning). (38)

## Quran 8:45-46

يَـٰٓأَيُّهَا ٱلَّذِينَ ءَامَنُوٓاْ إِذَا لَقِيتُمْ فِئَةً فَٱثْبُتُواْ وَٱذْكُرُواْ ٱللَّهَ كَثِيرًا لَّعَلَّكُمْ تُفْلِحُونَ (٤٥) وَأَطِيعُواْ ٱللَّهَ وَرَسُولَهُۥ وَلَا تَنَـٰزَعُواْ فَتَفْشَلُواْ وَتَذْهَبَ رِيحُكُمْۖ وَٱصْبِرُوٓاْ إِنَّ ٱللَّهَ مَعَ ٱلصَّـٰبِرِينَ (٤٦)

O you who believe! When you meet (an enemy) force, take a firm stand against them and remember the Name of Allâh much (both with tongue and mind), so that you may be successful. (45)And obey Allâh and His Messenger, and do not dispute (with one another) lest you lose courage and your strength departs, and be patient. Surely, Allâh is with those who are As-Sâbirûn (the patient). (46)

## Quran 8:50-51

وَلَوْ تَرَىٰٓ إِذْ يَتَوَفَّى ٱلَّذِينَ كَفَرُواْ ٱلْمَلَـٰٓئِكَةُ يَضْرِبُونَ وُجُوهَهُمْ وَأَدْبَـٰرَهُمْ وَذُوقُواْ عَذَابَ ٱلْحَرِيقِ (٥٠) ذَٰلِكَ بِمَا قَدَّمَتْ أَيْدِيكُمْ وَأَنَّ ٱللَّهَ لَيْسَ بِظَلَّـٰمٍ لِّلْعَبِيدِ (٥١)

And if you could see when the angels take away the souls of those who disbelieve (at death), they smite their faces and their backs, (saying): "Taste the punishment of the blazing Fire." (50)"This is because of that which your hands had forwarded. And verily, Allâh is not unjust to His slaves." (51)

## Quran 8:53

ذَٰلِكَ بِأَنَّ ٱللَّهَ لَمْ يَكُ مُغَيِّرًا نِّعْمَةً أَنْعَمَهَا عَلَىٰ قَوْمٍ حَتَّىٰ يُغَيِّرُوا۟ مَا بِأَنفُسِهِمْ ۙ وَأَنَّ ٱللَّهَ سَمِيعٌ عَلِيمٌ

*That is so because Allâh will never change a grace which*
*He has bestowed on a people until they change what is in*
*their ownselves. And verily, Allâh is All-Hearer, All-*
*Knower. (53)*

## Quran 8:55-56

إِنَّ شَرَّ ٱلدَّوَابِّ عِندَ ٱللَّهِ ٱلَّذِينَ كَفَرُوا۟ فَهُمْ لَا يُؤْمِنُونَ (٥٥) ٱلَّذِينَ عَٰهَدتَّ مِنْهُمْ ثُمَّ يَنقُضُونَ عَهْدَهُمْ فِى كُلِّ مَرَّةٍ وَهُمْ لَا يَتَّقُونَ (٥٦)

*Verily, The worst of moving (living) creatures before*
*Allâh are those who disbelieve, - so they shall not believe.*
*(55)They are those with whom you made a covenant, but*
*they break their covenant every time and they do not fear*
*Allâh. (56)*

## Quran 8:64-66

يَٰٓأَيُّهَا ٱلنَّبِىُّ حَسْبُكَ ٱللَّهُ وَمَنِ ٱتَّبَعَكَ مِنَ ٱلْمُؤْمِنِينَ (٦٤) يَٰٓأَيُّهَا ٱلنَّبِىُّ حَرِّضِ ٱلْمُؤْمِنِينَ عَلَى ٱلْقِتَالِ ۚ إِن يَكُن مِّنكُمْ عِشْرُونَ صَٰبِرُونَ يَغْلِبُوا۟ مِا۟ئَتَيْنِ ۚ وَإِن يَكُن مِّنكُم مِّا۟ئَةٌ يَغْلِبُوٓا۟ أَلْفًا مِّنَ ٱلَّذِينَ كَفَرُوا۟ بِأَنَّهُمْ قَوْمٌ لَّا يَفْقَهُونَ (٦٥) ٱلْـَٰٔنَ خَفَّفَ ٱللَّهُ عَنكُمْ وَعَلِمَ أَنَّ فِيكُمْ ضَعْفًا ۚ فَإِن يَكُن مِّنكُم مِّا۟ئَةٌ صَابِرَةٌ يَغْلِبُوا۟ مِا۟ئَتَيْنِ ۚ وَإِن يَكُن مِّنكُمْ أَلْفٌ يَغْلِبُوٓا۟ أَلْفَيْنِ بِإِذْنِ ٱللَّهِ ۗ وَٱللَّهُ مَعَ ٱلصَّٰبِرِينَ (٦٦)

*O Prophet (Muhammad)! Allâh is Sufficient for you and*
*for the believers who follow you. (64)O Prophet*
*(Muhammad)! Urge the believers to fight. If there are*

twenty steadfast persons amongst you, they will overcome two hundred, and if there be a hundred steadfast persons they will overcome a thousand of those who disbelieve, because they (the disbelievers) are people who do not understand. (65)Now Allâh has lightened your (task), for He knows that there is weakness in you. So if there are of you a hundred steadfast persons, they shall overcome two hundreds, and if there are a thousand of you, they shall overcome two thousand with the Leave of Allâh. And Allâh is with As-Sâbirûn (the patient). (66)

## Quran 8:70

يَـٰٓأَيُّهَا ٱلنَّبِىُّ قُل لِّمَن فِىٓ أَيْدِيكُم مِّنَ ٱلْأَسْرَىٰٓ إِن يَعْلَمِ ٱللَّهُ فِى قُلُوبِكُمْ خَيْرًا يُؤْتِكُمْ خَيْرًا مِّمَّآ أُخِذَ مِنكُمْ وَيَغْفِرْ لَكُمْ وَٱللَّهُ غَفُورٌ رَّحِيمٌ

O Prophet! (Muhammad)Say to the captives that are in your hands: "If Allâh knows any good in your hearts, He will give you something better than what has been taken from you, and He will forgive you, and Allâh is Oft-Forgiving, Most Merciful." (70)

## Quran 8:73-74

وَٱلَّذِينَ كَفَرُواْ بَعْضُهُمْ أَوْلِيَآءُ بَعْضٍ إِلَّا تَفْعَلُوهُ تَكُن فِتْنَةٌ فِى ٱلْأَرْضِ وَفَسَادٌ كَبِيرٌ (٧٣) وَٱلَّذِينَ ءَامَنُواْ وَهَاجَرُواْ

وَجَٰهَدُواْ فِى سَبِيلِ ٱللَّهِ وَٱلَّذِينَ ءَاوَواْ وَّنَصَرُوٓاْ أُوْلَٰٓئِكَ هُمُ
ٱلْمُؤْمِنُونَ حَقًّا لَّهُم مَّغْفِرَةٌ وَرِزْقٌ كَرِيمٌ (٧٤)

*And those who disbelieve are allies of one another, (and)
if you (Muslims of the whole world collectively) do not
do so [i.e. become allies, as one united block under one
Khalifah (a chief Muslim ruler for the whole Muslim
world) to make victorious Allâh's religion of Islâmic
Monotheism], there will be Fitnah (wars, battles,
polytheism) and oppression on the earth, and a great
mischief and corruption (appearance of polytheism).[]
(73) And those who believed, and emigrated and strove
hard in the Cause of Allâh (Al-Jihâd), as well as those
who gave (them) asylum and aid; - these are the believers
in truth, for them is forgiveness and Rizqun Karîm (a
generous provision i.e. Paradise). (74)*

## Quran 9:2-3

فَسِيحُواْ فِى ٱلْأَرْضِ أَرْبَعَةَ أَشْهُرٍ وَٱعْلَمُوٓاْ أَنَّكُمْ غَيْرُ مُعْجِزِى
ٱللَّهِ وَأَنَّ ٱللَّهَ مُخْزِى ٱلْكَٰفِرِينَ (٢) وَأَذَٰنٌ مِّنَ ٱللَّهِ وَرَسُولِهِ
إِلَى ٱلنَّاسِ يَوْمَ ٱلْحَجِّ ٱلْأَكْبَرِ أَنَّ ٱللَّهَ بَرِىٓءٌ مِّنَ ٱلْمُشْرِكِينَ
وَرَسُولُهُ فَإِن تُبْتُمْ فَهُوَ خَيْرٌ لَّكُمْ وَإِن تَوَلَّيْتُمْ فَٱعْلَمُوٓاْ أَنَّكُمْ
غَيْرُ مُعْجِزِى ٱللَّهِ وَبَشِّرِ ٱلَّذِينَ كَفَرُواْ بِعَذَابٍ أَلِيمٍ (٣)

*So travel freely (O Mushrikûn) for four months (as you
will) throughout the land, but know that you cannot
escape (from the Punishment of) Allâh, and Allâh will*

disgrace the disbelievers. (2)And a declaration from Allâh and His Messenger to mankind on the greatest day (the 10th of Dhul-Hijjah - the 12th month of Islâmic calendar) that Allâh is free from (all) obligations to the Mushrikûn and so is His Messenger. So if you (Mushrikûn) repent, it is better for you, but if you turn away, then know that you cannot escape (from the Punishment of) Allâh. And give tidings (O Muhammad) of a painful torment to those who disbelieve. (3)

## Quran 9:17-22

مَا كَانَ لِلْمُشْرِكِينَ أَن يَعْمُرُواْ مَسَٰجِدَ ٱللَّهِ شَٰهِدِينَ عَلَىٰٓ أَنفُسِهِم بِٱلْكُفْرِ أُوْلَٰٓئِكَ حَبِطَتْ أَعْمَٰلُهُمْ وَفِى ٱلنَّارِ هُمْ خَٰلِدُونَ (١٧) إِنَّمَا يَعْمُرُ مَسَٰجِدَ ٱللَّهِ مَنْ ءَامَنَ بِٱللَّهِ وَٱلْيَوْمِ ٱلْأَخِرِ وَأَقَامَ ٱلصَّلَوٰةَ وَءَاتَى ٱلزَّكَوٰةَ وَلَمْ يَخْشَ إِلَّا ٱللَّهَ فَعَسَىٰٓ أُوْلَٰٓئِكَ أَن يَكُونُواْ مِنَ ٱلْمُهْتَدِينَ (١٨) ۞ أَجَعَلْتُمْ سِقَايَةَ ٱلْحَاجِّ وَعِمَارَةَ ٱلْمَسْجِدِ ٱلْحَرَامِ كَمَنْ ءَامَنَ بِٱللَّهِ وَٱلْيَوْمِ ٱلْأَخِرِ وَجَٰهَدَ فِى سَبِيلِ ٱللَّهِ لَا يَسْتَوُۥنَ عِندَ ٱللَّهِ وَٱللَّهُ لَا يَهْدِى ٱلْقَوْمَ ٱلظَّٰلِمِينَ (١٩) ٱلَّذِينَ ءَامَنُواْ وَهَاجَرُواْ وَجَٰهَدُواْ فِى سَبِيلِ ٱللَّهِ بِأَمْوَٰلِهِمْ وَأَنفُسِهِمْ أَعْظَمُ دَرَجَةً عِندَ ٱللَّهِ وَأُوْلَٰٓئِكَ هُمُ ٱلْفَآئِزُونَ (٢٠) يُبَشِّرُهُمْ رَبُّهُم بِرَحْمَةٍ مِّنْهُ وَرِضْوَٰنٍ وَجَنَّٰتٍ لَّهُمْ فِيهَا نَعِيمٌ مُّقِيمٌ (٢١) خَٰلِدِينَ فِيهَآ أَبَدًا إِنَّ ٱللَّهَ عِندَهُۥٓ أَجْرٌ عَظِيمٌ (٢٢)

*It is not for the Mushrikûn (polytheists, idolaters, pagans, disbelievers in the Oneness of Allâh), to maintain the Mosques of Allâh (i.e. to pray and worship Allâh therein, to look after their cleanliness and their building), while they witness against their ownselves of disbelief. The works of such are in vain and in Fire shall they abide. (17)The Mosques of Allâh shall be maintained only by those who believe in Allâh and the Last Day; perform As-Salât (Iqâmat-as-Salât), and give Zakât and fear none but Allâh. It is they who are on true guidance. (18)Do you consider the providing of drinking water to the pilgrims and the maintenance of Al-Masjid-al-Harâm (at Makkah) as equal to the worth of those who believe in Allâh and the Last Day, and strive hard and fight in the Cause of Allâh? They are not equal before Allâh. And Allâh guides not those people who are the Zâlimûn (polytheists and wrong-doers). (19)Those who believed (in the Oneness of Allâh - Islâmic Monotheism) and emigrated and strove hard and fought in Allâh's Cause with their wealth and their lives are far higher in degree with Allâh. They are the successful. (20)Their Lord gives them glad tidings of Mercy from Him, and that His being pleased (with them), and of Gardens (Paradise) for them wherein are everlasting delights. (21)They will dwell therein forever. Verily, with Allâh is a great reward. (22)*

**Quran 9:27-28**

ثُمَّ يَتُوبُ ٱللَّهُ مِنۢ بَعْدِ ذَٰلِكَ عَلَىٰ مَن يَشَآءُ ۗ وَٱللَّهُ غَفُورٌ رَّحِيمٌ

(٢٧) يَـٰٓأَيُّهَا ٱلَّذِينَ ءَامَنُوٓا۟ إِنَّمَا ٱلْمُشْرِكُونَ نَجَسٌ فَلَا يَقْرَبُوا۟

ٱلْمَسْجِدَ ٱلْحَرَامَ بَعْدَ عَامِهِمْ هَٰذَا ۚ وَإِنْ خِفْتُمْ عَيْلَةً فَسَوْفَ

يُغْنِيكُمُ ٱللَّهُ مِن فَضْلِهِۦٓ إِن شَآءَ ۚ إِنَّ ٱللَّهَ عَلِيمٌ حَكِيمٌ (٢٨)

*Then after that Allâh will accept the repentance of whom
He wills. And Allâh is Oft-Forgiving, Most Merciful.
(27)O you who believe (in Allâh's Oneness and in His
Messenger (Muhammad)! Verily, the Mushrikûn
(polytheists, pagans, idolaters, disbelievers in the
Oneness of Allâh, and in the Message of Muhammad) are
Najasun (impure). So let them not come near Al-Masjid-
al-Harâm (at Makkah) after this year, and if you fear
poverty, Allâh will enrich you if He wills, out of His
Bounty. Surely, Allâh is All-Knowing, All-Wise. (28)*

## Quran 9:32-35

يُرِيدُونَ أَن يُطْفِـُٔوا۟ نُورَ ٱللَّهِ بِأَفْوَٰهِهِمْ وَيَأْبَى ٱللَّهُ إِلَّآ أَن يُتِمَّ

نُورَهُۥ وَلَوْ كَرِهَ ٱلْكَٰفِرُونَ (٣٢) هُوَ ٱلَّذِىٓ أَرْسَلَ رَسُولَهُۥ

بِٱلْهُدَىٰ وَدِينِ ٱلْحَقِّ لِيُظْهِرَهُۥ عَلَى ٱلدِّينِ كُلِّهِۦ وَلَوْ كَرِهَ

ٱلْمُشْرِكُونَ (٣٣) يَـٰٓأَيُّهَا ٱلَّذِينَ ءَامَنُوٓا۟ إِنَّ كَثِيرًا مِّنَ

ٱلْأَحْبَارِ وَٱلرُّهْبَانِ لَيَأْكُلُونَ أَمْوَٰلَ ٱلنَّاسِ بِٱلْبَٰطِلِ وَيَصُدُّونَ

عَن سَبِيلِ ٱللَّهِ ۗ وَٱلَّذِينَ يَكْنِزُونَ ٱلذَّهَبَ وَٱلْفِضَّةَ وَلَا يُنفِقُونَهَا

فِى سَبِيلِ ٱللَّهِ فَبَشِّرْهُم بِعَذَابٍ أَلِيمٍ (٣٤) يَوْمَ يُحْمَىٰ عَلَيْهَا فِى

نَارِ جَهَنَّمَ فَتُكْوَىٰ بِهَا جِبَاهُهُمْ وَجُنُوبُهُمْ وَظُهُورُهُمْۚ هَٰذَا مَا كَنَزْتُمْ لِأَنفُسِكُمْ فَذُوقُواْ مَا كُنتُمْ تَكْنِزُونَ (٣٥)

*They (the disbelievers, the Jews and the Christians) want to extinguish Allâh's Light (with which Muhammad has been sent - Islâmic Monotheism) with their mouths, but Allâh will not allow except that His Light should be perfected even though the Kâfirûn (disbelievers) hate (it). (32)It is He Who has sent His Messenger (Muhammad) with guidance and the religion of truth (Islâm), to make it superior over all religions even though the Mushrikûn (polytheists, pagans, idolaters, disbelievers in the Oneness of Allâh) hate (it). (33)O you who believe! Verily, there are many of the (Jewish) rabbis and the (Christian) monks who devour the wealth of mankind in falsehood, and hinder (them) from the Way of Allâh (i.e. Allâh's religion of Islâmic Monotheism). And those who hoard up gold and silver [Al-Kanz: the money, the Zakât of which has not been paid], and spend them not in the Way of Allâh, -announce unto them a painful torment. (34)On the Day when that (Al-Kanz: money, gold and silver, the Zakât of which has not been paid) will be heated in the Fire of Hell and with it will be branded their foreheads, their flanks, and their backs, (and it will be said unto them):-"This is the treasure which you hoarded for yourselves. Now taste of what you used to hoard." (35)*

## Quran 9:39-41

إِلَّا تَنفِرُواْ يُعَذِّبْكُمْ عَذَابًا أَلِيمًا وَيَسْتَبْدِلْ قَوْمًا غَيْرَكُمْ وَلَا
تَضُرُّوهُ شَيْئًا وَٱللَّهُ عَلَىٰ كُلِّ شَىْءٍ قَدِيرٌ (٣٩) إِلَّا تَنصُرُوهُ
فَقَدْ نَصَرَهُ ٱللَّهُ إِذْ أَخْرَجَهُ ٱلَّذِينَ كَفَرُواْ ثَانِىَ ٱثْنَيْنِ إِذْ هُمَا
فِى ٱلْغَارِ إِذْ يَقُولُ لِصَـٰحِبِهِ لَا تَحْزَنْ إِنَّ ٱللَّهَ مَعَنَا فَأَنزَلَ ٱللَّهُ
سَكِينَتَهُ عَلَيْهِ وَأَيَّدَهُ بِجُنُودٍ لَّمْ تَرَوْهَا وَجَعَلَ كَلِمَةَ ٱلَّذِينَ
كَفَرُواْ ٱلسُّفْلَىٰ وَكَلِمَةُ ٱللَّهِ هِىَ ٱلْعُلْيَا وَٱللَّهُ عَزِيزٌ حَكِيمٌ
(٤٠) ٱنفِرُواْ خِفَافًا وَثِقَالاً وَجَـٰهِدُواْ بِأَمْوَٰلِكُمْ وَأَنفُسِكُمْ فِى
سَبِيلِ ٱللَّهِ ذَٰلِكُمْ خَيْرٌ لَّكُمْ إِن كُنتُمْ تَعْلَمُونَ (٤١)

*If you march not forth, He will punish you with a painful torment and will replace you by another people, and you cannot harm Him at all, and Allâh is Able to do all things (39)If you help him (Muhammad) not (it does not matter), for Allâh did indeed help him when the disbelievers drove him out, the second of two, when they (Muhammad and Abu Bakr) were in the cave, and he said to his companion (Abu Bakr): "Be not sad (or afraid), surely Allâh is with us." Then Allâh sent down His Sakînah (calmness, tranquillity, peace) upon him, and strengthened him with forces (angels) which you saw not, and made the word of those who disbelieved the lowermost, while the Word of Allâh that became the uppermost, and Allâh is All-Mighty, All-Wise. (40)March forth, whether you are light (being healthy, young and wealthy) or heavy (being ill, old and poor), strive hard with your wealth and your lives in the Cause of Allâh. This is better for you, if you but knew. (41)*

## Quran 9:44-48

لَا يَسْتَـْٔذِنُكَ ٱلَّذِينَ يُؤْمِنُونَ بِٱللَّهِ وَٱلْيَوْمِ ٱلْأَخِرِ أَن يُجَـٰهِدُواْ بِأَمْوَٰلِهِمْ وَأَنفُسِهِمْ وَٱللَّهُ عَلِيمٌ بِٱلْمُتَّقِينَ (٤٤) إِنَّمَا يَسْتَـْٔذِنُكَ ٱلَّذِينَ لَا يُؤْمِنُونَ بِٱللَّهِ وَٱلْيَوْمِ ٱلْأَخِرِ وَٱرْتَابَتْ قُلُوبُهُمْ فَهُمْ فِى رَيْبِهِمْ يَتَرَدَّدُونَ (٤٥) ۞ وَلَوْ أَرَادُواْ ٱلْخُرُوجَ لَأَعَدُّواْ لَهُۥ عُدَّةً وَلَـٰكِن كَرِهَ ٱللَّهُ ٱنۢبِعَاثَهُمْ فَثَبَّطَهُمْ وَقِيلَ ٱقْعُدُواْ مَعَ ٱلْقَـٰعِدِينَ (٤٦) لَوْ خَرَجُواْ فِيكُم مَّا زَادُوكُمْ إِلَّا خَبَالاً وَلَأَوْضَعُواْ خِلَـٰلَكُمْ يَبْغُونَكُمُ ٱلْفِتْنَةَ وَفِيكُمْ سَمَّـٰعُونَ لَهُمْۗ وَٱللَّهُ عَلِيمٌ بِٱلظَّـٰلِمِينَ (٤٧) لَقَدِ ٱبْتَغَوُاْ ٱلْفِتْنَةَ مِن قَبْلُ وَقَلَّبُواْ لَكَ ٱلْأُمُورَ حَتَّىٰ جَاءَ ٱلْحَقُّ وَظَهَرَ أَمْرُ ٱللَّهِ وَهُمْ كَـٰرِهُونَ (٤٨)

*Those who believe in Allâh and the Last Day would not ask your leave to be exempted from fighting with their properties and their lives, and Allâh is the All-Knower of Al-Muttaqûn (the pious) (44)It is only those who believe not in Allâh and the Last Day and whose hearts are in doubt that ask your leave (to be exempted from Jihâd). So in their doubts they waver. (45)And if they had intended to march out, certainly, they would have made some preparation for it, but Allâh was averse to their being sent forth, so He made them lag behind, and it was said (to them), "Sit you among those who sit (at home)."*

(46) Had they marched out with you, they would have added to you nothing except disorder, and they would have hurried about in your midst (spreading corruption) and sowing sedition among you, and there are some among you who would have listened to them. And Allâh is the All-Knower of the Zâlimûn (polytheists and wrong-doers). (47) Verily, they had plotted sedition before, and had upset matters for you, - until the truth (victory) came and the Decree of Allâh (His religion, Islâm) became manifest though they hated it (48)

## Quran 9:52

قُلْ هَلْ تَرَبَّصُونَ بِنَآ إِلَّآ إِحْدَى ٱلْحُسْنَيَيْنِّ وَنَحْنُ نَتَرَبَّصُ بِكُمْ أَن يُصِيبَكُمُ ٱللَّهُ بِعَذَابٍ مِّنْ عِندِهِۦٓ أَوْ بِأَيْدِينَاۖ فَتَرَبَّصُوٓاْ إِنَّا مَعَكُم مُّتَرَبِّصُونَ

Say: "Do you wait for us (anything) except one of the two best things (martyrdom or victory); while we await for you either that Allâh will afflict you with a punishment from Himself or at our hands. So wait, we too are waiting with you." (52)

## Quran 9:55

فَلَا تُعْجِبْكَ أَمْوَٰلُهُمْ وَلَآ أَوْلَٰدُهُمّْ إِنَّمَا يُرِيدُ ٱللَّهُ لِيُعَذِّبَهُم بِهَا فِى ٱلْحَيَوٰةِ ٱلدُّنْيَا وَتَزْهَقَ أَنفُسُهُمْ وَهُمْ كَٰفِرُونَ

So let not their wealth or their children amaze you; in reality Allâh's Plan is to punish them with these things *in the life of the this world, and that their souls shall depart (die) while they are disbelievers. (55)*

## Quran 9:61

وَمِنْهُمُ ٱلَّذِينَ يُؤْذُونَ ٱلنَّبِىَّ وَيَقُولُونَ هُوَ أُذُنٌ قُلْ أُذُنُ خَيْرٍ
لَّكُمْ يُؤْمِنُ بِٱللَّهِ وَيُؤْمِنُ لِلْمُؤْمِنِينَ وَرَحْمَةٌ لِّلَّذِينَ ءَامَنُواْ
مِنكُمْ وَٱلَّذِينَ يُؤْذُونَ رَسُولَ ٱللَّهِ لَهُمْ عَذَابٌ أَلِيمٌ

*And among them are men who annoy the Prophet (Muhammad) and say: "He is (lending his) ear (to every news)." Say: "He listens to what is best for you; he believes in Allâh; has faith in the believers; and is a mercy to those of you who believe." But those who hurt Allâh's Messenger (Muhammad) will have a painful torment.*

## Quran 9:63-64

أَلَمْ يَعْلَمُواْ أَنَّهُۥ مَن يُحَادِدِ ٱللَّهَ وَرَسُولَهُۥ فَأَنَّ لَهُۥ نَارَ جَهَنَّمَ
خَٰلِدًا فِيهَآ ذَٰلِكَ ٱلْخِزْىُ ٱلْعَظِيمُ (٦٣) يَحْذَرُ ٱلْمُنَٰفِقُونَ أَن
تُنَزَّلَ عَلَيْهِمْ سُورَةٌ تُنَبِّئُهُم بِمَا فِى قُلُوبِهِمْ قُلِ ٱسْتَهْزِءُوٓاْ إِنَّ ٱللَّهَ
مُخْرِجٌ مَّا تَحْذَرُونَ (٦٤)

*Know they not that whoever opposes and shows hostility to Allâh and His Messenger, certainly for him will be the Fire of Hell to abide therein. That is extreme disgrace. (63) The hypocrites fear lest a Sûrah (chapter of the Qur'ân) should be revealed about them, showing them what is in their hearts. Say: "(Go ahead and) mock! But certainly Allâh will bring to light all that you fear." (64)*

## Quran 9:68-69

وَعَدَ ٱللَّهُ ٱلْمُنَـٰفِقِينَ وَٱلْمُنَـٰفِقَـٰتِ وَٱلْكُفَّارَ نَارَ جَهَنَّمَ خَـٰلِدِينَ فِيهَاۚ هِىَ حَسْبُهُمْۚ وَلَعَنَهُمُ ٱللَّهُۖ وَلَهُمْ عَذَابٌ مُّقِيمٌ (٦٨) كَٱلَّذِينَ مِن قَبْلِكُمْ كَانُوٓا۟ أَشَدَّ مِنكُمْ قُوَّةً وَأَكْثَرَ أَمْوَٰلًا وَأَوْلَـٰدًا فَٱسْتَمْتَعُوا۟ بِخَلَـٰقِهِمْ فَٱسْتَمْتَعْتُم بِخَلَـٰقِكُمْ كَمَا ٱسْتَمْتَعَ ٱلَّذِينَ مِن قَبْلِكُم بِخَلَـٰقِهِمْ وَخُضْتُمْ كَٱلَّذِى خَاضُوٓا۟ۚ أُو۟لَـٰٓئِكَ حَبِطَتْ أَعْمَـٰلُهُمْ فِى ٱلدُّنْيَا وَٱلْـَٔاخِرَةِۖ وَأُو۟لَـٰٓئِكَ هُمُ ٱلْخَـٰسِرُونَ (٦٩)

*Allâh has promised the hypocrites — men and women — and the disbelievers, the Fire of Hell, therein shall they abide. It will suffice them. Allâh has cursed them and for them is the lasting torment. (68)Like those before you: they were mightier than you in power, and more abundant in wealth and children. They had enjoyed their portion (awhile), so enjoy your portion (awhile) as those before you enjoyed their portion (awhile); and you indulged in play and pastime (and in telling lies against Allâh and His Messenger Muhammad) as they indulged in play and pastime. Such are they whose deeds are in vain in this world and in the Hereafter. Such are they who are the losers. (69)*

## Quran 9:71-74

وَٱلْمُؤْمِنُونَ وَٱلْمُؤْمِنَـٰتُ بَعْضُهُمْ أَوْلِيَآءُ بَعْضٍ يَأْمُرُونَ
بِٱلْمَعْرُوفِ وَيَنْهَوْنَ عَنِ ٱلْمُنكَرِ وَيُقِيمُونَ ٱلصَّلَوٰةَ وَيُؤْتُونَ
ٱلزَّكَوٰةَ وَيُطِيعُونَ ٱللَّهَ وَرَسُولَهُ أُوْلَـٰٓئِكَ سَيَرْحَمُهُمُ ٱللَّهُ إِنَّ ٱللَّهَ
عَزِيزٌ حَكِيمٌ (٧١) وَعَدَ ٱللَّهُ ٱلْمُؤْمِنِينَ وَٱلْمُؤْمِنَـٰتِ جَنَّـٰتٍ
تَجْرِى مِن تَحْتِهَا ٱلْأَنْهَـٰرُ خَـٰلِدِينَ فِيهَا وَمَسَـٰكِنَ طَيِّبَةً فِى
جَنَّـٰتِ عَدْنٍ وَرِضْوَٰنٌ مِّنَ ٱللَّهِ أَكْبَرُ ذَٰلِكَ هُوَ ٱلْفَوْزُ ٱلْعَظِيمُ
(٧٢) يَـٰٓأَيُّهَا ٱلنَّبِىُّ جَـٰهِدِ ٱلْكُفَّارَ وَٱلْمُنَـٰفِقِينَ وَٱغْلُظْ عَلَيْهِمْ
وَمَأْوَىٰهُمْ جَهَنَّمُ وَبِئْسَ ٱلْمَصِيرُ (٧٣) يَحْلِفُونَ بِٱللَّهِ مَا قَالُواْ
وَلَقَدْ قَالُواْ كَلِمَةَ ٱلْكُفْرِ وَكَفَرُواْ بَعْدَ إِسْلَـٰمِهِمْ وَهَمُّواْ بِمَا لَمْ
يَنَالُواْ وَمَا نَقَمُوٓاْ إِلَّا أَنْ أَغْنَـٰهُمُ ٱللَّهُ وَرَسُولُهُ مِن فَضْلِهِ فَإِن
يَتُوبُواْ يَكُ خَيْرًا لَّهُمْ وَإِن يَتَوَلَّوْاْ يُعَذِّبْهُمُ ٱللَّهُ عَذَابًا أَلِيمًا فِى
ٱلدُّنْيَا وَٱلْأَخِرَةِ وَمَا لَهُمْ فِى ٱلْأَرْضِ مِن وَلِىٍّ وَلَا نَصِيرٍ
(٧٤)

*The believers, men and women, are Auliyâ' (helpers, supporters, friends, protectors) of one another; they enjoin (on the people) Al-Ma'rûf (i.e. Islâmic Monotheism and all that Islâm orders one to do), and forbid (people) from Al-Munkar (i.e. polytheism and disbelief of all kinds, and all that Islâm has forbidden); they perform As-Salât (Iqâmat-as-Salât), and give the Zakât, and obey Allâh and His Messenger. Allâh will have His Mercy on them. Surely Allâh is All-Mighty, All-Wise. (71)Allâh has promised the believers -men and women, - Gardens under which rivers flow to dwell*

therein forever, and beautiful mansions in Gardens of
'Adn (Eden Paradise). But the greatest bliss is the Good
Pleasure of Allâh. That is the supreme success. (72)O
Prophet (Muhammad)! Strive hard against the
disbelievers and the hypocrites, and be harsh against
them, their abode is Hell, - and worst indeed is that
destination. (73)They swear by Allâh that they said
nothing (bad), but really they said the word of disbelief,
and they disbelieved after accepting Islâm, and they
resolved that (plot to murder Prophet Muhammad)
which they were unable to carry out, and they could not
find any cause to do so except that Allâh and His
Messenger had enriched them of His Bounty. If then they
repent, it will be better for them, but if they turn away,
Allâh will punish them with a painful torment in this
worldly life and in the Hereafter. And there is none for
them on earth as a Walî (supporter, protector) or a
helper. (74)

## Quran 10:4

إِلَيْهِ مَرْجِعُكُمْ جَمِيعًا وَعْدَ ٱللَّهِ حَقًّا إِنَّهُ يَبْدَؤُا۟ ٱلْخَلْقَ ثُمَّ يُعِيدُهُ
لِيَجْزِىَ ٱلَّذِينَ ءَامَنُوا۟ وَعَمِلُوا۟ ٱلصَّٰلِحَٰتِ بِٱلْقِسْطِ وَٱلَّذِينَ
كَفَرُوا۟ لَهُمْ شَرَابٌ مِّنْ حَمِيمٍ وَعَذَابٌ أَلِيمٌ بِمَا كَانُوا۟
يَكْفُرُونَ

To Him is the return of all of you. The Promise of Allâh
is true. It is He Who begins the creation and then will

repeat it, that He may reward with justice those who believed (in the Oneness of Allâh - Islâmic Monotheism) and did deeds of righteousness. But those who disbelieved will have a drink of boiling fluids and painful torment because they used to disbelieve. (4)

## Quran 10:7-9

إِنَّ ٱلَّذِينَ لَا يَرْجُونَ لِقَآءَنَا وَرَضُوا۟ بِٱلْحَيَوٰةِ ٱلدُّنْيَا وَٱطْمَأَنُّوا۟ بِهَا وَٱلَّذِينَ هُمْ عَنْ ءَايَٰتِنَا غَٰفِلُونَ (٧) أُو۟لَٰٓئِكَ مَأْوَىٰهُمُ ٱلنَّارُ بِمَا كَانُوا۟ يَكْسِبُونَ (٨) إِنَّ ٱلَّذِينَ ءَامَنُوا۟ وَعَمِلُوا۟ ٱلصَّٰلِحَٰتِ يَهْدِيهِمْ رَبُّهُم بِإِيمَٰنِهِمْ تَجْرِى مِن تَحْتِهِمُ ٱلْأَنْهَٰرُ فِى جَنَّٰتِ ٱلنَّعِيمِ (٩)

Verily, those who hope not for their meeting with Us, but are pleased and satisfied with the life of the present world, and those who are heedless of Our Ayât (proofs, evidences, verses, lessons, signs, revelations, etc.), (7)Those, their abode will be the Fire, because of what they used to earn. (8)Verily, those who believe and do deeds of righteousness, their Lord will guide them through their Faith; under them will flow rivers in the Gardens of Delight (Paradise). (9)

## Quran 10:13

وَلَقَدْ أَهْلَكْنَا ٱلْقُرُونَ مِن قَبْلِكُمْ لَمَّا ظَلَمُوا۟ وَجَآءَتْهُمْ رُسُلُهُم بِٱلْبَيِّنَٰتِ وَمَا كَانُوا۟ لِيُؤْمِنُوا۟ كَذَٰلِكَ نَجْزِى ٱلْقَوْمَ ٱلْمُجْرِمِينَ

*And indeed, We destroyed generations before you, when*
*they did wrong while their Messengers came to them*
*with clear proofs, but they were not such as to believe!*
*Thus do We requite the people who are Mujrimûn*
*(disbelievers, polytheists, sinners, criminals). (13)*

## Quran 10:17

فَمَنْ أَظْلَمُ مِمَّنِ ٱفْتَرَىٰ عَلَى ٱللَّهِ كَذِبًا أَوْ كَذَّبَ بِـَٔايَـٰتِهِۦٓ
إِنَّهُۥ لَا يُفْلِحُ ٱلْمُجْرِمُونَ

*So who does more wrong than he who forges a lie against*
*Allâh or denies His Ayât (proofs, evidences, verses,*
*lessons, signs, revelations, etc.)? Surely, the Mujrimûn*
*(criminals, sinners, disbelievers and polytheists) will*
*never be successful! (17)*

## Quran 10:23

فَلَمَّآ أَنجَىٰهُمْ إِذَا هُمْ يَبْغُونَ فِى ٱلْأَرْضِ بِغَيْرِ ٱلْحَقِّ يَـٰٓأَيُّهَا
ٱلنَّاسُ إِنَّمَا بَغْيُكُمْ عَلَىٰٓ أَنفُسِكُم مَّتَـٰعَ ٱلْحَيَوٰةِ ٱلدُّنْيَا ثُمَّ إِلَيْنَا
مَرْجِعُكُمْ فَنُنَبِّئُكُم بِمَا كُنتُمْ تَعْمَلُونَ

*But when He delivers them, behold! they rebel (disobey*
*Allâh) in the earth wrongfully. O mankind! Your*
*rebellion (disobedience to Allâh) is only against your*
*ownselves, - a brief enjoyment of this worldly life, then*
*(in the end) unto Us is your return, and We shall inform*
*you that which you used to do. (23)*

۞ لِّلَّذِينَ أَحْسَنُوا۟ ٱلْحُسْنَىٰ وَزِيَادَةٌۖ وَلَا يَرْهَقُ وُجُوهَهُمْ قَتَرٌ
وَلَا ذِلَّةٌۚ أُو۟لَٰٓئِكَ أَصْحَٰبُ ٱلْجَنَّةِۖ هُمْ فِيهَا خَٰلِدُونَ (٢٦) وَٱلَّذِينَ
كَسَبُوا۟ ٱلسَّيِّـَٔاتِ جَزَآءُ سَيِّئَةٍ بِمِثْلِهَا وَتَرْهَقُهُمْ ذِلَّةٌۖ مَّا لَهُم مِّنَ
ٱللَّهِ مِنْ عَاصِمٍۖ كَأَنَّمَآ أُغْشِيَتْ وُجُوهُهُمْ قِطَعًا مِّنَ ٱلَّيْلِ مُظْلِمًاۚ
أُو۟لَٰٓئِكَ أَصْحَٰبُ ٱلنَّارِۖ هُمْ فِيهَا خَٰلِدُونَ (٢٧) وَيَوْمَ نَحْشُرُهُمْ
جَمِيعًا ثُمَّ نَقُولُ لِلَّذِينَ أَشْرَكُوا۟ مَكَانَكُمْ أَنتُمْ وَشُرَكَآؤُكُمْۚ فَزَيَّلْنَا
بَيْنَهُمْۖ وَقَالَ شُرَكَآؤُهُم مَّا كُنتُمْ إِيَّانَا تَعْبُدُونَ (٢٨) فَكَفَىٰ بِٱللَّهِ
شَهِيدًۢا بَيْنَنَا وَبَيْنَكُمْ إِن كُنَّا عَنْ عِبَادَتِكُمْ لَغَٰفِلِينَ (٢٩) هُنَالِكَ
تَبْلُوا۟ كُلُّ نَفْسٍ مَّآ أَسْلَفَتْۚ وَرُدُّوٓا۟ إِلَى ٱللَّهِ مَوْلَٰهُمُ ٱلْحَقِّۖ وَضَلَّ
عَنْهُم مَّا كَانُوا۟ يَفْتَرُونَ (٣٠)

*For those who have done good is the best (reward, i.e.
Paradise) and even more (i.e. having the honour of
glancing at the Countenance of Allâh) Neither darkness
nor dust nor any humiliating disgrace shall cover their
faces. They are the dwellers of Paradise, they will abide
therein forever. (26) And those who have earned evil
deeds, the recompense of an evil deed is the like thereof,
and humiliating disgrace will cover them (their faces).
No defender will they have from Allâh. Their faces will be
covered, as it were with pieces from the darkness of night.
They are dwellers of the Fire, they will abide therein
forever. (27)And the Day whereon We shall gather them
all together, then We shall say to those who did set*

partners in worship with Us: "Stop at your place! You
and your partners (whom you had worshipped in the
worldly life)." then We shall separate them, and their
(Allâh's so-called) partners shall say: "It was not us that
you used to worship." (28) "So sufficient is Allâh for a
witness between us and you, that We indeed knew
nothing of your worship of us." (29) There! Every person
will know (exactly) what he had earned before, and they
will be brought back to Allâh, their rightful Maula
(Lord), and their invented false deities will vanish from
them. (30)

## Quran 10:48-52

وَيَقُولُونَ مَتَىٰ هَٰذَا ٱلْوَعْدُ إِن كُنتُمْ صَٰدِقِينَ (٤٨) قُل لَّآ أَمْلِكُ
لِنَفْسِى ضَرًّا وَلَا نَفْعًا إِلَّا مَا شَآءَ ٱللَّهُ لِكُلِّ أُمَّةٍ أَجَلٌ إِذَا جَآءَ
أَجَلُهُمْ فَلَا يَسْتَـْٔخِرُونَ سَاعَةً وَلَا يَسْتَقْدِمُونَ (٤٩) قُلْ أَرَءَيْتُمْ
إِنْ أَتَىٰكُمْ عَذَابُهُۥ بَيَٰتًا أَوْ نَهَارًا مَّاذَا يَسْتَعْجِلُ مِنْهُ ٱلْمُجْرِمُونَ
(٥٠) أَثُمَّ إِذَا مَا وَقَعَ ءَامَنتُم بِهِۦٓ ءَآلْـَٰٔنَ وَقَدْ كُنتُم بِهِۦ تَسْتَعْجِلُونَ
(٥١) ثُمَّ قِيلَ لِلَّذِينَ ظَلَمُواْ ذُوقُواْ عَذَابَ ٱلْخُلْدِ هَلْ تُجْزَوْنَ
إِلَّا بِمَا كُنتُمْ تَكْسِبُونَ (٥٢)

And they say: "When will be this promise (the torment
or the Day of Resurrection), - if you speak the truth?"
(48) Say (O Muhammad): "I have no power over any
harm or profit to myself except what Allâh may will. For
every Ummah (a community or a nation), there is a term

appointed; when their term comes, neither can they delay it nor can they advance it an hour (or a moment)." (49) Say: "Tell me, - if His torment should come to you by night or by day, - which portion thereof would the Mujrimûn (disbelievers, polytheists, sinners, criminals) hasten on ?" (50) Is it then, that when it has actually befallen, you will believe in it? What! Now (you believe)? And you used (aforetime) to hasten it on!" (51) Then it will be said to them who wronged themselves: "Taste you the everlasting torment! Are you recompensed (aught) save what you used to earn?" (52)

## Quran 10:54-56

وَلَوْ أَنَّ لِكُلِّ نَفْسٍ ظَلَمَتْ مَا فِى ٱلْأَرْضِ لَٱفْتَدَتْ بِهِۦ وَأَسَرُّواْ ٱلنَّدَامَةَ لَمَّا رَأَوُاْ ٱلْعَذَابَ وَقُضِىَ بَيْنَهُم بِٱلْقِسْطِ وَهُمْ لَا يُظْلَمُونَ (٥٤) أَلَا إِنَّ لِلَّهِ مَا فِى ٱلسَّمَـٰوَٰتِ وَٱلْأَرْضِ أَلَا إِنَّ وَعْدَ ٱللَّهِ حَقٌّ وَلَـٰكِنَّ أَكْثَرَهُمْ لَا يَعْلَمُونَ (٥٥) هُوَ يُحْىِۦ وَيُمِيتُ وَإِلَيْهِ تُرْجَعُونَ (٥٦)

And if every person who had wronged (by disbelieving in Allâh and by worshipping others besides Allâh), possessed all that is on earth, and sought to ransom himself therewith (it will not be accepted), and they would feel in their hearts regret when they see the torment, and they will be judged with justice, and no wrong will be done unto them. (54) No doubt, surely, all that is in the heavens and the earth belongs to Allâh. No

*doubt, surely, Allâh's Promise is true. But most of them*
*know not. (55) It is He Who gives life, and causes death,*
*and to Him you (all) shall return. (56)*

## Quran 10:62-64

أَلَا إِنَّ أَوْلِيَاءَ ٱللَّهِ لَا خَوْفٌ عَلَيْهِمْ وَلَا هُمْ يَحْزَنُونَ
(٦٢) ٱلَّذِينَ ءَامَنُواْ وَكَانُواْ يَتَّقُونَ (٦٣) لَهُمُ ٱلْبُشْرَىٰ فِى
ٱلْحَيَوٰةِ ٱلدُّنْيَا وَفِى ٱلْأَخِرَةِ لَا تَبْدِيلَ لِكَلِمَٰتِ ٱللَّهِ ذَٰلِكَ هُوَ
ٱلْفَوْزُ ٱلْعَظِيمُ (٦٤)

*No doubt! Verily, the Auliyâ' of Allâh [i.e. those who*
*believe in the Oneness of Allâh and fear Allâh much*
*(abstain from all kinds of sins and evil deeds which he has*
*forbidden), and love Allâh much (perform all kinds of*
*good deeds which He has ordained)], no fear shall come*
*upon them nor shall they grieve, - (62)Those who*
*believed (in the Oneness of Allâh - Islâmic Monotheism),*
*and used to fear Allâh much (by abstaining from evil*
*deeds and sins and by doing righteous deeds) (63)For*
*them are glad tidings, in the life of the present world (i.e.*
*through a righteous dream seen by the person himself or*
*shown to others), and in the Hereafter. No change can*
*there be in the Words of Allâh, this is indeed the supreme*
*success. (64)*

## Quran 10:69-70

قُلْ إِنَّ ٱلَّذِينَ يَفْتَرُونَ عَلَى ٱللَّهِ ٱلْكَذِبَ لَا يُفْلِحُونَ (٦٩) مَتَـٰعٌ فِى ٱلدُّنْيَا ثُمَّ إِلَيْنَا مَرْجِعُهُمْ ثُمَّ نُذِيقُهُمُ ٱلْعَذَابَ ٱلشَّدِيدَ بِمَا كَانُواْ يَكْفُرُونَ (٧٠)

*Say: "Verily, those who invent a lie against Allâh will never be successful" - (69)(A brief) enjoyment in this world! - and then unto Us will be their return, then We shall make them taste the severest torment because they used to disbelieve [in Allâh, belie His Messengers, deny and challenge His Ayât (proofs, signs, verses, etc.)]. (70)*

## Quran 10:93

وَلَقَدْ بَوَّأْنَا بَنِىٓ إِسْرَٰٓءِيلَ مُبَوَّأَ صِدْقٍ وَرَزَقْنَـٰهُم مِّنَ ٱلطَّيِّبَـٰتِ فَمَا ٱخْتَلَفُواْ حَتَّىٰ جَآءَهُمُ ٱلْعِلْمُ إِنَّ رَبَّكَ يَقْضِى بَيْنَهُمْ يَوْمَ ٱلْقِيَـٰمَةِ فِيمَا كَانُواْ فِيهِ يَخْتَلِفُونَ

*And indeed We settled the Children of Israel in an honourable dwelling place (Shâm and Misr), and provided them with good things, and they differed not until the knowledge came to them. Verily, Allâh will judge between them on the Day of Resurrection in that in which they used to differ. (93)*

## Quran 10:95-97

وَلَا تَكُونَنَّ مِنَ ٱلَّذِينَ كَذَّبُواْ بِـَٔايَـٰتِ ٱللَّهِ فَتَكُونَ مِنَ ٱلْخَـٰسِرِينَ (٩٥) إِنَّ ٱلَّذِينَ حَقَّتْ عَلَيْهِمْ كَلِمَتُ رَبِّكَ لَا يُؤْمِنُونَ (٩٦) وَلَوْ جَآءَتْهُمْ كُلُّ ءَايَةٍ حَتَّىٰ يَرَوُاْ ٱلْعَذَابَ ٱلْأَلِيمَ (٩٧)

*And be not one of those who belie the Ayât (proofs, evidences, verses, lessons, signs, revelations, etc.) of Allâh, for then you shall be one of the losers. (95)Truly! Those, against whom the Word (Wrath) of your Lord has been justified, will not believe. (96)Even if every sign should come to them, - until they see the painful torment.*

## Quran 10:100-101

وَمَا كَانَ لِنَفْسٍ أَن تُؤْمِنَ إِلَّا بِإِذْنِ ٱللَّهِ وَيَجْعَلُ ٱلرِّجْسَ عَلَى ٱلَّذِينَ لَا يَعْقِلُونَ (١٠٠) قُلِ ٱنظُرُواْ مَاذَا فِى ٱلسَّمَـٰوَٰتِ وَٱلْأَرْضِ وَمَا تُغْنِى ٱلْأَيَـٰتُ وَٱلنُّذُرُ عَن قَوْمٍ لَّا يُؤْمِنُونَ (١٠١)

*It is not for any person to believe, except by the Leave of Allâh, and He will put the wrath on those who are heedless. (100)Say: "Behold all that is in the heavens and the earth," but neither Ayât (proofs, evidences, verses, lessons, signs, revelations, etc.) nor warners benefit those who believe not. (101)*

## Quran 10:103

ثُمَّ نُنَجِّى رُسُلَنَا وَٱلَّذِينَ ءَامَنُواْ كَذَٰلِكَ حَقًّا عَلَيْنَا نُنجِ ٱلْمُؤْمِنِينَ

*Then (in the end) We save Our Messengers and those who believe! Thus it is incumbent upon Us to save the believers. (103)*

## Quran 10:107

وَإِن يَمْسَسْكَ ٱللَّهُ بِضُرٍّ فَلَا كَاشِفَ لَهُ ۥ إِلَّا هُوَ ۖ وَإِن يُرِدْكَ بِخَيْرٍ فَلَا رَادَّ لِفَضْلِهِ ۦ يُصِيبُ بِهِ ۦ مَن يَشَآءُ مِنْ عِبَادِهِ ۦ وَهُوَ ٱلْغَفُورُ ٱلرَّحِيمُ

*And if Allâh touches you with hurt, there is none who can remove it but He; and if He intends any good for you, there is none who can repel His Favour which He causes it to reach whomsoever of His slaves He wills. And He is the Oft-Forgiving, Most Merciful. (107)*

## Quran 11:4

إِلَى ٱللَّهِ مَرْجِعُكُمْ ۖ وَهُوَ عَلَىٰ كُلِّ شَيْءٍ قَدِيرٌ

*To Allâh is your return, and He is Able to do all things.*

## Quran 11:11

إِلَّا ٱلَّذِينَ صَبَرُواْ وَعَمِلُواْ ٱلصَّـٰلِحَـٰتِ أُوْلَـٰئِكَ لَهُم مَّغْفِرَةٌ وَأَجْرٌ كَبِيرٌ

*Except those who show patience and do righteous good deeds, those: theirs will be forgiveness and a great reward (Paradise). (11)*

## Quran 11:15-21

مَن كَانَ يُرِيدُ ٱلْحَيَوٰةَ ٱلدُّنْيَا وَزِينَتَهَا نُوَفِّ إِلَيْهِمْ أَعْمَـٰلَهُمْ فِيهَا وَهُمْ فِيهَا لَا يُبْخَسُونَ (١٥) أُوْلَـٰئِكَ ٱلَّذِينَ لَيْسَ لَهُمْ فِى

الْأَخِرَةِ إِلَّا ٱلنَّارُ وَحَبِطَ مَا صَنَعُوا۟ فِيهَا وَبَٰطِلٌ مَّا كَانُوا۟ يَعْمَلُونَ (١٦) أَفَمَن كَانَ عَلَىٰ بَيِّنَةٍ مِّن رَّبِّهِۦ وَيَتْلُوهُ شَاهِدٌ مِّنْهُ وَمِن قَبْلِهِۦ كِتَٰبُ مُوسَىٰٓ إِمَامًا وَرَحْمَةً أُو۟لَٰٓئِكَ يُؤْمِنُونَ بِهِۦ وَمَن يَكْفُرْ بِهِۦ مِنَ ٱلْأَحْزَابِ فَٱلنَّارُ مَوْعِدُهُۥ فَلَا تَكُ فِى مِرْيَةٍ مِّنْهُ إِنَّهُ ٱلْحَقُّ مِن رَّبِّكَ وَلَٰكِنَّ أَكْثَرَ ٱلنَّاسِ لَا يُؤْمِنُونَ (١٧) وَمَنْ أَظْلَمُ مِمَّنِ ٱفْتَرَىٰ عَلَى ٱللَّهِ كَذِبًا أُو۟لَٰٓئِكَ يُعْرَضُونَ عَلَىٰ رَبِّهِمْ وَيَقُولُ ٱلْأَشْهَٰدُ هَٰٓؤُلَآءِ ٱلَّذِينَ كَذَبُوا۟ عَلَىٰ رَبِّهِمْ أَلَا لَعْنَةُ ٱللَّهِ عَلَى ٱلظَّٰلِمِينَ (١٨) ٱلَّذِينَ يَصُدُّونَ عَن سَبِيلِ ٱللَّهِ وَيَبْغُونَهَا عِوَجًا وَهُم بِٱلْأَخِرَةِ هُمْ كَٰفِرُونَ (١٩) أُو۟لَٰٓئِكَ لَمْ يَكُونُوا۟ مُعْجِزِينَ فِى ٱلْأَرْضِ وَمَا كَانَ لَهُم مِّن دُونِ ٱللَّهِ مِنْ أَوْلِيَآءَ يُضَٰعَفُ لَهُمُ ٱلْعَذَابُ مَا كَانُوا۟ يَسْتَطِيعُونَ ٱلسَّمْعَ وَمَا كَانُوا۟ يُبْصِرُونَ (٢٠) أُو۟لَٰٓئِكَ ٱلَّذِينَ خَسِرُوٓا۟ أَنفُسَهُمْ وَضَلَّ عَنْهُم مَّا كَانُوا۟ يَفْتَرُونَ (٢١)

Whosoever desires the life of the world and its glitter; to them We shall pay in full (the wages of) their deeds therein, and they will have no diminution therein. (15)They are those for whom there is nothing in the Hereafter but Fire; and vain are the deeds they did therein. And of no effect is that which they used to do (16)Can they (Muslims) who rely on a clear proof (the Qur'ân) from their Lord, and whom a witness [Jibrail (Gabriel )] from Him recites (follows) it (can they be equal with the disbelievers); and before it, came the Book of Mûsa (Moses), a guidance and a mercy, they believe

therein, but those of the sects (Jews, Christians and all
the other non-Muslim nations) that reject it (the
Qur'ân), the Fire will be their promised meeting-place.
So be not in doubt about it (i.e. those who denied Prophet
Muhammad and also denied all that which he brought
from Allâh, surely, they will enter Hell). Verily, it is the
truth from your Lord, but most of the mankind believe
not (17)And who does more wrong than he who invents a
lie against Allâh. Such will be brought before their Lord,
and the witnesses will say, "These are the ones who lied
against their Lord!" No doubt! the curse of Allâh is on
the Zâlimûn (polytheists, wrong-doers, oppressors)
(18)Those who hinder (others) from the Path of Allâh
(Islâmic Monotheism), and seek a crookedness therein,
while they are disbelievers in the Hereafter. (19)By no
means will they escape (from Allâh's Torment) on earth,
nor have they protectors besides Allâh! Their torment
will be doubled! They could not bear to hear (the
preachers of the truth) and they used not to see (the truth
because of their severe aversoin, inspite of the fact that
they had the sense of hearing and sight). (20)They are
those who have lost their ownselves, and their invented
false deities will vanish from them. (21)

## Quran 11:23

إِنَّ ٱلَّذِينَ ءَامَنُواْ وَعَمِلُواْ ٱلصَّٰلِحَٰتِ وَأَخْبَتُوٓاْ إِلَىٰ رَبِّهِمْ أُوْلَٰٓئِكَ أَصْحَٰبُ
ٱلْجَنَّةِ هُمْ فِيهَا خَٰلِدُونَ

*Verily, those who believe (in the Oneness of Allâh -*
*Islâmic Monotheism) and do righteous good deeds, and*
*humble themselves (in repentance and obedience) before*
*their Lord, - they will be dwellers of Paradise to dwell*
*therein forever. (23)*

## Quran 11:60

وَأُتْبِعُواْ فِى هَـٰذِهِ ٱلدُّنْيَا لَعْنَةً وَيَوْمَ ٱلْقِيَـٰمَةِ أَلَا إِنَّ عَادًا
كَفَرُواْ رَبَّهُمْ أَلَا بُعْدًا لِّعَادٍ قَوْمِ هُودٍ

*And they were pursued by a curse in this world and (so*
*they will be) on the Day of Resurrection. No doubt!*
*Verily, 'Ad disbelieved in their Lord. So away with 'Ad,*
*the people of Hûd (60)*

## Quran 11:98-99

يَقْدُمُ قَوْمَهُ يَوْمَ ٱلْقِيَـٰمَةِ فَأَوْرَدَهُمُ ٱلنَّارَ وَبِئْسَ ٱلْوِرْدُ ٱلْمَوْرُودُ
(٩٨) وَأُتْبِعُواْ فِى هَـٰذِهِ لَعْنَةً وَيَوْمَ ٱلْقِيَـٰمَةِ بِئْسَ ٱلرِّفْدُ ٱلْمَرْفُودُ
(٩٩)

*He (Pharaoh) will go ahead of his people on the Day of*
*Resurrection, and will lead them into the Fire, and evil*
*indeed is the place to which they are led. (98)They were*
*pursued by a curse in this (deceiving life of this world)*
*and (so they will be pursued by a curse) on the Day of*
*Resurrection. Evil indeed is the gift gifted [i.e., the curse*

*(in this world) pursued by another curse (in the Hereafter)]. (99)*

## Quran 11:103-109

إِنَّ فِى ذَٰلِكَ لَءَايَةً لِّمَنْ خَافَ عَذَابَ ٱلْأَخِرَةِ ذَٰلِكَ يَوْمٌ مَّجْمُوعٌ لَّهُ ٱلنَّاسُ وَذَٰلِكَ يَوْمٌ مَّشْهُودٌ (١٠٣) وَمَا نُؤَخِّرُهُ إِلَّا لِأَجَلٍ مَّعْدُودٍ (١٠٤) يَوْمَ يَأْتِ لَا تَكَلَّمُ نَفْسٌ إِلَّا بِإِذْنِهِ فَمِنْهُمْ شَقِىٌّ وَسَعِيدٌ (١٠٥) فَأَمَّا ٱلَّذِينَ شَقُوا۟ فَفِى ٱلنَّارِ لَهُمْ فِيهَا زَفِيرٌ وَشَهِيقٌ (١٠٦) خَٰلِدِينَ فِيهَا مَا دَامَتِ ٱلسَّمَٰوَٰتُ وَٱلْأَرْضُ إِلَّا مَا شَاءَ رَبُّكَ إِنَّ رَبَّكَ فَعَّالٌ لِّمَا يُرِيدُ (١٠٧) ۞ وَأَمَّا ٱلَّذِينَ سُعِدُوا۟ فَفِى ٱلْجَنَّةِ خَٰلِدِينَ فِيهَا مَا دَامَتِ ٱلسَّمَٰوَٰتُ وَٱلْأَرْضُ إِلَّا مَا شَاءَ رَبُّكَ عَطَاءً غَيْرَ مَجْذُوذٍ (١٠٨) فَلَا تَكُ فِى مِرْيَةٍ مِّمَّا يَعْبُدُ هَٰؤُلَاءِ مَا يَعْبُدُونَ إِلَّا كَمَا يَعْبُدُ ءَابَاؤُهُم مِّن قَبْلُ وَإِنَّا لَمُوَفُّوهُمْ نَصِيبَهُمْ غَيْرَ مَنقُوصٍ (١٠٩)

*Indeed in that (there) is a sure lesson for those who fear the torment of the Hereafter. That is a Day whereon mankind will be gathered together, and that is a Day when all (the dwellers of the heavens and the earth) will be present. (103)And We delay it only for a term (already) fixed. (104)On the Day when it comes, no person shall speak except by His (Allâh's) Leave. Some among them will be wretched and (others) blessed. (105)As for those who are wretched, they will be in the*

*Fire, sighing in a high and low tone. (106)They will dwell therein for all the time that the heavens and the earth endure, except as your Lord wills. Verily, your Lord is the Doer of whatsoever He intends (or wills). (107)And those who are blessed, they will be in Paradise, abiding therein for all the time that the heavens and the earth endure, except as your Lord wills, a gift without an end. (108)So be not in doubt (O Muhammad) as to what these people (pagans and polytheists) worship. They worship nothing but what their fathers worshipped before (them). And verily, We shall repay them in full their portion without diminution. (109)*

## Quran 11:111

وَإِنَّ كُلاًّ لَّمَّا لَيُوَفِّيَنَّهُمْ رَبُّكَ أَعْمَالَهُمْ إِنَّهُ بِمَا يَعْمَلُونَ خَبِيرٌ

*And verily, to each of them your Lord will repay their works in full. Surely, He is All-Aware of what they do.*

## Quran 11:115

وَٱصْبِرْ فَإِنَّ ٱللَّهَ لَا يُضِيعُ أَجْرَ ٱلْمُحْسِنِينَ

*And be patient; verily, Allâh wastes not the reward of the good-doers. (115)*

## Quran 11:118-119

وَلَوۡ شَآءَ رَبُّكَ لَجَعَلَ ٱلنَّاسَ أُمَّةً وَٰحِدَةً وَلَا يَزَالُونَ مُخۡتَلِفِينَ
(١١٨) إِلَّا مَن رَّحِمَ رَبُّكَ وَلِذَٰلِكَ خَلَقَهُمۡ وَتَمَّتۡ كَلِمَةُ رَبِّكَ
لَأَمۡلَأَنَّ جَهَنَّمَ مِنَ ٱلۡجِنَّةِ وَٱلنَّاسِ أَجۡمَعِينَ (١١٩)

*And if your Lord had so willed, He could surely have made mankind one Ummah [nation or community (following one religion only i.e. Islâm)], but they will not cease to disagree, (118)Except him on whom your Lord has bestowed His Mercy (the follower of truth - Islâmic Monotheism) and for that did He create them. And the Word of your Lord has been fulfilled (i.e. His Saying): "Surely, I shall fill Hell with jinn and men all together."*

## Quran 12:103

وَمَآ أَكۡثَرُ ٱلنَّاسِ وَلَوۡ حَرَصۡتَ بِمُؤۡمِنِينَ

*And most of mankind will not believe even if you desire it eagerly (103)*

## Quran 12:110

حَتَّىٰٓ إِذَا ٱسۡتَيۡـَٔسَ ٱلرُّسُلُ وَظَنُّوٓاْ أَنَّهُمۡ قَدۡ كُذِبُواْ جَآءَهُمۡ
نَصۡرُنَا فَنُجِّیَ مَن نَّشَآءُ وَلَا يُرَدُّ بَأۡسُنَا عَنِ ٱلۡقَوۡمِ
ٱلۡمُجۡرِمِينَ

*(They were reprieved) until, when the Messengers gave up hope and thought that they were denied (by their people), then came to them Our Help, and whomsoever We willed were rescued. And Our Punishment cannot be*

*warded off from the people who are Mujrimûn*
*(criminals, sinners, disbelievers, polytheists). (110)*

## Quran 13:5

وَإِن تَعْجَبْ فَعَجَبٌ قَوْلُهُمْ أَءِذَا كُنَّا تُرَابًا أَءِنَّا لَفِى خَلْقٍ ۞
جَدِيدٍ أُوْلَـٰٓئِكَ ٱلَّذِينَ كَفَرُواْ بِرَبِّهِمْ وَأُوْلَـٰٓئِكَ ٱلْأَغْلَـٰلُ فِىٓ
أَعْنَاقِهِمْ وَأُوْلَـٰٓئِكَ أَصْحَـٰبُ ٱلنَّارِ هُمْ فِيهَا خَـٰلِدُونَ

*And if you (O Muhammad) wonder (at these polytheists
who deny your message of Islâmic Monotheism and have
taken besides Allâh others for worship who can neither
harm nor benefit), then wondrous is their saying: "When
we are dust, shall we indeed then be (raised) in a new
creation?" They are those who disbelieved in their Lord!
They are those who will have iron chains tying their
hands to their necks. They will be dwellers of the Fire to
abide therein. (5)*

## Quran 13:11

لَهُۥ مُعَقِّبَـٰتٌ مِّنۢ بَيْنِ يَدَيْهِ وَمِنْ خَلْفِهِۦ يَحْفَظُونَهُۥ مِنْ أَمْرِ
ٱللَّهِ إِنَّ ٱللَّهَ لَا يُغَيِّرُ مَا بِقَوْمٍ حَتَّىٰ يُغَيِّرُواْ مَا بِأَنفُسِهِمْ وَإِذَآ
أَرَادَ ٱللَّهُ بِقَوْمٍ سُوٓءًا فَلَا مَرَدَّ لَهُۥ وَمَا لَهُم مِّن دُونِهِۦ مِن وَالٍ

*For him (each person), there are angels in succession,
before and behind him. They guard him by the Command
of Allâh. Verily! Allâh will not change the (good)
condition of a people as long as they do not change their*

state (of goodness) themselves (by committing sins and by being ungrateful and disobedient to Allâh). But when Allâh wills a people's punishment, there can be no turning back of it, and they will find besides Him no protector. (11)

## Quran 13:18

لِلَّذِينَ ٱسْتَجَابُوا۟ لِرَبِّهِمُ ٱلْحُسْنَىٰ ۚ وَٱلَّذِينَ لَمْ يَسْتَجِيبُوا۟ لَهُۥ لَوْ أَنَّ لَهُم مَّا فِى ٱلْأَرْضِ جَمِيعًا وَمِثْلَهُۥ مَعَهُۥ لَٱفْتَدَوْا۟ بِهِۦٓ أُو۟لَٰٓئِكَ لَهُمْ سُوٓءُ ٱلْحِسَابِ وَمَأْوَىٰهُمْ جَهَنَّمُ ۖ وَبِئْسَ ٱلْمِهَادُ

For those who answered their Lord's Call [believed in the Oneness of Allâh and followed His Messenger Muhammad i.e. Islâmic Monotheism] is Al-Husna (i.e. Paradise). But those who answered not His Call (disbelieved in the Oneness of Allâh and followed not His Messenger Muhammad), if they had all that is in the earth together with its like, they would offer it in order to save themselves (from the torment, but it will be in vain). For them there will be the terrible reckoning. Their dwelling - place will be Hell; - and worst indeed is that place for rest. (18)

## Quran 13:20-25

ٱلَّذِينَ يُوفُونَ بِعَهْدِ ٱللَّهِ وَلَا يَنقُضُونَ ٱلْمِيثَٰقَ (٢٠) وَٱلَّذِينَ يَصِلُونَ مَآ أَمَرَ ٱللَّهُ بِهِۦٓ أَن يُوصَلَ وَيَخْشَوْنَ رَبَّهُمْ وَيَخَافُونَ سُوٓءَ ٱلْحِسَابِ (٢١) وَٱلَّذِينَ صَبَرُوا۟ ٱبْتِغَآءَ وَجْهِ رَبِّهِمْ

وَأَقَامُوا۟ ٱلصَّلَوٰةَ وَأَنفَقُوا۟ مِمَّا رَزَقْنَاهُمْ سِرًّا وَعَلَانِيَةً وَيَدْرَءُونَ بِٱلْحَسَنَةِ ٱلسَّيِّئَةَ أُو۟لَٰئِكَ لَهُمْ عُقْبَى ٱلدَّارِ (٢٢) جَنَّاتُ عَدْنٍ يَدْخُلُونَهَا وَمَن صَلَحَ مِنْ ءَابَآئِهِمْ وَأَزْوَاجِهِمْ وَذُرِّيَّاتِهِمْ وَٱلْمَلَٰئِكَةُ يَدْخُلُونَ عَلَيْهِم مِّن كُلِّ بَابٍ (٢٣) سَلَٰمٌ عَلَيْكُم بِمَا صَبَرْتُمْ فَنِعْمَ عُقْبَى ٱلدَّارِ (٢٤) وَٱلَّذِينَ يَنقُضُونَ عَهْدَ ٱللَّهِ مِنۢ بَعْدِ مِيثَٰقِهِۦ وَيَقْطَعُونَ مَآ أَمَرَ ٱللَّهُ بِهِۦٓ أَن يُوصَلَ وَيُفْسِدُونَ فِى ٱلْأَرْضِ أُو۟لَٰئِكَ لَهُمُ ٱللَّعْنَةُ وَلَهُمْ سُوٓءُ ٱلدَّارِ (٢٥)

*Those who fulfil the Covenant of Allâh and break not the Mîthâq (bond, treaty, covenant); (20)And those who join that which Allâh has commanded to be joined (i.e. they are good to their relatives and do not sever the bond of kinship), and fear their Lord, and dread the terrible reckoning (i.e. abstain from all kinds of sins and evil deeds which Allâh has forbidden and perform all kinds of good deeds which Allâh has ordained). (21)And those who remain patient, seeking their Lord's Countenance, perform As-Salât (Iqâmat-as-Salât), and spend out of that which We have bestowed on them, secretly and openly, and defend evil with good, for such there is a good end; (22)'Adn (Eden) Paradise (everlasting Gardens), which they shall enter and (also) those who acted righteously from among their fathers, and their wives, and their offspring. And angels shall enter unto them from every gate (saying): (23)"Salâmun 'Alaikum*

(peace be upon you) for that you persevered in patience!
Excellent indeed is the final home!" (24)And those who
break the Covenant of Allâh, after its ratification, and
sever that which Allâh has commanded to be joined (i.e.
they sever the bond of kinship and are not good to their
relatives), and work mischief in the land, on them is the
curse (i.e. they will be far away from Allâh's Mercy); and
for them is the unhappy (evil) home (i.e. Hell) (25)

## Quran 13:28-29

ٱلَّذِينَ ءَامَنُواْ وَتَطْمَئِنُّ قُلُوبُهُم بِذِكْرِ ٱللَّهِ أَلَا بِذِكْرِ ٱللَّهِ تَطْمَئِنُّ ٱلْقُلُوبُ
(٢٨) ٱلَّذِينَ ءَامَنُواْ وَعَمِلُواْ ٱلصَّـٰلِحَـٰتِ طُوبَىٰ لَهُمْ وَحُسْنُ مَـَٔابٍ (٢٩)

Those who believed (in the Oneness of Allâh - Islâmic
Monotheism), and whose hearts find rest in the
remembrance of Allâh, Verily, in the remembrance of
Allâh do hearts find rest(28)Those who believed (in the
Oneness of Allâh - Islâmic Monotheism), and work
righteousness, Tûbâ (all kinds of happiness or name of a
tree in Paradise) is for them and a beautiful place of
(final) return. (29)

## Quran 13:31

وَلَوْ أَنَّ قُرْءَانًا سُيِّرَتْ بِهِ ٱلْجِبَالُ أَوْ قُطِّعَتْ بِهِ ٱلْأَرْضُ أَوْ
كُلِّمَ بِهِ ٱلْمَوْتَىٰ بَل لِّلَّهِ ٱلْأَمْرُ جَمِيعًا أَفَلَمْ يَأْيْـَٔسِ ٱلَّذِينَ ءَامَنُوٓاْ
أَن لَّوْ يَشَآءُ ٱللَّهُ لَهَدَى ٱلنَّاسَ جَمِيعًا وَلَا يَزَالُ ٱلَّذِينَ

كَفَرُواْ تُصِيبُهُم بِمَا صَنَعُواْ قَارِعَةٌ أَوْ تَحُلُّ قَرِيبًا مِّن
دَارِهِمْ حَتَّىٰ يَأْتِيَ وَعْدُ ٱللَّهِ إِنَّ ٱللَّهَ لَا يُخْلِفُ ٱلْمِيعَادَ

*And if there had been a Qur'ân with which mountains could be moved (from their places), or the earth could be cloven asunder, or the dead could be made to speak (it would not have been other than this Qur'ân). But the decision of all things is certainly with Allâh. Have not then those who believed yet known that had Allâh willed, He could have guided all mankind? And a disaster will not cease to strike those who disbelieve because of their (evil) deeds or it (i.e. the disaster) settle close to their homes, until the Promise of Allâh comes to pass. Certainly, Allâh does not fail in His Promise. (31)*

## Quran 13:33-35

أَفَمَنْ هُوَ قَآئِمٌ عَلَىٰ كُلِّ نَفْسٍۭ بِمَا كَسَبَتْ وَجَعَلُواْ لِلَّهِ شُرَكَآءَ
قُلْ سَمُّوهُمْ أَمْ تُنَبِّئُونَهُ بِمَا لَا يَعْلَمُ فِى ٱلْأَرْضِ أَم بِظَٰهِرٍ مِّنَ
ٱلْقَوْلِ بَلْ زُيِّنَ لِلَّذِينَ كَفَرُواْ مَكْرُهُمْ وَصُدُّواْ عَنِ ٱلسَّبِيلِ وَمَن
يُضْلِلِ ٱللَّهُ فَمَا لَهُ مِنْ هَادٍ (٣٣) لَّهُمْ عَذَابٌ فِى ٱلْحَيَوٰةِ ٱلدُّنْيَا
وَلَعَذَابُ ٱلْأَخِرَةِ أَشَقُّ وَمَا لَهُم مِّنَ ٱللَّهِ مِن وَاقٍ (٣٤) ۞
مَّثَلُ ٱلْجَنَّةِ ٱلَّتِى وُعِدَ ٱلْمُتَّقُونَ تَجْرِى مِن تَحْتِهَا ٱلْأَنْهَٰرُ
أُكُلُهَا دَآئِمٌ وَظِلُّهَا تِلْكَ عُقْبَى ٱلَّذِينَ ٱتَّقَواْ وَّعُقْبَى ٱلْكَٰفِرِينَ
ٱلنَّارُ (٣٥)

Is then He (Allâh) Who takes charge (guards, maintains, provides) of every person and knows all that he has earned (like any other deities who know nothing)? Yet they ascribe partners to Allâh. Say: "Name them! Is it that you will inform Him of something He knows not in the earth or is it (just) a show of false words." Nay! To those who disbelieved, their plotting is made fairseeming, and they have been hindered from the Right Path, and whom Allâh sends astray, for him, there is no guide. (33)For them is a torment in the life of this world, and certainly, harder is the torment of the Hereafter. And they have no Waq (defender or protector) against Allâh (34)The description of the Paradise which the Muttaqûn (pious): have been promised! -Underneath it rivers flow, its provision is eternal and so is its shade, this is the end (final destination) of the Muttaqûn (pious), and the end (final destination) of the disbelievers is Fire. (35)

## Quran 13:41-42

أَوَلَمْ يَرَوْاْ أَنَّا نَأْتِى ٱلْأَرْضَ نَنقُصُهَا مِنْ أَطْرَافِهَا وَٱللَّهُ يَحْكُمُ لَا مُعَقِّبَ لِحُكْمِهِ وَهُوَ سَرِيعُ ٱلْحِسَابِ (٤١) وَقَدْ مَكَرَ ٱلَّذِينَ مِن قَبْلِهِمْ فَلِلَّهِ ٱلْمَكْرُ جَمِيعًا يَعْلَمُ مَا تَكْسِبُ كُلُّ نَفْسٍ وَسَيَعْلَمُ ٱلْكُفَّارُ لِمَنْ عُقْبَى ٱلدَّارِ (٤٢)

See they not that We gradually reduce the land (of disbelievers, by giving it to the believers, in war victories) from its outlying borders. And Allâh judges, there is none to put back His Judgement and He is Swift at reckoning. (41)And verily, those before them did devise plots, but all planning is Allâh's. He knows what every person earns, and the disbelievers will know who gets the good end (final destination). (42)

## Quran 14:16-18

مِّن وَرَآئِهِۦ جَهَنَّمُ وَيُسْقَىٰ مِن مَّآءٍ صَدِيدٍ (١٦) يَتَجَرَّعُهُۥ وَلَا يَكَادُ يُسِيغُهُۥ وَيَأْتِيهِ ٱلْمَوْتُ مِن كُلِّ مَكَانٍ وَمَا هُوَ بِمَيِّتٍ وَمِن وَرَآئِهِۦ عَذَابٌ غَلِيظٌ (١٧) مَّثَلُ ٱلَّذِينَ كَفَرُوا۟ بِرَبِّهِمْ أَعْمَٰلُهُمْ كَرَمَادٍ ٱشْتَدَّتْ بِهِ ٱلرِّيحُ فِى يَوْمٍ عَاصِفٍ لَّا يَقْدِرُونَ مِمَّا كَسَبُوا۟ عَلَىٰ شَىْءٍ ذَٰلِكَ هُوَ ٱلضَّلَٰلُ ٱلْبَعِيدُ (١٨)

In front of him (every obstinate, arrogant dictator) is Hell, and he will be made to drink boiling, festering water. (16)He will sip it unwillingly, and he will find a great difficulty to swallow it down his throat, and death will come to him from every side, yet he will not die and in front of him, will be a great torment. (17)The parable of those who disbelieve in their Lord is that their works are as ashes, on which the wind blows furiously on a stormy day, they shall not be able to get aught of what they have earned. That is the straying, far away (from the Right Path). (18)

## Quran 14:21-23

وَبَرَزُواْ لِلَّهِ جَمِيعًا فَقَالَ ٱلضُّعَفَـٰٓؤُاْ لِلَّذِينَ ٱسْتَكْبَرُوٓاْ إِنَّا كُنَّا لَكُمْ تَبَعًا فَهَلْ أَنتُم مُّغْنُونَ عَنَّا مِنْ عَذَابِ ٱللَّهِ مِن شَىْءٍ قَالُواْ لَوْ هَدَىٰنَا ٱللَّهُ لَهَدَيْنَـٰكُمْ سَوَآءٌ عَلَيْنَآ أَجَزِعْنَآ أَمْ صَبَرْنَا مَا لَنَا مِن مَّحِيصٍ (٢١) وَقَالَ ٱلشَّيْطَـٰنُ لَمَّا قُضِىَ ٱلْأَمْرُ إِنَّ ٱللَّهَ وَعَدَكُمْ وَعْدَ ٱلْحَقِّ وَوَعَدتُّكُمْ فَأَخْلَفْتُكُمْ وَمَا كَانَ لِىَ عَلَيْكُم مِّن سُلْطَـٰنٍ إِلَّآ أَن دَعَوْتُكُمْ فَٱسْتَجَبْتُمْ لِى فَلَا تَلُومُونِى وَلُومُوٓاْ أَنفُسَكُم مَّآ أَنَا۠ بِمُصْرِخِكُمْ وَمَآ أَنتُم بِمُصْرِخِىَّ إِنِّى كَفَرْتُ بِمَآ أَشْرَكْتُمُونِ مِن قَبْلُ إِنَّ ٱلظَّـٰلِمِينَ لَهُمْ عَذَابٌ أَلِيمٌ (٢٢) وَأُدْخِلَ ٱلَّذِينَ ءَامَنُواْ وَعَمِلُواْ ٱلصَّـٰلِحَـٰتِ جَنَّـٰتٍ تَجْرِى مِن تَحْتِهَا ٱلْأَنْهَـٰرُ خَـٰلِدِينَ فِيهَا بِإِذْنِ رَبِّهِمْ تَحِيَّتُهُمْ فِيهَا سَلَـٰمٌ (٢٣)

And they all shall appear before Allâh (on the Day of Resurrection) then the weak will say to those who were arrogant (chiefs): "Verily, we were following you; can you avail us anything against Allâh's Torment?" They will say: "Had Allâh guided us, we would have guided you. It makes no difference to us (now) whether we rage, or bear (these torments) with patience, there is no place of refuge for us." (21)And Shaitân (Satan) will say when the matter has been decided: "Verily, Allâh promised you a promise of truth. And I too promised you, but I betrayed you. I had no authority over you except that I called you, so you responded to me. So blame me not, but blame yourselves. I cannot help you, nor can you help me. I deny your former act in associating me (Satan) as a partner with Allâh (by obeying me in the life of the world). Verily, there is a painful torment for the Zâlimûn (polytheists and wrong-doers)." (22)And those who believed (in the Oneness of Allâh and His Messengers and whatever they brought) and did righteous deeds, will be made to enter Gardens under which rivers flow, - to dwell therein forever (i.e.in Paradise), with the permission of their Lord. Their greeting therein will be: Salâm (peace!) (23)

## Quran 14:27-31

يُثَبِّتُ ٱللَّهُ ٱلَّذِينَ ءَامَنُواْ بِٱلْقَوْلِ ٱلثَّابِتِ فِى ٱلْحَيَوٰةِ ٱلدُّنْيَا وَفِى ٱلْأَخِرَةِۖ وَيُضِلُّ ٱللَّهُ ٱلظَّٰلِمِينَۚ وَيَفْعَلُ ٱللَّهُ مَا يَشَآءُ (٢٧) ۞ أَلَمْ تَرَ إِلَى ٱلَّذِينَ بَدَّلُواْ نِعْمَتَ ٱللَّهِ كُفْرًا وَأَحَلُّواْ قَوْمَهُمْ دَارَ ٱلْبَوَارِ (٢٨) جَهَنَّمَ يَصْلَوْنَهَاۖ وَبِئْسَ ٱلْقَرَارُ (٢٩) وَجَعَلُواْ لِلَّهِ أَندَادًا لِّيُضِلُّواْ عَن سَبِيلِهِۦۗ قُلْ تَمَتَّعُواْ فَإِنَّ مَصِيرَكُمْ إِلَى ٱلنَّارِ (٣٠) قُل لِّعِبَادِىَ ٱلَّذِينَ ءَامَنُواْ يُقِيمُواْ ٱلصَّلَوٰةَ وَيُنفِقُواْ مِمَّا رَزَقْنَٰهُمْ سِرًّا وَعَلَانِيَةً مِّن قَبْلِ أَن يَأْتِىَ يَوْمٌ لَّا بَيْعٌ فِيهِ وَلَا خِلَٰلٌ (٣١)

Allâh will keep firm those who believe, with the word that stands firm in this world (i.e. they will keep on worshipping Allâh Alone and none else), and in the Hereafter. And Allâh will cause to go astray those who are Zâlimûn (polytheists and wrong-doers, etc.), and

*Allâh does what He wills. (27)Have you not seen those who have changed the Blessings of Allâh into disbelief (by denying Prophet Muhammad and his Message of Islâm), and caused their people to dwell in the house of destruction? (28)Hell, in which they will burn, - and what an evil place to settle in! (29)And they set up rivals to Allâh, to mislead (men) from His Path! Say: "Enjoy (your brief life)! But certainly, your destination is the (Hell) Fire!" (30)Say (O Muhammad) to 'Ibâdî (My slaves) who have believed, that they should perform As-Salât (Iqâmat-as-Salât), and spend in charity out of the sustenance We have given them, secretly and openly, before the coming of a Day on which there will be neither mutual bargaining nor befriending. (31)*

## Quran 14:42-44

وَلَا تَحْسَبَنَّ ٱللَّهَ غَٰفِلًا عَمَّا يَعْمَلُ ٱلظَّٰلِمُونَ إِنَّمَا يُؤَخِّرُهُمْ لِيَوْمٍ تَشْخَصُ فِيهِ ٱلْأَبْصَٰرُ (٤٢) مُهْطِعِينَ مُقْنِعِى رُءُوسِهِمْ لَا يَرْتَدُّ إِلَيْهِمْ طَرْفُهُمْ ۖ وَأَفْـِٔدَتُهُمْ هَوَآءٌ (٤٣) وَأَنذِرِ ٱلنَّاسَ يَوْمَ يَأْتِيهِمُ ٱلْعَذَابُ فَيَقُولُ ٱلَّذِينَ ظَلَمُوا رَبَّنَا أَخِّرْنَا إِلَىٰ أَجَلٍ قَرِيبٍ نُّجِبْ دَعْوَتَكَ وَنَتَّبِعِ ٱلرُّسُلَ ۗ أَوَلَمْ تَكُونُوا أَقْسَمْتُم مِّن قَبْلُ مَا لَكُم مِّن زَوَالٍ (٤٤)

*Consider not that Allâh is unaware of that which the Zâlimûn (polytheists, wrong-doers) do, but He gives them respite up to a Day when the eyes will stare in horror. (42)(They will be) hastening forward with necks* outstretched, their heads raised up (towards the sky), their gaze returning not towards them and their hearts empty (from thinking because of extreme fear). (43)And warn (O Muhammad) mankind of the Day when the torment will come unto them; then the wrong-doers will say: "Our Lord! Respite us for a little while, we will answer Your Call and follow the Messengers!" (It will be said): "Had you not sworn aforetime that you would not leave (the world for the Hereafter). (44)

## Quran 14:47-51

فَلَا تَحْسَبَنَّ ٱللَّهَ مُخْلِفَ وَعْدِهِ رُسُلَهُ ۗ إِنَّ ٱللَّهَ عَزِيزٌ ذُو ٱنتِقَامٍ (٤٧) يَوْمَ تُبَدَّلُ ٱلْأَرْضُ غَيْرَ ٱلْأَرْضِ وَٱلسَّمَٰوَٰتُ ۖ وَبَرَزُوا۟ لِلَّهِ ٱلْوَٰحِدِ ٱلْقَهَّارِ (٤٨) وَتَرَى ٱلْمُجْرِمِينَ يَوْمَئِذٍ مُّقَرَّنِينَ فِى ٱلْأَصْفَادِ (٤٩) سَرَابِيلُهُم مِّن قَطِرَانٍ وَتَغْشَىٰ وُجُوهَهُمُ ٱلنَّارُ (٥٠) لِيَجْزِىَ ٱللَّهُ كُلَّ نَفْسٍ مَّا كَسَبَتْ ۚ إِنَّ ٱللَّهَ سَرِيعُ ٱلْحِسَابِ (٥١)

So think not that Allâh will fail to keep His Promise to His Messengers. Certainly, Allâh is All-Mighty, - All-Able of Retribution. (47)On the Day when the earth will be changed to another earth and so will be the heavens, and they (all creatures) will appear before Allâh, the One, the Irresistible. (48)And you will see the Mujrimûn (criminals, disbelievers in the Oneness of Allâh — Islâmic Monotheism, polytheists) that Day Muqarranûn (bound together) in fetters. (49)Their garments will be of pitch, and fire will cover their faces. (50)That Allâh may requite each person according to what he has earned. Truly, Allâh is Swift at reckoning. (51)

## Quran 15:2-3

رُّبَمَا يَوَدُّ ٱلَّذِينَ كَفَرُواْ لَوْ كَانُواْ مُسْلِمِينَ (٢) ذَرْهُمْ يَأْكُلُواْ وَيَتَمَتَّعُواْ وَيُلْهِهِمُ ٱلْأَمَلُ فَسَوْفَ يَعْلَمُونَ (٣)

How much will those who disbelieve desire that they were Muslims [those who have submitted themselves to Allâh's Will in Islâm i.e. Islâmic Monotheism, this will be on the Day of Resurrection when they will see the disbelievers going to Hell and the Muslims going to Paradise]. (2)Leave them to eat and enjoy, and let them be preoccupied with (false) hope. They will come to know!

## Quran 15:24-25

وَلَقَدْ عَلِمْنَا ٱلْمُسْتَقْدِمِينَ مِنكُمْ وَلَقَدْ عَلِمْنَا ٱلْمُسْتَخِرِينَ (٢٤) وَإِنَّ رَبَّكَ هُوَ يَحْشُرُهُمْ إِنَّهُ حَكِيمٌ عَلِيمٌ (٢٥)

And indeed, We know the first generations of you who had passed away, and indeed, We know the present generations of you (mankind), and also those who will come afterwards (24)And verily, your Lord will gather them together. Truly, He is All-Wise, All-Knowing (25)

## Quran 15:34-48

قَالَ فَٱخْرُجْ مِنْهَا فَإِنَّكَ رَجِيمٌ (٣٤) وَإِنَّ عَلَيْكَ ٱللَّعْنَةَ إِلَىٰ يَوْمِ ٱلدِّينِ (٣٥) قَالَ رَبِّ فَأَنظِرْنِىٓ إِلَىٰ يَوْمِ يُبْعَثُونَ (٣٦) قَالَ فَإِنَّكَ مِنَ ٱلْمُنظَرِينَ (٣٧) إِلَىٰ يَوْمِ ٱلْوَقْتِ ٱلْمَعْلُومِ (٣٨) قَالَ رَبِّ بِمَآ أَغْوَيْتَنِى لَأُزَيِّنَنَّ لَهُمْ فِى ٱلْأَرْضِ وَلَأُغْوِيَنَّهُمْ أَجْمَعِينَ (٣٩) إِلَّا عِبَادَكَ مِنْهُمُ ٱلْمُخْلَصِينَ (٤٠) قَالَ هَـٰذَا صِرَٰطٌ عَلَىَّ مُسْتَقِيمٌ (٤١) إِنَّ عِبَادِى لَيْسَ لَكَ عَلَيْهِمْ سُلْطَـٰنٌ إِلَّا مَنِ ٱتَّبَعَكَ مِنَ ٱلْغَاوِينَ (٤٢) وَإِنَّ جَهَنَّمَ لَمَوْعِدُهُمْ أَجْمَعِينَ (٤٣) لَهَا سَبْعَةُ أَبْوَٰبٍ لِّكُلِّ بَابٍ مِّنْهُمْ جُزْءٌ مَّقْسُومٌ (٤٤) إِنَّ ٱلْمُتَّقِينَ فِى جَنَّـٰتٍ وَعُيُونٍ (٤٥) ٱدْخُلُوهَا بِسَلَٰمٍ ءَامِنِينَ (٤٦) وَنَزَعْنَا مَا فِى صُدُورِهِم مِّنْ غِلٍّ إِخْوَٰنًا عَلَىٰ سُرُرٍ مُّتَقَـٰبِلِينَ (٤٧) لَا يَمَسُّهُمْ فِيهَا نَصَبٌ وَمَا هُم مِّنْهَا بِمُخْرَجِينَ (٤٨)

(Allâh) said: "Then, get out from here, for verily, you are Rajîm (an outcast or a cursed one)." (34)"And verily, the curse shall be upon you till the Day of Recompense (i.e. the Day of Resurrection)." (35)[Iblîs (Satan)] said: "O my Lord! Give me then respite till the Day they (the dead) will be resurrected." (36)Allâh said: "Then, verily, you are of those reprieved, (37)"Till the Day of the time appointed." (38)[Iblîs (Satan)] said: "O my Lord! Because you misled me, I shall indeed adorn the path of error for them (mankind) on the earth, and I shall mislead them all. (39)"Except Your chosen, (guided) slaves among them." (40)(Allâh) said: "This is the Way which will lead straight to Me." (41)"Certainly, you shall have no authority over My slaves, except those who follow you of the Ghâwun (Mushrikûn and those who go astray, criminals, polytheists, and evil-doers) (42)"And surely, Hell is the promised place for them all. (43)"It (Hell) has seven gates, for each of those gates is a (special) class (of sinners) assigned. (44)"Truly! The Muttaqûn (pious and righteous persons) will be amidst Gardens and water-springs (Paradise). (45)"(It will be said to them): 'Enter therein (Paradise), in peace and security.' (46)"And We shall remove from their breasts any deep feeling of bitterness (that they may have), (So they will be like) brothers facing each other on thrones. (47)"No sense of fatigue shall touch them, nor shall they (ever) be asked to leave it." (48)

## Quran 15:92-96

فَوَرَبِّكَ لَنَسْـَٔلَنَّهُمْ أَجْمَعِينَ (٩٢) عَمَّا كَانُوا۟ يَعْمَلُونَ (٩٣) فَٱصْدَعْ بِمَا تُؤْمَرُ وَأَعْرِضْ عَنِ ٱلْمُشْرِكِينَ (٩٤) إِنَّا كَفَيْنَٰكَ ٱلْمُسْتَهْزِءِينَ (٩٥) ٱلَّذِينَ يَجْعَلُونَ مَعَ ٱللَّهِ إِلَٰهًا ءَاخَرَ فَسَوْفَ يَعْلَمُونَ (٩٦)

So, by your Lord (O Muhammad), We shall certainly call all of them to account. (92)For all that they used to do. (93)Therefore proclaim openly (Allâh's Message - Islâmic Monotheism) that which you are commanded, and turn away from Al-Mushrikûn (polytheists, idolaters, and disbelievers, etc.). (94)Truly! We will suffice you against the scoffers. (95)Who set up along with Allâh another ilâh (god), but they will come to know. (96)

## Quran 16:1

أَتَىٰ أَمْرُ ٱللَّهِ فَلَا تَسْتَعْجِلُوهُ سُبْحَٰنَهُۥ وَتَعَٰلَىٰ عَمَّا يُشْرِكُونَ

The Event (the Hour or the punishment of disbelievers and polytheists or the Islâmic laws or commandments), ordained by Allâh will come to pass, so seek not to hasten it. Glorified and Exalted be He above all that they associate as partners with Him. (1)

## Quran 16:25-32

لِيَحْمِلُوٓاْ أَوْزَارَهُمْ كَامِلَةً يَوْمَ ٱلْقِيَٰمَةِ وَمِنْ أَوْزَارِ ٱلَّذِينَ يُضِلُّونَهُم بِغَيْرِ عِلْمٍ أَلَا سَآءَ مَا يَزِرُونَ (٢٥) قَدْ مَكَرَ ٱلَّذِينَ مِن قَبْلِهِمْ فَأَتَى ٱللَّهُ بُنْيَٰنَهُم مِّنَ ٱلْقَوَاعِدِ فَخَرَّ عَلَيْهِمُ ٱلسَّقْفُ مِن فَوْقِهِمْ وَأَتَىٰهُمُ ٱلْعَذَابُ مِنْ حَيْثُ لَا يَشْعُرُونَ (٢٦) ثُمَّ يَوْمَ ٱلْقِيَٰمَةِ يُخْزِيهِمْ وَيَقُولُ أَيْنَ شُرَكَآءِىَ ٱلَّذِينَ كُنتُمْ تُشَٰقُّونَ فِيهِمْ قَالَ ٱلَّذِينَ أُوتُواْ ٱلْعِلْمَ إِنَّ ٱلْخِزْىَ ٱلْيَوْمَ وَٱلسُّوٓءَ عَلَى ٱلْكَٰفِرِينَ (٢٧) ٱلَّذِينَ تَتَوَفَّىٰهُمُ ٱلْمَلَٰٓئِكَةُ ظَالِمِىٓ أَنفُسِهِمْ فَأَلْقَوُاْ ٱلسَّلَمَ مَا كُنَّا نَعْمَلُ مِن سُوٓءٍ بَلَىٰٓ إِنَّ ٱللَّهَ عَلِيمٌۢ بِمَا كُنتُمْ تَعْمَلُونَ (٢٨) فَٱدْخُلُوٓاْ أَبْوَٰبَ جَهَنَّمَ خَٰلِدِينَ فِيهَا فَلَبِئْسَ مَثْوَى ٱلْمُتَكَبِّرِينَ (٢٩) ۞ وَقِيلَ لِلَّذِينَ ٱتَّقَوْاْ مَاذَآ أَنزَلَ رَبُّكُمْ قَالُواْ خَيْرًا لِّلَّذِينَ أَحْسَنُواْ فِى هَٰذِهِ ٱلدُّنْيَا حَسَنَةٌ

وَلَدَارُ ٱلْأَخِرَةِ خَيْرٌ وَلَنِعْمَ دَارُ ٱلْمُتَّقِينَ (٣٠) جَنَّتُ عَدْنٍ
يَدْخُلُونَهَا تَجْرِى مِن تَحْتِهَا ٱلْأَنْهَارُ لَهُمْ فِيهَا مَا يَشَآءُونَ
كَذَٰلِكَ يَجْزِى ٱللَّهُ ٱلْمُتَّقِينَ (٣١) ٱلَّذِينَ تَتَوَفَّىٰهُمُ ٱلْمَلَـٰئِكَةُ
طَيِّبِينَ يَقُولُونَ سَلَـٰمٌ عَلَيْكُمُ ٱدْخُلُوا ٱلْجَنَّةَ بِمَا كُنتُمْ تَعْمَلُونَ

*They may bear their own burdens in full on the Day of Resurrection, and also of the burdens of those whom they misled without knowledge. Evil indeed is that which they shall bear! (25) Those before them indeed plotted, but Allâh struck at the foundation of their building, and then the roof fell down upon them, from above them, and the torment overtook them from directions they did not perceive. (26) Then, on the Day of Resurrection, He will disgrace them and will say: "Where are My (so called) 'partners' concerning whom you used to disagree and dispute (with the believers, by defying and disobeying Allâh)?" Those who have been given the knowledge (about the Torment of Allâh for the disbelievers) will say: "Verily! Disgrace this Day and misery this Day are upon the disbelievers. (27) "Those whose lives the angels take while they are doing wrong to themselves (by disbelief and by associating partners in worship with Allâh and by committing all kinds of crimes and evil deeds)." Then, they will make (false) submission (saying): "We used not to do any evil." (The angels will reply): "Yes! Truly, Allâh is All-Knower of what you used to do. (28) "So enter the gates of Hell, to abide* therein, and indeed, what an evil abode will be for the arrogant." (29)And (when) it is said to those who are the Muttaqûn (pious ) "What is it that your Lord has sent down?" They say: "That which is good." For those who do good in this world, there is good, and the home of the Hereafter will be better. And excellent indeed will be the home (i.e. Paradise) of the Muttaqûn (pious ). (30)'Adn (Eden) Paradise (Gardens of Eternity) which they will enter, under which rivers flow, they will have therein all that they wish. Thus Allâh rewards the Muttaqûn (pious). (31) Those whose lives the angels take while they are in a pious state (i.e. pure from all evil, and worshipping none but Allâh Alone) saying (to them): Salâmun 'Alaikum (peace be on you) enter you Paradise, because of that (the good) which you used to do (in the world)." (32)

## Quran 16:38-39

وَأَقْسَمُواْ بِٱللَّهِ جَهْدَ أَيْمَٰنِهِمْ لَا يَبْعَثُ ٱللَّهُ مَن يَمُوتُۚ بَلَىٰ وَعْدًا عَلَيْهِ حَقًّا وَلَٰكِنَّ أَكْثَرَ ٱلنَّاسِ لَا يَعْلَمُونَ (٣٨) لِيُبَيِّنَ لَهُمُ ٱلَّذِى يَخْتَلِفُونَ فِيهِ وَلِيَعْلَمَ ٱلَّذِينَ كَفَرُوٓاْ أَنَّهُمْ كَانُواْ كَٰذِبِينَ

And they swear by Allâh their strongest oaths, that Allâh will not raise up him who dies. Yes, (He will raise them up), a promise (binding) upon Him in truth, but most of mankind know not. (38)In order that He may make manifest to them the truth of that wherein they differ, and that those who disbelieved (in Resurrection, and in the Oneness of Allâh) may know that they were liars.

## Quran 16:62

وَيَجْعَلُونَ لِلَّهِ مَا يَكْرَهُونَ وَتَصِفُ أَلْسِنَتُهُمُ ٱلْكَذِبَ أَنَّ لَهُمُ ٱلْحُسْنَىٰ لَا جَرَمَ أَنَّ لَهُمُ ٱلنَّارَ وَأَنَّهُم مُّفْرَطُونَ

They assign to Allâh that which they dislike (for themselves), and their tongues assert the falsehood that the better things will be theirs. No doubt for them is the Fire, and they will be the first to be hastened on into it, and left there neglected. (62)

## Quran 16:70

وَٱللَّهُ خَلَقَكُمْ ثُمَّ يَتَوَفَّىٰكُمْ وَمِنكُم مَّن يُرَدُّ إِلَىٰ أَرْذَلِ ٱلْعُمُرِ لِكَىْ لَا يَعْلَمَ بَعْدَ عِلْمٍ شَيْئًا إِنَّ ٱللَّهَ عَلِيمٌ قَدِيرٌ

And Allâh has created you and then He will cause you to die, and of you there are some who are sent back to senility, so that they know nothing after having known (much). Truly! Allâh is All-Knowing, All-Powerful. (70)

## Quran 16:84-89

وَيَوْمَ نَبْعَثُ مِن كُلِّ أُمَّةٍ شَهِيدًا ثُمَّ لَا يُؤْذَنُ لِلَّذِينَ كَفَرُواْ وَلَا هُمْ يُسْتَعْتَبُونَ (٨٤) وَإِذَا رَءَا ٱلَّذِينَ ظَلَمُواْ ٱلْعَذَابَ فَلَا يُخَفَّفُ عَنْهُمْ وَلَا هُمْ يُنظَرُونَ (٨٥) وَإِذَا رَءَا ٱلَّذِينَ أَشْرَكُواْ شُرَكَآءَهُمْ قَالُواْ رَبَّنَا هَٰؤُلَآءِ شُرَكَآؤُنَا ٱلَّذِينَ كُنَّا نَدْعُواْ

مِن دُونِكَ فَأَلْقَوُاْ إِلَيْهِمُ ٱلْقَوْلَ إِنَّكُمْ لَكَـٰذِبُونَ ﴿٨٦﴾ وَأَلْقَوُاْ إِلَى ٱللَّهِ يَوْمَئِذٍ ٱلسَّلَمَّ وَضَلَّ عَنْهُم مَّا كَانُواْ يَفْتَرُونَ ﴿٨٧﴾ ٱلَّذِينَ كَفَرُواْ وَصَدُّواْ عَن سَبِيلِ ٱللَّهِ زِدْنَـٰهُمْ عَذَابًا فَوْقَ ٱلْعَذَابِ بِمَا كَانُواْ يُفْسِدُونَ ﴿٨٨﴾ وَيَوْمَ نَبْعَثُ فِى كُلِّ أُمَّةٍ شَهِيدًا عَلَيْهِم مِّنْ أَنفُسِهِمْ وَجِئْنَا بِكَ شَهِيدًا عَلَىٰ هَـٰؤُلَاءِ وَنَزَّلْنَا عَلَيْكَ ٱلْكِتَـٰبَ تِبْيَـٰنًا لِّكُلِّ شَىْءٍ وَهُدًى وَرَحْمَةً وَبُشْرَىٰ لِلْمُسْلِمِينَ

*And (remember) the Day when We shall raise up from each nation a witness (their Messenger), then, those who have disbelieved will not be given leave (to put forward excuses), nor will they be allowed (to return to the world) to repent and ask for Allâh's Forgiveness (of their sins). (84) And when those who did wrong (the disbelievers) will see the torment, then it will not be lightened unto them, nor will they be given respite. (85)And when those who associated partners with Allâh see their (Allâh's so-called) partners, they will say: "Our Lord! These are our partners whom we used to invoke besides you." But they will throw back their word at them (and say): "Surely! You indeed are liars!" (86)And they will offer (their full) submission to Allâh (Alone) on that Day, and their invented false deities [all that they used to invoke besides Allâh, e.g. idols, saints, priests, monks, angels, jinn, Jibrael (Gabriel), Messengers] will vanish from them. (87)Those who disbelieved and hinder (men) from the Path of Allâh, for them We will add torment to the* torment; because they used to spread corruption [by disobeying Allâh themselves, as well as ordering others (mankind) to do so]. (88)And (remember) the Day when We shall raise up from every nation a witness against them from amongst themselves. And We shall bring you (O Muhammad) as a witness against these. And We have sent down to you the Book (the Qur'an) as an exposition of everything, a guidance, a mercy, and glad tidings for those who have submitted themselves (to Allâh as Muslims). (89)

## Quran 16:92-97

وَلَا تَكُونُواْ كَٱلَّتِى نَقَضَتْ غَزْلَهَا مِنْ بَعْدِ قُوَّةٍ أَنكَـٰثًا تَتَّخِذُونَ أَيْمَـٰنَكُمْ دَخَلًا بَيْنَكُمْ أَن تَكُونَ أُمَّةٌ هِىَ أَرْبَىٰ مِنْ أُمَّةٍ إِنَّمَا يَبْلُوكُمُ ٱللَّهُ بِهِۦ وَلَيُبَيِّنَنَّ لَكُمْ يَوْمَ ٱلْقِيَـٰمَةِ مَا كُنتُمْ فِيهِ تَخْتَلِفُونَ (٩٢) وَلَوْ شَآءَ ٱللَّهُ لَجَعَلَكُمْ أُمَّةً وَٰحِدَةً وَلَـٰكِن يُضِلُّ مَن يَشَآءُ وَيَهْدِى مَن يَشَآءُ وَلَتُسْـَٔلُنَّ عَمَّا كُنتُمْ تَعْمَلُونَ (٩٣) وَلَا تَتَّخِذُواْ أَيْمَـٰنَكُمْ دَخَلًا بَيْنَكُمْ فَتَزِلَّ قَدَمٌ بَعْدَ ثُبُوتِهَا وَتَذُوقُواْ ٱلسُّوٓءَ بِمَا صَدَدتُّمْ عَن سَبِيلِ ٱللَّهِ وَلَكُمْ عَذَابٌ عَظِيمٌ (٩٤) وَلَا تَشْتَرُواْ بِعَهْدِ ٱللَّهِ ثَمَنًا قَلِيلًا إِنَّمَا عِندَ ٱللَّهِ هُوَ خَيْرٌ لَّكُمْ إِن كُنتُمْ تَعْلَمُونَ (٩٥) مَا عِندَكُمْ يَنفَدُ وَمَا عِندَ ٱللَّهِ بَاقٍ وَلَنَجْزِيَنَّ ٱلَّذِينَ صَبَرُوٓاْ أَجْرَهُم بِأَحْسَنِ مَا كَانُواْ يَعْمَلُونَ (٩٦) مَنْ عَمِلَ صَـٰلِحًا مِّن ذَكَرٍ أَوْ أُنثَىٰ وَهُوَ مُؤْمِنٌ

فَلَنُحْيِيَنَّهُۥ حَيَوٰةً طَيِّبَةًۖ وَلَنَجْزِيَنَّهُمْ أَجْرَهُم بِأَحْسَنِ مَا كَانُوا۟ يَعْمَلُونَ (٩٧)

*And be not like her who undoes the thread which she has spun after it has become strong, by taking your oaths as a means of deception among yourselves, lest a nation should be more numerous than another nation. Allâh only tests you by this [i.e who obeys Allâh and fulfills Allâh's Covenant and who disobeys Allâh and breaks Allâh's Covenant]. And on the Day of Resurrection, He will certainly make clear to you that wherein you used to differ [i.e. a believer confesses and believes in the Oneness of Allâh and in the Prophethood of Prophet Muhammad which the disbeliever denies it and that was their difference amongst them in the life of this world] (92)And had Allâh willed, He could have made you (all) one nation, but He sends astray whom He wills and guides whom He wills. But you shall certainly be called to account for what you used to do. (93)And make not your oaths, a means of deception among yourselves, lest a foot should slip after being firmly planted, and you may have to taste the evil (punishment in this world) of having hindered (men) from the Path of Allâh (i.e. Belief in the Oneness of Allâh and His Messenger, Muhammad), and yours will be a great torment (i.e. the Fire of Hell in the Hereafter). (94)And purchase not a small gain at the cost of Allâh's Covenant. Verily! What*

is with Allâh is better for you if you did but know.
(95)Whatever is with you, will be exhausted, and
whatever is with Allâh (of good deeds) will remain. And
those who are patient, We will certainly pay them a
reward in proportion to the best of what they used to
do[]. (96)Whoever works righteousness, whether male or
female, while he (or she) is a true believer (of Islâmic
Monotheism) verily, to him We will give a good life (in
this world with respect, contentment and lawful
provision), and We shall pay them certainly a reward in
proportion to the best of what they used to do (i.e.
Paradise in the Hereafter). (97)

## Quran 16:99-100

إِنَّهُ لَيْسَ لَهُ سُلْطَـٰنٌ عَلَى ٱلَّذِينَ ءَامَنُواْ وَعَلَىٰ رَبِّهِمْ
يَتَوَكَّلُونَ (٩٩) إِنَّمَا سُلْطَـٰنُهُ عَلَى ٱلَّذِينَ يَتَوَلَّوْنَهُ وَٱلَّذِينَ
هُم بِهِۦ مُشْرِكُونَ (١٠٠)

Verily! He has no power over those who believe and put
their trust only in their Lord (Allâh). (99)His power is
only over those who obey and follow him (Satan), and
those who join partners with Him (Allâh) [i.e. those who
are Mushrikûn - polytheists] (100)

## Quran 16:104

إِنَّ ٱلَّذِينَ لَا يُؤْمِنُونَ بِـَٔايَـٰتِ ٱللَّهِ لَا يَهْدِيهِمُ ٱللَّهُ وَلَهُمْ عَذَابٌ
أَلِيمٌ

*Verily! Those who believe not in the Ayât (proofs,*
*evidences, verses, lessons, signs, revelations, etc.) of*
*Allâh, Allâh will not guide them and theirs will be a*
*painful torment (104)*

## Quran 16:106-111

مَن كَفَرَ بِٱللَّهِ مِنۢ بَعْدِ إِيمَٰنِهِ إِلَّا مَنْ أُكْرِهَ وَقَلْبُهُۥ مُطْمَئِنٌّۢ
بِٱلْإِيمَٰنِ وَلَٰكِن مَّن شَرَحَ بِٱلْكُفْرِ صَدْرًا فَعَلَيْهِمْ غَضَبٌ مِّنَ
ٱللَّهِ وَلَهُمْ عَذَابٌ عَظِيمٌ (١٠٦) ذَٰلِكَ بِأَنَّهُمُ ٱسْتَحَبُّوا۟ ٱلْحَيَوٰةَ
ٱلدُّنْيَا عَلَى ٱلْأَخِرَةِ وَأَنَّ ٱللَّهَ لَا يَهْدِى ٱلْقَوْمَ ٱلْكَٰفِرِينَ
(١٠٧) أُو۟لَٰٓئِكَ ٱلَّذِينَ طَبَعَ ٱللَّهُ عَلَىٰ قُلُوبِهِمْ وَسَمْعِهِمْ
وَأَبْصَٰرِهِمْ وَأُو۟لَٰٓئِكَ هُمُ ٱلْغَٰفِلُونَ (١٠٨) لَا جَرَمَ أَنَّهُمْ فِى
ٱلْأَخِرَةِ هُمُ ٱلْخَٰسِرُونَ (١٠٩) ثُمَّ إِنَّ رَبَّكَ لِلَّذِينَ هَاجَرُوا۟ مِنۢ
بَعْدِ مَا فُتِنُوا۟ ثُمَّ جَٰهَدُوا۟ وَصَبَرُوٓا۟ إِنَّ رَبَّكَ مِنۢ بَعْدِهَا لَغَفُورٌ
رَّحِيمٌ (١١٠) ۞ يَوْمَ تَأْتِى كُلُّ نَفْسٍ تُجَٰدِلُ عَن نَّفْسِهَا
وَتُوَفَّىٰ كُلُّ نَفْسٍ مَّا عَمِلَتْ وَهُمْ لَا يُظْلَمُونَ (١١١)

*Whoever disbelieved in Allâh after his belief, except him*
*who is forced thereto and whose heart is at rest with*
*Faith, but such as open their breasts to disbelief, on them*
*is wrath from Allâh, and theirs will be a great torment.*
*(106)That is because they loved and preferred the life of*
*this world over that of the Hereafter. And Allâh guides*
*not the people who disbelieve. (107)They are those upon*
*whose hearts, hearing (ears) and sight (eyes) Allâh has*
*set a seal. And they are the heedless! (108)No doubt, in*

the Hereafter, they will be the losers. (109)Then, verily!
Your Lord for those who emigrated after they had been
put to trials and thereafter strove hard and fought (for
the Cause of Allâh) and were patient, verily, your Lord
afterward is, Oft-Forgiving, Most Merciful.
(110)(Remember) the Day when every person will come
up pleading for himself, and every one will be paid in full
for what he did (good or evil, belief or disbelief in the life
of this world) and they will not be dealt with unjustly.

## Quran 16:116-117

وَلَا تَقُولُواْ لِمَا تَصِفُ أَلْسِنَتُكُمُ ٱلْكَذِبَ هَٰذَا حَلَٰلٌ وَهَٰذَا
حَرَامٌ لِّتَفْتَرُواْ عَلَى ٱللَّهِ ٱلْكَذِبَ إِنَّ ٱلَّذِينَ يَفْتَرُونَ عَلَى ٱللَّهِ
ٱلْكَذِبَ لَا يُفْلِحُونَ (١١٦) مَتَٰعٌ قَلِيلٌ وَلَهُمْ عَذَابٌ أَلِيمٌ

And say not concerning that which your tongues put
forth falsely: "This is lawful and this is forbidden," so as
to invent lies against Allâh. Verily, those who invent lies
against Allâh will never prosper. (116)A passing brief
enjoyment (will be theirs), but they will have a painful
torment. (117)

## Quran 16:119

ثُمَّ إِنَّ رَبَّكَ لِلَّذِينَ عَمِلُواْ ٱلسُّوٓءَ بِجَهَٰلَةٍ ثُمَّ تَابُواْ مِنۢ بَعْدِ
ذَٰلِكَ وَأَصْلَحُوٓاْ إِنَّ رَبَّكَ مِنۢ بَعْدِهَا لَغَفُورٌ رَّحِيمٌ

*Then, verily! Your Lord — for those who do evil (commit sins and are disobedient to Allâh) in ignorance and afterward repent and do righteous deeds, verily, your Lord thereafter, (to such) is Oft-Forgiving, Most Merciful. (119)*

## Quran 16:124

إِنَّمَا جُعِلَ ٱلسَّبْتُ عَلَى ٱلَّذِينَ ٱخْتَلَفُواْ فِيهِ وَإِنَّ رَبَّكَ لَيَحْكُمُ بَيْنَهُمْ يَوْمَ ٱلْقِيَـٰمَةِ فِيمَا كَانُواْ فِيهِ يَخْتَلِفُونَ

*The Sabbath was only prescribed for those who differed concerning it, and verily, your Lord will judge between them on the Day of Resurrection about that wherein they used to differ (124)*

## Quran 16:128

إِنَّ ٱللَّهَ مَعَ ٱلَّذِينَ ٱتَّقَواْ وَّٱلَّذِينَ هُم مُّحْسِنُونَ

*Truly, Allâh is with those who fear Him (keep their duty unto Him), and those who are Muhsinûn (good-doers).*

## Quran 17:4-10

وَقَضَيْنَآ إِلَىٰ بَنِىٓ إِسْرَٰٓءِيلَ فِى ٱلْكِتَـٰبِ لَتُفْسِدُنَّ فِى ٱلْأَرْضِ مَرَّتَيْنِ وَلَتَعْلُنَّ عُلُوًّا كَبِيرًا (٤) فَإِذَا جَآءَ وَعْدُ أُولَىٰهُمَا بَعَثْنَا عَلَيْكُمْ عِبَادًا لَّنَآ أُوْلِى بَأْسٍ شَدِيدٍ فَجَاسُواْ خِلَـٰلَ ٱلدِّيَارِ وَكَانَ وَعْدًا مَّفْعُولاً (٥) ثُمَّ رَدَدْنَا لَكُمُ ٱلْكَرَّةَ عَلَيْهِمْ وَأَمْدَدْنَـٰكُم بِأَمْوَٰلٍ وَبَنِينَ وَجَعَلْنَـٰكُمْ أَكْثَرَ نَفِيرًا (٦) إِنْ أَحْسَنتُمْ أَحْسَنتُمْ

لِأَنفُسِكُمْ ۚ وَإِنْ أَسَأْتُمْ فَلَهَا ۚ فَإِذَا جَآءَ وَعْدُ ٱلْآخِرَةِ لِيَسُوٓءُوا۟
وُجُوهَكُمْ وَلِيَدْخُلُوا۟ ٱلْمَسْجِدَ كَمَا دَخَلُوهُ أَوَّلَ مَرَّةٍ وَلِيُتَبِّرُوا۟
مَا عَلَوْا۟ تَتْبِيرًا (٧) عَسَىٰ رَبُّكُمْ أَن يَرْحَمَكُمْ ۚ وَإِنْ عُدتُّمْ عُدْنَا ۘ
وَجَعَلْنَا جَهَنَّمَ لِلْكَٰفِرِينَ حَصِيرًا (٨) إِنَّ هَٰذَا ٱلْقُرْءَانَ يَهْدِى
لِلَّتِى هِىَ أَقْوَمُ وَيُبَشِّرُ ٱلْمُؤْمِنِينَ ٱلَّذِينَ يَعْمَلُونَ ٱلصَّٰلِحَٰتِ أَنَّ
لَهُمْ أَجْرًا كَبِيرًا (٩) وَأَنَّ ٱلَّذِينَ لَا يُؤْمِنُونَ بِٱلْآخِرَةِ أَعْتَدْنَا
لَهُمْ عَذَابًا أَلِيمًا (١٠)

*And We decreed for the Children of Israel in the Scripture, indeed you would do mischief in land twice and you will become tyrants and extremely arrogant! (4)So, when the promise came for the first of the two, We sent against you slaves of Ours given to terrible warfare. They entered the very innermost parts of your homes. And it was a promise (completely) fulfilled. (5)Then We gave you, a return of victory over them. And We helped you with wealth and children and made you more numerous in man - power. (6)(And We said): "If you do good, you do good for your ownselves, and if you do evil (you do it) against yourselves." Then, when the second promise came to pass, (We permitted your enemies) to disgrace your faces and to enter the mosque (of Jerusalem) as they had entered it before, and to destroy with utter destruction all that fell in their hands. (7)[And We said in the Taurât (Torah)]: "It may be that your Lord may show mercy unto you, but if you return (to* sins), We shall return (to Our Punishment). And We have made Hell a prison for the disbelievers. (8) Verily, this Qur'ân guides to that which is most just and right and gives glad tidings to the believers (in the Oneness of Allâh and His Messenger, Muhammad). who work deeds of righteousness, that they shall have a great reward (Paradise). (9) And that those who believe not in the Hereafter, for them We have prepared a painful torment (Hell). (10)

## Quran 17:13-16

وَكُلَّ إِنسَـٰنٍ أَلْزَمْنَـٰهُ طَـٰٓئِرَهُۥ فِى عُنُقِهِۦ وَنُخْرِجُ لَهُۥ يَوْمَ ٱلْقِيَـٰمَةِ كِتَـٰبًا يَلْقَىٰهُ مَنشُورًا (١٣) ٱقْرَأْ كِتَـٰبَكَ كَفَىٰ بِنَفْسِكَ ٱلْيَوْمَ عَلَيْكَ حَسِيبًا (١٤) مَّنِ ٱهْتَدَىٰ فَإِنَّمَا يَهْتَدِى لِنَفْسِهِۦ وَمَن ضَلَّ فَإِنَّمَا يَضِلُّ عَلَيْهَا وَلَا تَزِرُ وَازِرَةٌ وِزْرَ أُخْرَىٰ وَمَا كُنَّا مُعَذِّبِينَ حَتَّىٰ نَبْعَثَ رَسُولاً (١٥) وَإِذَآ أَرَدْنَآ أَن نُّهْلِكَ قَرْيَةً أَمَرْنَا مُتْرَفِيهَا فَفَسَقُواْ فِيهَا فَحَقَّ عَلَيْهَا ٱلْقَوْلُ فَدَمَّرْنَـٰهَا تَدْمِيرًا (١٦)

And We have fastened every man's deeds to his neck, and on the Day of Resurrection, We shall bring out for him a book which he will find wide open. (13) (It will be said to him): "Read your book. You yourself are sufficient as a reckoner against you this Day." (14) Whoever goes right, then he goes right only for the benefit of his ownself. And whoever goes astray, then he goes astray to his own loss.

*No one laden with burdens can bear another's burden. And We never punish until We have sent a Messenger (to give warning). (15)And when We decide to destroy a town (population), We (first) send a definite order (to obey Allâh and be righteous) to those among them [or We (first) increase in number those of its population] who lead a life of luxury. Then, they transgress therein, and thus the word (of torment) is justified against it (them). Then We destroy it with complete destruction (16)*

## Quran 17:18-22

مَّن كَانَ يُرِيدُ ٱلْعَاجِلَةَ عَجَّلْنَا لَهُ فِيهَا مَا نَشَاءُ لِمَن نُّرِيدُ ثُمَّ جَعَلْنَا لَهُ جَهَنَّمَ يَصْلَلْهَا مَذْمُومًا مَّدْحُورًا (١٨) وَمَنْ أَرَادَ ٱلْآخِرَةَ وَسَعَىٰ لَهَا سَعْيَهَا وَهُوَ مُؤْمِنٌ فَأُو۟لَـٰئِكَ كَانَ سَعْيُهُم مَّشْكُورًا (١٩) كُلاًّ نُّمِدُّ هَـٰؤُلَآءِ وَهَـٰؤُلَآءِ مِنْ عَطَاءِ رَبِّكَ وَمَا كَانَ عَطَاءُ رَبِّكَ مَحْظُورًا (٢٠) ٱنظُرْ كَيْفَ فَضَّلْنَا بَعْضَهُمْ عَلَىٰ بَعْضٍ وَلَلْآخِرَةُ أَكْبَرُ دَرَجَـٰتٍ وَأَكْبَرُ تَفْضِيلاً (٢١) لَّا تَجْعَلْ مَعَ ٱللَّهِ إِلَـٰهًا ءَاخَرَ فَتَقْعُدَ مَذْمُومًا مَّخْذُولاً (٢٢)

*Whoever desires the quick-passing (transitory enjoyment of this world), We readily grant him what We will for whom We like. Then, afterwards, We have appointed for him Hell, he will burn therein disgraced and rejected, - (far away from Allâhs Mercy). (18)And whoever desires the Hereafter and strives for it, with the necessary effort due for it (i.e. do righteous deeds of Allâh's Obedience)* while he is a believer (in the Oneness of Allâh — Islâmic Monotheism), then such are the ones whose striving shall be appreciated, (thanked and rewarded by Allâh). (19)On - each these as well as those - We bestow from the Bounties of your Lord. And the Bounties of your Lord can never be forbidden. (20)See how We prefer one above another (in this world) and verily, the Hereafter will be greater in degrees and greater in preference (21)Set not up with Allâh any other ilâh (god), (O man) or you will sit down reproved, forsaken (in the Hell-fire). (22)

## Quran 17:25

رَّبُّكُمْ أَعْلَمُ بِمَا فِى نُفُوسِكُمْ إِن تَكُونُوا صَٰلِحِينَ فَإِنَّهُ كَانَ لِلْأَوَّٰبِينَ غَفُورًا

Your Lord knows best what is in your inner-selves. If you are righteous, then, verily, He is Ever Most Forgiving to those who turn unto Him again and again in obedience, and in repentance. (25)

## Quran 17:31

وَلَا تَقْتُلُوا أَوْلَٰدَكُمْ خَشْيَةَ إِمْلَٰقٍ نَّحْنُ نَرْزُقُهُمْ وَإِيَّاكُمْ إِنَّ قَتْلَهُمْ كَانَ خِطْئًا كَبِيرًا

And kill not your children for fear of poverty. We shall provide for them as well as for you. Surely, the killing of them is a great sin. (31)

## Quran 17:34-36

وَلَا تَقْرَبُواْ مَالَ ٱلْيَتِيمِ إِلَّا بِٱلَّتِى هِىَ أَحْسَنُ حَتَّىٰ يَبْلُغَ أَشُدَّهُۥ وَأَوْفُواْ بِٱلْعَهْدِ إِنَّ ٱلْعَهْدَ كَانَ مَسْـُٔولاً (٣٤) وَأَوْفُواْ ٱلْكَيْلَ إِذَا كِلْتُمْ وَزِنُواْ بِٱلْقِسْطَاسِ ٱلْمُسْتَقِيمِ ذَٰلِكَ خَيْرٌ وَأَحْسَنُ تَأْوِيلاً (٣٥) وَلَا تَقْفُ مَا لَيْسَ لَكَ بِهِۦ عِلْمٌ إِنَّ ٱلسَّمْعَ وَٱلْبَصَرَ وَٱلْفُؤَادَ كُلُّ أُوْلَٰٓئِكَ كَانَ عَنْهُ مَسْـُٔولاً (٣٦)

*And come not near to the orphan's property except to improve it, until he attains the age of full strength. And fulfil (every) covenant. Verily! the covenant, will be questioned about. (34)And give full measure when you measure, and weigh with a balance that is straight. That is good (advantageous) and better in the end. (35)And follow not (O man i.e., say not, or do not or witness not) that of which you have no knowledge. Verily! The hearing, and the sight, and the heart, of each of those one will be questioned (by Allâh). (36)*

## Quran 17:39

ذَٰلِكَ مِمَّآ أَوْحَىٰٓ إِلَيْكَ رَبُّكَ مِنَ ٱلْحِكْمَةِ وَلَا تَجْعَلْ مَعَ ٱللَّهِ إِلَٰهًا ءَاخَرَ فَتُلْقَىٰ فِى جَهَنَّمَ مَلُومًا مَّدْحُورًا

*This is (part) of Al-Hikmah (wisdom, good manners and high character) which your Lord has revealed to you (O Muhammad). And set not up with Allâh any other ilâh (god) lest you should be thrown into Hell, blameworthy and rejected, (from Allâh's Mercy). (39)*

## Quran 17:45-46

وَإِذَا قَرَأْتَ ٱلْقُرْءَانَ جَعَلْنَا بَيْنَكَ وَبَيْنَ ٱلَّذِينَ لَا يُؤْمِنُونَ
بِٱلْأَخِرَةِ حِجَابًا مَّسْتُورًا (٤٥) وَجَعَلْنَا عَلَىٰ قُلُوبِهِمْ أَكِنَّةً أَن
يَفْقَهُوهُ وَفِىٓ ءَاذَانِهِمْ وَقْرًا وَإِذَا ذَكَرْتَ رَبَّكَ فِى ٱلْقُرْءَانِ
وَحْدَهُۥ وَلَّوْا۟ عَلَىٰٓ أَدْبَٰرِهِمْ نُفُورًا (٤٦)

*And when you (Muhammad) recite the Qur'ân, We put
between you and those who believe not in the Hereafter,
an invisible veil (or screen their hearts, so they hear or
understand it not). (45)And We have put coverings over
their hearts lest, they should understand it (the Qur'ân),
and in their ears deafness. And when you make mention
of your Lord Alone [Lâ ilâha ill-allâh (none has the right
to be worshipped but Allâh) Islâmic Monotheism] in the
Qur'ân, they turn on their backs, fleeing in extreme
dislike. (46)*

## Quran 17:49-53

وَقَالُوٓا۟ أَءِذَا كُنَّا عِظَٰمًا وَرُفَٰتًا أَءِنَّا لَمَبْعُوثُونَ خَلْقًا جَدِيدًا
(٤٩) ۞ قُلْ كُونُوا۟ حِجَارَةً أَوْ حَدِيدًا (٥٠) أَوْ خَلْقًا مِّمَّا
يَكْبُرُ فِى صُدُورِكُمْ فَسَيَقُولُونَ مَن يُعِيدُنَا قُلِ ٱلَّذِى فَطَرَكُمْ
أَوَّلَ مَرَّةٍ فَسَيُنْغِضُونَ إِلَيْكَ رُءُوسَهُمْ وَيَقُولُونَ مَتَىٰ هُوَ قُلْ
عَسَىٰٓ أَن يَكُونَ قَرِيبًا (٥١) يَوْمَ يَدْعُوكُمْ فَتَسْتَجِيبُونَ بِحَمْدِهِ
وَتَظُنُّونَ إِن لَّبِثْتُمْ إِلَّا قَلِيلًا (٥٢) وَقُل لِّعِبَادِى يَقُولُوا۟ ٱلَّتِى
هِىَ أَحْسَنُ إِنَّ ٱلشَّيْطَٰنَ يَنزَغُ بَيْنَهُمْ إِنَّ ٱلشَّيْطَٰنَ كَانَ لِلْإِنسَٰنِ
عَدُوًّا مُّبِينًا (٥٣)

And they say: "When we are bones and fragments (destroyed), should we really be resurrected (to be) a new creation?" (49)Say"Be you stones or iron," (50)"Or some created thing that is yet greater (or harder) in your breasts (thoughts to be resurrected, even then you shall be resurrected)" Then, they will say: "Who shall bring us back (to life)?" Say: "He Who created you first!" Then, they will shake their heads at you and say: "When will that be?" Say: "Perhaps it is near!" (51)On the Day when He will call you, and you will answer (His Call) with (words of) His Praise and Obedience, and you will think that you have stayed (in this world) but a little while! (52)And say to My slaves (i.e. the true believers of Islâmic Monotheism) that they should (only) say those words that are the best. (Because) Shaitân (Satan) verily, sows state of conflicit and disagreements among them. Surely, Shaitân (Satan) is to man a plain enemy. (53)

## Quran 17:62-65

قَالَ أَرَءَيْتَكَ هَـٰذَا ٱلَّذِى كَرَّمْتَ عَلَىَّ لَئِنْ أَخَّرْتَنِ إِلَىٰ يَوْمِ ٱلْقِيَمَةِ لَأَحْتَنِكَنَّ ذُرِّيَّتَهُ إِلَّا قَلِيلًا (٦٢) قَالَ ٱذْهَبْ فَمَن تَبِعَكَ مِنْهُمْ فَإِنَّ جَهَنَّمَ جَزَآؤُكُمْ جَزَآءً مَّوْفُورًا (٦٣) وَٱسْتَفْزِزْ مَنِ ٱسْتَطَعْتَ مِنْهُم بِصَوْتِكَ وَأَجْلِبْ عَلَيْهِم بِخَيْلِكَ وَرَجِلِكَ وَشَارِكْهُمْ فِى ٱلْأَمْوَٰلِ وَٱلْأَوْلَٰدِ وَعِدْهُمْ وَمَا يَعِدُهُمُ ٱلشَّيْطَٰنُ إِلَّا غُرُورًا (٦٤) إِنَّ عِبَادِى لَيْسَ لَكَ عَلَيْهِمْ سُلْطَٰنٌ وَكَفَىٰ بِرَبِّكَ وَكِيلًا (٦٥)

[Iblîs (Satan)] said: "See this one whom You have honoured above me, if You give me respite (keep me alive) to the Day of Resurrection, I will surely seize and mislead his offspring (by sending them astray) all but a few!" (62)(Allâh) said: "Go, and whosoever of them follows you, surely! Hell will be the recompense of you (all) - an ample recompense. (63)"And befool them gradually those whom you can among them with your voice (i.e. songs, music, and any other call for Allâh's disobedience), make assaults on them with your cavalry and your infantry, share with them wealth and children (by tempting them to earn money by illegal ways - usury or by committing illegal sexual intercourse), and make promises to them." But Satan promises them nothing but deceit (64)"Verily! My slaves (i.e the true believers of Islâmic Monotheism), - you have no authority over them. And All-Sufficient is your Lord as a Guardian." (65)

## Quran 17:71-72

يَوۡمَ نَدۡعُواْ كُلَّ أُنَاسِۭ بِإِمَـٰمِهِمۡۖ فَمَنۡ أُوتِىَ كِتَـٰبَهُۥ بِيَمِينِهِۦ فَأُوْلَـٰٓئِكَ يَقۡرَءُونَ كِتَـٰبَهُمۡ وَلَا يُظۡلَمُونَ فَتِيلاً (٧١) وَمَن كَانَ فِى هَـٰذِهِۦٓ أَعۡمَىٰ فَهُوَ فِى ٱلۡأَخِرَةِ أَعۡمَىٰ وَأَضَلُّ سَبِيلاً (٧٢)

(And remember) the Day when We shall call together all human beings with their (respective) Imâm [their Prophets, or their records of good and bad deeds, or their Holy Books like the Qur'ân, the Taurât (Torah), the Injeel the readers whom the people followed in this world)]. So whosoever is given his record in his right hand, such will read their records, and they will not be dealt with unjustly in the least. (71) And whoever is blind in this world (i.e., does not see Allâh's Signs and believes not in Him), will be blind in the Hereafter, and more astray from the Path. (72)

## Quran 17:81-83

وَقُلْ جَاءَ ٱلْحَقُّ وَزَهَقَ ٱلْبَٰطِلُ إِنَّ ٱلْبَٰطِلَ كَانَ زَهُوقًا (٨١) وَنُنَزِّلُ مِنَ ٱلْقُرْءَانِ مَا هُوَ شِفَآءٌ وَرَحْمَةٌ لِّلْمُؤْمِنِينَ وَلَا يَزِيدُ ٱلظَّٰلِمِينَ إِلَّا خَسَارًا (٨٢) وَإِذَآ أَنْعَمْنَا عَلَى ٱلْإِنسَٰنِ أَعْرَضَ وَنَٔا بِجَانِبِهِۦ وَإِذَا مَسَّهُ ٱلشَّرُّ كَانَ يَـُٔوسًا (٨٣)

And say: "Truth (i.e. Islâmic Monotheism or this Qur'ân or Jihâd against polytheists) has come and Bâtil (falsehood, i.e. Satan or polytheism) has vanished. Surely! Bâtil is ever bound to vanish." (81) And We send down of the Qur'ân that which is a healing and a mercy to those who believe (in Islâmic Monotheism and act on it), and it increases the Zâlimûn (polytheists and wrong-doers) nothing but loss. (82) And when We bestow Our Grace on man (the disbeliever), he turns away and becomes arrogant, (far away from the Right Path). And when evil touches him he is in great despair (83)

## Quran 17:88-89

قُل لَّئِنِ ٱجْتَمَعَتِ ٱلْإِنسُ وَٱلْجِنُّ عَلَىٰٓ أَن يَأْتُوا۟ بِمِثْلِ هَٰذَا ٱلْقُرْءَانِ لَا يَأْتُونَ بِمِثْلِهِۦ وَلَوْ كَانَ بَعْضُهُمْ لِبَعْضٍ ظَهِيرًا (٨٨) وَلَقَدْ صَرَّفْنَا لِلنَّاسِ فِى هَٰذَا ٱلْقُرْءَانِ مِن كُلِّ مَثَلٍ فَأَبَىٰٓ أَكْثَرُ ٱلنَّاسِ إِلَّا كُفُورًا (٨٩)

Say: "If the mankind and the jinn were together to produce the like of this Qur'ân, they could not produce the like thereof, even if they helped one another." (88)And indeed We have fully explained to mankind, in this Qur'ân, every kind of similitude, but most of mankind refuse (the truth and accept nothing) but disbelief. (89)

## Quran 17:97-99

وَمَن يَهْدِ ٱللَّهُ فَهُوَ ٱلْمُهْتَدِ وَمَن يُضْلِلْ فَلَن تَجِدَ لَهُمْ أَوْلِيَآءَ مِن دُونِهِ وَنَحْشُرُهُمْ يَوْمَ ٱلْقِيَـٰمَةِ عَلَىٰ وُجُوهِهِمْ عُمْيًا وَبُكْمًا وَصُمًّا مَّأْوَىٰهُمْ جَهَنَّمُ كُلَّمَا خَبَتْ زِدْنَـٰهُمْ سَعِيرًا (٩٧) ذَٰلِكَ جَزَآؤُهُم بِأَنَّهُمْ كَفَرُواْ بِـَٔايَـٰتِنَا وَقَالُوٓاْ أَءِذَا كُنَّا عِظَـٰمًا وَرُفَـٰتًا أَءِنَّا لَمَبْعُوثُونَ خَلْقًا جَدِيدًا (٩٨) ۞ أَوَلَمْ يَرَوْاْ أَنَّ ٱللَّهَ ٱلَّذِى خَلَقَ ٱلسَّمَـٰوَٰتِ وَٱلْأَرْضَ قَادِرٌ عَلَىٰٓ أَن يَخْلُقَ مِثْلَهُمْ وَجَعَلَ لَهُمْ أَجَلًا لَّا رَيْبَ فِيهِ فَأَبَى ٱلظَّـٰلِمُونَ إِلَّا كُفُورًا (٩٩)

And he whom Allâh guides, he is led aright; but he whom He sends astray for such you will find no Auliyâ' (helpers and protectors), besides Him, and We shall gather them together on the Day of Resurrection on their faces, blind, dumb and deaf, their abode will be Hell; whenever it abates, We shall increase for them the fierceness of the Fire (97) That is their recompense, because they denied Our Ayât (proofs, evidences, verses, lessons, signs, revelations, etc.) and said: "When we are bones and fragments, shall we really be raised up as a new creation?" (98)See they not that Allâh, Who created the heavens and the earth, is Able to create the like of them. And He has decreed for them an appointed term, whereof there is not doubt. But the Zâlimûn (polytheists and wrong-doers) refuse (the truth – the – Message of Islâmic Monotheism, and accept nothing) but disbelief.

## Quran 17:104

وَقُلْنَا مِنْ بَعْدِهِ لِبَنِىٓ إِسْرَٰٓءِيلَ ٱسْكُنُواْ ٱلْأَرْضَ فَإِذَا جَآءَ وَعْدُ ٱلْءَاخِرَةِ جِئْنَا بِكُمْ لَفِيفًا

And We said to the Children of Israel after him: "Dwell in the land, then, when the final and the last promise comes near [i.e. the Day of Resurrection or the descent of Christ ['Īsā (Jesus), son of Maryam (Mary) on the earth]. We shall bring you altogether as mixed crowd (gathered out of various nations). (104)

## Quran 18:2-3

قَيِّمًا لِّيُنذِرَ بَأْسًا شَدِيدًا مِّن لَّدُنْهُ وَيُبَشِّرَ ٱلْمُؤْمِنِينَ ٱلَّذِينَ يَعْمَلُونَ ٱلصَّٰلِحَٰتِ أَنَّ لَهُمْ أَجْرًا حَسَنًا (٢) مَّٰكِثِينَ فِيهِ أَبَدًا

(He has made it) Straight to give warning (to the disbelievers) of a severe punishment from Him, and to give glad tidings to the believers (in the Oneness of Allâh Islâmic Monotheism), who do righteous - deeds, that they shall have a fair reward (i.e. Paradise). (2)They shall abide therein forever. (3)

## Quran 18:29-31

وَقُلِ ٱلْحَقُّ مِن رَّبِّكُمْ فَمَن شَاءَ فَلْيُؤْمِن وَمَن شَاءَ فَلْيَكْفُرْ إِنَّا
أَعْتَدْنَا لِلظَّٰلِمِينَ نَارًا أَحَاطَ بِهِمْ سُرَادِقُهَا وَإِن يَسْتَغِيثُوا يُغَاثُوا
بِمَاءٍ كَٱلْمُهْلِ يَشْوِى ٱلْوُجُوهَ بِئْسَ ٱلشَّرَابُ وَسَاءَتْ مُرْتَفَقًا
(٢٩) إِنَّ ٱلَّذِينَ ءَامَنُوا وَعَمِلُوا ٱلصَّٰلِحَٰتِ إِنَّا لَا نُضِيعُ أَجْرَ
مَنْ أَحْسَنَ عَمَلًا (٣٠) أُولَٰئِكَ لَهُمْ جَنَّٰتُ عَدْنٍ تَجْرِى مِن
تَحْتِهِمُ ٱلْأَنْهَٰرُ يُحَلَّوْنَ فِيهَا مِنْ أَسَاوِرَ مِن ذَهَبٍ وَيَلْبَسُونَ ثِيَابًا
خُضْرًا مِّن سُنْدُسٍ وَإِسْتَبْرَقٍ مُّتَّكِئِينَ فِيهَا عَلَى ٱلْأَرَائِكِ نِعْمَ
ٱلثَّوَابُ وَحَسُنَتْ مُرْتَفَقًا (٣١)

*And say: "The truth is from your Lord." Then whosoever
wills, let him believe, and whosoever wills, let him
disbelieve. Verily, We have prepared for the Zâlimûn
(polytheists and wrong-doers), a Fire whose walls will be
surrounding them (disbelievers in the Oneness of Allâh).
And if they ask for help (relief, water) they will be
granted water like boiling oil, that will scald their faces.
Terrible is the drink, and an evil Murtafaq (dwelling,
resting place)! (29) Verily As for those who believed and
did righteous deeds, certainly We shall not make to be
lost the reward of anyone who does his (righteous) deeds
in the most perfect manner. (30) These! For them will be
'Adn (Eden) Paradise (everlasting Gardens); wherein
rivers flow underneath them, therein they will be adorned
with bracelets of gold, and they will wear green garments
of fine and thick silk. They will recline therein on raised*

thrones. How good is the reward, and what an excellent Murtafaq (dwelling, resting place)! (31)

## Quran 18:46-49

ٱلْمَالُ وَٱلْبَنُونَ زِينَةُ ٱلْحَيَوٰةِ ٱلدُّنْيَا وَٱلْبَٰقِيَٰتُ ٱلصَّٰلِحَٰتُ خَيْرٌ عِندَ رَبِّكَ ثَوَابًا وَخَيْرٌ أَمَلاً (٤٦) وَيَوْمَ نُسَيِّرُ ٱلْجِبَالَ وَتَرَى ٱلْأَرْضَ بَارِزَةً وَحَشَرْنَٰهُمْ فَلَمْ نُغَادِرْ مِنْهُمْ أَحَدًا (٤٧) وَعُرِضُوا عَلَىٰ رَبِّكَ صَفًّا لَّقَدْ جِئْتُمُونَا كَمَا خَلَقْنَٰكُمْ أَوَّلَ مَرَّةٍ بَلْ زَعَمْتُمْ أَلَّن نَّجْعَلَ لَكُم مَّوْعِدًا (٤٨) وَوُضِعَ ٱلْكِتَٰبُ فَتَرَى ٱلْمُجْرِمِينَ مُشْفِقِينَ مِمَّا فِيهِ وَيَقُولُونَ يَٰوَيْلَتَنَا مَالِ هَٰذَا ٱلْكِتَٰبِ لَا يُغَادِرُ صَغِيرَةً وَلَا كَبِيرَةً إِلَّا أَحْصَىٰهَا وَوَجَدُوا مَا عَمِلُوا حَاضِرًا وَلَا يَظْلِمُ رَبُّكَ أَحَدًا (٤٩)

*Wealth and children are the adornment of the life of this world. But the good righteous deeds, that last, are better with your Lord for rewards and better in respect of hope. (46) And (remember) the Day We shall cause the mountains to pass away (like clouds of dust), and you will see the earth as a levelled plain, and we shall gather them all together so as to leave not one of them behind. (47) And they will be set before your Lord in (lines as) rows, (and Allâh will say): "Now indeed, you have come to Us as We created you the first time. Nay, but you thought that We had appointed no meeting for you (with Us)." (48) And the Book (one's Record) will be placed (in the right hand for a believer in the Oneness of Allâh, and* in the left hand for a disbeliever in the Oneness of Allâh), and you will see the Mujrimûn (criminals, polytheists, sinners), fearful of that which is (recorded) therein. They will say: "Woe to us! What sort of Book is this that leaves neither a small thing nor a big thing, but has recorded it with numbers!" And they will find all that they did, placed before them, and your Lord treats no one with injustice. (49)

## Quran 18:52-53

وَيَوْمَ يَقُولُ نَادُواْ شُرَكَاءِىَ ٱلَّذِينَ زَعَمْتُمْ فَدَعَوْهُمْ فَلَمْ يَسْتَجِيبُواْ لَهُمْ وَجَعَلْنَا بَيْنَهُم مَّوْبِقًا (٥٢) وَرَءَا ٱلْمُجْرِمُونَ ٱلنَّارَ فَظَنُّواْ أَنَّهُم مُّوَاقِعُوهَا وَلَمْ يَجِدُواْ عَنْهَا مَصْرِفًا (٥٣)

And (remember) the Day He will say: "Call those (so-called) partners of Mine whom you pretended." Then they will cry unto them, but they will not answer them, and We shall put Maubiq (barrier) between them. (52)And the Mujrimûn (criminals, polytheists, sinners), shall see the Fire and apprehend that they have to fall therein. And they will find no way of escape from there.

## Quran 18:57-58

وَمَنْ أَظْلَمُ مِمَّن ذُكِّرَ بِـَٔايَـٰتِ رَبِّهِ فَأَعْرَضَ عَنْهَا وَنَسِىَ مَا قَدَّمَتْ يَدَاهُ إِنَّا جَعَلْنَا عَلَىٰ قُلُوبِهِمْ أَكِنَّةً أَن يَفْقَهُوهُ وَفِى ءَاذَانِهِمْ وَقْرًا وَإِن تَدْعُهُمْ إِلَى ٱلْهُدَىٰ فَلَن يَهْتَدُواْ إِذًا أَبَدًا

(٥٧) وَرَبُّكَ ٱلْغَفُورُ ذُو ٱلرَّحْمَةِ لَوْ يُؤَاخِذُهُم بِمَا كَسَبُوا۟ لَعَجَّلَ لَهُمُ ٱلْعَذَابَ بَل لَّهُم مَّوْعِدٌ لَّن يَجِدُوا۟ مِن دُونِهِ مَوْئِلاً

*And who does more wrong than he who is reminded of the Ayât (proofs, verses, lessons, signs, revelations, etc.) of his Lord, but turns away from them forgetting what (deeds) his hands have sent forth. Truly, We have set veils over their hearts lest they should understand this (the Qur'ân), and in their ears, deafness. And if you (O Muhammad) call them to guidance, even then they will never be guided. (57) And your Lord is Most Forgiving, Owner of Mercy. Were He to call them to account for what they have earned, then surely, He would have hastened their punishment. But they have their appointed time, beyond which they will find no escape. (58)*

## Quran 18:87-88

قَالَ أَمَّا مَن ظَلَمَ فَسَوْفَ نُعَذِّبُهُ ثُمَّ يُرَدُّ إِلَىٰ رَبِّهِ فَيُعَذِّبُهُ عَذَابًا نُّكْرًا (٨٧) وَأَمَّا مَنْ ءَامَنَ وَعَمِلَ صَٰلِحًا فَلَهُ جَزَآءً ٱلْحُسْنَىٰ وَسَنَقُولُ لَهُ مِنْ أَمْرِنَا يُسْرًا (٨٨)

*He said: "As for him (a disbeliever) who does wrong, we shall punish him; and then he will be brought back unto his Lord; Who will punish him with a terrible torment (Hell). (87) "But as for him who believes (in Allâh's Oneness) and works righteousness, he shall have the best reward, (Paradise), and we (Dhul-Qarnain) shall speak unto him mild words (as instructions)." (88)*

Quran 18:98-102

قَالَ هَـٰذَا رَحْمَةٌ مِّن رَّبِّى ۖ فَإِذَا جَاءَ وَعْدُ رَبِّى جَعَلَهُ دَكَّاءَ ۖ وَكَانَ وَعْدُ رَبِّى حَقًّا (٩٨) ۞ وَتَرَكْنَا بَعْضَهُمْ يَوْمَئِذٍ يَمُوجُ فِى بَعْضٍ ۖ وَنُفِخَ فِى ٱلصُّورِ فَجَمَعْنَاهُمْ جَمْعًا (٩٩) وَعَرَضْنَا جَهَنَّمَ يَوْمَئِذٍ لِّلْكَافِرِينَ عَرْضًا (١٠٠) ٱلَّذِينَ كَانَتْ أَعْيُنُهُمْ فِى غِطَاءٍ عَن ذِكْرِى وَكَانُوا لَا يَسْتَطِيعُونَ سَمْعًا (١٠١) أَفَحَسِبَ ٱلَّذِينَ كَفَرُوا أَن يَتَّخِذُوا عِبَادِى مِن دُونِى أَوْلِيَاءَ ۚ إِنَّا أَعْتَدْنَا جَهَنَّمَ لِلْكَافِرِينَ نُزُلًا (١٠٢)

*(Dhul-Qarnain) said: "This is a mercy from my Lord, but when the Promise of my Lord comes, He shall level it down to the ground. And the Promise of my Lord is ever true." (98)And on that Day [i.e. the Day Ya'jûj and Ma'jûj (Gog and Magog) will come out], We shall leave them to surge like waves on one another, and the Trumpet will be blown, and We shall collect them (the creatures) all together. (99)And on that Day We shall present Hell to the disbelievers, plain to view, — (100)(To) those whose eyes had been under a covering from My Reminder (this Qur'ân), and who could not bear to hear (it). (101)Do then those who disbelieved think that they can take My slaves [i.e., the angels, Allâh's Messengers, 'Īsā (Jesus), son of Maryam (Mary)]*

as Auliyâ' (lords, gods, protectors) besides Me? Verily, We have prepared Hell as an entertainment for the disbelievers (in the Oneness of Allâh Islâmic Monotheism). (102)

## Quran 18:105-108

أُوْلَـٰٓئِكَ ٱلَّذِينَ كَفَرُواْ بِـَٔايَـٰتِ رَبِّهِمْ وَلِقَآئِهِۦ فَحَبِطَتْ أَعْمَـٰلُهُمْ فَلَا
نُقِيمُ لَهُمْ يَوْمَ ٱلْقِيَـٰمَةِ وَزْنًا (١٠٥) ذَٰلِكَ جَزَآؤُهُمْ جَهَنَّمُ بِمَا
كَفَرُواْ وَٱتَّخَذُوٓاْ ءَايَـٰتِى وَرُسُلِى هُزُوًا (١٠٦) إِنَّ ٱلَّذِينَ
ءَامَنُواْ وَعَمِلُواْ ٱلصَّـٰلِحَـٰتِ كَانَتْ لَهُمْ جَنَّـٰتُ ٱلْفِرْدَوْسِ نُزُلاً
(١٠٧) خَـٰلِدِينَ فِيهَا لَا يَبْغُونَ عَنْهَا حِوَلاً (١٠٨)

"They are those who deny the Ayât (proofs, evidences, verses, lessons, signs, revelations, etc.) of their Lord and the Meeting with Him (in the Hereafter). So their works are in vain, and on the Day of Resurrection, We shall assign not weight for them. (105)"That shall be their recompense, Hell; because they disbelieved and took My Ayât (proofs, evidences, verses, lessons, signs, revelations, etc.) and My Messengers by way of jest and mockery. (106)"Verily! those who believe (in the Oneness of Allâh - Islâmic Monotheism) and do righteous deeds, shall have the Gardens of Al-Firdaus (the Paradise) for their entertainment. (107)"Wherein they shall dwell (forever). No desire will they have for removal therefrom." (108)

## Quran 19:38-40

أَسْمِعْ بِهِمْ وَأَبْصِرْ يَوْمَ يَأْتُونَنَا ۖ لَكِنِ ٱلظَّٰلِمُونَ ٱلْيَوْمَ فِى ضَلَٰلٍ مُّبِينٍ (٣٨) وَأَنذِرْهُمْ يَوْمَ ٱلْحَسْرَةِ إِذْ قُضِىَ ٱلْأَمْرُ وَهُمْ فِى غَفْلَةٍ وَهُمْ لَا يُؤْمِنُونَ (٣٩) إِنَّا نَحْنُ نَرِثُ ٱلْأَرْضَ وَمَنْ عَلَيْهَا وَإِلَيْنَا يُرْجَعُونَ (٤٠)

*How clearly will they (polytheists and disbelievers in the Oneness of Allâh) see and hear, the Day when they will appear before Us! But the Zalimûn (polytheists and wrong-doers) today are in plain error (38) And warn them (O Muhammad) of the Day of grief and regrets, when the case has been decided, while (now) they are in a state of carelessness, and they believe not (39) Verily! We will inherit the earth and whatsoever is thereon. And to Us they all shall be returned, (40)*

## Quran 19:59-62

۞ فَخَلَفَ مِنۢ بَعْدِهِمْ خَلْفٌ أَضَاعُوا۟ ٱلصَّلَوٰةَ وَٱتَّبَعُوا۟ ٱلشَّهَوَٰتِ ۖ فَسَوْفَ يَلْقَوْنَ غَيًّا (٥٩) إِلَّا مَن تَابَ وَءَامَنَ وَعَمِلَ صَٰلِحًا فَأُو۟لَٰٓئِكَ يَدْخُلُونَ ٱلْجَنَّةَ وَلَا يُظْلَمُونَ شَيْـًٔا (٦٠) جَنَّٰتِ عَدْنٍ ٱلَّتِى وَعَدَ ٱلرَّحْمَٰنُ عِبَادَهُۥ بِٱلْغَيْبِ ۚ إِنَّهُۥ كَانَ وَعْدُهُۥ مَأْتِيًّا (٦١) لَّا يَسْمَعُونَ فِيهَا لَغْوًا إِلَّا سَلَٰمًا ۖ وَلَهُمْ رِزْقُهُمْ فِيهَا بُكْرَةً وَعَشِيًّا (٦٢)

*Then, there has succeeded them a posterity who have given up As-Salât (the prayers) [i.e. made their Salât (prayers) to be lost, either by not offering them or by not offering them perfectly or by not offering them in their proper fixed times] and have followed lusts. So they will be thrown in Hell. (59)Except those who repent and believe (in the Oneness of Allâh and His Messenger Muhammad), and work righteousness. Such will enter Paradise and they will not be wronged in aught. (60)(They will enter) 'Adn (Eden) Paradise (everlasting Gardens), which the Most Gracious (Allâh) has promised to His slaves in the unseen: Verily! His Promise must come to pass. (61)They shall not hear therein (in Paradise) any Laghw (dirty, false, evil vain talk), but only Salâm (salutations of peace). And they will have therein their sustenance, morning and afternoon. (62)*

## Quran 19:68-72

فَوَرَبِّكَ لَنَحْشُرَنَّهُمْ وَٱلشَّيَـٰطِينَ ثُمَّ لَنُحْضِرَنَّهُمْ حَوْلَ جَهَنَّمَ جِثِيًّا (٦٨) ثُمَّ لَنَنزِعَنَّ مِن كُلِّ شِيعَةٍ أَيُّهُمْ أَشَدُّ عَلَى ٱلرَّحْمَـٰنِ عِتِيًّا (٦٩) ثُمَّ لَنَحْنُ أَعْلَمُ بِٱلَّذِينَ هُمْ أَوْلَىٰ بِهَا صِلِيًّا (٧٠) وَإِن مِّنكُمْ إِلَّا وَارِدُهَاۚ كَانَ عَلَىٰ رَبِّكَ حَتْمًا مَّقْضِيًّا (٧١) ثُمَّ نُنَجِّى ٱلَّذِينَ ٱتَّقَواْ وَّنَذَرُ ٱلظَّـٰلِمِينَ فِيهَا جِثِيًّا (٧٢)

*So by your Lord, surely, We shall gather them together, and (also) the Shayâtin (devils) (with them), then We shall bring them round Hell on their knees. (68)Then indeed We shall drag out from every sect all those who were worst in obstinate rebellion against the Most*

Gracious (Allâh). (69)Then, verily, We know best those
who are most worthy of being burnt therein. (70)There is
not one of you but will pass over it (Hell); this is with
your Lord; a Decree which must be accomplished
(71)Then We shall save those who use to fear Allâh and
were dutiful to Him. And We shall leave the Zâlimûn
(polytheists and wrongdoers) therein (humbled) to their
knees (in Hell). (72)

**Quran 19:75-80**

قُلْ مَن كَانَ فِى ٱلضَّلَالَةِ فَلْيَمْدُدْ لَهُ ٱلرَّحْمَـٰنُ مَدًّا حَتَّىٰ إِذَا
رَأَوْاْ مَا يُوعَدُونَ إِمَّا ٱلْعَذَابَ وَإِمَّا ٱلسَّاعَةَ فَسَيَعْلَمُونَ مَنْ هُوَ
شَرٌّ مَّكَانًا وَأَضْعَفُ جُندًا (٧٥) وَيَزِيدُ ٱللَّهُ ٱلَّذِينَ ٱهْتَدَوْاْ هُدًى
وَٱلْبَـٰقِيَـٰتُ ٱلصَّـٰلِحَـٰتُ خَيْرٌ عِندَ رَبِّكَ ثَوَابًا وَخَيْرٌ مَّرَدًّا
(٧٦) أَفَرَءَيْتَ ٱلَّذِى كَفَرَ بِـَٔايَـٰتِنَا وَقَالَ لَأُوتَيَنَّ مَالاً وَوَلَدًا
(٧٧) أَطَّلَعَ ٱلْغَيْبَ أَمِ ٱتَّخَذَ عِندَ ٱلرَّحْمَـٰنِ عَهْدًا (٧٨) كَلَّا
سَنَكْتُبُ مَا يَقُولُ وَنَمُدُّ لَهُ مِنَ ٱلْعَذَابِ مَدًّا (٧٩) وَنَرِثُهُ مَا
يَقُولُ وَيَأْتِينَا فَرْدًا (٨٠)

Say (O Muhammad) whoever is in error, the Most
Gracious (Allâh) will extend (the rope) to him, until,
when they see that which they were promised, either the
torment or the Hour, they will come to know who is
worst in position, and who is weaker in forces. (75)And
Allâh increases in guidance those who walk aright. And
the righteous good deeds that last, are better with your

Lord, for reward and better for resort. (76)Have you seen him who disbelieved in Our Ayât (this Qur'ân and Muhammad) and said: "I shall certainly be given wealth and children [if I will be alive (again)]," (77)Has he known the unseen or has he taken a covenant from the Most Gracious (Allâh)? (78)Nay! We shall record what he says, and We shall increase his torment (in the Hell); (79)And We shall inherit from him (at his death) all that he talks of (i.e. wealth and children which We have bestowed upon him in this world), and he shall come to Us alone (80)

**Quran 19:82-87**

كَلَّا سَيَكْفُرُونَ بِعِبَادَتِهِمْ وَيَكُونُونَ عَلَيْهِمْ ضِدًّا (٨٢) أَلَمْ تَرَ أَنَّا أَرْسَلْنَا الشَّيَاطِينَ عَلَى الْكَافِرِينَ تَؤُزُّهُمْ أَزًّا (٨٣) فَلَا تَعْجَلْ عَلَيْهِمْ إِنَّمَا نَعُدُّ لَهُمْ عَدًّا (٨٤) يَوْمَ نَحْشُرُ الْمُتَّقِينَ إِلَى الرَّحْمَٰنِ وَفْدًا (٨٥) وَنَسُوقُ الْمُجْرِمِينَ إِلَىٰ جَهَنَّمَ وِرْدًا (٨٦) لَّا يَمْلِكُونَ الشَّفَاعَةَ إِلَّا مَنِ اتَّخَذَ عِندَ الرَّحْمَٰنِ عَهْدًا

Nay, but they (the so-called gods) will deny their worship of them, and become opponents to them (on the Day of Resurrection). (82) See you not that We have sent the Shayâtin (devils) against the disbelievers to push them to do evil. (83) So make no haste against them; We only count out to them a (limited) number (of the days of the life of this world and delay their term so that they may increase in evil and sins). (84) The Day We shall gather

the Muttaqûn (pious and righteous Persons) unto the
Most Gracious (Allâh), like a delegatation (presented
before a king for honour). (85)And We shall drive the
Mujrimûn (polytheists, sinners, criminals, disbelievers
in the Oneness of Allâh) to Hell, in a thirsty state (like a
thirsty herd driven down to water), (86)None shall have
the power of intercession, but such a one as has received
permission (or promise) from the Most Gracious (Allâh).

## Quran 19:95-96

وَكُلُّهُمْ ءَاتِيهِ يَوْمَ ٱلْقِيَـٰمَةِ فَرْدًا (٩٥) إِنَّ ٱلَّذِينَ ءَامَنُوا۟ وَعَمِلُوا۟
ٱلصَّـٰلِحَـٰتِ سَيَجْعَلُ لَهُمُ ٱلرَّحْمَـٰنُ وُدًّا (٩٦)

And everyone of them will come to Him alone on the Day
of Resurrection (without any helper, or protector or
defender). (95) Verily, those who believe [in the Oneness
of Allâh and in His Messenger (Muhammad)] and work
deeds of righteousness, the Most Gracious (Allâh) will
bestow love for them(in the hearts of the believers). (96)

## Quran 20:15

إِنَّ ٱلسَّاعَةَ ءَاتِيَةٌ أَكَادُ أُخْفِيهَا لِتُجْزَىٰ كُلُّ نَفْسٍ بِمَا تَسْعَىٰ

"Verily, the Hour is coming and I am almost hiding it
from myself - that every person may be rewarded for that
which he strives. (15)

## Quran 20:47-48

فَأْتِيَاهُ فَقُولَا إِنَّا رَسُولَا رَبِّكَ فَأَرْسِلْ مَعَنَا بَنِىٓ إِسْرَٰٓءِيلَ وَلَا
تُعَذِّبْهُمْۖ قَدْ جِئْنَٰكَ بِـَٔايَةٍ مِّن رَّبِّكَۖ وَٱلسَّلَٰمُ عَلَىٰ مَنِ ٱتَّبَعَ ٱلْهُدَىٰٓ
(٤٧) إِنَّا قَدْ أُوحِىَ إِلَيْنَآ أَنَّ ٱلْعَذَابَ عَلَىٰ مَن كَذَّبَ وَتَوَلَّىٰ

"So go you both to him, and say: 'Verily, we are
Messengers of your Lord, so let the Children of Israel go
with us, and torment them not; indeed, we have come
with a sign from your Lord! And peace will be upon him
who follows the guidance! (47)'Truly, it has been
revealed to us that the torment will be for him who denies
[believes not in the Oneness of Allâh, and in His
Messengers], and turns away.'(from the truth and
obedience of Allâh)" (48)

## Quran 20:68-69

قُلْنَا لَا تَخَفْ إِنَّكَ أَنتَ ٱلْأَعْلَىٰ (٦٨) وَأَلْقِ مَا فِى يَمِينِكَ تَلْقَفْ
مَا صَنَعُوٓا۟ۖ إِنَّمَا صَنَعُوا۟ كَيْدُ سَٰحِرٍۖ وَلَا يُفْلِحُ ٱلسَّاحِرُ حَيْثُ
أَتَىٰ (٦٩)

We (Allâh) said: "Fear not! Surely, you will have the
upper hand. (68) "And throw that which is in your right
hand! It will swallow up that which they have made.
That which they have made is only a magician's trick,
and the magician will never be successful, to whatever
amount (of skill) he may attain." (69)

## Quran 20:74-76

إِنَّهُ مَن يَأْتِ رَبَّهُ مُجْرِمًا فَإِنَّ لَهُۥ جَهَنَّمَ لَا يَمُوتُ فِيهَا وَلَا يَحْيَىٰ (٧٤) وَمَن يَأْتِهِۦ مُؤْمِنًا قَدْ عَمِلَ ٱلصَّٰلِحَٰتِ فَأُوْلَٰٓئِكَ لَهُمُ ٱلدَّرَجَٰتُ ٱلْعُلَىٰ (٧٥) جَنَّٰتُ عَدْنٍ تَجْرِى مِن تَحْتِهَا ٱلْأَنْهَٰرُ خَٰلِدِينَ فِيهَا ۚ وَذَٰلِكَ جَزَآءُ مَن تَزَكَّىٰ (٧٦)

*Verily! whoever comes to his Lord as a Mujrim (criminal, polytheist, disbeliever in the Oneness of Allâh and His Messengers), then surely, for him is Hell, wherein he will neither die nor live (74)But whoever comes to Him (Allâh) as a believer (in the Oneness of Allâh), and has done righteous good deeds, for such are the high ranks (in the Hereafter), – (75)'Adn (Eden) Paradise (everlasting Gardens), under which rivers flow, wherein they will abide forever: such is the reward of those who purify themselves (by abstaining from all kinds of sins and evil deeds which Allâh has forbidden and by doing all that which Allâh has ordained). (76)*

## Quran 20:82

وَإِنِّى لَغَفَّارٌ لِّمَن تَابَ وَءَامَنَ وَعَمِلَ صَٰلِحًا ثُمَّ ٱهْتَدَىٰ

*And verily, I am indeed forgiving to him who repents, believes (in My Oneness, and associates none in worship with Me) and does righteous good deeds, and then remains constant in doing them, (till his death). (82)*

## Quran 20:100-112

مَّنْ أَعْرَضَ عَنْهُ فَإِنَّهُ يَحْمِلُ يَوْمَ ٱلْقِيَمَةِ وِزْرًا
(١٠٠) خَٰلِدِينَ فِيهِ وَسَاءَ لَهُمْ يَوْمَ ٱلْقِيَمَةِ حِمْلاً (١٠١) يَوْمَ
يُنفَخُ فِى ٱلصُّورِ وَنَحْشُرُ ٱلْمُجْرِمِينَ يَوْمَئِذٍ زُرْقًا
(١٠٢) يَتَخَٰفَتُونَ بَيْنَهُمْ إِن لَّبِثْتُمْ إِلَّا عَشْرًا (١٠٣) نَّحْنُ أَعْلَمُ
بِمَا يَقُولُونَ إِذْ يَقُولُ أَمْثَلُهُمْ طَرِيقَةً إِن لَّبِثْتُمْ إِلَّا يَوْمًا
(١٠٤) وَيَسْـَٔلُونَكَ عَنِ ٱلْجِبَالِ فَقُلْ يَنسِفُهَا رَبِّى نَسْفًا
(١٠٥) فَيَذَرُهَا قَاعًا صَفْصَفًا (١٠٦) لَّا تَرَىٰ فِيهَا عِوَجًا
وَلَا أَمْتًا (١٠٧) يَوْمَئِذٍ يَتَّبِعُونَ ٱلدَّاعِىَ لَا عِوَجَ لَهُ وَخَشَعَتِ
ٱلْأَصْوَاتُ لِلرَّحْمَٰنِ فَلَا تَسْمَعُ إِلَّا هَمْسًا (١٠٨) يَوْمَئِذٍ لَّا
تَنفَعُ ٱلشَّفَٰعَةُ إِلَّا مَنْ أَذِنَ لَهُ ٱلرَّحْمَٰنُ وَرَضِىَ لَهُ قَوْلًا
(١٠٩) يَعْلَمُ مَا بَيْنَ أَيْدِيهِمْ وَمَا خَلْفَهُمْ وَلَا يُحِيطُونَ بِهِ عِلْمًا
(١١٠) ۞ وَعَنَتِ ٱلْوُجُوهُ لِلْحَىِّ ٱلْقَيُّومِ وَقَدْ خَابَ مَنْ حَمَلَ
ظُلْمًا (١١١) وَمَن يَعْمَلْ مِنَ ٱلصَّٰلِحَٰتِ وَهُوَ مُؤْمِنٌ فَلَا
يَخَافُ ظُلْمًا وَلَا هَضْمًا (١١٢)

Whoever turns away from it (this Qur'ân i.e. does not believe in it, nor acts on its orders), verily, they will bear a heavy burden (of sins) on the Day of Resurrection, (100)They will abide in that (state in the Fire of Hell), — and evil indeed will it be that load for them on the Day of Resurrection; (101)The Day when the Trumpet will be blown (the second blowing): that Day, We shall gather the Mujrimûn (criminals, polytheists, sinners, disbelievers in the Oneness of Allâh) blue or blind eyed with thirst. (102)In whispers will they speak in a very *low voice to each other (saying): "You stayed not longer than ten (days)." (103)We know very well what they will say, when the best among them in knowledge and wisdom will say: "You stayed no longer than a day!" (104)And they ask you concerning the mountains, say;"My Lord will blast them and scatter them as particles of dust. (105)"Then He shall leave them as a level smooth plain. (106)"You will see therein nothing crooked or curved." (107)On that Day mankind will follow strictly (the voice of) Allâh's caller, no crookedness (that is without going to the right or left of that voice) will they show him (Allâh's caller). And all voices will be humbled for the Most Gracious (Allâh), and nothing shall you hear but the low voice of their footsteps (108)On that day no intercession shall avail, except the one for whom the Most Gracious (Allâh) has given permission and whose word is acceptable to Him. (109)He (Allâh) knows what happens to them (His creatures) in this world, and what will happen to them (in the Hereafter), but they will never compass anything of His Knowledge. (110)And (all) faces shall be humbled before (Allâh), the Ever Living, the One Who sustains and protects all that exists. And he who carried (a burden of) wrongdoing (i.e. he who disbelieved in Allâh, ascribed partners to Him, and did deeds of His disobedience), will be indeed a complete failure (on that Day). (111)And he who works deeds of righteousness, while he is a believer (in Islâmic Monotheism) then he will have no fear of injustice, nor of any curtailment (of his reward). (112)*

## Quran 20:123-127

قَالَ ٱهۡبِطَا مِنۡهَا جَمِيعَۢاۖ بَعۡضُكُمۡ لِبَعۡضٍ عَدُوّٞۖ فَإِمَّا يَأۡتِيَنَّكُم مِّنِّى هُدٗى فَمَنِ ٱتَّبَعَ هُدَاىَ فَلَا يَضِلُّ وَلَا يَشۡقَىٰ (١٢٣) وَمَنۡ أَعۡرَضَ عَن ذِكۡرِى فَإِنَّ لَهُۥ مَعِيشَةٗ ضَنكٗا وَنَحۡشُرُهُۥ يَوۡمَ ٱلۡقِيَٰمَةِ أَعۡمَىٰ (١٢٤) قَالَ رَبِّ لِمَ حَشَرۡتَنِىٓ أَعۡمَىٰ وَقَدۡ كُنتُ بَصِيرٗا (١٢٥) قَالَ كَذَٰلِكَ أَتَتۡكَ ءَايَٰتُنَا فَنَسِيتَهَاۖ وَكَذَٰلِكَ ٱلۡيَوۡمَ تُنسَىٰ (١٢٦) وَكَذَٰلِكَ نَجۡزِى مَنۡ أَسۡرَفَ وَلَمۡ يُؤۡمِنۢ بِـَٔايَٰتِ رَبِّهِۦۚ وَلَعَذَابُ ٱلۡأٓخِرَةِ أَشَدُّ وَأَبۡقَىٰٓ (١٢٧)

*He (Allâh) said:"Get you down (from the Paradise to the earth), both of you, together, some of you are an enemy to some others. Then if there comes to you guidance from Me, then whoever follows My Guidance he shall neither go astray, nor shall be distressed. (123)"But whosoever turns away from My Reminder (i.e. neither believes in this Qur'ân nor acts on its teachings) verily, for him is a life of hardship, and We shall raise him up blind on the Day of Resurrection." (124)He will say:"O my Lord! Why have you raised me up blind, while I had sight (before)." (125)(Allâh) will say: "Like this, Our Ayât (proofs, evidences, verses, lessons, signs, revelations, etc.) came unto you, but you disregarded them (i.e. you left them, did not think deeply in them, and you turned away* from them), and so this Day, you will be neglected (in the Hell-fire, away from Allâh's Mercy)." (126)And thus do We requite him who transgresses beyond bounds [i.e. commits the great sins and disobeys his Lord (Allâh) and believes not in His Messengers, and His revealed Books, like this Qur'ân, etc.], and believes not in the Ayât (proofs, evidences, verses, lessons, signs, revelations) of his Lord, and the torment of the Hereafter is far more severe and more lasting. (127)

## Quran 20:129-130

وَلَوْلَا كَلِمَةٌ سَبَقَتْ مِن رَّبِّكَ لَكَانَ لِزَامًا وَأَجَلٌ مُّسَمًّى
(١٢٩) فَٱصْبِرْ عَلَىٰ مَا يَقُولُونَ وَسَبِّحْ بِحَمْدِ رَبِّكَ قَبْلَ طُلُوعِ
ٱلشَّمْسِ وَقَبْلَ غُرُوبِهَا وَمِنْ ءَانَآئِ ٱلَّيْلِ فَسَبِّحْ وَأَطْرَافَ
ٱلنَّهَارِ لَعَلَّكَ تَرْضَىٰ (١٣٠)

And had it not been for a Word that went forth before from your Lord, and a term determined, (their punishment) must necessarily have come (in this world). (129) So bear patiently what they say, and glorify the praises of your Lord before the rising of the sun, and before its setting, and during some hours of the night, and at the ends of the day (an indication for the five compulsory congregational prayers), that you may become pleased with the reward which Allâh shall give you. (130)

## Quran 20:132

وَأْمُرْ أَهْلَكَ بِٱلصَّلَوٰةِ وَٱصْطَبِرْ عَلَيْهَا ۖ لَا نَسْـَٔلُكَ رِزْقًا ۖ نَّحْنُ نَرْزُقُكَ ۗ وَٱلْعَـٰقِبَةُ لِلتَّقْوَىٰ

And enjoin As-Salât (the prayer) on your family, and be patient in offering them [i.e. the Salât (prayers)]. We ask not of you a provision (i.e. to give Us something: money); We provide for you. And the good end (i.e. Paradise) is for the Muttaqûn (pious and righteous persons ). (132)

## Quran 20:135

قُلْ كُلٌّ مُّتَرَبِّصٌ فَتَرَبَّصُوا ۖ فَسَتَعْلَمُونَ مَنْ أَصْحَـٰبُ ٱلصِّرَٰطِ ٱلسَّوِيِّ وَمَنِ ٱهْتَدَىٰ

Say: "Each one (believer and disbeliever) is waiting, so wait you too, and you shall know who are they that are on the Straight and Even Path (i.e. Allâh's religion of Islâmic Monotheism), and who are they that have let themselves be guided (on the Right Path).

## Quran 21:1

ٱقْتَرَبَ لِلنَّاسِ حِسَابُهُمْ وَهُمْ فِى غَفْلَةٍ مُّعْرِضُونَ

Draws near for mankind their reckoning, while they turn away in heedlessness. (1)

## Quran 21:18

بَلْ نَقْذِفُ بِٱلْحَقِّ عَلَى ٱلْبَـٰطِلِ فَيَدْمَغُهُ فَإِذَا هُوَ زَاهِقٌ ۚ وَلَكُمُ ٱلْوَيْلُ مِمَّا تَصِفُونَ

*Nay, We fling (send down) the truth (this Qur'ân) against the falsehood (disbelief), so it destroys it, and behold, it (falsehood) is vanished. And woe to you for that (lie) which you ascribe (to Allâh by uttering that Allâh has a wife and a son). (18)*

## Quran 21:23

لَا يُسۡـَٔلُ عَمَّا يَفۡعَلُ وَهُمۡ يُسۡـَٔلُونَ

*He cannot be questioned as to what He does, while they will be questioned. (23)*

## Quran 21:35

كُلُّ نَفۡسٍ ذَآئِقَةُ ٱلۡمَوۡتِۗ وَنَبۡلُوكُم بِٱلشَّرِّ وَٱلۡخَيۡرِ فِتۡنَةًۖ وَإِلَيۡنَا تُرۡجَعُونَ

*Everyone is going to taste death, and We shall make a trial of you with evil and with good, and to Us you will be returned. (35)*

## Quran 21:38-40

وَيَقُولُونَ مَتَىٰ هَٰذَا ٱلۡوَعۡدُ إِن كُنتُمۡ صَٰدِقِينَ (٣٨) لَوۡ يَعۡلَمُ ٱلَّذِينَ كَفَرُواْ حِينَ لَا يَكُفُّونَ عَن وُجُوهِهِمُ ٱلنَّارَ وَلَا عَن ظُهُورِهِمۡ وَلَا هُمۡ يُنصَرُونَ (٣٩) بَلۡ تَأۡتِيهِم بَغۡتَةً فَتَبۡهَتُهُمۡ فَلَا يَسۡتَطِيعُونَ رَدَّهَا وَلَا هُمۡ يُنظَرُونَ (٤٠)

*And they say: "When will this promise (come to pass), if you are truthful." (38) If only those who disbelieved*

knew (the time) when they will not be able to ward off the
Fire from their faces, nor from their backs; and they will
not be helped. (39) Nay, it (the Fire or the Day of
Resurrection) will come upon them all of a sudden and
will perplex them, and they will have no power to avert
it, nor will they get respite. (40)

## Quran 21:44

بَلْ مَتَّعْنَا هَٰؤُلَآءِ وَءَابَاءَهُمْ حَتَّىٰ طَالَ عَلَيْهِمُ ٱلْعُمُرُۗ أَفَلَا
يَرَوْنَ أَنَّا نَأْتِى ٱلْأَرْضَ نَنقُصُهَا مِنْ أَطْرَافِهَآ أَفَهُمُ ٱلْغَٰلِبُونَ

Nay, We gave the luxuries of this life to these men and
their fathers until the period grew long for them. See they
not that We gradually reduce the land (in their control)
from its outlying borders? Is it then they who will
overcome. (44)

## Quran 21:47

وَنَضَعُ ٱلْمَوَٰزِينَ ٱلْقِسْطَ لِيَوْمِ ٱلْقِيَٰمَةِ فَلَا تُظْلَمُ نَفْسٌ شَيْئًاۖ وَإِن
كَانَ مِثْقَالَ حَبَّةٍ مِّنْ خَرْدَلٍ أَتَيْنَا بِهَاۗ وَكَفَىٰ بِنَا حَٰسِبِينَ

And We shall set up balances of justice on the Day of
Resurrection, then none will be dealt with unjustly in
anything. And if there be the weight of a mustard seed,
We will bring it. And Sufficient are We to take account.
(47)

## Quran 21:88

فَٱسْتَجَبْنَا لَهُ ۥ وَنَجَّيْنَـٰهُ مِنَ ٱلْغَمِّ ۚ وَكَذَٰلِكَ نُـۧجِى ٱلْمُؤْمِنِينَ

*So We answered his call, and delivered him from the distress. And thus We do deliver the believers (who believe in the Oneness of Allâh, abstain from evil and work righteousness) (88)*

## Quran 21:93-105

وَتَقَطَّعُوٓا۟ أَمْرَهُم بَيْنَهُمْ ۖ كُلٌّ إِلَيْنَا رَٰجِعُونَ (٩٣) فَمَن يَعْمَلْ مِنَ ٱلصَّـٰلِحَـٰتِ وَهُوَ مُؤْمِنٌ فَلَا كُفْرَانَ لِسَعْيِهِۦ وَإِنَّا لَهُ ۥ كَـٰتِبُونَ (٩٤) وَحَرَٰمٌ عَلَىٰ قَرْيَةٍ أَهْلَكْنَـٰهَآ أَنَّهُمْ لَا يَرْجِعُونَ (٩٥) حَتَّىٰٓ إِذَا فُتِحَتْ يَأْجُوجُ وَمَأْجُوجُ وَهُم مِّن كُلِّ حَدَبٍ يَنسِلُونَ (٩٦) وَٱقْتَرَبَ ٱلْوَعْدُ ٱلْحَقُّ فَإِذَا هِىَ شَـٰخِصَةٌ أَبْصَـٰرُ ٱلَّذِينَ كَفَرُوا۟ يَـٰوَيْلَنَا قَدْ كُنَّا فِى غَفْلَةٍ مِّنْ هَـٰذَا بَلْ كُنَّا ظَـٰلِمِينَ (٩٧) إِنَّكُمْ وَمَا تَعْبُدُونَ مِن دُونِ ٱللَّهِ حَصَبُ جَهَنَّمَ أَنتُمْ لَهَا وَٰرِدُونَ (٩٨) لَوْ كَانَ هَـٰٓؤُلَآءِ ءَالِهَةً مَّا وَرَدُوهَا ۖ وَكُلٌّ فِيهَا خَـٰلِدُونَ (٩٩) لَهُمْ فِيهَا زَفِيرٌ وَهُمْ فِيهَا لَا يَسْمَعُونَ (١٠٠) إِنَّ ٱلَّذِينَ سَبَقَتْ لَهُم مِّنَّا ٱلْحُسْنَىٰٓ أُو۟لَـٰٓئِكَ عَنْهَا مُبْعَدُونَ (١٠١) لَا يَسْمَعُونَ حَسِيسَهَا ۖ وَهُمْ فِى مَا ٱشْتَهَتْ أَنفُسُهُمْ خَـٰلِدُونَ (١٠٢) لَا يَحْزُنُهُمُ ٱلْفَزَعُ ٱلْأَكْبَرُ وَتَتَلَقَّـٰهُمُ ٱلْمَلَـٰٓئِكَةُ هَـٰذَا يَوْمُكُمُ ٱلَّذِى كُنتُمْ تُوعَدُونَ (١٠٣) يَوْمَ نَطْوِى ٱلسَّمَآءَ كَطَىِّ ٱلسِّجِلِّ لِلْكُتُبِ ۚ كَمَا بَدَأْنَآ أَوَّلَ خَلْقٍ نُّعِيدُهُ ۥ ۚ وَعْدًا عَلَيْنَآ ۚ إِنَّا كُنَّا فَـٰعِلِينَ (١٠٤) وَلَقَدْ

كَتَبْنَا فِى ٱلزَّبُورِ مِنۢ بَعْدِ ٱلذِّكْرِ أَنَّ ٱلْأَرْضَ يَرِثُهَا عِبَادِىَ ٱلصَّٰلِحُونَ (١٠٥)

*But they have broken up and differed as regards their religion among themselves. (And) they all shall return to Us. (93)So whoever does righteous good deeds while he is a believer (in the Oneness of Allâh Islâmic Monotheism), his efforts will not be rejected. Verily! We record it for him (in his Book of deeds). (94)And a ban is laid on every town (population) which We have destroyed that they shall not return (to this world again, nor repent to Us). (95)Until, when Ya'jûj and Ma'jûj (Gog and Magog) are let loose (from their barrier), and they swoop down from every mound. (96)And the true promise (Day of Resurrection) shall draw near (of fulfillment). Then (when mankind is resurrected from their graves), you shall see the eyes of the disbelievers fixedly staring in horror. (They will say): "Woe to us! We were indeed heedless of this; nay, but we were Zâlimûn (polytheists and wrong-doers)." (97)Certainly! You (disbelievers) and that which you are worshipping now besides Allâh, are (but) fuel for Hell! (Surely), you will enter it. (98)Had these (idols) been âlihah (gods), they would not have entered there (Hell), and all of them will abide therein. (99)Therein they will be breathing out with deep sighs and roaring, and therein they will hear not. (100)Verily those for whom the good has preceded from*

Us, they will be removed far therefrom (Hell) [e.g. 'Īsā (Jesus), son of Maryam (Mary); 'Uzair (Ezra)]. (101)They shall not hear the slightest sound of it (Hell), while they abide in that which their ownselves desire. (102)The greatest terror (on the Day of Resurrection) will not grieve them, and the angels will meet them, (with the greeting): "This is your Day which you were promised." (103)And (remember) the Day when We shall roll up the heaven like a scroll rolled up for books, As We began the first creation, We shall repeat it, (it is) a promise binding upon Us. Truly, We shall do it. (104) And indeed We have written in Az-Zabûr [i.e. all the revealed Holy Books - the Taurât (Torah), the Injeel, the Zabur, the Qur'ân] after (We have already written in) Al-Lauh Al-Mahfûz (the Book, that is in the heaven with Allâh), that My righteous slaves shall inherit the land (i.e. the land of Paradise). (105)

## Quran 22:1-2

يَـٰٓأَيُّهَا ٱلنَّاسُ ٱتَّقُواْ رَبَّكُمْ إِنَّ زَلْزَلَةَ ٱلسَّاعَةِ شَىْءٌ عَظِيمٌ (١) يَوْمَ تَرَوْنَهَا تَذْهَلُ كُلُّ مُرْضِعَةٍ عَمَّآ أَرْضَعَتْ وَتَضَعُ كُلُّ ذَاتِ حَمْلٍ حَمْلَهَا وَتَرَى ٱلنَّاسَ سُكَـٰرَىٰ وَمَا هُم بِسُكَـٰرَىٰ وَلَـٰكِنَّ عَذَابَ ٱللَّهِ شَدِيدٌ (٢)

O mankind! Fear your Lord and be dutiful to Him! Verily, the earthquake of the Hour (of Judgement) is a terrible thing. (1)The Day you shall see it, every nursing *mother will forget her nursling, and every pregnant one will drop her load, and you shall see mankind as in a drunken state, yet they will not be drunken, but severe will be the Torment of Allâh. (2)*

## Quran 22:4-7

كُتِبَ عَلَيْهِ أَنَّهُ مَن تَوَلَّاهُ فَأَنَّهُ يُضِلُّهُ وَيَهْدِيهِ إِلَىٰ عَذَابِ ٱلسَّعِيرِ (٤) يَـٰٓأَيُّهَا ٱلنَّاسُ إِن كُنتُمْ فِى رَيْبٍ مِّنَ ٱلْبَعْثِ فَإِنَّا خَلَقْنَـٰكُم مِّن تُرَابٍ ثُمَّ مِن نُّطْفَةٍ ثُمَّ مِنْ عَلَقَةٍ ثُمَّ مِن مُّضْغَةٍ مُّخَلَّقَةٍ وَغَيْرِ مُخَلَّقَةٍ لِّنُبَيِّنَ لَكُمْ وَنُقِرُّ فِى ٱلْأَرْحَامِ مَا نَشَاءُ إِلَىٰ أَجَلٍ مُّسَمًّى ثُمَّ نُخْرِجُكُمْ طِفْلاً ثُمَّ لِتَبْلُغُوٓاْ أَشُدَّكُمْ وَمِنكُم مَّن يُتَوَفَّىٰ وَمِنكُم مَّن يُرَدُّ إِلَىٰٓ أَرْذَلِ ٱلْعُمُرِ لِكَيْلَا يَعْلَمَ مِنْ بَعْدِ عِلْمٍ شَيْئاً وَتَرَى ٱلْأَرْضَ هَامِدَةً فَإِذَآ أَنزَلْنَا عَلَيْهَا ٱلْمَآءَ ٱهْتَزَّتْ وَرَبَتْ وَأَنۢبَتَتْ مِن كُلِّ زَوْجٍ بَهِيجٍ (٥) ذَٰلِكَ بِأَنَّ ٱللَّهَ هُوَ ٱلْحَقُّ وَأَنَّهُ يُحْىِ ٱلْمَوْتَىٰ وَأَنَّهُ عَلَىٰ كُلِّ شَىْءٍ قَدِيرٌ (٦) وَأَنَّ ٱلسَّاعَةَ ءَاتِيَةٌ لَّا رَيْبَ فِيهَا وَأَنَّ ٱللَّهَ يَبْعَثُ مَن فِى ٱلْقُبُورِ (٧)

*For him (the devil) it is decreed that whosoever follows him, he will mislead him, and will drive him to the torment of the Fire. (4)O mankind! If you are in doubt about the Resurrection, then verily! We have created you (i.e. Adam) from dust, then from a Nutfah (mixed drops of male and female sexual discharge i.e. offspring of Adam), then from a clot (a piece of thick coagulated*

blood) then from a little lump of flesh, — some formed
and some unformed (as in the case of miscarriage), that
We may make (it) clear to you (i.e. to show you Our
Power and Ability to do what We will). And We cause
whom We will to remain in the wombs for an appointed
term, then We bring you out as infants, then (give you
growth) that you may reach your age of full strength.
And among you there is he who dies (young), and among
you there is he who is brought back to the miserable old
age, so that he knows nothing after having known. And
you see the earth barren, but when We send down water
(rain) on it, it is stirred (to life), it swells and puts forth
every lovely kind (of growth). (5)That is because Allâh,
He is the Truth, and it is He Who gives life to the dead,
and it is He Who is Able to do all things. (6)And surely,
the Hour is coming, there is no doubt about it, and
certainly, Allâh will resurrect those who are in the
graves. (7)

## Quran 22:8-9

وَمِنَ ٱلنَّاسِ مَن يُجَٰدِلُ فِى ٱللَّهِ بِغَيْرِ عِلْمٍ وَلَا هُدًى وَلَا كِتَٰبٍ
مُّنِيرٍ (٨) ثَانِىَ عِطْفِهِ لِيُضِلَّ عَن سَبِيلِ ٱللَّهِ ۖ لَهُۥ فِى ٱلدُّنْيَا
خِزْىٌ ۖ وَنُذِيقُهُۥ يَوْمَ ٱلْقِيَٰمَةِ عَذَابَ ٱلْحَرِيقِ (٩)

And among men is he who disputes about Allâh, without
knowledge or guidance, or a Book giving light (from
Allâh), (8)Bending his neck in pride (far astray from the

Path of Allâh), and leading (others) too (far) astray from the Path of Allâh. For him there is disgrace in this worldly life, and on the Day of Resurrection We shall make him taste the torment of burning (Fire). (9)

## Quran 22:11

وَمِنَ ٱلنَّاسِ مَن يَعْبُدُ ٱللَّهَ عَلَىٰ حَرْفٍ فَإِنْ أَصَابَهُۥ خَيْرٌ ٱطْمَأَنَّ بِهِۦ وَإِنْ أَصَابَتْهُ فِتْنَةٌ ٱنقَلَبَ عَلَىٰ وَجْهِهِۦ خَسِرَ ٱلدُّنْيَا وَٱلْءَاخِرَةَ ذَٰلِكَ هُوَ ٱلْخُسْرَانُ ٱلْمُبِينُ

And among mankind is he who worships Allâh as it were, upon the edge (i.e. in doubt); if good befalls him, he is content therewith; but if a trial befalls him, he turns back on his face (i.e. reverts back to disbelief after embracing Islâm). He loses both this world and the Hereafter. That is the evident loss. (11)

## Quran 22:14-15

إِنَّ ٱللَّهَ يُدْخِلُ ٱلَّذِينَ ءَامَنُوا۟ وَعَمِلُوا۟ ٱلصَّـٰلِحَـٰتِ جَنَّـٰتٍ تَجْرِى مِن تَحْتِهَا ٱلْأَنْهَـٰرُ إِنَّ ٱللَّهَ يَفْعَلُ مَا يُرِيدُ (١٤) مَن كَانَ يَظُنُّ أَن لَّن يَنصُرَهُ ٱللَّهُ فِى ٱلدُّنْيَا وَٱلْءَاخِرَةِ فَلْيَمْدُدْ بِسَبَبٍ إِلَى ٱلسَّمَآءِ ثُمَّ لْيَقْطَعْ فَلْيَنظُرْ هَلْ يُذْهِبَنَّ كَيْدُهُۥ مَا يَغِيظُ (١٥)

Truly, Allâh will admit those who believe (in Islâmic Monotheism) and do righteous good deeds (according to the Qur'ân and the Sunnah) to Gardens underneath which rivers flow (in Paradise). Verily, Allâh does what

*He wills. (14)Whoever thinks that Allâh will not help him (Muhammad) in this world and in the Hereafter, let him stretch out a rope to the ceiling and let him strangle himself. Then let him see whether his plan will remove that whereat he rages! (15)*

## Quran 22:17-25

إِنَّ ٱلَّذِينَ ءَامَنُوا۟ وَٱلَّذِينَ هَادُوا۟ وَٱلصَّٰبِـِٔينَ وَٱلنَّصَٰرَىٰ وَٱلْمَجُوسَ وَٱلَّذِينَ أَشْرَكُوٓا۟ إِنَّ ٱللَّهَ يَفْصِلُ بَيْنَهُمْ يَوْمَ ٱلْقِيَٰمَةِ إِنَّ ٱللَّهَ عَلَىٰ كُلِّ شَىْءٍ شَهِيدٌ (١٧) أَلَمْ تَرَ أَنَّ ٱللَّهَ يَسْجُدُ لَهُۥ مَن فِى ٱلسَّمَٰوَٰتِ وَمَن فِى ٱلْأَرْضِ وَٱلشَّمْسُ وَٱلْقَمَرُ وَٱلنُّجُومُ وَٱلْجِبَالُ وَٱلشَّجَرُ وَٱلدَّوَآبُّ وَكَثِيرٌ مِّنَ ٱلنَّاسِ وَكَثِيرٌ حَقَّ عَلَيْهِ ٱلْعَذَابُ وَمَن يُهِنِ ٱللَّهُ فَمَا لَهُۥ مِن مُّكْرِمٍ إِنَّ ٱللَّهَ يَفْعَلُ مَا يَشَآءُ ۩ (١٨) ۞ هَٰذَانِ خَصْمَانِ ٱخْتَصَمُوا۟ فِى رَبِّهِمْ فَٱلَّذِينَ كَفَرُوا۟ قُطِّعَتْ لَهُمْ ثِيَابٌ مِّن نَّارٍ يُصَبُّ مِن فَوْقِ رُءُوسِهِمُ ٱلْحَمِيمُ (١٩) يُصْهَرُ بِهِۦ مَا فِى بُطُونِهِمْ وَٱلْجُلُودُ (٢٠) وَلَهُم مَّقَٰمِعُ مِنْ حَدِيدٍ (٢١) كُلَّمَآ أَرَادُوٓا۟ أَن يَخْرُجُوا۟ مِنْهَا مِنْ غَمٍّ أُعِيدُوا۟ فِيهَا وَذُوقُوا۟ عَذَابَ ٱلْحَرِيقِ (٢٢) إِنَّ ٱللَّهَ يُدْخِلُ ٱلَّذِينَ ءَامَنُوا۟ وَعَمِلُوا۟ ٱلصَّٰلِحَٰتِ جَنَّٰتٍ تَجْرِى مِن تَحْتِهَا ٱلْأَنْهَٰرُ يُحَلَّوْنَ فِيهَا مِنْ أَسَاوِرَ مِن ذَهَبٍ وَلُؤْلُؤًا وَلِبَاسُهُمْ فِيهَا حَرِيرٌ (٢٣) وَهُدُوٓا۟ إِلَى ٱلطَّيِّبِ مِنَ ٱلْقَوْلِ وَهُدُوٓا۟ إِلَىٰ صِرَٰطِ ٱلْحَمِيدِ (٢٤) إِنَّ ٱلَّذِينَ كَفَرُوا۟ وَيَصُدُّونَ عَن سَبِيلِ ٱللَّهِ وَٱلْمَسْجِدِ ٱلْحَرَامِ ٱلَّذِى جَعَلْنَٰهُ لِلنَّاسِ

سَوَآءً ٱلْعَـٰكِفُ فِيهِ وَٱلْبَادِ وَمَن يُرِدْ فِيهِ بِإِلْحَادٍ بِظُلْمٍ نُّذِقْهُ مِنْ عَذَابٍ أَلِيمٍ (٢٥)

*Verily, those who believe (in Allâh and in His Messenger Muhammad), and those who are Jews, and the Sabians, and the Christians, and the Majus, and those who worship others besides Allâh, truly, Allâh will judge between them on the Day of Resurrection. Verily! Allâh is Witness over all things awitness. (17)See you not that whoever is in the heavens and whoever is on the earth, and the sun, and the moon, and the stars, and the mountains, and the trees, and Ad-Dawâb moving (living creatures, beasts), and many of mankind prostrate themselves to Allah? But there are many (men) on whom the punishment is justified. And whomsoever Allâh disgraces, none can honour him. Verily! Allâh does what He wills. (18)These two opponents (believers and disbelievers) dispute with each other about their Lord; then as for those who disbelieved, garments of fire will be cut out for them, boiling water will be poured down over their heads. (19)With it will melt (or vanish away) what is within their bellies, as well as (their) skins. (20) And for them are hooked rods of iron (to punish them). (21)Every time they seek to get away therefrom, from anguish, they will be driven back therein, and (it will be) said to them: "Taste the torment of burning!" (22)Truly, Allâh will admit those who believe (in the Oneness of*

Allâh - Islâmic Monotheism) and do righteous good deeds, to Gardens underneath which rivers flow (in Paradise), wherein they will be adorned with bracelets of gold and pearls and their garments therein will be of silk. (23)And they are guided (in this world) unto goodly speech (i.e. Lâ ilâha ill-allâh, Alhamdu lillâh, recitation of the Qur'ân, etc.) and they are guided to the Path of Him (i.e. Allâh's religion of Islâmic Monotheism), Who is Worthy of all praises. (24)Verily! those who disbelieved and hinder (men) from the Path of Allâh, and from Al-Masjid-al-Harâm (at Makkah) which We have made (open) to (all) men, the dweller in it and the visitor from the country are equal there [as regards its sanctity and pilgrimage (Hajj and 'Umrah)]. And whoever inclines to evil actions therein or to do wrong (i.e. practise polytheism and leave Islâmic Monotheism), him We shall cause to taste from a painful torment. (25)

## Quran 22:27

وَأَذِّن فِى ٱلنَّاسِ بِٱلْحَجِّ يَأْتُوكَ رِجَالاً وَعَلَىٰ كُلِّ ضَامِرٍ يَأْتِينَ مِن كُلِّ فَجٍّ عَمِيقٍ

And proclaim to mankind the Hajj (pilgrimage). They will come to you on foot and on every lean camel, they will come from every deep and distant (wide) mountain highway (to perform Hajj). (27)

## Quran 22:38-41

۞ إِنَّ ٱللَّهَ يُدَٰفِعُ عَنِ ٱلَّذِينَ ءَامَنُوٓاْ إِنَّ ٱللَّهَ لَا يُحِبُّ كُلَّ خَوَّانٍ كَفُورٍ (٣٨) أُذِنَ لِلَّذِينَ يُقَٰتَلُونَ بِأَنَّهُمْ ظُلِمُوٓاْ وَإِنَّ ٱللَّهَ عَلَىٰ نَصْرِهِمْ لَقَدِيرٌ (٣٩) ٱلَّذِينَ أُخْرِجُواْ مِن دِيَٰرِهِم بِغَيْرِ حَقٍّ إِلَّآ أَن يَقُولُواْ رَبُّنَا ٱللَّهُ وَلَوْلَا دَفْعُ ٱللَّهِ ٱلنَّاسَ بَعْضَهُم بِبَعْضٍ لَّهُدِّمَتْ صَوَٰمِعُ وَبِيَعٌ وَصَلَوَٰتٌ وَمَسَٰجِدُ يُذْكَرُ فِيهَا ٱسْمُ ٱللَّهِ كَثِيرًا وَلَيَنصُرَنَّ ٱللَّهُ مَن يَنصُرُهُ إِنَّ ٱللَّهَ لَقَوِيٌّ عَزِيزٌ (٤٠) ٱلَّذِينَ إِن مَّكَّنَّٰهُمْ فِى ٱلْأَرْضِ أَقَامُواْ ٱلصَّلَوٰةَ وَءَاتَوُاْ ٱلزَّكَوٰةَ وَأَمَرُواْ بِٱلْمَعْرُوفِ وَنَهَوْاْ عَنِ ٱلْمُنكَرِ وَلِلَّهِ عَٰقِبَةُ ٱلْأُمُورِ (٤١)

*Truly, Allâh defends those who believe. Verily! Allâh likes not any treacherous ingrate to Allâh [those who disobey Allâh but obey Shaitân (Satan)]. (38)Permission to fight is (against disbelievers) is given to those (believers), who are fought against, because they (believers) have been wronged, and surely, Allâh is Able to give them victory. (39)Those who have been expelled from their homes unjustly only because they said: "Our Lord is Allâh." - For had it not been that Allâh checks one set of people by means of another, monasteries, churches, synagogues, and mosques, wherein the Name of Allâh is mentioned much would surely have been pulled down. Verily, Allâh will help those who help His (Cause). Truly, Allâh is All-Strong, All-Mighty. (40)Those (Muslim rulers) who, if We give them power in the land, (they) enjoin Iqamat-as-Salât. [i.e. to perform*

the five compulsory congregational Salât (prayers)], to
pay the Zakât and they enjoin Al-Ma'rûf (i.e. Islâmic
Monotheism and all that Islâm orders one to do), and
forbid Al-Munkar (i.e. disbelief, polytheism and all that
Islâm has forbidden) [i.e. they make the Qur'ân and
Sunnah the law of their country in all the spheres of life].
And with Allâh rests the end of (all) matters. (41)

## Quran 22:47

وَيَسْتَعْجِلُونَكَ بِٱلْعَذَابِ وَلَن يُخْلِفَ ٱللَّهُ وَعْدَهُۥ ۚ وَإِنَّ يَوْمًا
عِندَ رَبِّكَ كَأَلْفِ سَنَةٍ مِّمَّا تَعُدُّونَ

And they ask you to hasten on the torment! And Allâh
fails not His Promise. And verily, a day with your Lord
is as a thousand years of what you reckon. (47)

## Quran 22:51-60

وَٱلَّذِينَ سَعَوْاْ فِىٓ ءَايَٰتِنَا مُعَٰجِزِينَ أُوْلَٰٓئِكَ أَصْحَٰبُ ٱلْجَحِيمِ
(٥١) وَمَآ أَرْسَلْنَا مِن قَبْلِكَ مِن رَّسُولٍ وَلَا نَبِىٍّ إِلَّآ إِذَا تَمَنَّىٰٓ
أَلْقَى ٱلشَّيْطَٰنُ فِىٓ أُمْنِيَّتِهِۦ فَيَنسَخُ ٱللَّهُ مَا يُلْقِى ٱلشَّيْطَٰنُ ثُمَّ
يُحْكِمُ ٱللَّهُ ءَايَٰتِهِۦ ۗ وَٱللَّهُ عَلِيمٌ حَكِيمٌ (٥٢) لِّيَجْعَلَ مَا يُلْقِى
ٱلشَّيْطَٰنُ فِتْنَةً لِّلَّذِينَ فِى قُلُوبِهِم مَّرَضٌ وَٱلْقَاسِيَةِ قُلُوبُهُمْ ۗ وَإِنَّ
ٱلظَّٰلِمِينَ لَفِى شِقَاقٍ بَعِيدٍ (٥٣) وَلِيَعْلَمَ ٱلَّذِينَ أُوتُواْ ٱلْعِلْمَ أَنَّهُ
ٱلْحَقُّ مِن رَّبِّكَ فَيُؤْمِنُواْ بِهِۦ فَتُخْبِتَ لَهُۥ قُلُوبُهُمْ ۗ وَإِنَّ ٱللَّهَ لَهَادِ
ٱلَّذِينَ ءَامَنُوٓاْ إِلَىٰ صِرَٰطٍ مُّسْتَقِيمٍ (٥٤) وَلَا يَزَالُ ٱلَّذِينَ

كَفَرُواْ فِى مِرْيَةٍ مِّنْهُ حَتَّىٰ تَأْتِيَهُمُ ٱلسَّاعَةُ بَغْتَةً أَوْ يَأْتِيَهُمْ

عَذَابُ يَوْمٍ عَقِيمٍ (٥٥) ٱلْمُلْكُ يَوْمَئِذٍ لِّلَّهِ يَحْكُمُ بَيْنَهُمْ فَٱلَّذِينَ

ءَامَنُواْ وَعَمِلُواْ ٱلصَّٰلِحَٰتِ فِى جَنَّٰتِ ٱلنَّعِيمِ (٥٦) وَٱلَّذِينَ

كَفَرُواْ وَكَذَّبُواْ بِـَٔايَٰتِنَا فَأُوْلَٰٓئِكَ لَهُمْ عَذَابٌ مُّهِينٌ

(٥٧) وَٱلَّذِينَ هَاجَرُواْ فِى سَبِيلِ ٱللَّهِ ثُمَّ قُتِلُوٓاْ أَوْ مَاتُواْ

لَيَرْزُقَنَّهُمُ ٱللَّهُ رِزْقًا حَسَنًا وَإِنَّ ٱللَّهَ لَهُوَ خَيْرُ ٱلرَّٰزِقِينَ

(٥٨) لَيُدْخِلَنَّهُم مُّدْخَلًا يَرْضَوْنَهُ وَإِنَّ ٱللَّهَ لَعَلِيمٌ حَلِيمٌ

(٥٩) ۞ ذَٰلِكَ وَمَنْ عَاقَبَ بِمِثْلِ مَا عُوقِبَ بِهِ ثُمَّ بُغِىَ عَلَيْهِ

لَيَنصُرَنَّهُ ٱللَّهُ إِنَّ ٱللَّهَ لَعَفُوٌّ غَفُورٌ (٦٠)

*But those who strive against Our Ayât (proofs,*
*evidences, verses, lessons, signs, revelations, etc.), to*
*frustrate them, they will be dwellers of the Hell-fire.*
*(51)Never did We send a Messenger or a Prophet before*
*you, but; when he did recite the revelation or narrated or*
*spoke, Shaitân (Satan) threw (some falsehood) in it. But*
*Allâh abolishes that which Shaitân (Satan) throws in.*
*Then Allâh establishes His Revelations. And Allâh is*
*All-Knower, All-Wise: (52)That He (Allâh) may make*
*what is thrown in by Shaitân (Satan) a trial for those in*
*whose hearts is a disease (of hypocrisy and disbelief) and*
*whose hearts are hardened. And certainly, the Zalimûn*
*(polytheists and wrong-doers) are in an opposition far-off*
*(from the truth against Allâh's Messenger and the*
*believers). (53)And that those who have been given*
*knowledge may know that it (this Qur'ân) is the truth*

*from your Lord, so that they may believe therein, and their hearts may submit to it with humility. And verily, Allâh is the Guide of those who believe, to the Straight Path. (54)And those who disbelieved will not cease to be in doubt about it (this Qur'ân) until the Hour comes suddenly upon them, or there comes to them the torment of the Day after which there will be no night (i.e. the Day of Resurrection). (55)The sovereignty on that Day will be that of Allâh (the one Who has no partners). He will judge between them. So those who believed (in the Oneness of Allâh Islâmic Monotheism) and did righteous good deeds will be in Gardens of delight (Paradise). (56) And those who disbelieved and belied Our Verses (of this Qur'ân), for them will be a humiliating torment (in Hell). (57)Those who emigrated in the Cause of Allâh and after that were killed or died, surely, Allâh will provide a good provision for them. And verily, it is Allâh Who indeed is the Best of those who make provision. (58)Truly, He will make them enter an entrance with which they shall be well-pleased, and verily, Allâh indeed is All-Knowing, Most Forbearing. (59)That is so. And whoever has retaliated with the like of that which he was made to suffer, and then has again been wronged, Allâh will surely help him. Verily! Allâh indeed is Oft-Pardoning, Oft-Forgiving. (60)*

**Quran 22:66**

وَهُوَ ٱلَّذِىٓ أَحْيَاكُمْ ثُمَّ يُمِيتُكُمْ ثُمَّ يُحْيِيكُمْ إِنَّ ٱلْإِنسَـٰنَ لَكَفُورٌ

*It is He, Who gave you life, and then will cause you to die, and will again give you life (on the Day of Resurrection). Verily! man is indeed an ingrate. (66)*

## Quran 22:69

ٱللَّهُ يَحْكُمُ بَيْنَكُمْ يَوْمَ ٱلْقِيَـٰمَةِ فِيمَا كُنتُمْ فِيهِ تَخْتَلِفُونَ

*"Allâh will judge between you on the Day of Resurrection about that wherein you used to differ." (69)*

## Quran 22:71-72

وَيَعْبُدُونَ مِن دُونِ ٱللَّهِ مَا لَمْ يُنَزِّلْ بِهِ سُلْطَـٰنًا وَمَا لَيْسَ لَهُم بِهِۦ عِلْمٌ وَمَا لِلظَّـٰلِمِينَ مِن نَّصِيرٍ ( ٧١ ) وَإِذَا تُتْلَىٰ عَلَيْهِمْ ءَايَـٰتُنَا بَيِّنَـٰتٍ تَعْرِفُ فِى وُجُوهِ ٱلَّذِينَ كَفَرُواْ ٱلْمُنكَرَ يَكَادُونَ يَسْطُونَ بِٱلَّذِينَ يَتْلُونَ عَلَيْهِمْ ءَايَـٰتِنَا قُلْ أَفَأُنَبِّئُكُم بِشَرٍّ مِّن ذَٰلِكُمُ ٱلنَّارُ وَعَدَهَا ٱللَّهُ ٱلَّذِينَ كَفَرُواْ وَبِئْسَ ٱلْمَصِيرُ ( ٧٢ )

*And they worship besides Allâh others for which He has sent down no authority, and of which they have no knowledge and for the Zâlimûn (wrong-doers, polytheists and disbelievers in the Oneness of Allâh) there is no helper. (71)And when Our Clear Verses are recited to them, you will notice a denial on the faces of the disbelievers! They are nearly ready to attack with violence those who recite Our Verses to them. Say: "Shall*

I tell you of something worse than that? The Fire (of Hell) which Allâh has promised to those who disbelieved, and worst indeed is that destination!" (72)

## Quran 23:1-11

قَدْ أَفْلَحَ ٱلْمُؤْمِنُونَ (١) ٱلَّذِينَ هُمْ فِى صَلَاتِهِمْ خَـٰشِعُونَ (٢) وَٱلَّذِينَ هُمْ عَنِ ٱللَّغْوِ مُعْرِضُونَ (٣) وَٱلَّذِينَ هُمْ لِلزَّكَوٰةِ فَـٰعِلُونَ (٤) وَٱلَّذِينَ هُمْ لِفُرُوجِهِمْ حَـٰفِظُونَ (٥) إِلَّا عَلَىٰ أَزْوَٰجِهِمْ أَوْ مَا مَلَكَتْ أَيْمَـٰنُهُمْ فَإِنَّهُمْ غَيْرُ مَلُومِينَ (٦) فَمَنِ ٱبْتَغَىٰ وَرَآءَ ذَٰلِكَ فَأُوْلَـٰئِكَ هُمُ ٱلْعَادُونَ (٧) وَٱلَّذِينَ هُمْ لِأَمَـٰنَـٰتِهِمْ وَعَهْدِهِمْ رَٰعُونَ (٨) وَٱلَّذِينَ هُمْ عَلَىٰ صَلَوَٰتِهِمْ يُحَافِظُونَ (٩) أُوْلَـٰئِكَ هُمُ ٱلْوَٰرِثُونَ (١٠) ٱلَّذِينَ يَرِثُونَ ٱلْفِرْدَوْسَ هُمْ فِيهَا خَـٰلِدُونَ (١١)

Successful indeed are the believers. (1) Those who offer their Salât (prayers) with all solemnity and full submissiveness. (2) And those who turn away from Al-Laghw (dirty, false, evil vain talk, falsehood, and all that Allâh has forbidden). (3) And those who pay the Zakât. (4) And those who guard their chastity (i.e. private parts, from illegal sexual acts). (5) Except from their wives or (slaves) that their right hands possess, - for then, they are free from blame; (6) But whoever seeks beyond that, then those are the transgressors; (7) Those who are faithfully true to their Amanât (all the duties which Allâh has ordained, honesty, moral responsibility and trusts) and

to their covenants; (8) And those who strictly guard their
(five compulsory congregational) Salawât (prayers) (at
their fixed stated hours). (9) These are indeed the
inheritors. (10) Who shall inherit the Firdaus (Paradise).
They shall dwell therein forever. (11)

## Quran 23:15-16

ثُمَّ إِنَّكُم بَعْدَ ذَٰلِكَ لَمَيِّتُونَ (١٥) ثُمَّ إِنَّكُمْ يَوْمَ ٱلْقِيَٰمَةِ تُبْعَثُونَ
(١٦)

After that, surely, you will die. (15) Then (again), surely,
you will be resurrected on the Day of Resurrection. (16)

## Quran 23:33-40

وَقَالَ ٱلْمَلَأُ مِن قَوْمِهِ ٱلَّذِينَ كَفَرُوا۟ وَكَذَّبُوا۟ بِلِقَآءِ ٱلْأَخِرَةِ
وَأَتْرَفْنَٰهُمْ فِى ٱلْحَيَوٰةِ ٱلدُّنْيَا مَا هَٰذَآ إِلَّا بَشَرٌ مِّثْلُكُمْ يَأْكُلُ مِمَّا
تَأْكُلُونَ مِنْهُ وَيَشْرَبُ مِمَّا تَشْرَبُونَ (٣٣) وَلَئِنْ أَطَعْتُم بَشَرًا
مِّثْلَكُمْ إِنَّكُمْ إِذًا لَّخَٰسِرُونَ (٣٤) أَيَعِدُكُمْ أَنَّكُمْ إِذَا مِتُّمْ وَكُنتُمْ
تُرَابًا وَعِظَٰمًا أَنَّكُم مُّخْرَجُونَ (٣٥) ۞ هَيْهَاتَ هَيْهَاتَ لِمَا
تُوعَدُونَ (٣٦) إِنْ هِىَ إِلَّا حَيَاتُنَا ٱلدُّنْيَا نَمُوتُ وَنَحْيَا وَمَا
نَحْنُ بِمَبْعُوثِينَ (٣٧) إِنْ هُوَ إِلَّا رَجُلٌ ٱفْتَرَىٰ عَلَى ٱللَّهِ كَذِبًا
وَمَا نَحْنُ لَهُۥ بِمُؤْمِنِينَ (٣٨) قَالَ رَبِّ ٱنصُرْنِى بِمَا كَذَّبُونِ
(٣٩) قَالَ عَمَّا قَلِيلٍ لَّيُصْبِحُنَّ نَٰدِمِينَ (٤٠)

And the chiefs of his people, who disbelieved and denied
the Meeting in the Hereafter, and whom We had given

the luxuries and comforts of this life, said: "He is no more than a human being like you, he eats of that which you eat, and drinks of what you drink (33) "If you were to obey a human being like yourselves, then verily! You indeed would be losers. (34) "Does he promise you that when you have died and have become dust and bones, you shall come out alive (resurrected)? (35) "Far, very far is that which you are promised! (36) "There is nothing but our life of this world! We die and we live! And we are not going to be resurrected! (37) "He is only a man who has invented a lie against Allâh, and we are not going to believe in him." (38) He said: "O my Lord! Help me because they deny me." (39) (Allâh) said: "In a little while, they are sure to be regretful." (40)

## Quran 23:43

مَا تَسْبِقُ مِنْ أُمَّةٍ أَجَلَهَا وَمَا يَسْتَـٔخِرُونَ

No nation can advance their term, nor can they delay it.

## Quran 23:55-56

أَيَحْسَبُونَ أَنَّمَا نُمِدُّهُم بِهِۦ مِن مَّالٍ وَبَنِينَ (٥٥) نُسَارِعُ لَهُمْ فِى ٱلْخَيْرَٰتِ بَل لَّا يَشْعُرُونَ (٥٦)

Do they think that in wealth and children with which We enlarge them (55) We hasten unto them with good things (Nay it is Fitnah (trial) in this worldly life so that they

*will have no share of good things in the Hereafter)? but*
*they perceive not.  (56)*

## Quran 23:63-66

بَلْ قُلُوبُهُمْ فِى غَمْرَةٍ مِّنْ هَـٰذَا وَلَهُمْ أَعْمَـٰلٌ مِّن دُونِ ذَٰلِكَ هُمْ
لَهَا عَـٰمِلُونَ (٦٣) حَتَّىٰٓ إِذَآ أَخَذْنَا مُتْرَفِيهِم بِٱلْعَذَابِ إِذَا هُمْ
يَجْـَٔرُونَ (٦٤) لَا تَجْـَٔرُوا۟ ٱلْيَوْمَ ۖ إِنَّكُم مِّنَّا لَا تُنصَرُونَ
(٦٥) قَدْ كَانَتْ ءَايَـٰتِى تُتْلَىٰ عَلَيْكُمْ فَكُنتُمْ عَلَىٰٓ أَعْقَـٰبِكُمْ
تَنكِصُونَ (٦٦)

*Nay, but their hearts are covered from (understanding)*
*this (the Qur'ân), and they have other (evil) deeds,*
*besides, which they are doing. (63) Until, when We seize*
*those of them who lead a luxurious life with punishment,*
*behold! they make humble invocation with a loud voice.*
*(64) Invoke not loudly this day! Certainly, you shall not*
*be helped by Us. (65) Indeed My Verses used to be recited*
*to you, but you used to turn back on your heels (denying*
*them, and refusing with hatred to listen to them). (66)*

## Quran 23:79-83

وَهُوَ ٱلَّذِى ذَرَأَكُمْ فِى ٱلْأَرْضِ وَإِلَيْهِ تُحْشَرُونَ (٧٩) وَهُوَ
ٱلَّذِى يُحْىِۦ وَيُمِيتُ وَلَهُ ٱخْتِلَـٰفُ ٱلَّيْلِ وَٱلنَّهَارِ ۚ أَفَلَا تَعْقِلُونَ
(٨٠) بَلْ قَالُوا۟ مِثْلَ مَا قَالَ ٱلْأَوَّلُونَ (٨١) قَالُوٓا۟ أَءِذَا مِتْنَا
وَكُنَّا تُرَابًا وَعِظَـٰمًا أَءِنَّا لَمَبْعُوثُونَ (٨٢) لَقَدْ وُعِدْنَا نَحْنُ
وَءَابَآؤُنَا هَـٰذَا مِن قَبْلُ إِنْ هَـٰذَآ إِلَّآ أَسَـٰطِيرُ ٱلْأَوَّلِينَ (٨٣)

And it is He Who has created you on the earth, and to Him you shall be gathered back. (79) And it is He Who gives life and causes death, and His is the alternation of night and day. Will you not then understand? (80) Nay, but they say the like of what the men of old said. (81) They said: "When we are dead and have become dust and bones, shall we be resurrected indeed? (82) "Verily, this we have been promised, - we and our fathers before (us)! This is only the tales of the ancients!" (83)

## Quran 23:99-115

حَتَّىٰ إِذَا جَاءَ أَحَدَهُمُ ٱلْمَوْتُ قَالَ رَبِّ ٱرْجِعُونِ (٩٩) لَعَلِّىٓ
أَعْمَلُ صَٰلِحًا فِيمَا تَرَكْتُ كَلَّآ إِنَّهَا كَلِمَةٌ هُوَ قَآئِلُهَا وَمِن
وَرَآئِهِم بَرْزَخٌ إِلَىٰ يَوْمِ يُبْعَثُونَ (١٠٠) فَإِذَا نُفِخَ فِى ٱلصُّورِ
فَلَآ أَنسَابَ بَيْنَهُمْ يَوْمَئِذٍ وَلَا يَتَسَآءَلُونَ (١٠١) فَمَن ثَقُلَتْ
مَوَٰزِينُهُ فَأُوْلَٰٓئِكَ هُمُ ٱلْمُفْلِحُونَ (١٠٢) وَمَنْ خَفَّتْ مَوَٰزِينُهُ
فَأُوْلَٰٓئِكَ ٱلَّذِينَ خَسِرُوٓا أَنفُسَهُمْ فِى جَهَنَّمَ خَٰلِدُونَ (١٠٣) تَلْفَحُ
وُجُوهَهُمُ ٱلنَّارُ وَهُمْ فِيهَا كَٰلِحُونَ (١٠٤) أَلَمْ تَكُنْ ءَايَٰتِى
تُتْلَىٰ عَلَيْكُمْ فَكُنتُم بِهَا تُكَذِّبُونَ (١٠٥) قَالُوا رَبَّنَا غَلَبَتْ عَلَيْنَا
شِقْوَتُنَا وَكُنَّا قَوْمًا ضَآلِّينَ (١٠٦) رَبَّنَآ أَخْرِجْنَا مِنْهَا فَإِنْ
عُدْنَا فَإِنَّا ظَٰلِمُونَ (١٠٧) قَالَ ٱخْسَـُٔوا فِيهَا وَلَا تُكَلِّمُونِ
(١٠٨) إِنَّهُ كَانَ فَرِيقٌ مِّنْ عِبَادِى يَقُولُونَ رَبَّنَآ ءَامَنَّا فَٱغْفِرْ
لَنَا وَٱرْحَمْنَا وَأَنتَ خَيْرُ ٱلرَّٰحِمِينَ (١٠٩) فَٱتَّخَذْتُمُوهُمْ
سِخْرِيًّا حَتَّىٰٓ أَنسَوْكُمْ ذِكْرِى وَكُنتُم مِّنْهُمْ تَضْحَكُونَ

إِنِّى جَزَيْتُهُمُ ٱلْيَوْمَ بِمَا صَبَرُوٓا۟ أَنَّهُمْ هُمُ ٱلْفَآئِزُونَ (١١٠) قَالَ كَمْ لَبِثْتُمْ فِى ٱلْأَرْضِ عَدَدَ سِنِينَ (١١١) قَالُوا۟ لَبِثْنَا يَوْمًا أَوْ بَعْضَ يَوْمٍ فَسْئَلِ ٱلْعَآدِّينَ (١١٣) قَالَ إِن لَّبِثْتُمْ إِلَّا قَلِيلًا ۖ لَّوْ أَنَّكُمْ كُنتُمْ تَعْلَمُونَ (١١٤) أَفَحَسِبْتُمْ أَنَّمَا خَلَقْنَٰكُمْ عَبَثًا وَأَنَّكُمْ إِلَيْنَا لَا تُرْجَعُونَ (١١٥)

Until, when death comes to one of them (those who join partners with Allâh), he says: "My Lord! Send me back, (99) "So that I may do good in that which I have left behind!" No! It is but a word that he speaks, and behind them is Barzakh (a barrier) until the Day when they will be resurrected. (100) Then, when the Trumpet is blown, there will be no kinship among them that Day, nor will they ask of one another. (101) Then, those whose scales (of good deeds) are heavy, - these, they are the successful. (102) And those whose scales (of good deeds) are light, they are those who lose their ownselves, in Hell will they abide. (103) The Fire will burn their faces, and therein they will grin, with displaced lips (disfigured).
(104) "Were not My Verses (this Qur'ân) recited to you, and then you used to deny them?" (105) They will say: "Our Lord! Our wretchedness overcame us, and we were (an) erring people. (106) "Our Lord! Bring us out of this; if ever we return (to evil), then indeed we shall be Zâlimûn: (polytheists, oppressors, unjust, and wrong-

doers)." (107) He (Allâh) will say: "Remain you in it with ignominy! And speak you not to Me!" (108) Verily! there was a party of My slaves, who used to say: "Our Lord! We believe, so forgive us, and have mercy on us, for You are the Best of all who show mercy!" (109) But you took them for a laughingstock, so much so that they made you forget My Remembrance while you used to laugh at them! (110) Verily! I have rewarded them this Day for their patience, they are indeed the ones that are successful. (111) He (Allâh) will say: "What number of years did you stay on earth?" (112) They will say: "We stayed a day or part of a day. Ask of those who keep account." (113) He (Allâh) will say: "You stayed not but a little, if you had only known! (114) "Did you think that We had created you in play (without any purpose), and that you would not be brought back to Us?" (115)

## Quran 23:117

وَمَن يَدْعُ مَعَ ٱللَّهِ إِلَٰهًا ءَاخَرَ لَا بُرْهَٰنَ لَهُۥ بِهِۦ فَإِنَّمَا حِسَابُهُۥ عِندَ رَبِّهِۦٓ إِنَّهُۥ لَا يُفْلِحُ ٱلْكَٰفِرُونَ

And whoever invokes (or worships), besides Allâh, any other ilâh (god), of whom he has no proof, then his reckoning is only with his Lord. Surely! Al-Kâfirûn (the disbelievers in Allâh and in the Oneness of Allâh, polytheists, pagans, idolaters) will not be successful (117)

## Quran 24:19

إِنَّ ٱلَّذِينَ يُحِبُّونَ أَن تَشِيعَ ٱلْفَٰحِشَةُ فِى ٱلَّذِينَ ءَامَنُوا۟ لَهُمْ عَذَابٌ أَلِيمٌ فِى ٱلدُّنْيَا وَٱلْءَاخِرَةِ ۚ وَٱللَّهُ يَعْلَمُ وَأَنتُمْ لَا تَعْلَمُونَ

*Verily, those who like that (the crime of) illegal sexual intercourse should be propagated among those who believe, they will have a painful torment in this world and in the Hereafter. And Allâh knows and you know not. (19)*

## Quran 24:21

يَٰٓأَيُّهَا ٱلَّذِينَ ءَامَنُوا۟ لَا تَتَّبِعُوا۟ خُطُوَٰتِ ٱلشَّيْطَٰنِ ۚ وَمَن يَتَّبِعْ خُطُوَٰتِ ٱلشَّيْطَٰنِ فَإِنَّهُۥ يَأْمُرُ بِٱلْفَحْشَآءِ وَٱلْمُنكَرِ ۚ وَلَوْلَا فَضْلُ ٱللَّهِ عَلَيْكُمْ وَرَحْمَتُهُۥ مَا زَكَىٰ مِنكُم مِّنْ أَحَدٍ أَبَدًا وَلَٰكِنَّ ٱللَّهَ يُزَكِّى مَن يَشَآءُ ۗ وَٱللَّهُ سَمِيعٌ عَلِيمٌ

*O you who believe! Follow not the footsteps of Shaitân (Satan). And whosoever follows the footsteps of Shaitân (Satan), then, verily he commands Al-Fahshâ' [i.e. to commit indecency (illegal sexual intercourse)], and Al-Munkar [disbelief and polytheism (i.e. to do evil and wicked deeds; and to speak or to do what is forbidden in Islâm)]. And had it not been for the Grace of Allâh and His Mercy on you, not one of you would ever have been pure from sins. But Allâh purifies (guides to Islâm) whom He wills, and Allâh is All-Hearer, All-Knower. (21)*

# Quran 23:28

إِنَّ ٱلَّذِينَ يَرْمُونَ ٱلْمُحْصَنَـٰتِ ٱلْغَـٰفِلَـٰتِ ٱلْمُؤْمِنَـٰتِ لُعِنُواْ فِى ٱلدُّنْيَا وَٱلْءَاخِرَةِ وَلَهُمْ عَذَابٌ عَظِيمٌ (٢٣) يَوْمَ تَشْهَدُ عَلَيْهِمْ أَلْسِنَتُهُمْ وَأَيْدِيهِمْ وَأَرْجُلُهُم بِمَا كَانُواْ يَعْمَلُونَ (٢٤) يَوْمَئِذٍ يُوَفِّيهِمُ ٱللَّهُ دِينَهُمُ ٱلْحَقَّ وَيَعْلَمُونَ أَنَّ ٱللَّهَ هُوَ ٱلْحَقُّ ٱلْمُبِينُ (٢٥) ٱلْخَبِيثَـٰتُ لِلْخَبِيثِينَ وَٱلْخَبِيثُونَ لِلْخَبِيثَـٰتِ وَٱلطَّيِّبَـٰتُ لِلطَّيِّبِينَ وَٱلطَّيِّبُونَ لِلطَّيِّبَـٰتِ أُوْلَـٰئِكَ مُبَرَّءُونَ مِمَّا يَقُولُونَ لَهُم مَّغْفِرَةٌ وَرِزْقٌ كَرِيمٌ (٢٦) يَـٰٓأَيُّهَا ٱلَّذِينَ ءَامَنُواْ لَا تَدْخُلُواْ بُيُوتًا غَيْرَ بُيُوتِكُمْ حَتَّىٰ تَسْتَأْنِسُواْ وَتُسَلِّمُواْ عَلَىٰٓ أَهْلِهَا ذَٰلِكُمْ خَيْرٌ لَّكُمْ لَعَلَّكُمْ تَذَكَّرُونَ (٢٧) فَإِن لَّمْ تَجِدُواْ فِيهَآ أَحَدًا فَلَا تَدْخُلُوهَا حَتَّىٰ يُؤْذَنَ لَكُمْ وَإِن قِيلَ لَكُمُ ٱرْجِعُواْ فَٱرْجِعُواْ هُوَ أَزْكَىٰ لَكُمْ وَٱللَّهُ بِمَا تَعْمَلُونَ عَلِيمٌ (٢٨)

*Verily, those who accuse chaste women, who never even think of anything touching their chastity and are good believers, — are cursed in this life and in the Hereafter, and for them will be a great torment, — (23) On the Day when their tongues, their hands, and their legs (or feet) will bear witness against them as to what they used to do. (24) On that Day Allâh will pay them the recompense of their deeds in full, and they will know that Allâh, He is the Manifest Truth. (25) Bad statements are for bad people (or bad women for bad men) and bad people for bad statements (or bad men for bad women). Good statements are for good people (or good women for good* men) and good people for good statements (or good men for good women), such (good people) are innocent of (every) bad statement which they say, for them is Forgiveness, and Rizqun Karîm (generous provision i.e.Paradise). (26) O you who believe! Enter not houses other than your own, until you have asked permission and greeted those in them, that is better for you, in order that you may remember. (27) And if you find no one therein, still, enter not until permission has been given. And if you are asked to go back, go back, for it is purer for you, and Allâh is All-Knower of what you do. (28)

## Quran 24:30

قُل لِّلْمُؤْمِنِينَ يَغُضُّوا مِنْ أَبْصَـٰرِهِمْ وَيَحْفَظُوا فُرُوجَهُمْ ذَٰلِكَ أَزْكَىٰ لَهُمْ إِنَّ ٱللَّهَ خَبِيرٌ بِمَا يَصْنَعُونَ

Tell the believing men to lower their gaze (from looking at forbidden things), and protect their private parts (from illegal sexual acts). That is purer for them. Verily, Allâh is All-Aware of what they do. (30)

## Quran 24:32-34

وَأَنكِحُوا ٱلْأَيَـٰمَىٰ مِنكُمْ وَٱلصَّـٰلِحِينَ مِنْ عِبَادِكُمْ وَإِمَآئِكُمْ إِن يَكُونُوا فُقَرَآءَ يُغْنِهِمُ ٱللَّهُ مِن فَضْلِهِ وَٱللَّهُ وَٰسِعٌ عَلِيمٌ (٣٢) وَلْيَسْتَعْفِفِ ٱلَّذِينَ لَا يَجِدُونَ نِكَاحًا حَتَّىٰ يُغْنِيَهُمُ ٱللَّهُ مِن فَضْلِهِ وَٱلَّذِينَ يَبْتَغُونَ ٱلْكِتَـٰبَ مِمَّا مَلَكَتْ أَيْمَـٰنُكُمْ فَكَاتِبُوهُمْ إِنْ

عَلِمْتُمْ فِيهِمْ خَيْرًا وَءَاتُوهُم مِّن مَّالِ اللَّهِ الَّذِىٓ ءَاتَىٰكُمْ وَلَا
تُكْرِهُوا۟ فَتَيَـٰتِكُمْ عَلَى الْبِغَآءِ إِنْ أَرَدْنَ تَحَصُّنًا لِّتَبْتَغُوا۟ عَرَضَ
الْحَيَوٰةِ الدُّنْيَا وَمَن يُكْرِههُنَّ فَإِنَّ اللَّهَ مِنۢ بَعْدِ إِكْرَٰهِهِنَّ غَفُورٌ
رَّحِيمٌ (٣٣) وَلَقَدْ أَنزَلْنَآ إِلَيْكُمْ ءَايَـٰتٍ مُّبَيِّنَـٰتٍ وَمَثَلًا مِّنَ الَّذِينَ
خَلَوْا۟ مِن قَبْلِكُمْ وَمَوْعِظَةً لِّلْمُتَّقِينَ (٣٤)

And marry those among you who are single (i.e. a man who has no wife and the woman who has no husband) and (also marry) the Sâlihûn (pious, fit and capable ones) of your (male) slaves and maid-servants (female slaves). If they be poor, Allâh will enrich them out of His Bounty. And Allâh is All-Suffecent for His creatures' needs, All-Knowing (about the state of the people). (32) And let those who find not the financial means for marriage keep themselves chaste, until Allâh enriches them of His Bounty. And such of your slaves as seek a writing (of emancipation), give them such writing, if you find that there is good and honesty in them. And give them something (yourselves) out of the wealth of Allâh which He has bestowed upon you. And force not your maids to prostitution, if they desire chastity, in order that you may make a gain in the (perishable) goods of this worldly life. But if anyone compels them (to prostitution), then after such compulsion, Allâh is Oft-Forgiving, Most Merciful (to those women, i.e. He will forgive them because they have been forced to do this evil act unwillingly). (33) And indeed We have sent down for you Ayât (proofs, evidences, verses, lessons, signs, revelations, etc.) that make things plain, and the example of those who passed away before you, and an admonition for those who are Al-Muttaqûn (the pious and righteous persons). (34)

## Quran 24:39-40

وَٱلَّذِينَ كَفَرُوٓاْ أَعْمَٰلُهُمْ كَسَرَابٍ بِقِيعَةٍ يَحْسَبُهُ ٱلظَّمْـَٔانُ مَآءً حَتَّىٰٓ إِذَا جَآءَهُۥ لَمْ يَجِدْهُ شَيْـًٔا وَوَجَدَ ٱللَّهَ عِندَهُۥ فَوَفَّىٰهُ حِسَابَهُۥ وَٱللَّهُ سَرِيعُ ٱلْحِسَابِ (٣٩) أَوْ كَظُلُمَٰتٍ فِى بَحْرٍ لُّجِّىٍّ يَغْشَىٰهُ مَوْجٌ مِّن فَوْقِهِۦ مَوْجٌ مِّن فَوْقِهِۦ سَحَابٌ ظُلُمَٰتٌ بَعْضُهَا فَوْقَ بَعْضٍ إِذَآ أَخْرَجَ يَدَهُۥ لَمْ يَكَدْ يَرَىٰهَا وَمَن لَّمْ يَجْعَلِ ٱللَّهُ لَهُۥ نُورًا فَمَا لَهُۥ مِن نُّورٍ (٤٠)

As for those who disbelieve, their deeds are like a mirage in a desert. The thirsty one thinks it to be water, until he comes up to it, he finds it to be nothing, but he finds Allâh with him, Who will pay him his due (Hell). And Allâh is Swift in taking account. (39) Or [the state of a disbeliever] is like the darkness in a vast deep sea, overwhelmed with waves topped by waves, topped by dark clouds, (layers of) darkness upon darkness: if a man stretches out his hand, he can hardly see it! And he for whom Allâh has not appointed light, for him there is no light. (40)

## Quran 24:46-47

لَّقَدْ أَنزَلْنَآ ءَايَٰتٍ مُّبَيِّنَٰتٍ وَٱللَّهُ يَهْدِى مَن يَشَآءُ إِلَىٰ صِرَٰطٍ مُّسْتَقِيمٍ (٤٦) وَيَقُولُونَ ءَامَنَّا بِٱللَّهِ وَبِٱلرَّسُولِ وَأَطَعْنَا ثُمَّ يَتَوَلَّىٰ فَرِيقٌ مِّنْهُم مِّنۢ بَعْدِ ذَٰلِكَ وَمَآ أُوْلَٰٓئِكَ بِٱلْمُؤْمِنِينَ (٤٧)

*We have indeed sent down (in this Qur'ân) manifest Ayât (proofs, evidences, verses, lessons, signs, revelations, lawful and unlawful things, and the set boundries of Islâmic religion, etc. that make things clear showing the Right Path of Allâh). And Allâh guides whom He wills to a Straight Path (i.e. to Allâh's religion of Islâmic Monotheism). (46) They (hypocrites) say: "We have believed in Allâh and in the Messenger (Muhammad), and we obey," then a party of them turn away thereafter, such are not believers. (47)*

## Quran 24:51-52

إِنَّمَا كَانَ قَوْلَ ٱلْمُؤْمِنِينَ إِذَا دُعُوٓاْ إِلَى ٱللَّهِ وَرَسُولِهِۦ لِيَحْكُمَ بَيْنَهُمْ أَن يَقُولُواْ سَمِعْنَا وَأَطَعْنَا وَأُوْلَٰٓئِكَ هُمُ ٱلْمُفْلِحُونَ (٥١) وَمَن يُطِعِ ٱللَّهَ وَرَسُولَهُۥ وَيَخْشَ ٱللَّهَ وَيَتَّقْهِ فَأُوْلَٰٓئِكَ هُمُ ٱلْفَآئِزُونَ (٥٢)

*The only saying of the faithful believers, when they are called to Allâh (His Words, the Qur'ân) and His Messenger, to judge between them, is that they say: "We hear and we obey." And such are the successful (who will live forever in Paradise). (51) And whosoever obeys Allâh* and His Messenger, fears Allâh, and keeps his duty (to Him), such are the successful. (52)

## Quran 24:54-55

قُلْ أَطِيعُواْ ٱللَّهَ وَأَطِيعُواْ ٱلرَّسُولَ ۖ فَإِن تَوَلَّوْاْ فَإِنَّمَا عَلَيْهِ مَا حُمِّلَ وَعَلَيْكُم مَّا حُمِّلْتُمْ ۖ وَإِن تُطِيعُوهُ تَهْتَدُواْ ۚ وَمَا عَلَى ٱلرَّسُولِ إِلَّا ٱلْبَلَٰغُ ٱلْمُبِينُ (٥٤) وَعَدَ ٱللَّهُ ٱلَّذِينَ ءَامَنُواْ مِنكُمْ وَعَمِلُواْ ٱلصَّٰلِحَٰتِ لَيَسْتَخْلِفَنَّهُمْ فِى ٱلْأَرْضِ كَمَا ٱسْتَخْلَفَ ٱلَّذِينَ مِن قَبْلِهِمْ وَلَيُمَكِّنَنَّ لَهُمْ دِينَهُمُ ٱلَّذِى ٱرْتَضَىٰ لَهُمْ وَلَيُبَدِّلَنَّهُم مِّنۢ بَعْدِ خَوْفِهِمْ أَمْنًا ۚ يَعْبُدُونَنِى لَا يُشْرِكُونَ بِى شَيْئًا ۚ وَمَن كَفَرَ بَعْدَ ذَٰلِكَ فَأُوْلَٰٓئِكَ هُمُ ٱلْفَٰسِقُونَ (٥٥)

Say: "Obey Allâh and obey the Messenger, but if you turn away, he (Messenger Muhammad) is only responsible for the duty placed on him (i.e. to convey Allâh's Message) and you for that placed on you. If you obey him, you shall be on the right guidance. The Messenger's duty is only to convey (the message) in a clear way (i.e. to preach in a plain way)." (54) Allâh has promised those among you who believe, and do righteous good deeds, that He will certainly grant them succession to (the present rulers) in the land, as He granted it to those before them, and that He will grant them the authority to practise their religion, which He has chosen for them (i.e. Islâm). And He will surely give them in exchange a safe security after their fear (provided) they (believers) worship Me and do not associate anything (in worship) with Me. But whoever disbelieves after this, they are the Fâsiqûn (rebellious, disobedient to Allâh). (55)

**Quran 24:57**

لَا تَحْسَبَنَّ ٱلَّذِينَ كَفَرُواْ مُعْجِزِينَ فِى ٱلْأَرْضِ وَمَأْوَىٰهُمُ ٱلنَّارُ وَلَبِئْسَ ٱلْمَصِيرُ

Consider not that the disbelievers can escape in the land. Their abode shall be the Fire,- and worst indeed is that destination. (57)

**Quran 24:62**

إِنَّمَا ٱلْمُؤْمِنُونَ ٱلَّذِينَ ءَامَنُواْ بِٱللَّهِ وَرَسُولِهِ وَإِذَا كَانُواْ مَعَهُ عَلَىٰ أَمْرٍ جَامِعٍ لَّمْ يَذْهَبُواْ حَتَّىٰ يَسْتَـْٔذِنُوهُ إِنَّ ٱلَّذِينَ يَسْتَـْٔذِنُونَكَ أُوْلَـٰئِكَ ٱلَّذِينَ يُؤْمِنُونَ بِٱللَّهِ وَرَسُولِهِ فَإِذَا ٱسْتَـْٔذَنُوكَ لِبَعْضِ شَأْنِهِمْ فَأْذَن لِّمَن شِئْتَ مِنْهُمْ وَٱسْتَغْفِرْ لَهُمُ ٱللَّهَ إِنَّ ٱللَّهَ غَفُورٌ رَّحِيمٌ

The true believers are only those, who believe in (the Oneness of) Allâh and His Messenger (Muhammad), and when they are with him on some common matter, they go not away until they have asked his permission. Verily! those who ask your permission, those are they who (really) believe in Allâh and His Messenger. So if they ask your permission for some affairs of theirs, give permission to whom you will of them, and ask Allâh for their forgiveness. Truly, Allâh is Oft-Forgiving, Most Merciful. (62)

## Quran 24:64

أَلَا إِنَّ لِلَّهِ مَا فِى ٱلسَّمَـٰوَٰتِ وَٱلْأَرْضِ ۖ قَدْ يَعْلَمُ مَآ أَنتُمْ عَلَيْهِ وَيَوْمَ يُرْجَعُونَ إِلَيْهِ فَيُنَبِّئُهُم بِمَا عَمِلُواْ ۗ وَٱللَّهُ بِكُلِّ شَىْءٍ عَلِيمٌ

Certainly, to Allâh belongs all that is in the heavens and the earth. Surely, He knows your condition and (He knows) the Day when they will be brought back to Him, then He will inform them of what they did. And Allâh is All-Knower of everything. (64)

## Quran 25:10-13

تَبَارَكَ ٱلَّذِىٓ إِن شَآءَ جَعَلَ لَكَ خَيْرًا مِّن ذَٰلِكَ جَنَّـٰتٍ تَجْرِى مِن تَحْتِهَا ٱلْأَنْهَـٰرُ وَيَجْعَل لَّكَ قُصُورًا (١٠) بَلْ كَذَّبُواْ بِٱلسَّاعَةِ ۖ وَأَعْتَدْنَا لِمَن كَذَّبَ بِٱلسَّاعَةِ سَعِيرًا (١١) إِذَا رَأَتْهُم مِّن مَّكَانٍ بَعِيدٍ سَمِعُواْ لَهَا تَغَيُّظًا وَزَفِيرًا (١٢) وَإِذَآ أُلْقُواْ مِنْهَا مَكَانًا ضَيِّقًا مُّقَرَّنِينَ دَعَوْاْ هُنَالِكَ ثُبُورًا (١٣)

Blessed is He Who, if He wills, will assign you better than (all) that, - Gardens under which rivers flow (Paradise) and will assign you palaces (i.e. in Paradise). (10) Nay, they deny the Hour (the Day of Resurrection), and for those who deny the Hour, We have prepared a

*flaming Fire (i.e. Hell). (11) When it (Hell) sees them*
*from a far place, they will hear its raging and its roaring.*
*(12) And when they shall be thrown into a narrow place*
*thereof, chained together, they will exclaim therein for*
*destruction. (13)*

## Quran 25:15-20

قُلْ أَذَٰلِكَ خَيْرٌ أَمْ جَنَّةُ ٱلْخُلْدِ ٱلَّتِى وُعِدَ ٱلْمُتَّقُونَ كَانَتْ لَهُمْ
جَزَآءً وَمَصِيرًا (١٥) لَّهُمْ فِيهَا مَا يَشَآءُونَ خَٰلِدِينَ كَانَ عَلَىٰ
رَبِّكَ وَعْدًا مَّسْئُولاً (١٦) وَيَوْمَ يَحْشُرُهُمْ وَمَا يَعْبُدُونَ مِن
دُونِ ٱللَّهِ فَيَقُولُ ءَأَنتُمْ أَضْلَلْتُمْ عِبَادِى هَٰؤُلَآءِ أَمْ هُمْ ضَلُّواْ
ٱلسَّبِيلَ (١٧) قَالُواْ سُبْحَٰنَكَ مَا كَانَ يَنۢبَغِى لَنَآ أَن نَّتَّخِذَ مِن
دُونِكَ مِنْ أَوْلِيَآءَ وَلَٰكِن مَّتَّعْتَهُمْ وَءَابَآءَهُمْ حَتَّىٰ نَسُواْ ٱلذِّكْرَ
وَكَانُواْ قَوْمًا بُورًا (١٨) فَقَدْ كَذَّبُوكُم بِمَا تَقُولُونَ فَمَا
تَسْتَطِيعُونَ صَرْفًا وَلَا نَصْرًا وَمَن يَظْلِم مِّنكُمْ نُذِقْهُ عَذَابًا
كَبِيرًا (١٩) وَمَآ أَرْسَلْنَا قَبْلَكَ مِنَ ٱلْمُرْسَلِينَ إِلَّا إِنَّهُمْ
لَيَأْكُلُونَ ٱلطَّعَامَ وَيَمْشُونَ فِى ٱلْأَسْوَاقِ وَجَعَلْنَا بَعْضَكُمْ
لِبَعْضٍ فِتْنَةً أَتَصْبِرُونَ وَكَانَ رَبُّكَ بَصِيرًا (٢٠)

*Say: (O Muhammad) "Is that (torment) better or the*
*Paradise of Eternity which is promised to the Muttaqûn*
*(pious and righteous persons)?" It will be theirs as a*
*reward and as a final destination. (15) For them there*
*will be therein all that they desire, and they will abide*
*(there forever). It is a promise binding upon your Lord*

that must be fulfilled. (16) And on the Day when He will gather them together and that which they worship besides Allâh [idols, angels, pious men, saints, 'Īsā (Jesus) son of Maryam (Mary), etc.]. He will say: "Was it you who misled these My slaves or did they (themselves) stray from the (Right) Path?" (17) They will say: "Glorified are You! It was not for us to take any Auliyâ' (Protectors, Helpers) besides You, but You gave them and their fathers comfort till they forgot the warning, and became a lost people (doomed to total loss). (18) Thus they (false gods — all deities other than Allâh) will belie you (polytheists) regarding what you say (that they are gods besides Allâh), then you can neither avert (the punishment), nor get help. And whoever among you does wrong (i.e. sets up rivals to Allâh), We shall make him taste a great torment. (19) And We never sent before you (O Muhammad) any of the Messengers but verily, they ate food and walked in the markets. And We have made some of you as a trial for others: will you have patience? And your Lord is Ever All-Seer (of everything). (20)

**Quran 25:33-34**

وَلَا يَأْتُونَكَ بِمَثَلٍ إِلَّا جِئْنَاكَ بِالْحَقِّ وَأَحْسَنَ تَفْسِيرًا
(٣٣) ٱلَّذِينَ يُحْشَرُونَ عَلَىٰ وُجُوهِهِمْ إِلَىٰ جَهَنَّمَ أُوْلَٰٓئِكَ شَرٌّ
مَّكَانًا وَأَضَلُّ سَبِيلًا (٣٤)

*And no example or similitude do they bring (to oppose or to find fault in you or in this Qur'ân), but We reveal to you the truth (against that similitude or example), and the better explanation thereof. (33) Those who will be gathered to Hell (prone) on their faces, such will be in an evil state, and most astray from the (Straight) Path. (34)*

## Quran 25:37

وَقَوْمَ نُوحٍ لَّمَّا كَذَّبُوا۟ ٱلرُّسُلَ أَغْرَقْنَٰهُمْ وَجَعَلْنَٰهُمْ لِلنَّاسِ ءَايَةً وَأَعْتَدْنَا لِلظَّٰلِمِينَ عَذَابًا أَلِيمًا

*And Nûh's (Noah) people, when they denied the Messengers We drowned them, and We made them as a sign for mankind. And We have prepared a painful torment for the Zâlimûn (polytheists and wrong-doers). (37)*

## Quran 25:40-42

وَلَقَدْ أَتَوْا۟ عَلَى ٱلْقَرْيَةِ ٱلَّتِىٓ أُمْطِرَتْ مَطَرَ ٱلسَّوْءِ أَفَلَمْ يَكُونُوا۟ يَرَوْنَهَا بَلْ كَانُوا۟ لَا يَرْجُونَ نُشُورًا ( ٤٠ ) وَإِذَا رَأَوْكَ إِن يَتَّخِذُونَكَ إِلَّا هُزُوًا أَهَٰذَا ٱلَّذِى بَعَثَ ٱللَّهُ رَسُولاً ( ٤١ ) إِن كَادَ لَيُضِلُّنَا عَنْ ءَالِهَتِنَا لَوْلَآ أَن صَبَرْنَا عَلَيْهَآ وَسَوْفَ يَعْلَمُونَ حِينَ يَرَوْنَ ٱلْعَذَابَ مَنْ أَضَلُّ سَبِيلاً ( ٤٢ )

*And indeed they have passed by the town [of Prophet Lut (Lot)] on which was rained the evil rain. Did they (disbelievers) not then see it (with their own eyes)? Nay ! But they used not to expect any resurrection. (40) And*

when they see you (O Muhammad), they treat you only in mockery (saying):"Is this the one whom Allâh has sent as a Messenger? (41) "He would have nearly misled us from our âlihah (gods), had it not been that we were patient and constant in their worship!" And they will know when they see the torment, who it is that is most astray from the (Right) Path! (42)

## Quran 25:55-56

وَيَعْبُدُونَ مِن دُونِ ٱللَّهِ مَا لَا يَنفَعُهُمْ وَلَا يَضُرُّهُمْ وَكَانَ ٱلْكَافِرُ عَلَىٰ رَبِّهِ ظَهِيرًا (٥٥) وَمَا أَرْسَلْنَٰكَ إِلَّا مُبَشِّرًا وَنَذِيرًا (٥٦)

And they (disbelievers, polytheists) worship besides Allâh, that which can neither profit them nor harm them, and the disbeliever is ever a helper (of the Satan) against his Lord. (55) And We have sent you (O Muhammad) only as a bearer of glad tidings and a warner. (56)

## Quran 25:63-77

وَعِبَادُ ٱلرَّحْمَٰنِ ٱلَّذِينَ يَمْشُونَ عَلَى ٱلْأَرْضِ هَوْنًا وَإِذَا خَاطَبَهُمُ ٱلْجَٰهِلُونَ قَالُوا سَلَٰمًا (٦٣) وَٱلَّذِينَ يَبِيتُونَ لِرَبِّهِمْ سُجَّدًا وَقِيَٰمًا (٦٤) وَٱلَّذِينَ يَقُولُونَ رَبَّنَا ٱصْرِفْ عَنَّا عَذَابَ جَهَنَّمَ إِنَّ عَذَابَهَا كَانَ غَرَامًا (٦٥) إِنَّهَا سَآءَتْ مُسْتَقَرًّا وَمُقَامًا (٦٦) وَٱلَّذِينَ إِذَآ أَنفَقُوا لَمْ يُسْرِفُوا وَلَمْ يَقْتُرُوا وَكَانَ بَيْنَ ذَٰلِكَ قَوَامًا (٦٧) وَٱلَّذِينَ لَا يَدْعُونَ مَعَ ٱللَّهِ إِلَٰهًا ءَاخَرَ

وَلَا يَقْتُلُونَ ٱلنَّفْسَ ٱلَّتِى حَرَّمَ ٱللَّهُ إِلَّا بِٱلْحَقِّ وَلَا يَزْنُونَ وَمَن يَفْعَلْ ذَٰلِكَ يَلْقَ أَثَامًا (٦٨) يُضَٰعَفْ لَهُ ٱلْعَذَابُ يَوْمَ ٱلْقِيَٰمَةِ وَيَخْلُدْ فِيهِۦ مُهَانًا (٦٩) إِلَّا مَن تَابَ وَءَامَنَ وَعَمِلَ عَمَلًا صَٰلِحًا فَأُوْلَٰٓئِكَ يُبَدِّلُ ٱللَّهُ سَيِّـَٔاتِهِمْ حَسَنَٰتٍ وَكَانَ ٱللَّهُ غَفُورًا رَّحِيمًا (٧٠) وَمَن تَابَ وَعَمِلَ صَٰلِحًا فَإِنَّهُۥ يَتُوبُ إِلَى ٱللَّهِ مَتَابًا (٧١) وَٱلَّذِينَ لَا يَشْهَدُونَ ٱلزُّورَ وَإِذَا مَرُّواْ بِٱللَّغْوِ مَرُّواْ كِرَامًا (٧٢) وَٱلَّذِينَ إِذَا ذُكِّرُواْ بِـَٔايَٰتِ رَبِّهِمْ لَمْ يَخِرُّواْ عَلَيْهَا صُمًّا وَعُمْيَانًا (٧٣) وَٱلَّذِينَ يَقُولُونَ رَبَّنَا هَبْ لَنَا مِنْ أَزْوَٰجِنَا وَذُرِّيَّٰتِنَا قُرَّةَ أَعْيُنٍ وَٱجْعَلْنَا لِلْمُتَّقِينَ إِمَامًا (٧٤) أُوْلَٰٓئِكَ يُجْزَوْنَ ٱلْغُرْفَةَ بِمَا صَبَرُواْ وَيُلَقَّوْنَ فِيهَا تَحِيَّةً وَسَلَٰمًا (٧٥) خَٰلِدِينَ فِيهَآ حَسُنَتْ مُسْتَقَرًّا وَمُقَامًا (٧٦) قُلْ مَا يَعْبَؤُاْ بِكُمْ رَبِّى لَوْلَا دُعَآؤُكُمْ فَقَدْ كَذَّبْتُمْ فَسَوْفَ يَكُونُ لِزَامًا (٧٧)

And the (faithful) slaves of the Most Gracious (Allâh) are those who walk on the earth in humility and sedateness, and when the foolish address them (with bad words) they reply back with mild words of gentleness. (63) And those who spend the night in worship of their Lord, prostrate and standing (64) And those who say: "Our Lord! Avert from us the torment of Hell. Verily! Its torment is ever an inseparable, permanent punishment." (65) Evil indeed it (Hell) is as an abode and as a place to rest in. (66) And those, who, when they spend, are neither extravagant nor niggardly, but hold a medium (way) between those *(extremes). (67) And those who invoke not any other ilâh (god) along with Allâh, nor kill such person as Allâh has forbidden, except for just cause, nor commit illegal sexual intercourse - and whoever does this shall receive the punishment(68) The torment will be doubled to him on the Day of Resurrection, and he will abide therein in disgrace; (69) Except those who repent and believe (in Islâmic Monotheism), and do righteous deeds, for those, Allâh will change their sins into good deeds, and Allâh is Oft-Forgiving, Most Merciful (70) And whosoever repents and does righteous good deeds, then verily, he repents towards Allâh with true repentance. (71) And those who do not witness to falsehood, and if they pass by some evil play or evil talk, they pass by it with dignity. (72) And those who, when they are reminded of the Ayât (proofs, evidences, verses, lessons, signs, revelations, etc.) of their Lord, fall not deaf and blind thereat. (73) And those who say: "Our Lord! Bestow on us from our wives and our offspring the comfort of our eyes, and make us leaders for the Muttaqûn" (pious)." (74) Those will be rewarded with the highest place (in Paradise) because of their patience. Therein they shall be met with greetings and the word of peace and respect. (75) Abiding therein; — excellent it is as an abode, and as a place to dwell. (76) Say (O Muhammad to the disbelievers): "My Lord pays attention to you only because of your invocation to Him. But now you have indeed denied*

(Him). So the torment will be yours forever (inseparable permanent punishment)." (77)

## Quran 26:5-6

وَمَا يَأْتِيهِم مِّن ذِكْرٍ مِّنَ ٱلرَّحْمَـٰنِ مُحْدَثٍ إِلَّا كَانُواْ عَنْهُ مُعْرِضِينَ (٥) فَقَدْ كَذَّبُواْ فَسَيَأْتِيهِمْ أَنۢبَـٰٓؤُاْ مَا كَانُواْ بِهِۦ يَسْتَهْزِءُونَ (٦)

And never comes there unto them a Reminder as a recent revelation from the Most Gracious (Allâh), but they turn away therefrom. (5) So they have indeed denied (the truth — this Qur'ân), then the news of what they mocked at, will come to them. (6)

## Quran 26:87-102

وَلَا تُخْزِنِى يَوْمَ يُبْعَثُونَ (٨٧) يَوْمَ لَا يَنفَعُ مَالٌ وَلَا بَنُونَ (٨٨) إِلَّا مَنْ أَتَى ٱللَّهَ بِقَلْبٍ سَلِيمٍ (٨٩) وَأُزْلِفَتِ ٱلْجَنَّةُ لِلْمُتَّقِينَ (٩٠) وَبُرِّزَتِ ٱلْجَحِيمُ لِلْغَاوِينَ (٩١) وَقِيلَ لَهُمْ أَيْنَ مَا كُنتُمْ تَعْبُدُونَ (٩٢) مِن دُونِ ٱللَّهِ هَلْ يَنصُرُونَكُمْ أَوْ يَنتَصِرُونَ (٩٣) فَكُبْكِبُواْ فِيهَا هُمْ وَٱلْغَاوُۥنَ (٩٤) وَجُنُودُ إِبْلِيسَ أَجْمَعُونَ (٩٥) قَالُواْ وَهُمْ فِيهَا يَخْتَصِمُونَ (٩٦) تَٱللَّهِ إِن كُنَّا لَفِى ضَلَـٰلٍ مُّبِينٍ (٩٧) إِذْ نُسَوِّيكُم بِرَبِّ ٱلْعَـٰلَمِينَ (٩٨) وَمَآ أَضَلَّنَآ إِلَّا ٱلْمُجْرِمُونَ (٩٩) فَمَا لَنَا مِن شَـٰفِعِينَ (١٠٠) وَلَا صَدِيقٍ حَمِيمٍ (١٠١) فَلَوْ أَنَّ لَنَا كَرَّةً فَنَكُونَ مِنَ ٱلْمُؤْمِنِينَ (١٠٢)

*And disgrace me not on the Day when (all the creatures) will be resurrected; (87) The Day whereon neither wealth nor sons will avail, (88) Except him who brings to Allâh a clean heart [clean from Shirk (polytheism) and Nifâq (hypocrisy)]. (89) And Paradise will be brought near to the Muttaqûn (pious and righteous persons). (90) And the (Hell) Fire will be placed in full view of the erring. (91) And it will be said to them: "Where are those (the false gods whom you used to set up as rivals with Allâh) that you used to worship. (92) "Instead of Allâh? Can they help you or (even) help themselves?" (93) Then they will be thrown on their faces into the (Fire), They and the Ghâwûn (devils, and those who were in error). (94) And the whole hosts of Iblîs (Satan) together. (95) They will say while contending therein, (96) By Allâh, we were truly in a manifest error, (97) When We held you (false gods) as equals (in worship) with the Lord of the 'Alamîn (mankind, jinn and all that exists); (98) And none has brought us into error except the Mujrimûn [Iblîs (Satan) and those of human beings who commit crimes, murderers, polytheists, oppressors], (99) Now we have no intercessors, (100) Nor a close friend (to help us). (101) (Alas!) If we only had a chance to return (to the world), we shall truly be among the believers! (102)*

**Quran 26:200-212**

كَذَٰلِكَ سَلَكْنَـٰهُ فِى قُلُوبِ ٱلْمُجْرِمِينَ (٢٠٠) لَا يُؤْمِنُونَ بِهِ حَتَّىٰ يَرَوُاْ ٱلْعَذَابَ ٱلْأَلِيمَ (٢٠١) فَيَأْتِيَهُم بَغْتَةً وَهُمْ لَا يَشْعُرُونَ (٢٠٢) فَيَقُولُواْ هَلْ نَحْنُ مُنظَرُونَ (٢٠٣) أَفَبِعَذَابِنَا يَسْتَعْجِلُونَ (٢٠٤) أَفَرَءَيْتَ إِن مَّتَّعْنَـٰهُمْ سِنِينَ (٢٠٥) ثُمَّ جَآءَهُم مَّا كَانُواْ يُوعَدُونَ (٢٠٦) مَآ أَغْنَىٰ عَنْهُم مَّا كَانُواْ يُمَتَّعُونَ (٢٠٧) وَمَآ أَهْلَكْنَا مِن قَرْيَةٍ إِلَّا لَهَا مُنذِرُونَ (٢٠٨) ذِكْرَىٰ وَمَا كُنَّا ظَـٰلِمِينَ (٢٠٩) وَمَا تَنَزَّلَتْ بِهِ ٱلشَّيَـٰطِينُ (٢١٠) وَمَا يَنۢبَغِى لَهُمْ وَمَا يَسْتَطِيعُونَ (٢١١) إِنَّهُمْ عَنِ ٱلسَّمْعِ لَمَعْزُولُونَ (٢١٢)

Thus have We caused it (the denial of the Qur'ân) to enter the hearts of the Mûjrimûn (criminals, polytheists, sinners). (200) They will not believe in it until they see the painful torment, (201) It shall come to them of a sudden, while they perceive it not. (202) Then they will say: "Can we be respited?" (203) Would they then wish for Our Torment to be hastened on? (204) Tell Me, (even) if We do let them enjoy for years, (205) And afterwards comes to them that (punishment) which they had been promised! (206) All that with which they used to enjoy shall not avail them. (207) And never did We destroy a township, but it had its warners (208) By way of reminder, and We have never been unjust. (209) And it is not the Shayâtin (devils) who have brought it (this Qur'ân) down, (210) Neither would it suit them, nor *they can (produce it). (211) Verily, they have been removed far from hearing it. (212)*

## Quran 26:221-227

هَلۡ أُنَبِّئُكُمۡ عَلَىٰ مَن تَنَزَّلُ ٱلشَّيَٰطِينُ (٢٢١) تَنَزَّلُ عَلَىٰ كُلِّ أَفَّاكٍ أَثِيمٍ (٢٢٢) يُلۡقُونَ ٱلسَّمۡعَ وَأَكۡثَرُهُمۡ كَٰذِبُونَ (٢٢٣) وَٱلشُّعَرَآءُ يَتَّبِعُهُمُ ٱلۡغَاوُۥنَ (٢٢٤) أَلَمۡ تَرَ أَنَّهُمۡ فِى كُلِّ وَادٍ يَهِيمُونَ (٢٢٥) وَأَنَّهُمۡ يَقُولُونَ مَا لَا يَفۡعَلُونَ (٢٢٦) إِلَّا ٱلَّذِينَ ءَامَنُواْ وَعَمِلُواْ ٱلصَّٰلِحَٰتِ وَذَكَرُواْ ٱللَّهَ كَثِيرًا وَٱنتَصَرُواْ مِنۢ بَعۡدِ مَا ظُلِمُواْۗ وَسَيَعۡلَمُ ٱلَّذِينَ ظَلَمُوٓاْ أَىَّ مُنقَلَبٍ يَنقَلِبُونَ (٢٢٧)

*Shall I inform you (O people!) upon whom the Shayâtin (devils) descend? (221) They descend on every lying, sinful person. (222) Who gives ear (to the devils and they pour what they may have heard of the unseen from the angels), and most of them are liars. (223) As for the poets, the erring ones follow them, (224) See you not that they speak about every subject (praising people - right or wrong) in their poetry? (225) And that they say what they do not do. (226) Except those who believe (in the Oneness of Allâh — Islâmic Monotheism), and do righteous deeds, and remember Allâh much and vindicate themselves after they have been wronged [by replying back in the poetry to the unjust poetry (which the pagan poets utter against the Muslims)]. And those who do*

*wrong will come to know by what overturning they will
be overturned. (227)*

## Quran 27:1-5

طسٓ تِلْكَ ءَايَٰتُ ٱلْقُرْءَانِ وَكِتَابٍ مُّبِينٍ (١) هُدًى وَبُشْرَىٰ
لِلْمُؤْمِنِينَ (٢) ٱلَّذِينَ يُقِيمُونَ ٱلصَّلَوٰةَ وَيُؤْتُونَ ٱلزَّكَوٰةَ وَهُم
بِٱلْأَخِرَةِ هُمْ يُوقِنُونَ (٣) إِنَّ ٱلَّذِينَ لَا يُؤْمِنُونَ بِٱلْأَخِرَةِ زَيَّنَّا
لَهُمْ أَعْمَٰلَهُمْ فَهُمْ يَعْمَهُونَ (٤) أُوْلَٰٓئِكَ ٱلَّذِينَ لَهُمْ سُوٓءُ ٱلْعَذَابِ
وَهُمْ فِى ٱلْأَخِرَةِ هُمُ ٱلْأَخْسَرُونَ (٥)

*Tâ¬Sîn. These are the Verses of the Qur'ân, and (it is) a
Book (that makes things) clear; (1) A guide (to the Right
Path); and glad tidings for the believers [who believe in
the Oneness of Allâh (i.e. Islâmic Monotheism)].
(2) Those who perform As¬Salât (Iqâmat¬as¬Salât) and
give Zakât and they believe with certainty in the
Hereafter (resurrection, recompense of their good and bad
deeds, Paradise and Hell). (3) Verily, those who believe
not in the Hereafter, We have made their deeds fair-
seeming to them, so that they wander about blindly
(4) They are those for whom there will be an evil torment
(in this world). And in the Hereafter they will be the
greatest losers. (5)*

## Quran 27:65-68

قُل لَّا يَعْلَمُ مَن فِى ٱلسَّمَـٰوَٰتِ وَٱلْأَرْضِ ٱلْغَيْبَ إِلَّا ٱللَّهُ ۚ وَمَا يَشْعُرُونَ أَيَّانَ يُبْعَثُونَ ﴿٦٥﴾ بَلِ ٱدَّٰرَكَ عِلْمُهُمْ فِى ٱلْأَخِرَةِ ۚ بَلْ هُمْ فِى شَكٍّ مِّنْهَا ۖ بَلْ هُم مِّنْهَا عَمُونَ ﴿٦٦﴾ وَقَالَ ٱلَّذِينَ كَفَرُوٓا۟ أَءِذَا كُنَّا تُرَٰبًا وَءَابَآؤُنَآ أَئِنَّا لَمُخْرَجُونَ ﴿٦٧﴾ لَقَدْ وُعِدْنَا هَـٰذَا نَحْنُ وَءَابَآؤُنَا مِن قَبْلُ إِنْ هَـٰذَآ إِلَّآ أَسَـٰطِيرُ ٱلْأَوَّلِينَ ﴿٦٨﴾

Say: "None in the heavens and the earth knows the Ghaib (unseen) except Allâh, nor can they perceive when they shall be resurrected." (65) Nay, they have no knowledge of the Hereafter. Nay, they are in doubt about it. Nay, they are in complete blindness about it. (66) And those who disbelieve say: "When we have become dust — we and our fathers — shall we really be brought forth (again)? (67) "Indeed we were promised this, we and our forefathers before (us), Verily, these are nothing but tales of ancients." (68)

## Quran 27:71-72

وَيَقُولُونَ مَتَىٰ هَـٰذَا ٱلْوَعْدُ إِن كُنتُمْ صَـٰدِقِينَ ﴿٧١﴾ قُلْ عَسَىٰٓ أَن يَكُونَ رَدِفَ لَكُم بَعْضُ ٱلَّذِى تَسْتَعْجِلُونَ ﴿٧٢﴾

And they (the disbelievers in the Oneness of Allâh) say: "When (will) this promise (be fulfilled), if you are truthful?" (71) Say: "Perhaps that which you wish to hasten on, may be close behind you (72)

## Quran 27:75-85

وَمَا مِنْ غَآئِبَةٍ فِى ٱلسَّمَآءِ وَٱلْأَرْضِ إِلَّا فِى كِتَٰبٍ مُّبِينٍ
(٧٥) إِنَّ هَٰذَا ٱلْقُرْءَانَ يَقُصُّ عَلَىٰ بَنِىٓ إِسْرَٰٓءِيلَ أَكْثَرَ
ٱلَّذِى هُمْ فِيهِ يَخْتَلِفُونَ (٧٦) وَإِنَّهُ لَهُدًى وَرَحْمَةٌ لِّلْمُؤْمِنِينَ
(٧٧) إِنَّ رَبَّكَ يَقْضِى بَيْنَهُم بِحُكْمِهِۦ وَهُوَ ٱلْعَزِيزُ ٱلْعَلِيمُ
(٧٨) فَتَوَكَّلْ عَلَى ٱللَّهِ إِنَّكَ عَلَى ٱلْحَقِّ ٱلْمُبِينِ (٧٩) إِنَّكَ لَا
تُسْمِعُ ٱلْمَوْتَىٰ وَلَا تُسْمِعُ ٱلصُّمَّ ٱلدُّعَآءَ إِذَا وَلَّوْا۟ مُدْبِرِينَ
(٨٠) وَمَآ أَنتَ بِهَٰدِى ٱلْعُمْىِ عَن ضَلَٰلَتِهِمْ إِن تُسْمِعُ إِلَّا مَن
يُؤْمِنُ بِـَٔايَٰتِنَا فَهُم مُّسْلِمُونَ (٨١) ۞ وَإِذَا وَقَعَ ٱلْقَوْلُ عَلَيْهِمْ
أَخْرَجْنَا لَهُمْ دَآبَّةً مِّنَ ٱلْأَرْضِ تُكَلِّمُهُمْ أَنَّ ٱلنَّاسَ كَانُوا۟ بِـَٔايَٰتِنَا
لَا يُوقِنُونَ (٨٢) وَيَوْمَ نَحْشُرُ مِن كُلِّ أُمَّةٍ فَوْجًا مِّمَّن يُكَذِّبُ
بِـَٔايَٰتِنَا فَهُمْ يُوزَعُونَ (٨٣) حَتَّىٰٓ إِذَا جَآءُو قَالَ أَكَذَّبْتُم
بِـَٔايَٰتِى وَلَمْ تُحِيطُوا۟ بِهَا عِلْمًا أَمَّاذَا كُنتُمْ تَعْمَلُونَ (٨٤) وَوَقَعَ
ٱلْقَوْلُ عَلَيْهِم بِمَا ظَلَمُوا۟ فَهُمْ لَا يَنطِقُونَ (٨٥)

And there is nothing hidden in the heaven and the earth,
but is in a Clear Book (i.e. Al-Lauh Al-Mahfûz)
(75) Verily, this Qur'ân narrates to the Children of Israel
most of that in which they differ. (76) And truly, it (this
Qur'ân) is a guide and a mercy for the believers.
(77) Verily, your Lord will decide between them (various
sects) by His Judgement. And He is the All-Mighty, the
All-Knowing. (78) So put your trust in Allâh; surely,
you (O Muhammad) are on manifest truth. (79) Verily,
you cannot make the dead to hear nor can you make the
deaf to hear the call (i.e. benefit them and similarly the

disbelievers). when they flee, turning their backs.
(80) Nor can you lead the blind out of their error, you
can only make to hear those who believe in Our Ayât
(proofs, evidences, verses, lessons, signs, revelations,
etc.), and who have submitted (themselves to Allâh in
Islâm as Muslims) (81) And when the Word (of torment)
is fulfilled against them, We shall bring out from the
earth a beast for them, to speak to them because mankind
believed not with certainty in Our Ayât (Verses of the
Qur'ân and Prophet Muhammad) (82) And (remember)
the Day when We shall gather out of every nation a troop
of those who denied Our Ayât (proofs, evidences, verses,
lessons, signs, revelations, etc.), and (then) they (all)
shall be set in array (gathered and driven to the place of
reckoning), (83) Till, when they come (before their Lord
at the place of reckoning), He will say: "Did you deny
My Ayât (proofs, evidences, verses, lessons, signs,
revelations, etc.) where as you comprehended them not by
knowledge (of their truth or falsehood), or what (else) was
it that you used to do?" (84) And the Word (of torment)
will be fulfilled against them, because they have done
wrong, and they will be unable to speak (in order to
defend themselves). (85)

## Quran 27:87-90

وَيَوْمَ يُنفَخُ فِى ٱلصُّورِ فَفَزِعَ مَن فِى ٱلسَّمَٰوَٰتِ وَمَن فِى
ٱلْأَرْضِ إِلَّا مَن شَآءَ ٱللَّهُ وَكُلٌّ أَتَوْهُ دَٰخِرِينَ (٨٧) وَتَرَى

ٱلْجِبَالَ تَحْسَبُهَا جَامِدَةً وَهِىَ تَمُرُّ مَرَّ ٱلسَّحَابِ صُنْعَ ٱللَّهِ ٱلَّذِىٓ
أَتْقَنَ كُلَّ شَىْءٍ إِنَّهُۥ خَبِيرٌۢ بِمَا تَفْعَلُونَ (٨٨) مَن جَآءَ بِٱلْحَسَنَةِ
فَلَهُۥ خَيْرٌ مِّنْهَا وَهُم مِّن فَزَعٍ يَوْمَئِذٍ ءَامِنُونَ (٨٩) وَمَن جَآءَ
بِٱلسَّيِّئَةِ فَكُبَّتْ وُجُوهُهُمْ فِى ٱلنَّارِ هَلْ تُجْزَوْنَ إِلَّا مَا كُنتُمْ
تَعْمَلُونَ (٩٠)

And (remember) the Day on which the Trumpet will be
blown — and all who are in the heavens and all who are
on the earth, will be terrified except him whom Allâh will
(exempt). And all shall come to Him humbled. (87) And
you will see the mountains and think them solid, but they
shall pass away as the passing away of the clouds. The
Work of Allâh, Who perfected all things, verily! He is
Well-Acquainted with what you do. (88) Whoever brings
a good deed (i.e. Belief in the Oneness of Allâh along with
every deed of righteousness), will have better than its
worth, and they will be safe from the terror on that Day.
(89) And whoever brings an evil deed (i.e. Shirk —
polytheism, disbelief in the Oneness of Allâh and every
evil sinful deed), they will be cast down (prone) on their
faces in the Fire. (And it will be said to them) "Are you
being recompensed anything except what you used to
do?" (90)

**Quran 27:93**

وَقُلِ ٱلْحَمْدُ لِلَّهِ سَيُرِيكُمْ ءَايَـٰتِهِۦ فَتَعْرِفُونَهَا ۚ وَمَا رَبُّكَ بِغَـٰفِلٍ عَمَّا تَعْمَلُونَ

*And say [(O Muhammad) to these polytheists and pagans]: "All the praises and thanks are to Allâh. He will show you His Ayât (signs, in yourselves, and in the universe or punishments), and you shall recognize them. And your Lord is not unaware of what you do." (93)*

## Quran 28:41-42

وَجَعَلْنَـٰهُمْ أَئِمَّةً يَدْعُونَ إِلَى ٱلنَّارِ ۖ وَيَوْمَ ٱلْقِيَـٰمَةِ لَا يُنصَرُونَ (٤١) وَأَتْبَعْنَـٰهُمْ فِى هَـٰذِهِ ٱلدُّنْيَا لَعْنَةً ۖ وَيَوْمَ ٱلْقِيَـٰمَةِ هُم مِّنَ ٱلْمَقْبُوحِينَ (٤٢)

*And We made them leaders inviting to the Fire, and on the Day of Resurrection, they will not be helped. (41) And We made a curse to follow them in this world, and on the Day of Resurrection, they will be among Al-Maqbuhûn (those who are prevented to receive Allâh's Mercy or any good, despised or destroyed). (42)*

## Quran 28:59-67

وَمَا كَانَ رَبُّكَ مُهْلِكَ ٱلْقُرَىٰ حَتَّىٰ يَبْعَثَ فِىٓ أُمِّهَا رَسُولاً يَتْلُوا۟ عَلَيْهِمْ ءَايَـٰتِنَا ۚ وَمَا كُنَّا مُهْلِكِى ٱلْقُرَىٰٓ إِلَّا وَأَهْلُهَا ظَـٰلِمُونَ (٥٩) وَمَآ أُوتِيتُم مِّن شَىْءٍ فَمَتَـٰعُ ٱلْحَيَوٰةِ ٱلدُّنْيَا وَزِينَتُهَا ۚ وَمَا عِندَ ٱللَّهِ خَيْرٌ وَأَبْقَىٰٓ ۚ أَفَلَا تَعْقِلُونَ (٦٠) أَفَمَن وَعَدْنَـٰهُ وَعْدًا

حَسَنًا فَهُوَ لَٰقِيهِ كَمَن مَّتَّعْنَٰهُ مَتَٰعَ ٱلْحَيَوٰةِ ٱلدُّنْيَا ثُمَّ هُوَ يَوْمَ
ٱلْقِيَٰمَةِ مِنَ ٱلْمُحْضَرِينَ (٦١) وَيَوْمَ يُنَادِيهِمْ فَيَقُولُ أَيْنَ
شُرَكَآءِىَ ٱلَّذِينَ كُنتُمْ تَزْعُمُونَ (٦٢) قَالَ ٱلَّذِينَ حَقَّ عَلَيْهِمُ
ٱلْقَوْلُ رَبَّنَا هَٰٓؤُلَآءِ ٱلَّذِينَ أَغْوَيْنَا أَغْوَيْنَٰهُمْ كَمَا غَوَيْنَا تَبَرَّأْنَا
إِلَيْكَ مَا كَانُوٓا۟ إِيَّانَا يَعْبُدُونَ (٦٣) وَقِيلَ ٱدْعُوا۟ شُرَكَآءَكُمْ
فَدَعَوْهُمْ فَلَمْ يَسْتَجِيبُوا۟ لَهُمْ وَرَأَوُا۟ ٱلْعَذَابَ لَوْ أَنَّهُمْ كَانُوا۟
يَهْتَدُونَ (٦٤) وَيَوْمَ يُنَادِيهِمْ فَيَقُولُ مَاذَآ أَجَبْتُمُ ٱلْمُرْسَلِينَ
(٦٥) فَعَمِيَتْ عَلَيْهِمُ ٱلْأَنۢبَآءُ يَوْمَئِذٍ فَهُمْ لَا يَتَسَآءَلُونَ
(٦٦) فَأَمَّا مَن تَابَ وَءَامَنَ وَعَمِلَ صَٰلِحًا فَعَسَىٰٓ أَن يَكُونَ
مِنَ ٱلْمُفْلِحِينَ (٦٧)

And never will your Lord destroy the towns
(populations) until He sends to their mother town a
Messenger reciting to them Our Verses. And never
would We destroy the towns unless the people thereof are
Zâlimûn (polytheists, wrong-doers, disbelievers in the
Oneness of Allâh, oppressors and tyrants). (59) And
whatever you have been given is an enjoyment of the life
of (this) world and its adornment, and that (Hereafter)
which is with Allâh is better and will remain forever.
Have you then no sense? (60) Is he whom We have
promised an excellent promise (Paradise), – which he
will find true, - like him whom We have made to enjoy
the luxuries of the life of (this) world, then on the Day of
Resurrection, he will be among those brought up (to be
punished in the Hell-fire)? (61) And (remember) the Day

when He will call to them, and say: "Where are My (so-called) partners whom you used to assert?" (62) Those about whom the Word will have come true (to be punished) will say: "Our Lord! These are they whom we led astray. We led them astray, as we were astray ourselves. We declare our innocence (from them) before You. It was not us they worshipped." (63) And it will be said (to them): "Call upon your (so-called) partners (of Allâh), and they will call upon them, but they will give no answer to them, and they will see the torment. (They will then wish) if only they had been guided! (64) And (remember) the Day (Allâh) will call to them, and say: "What answer gave you to the Messengers?" (65) Then the news of a good answer will be obscured to them on that day, and they will not be able to ask one another. (66) But as for him who repented (from polytheism and sins), believed (in the Oneness of Allâh, and in His Messenger Muhammad), and did righteous deeds (in the life of this world), then he will be among those who are successful. (67)

## Quran 28:70-72

وَهُوَ ٱللَّهُ لَآ إِلَـٰهَ إِلَّا هُوَ لَهُ ٱلْحَمْدُ فِى ٱلْأُولَىٰ وَٱلْأَخِرَةِ وَلَهُ ٱلْحُكْمُ وَإِلَيْهِ تُرْجَعُونَ (٧٠) قُلْ أَرَءَيْتُمْ إِن جَعَلَ ٱللَّهُ عَلَيْكُمُ ٱلَّيْلَ سَرْمَدًا إِلَىٰ يَوْمِ ٱلْقِيَـٰمَةِ مَنْ إِلَـٰهٌ غَيْرُ ٱللَّهِ يَأْتِيكُم بِضِيَآءٍ أَفَلَا تَسْمَعُونَ (٧١) قُلْ أَرَءَيْتُمْ إِن جَعَلَ ٱللَّهُ عَلَيْكُمُ ٱلنَّهَارَ

سَرْمَدًا إِلَىٰ يَوْمِ ٱلْقِيَـٰمَةِ مَنْ إِلَـٰهٌ غَيْرُ ٱللَّهِ يَأْتِيكُم بِلَيْلٍ
تَسْكُنُونَ فِيهِ أَفَلَا تُبْصِرُونَ (٧٢)

And He is Allâh; Lâ ilâha illa Huwa (none has the right
to be worshipped but He). all praises and thanks be to
Him (both) in the first (i.e. in this world) and in the last
(i.e.in the Hereafter). And for Him is the Decision, and to
Him shall you (all) be returned. (70) Say: "Tell me! If
Allâh made the night continuous for you till the Day of
Resurrection, which ilâh (god) besides Allâh could bring
you light? Will you not then hear?" (71) Say: "Tell me!
If Allâh made the day continuous for you till the Day of
Resurrection, which ilâh (god) besides Allâh could bring
you night wherein you rest? Will you not then see?" (72)

**Quran 28:74-75**

وَيَوْمَ يُنَادِيهِمْ فَيَقُولُ أَيْنَ شُرَكَآءِىَ ٱلَّذِينَ كُنتُمْ تَزْعُمُونَ
(٧٤) وَنَزَعْنَا مِن كُلِّ أُمَّةٍ شَهِيدًا فَقُلْنَا هَاتُوا بُرْهَـٰنَكُمْ
فَعَلِمُوٓا أَنَّ ٱلْحَقَّ لِلَّهِ وَضَلَّ عَنْهُم مَّا كَانُوا يَفْتَرُونَ (٧٥)

And (remember) the Day when He (your Lord – Allâh)
will call to them (those who worshipped others along
with Allâh), and will say: "Where are My (so-called)
partners, whom you used to assert?" (74) And We shall
take out from every nation a witness, and We shall say:
"Bring your proof." Then they shall know that the truth

is with Allâh (Alone), and the lies (false gods) which they invented will disappear from them. (75)

## Quran 28:78

قَالَ إِنَّمَآ أُوتِيتُهُ عَلَىٰ عِلْمٍ عِندِىٓ أَوَلَمْ يَعْلَمْ أَنَّ ٱللَّهَ قَدْ أَهْلَكَ مِن قَبْلِهِ مِنَ ٱلْقُرُونِ مَنْ هُوَ أَشَدُّ مِنْهُ قُوَّةً وَأَكْثَرُ جَمْعًا وَلَا يُسْـَٔلُ عَن ذُنُوبِهِمُ ٱلْمُجْرِمُونَ

He said: "This has been given to me only because of knowledge I possess." Did he not know that Allâh had destroyed before him generations, men who were stronger than him in might and greater in the amount (of riches) they had collected? But the Mujrimûn (criminals, disbelievers, polytheists, sinners) will not be questioned of their sins (because Allâh knows them well, so they will be punished without being called to account). (78)

## Quran 28:80

وَقَالَ ٱلَّذِينَ أُوتُوا۟ ٱلْعِلْمَ وَيْلَكُمْ ثَوَابُ ٱللَّهِ خَيْرٌ لِّمَنْ ءَامَنَ وَعَمِلَ صَٰلِحًا وَلَا يُلَقَّىٰهَآ إِلَّا ٱلصَّٰبِرُونَ

But those who had been given (religious) knowledge said: "Woe to you! The Reward of Allâh (in the Hereafter) is better for those who believe and do righteous good deeds, and this none shall attain except those who are As-Sabirun (the patient in following the truth)." (80)

## Quran 28:82-85

وَأَصْبَحَ ٱلَّذِينَ تَمَنَّوْاْ مَكَانَهُ بِٱلْأَمْسِ يَقُولُونَ وَيْكَأَنَّ ٱللَّهَ يَبْسُطُ
ٱلرِّزْقَ لِمَن يَشَاءُ مِنْ عِبَادِهِ وَيَقْدِرُ لَوْلَا أَن مَّنَّ ٱللَّهُ عَلَيْنَا
لَخَسَفَ بِنَا وَيْكَأَنَّهُ لَا يُفْلِحُ ٱلْكَافِرُونَ (٨٢) تِلْكَ ٱلدَّارُ
ٱلْآخِرَةُ نَجْعَلُهَا لِلَّذِينَ لَا يُرِيدُونَ عُلُوًّا فِى ٱلْأَرْضِ وَلَا فَسَادًا
وَٱلْعَاقِبَةُ لِلْمُتَّقِينَ (٨٣) مَن جَاءَ بِٱلْحَسَنَةِ فَلَهُ خَيْرٌ مِّنْهَا وَمَن
جَاءَ بِٱلسَّيِّئَةِ فَلَا يُجْزَى ٱلَّذِينَ عَمِلُواْ ٱلسَّيِّئَاتِ إِلَّا مَا كَانُواْ
يَعْمَلُونَ (٨٤) إِنَّ ٱلَّذِى فَرَضَ عَلَيْكَ ٱلْقُرْءَانَ لَرَادُّكَ إِلَىٰ
مَعَادٍ قُل رَّبِّى أَعْلَمُ مَن جَاءَ بِٱلْهُدَىٰ وَمَنْ هُوَ فِى ضَلَلٍ مُّبِينٍ
(٨٥)

And those who had desired (for a position like) his
position the day before, began to say: "Know you not that
it is Allâh Who enlarges the provision or restricts it to
whomsoever He pleases of His slaves. Had it not been
that Allâh was Gracious to us, He could have caused the
earth to swallow us up (also)! Know you not that the
disbelievers will never be successful. (82) That home of
the Hereafter (i.e. Paradise), We shall assign to those who
rebel not against the truth with pride and oppression in
the land nor do mischief by committing crimes. And the
good end is for the Muttaqûn (pious righteous persons).
(83) Whosoever brings good (Islâmic Monotheism along
with righteous deeds), he shall have the better thereof,
and whosoever brings evil (polytheism along with evil
deeds) then, those who do evil deeds will only be requited
for what they used to do. (84) Verily, He Who has given

you (O Muhammad) the Qur'an (i.e. ordered you to act on its laws and to preach it to others) will surely bring you back to the Ma'âd (place of return, either to Makkah or to Paradise after your death, etc.). Say (O Muhammad): "My Lord is Aware of him who brings guidance, and of him who is in manifest error." (85)

**Quran 28:88**

وَلَا تَدْعُ مَعَ ٱللَّهِ إِلَٰهًا ءَاخَرَ لَآ إِلَٰهَ إِلَّا هُوَ كُلُّ شَىْءٍ هَالِكٌ إِلَّا وَجْهَهُ لَهُ ٱلْحُكْمُ وَإِلَيْهِ تُرْجَعُونَ

And invoke not any other ilâh (god) along with Allâh, Lâ ilâha illa Huwa (none has the right to be worshipped but He). Everything will perish save His Face. His is the Decision, and to Him you (all) shall be returned. (88)

**Quran 29:2-3**

أَحَسِبَ ٱلنَّاسُ أَن يُتْرَكُوٓاْ أَن يَقُولُوٓاْ ءَامَنَّا وَهُمْ لَا يُفْتَنُونَ (٢) وَلَقَدْ فَتَنَّا ٱلَّذِينَ مِن قَبْلِهِمْ فَلَيَعْلَمَنَّ ٱللَّهُ ٱلَّذِينَ صَدَقُواْ وَلَيَعْلَمَنَّ ٱلْكَٰذِبِينَ (٣)

Do people think that they will be left alone because they say: "We believe," and will not be tested (2) And We indeed tested those who were before them. And Allâh will certainly make (it) known (the truth of) those who are true, and will certainly make (it) known (the falsehood of) those who are liars, (although Allâh knows all that before putting them to test). (3)

## Quran 29:5

مَن كَانَ يَرْجُواْ لِقَآءَ ٱللَّهِ فَإِنَّ أَجَلَ ٱللَّهِ لَأَتٍ وَهُوَ ٱلسَّمِيعُ ٱلْعَلِيمُ

*Whoever hopes for the Meeting with Allâh, then Allâh's Term is surely coming. and He is the All-Hearer, the All-Knower. (5)*

## Quran 29:7-9

وَٱلَّذِينَ ءَامَنُواْ وَعَمِلُواْ ٱلصَّٰلِحَٰتِ لَنُكَفِّرَنَّ عَنْهُمْ سَيِّئَاتِهِمْ وَلَنَجْزِيَنَّهُمْ أَحْسَنَ ٱلَّذِى كَانُواْ يَعْمَلُونَ (٧) وَوَصَّيْنَا ٱلْإِنسَٰنَ بِوَٰلِدَيْهِ حُسْنًا وَإِن جَٰهَدَاكَ لِتُشْرِكَ بِى مَا لَيْسَ لَكَ بِهِۦ عِلْمٌ فَلَا تُطِعْهُمَآ إِلَىَّ مَرْجِعُكُمْ فَأُنَبِّئُكُم بِمَا كُنتُمْ تَعْمَلُونَ (٨) وَٱلَّذِينَ ءَامَنُواْ وَعَمِلُواْ ٱلصَّٰلِحَٰتِ لَنُدْخِلَنَّهُمْ فِى ٱلصَّٰلِحِينَ (٩)

*Those who believe [in the Oneness of Allâh (Monotheism) and in Messenger Muhammad, and do not give up their faith because of the harm they receive from the polytheists], and do righteous good deeds, surely, We shall expiate from them their evil deeds and shall reward them according to the best of that which they used to do.(7) And We have enjoined on man to be good and dutiful to his parents, but if they strive to make you join with Me (in worship) anything (as a partner) of which you have no knowledge, then obey them not. Unto Me is*

your return, and I shall tell you what you used to do.
(8) And for those who believe (in the Oneness of Allâh
and other articles of Faith) and do righteous good deeds,
surely, We shall make them enter with (in the entrance
of) the righteous (in Paradise). (9)

## Quran 29:12-13

وَقَالَ ٱلَّذِينَ كَفَرُواْ لِلَّذِينَ ءَامَنُواْ ٱتَّبِعُواْ سَبِيلَنَا وَلْنَحْمِلْ
خَطَٰيَٰكُمْ وَمَا هُم بِحَٰمِلِينَ مِنْ خَطَٰيَٰهُم مِّن شَىْءٍ إِنَّهُمْ
لَكَٰذِبُونَ (١٢) وَلَيَحْمِلُنَّ أَثْقَالَهُمْ وَأَثْقَالًا مَّعَ أَثْقَالِهِمْ وَلَيُسْـَٔلُنَّ
يَوْمَ ٱلْقِيَٰمَةِ عَمَّا كَانُواْ يَفْتَرُونَ (١٣)

And those who disbelieve say to those who believe:
"Follow our way and we will verily bear your sins,"
never will they bear anything of their sins. Surely, they
are liars. (12) And verily, they shall bear their own loads,
and other loads besides their own, and verily, they shall
be questioned on the Day of Resurrection about that
which they used to fabricate. (13)

## Quran 29:23

وَٱلَّذِينَ كَفَرُواْ بِـَٔايَٰتِ ٱللَّهِ وَلِقَآئِهِۦ أُوْلَٰٓئِكَ يَئِسُواْ مِن
رَّحْمَتِى وَأُوْلَٰٓئِكَ لَهُمْ عَذَابٌ أَلِيمٌ

And those who disbelieve in the Ayât (proofs, evidences,
verses, lessons, signs, revelations, etc.) of Allâh and the
Meeting with Him, it is they who have no hope of My

Mercy, and it is they who will have a painful torment. (23)

## Quran 29:25

$$وَقَالَ إِنَّمَا ٱتَّخَذْتُم مِّن دُونِ ٱللَّهِ أَوْثَـٰنًا مَّوَدَّةَ بَيْنِكُمْ فِى ٱلْحَيَوٰةِ ٱلدُّنْيَا ثُمَّ يَوْمَ ٱلْقِيَـٰمَةِ يَكْفُرُ بَعْضُكُم بِبَعْضٍ وَيَلْعَنُ بَعْضُكُم بَعْضًا وَمَأْوَىٰكُمُ ٱلنَّارُ وَمَا لَكُم مِّن نَّـٰصِرِينَ$$

And [Ibrâhim (Abraham)] said: "You have taken (for worship) idols instead of Allâh, The love between you is only in the life of this world, but on the Day of Resurrection, you shall disown each other, and curse each other, and your abode will be the Fire, and you shall have no helper." (25)

## Quran 29:51-55

$$أَوَلَمْ يَكْفِهِمْ أَنَّا أَنزَلْنَا عَلَيْكَ ٱلْكِتَـٰبَ يُتْلَىٰ عَلَيْهِمْ إِنَّ فِى ذَٰلِكَ لَرَحْمَةً وَذِكْرَىٰ لِقَوْمٍ يُؤْمِنُونَ (٥١) قُلْ كَفَىٰ بِٱللَّهِ بَيْنِى وَبَيْنَكُمْ شَهِيدًا يَعْلَمُ مَا فِى ٱلسَّمَـٰوَٰتِ وَٱلْأَرْضِ وَٱلَّذِينَ ءَامَنُوا۟ بِٱلْبَـٰطِلِ وَكَفَرُوا۟ بِٱللَّهِ أُو۟لَـٰٓئِكَ هُمُ ٱلْخَـٰسِرُونَ (٥٢) وَيَسْتَعْجِلُونَكَ بِٱلْعَذَابِ وَلَوْلَآ أَجَلٌ مُّسَمًّى لَّجَآءَهُمُ ٱلْعَذَابُ وَلَيَأْتِيَنَّهُم بَغْتَةً وَهُمْ لَا يَشْعُرُونَ (٥٣) يَسْتَعْجِلُونَكَ بِٱلْعَذَابِ وَإِنَّ جَهَنَّمَ لَمُحِيطَةٌ بِٱلْكَـٰفِرِينَ (٥٤) يَوْمَ يَغْشَـٰهُمُ ٱلْعَذَابُ مِن فَوْقِهِمْ وَمِن تَحْتِ أَرْجُلِهِمْ وَيَقُولُ ذُوقُوا۟ مَا كُنتُمْ تَعْمَلُونَ (٥٥)$$

Is it not sufficient for them that We have sent down to you the Book (the Qur'ân) which is recited to them? Verily, herein is mercy and a reminder (or an admonition) for a people who believe. (51) Say (to them O Muhammad): "Sufficient is Allâh for a witness between me and you. He knows what is in the heavens and on earth." And those who believe in Bâtil (all false deities other than Allâh), and disbelieve in Allâh and (in His Oneness), it is they who are the losers. (52) And they ask you to hasten on the torment (for them), and had it not been for a term appointed, the torment would certainly have come to them. And surely, it will come upon them suddenly while they perceive not! (53) They ask you to hasten on the torment. And verily! Hell, of a surety, will encompass the disbelievers. (54) On the Day when the torment (Hell-fire) shall cover them from above them and from underneath their feet, and it will be said: "Taste what you used to do." (55)

## Quran 29:57-60

كُلُّ نَفْسٍ ذَآئِقَةُ ٱلْمَوْتِ ۖ ثُمَّ إِلَيْنَا تُرْجَعُونَ (٥٧) وَٱلَّذِينَ ءَامَنُواْ وَعَمِلُواْ ٱلصَّٰلِحَٰتِ لَنُبَوِّئَنَّهُم مِّنَ ٱلْجَنَّةِ غُرَفًا تَجْرِى مِن تَحْتِهَا ٱلْأَنْهَٰرُ خَٰلِدِينَ فِيهَا ۚ نِعْمَ أَجْرُ ٱلْعَٰمِلِينَ (٥٨) ٱلَّذِينَ صَبَرُواْ وَعَلَىٰ رَبِّهِمْ يَتَوَكَّلُونَ (٥٩) وَكَأَيِّن مِّن دَآبَّةٍ لَّا تَحْمِلُ رِزْقَهَا ٱللَّهُ يَرْزُقُهَا وَإِيَّاكُمْ ۚ وَهُوَ ٱلسَّمِيعُ ٱلْعَلِيمُ (٦٠)

Everyone shall taste the death. Then unto Us you shall be returned. (57) And those who believe (in the Oneness of Allâh Islâmic Monotheism) and do righteous good deeds, to them We shall surely give lofty dwellings in Paradise, underneath which rivers flow, to live therein forever. Excellent is the reward of the workers. (58) Those who are patient, and put their trust (only) in their Lord (Allâh). (59) And so many a moving (living) creature carries not its own provision! Allâh provides for it and for you. And He is the All-Hearer, the All¬Knower. (60)

## Quran 29:64

وَمَا هَٰذِهِ ٱلْحَيَوٰةُ ٱلدُّنْيَآ إِلَّا لَهْوٌ وَلَعِبٌ ۚ وَإِنَّ ٱلدَّارَ
ٱلْأَخِرَةَ لَهِىَ ٱلْحَيَوَانُ ۚ لَوْ كَانُوا۟ يَعْلَمُونَ

And this life of the world is only an amusement and play! Verily, the home of the Hereafter, that is the life indeed (i.e. the eternal life that will never end), if they but knew. (64)

## Quran 29:68-69

وَمَنْ أَظْلَمُ مِمَّنِ ٱفْتَرَىٰ عَلَى ٱللَّهِ كَذِبًا أَوْ كَذَّبَ بِٱلْحَقِّ لَمَّا
جَآءَهُۥٓ ۚ أَلَيْسَ فِى جَهَنَّمَ مَثْوًى لِّلْكَٰفِرِينَ (٦٨) وَٱلَّذِينَ
جَٰهَدُوا۟ فِينَا لَنَهْدِيَنَّهُمْ سُبُلَنَا ۚ وَإِنَّ ٱللَّهَ لَمَعَ ٱلْمُحْسِنِينَ (٦٩)

And who does more wrong than he who invents a lie against Allâh or denies the truth (Muhammad and his doctrine of Islâmic Monotheism and this Qur'ân), when it comes to him? Is there not a dwelling in Hell for disbelievers (in the Oneness of Allâh and in His Messenger Muhammad)? (68) As for those who strive hard in Us (Our Cause), We will surely guide them to Our Paths (i.e. Allâh's religion - Islâmic Monotheism). And verily, Allâh is with the Muhsinûn (good doers)." (69)

## Quran 30:2-6

غُلِبَتِ ٱلرُّومُ (٢) فِىٓ أَدْنَى ٱلْأَرْضِ وَهُم مِّنۢ بَعْدِ غَلَبِهِمْ سَيَغْلِبُونَ (٣) فِى بِضْعِ سِنِينَ لِلَّهِ ٱلْأَمْرُ مِن قَبْلُ وَمِنۢ بَعْدُ وَيَوْمَئِذٍ يَفْرَحُ ٱلْمُؤْمِنُونَ (٤) بِنَصْرِ ٱللَّهِ يَنصُرُ مَن يَشَآءُ وَهُوَ ٱلْعَزِيزُ ٱلرَّحِيمُ (٥) وَعْدَ ٱللَّهِ لَا يُخْلِفُ ٱللَّهُ وَعْدَهُ وَلَٰكِنَّ أَكْثَرَ ٱلنَّاسِ لَا يَعْلَمُونَ (٦)

The Romans have been defeated. (2) In the nearer land (Syria, Iraq, Jordan, and Palestine), and they, after their defeat, will be victorious. (3) Within three to nine years. The decision of the matter, before and after (these events) is only with Allâh, (before the defeat of Romans by the Persians, and after, the defeat of the Persians by the Romans). And on that Day, the believers (i.e. Muslims) will rejoice (at the victory given by Allâh to the Romans against the Persians) — (4) With the help of Allâh, He helps whom He wills, and He is the All¬Mighty, the Most Merciful. (5) (It is) a Promise of Allâh (i.e. Allâh

will give victory to the Romans against the Persians),
and Allâh fails not in His Promise, but most of men
know not. (6)

## Quran 30:8

أَوَلَمْ يَتَفَكَّرُواْ فِىٓ أَنفُسِهِم مَّا خَلَقَ ٱللَّهُ ٱلسَّمَـٰوَٰتِ وَٱلْأَرْضَ
وَمَا بَيْنَهُمَآ إِلَّا بِٱلْحَقِّ وَأَجَلٍ مُّسَمًّى وَإِنَّ كَثِيرًا مِّنَ
ٱلنَّاسِ بِلِقَآئِ رَبِّهِمْ لَكَـٰفِرُونَ

Do they not think deeply (in their ownselves) about
themselves (how Allâh created them from nothing, and
similarly He will resurrect them)? Allâh has created not
the heavens and the earth, and all that is between them,
except with truth and for an appointed term. And indeed
many of mankind deny the Meeting with their Lord. (8)

## Quran 30:11-16

ٱللَّهُ يَبْدَؤُاْ ٱلْخَلْقَ ثُمَّ يُعِيدُهُۥ ثُمَّ إِلَيْهِ تُرْجَعُونَ (١١) وَيَوْمَ تَقُومُ
ٱلسَّاعَةُ يُبْلِسُ ٱلْمُجْرِمُونَ (١٢) وَلَمْ يَكُن لَّهُم مِّن شُرَكَآئِهِمْ
شُفَعَـٰٓؤُاْ وَكَانُواْ بِشُرَكَآئِهِمْ كَـٰفِرِينَ (١٣) وَيَوْمَ تَقُومُ
ٱلسَّاعَةُ يَوْمَئِذٍ يَتَفَرَّقُونَ (١٤) فَأَمَّا ٱلَّذِينَ ءَامَنُواْ وَعَمِلُواْ
ٱلصَّـٰلِحَـٰتِ فَهُمْ فِى رَوْضَةٍ يُحْبَرُونَ (١٥) وَأَمَّا ٱلَّذِينَ كَفَرُواْ
وَكَذَّبُواْ بِـَٔايَـٰتِنَا وَلِقَآئِ ٱلْأَخِرَةِ فَأُوْلَـٰٓئِكَ فِى ٱلْعَذَابِ مُحْضَرُونَ
(١٦)

Allâh (Alone) originates the creation, then He will repeat it, then to Him you will be returned. (11) And on the Day when the Hour will be established, the Mujrimûn (disbelievers, sinners, criminals, polytheists) will be plunged into destruction with (deep regrets, sorrows, and) despair. (12) No intercessors will they have from those whom they made equal with Allâh (partners i.e. their so¬called associate gods), and they will (themselves) reject and deny their partners. (13) And on the Day when the Hour will be established, that Day shall (all men) be separated (i.e the believers will be separated from the disbelievers). (14) Then as for those who believed (in the Oneness of Allâh - Islâmic Monotheism) and did righteous good deeds, such shall be honoured and made to enjoy luxurious life (forever) in a Garden of Delight (Paradise). (15) And as for those who disbelieved and belied Our Ayât (proofs, evidences, verses, lessons, signs, revelations, Allâh's Messengers, Resurrection, etc.), and the Meeting of the Hereafter, such shall be brought forth to the torment (in the Hell-fire). (16)

## Quran 30:19

يُخْرِجُ ٱلْحَىَّ مِنَ ٱلْمَيِّتِ وَيُخْرِجُ ٱلْمَيِّتَ مِنَ ٱلْحَيِّ وَيُحْيِ ٱلْأَرْضَ بَعْدَ مَوْتِهَآ وَكَذَٰلِكَ تُخْرَجُونَ

He brings out the living from the dead, and brings out the dead from the living. And He revives the earth after

*its death. And thus shall you be brought out*
*(resurrected). (19)*

## Quran 30:25

وَمِنْ ءَايَـٰتِهِۦٓ أَن تَقُومَ ٱلسَّمَآءُ وَٱلْأَرْضُ بِأَمْرِهِۦ ثُمَّ إِذَا دَعَاكُمْ
دَعْوَةً مِّنَ ٱلْأَرْضِ إِذَآ أَنتُمْ تَخْرُجُونَ

*And among His Signs is that the heaven and the earth*
*stand by His Command, Then afterwards when He will*
*call you by single call, behold, you will come out from the*
*earth (i.e from your graves for reckoning and*
*recompense). (25)*

## Quran 30:27

وَهُوَ ٱلَّذِى يَبْدَؤُاْ ٱلْخَلْقَ ثُمَّ يُعِيدُهُۥ وَهُوَ أَهْوَنُ عَلَيْهِ وَلَهُ ٱلْمَثَلُ
ٱلْأَعْلَىٰ فِى ٱلسَّمَـٰوَٰتِ وَٱلْأَرْضِ وَهُوَ ٱلْعَزِيزُ ٱلْحَكِيمُ

*And He it is Who originates the creation, then will repeat*
*it (after it has been perished), and this is easier for Him.*
*His is the highest description (i.e. none has the right to be*
*worshipped but He, and there is nothing comparable unto*
*Him) in the heavens and in the earth. And He is the*
*All¬Mighty, the All¬Wise. (27)*

## Quran 30:29-30

بَلِ ٱتَّبَعَ ٱلَّذِينَ ظَلَمُوٓاْ أَهْوَآءَهُم بِغَيْرِ عِلْمٍ فَمَن يَهْدِى مَنْ أَضَلَّ
ٱللَّهُ وَمَا لَهُم مِّن نَّـٰصِرِينَ (٢٩) فَأَقِمْ وَجْهَكَ لِلدِّينِ حَنِيفًا

فِطْرَتَ ٱللَّهِ ٱلَّتِى فَطَرَ ٱلنَّاسَ عَلَيْهَا لَا تَبْدِيلَ لِخَلْقِ ٱللَّهِ ذَٰلِكَ ٱلدِّينُ ٱلْقَيِّمُ وَلَٰكِنَّ أَكْثَرَ ٱلنَّاسِ لَا يَعْلَمُونَ (٣٠)

*Nay, but those who do wrong follow their own lusts without knowledge, Then who will guide him whom Allâh has sent astray? And for such there will be no helpers. (29) So set you (O Muhammad) your face towards the religion (of pure Islâmic Monotheism) Hanif (worship none but Allâh Alone) Allâh's Fitrah (i.e. Allâh's Islâmic Monotheism), with which He has created mankind. No change let there be in Khalq¬illâh (i.e. the religion of Allâh — Islâmic Monotheism), that is the straight religion, but most of men know not. (30)*

## Quran 30:38-41

فَـَٔاتِ ذَا ٱلْقُرْبَىٰ حَقَّهُ وَٱلْمِسْكِينَ وَٱبْنَ ٱلسَّبِيلِ ذَٰلِكَ خَيْرٌ لِّلَّذِينَ يُرِيدُونَ وَجْهَ ٱللَّهِ وَأُوْلَٰٓئِكَ هُمُ ٱلْمُفْلِحُونَ (٣٨) وَمَآ ءَاتَيْتُم مِّن رِّبًا لِّيَرْبُوَا۟ فِىٓ أَمْوَٰلِ ٱلنَّاسِ فَلَا يَرْبُوا۟ عِندَ ٱللَّهِ وَمَآ ءَاتَيْتُم مِّن زَكَوٰةٍ تُرِيدُونَ وَجْهَ ٱللَّهِ فَأُوْلَٰٓئِكَ هُمُ ٱلْمُضْعِفُونَ (٣٩) ٱللَّهُ ٱلَّذِى خَلَقَكُمْ ثُمَّ رَزَقَكُمْ ثُمَّ يُمِيتُكُمْ ثُمَّ يُحْيِيكُمْ هَلْ مِن شُرَكَآئِكُم مَّن يَفْعَلُ مِن ذَٰلِكُم مِّن شَىْءٍ سُبْحَٰنَهُ وَتَعَٰلَىٰ عَمَّا يُشْرِكُونَ (٤٠) ظَهَرَ ٱلْفَسَادُ فِى ٱلْبَرِّ وَٱلْبَحْرِ بِمَا كَسَبَتْ أَيْدِى ٱلنَّاسِ لِيُذِيقَهُم بَعْضَ ٱلَّذِى عَمِلُوا۟ لَعَلَّهُمْ يَرْجِعُونَ (٤١)

*So give to the kindred his due, and to Al¬Miskîn (the poor) and to the wayfarer; That is best for those who seek*

*Allâh's Countenance, and it is they who will be successful. (38) And that which you give in gift[] (to others), in order that it may increase (your wealth by expecting to get a better one in return) from other people's property, has no increase with Allâh, but that which you give in Zakât seeking Allâh's Countenance then those, they shall have manifold increase. (39) Allâh is He Who created you, then provided food for you, then will cause you to die, then (again) He will give you life (on the Day of Resurrection). Is there any of your (so¬called) partners (of Allâh) that do anything of that ? Glory is to Him! And Exalted is He above all that (evil) they associate (with Him). (40) Evil (sins and disobedience to Allâh) has appeared on land and sea because of what the hands of men have earned (by oppression and evil deeds), that He (Allâh) may make them taste a part of that which they have done, in order that they may return (by repenting to Allâh, and begging His Pardon). (41)*

## Quran 30:43-45

فَأَقِمْ وَجْهَكَ لِلدِّينِ ٱلْقَيِّمِ مِن قَبْلِ أَن يَأْتِىَ يَوْمٌ لَّا مَرَدَّ لَهُۥ مِنَ ٱللَّهِ يَوْمَئِذٍ يَصَّدَّعُونَ (٤٣) مَن كَفَرَ فَعَلَيْهِ كُفْرُهُۥ وَمَنْ عَمِلَ صَٰلِحًا فَلِأَنفُسِهِمْ يَمْهَدُونَ (٤٤) لِيَجْزِىَ ٱلَّذِينَ ءَامَنُواْ وَعَمِلُواْ ٱلصَّٰلِحَٰتِ مِن فَضْلِهِۦٓ إِنَّهُۥ لَا يُحِبُّ ٱلْكَٰفِرِينَ (٤٥)

So set you (O Muhammad) your face (in obedience to Allâh, your Lord) to the straight and right religion (Islâmic Monotheism), before there comes from Allâh a Day which none can avert it. On that Day men shall be divided [(in two groups), a group in Paradise and a group in Hell]. (43) Whosoever disbelieves will suffer from his disbelief, and whosoever does righteous good deeds (by practising Islâmic Monotheism), then such will prepare a good place (in Paradise) for themselves (and will be saved by Allâh from His Torment). (44) That He may reward those who believe (in the Oneness of Allâh Islâmic Monotheism), and do righteous good deeds, out of His Bounty. Verily, He likes not the disbelievers. (45)

## Quran 30:47

وَلَقَدْ أَرْسَلْنَا مِن قَبْلِكَ رُسُلاً إِلَىٰ قَوْمِهِمْ فَجَاءُوهُم بِالْبَيِّنَـٰتِ فَانتَقَمْنَا مِنَ الَّذِينَ أَجْرَمُواْ ۖ وَكَانَ حَقًّا عَلَيْنَا نَصْرُ الْمُؤْمِنِينَ

And indeed We did send Messengers before you (O Muhammad) to their own peoples. They came to them with clear proofs, then, We took vengeance on those who committed crimes (disbelief, setting partners in worship with Allâh, sins), and (as for) the believers it was incumbent upon Us to help (them). (47)

## Quran 30:50

فَٱنظُرۡ إِلَىٰٓ ءَاثَٰرِ رَحۡمَتِ ٱللَّهِ كَيۡفَ يُحۡىِ ٱلۡأَرۡضَ بَعۡدَ مَوۡتِهَآۚ إِنَّ ذَٰلِكَ لَمُحۡىِ ٱلۡمَوۡتَىٰۖ وَهُوَ عَلَىٰ كُلِّ شَىۡءٍ قَدِيرٌ

*Look then at the effects (results) of Allâh's Mercy, how He revives the earth after its death. Verily, that (Allâh) (Who revived the earth after its death) shall indeed raise the dead (on the Day of Resurrection), and He is Able to do all things. (50)*

## Quran 30:54-60

۞ ٱللَّهُ ٱلَّذِى خَلَقَكُم مِّن ضَعۡفٍ ثُمَّ جَعَلَ مِنۢ بَعۡدِ ضَعۡفٍ قُوَّةً ثُمَّ جَعَلَ مِنۢ بَعۡدِ قُوَّةٍ ضَعۡفًا وَشَيۡبَةًۚ يَخۡلُقُ مَا يَشَآءُۖ وَهُوَ ٱلۡعَلِيمُ ٱلۡقَدِيرُ (٥٤) وَيَوۡمَ تَقُومُ ٱلسَّاعَةُ يُقۡسِمُ ٱلۡمُجۡرِمُونَ مَا لَبِثُوا۟ غَيۡرَ سَاعَةٍۚ كَذَٰلِكَ كَانُوا۟ يُؤۡفَكُونَ (٥٥) وَقَالَ ٱلَّذِينَ أُوتُوا۟ ٱلۡعِلۡمَ وَٱلۡإِيمَٰنَ لَقَدۡ لَبِثۡتُمۡ فِى كِتَٰبِ ٱللَّهِ إِلَىٰ يَوۡمِ ٱلۡبَعۡثِۖ فَهَٰذَا يَوۡمُ ٱلۡبَعۡثِ وَلَٰكِنَّكُمۡ كُنتُمۡ لَا تَعۡلَمُونَ (٥٦) فَيَوۡمَئِذٍ لَّا يَنفَعُ ٱلَّذِينَ ظَلَمُوا۟ مَعۡذِرَتُهُمۡ وَلَا هُمۡ يُسۡتَعۡتَبُونَ (٥٧) وَلَقَدۡ ضَرَبۡنَا لِلنَّاسِ فِى هَٰذَا ٱلۡقُرۡءَانِ مِن كُلِّ مَثَلٍۚ وَلَئِن جِئۡتَهُم بِـَٔايَةٍ لَّيَقُولَنَّ ٱلَّذِينَ كَفَرُوٓا۟ إِنۡ أَنتُمۡ إِلَّا مُبۡطِلُونَ (٥٨) كَذَٰلِكَ يَطۡبَعُ ٱللَّهُ عَلَىٰ قُلُوبِ ٱلَّذِينَ لَا يَعۡلَمُونَ (٥٩) فَٱصۡبِرۡ إِنَّ وَعۡدَ ٱللَّهِ حَقٌّۖ وَلَا يَسۡتَخِفَّنَّكَ ٱلَّذِينَ لَا يُوقِنُونَ (٦٠)

*Allâh is He Who created you in (a state of) weakness, then gave you strength after weakness, then after strength gave (you) weakness and grey hair. He creates what He wills. And it is He Who is the All¬Knowing,*

277

*the All¬Powerful (i.e. Able to do all things). (54) And on the Day that the Hour will be established, the Mujrimûn (criminals, disbelievers, polytheists, sinners) will swear that they stayed not but an hour, thus were they ever deluded [away from the truth (i.e they used to tell lies and take false oaths, and turn away from the truth) in this life of the world]. (55) And those who have been bestowed with knowledge and faith will say: "Indeed you have stayed according to the Decree of Allâh, until the Day of Resurrection, so this is the Day of Resurrection, but you knew not." (56) So on that Day no excuse of theirs will avail those who did wrong (by associating partners in worship with Allâh, and by denying the Day of Resurrection), nor will they be allowed (then) to return to seek Allâh's Pleasure (by having Islâmic Faith with righteous deeds and by giving up polytheism, sins and crimes with repentance). (57) And indeed We have set forth for mankind, in this Qur'ân every kind of parable. But if you (O Muhammad) bring to them any sign or proof, (as an evidence for the truth of your Prophethood), the disbelievers are sure to say (to the believers): "You follow nothing but falsehood, and magic." (58) Thus does Allâh seal up the hearts of those who know not [the proofs and evidence of the Oneness of Allâh i.e. those who try not to understand true facts that which you (Muhammad) have brought to them]. (59) So be patient (O Muhammad). Verily, the Promise of Allâh* is true, and let not those who have no certainty of faith, discourage you from conveying Allâh's Message (which you are obliged to convey). (60)

## Quran 31:2-9

تِلْكَ ءَايَـٰتُ ٱلْكِتَـٰبِ ٱلْحَكِيمِ (٢) هُدًى وَرَحْمَةً لِّلْمُحْسِنِينَ (٣) ٱلَّذِينَ يُقِيمُونَ ٱلصَّلَوٰةَ وَيُؤْتُونَ ٱلزَّكَوٰةَ وَهُم بِٱلْأَخِرَةِ هُمْ يُوقِنُونَ (٤) أُوْلَـٰئِكَ عَلَىٰ هُدًى مِّن رَّبِّهِمْ وَأُوْلَـٰئِكَ هُمُ ٱلْمُفْلِحُونَ (٥) وَمِنَ ٱلنَّاسِ مَن يَشْتَرِى لَهْوَ ٱلْحَدِيثِ لِيُضِلَّ عَن سَبِيلِ ٱللَّهِ بِغَيْرِ عِلْمٍ وَيَتَّخِذَهَا هُزُوًا أُوْلَـٰئِكَ لَهُمْ عَذَابٌ مُّهِينٌ (٦) وَإِذَا تُتْلَىٰ عَلَيْهِ ءَايَـٰتُنَا وَلَّىٰ مُسْتَكْبِرًا كَأَن لَّمْ يَسْمَعْهَا كَأَنَّ فِى أُذُنَيْهِ وَقْرًا فَبَشِّرْهُ بِعَذَابٍ أَلِيمٍ (٧) إِنَّ ٱلَّذِينَ ءَامَنُوا وَعَمِلُوا ٱلصَّـٰلِحَـٰتِ لَهُمْ جَنَّـٰتُ ٱلنَّعِيمِ (٨) خَـٰلِدِينَ فِيهَا وَعْدَ ٱللَّهِ حَقًّا وَهُوَ ٱلْعَزِيزُ ٱلْحَكِيمُ (٩)

*These are Verses of the Wise Book (the Qur'ân). (2) A guide and a mercy for the Muhsinûn (good¬doers). (3) Those who perform As¬Salât (Iqamat¬as- Salât) and give Zakât and they have faith in the Hereafter with certainty. (4) Such are on guidance from their Lord, and such are the successful. (5) And of mankind is he who purchases idle talks (i.e.music, singing, etc.) to mislead (men) from the Path of Allâh without knowledge, and takes it (the Path of Allâh, or the Verses of the Qur'ân) by way of mockery. For such there will be a humiliating torment (in the Hell-fire). (6) And when Our Verses (of* the Qur'ân) are recited to such a one, he turns away in pride, as if he heard them not, — as if there were deafness in his ear. So announce to him a painful torment (7) Verily, those who believe (in Islâmic Monotheism) and do righteous good deeds, for them are Gardens of Delight (Paradise). (8) To abide therein. It is a Promise of Allâh in truth. And He is the All¬Mighty, the All¬Wise. (9)

## Quran 31:15-16

وَإِن جَٰهَدَاكَ عَلَىٰٓ أَن تُشْرِكَ بِى مَا لَيْسَ لَكَ بِهِۦ عِلْمٌ فَلَا تُطِعْهُمَا ۖ وَصَاحِبْهُمَا فِى ٱلدُّنْيَا مَعْرُوفًا ۖ وَٱتَّبِعْ سَبِيلَ مَنْ أَنَابَ إِلَىَّ ۚ ثُمَّ إِلَىَّ مَرْجِعُكُمْ فَأُنَبِّئُكُم بِمَا كُنتُمْ تَعْمَلُونَ (١٥) يَٰبُنَىَّ إِنَّهَآ إِن تَكُ مِثْقَالَ حَبَّةٍ مِّنْ خَرْدَلٍ فَتَكُن فِى صَخْرَةٍ أَوْ فِى ٱلسَّمَٰوَٰتِ أَوْ فِى ٱلْأَرْضِ يَأْتِ بِهَا ٱللَّهُ ۚ إِنَّ ٱللَّهَ لَطِيفٌ خَبِيرٌ (١٦)

But if they (both) strive with you to make you join in worship with Me others that of which you have no knowledge, then obey them not, but behave with them in the world kindly, and follow the path of him who turns to Me in repentance and in obedience. Then to Me will be your return, and I shall tell you what you used to do. (15) "O my son! If it be (anything) equal to the weight of a grain of mustard seed, and though it be in a rock, or in the heavens or in the earth, Allâh will bring it forth.

*Verily, Allâh is Subtle (in bringing out that grain),*
*Well¬Aware (of its place). (16)*

## Quran 31:18

وَلَا تُصَعِّرْ خَدَّكَ لِلنَّاسِ وَلَا تَمْشِ فِى ٱلْأَرْضِ مَرَحًا إِنَّ ٱللَّهَ لَا يُحِبُّ كُلَّ مُخْتَالٍ فَخُورٍ

*"And turn not your face away from men with pride, nor walk in insolence through the earth. Verily, Allâh likes not any arrogant boaster (18)*

## Quran 31:21-24

وَإِذَا قِيلَ لَهُمُ ٱتَّبِعُواْ مَآ أَنزَلَ ٱللَّهُ قَالُواْ بَلْ نَتَّبِعُ مَا وَجَدْنَا عَلَيْهِ ءَابَآءَنَآ أَوَلَوْ كَانَ ٱلشَّيْطَـٰنُ يَدْعُوهُمْ إِلَىٰ عَذَابِ ٱلسَّعِيرِ (٢١) ۞ وَمَن يُسْلِمْ وَجْهَهُۥ إِلَى ٱللَّهِ وَهُوَ مُحْسِنٌ فَقَدِ ٱسْتَمْسَكَ بِٱلْعُرْوَةِ ٱلْوُثْقَىٰ وَإِلَى ٱللَّهِ عَـٰقِبَةُ ٱلْأُمُورِ (٢٢) وَمَن كَفَرَ فَلَا يَحْزُنكَ كُفْرُهُۥ إِلَيْنَا مَرْجِعُهُمْ فَنُنَبِّئُهُم بِمَا عَمِلُوٓاْ إِنَّ ٱللَّهَ عَلِيمٌ بِذَاتِ ٱلصُّدُورِ (٢٣) نُمَتِّعُهُمْ قَلِيلاً ثُمَّ نَضْطَرُّهُمْ إِلَىٰ عَذَابٍ غَلِيظٍ (٢٤)

*And when it is said to them: "Follow that which Allâh has sent down", they say: "Nay, we shall follow that which we found our fathers (following)." (Would they do so) even if Shaitân (Satan) invites them to the torment of the Fire? (21) And whosoever submits his face (himself) to Allâh, while he is a Muhsin (good¬doer i.e. performs good deeds totally for Allâh's sake without any show - off*

or to gain praise or fame and does them in accordance
with the Sunnah of Allâh's Messenger Muhammad),
then he has grasped the most trustworthy hand¬hold [Lâ
ilâha illallâh (none has the right to be worshipped but
Allâh)]. And to Allâh return all matters for decision.
(22) And whosoever disbelieves, let not his disbelief
grieve you (O Muhammad). To Us is their return, and
We shall inform them what they have done. Verily, Allâh
is the All¬Knower of what is in the breasts (of men).
(23) We let them enjoy for a little while, then in the end
We shall oblige them to (enter) a great torment. (24)

## Quran 31:33-34

يَـٰٓأَيُّهَا ٱلنَّاسُ ٱتَّقُوا۟ رَبَّكُمْ وَٱخْشَوْا۟ يَوْمًا لَّا يَجْزِى وَالِدٌ عَن
وَلَدِهِۦ وَلَا مَوْلُودٌ هُوَ جَازٍ عَن وَالِدِهِۦ شَيْـًٔا إِنَّ وَعْدَ ٱللَّهِ حَقٌّ فَلَا
تَغُرَّنَّكُمُ ٱلْحَيَوٰةُ ٱلدُّنْيَا وَلَا يَغُرَّنَّكُم بِٱللَّهِ ٱلْغَرُورُ (٣٣) إِنَّ
ٱللَّهَ عِندَهُۥ عِلْمُ ٱلسَّاعَةِ وَيُنَزِّلُ ٱلْغَيْثَ وَيَعْلَمُ مَا فِى ٱلْأَرْحَامِ
وَمَا تَدْرِى نَفْسٌ مَّاذَا تَكْسِبُ غَدًا وَمَا تَدْرِى نَفْسٌۢ بِأَىِّ
أَرْضٍ تَمُوتُ إِنَّ ٱللَّهَ عَلِيمٌ خَبِيرٌ (٣٤)

O mankind! Be afraid of your Lord (by keeping your duty
to Him and avoiding all evil), and fear a Day when no
father can avail aught for his son, nor a son avail aught
for his father. Verily, the Promise of Allâh is true, let not
then this (worldly) present life deceive you, nor let the
chief deceiver (Satan) deceive you about Allâh.
(33) Verily, Allâh! With Him (Alone) is the knowledge of

the Hour, He sends down the rain, and knows that which is in the wombs. No person knows what he will earn tomorrow, and no person knows in what land he will die. Verily, Allâh is All¬Knower, All¬Aware (of things). (34)

## Quran 32:5

يُدَبِّرُ ٱلْأَمْرَ مِنَ ٱلسَّمَاءِ إِلَى ٱلْأَرْضِ ثُمَّ يَعْرُجُ إِلَيْهِ فِى يَوْمٍ كَانَ مِقْدَارُهُ أَلْفَ سَنَةٍ مِّمَّا تَعُدُّونَ

He manages and regulates (every) affair from the heavens to the earth, then it (affair) will go up to Him, in one Day, the space whereof is a thousand years of your reckoning (i.e. reckoning of our present worlds time). (5)

## Quran 32:10-22

وَقَالُوٓاْ أَءِذَا ضَلَلْنَا فِى ٱلْأَرْضِ أَءِنَّا لَفِى خَلْقٍ جَدِيدٍ بَلْ هُم بِلِقَآءِ رَبِّهِمْ كَـٰفِرُونَ (١٠) قُلْ يَتَوَفَّىٰكُم مَّلَكُ ٱلْمَوْتِ ٱلَّذِى وُكِّلَ بِكُمْ ثُمَّ إِلَىٰ رَبِّكُمْ تُرْجَعُونَ (١١) وَلَوْ تَرَىٰٓ إِذِ ٱلْمُجْرِمُونَ نَاكِسُواْ رُءُوسِهِمْ عِندَ رَبِّهِمْ رَبَّنَآ أَبْصَرْنَا وَسَمِعْنَا فَٱرْجِعْنَا نَعْمَلْ صَـٰلِحًا إِنَّا مُوقِنُونَ (١٢) وَلَوْ شِئْنَا لَـَٔاتَيْنَا كُلَّ نَفْسٍ هُدَىٰهَا وَلَـٰكِنْ حَقَّ ٱلْقَوْلُ مِنِّى لَأَمْلَأَنَّ جَهَنَّمَ مِنَ ٱلْجِنَّةِ وَٱلنَّاسِ أَجْمَعِينَ (١٣) فَذُوقُواْ بِمَا نَسِيتُمْ لِقَآءَ يَوْمِكُمْ هَـٰذَآ إِنَّا نَسِينَـٰكُمْ وَذُوقُواْ عَذَابَ ٱلْخُلْدِ بِمَا كُنتُمْ تَعْمَلُونَ (١٤) إِنَّمَا يُؤْمِنُ بِـَٔايَـٰتِنَا ٱلَّذِينَ إِذَا ذُكِّرُواْ بِهَا خَرُّواْ سُجَّدًا وَسَبَّحُواْ

بِحَمْدِ رَبِّهِمْ وَهُمْ لَا يَسْتَكْبِرُونَ ۩ (١٥) تَتَجَافَىٰ جُنُوبُهُمْ عَنِ
ٱلْمَضَاجِعِ يَدْعُونَ رَبَّهُمْ خَوْفًا وَطَمَعًا وَمِمَّا رَزَقْنَٰهُمْ
يُنفِقُونَ (١٦) فَلَا تَعْلَمُ نَفْسٌ مَّآ أُخْفِىَ لَهُم مِّن قُرَّةِ أَعْيُنٍ
جَزَآءًۢ بِمَا كَانُواْ يَعْمَلُونَ (١٧) أَفَمَن كَانَ مُؤْمِنًا كَمَن كَانَ
فَاسِقًا لَّا يَسْتَوُۥنَ (١٨) أَمَّا ٱلَّذِينَ ءَامَنُواْ وَعَمِلُواْ ٱلصَّٰلِحَٰتِ
فَلَهُمْ جَنَّٰتُ ٱلْمَأْوَىٰ نُزُلاًۢ بِمَا كَانُواْ يَعْمَلُونَ (١٩) وَأَمَّا ٱلَّذِينَ
فَسَقُواْ فَمَأْوَىٰهُمُ ٱلنَّارُ كُلَّمَآ أَرَادُوٓاْ أَن يَخْرُجُواْ مِنْهَآ أُعِيدُواْ
فِيهَا وَقِيلَ لَهُمْ ذُوقُواْ عَذَابَ ٱلنَّارِ ٱلَّذِى كُنتُم بِهِۦ تُكَذِّبُونَ
(٢٠) وَلَنُذِيقَنَّهُم مِّنَ ٱلْعَذَابِ ٱلْأَدْنَىٰ دُونَ ٱلْعَذَابِ ٱلْأَكْبَرِ
لَعَلَّهُمْ يَرْجِعُونَ (٢١) وَمَنْ أَظْلَمُ مِمَّن ذُكِّرَ بِـَٔايَٰتِ رَبِّهِۦ ثُمَّ
أَعْرَضَ عَنْهَآ إِنَّا مِنَ ٱلْمُجْرِمِينَ مُنتَقِمُونَ (٢٢)

And they say: "When we are (dead and become) lost in
the earth, shall we indeed be created anew?" Nay, but
they deny the Meeting with their Lord! (10) Say: "The
angel of death, who is set over you, will take your souls,
Then you shall be brought to your Lord." (11) And if you
only could see when the Mujrimûn (criminals,
disbelievers, polytheists, sinners, etc.) shall hang their
heads before their Lord (saying): "Our Lord! We have
now seen and heard, so send us back (to the world), that
we will do righteous good deeds. Verily! We now believe
with certainty." (12) And if We had willed, surely! We
would have given every person his guidance, but the
Word from Me took effect (about evil¬doers), that I will

fill Hell with jinn and mankind together (13) Then taste you (the torment of the Fire) because of your forgetting the Meeting of this Day of yours, surely! We too will forget you, so taste you the abiding torment for what you used to do (14) Only those believe in Our Ayât (proofs, evidences, verses, lessons, signs, revelations, etc.), who, when they are reminded of them fall down prostrate, and glorify the Praises of their Lord, and they are not proud. (15) Their sides forsake their beds, to invoke their Lord in fear and hope, and they spend (in charity in Allâh's Cause) out of what We have bestowed on them (16) No person knows what is kept hidden for them of joy as a reward for what they used to do (17) Is then he who is a believer like him who is Fâsiq (disbeliever and disobedient to Allâh)? Not equal are they (18) As for those who believe (in the Oneness of Allâh Islâmic Monotheism) and do righteous good deeds, for them are Gardens (Paradise) as an entertainment, for what they used to do (19) And as for those who are Fâsiqûn (disbelievers and disobedient to Allâh), their abode will be the Fire, everytime they wish to get away therefrom, they will be put back thereto, and it will be said to them: "Taste you the torment of the Fire which you used to deny."
(20) And verily, We will make them taste of the near torment (i.e. the torment in the life of this world, i.e. disasters, calamities, etc.) prior to the supreme torment (in the Hereafter), in order that they may (repent and)

return (i.e. accept Islâm). (21) And who does more wrong
than he who is reminded of the Ayât (proofs, evidences,
verses, lessons, signs, revelations, etc.) of his Lord, then
turns aside therefrom? Verily, We shall exact retribution
from the Mujrimûn (criminals, disbelievers, polytheists,
sinners, etc.) (22)

## Quran 32:25

إِنَّ رَبَّكَ هُوَ يَفْصِلُ بَيْنَهُمْ يَوْمَ ٱلْقِيَـٰمَةِ فِيمَا كَانُواْ فِيهِ
يَخْتَلِفُونَ

Verily, your Lord will judge between them on the Day of
Resurrection, concerning that wherein they used to differ
(25)

## Quran 32:28-29

وَيَقُولُونَ مَتَىٰ هَـٰذَا ٱلْفَتْحُ إِن كُنتُمْ صَـٰدِقِينَ (٢٨) قُلْ يَوْمَ
ٱلْفَتْحِ لَا يَنفَعُ ٱلَّذِينَ كَفَرُواْ إِيمَـٰنُهُمْ وَلَا هُمْ يُنظَرُونَ (٢٩)

They say: "When will this Fath (Decision) be (between
us and you, i.e. the Day of Resurrection), if you are
telling the truth?" (28) Say: "On the Day of Al¬Fath
(Decision), no profit will it be to those who disbelieve if
they (then) believe! Nor will they be granted a respite."
(29)

## Quran 33:8

لِّيَسْـَٔلَ ٱلصَّـٰدِقِينَ عَن صِدْقِهِمْ وَأَعَدَّ لِلْكَـٰفِرِينَ عَذَابًا أَلِيمًا

*That He may ask the truthful (Allâh's Messengers and*
*His Prophets) about their truth (i.e. the conveyance of*
*Allâh's Message that which they were charged with).*
*And He has prepared for the disbelievers a painful*
*torment (Hell-fire). (8)*

## Quran 33:21-22

لَّقَدْ كَانَ لَكُمْ فِى رَسُولِ ٱللَّهِ أُسْوَةٌ حَسَنَةٌ لِّمَن كَانَ يَرْجُواْ ٱللَّهَ
وَٱلْيَوْمَ ٱلْأَخِرَ وَذَكَرَ ٱللَّهَ كَثِيرًا (٢١) وَلَمَّا رَءَا ٱلْمُؤْمِنُونَ
ٱلْأَحْزَابَ قَالُواْ هَـٰذَا مَا وَعَدَنَا ٱللَّهُ وَرَسُولُهُ وَصَدَقَ ٱللَّهُ
وَرَسُولُهُ وَمَا زَادَهُمْ إِلَّآ إِيمَـٰنًا وَتَسْلِيمًا (٢٢)

*Indeed in the Messenger of Allâh (Muhammad) you have*
*a good example to follow for him who hopes for (the*
*Meeting with) Allâh and the Last Day and remembers*
*Allâh much. (21) And when the believers saw Al¬Ahzâb*
*(the Confederates), they said: "This is what Allâh and*
*His Messenger (Muhammad) had promised us, and*
*Allâh and His Messenger (Muhammad) had spoken the*
*truth, And it only added to their faith and to their*
*submissiveness (to Allâh). (22)*

## Quran 33:29-31

وَإِن كُنتُنَّ تُرِدْنَ ٱللَّهَ وَرَسُولَهُ وَٱلدَّارَ ٱلْأَخِرَةَ فَإِنَّ ٱللَّهَ أَعَدَّ
لِلْمُحْسِنَـٰتِ مِنكُنَّ أَجْرًا عَظِيمًا (٢٩) يَـٰنِسَآءَ ٱلنَّبِيِّ مَن يَأْتِ
مِنكُنَّ بِفَـٰحِشَةٍ مُّبَيِّنَةٍ يُضَـٰعَفْ لَهَا ٱلْعَذَابُ ضِعْفَيْنِ وَكَانَ ذَٰلِكَ

عَلَى ٱللَّهِ يَسِيرًا (٣٠) ۞ وَمَن يَقْنُتْ مِنكُنَّ لِلَّهِ وَرَسُولِهِۦ
وَتَعْمَلْ صَلِحًا نُّؤْتِهَآ أَجْرَهَا مَرَّتَيْنِ وَأَعْتَدْنَا لَهَا رِزْقًا
كَرِيمًا (٣١)

But if you desire Allâh and His Messenger, and the home
of the Hereafter, then verily, Allâh has prepared for
Al¬Muhsinât (good¬doers) amongst you an enormous
reward. (29) O wives of the Prophet! Whoever of you
commits an open illegal sexual intercourse, the torment
for her will be doubled, and that is ever easy for Allâh.
(30) And whosoever of you is obedient to Allâh and His
Messenger, and does righteous good deeds, We shall give
her, her reward twice over, and We have prepared for her
Rizqan Karim (a noble provision -Paradise). (31)

## Quran 33:35-36

إِنَّ ٱلْمُسْلِمِينَ وَٱلْمُسْلِمَٰتِ وَٱلْمُؤْمِنِينَ وَٱلْمُؤْمِنَٰتِ وَٱلْقَٰنِتِينَ
وَٱلْقَٰنِتَٰتِ وَٱلصَّٰدِقِينَ وَٱلصَّٰدِقَٰتِ وَٱلصَّٰبِرِينَ وَٱلصَّٰبِرَٰتِ
وَٱلْخَٰشِعِينَ وَٱلْخَٰشِعَٰتِ وَٱلْمُتَصَدِّقِينَ وَٱلْمُتَصَدِّقَٰتِ
وَٱلصَّٰٓئِمِينَ وَٱلصَّٰٓئِمَٰتِ وَٱلْحَٰفِظِينَ فُرُوجَهُمْ وَٱلْحَٰفِظَٰتِ
وَٱلذَّٰكِرِينَ ٱللَّهَ كَثِيرًا وَٱلذَّٰكِرَٰتِ أَعَدَّ ٱللَّهُ لَهُم مَّغْفِرَةً
وَأَجْرًا عَظِيمًا (٣٥) وَمَا كَانَ لِمُؤْمِنٍ وَلَا مُؤْمِنَةٍ إِذَا قَضَى
ٱللَّهُ وَرَسُولُهُۥٓ أَمْرًا أَن يَكُونَ لَهُمُ ٱلْخِيَرَةُ مِنْ أَمْرِهِمْ وَمَن
يَعْصِ ٱللَّهَ وَرَسُولَهُۥ فَقَدْ ضَلَّ ضَلَٰلًا مُّبِينًا (٣٦)

Verily, the Muslims (those who submit to Allâh in Islâm) men and women, the believers men and women (who believe in Islâmic Monotheism), the men and the women who are obedient (to Allâh), the men and women who are truthful (in their speech and deeds), the men and the women who are patient (in performing all the duties which Allâh has ordered and in abstaining from all that Allâh has forbidden), the men and the women who are humble (before their Lord Allâh), the men and the women who give Sadaqât (i.e. Zakât, and alms), the men and the women who observe Saum (fast) (the obligatory fasting during the month of Ramadân, and the optional Nawâfil fasting), the men and the women who guard their chastity (from illegal sexual acts) and the men and the women who remember Allâh much with their hearts and tongues. Allâh has prepared for them forgiveness and a great reward (i.e. Paradise). (35) It is not for a believer, man or woman, when Allâh and His Messenger have decreed a matter that they should have any option in their decision. And whoever disobeys Allâh and His Messenger, he has indeed strayed in to a plain error. (36)

## Quran 33:40

مَّا كَانَ مُحَمَّدٌ أَبَآ أَحَدٍ مِّن رِّجَالِكُمْ وَلَـٰكِن رَّسُولَ ٱللَّهِ وَخَاتَمَ ٱلنَّبِيِّـۧنَ وَكَانَ ٱللَّهُ بِكُلِّ شَىْءٍ عَلِيمًا

*Muhammad is not the father of any of your men, but he is the Messenger of Allâh and the last (end) of the Prophets. And Allâh is Ever All¬Aware of everything. (40)*

## Quran 33:43-47

هُوَ ٱلَّذِى يُصَلِّى عَلَيْكُمْ وَمَلَـٰٓئِكَتُهُۥ لِيُخْرِجَكُم مِّنَ ٱلظُّلُمَـٰتِ إِلَى ٱلنُّورِ ۚ وَكَانَ بِٱلْمُؤْمِنِينَ رَحِيمًا (٤٣) تَحِيَّتُهُمْ يَوْمَ يَلْقَوْنَهُۥ سَلَـٰمٌ ۚ وَأَعَدَّ لَهُمْ أَجْرًا كَرِيمًا (٤٤) يَـٰٓأَيُّهَا ٱلنَّبِىُّ إِنَّآ أَرْسَلْنَـٰكَ شَـٰهِدًا وَمُبَشِّرًا وَنَذِيرًا (٤٥) وَدَاعِيًا إِلَى ٱللَّهِ بِإِذْنِهِۦ وَسِرَاجًا مُّنِيرًا (٤٦) وَبَشِّرِ ٱلْمُؤْمِنِينَ بِأَنَّ لَهُم مِّنَ ٱللَّهِ فَضْلاً كَبِيرًا (٤٧)

*He it is Who sends Salât (His blessings) on you, and His angels too (ask Allâh to bless and forgive you), that He may bring you out from darkness (of disbelief and polytheism) into light (of Belief and Islâmic Monotheism). And He is Ever Most Merciful to the believers. (43) Their greeting on the Day they shall meet Him will be "Salâm: Peace (i.e. the angels will say to them: Salâmu 'Alaikum)!" And He has prepared for them a generous reward (i.e. Paradise). (44) O Prophet (Muhammad )! Verily, We have sent you as witness, and a bearer of glad tidings, and a warner, (45) And as one who invites to Allâh [Islâmic Monotheism, i.e. to worship none but Allâh (Alone)] by His Leave, and as a lamp spreading light (through your instructions from the*

Qur'ân and the Sunnah the legal ways of the Prophet).
(46) And announce to the believers (in the Oneness of
Allâh and in His Messenger Muhammad) the glad
tidings, that they will have from Allâh a Great Bounty.
(47)

## Quran 33:57-58

إِنَّ ٱلَّذِينَ يُؤْذُونَ ٱللَّهَ وَرَسُولَهُ لَعَنَهُمُ ٱللَّهُ فِى ٱلدُّنْيَا وَٱلْآخِرَةِ
وَأَعَدَّ لَهُمْ عَذَابًا مُّهِينًا (٥٧) وَٱلَّذِينَ يُؤْذُونَ ٱلْمُؤْمِنِينَ
وَٱلْمُؤْمِنَٰتِ بِغَيْرِ مَا ٱكْتَسَبُوا۟ فَقَدِ ٱحْتَمَلُوا۟ بُهْتَٰنًا وَإِثْمًا مُّبِينًا
(٥٨)

*Verily, those who annoy Allâh and His Messenger Allâh
has cursed them in this world, and in the Hereafter, and
has prepared for them a humiliating torment. (57) And
those who annoy believing men and women
undeservedly, they bear (on themselves) the crime of
slander and plain sin. (58)*

## Quran 33:60-68

۞ لَّئِن لَّمْ يَنتَهِ ٱلْمُنَٰفِقُونَ وَٱلَّذِينَ فِى قُلُوبِهِم مَّرَضٌ
وَٱلْمُرْجِفُونَ فِى ٱلْمَدِينَةِ لَنُغْرِيَنَّكَ بِهِمْ ثُمَّ لَا يُجَاوِرُونَكَ فِيهَآ
إِلَّا قَلِيلًا (٦٠) مَّلْعُونِينَ أَيْنَمَا ثُقِفُوا۟ أُخِذُوا۟ وَقُتِّلُوا۟ تَقْتِيلًا
(٦١) سُنَّةَ ٱللَّهِ فِى ٱلَّذِينَ خَلَوْا۟ مِن قَبْلُ وَلَن تَجِدَ لِسُنَّةِ ٱللَّهِ
تَبْدِيلًا (٦٢) يَسْـَٔلُكَ ٱلنَّاسُ عَنِ ٱلسَّاعَةِ قُلْ إِنَّمَا عِلْمُهَا عِندَ
ٱللَّهِ وَمَا يُدْرِيكَ لَعَلَّ ٱلسَّاعَةَ تَكُونُ قَرِيبًا (٦٣) إِنَّ ٱللَّهَ لَعَنَ

ٱلْكَـٰفِرِينَ وَأَعَدَّ لَهُمْ سَعِيرًا ﴿٦٤﴾ خَـٰلِدِينَ فِيهَآ أَبَدًا ۖ لَّا يَجِدُونَ
وَلِيًّا وَلَا نَصِيرًا ﴿٦٥﴾ يَوْمَ تُقَلَّبُ وُجُوهُهُمْ فِى ٱلنَّارِ يَقُولُونَ
يَـٰلَيْتَنَآ أَطَعْنَا ٱللَّهَ وَأَطَعْنَا ٱلرَّسُولَا۠ ﴿٦٦﴾ وَقَالُوا۟ رَبَّنَآ إِنَّآ أَطَعْنَا
سَادَتَنَا وَكُبَرَآءَنَا فَأَضَلُّونَا ٱلسَّبِيلَا۠ ﴿٦٧﴾ رَبَّنَآ ءَاتِهِمْ ضِعْفَيْنِ
مِنَ ٱلْعَذَابِ وَٱلْعَنْهُمْ لَعْنًا كَبِيرًا ﴿٦٨﴾

*If the hypocrites, and those in whose hearts is a disease
(evil desire for adultery), and those who spread false news
among the people in Al¬Madinah, stop not, We shall
certainly let you overpower them; then they will not be
able to stay in it as your neighbours but a little while.
(60) Accursed, they shall be seized wherever found and
killed with a (terrible) slaughter. (61) That was the Way
of Allâh in the case of those who passed away of old, and
you will not find any change in the Way of Allâh.
(62) People ask you concerning the Hour, say: "The
knowledge of it is with Allâh only. What do you know? It
may be that the Hour is near!" (63) Verily, Allâh has
cursed the disbelievers, and has prepared for them a
flaming Fire (Hell). (64) Wherein they will abide for ever,
and they will find neither a Walî (a protector) nor a
helper. (65) On the Day when their faces will be turned
over in the Fire, they will say: "Oh, would that we had
obeyed Allâh and obeyed the Messenger (Muhammad)."
(66) And they will say: "Our Lord! Verily, we obeyed
our chiefs and our great ones, and they misled us from*

the (Right) Way. (67) Our Lord! Give them double torment and curse them with a mighty curse!" (68)

## Quran 33:70-71

يَـٰٓأَيُّهَا ٱلَّذِينَ ءَامَنُوا۟ ٱتَّقُوا۟ ٱللَّهَ وَقُولُوا۟ قَوْلًا سَدِيدًا (٧٠) يُصْلِحْ لَكُمْ أَعْمَـٰلَكُمْ وَيَغْفِرْ لَكُمْ ذُنُوبَكُمْ وَمَن يُطِعِ ٱللَّهَ وَرَسُولَهُۥ فَقَدْ فَازَ فَوْزًا عَظِيمًا (٧١)

*O you who believe! Keep your duty to Allâh and fear Him, and speak (always) the truth. (70) He will direct you to do righteous good deeds and will forgive you your sins. And whosoever obeys Allâh and His Messenger he has indeed achieved a great achievement (i.e. he will be saved from the Hell-fire and will be admitted to Paradise). (71)*

## Quran 34:3-8

وَقَالَ ٱلَّذِينَ كَفَرُوا۟ لَا تَأْتِينَا ٱلسَّاعَةُ قُلْ بَلَىٰ وَرَبِّى لَتَأْتِيَنَّكُمْ عَـٰلِمِ ٱلْغَيْبِ لَا يَعْزُبُ عَنْهُ مِثْقَالُ ذَرَّةٍ فِى ٱلسَّمَـٰوَٰتِ وَلَا فِى ٱلْأَرْضِ وَلَآ أَصْغَرُ مِن ذَٰلِكَ وَلَآ أَكْبَرُ إِلَّا فِى كِتَـٰبٍ مُّبِينٍ (٣) لِّيَجْزِىَ ٱلَّذِينَ ءَامَنُوا۟ وَعَمِلُوا۟ ٱلصَّـٰلِحَـٰتِ أُو۟لَـٰٓئِكَ لَهُم مَّغْفِرَةٌ وَرِزْقٌ كَرِيمٌ (٤) وَٱلَّذِينَ سَعَوْ فِىٓ ءَايَـٰتِنَا مُعَـٰجِزِينَ أُو۟لَـٰٓئِكَ لَهُمْ عَذَابٌ مِّن رِّجْزٍ أَلِيمٌ (٥) وَيَرَى ٱلَّذِينَ أُوتُوا۟ ٱلْعِلْمَ ٱلَّذِىٓ أُنزِلَ إِلَيْكَ مِن رَّبِّكَ هُوَ ٱلْحَقَّ وَيَهْدِىٓ إِلَىٰ صِرَٰطِ ٱلْعَزِيزِ ٱلْحَمِيدِ (٦) وَقَالَ ٱلَّذِينَ كَفَرُوا۟ هَلْ نَدُلُّكُمْ عَلَىٰ رَجُلٍ

يُنَبِّئُكُمْ إِذَا مُزِّقْتُمْ كُلَّ مُمَزَّقٍ إِنَّكُمْ لَفِى خَلْقٍ جَدِيدٍ (٧) أَفْتَرَىٰ
عَلَى ٱللَّهِ كَذِبًا أَم بِهِۦ جِنَّةٌۢ بَلِ ٱلَّذِينَ لَا يُؤْمِنُونَ بِٱلْءَاخِرَةِ فِى
ٱلْعَذَابِ وَٱلضَّلَٰلِ ٱلْبَعِيدِ (٨)

*Those who disbelieve say: "The Hour will not come to us." Say: "Yes, by my Lord, the All¬Knower of the unseen, it will come to you." not even the weight of an atom (or a small ant) or less than that or greater, escapes His Knowledge in the heavens or in the earth, but it is in a Clear Book (Al¬Lauh Al¬Mahfûz). (3) That He may recompense those who believe (in the Oneness of Allâh Islâmic Monotheism) and do righteous good deeds. Those, theirs is forgiveness and Rizq Karîm (generous provision, i.e. Paradise). (4) But those who strive against Our Ayât (proofs, evidences, verses, lessons, signs, revelations, etc.) to frustrate them, those, for them will be a severe painful torment. (5) And those who have been given knowledge see that what is revealed to you (O Muhammad) from your Lord is the truth, and that it guides to the Path of the Exalted in Might, Owner of all praise. (6) Those who disbelieve say: "Shall we direct you to a man (Muhammad) who will tell you (that) when you have become fully disintegrated into dust with full dispersion, then, you will be created (again) anew?" (7) Has he (Muhammad) invented a lie against Allâh, or is there a madness in him? Nay, but those who disbelieve*

*in the Hereafter are (themselves) in a torment, and in far
error. (8)*

## Quran 34:17

ذَٰلِكَ جَزَيْنَـٰهُم بِمَا كَفَرُواۖ وَهَلْ نُجَـٰزِىٓ إِلَّا ٱلْكَفُورَ

*Like this We requited them because they were ungrateful
disbelievers. And never do We requite in such a way
except those who are ungrateful, (disbelievers). (17)*

## Quran 34:25-26

قُل لَّا تُسْـَٔلُونَ عَمَّآ أَجْرَمْنَا وَلَا نُسْـَٔلُ عَمَّا تَعْمَلُونَ (٢٥) قُلْ
يَجْمَعُ بَيْنَنَا رَبُّنَا ثُمَّ يَفْتَحُ بَيْنَنَا بِٱلْحَقِّ وَهُوَ ٱلْفَتَّاحُ ٱلْعَلِيمُ (٢٦)

*Say "You will not be asked about our sins, nor shall we
be asked of what you do." (25) Say: "Our Lord will
assemble us all together (on the Day of Resurrection),
then He will judge between us with truth. And He is the
Just judge, the All-Knower of the true state of affairs."
(26)*

## Quran 34:29-33

وَيَقُولُونَ مَتَىٰ هَـٰذَا ٱلْوَعْدُ إِن كُنتُمْ صَـٰدِقِينَ (٢٩) قُل لَّكُم
مِّيعَادُ يَوْمٍ لَّا تَسْتَـْٔخِرُونَ عَنْهُ سَاعَةً وَلَا تَسْتَقْدِمُونَ
(٣٠) وَقَالَ ٱلَّذِينَ كَفَرُواْ لَن نُّؤْمِنَ بِهَـٰذَا ٱلْقُرْءَانِ وَلَا بِٱلَّذِى
بَيْنَ يَدَيْهِۗ وَلَوْ تَرَىٰٓ إِذِ ٱلظَّـٰلِمُونَ مَوْقُوفُونَ عِندَ رَبِّهِمْ يَرْجِعُ
بَعْضُهُمْ إِلَىٰ بَعْضٍ ٱلْقَوْلَ يَقُولُ ٱلَّذِينَ ٱسْتُضْعِفُواْ لِلَّذِينَ

ٱسْتَكْبَرُوٓاْ لَوْلَآ أَنتُمْ لَكُنَّا مُؤْمِنِينَ (٣١) قَالَ ٱلَّذِينَ ٱسْتَكْبَرُواْ
لِلَّذِينَ ٱسْتُضْعِفُوٓاْ أَنَحْنُ صَدَدْنَٰكُمْ عَنِ ٱلْهُدَىٰ بَعْدَ إِذْ جَآءَكُمْ
بَلْ كُنتُم مُّجْرِمِينَ (٣٢) وَقَالَ ٱلَّذِينَ ٱسْتُضْعِفُواْ لِلَّذِينَ
ٱسْتَكْبَرُوٓاْ بَلْ مَكْرُ ٱلَّيْلِ وَٱلنَّهَارِ إِذْ تَأْمُرُونَنَآ أَن نَّكْفُرَ بِٱللَّهِ
وَنَجْعَلَ لَهُۥٓ أَندَادٗاْ وَأَسَرُّواْ ٱلنَّدَامَةَ لَمَّا رَأَوُاْ ٱلْعَذَابَ وَجَعَلْنَا
ٱلْأَغْلَٰلَ فِىٓ أَعْنَاقِ ٱلَّذِينَ كَفَرُواْ هَلْ يُجْزَوْنَ إِلَّا مَا كَانُواْ
يَعْمَلُونَ (٣٣)

*And they say: "When is this promise (i.e. the Day of Resurrection) if you are truthful?" (29) Say (O Muhammad): "The appointment to you is for a Day, which you cannot put back for an hour (or a moment) nor put forward." (30) And those who disbelieve say: "We believe not in this Qur'ân nor in that which was before it," but if you could see when the Zâlimûn (polytheists and wrong¬doers) will be made to stand before their Lord, how they will cast the (blaming) word one to another! Those who were deemed weak will say to those who were arrogant: "Had it not been for you, we should certainly have been believers!" (31) And those who were arrogant will say to those who were deemed weak: "Did we keep you back from guidance after it had come to you? Nay, but you were Mujrimûn (polytheists, sinners, disbeliveres, criminals). (32) Those who were deemed weak will say to those who were arrogant: "Nay, but it was your plotting by night and day, when you*

ordered us to disbelieve in Allâh and set up rivals to
Him!" And each of them (parties) will conceal their own
regrets (for disobeying Allâh during this worldly life),
when they behold the torment. And We shall put iron
collars round the necks of those who disbelieved. Are they
requited aught except what they used to do? (33)

## Quran 34:37-42

وَمَآ أَمْوَٰلُكُمْ وَلَآ أَوْلَٰدُكُم بِٱلَّتِى تُقَرِّبُكُمْ عِندَنَا زُلْفَىٰٓ إِلَّا مَنْ
ءَامَنَ وَعَمِلَ صَٰلِحًا فَأُوْلَٰٓئِكَ لَهُمْ جَزَآءُ ٱلضِّعْفِ بِمَا عَمِلُواْ
وَهُمْ فِى ٱلْغُرُفَٰتِ ءَامِنُونَ (٣٧) وَٱلَّذِينَ يَسْعَوْنَ فِىٓ ءَايَٰتِنَا
مُعَٰجِزِينَ أُوْلَٰٓئِكَ فِى ٱلْعَذَابِ مُحْضَرُونَ (٣٨) قُلْ إِنَّ رَبِّى
يَبْسُطُ ٱلرِّزْقَ لِمَن يَشَآءُ مِنْ عِبَادِهِ وَيَقْدِرُ لَهُۥ وَمَآ أَنفَقْتُم مِّن
شَىْءٍ فَهُوَ يُخْلِفُهُۥ وَهُوَ خَيْرُ ٱلرَّٰزِقِينَ (٣٩) وَيَوْمَ يَحْشُرُهُمْ
جَمِيعًا ثُمَّ يَقُولُ لِلْمَلَٰٓئِكَةِ أَهَٰٓؤُلَآءِ إِيَّاكُمْ كَانُواْ يَعْبُدُونَ
(٤٠) قَالُواْ سُبْحَٰنَكَ أَنتَ وَلِيُّنَا مِن دُونِهِم بَلْ كَانُواْ يَعْبُدُونَ
ٱلْجِنَّ أَكْثَرُهُم بِهِم مُّؤْمِنُونَ (٤١) فَٱلْيَوْمَ لَا يَمْلِكُ بَعْضُكُمْ
لِبَعْضٍ نَّفْعًا وَلَا ضَرًّا وَنَقُولُ لِلَّذِينَ ظَلَمُواْ ذُوقُواْ عَذَابَ ٱلنَّارِ
ٱلَّتِى كُنتُم بِهَا تُكَذِّبُونَ (٤٢)

And it is not your wealth, nor your children that bring
you nearer to Us (i.e. pleases Allâh), but only he who
believes (in the Islâmic Monotheism), and does righteous
deeds (will please us); as for such, there will be twofold
reward for what they did, and they will reside in the high

dwellings (Paradise) in peace and security. (37) And those who strive against Our Ayât (proofs, evidences, verses, lessons, signs, revelations, etc.), to frustrate them, will be brought to the torment. (38) Say: "Truly, my Lord enlarges the provision for whom He wills of His slaves, and (also) restricts (it) for him, and whatsoever you spend of anything (in Allâh's Cause), He will replace it. And He is the Best of providers." (39) And (remember) the Day when He will gather them all together, then He will say to the angels: "Was it you that these people used to worship?" (40) They (the angels) will say: "Glorified are You! You are our Walî (Lord) instead of them. Nay, but they used to worship the jinn; most of them were believers in them." (41) So Today (i.e. the Day of Resurrection), none of you can profit or harm one another. And We shall say to those who did wrong [i.e. worshipped others (like angels, jinn, prophets, saints, righteous persons) along with Allâh]: "Taste the torment of the Fire which you used to belie. (42)

## Quran 34:52-54

وَقَالُوٓاْ ءَامَنَّا بِهِۦ وَأَنَّىٰ لَهُمُ ٱلتَّنَاوُشُ مِن مَّكَانٍ بَعِيدٍ (٥٢) وَقَدْ كَفَرُواْ بِهِۦ مِن قَبْلُۖ وَيَقْذِفُونَ بِٱلْغَيْبِ مِن مَّكَانٍ بَعِيدٍ (٥٣) وَحِيلَ بَيْنَهُمْ وَبَيْنَ مَا يَشْتَهُونَ كَمَا فُعِلَ بِأَشْيَاعِهِم مِّن قَبْلُۚ إِنَّهُمْ كَانُواْ فِى شَكٍّ مُّرِيبٍ (٥٤)

*And they will say (in the Hereafter): "We do believe
(now);" but how could they receive (Faith and the
acceptance of their repentance by Allâh) from a place so
far off (i.e. to return to the worldly life again).
(52) Indeed they did disbelieve (in the Oneness of Allâh,
Islâm, the Qur'ân and Muhammad) before (in this
world), and they (used to) conjecture about the unseen
[i.e. the Hereafter, Hell, Paradise, Resurrection and the
Promise of Allâh (by saying) all that is untrue], from a
far place. (53) And a barrier will be set between them and
that which they desire [i.e. At-Taubah (turning to Allâh
in repentance) and the accepting of Faith], as was done in
the past with the people of their kind. Verily, they have
been in grave doubt. (54)*

## Quran 35:2

مَّا يَفْتَحِ ٱللَّهُ لِلنَّاسِ مِن رَّحْمَةٍ فَلَا مُمْسِكَ لَهَا وَمَا يُمْسِكْ فَلَا
مُرْسِلَ لَهُۥ مِنۢ بَعْدِهِۦ وَهُوَ ٱلْعَزِيزُ ٱلْحَكِيمُ

*Whatever of mercy (i.e.of good), Allâh may grant to
mankind, none can withhold it, and whatever He may
withhold, none can grant it thereafter. And He is the
All¬Mighty, the All¬Wise. (2)*

## Quran 35:5-10

يَـٰٓأَيُّهَا ٱلنَّاسُ إِنَّ وَعْدَ ٱللَّهِ حَقٌّ فَلَا تَغُرَّنَّكُمُ ٱلْحَيَوٰةُ ٱلدُّنْيَا وَلَا
يَغُرَّنَّكُم بِٱللَّهِ ٱلْغَرُورُ (٥) إِنَّ ٱلشَّيْطَـٰنَ لَكُمْ عَدُوٌّ فَٱتَّخِذُوهُ

عَدُوًّا إِنَّمَا يَدْعُوا حِزْبَهُ لِيَكُونُوا مِنْ أَصْحَـٰبِ ٱلسَّعِيرِ
(٦) ٱلَّذِينَ كَفَرُوا لَهُمْ عَذَابٌ شَدِيدٌ وَٱلَّذِينَ ءَامَنُوا وَعَمِلُوا
ٱلصَّـٰلِحَـٰتِ لَهُم مَّغْفِرَةٌ وَأَجْرٌ كَبِيرٌ (٧) أَفَمَن زُيِّنَ لَهُ سُوٓءُ
عَمَلِهِ فَرَءَاهُ حَسَنًا فَإِنَّ ٱللَّهَ يُضِلُّ مَن يَشَآءُ وَيَهْدِى مَن يَشَآءُ
فَلَا تَذْهَبْ نَفْسُكَ عَلَيْهِمْ حَسَرَٰتٍ إِنَّ ٱللَّهَ عَلِيمٌ بِمَا يَصْنَعُونَ
(٨) وَٱللَّهُ ٱلَّذِىٓ أَرْسَلَ ٱلرِّيَـٰحَ فَتُثِيرُ سَحَابًا فَسُقْنَـٰهُ إِلَىٰ بَلَدٍ
مَّيِّتٍ فَأَحْيَيْنَا بِهِ ٱلْأَرْضَ بَعْدَ مَوْتِهَا كَذَٰلِكَ ٱلنُّشُورُ (٩) مَن
كَانَ يُرِيدُ ٱلْعِزَّةَ فَلِلَّهِ ٱلْعِزَّةُ جَمِيعًا إِلَيْهِ يَصْعَدُ ٱلْكَلِمُ ٱلطَّيِّبُ
وَٱلْعَمَلُ ٱلصَّـٰلِحُ يَرْفَعُهُ وَٱلَّذِينَ يَمْكُرُونَ ٱلسَّيِّـَٔاتِ لَهُمْ عَذَابٌ
شَدِيدٌ وَمَكْرُ أُوْلَـٰٓئِكَ هُوَ يَبُورُ (١٠)

O mankind! Verily, the Promise of Allâh is true. So let
not this present life deceive you, and let not the chief
deceiver (Satan) deceive you about Allâh. (5) Surely,
Shaitân (Satan) is an enemy to you, so take (treat) him as
an enemy. He only invites his Hizb (followers) that they
may become the dwellers of the blazing Fire. (6) Those
who disbelieve, theirs will be a severe torment; and those
who believe (in the Oneness of Allâh Islâmic
Monotheism) and do righteous good deeds, theirs will be
forgiveness and a great reward (i.e. Paradise). (7) Is he,
then, to whom the evil of his deeds made fair¬seeming, so
that he considers it as good (equal to one who is rightly
guided)? Verily, Allâh sends astray whom He wills, and

guides whom He wills. So destroy not yourself (O Muhammad) in sorrow for them. Truly, Allâh is the All¬Knower of what they do! (8) And it is Allâh Who sends the winds, so that they raise up the clouds, and We drive them to a dead land, and revive therewith the earth after its death. As such (will be) the Resurrection! (9) Whosoever desires honour, (power and glory) then to Allâh belong all honour, power and glory [and one can get honour, power and glory only by obeying and worshipping Allâh (Alone)]. To Him ascend (all) the goodly words, and the righteous deeds exalt it (i.e. the goodly words are not accepted by Allâh unless and until they are followed by good deeds), but those who plot evils, theirs will be severe torment. And the plotting of such will perish. (10)

## Quran 35:14

إِن تَدْعُوهُمْ لَا يَسْمَعُواْ دُعَآءَكُمْ وَلَوْ سَمِعُواْ مَا ٱسْتَجَابُواْ لَكُمْ وَيَوْمَ ٱلْقِيَـٰمَةِ يَكْفُرُونَ بِشِرْكِكُمْ وَلَا يُنَبِّئُكَ مِثْلُ خَبِيرٍ

If you invoke (or call upon) them, they hear not your call, and if (in case) they were to hear, they could not grant it (your request) to you. And on the Day of Resurrection, they will disown your worshipping them. And none can inform you (O Muhammad) like Him Who is the All¬Knower (of everything). (14)

## Quran 35:18

وَلَا تَزِرُ وَازِرَةٌ وِزْرَ أُخْرَىٰ وَإِن تَدْعُ مُثْقَلَةٌ إِلَىٰ حِمْلِهَا لَا
يُحْمَلْ مِنْهُ شَىْءٌ وَلَوْ كَانَ ذَا قُرْبَىٰٓ إِنَّمَا تُنذِرُ ٱلَّذِينَ
يَخْشَوْنَ رَبَّهُم بِٱلْغَيْبِ وَأَقَامُوا ٱلصَّلَوٰةَ وَمَن تَزَكَّىٰ فَإِنَّمَا
يَتَزَكَّىٰ لِنَفْسِهِ وَإِلَى ٱللَّهِ ٱلْمَصِيرُ

And no bearer of burdens shall bear another's burden,
and if one heavily laden calls another to (bear) his load,
nothing of it will be lifted even though he be near of kin.
You (O Muhammad) can warn only those who fear their
Lord unseen, and perform As-Salât (Iqâmat¬as¬Salât).
And he who purifies himself (from all kinds of sins), then
he purifies only for the benefit of his ownself. And to
Allâh is the (final) Return (of all). (18)

## Quran 35:28-30

وَمِنَ ٱلنَّاسِ وَٱلدَّوَآبِّ وَٱلْأَنْعَٰمِ مُخْتَلِفٌ أَلْوَٰنُهُ كَذَٰلِكَ إِنَّمَا
يَخْشَى ٱللَّهَ مِنْ عِبَادِهِ ٱلْعُلَمَٰٓؤُا۟ إِنَّ ٱللَّهَ عَزِيزٌ غَفُورٌ (٢٨) إِنَّ
ٱلَّذِينَ يَتْلُونَ كِتَٰبَ ٱللَّهِ وَأَقَامُوا ٱلصَّلَوٰةَ وَأَنفَقُوا مِمَّا رَزَقْنَٰهُمْ
سِرًّا وَعَلَانِيَةً يَرْجُونَ تِجَٰرَةً لَّن تَبُورَ (٢٩) لِيُوَفِّيَهُمْ
أُجُورَهُمْ وَيَزِيدَهُم مِّن فَضْلِهِ إِنَّهُ غَفُورٌ شَكُورٌ (٣٠)

And likewise of men and Ad¬Dawâbb (moving (living)
creatures, beasts), and cattle, of various colours. It is only
those who have knowledge among His slaves that fear
Allâh. Verily, Allâh is All¬Mighty, Oft¬Forgiving.

(28) *Verily, those who recite the Book of Allâh (this Qur'ân), and perform As¬Salât (Iqâmat¬as¬Salât), and spend (in charity) out of what We have provided for them, secretly and openly, they hope for a (sure) trade¬gain that will never perish. (29) That He may pay them their wages in full, and give them (even) more, out of His Grace. Verily! He is Oft¬Forgiving, Most Ready to appreciate (good deeds and to recompense). (30)*

## Quran 35:33-37

جَنَّـٰتُ عَدْنٍ يَدْخُلُونَهَا يُحَلَّوْنَ فِيهَا مِنْ أَسَاوِرَ مِن ذَهَبٍ وَلُؤْلُؤًا ۖ وَلِبَاسُهُمْ فِيهَا حَرِيرٌ (٣٣) وَقَالُواْ ٱلْحَمْدُ لِلَّهِ ٱلَّذِىٓ أَذْهَبَ عَنَّا ٱلْحَزَنَ ۖ إِنَّ رَبَّنَا لَغَفُورٌ شَكُورٌ (٣٤) ٱلَّذِىٓ أَحَلَّنَا دَارَ ٱلْمُقَامَةِ مِن فَضْلِهِ لَا يَمَسُّنَا فِيهَا نَصَبٌ وَلَا يَمَسُّنَا فِيهَا لُغُوبٌ (٣٥) وَٱلَّذِينَ كَفَرُواْ لَهُمْ نَارُ جَهَنَّمَ لَا يُقْضَىٰ عَلَيْهِمْ فَيَمُوتُواْ وَلَا يُخَفَّفُ عَنْهُم مِّنْ عَذَابِهَا ۚ كَذَٰلِكَ نَجْزِى كُلَّ كَفُورٍ (٣٦) وَهُمْ يَصْطَرِخُونَ فِيهَا رَبَّنَآ أَخْرِجْنَا نَعْمَلْ صَٰلِحًا غَيْرَ ٱلَّذِى كُنَّا نَعْمَلُ ۚ أَوَلَمْ نُعَمِّرْكُم مَّا يَتَذَكَّرُ فِيهِ مَن تَذَكَّرَ وَجَآءَكُمُ ٱلنَّذِيرُ ۖ فَذُوقُواْ فَمَا لِلظَّٰلِمِينَ مِن نَّصِيرٍ (٣٧)

*'Adn (Eden) Paradise (everlasting Gardens) will they enter, therein will they be adorned with bracelets of gold and pearls, and their garments there will be of silk. (33) And they will say: "All the praises and thanks are to Allâh, Who has removed from us (all) grief. Verily, our*

Lord is indeed Oft¬Forgiving, Most Ready to appreciate (good deeds and to recompense). (34) Who, out of His Grace, has lodged us in a home that will last forever; where, toil will touch us not, nor weariness will touch us." (35) But those who disbelieve, (in the Oneness of Allâh - Islâmic Monotheism) for them will be the Fire of Hell. Neither will it have a complete killing effect on them so that they die, nor shall its torment be lightened for them. Thus do We requite every disbeliever! (36) Therein they will cry: "Our Lord! Bring us out, we shall do righteous good deeds, not (the evil deeds) that we used to do." (Allâh will reply): "Did We not give you lives long enough, so that whosoever would receive admonition, could receive it? And the warner came to you. So taste you (the evil of your deeds). For the Zâlimûn (polytheists and wrong¬doers) there is no helper." (37)

## Quran 35:39-40

هُوَ ٱلَّذِى جَعَلَكُمْ خَلَـٰٓئِفَ فِى ٱلْأَرْضِ فَمَن كَفَرَ فَعَلَيْهِ كُفْرُهُۥ
وَلَا يَزِيدُ ٱلْكَـٰفِرِينَ كُفْرُهُمْ عِندَ رَبِّهِمْ إِلَّا مَقْتًا وَلَا يَزِيدُ
ٱلْكَـٰفِرِينَ كُفْرُهُمْ إِلَّا خَسَارًا (٣٩) قُلْ أَرَءَيْتُمْ شُرَكَآءَكُمُ ٱلَّذِينَ
تَدْعُونَ مِن دُونِ ٱللَّهِ أَرُونِى مَاذَا خَلَقُوا۟ مِنَ ٱلْأَرْضِ أَمْ لَهُمْ
شِرْكٌ فِى ٱلسَّمَـٰوَٰتِ أَمْ ءَاتَيْنَـٰهُمْ كِتَـٰبًا فَهُمْ عَلَىٰ بَيِّنَتٍ مِّنْهُ بَلْ
إِن يَعِدُ ٱلظَّـٰلِمُونَ بَعْضُهُم بَعْضًا إِلَّا غُرُورًا (٤٠)

304

He it is Who has made you successors generations after generations in the earth, so whosoever disbelieves (in Islâmic Monotheism) on him will be his disbelief. And the disbelief of the disbelievers adds nothing but hatred of their Lord. And the disbelief of the disbelievers adds nothing but loss. (39) Say (O Muhammad): "Tell me or inform me (what) do you think about your (so¬called) partner¬gods to whom you call upon besides Allâh? show me, what they have created of the earth? Or have they any share in the heavens? Or have We given them a Book, so that they act on clear proof therefrom? Nay, the Zâlimûn (polytheists and wrong¬doers) promise one another nothing but delusions." (40)

## Quran 36:2-5

وَٱلْقُرْءَانِ ٱلْحَكِيمِ (٢) إِنَّكَ لَمِنَ ٱلْمُرْسَلِينَ (٣) عَلَىٰ صِرَٰطٍ مُّسْتَقِيمٍ (٤) تَنزِيلَ ٱلْعَزِيزِ ٱلرَّحِيمِ (٥)

By the Qur'ân, full of wisdom (i.e. full of laws, evidences, and proofs), (2) Truly, you (O Muhammad) are one of the Messengers, (3) On the Straight Path (i.e. on Allâh's religion of Islâmic Monotheism). (4) (This is a Revelation) sent down by the All¬Mighty, the Most Merciful, (5)

## Quran 36:7-12

لَقَدْ حَقَّ ٱلْقَوْلُ عَلَىٰ أَكْثَرِهِمْ فَهُمْ لَا يُؤْمِنُونَ (٧) إِنَّا جَعَلْنَا فِىٓ
أَعْنَٰقِهِمْ أَغْلَٰلًا فَهِىَ إِلَى ٱلْأَذْقَانِ فَهُم مُّقْمَحُونَ (٨) وَجَعَلْنَا
مِنۢ بَيْنِ أَيْدِيهِمْ سَدًّا وَمِنْ خَلْفِهِمْ سَدًّا فَأَغْشَيْنَٰهُمْ فَهُمْ لَا
يُبْصِرُونَ (٩) وَسَوَآءٌ عَلَيْهِمْ ءَأَنذَرْتَهُمْ أَمْ لَمْ تُنذِرْهُمْ لَا
يُؤْمِنُونَ (١٠) إِنَّمَا تُنذِرُ مَنِ ٱتَّبَعَ ٱلذِّكْرَ وَخَشِىَ ٱلرَّحْمَٰنَ
بِٱلْغَيْبِ فَبَشِّرْهُ بِمَغْفِرَةٍ وَأَجْرٍ كَرِيمٍ (١١) إِنَّا نَحْنُ نُحْىِ
ٱلْمَوْتَىٰ وَنَكْتُبُ مَا قَدَّمُوا۟ وَءَاثَٰرَهُمْ وَكُلَّ شَىْءٍ أَحْصَيْنَٰهُ
فِىٓ إِمَامٍ مُّبِينٍ (١٢)

Indeed the Word (of punishment) has proved true against
most of them, so they will not believe. (7) Verily! We
have put on their necks iron collars reaching to the chins,
so that their heads are raised up. (8) And We have put a
barrier before them, and a barrier behind them, and We
have covered them up, so that they cannot see. (9) It is
the same to them whether you warn them or you warn
them not, they will not believe. (10) You can only warn
him who follows the Reminder (the Qur'ân), and fears
the Most Gracious (Allâh) unseen. Bear you to such one
the glad tidings of forgiveness, and a generous reward
(i.e. Paradise). (11) Verily, We give life to the dead, and
We record that which they send before (them), and their
traces and all things We have recorded with numbers (as
a record) in a Clear Book. (12)

**Quran 36:31-32**

أَلَمْ يَرَوْاْ كَمْ أَهْلَكْنَا قَبْلَهُم مِّنَ ٱلْقُرُونِ أَنَّهُمْ إِلَيْهِمْ لَا يَرْجِعُونَ (٣١) وَإِن كُلٌّ لَّمَّا جَمِيعٌ لَّدَيْنَا مُحْضَرُونَ (٣٢)

*Do they not see how many of the generations We have destroyed before them? Verily, they will not return to them. (31) And surely, all, — everyone of them will be brought before Us. (32)*

## Quran 36:48-65

وَيَقُولُونَ مَتَىٰ هَـٰذَا ٱلْوَعْدُ إِن كُنتُمْ صَـٰدِقِينَ (٤٨) مَا يَنظُرُونَ إِلَّا صَيْحَةً وَٰحِدَةً تَأْخُذُهُمْ وَهُمْ يَخِصِّمُونَ (٤٩) فَلَا يَسْتَطِيعُونَ تَوْصِيَةً وَلَا إِلَىٰ أَهْلِهِمْ يَرْجِعُونَ (٥٠) وَنُفِخَ فِى ٱلصُّورِ فَإِذَا هُم مِّنَ ٱلْأَجْدَاثِ إِلَىٰ رَبِّهِمْ يَنسِلُونَ (٥١) قَالُوا يَـٰوَيْلَنَا مَنۢ بَعَثَنَا مِن مَّرْقَدِنَا هَـٰذَا مَا وَعَدَ ٱلرَّحْمَـٰنُ وَصَدَقَ ٱلْمُرْسَلُونَ (٥٢) إِن كَانَتْ إِلَّا صَيْحَةً وَٰحِدَةً فَإِذَا هُمْ جَمِيعٌ لَّدَيْنَا مُحْضَرُونَ (٥٣) فَٱلْيَوْمَ لَا تُظْلَمُ نَفْسٌ شَيْـًٔا وَلَا تُجْزَوْنَ إِلَّا مَا كُنتُمْ تَعْمَلُونَ (٥٤) إِنَّ أَصْحَـٰبَ ٱلْجَنَّةِ ٱلْيَوْمَ فِى شُغُلٍ فَـٰكِهُونَ (٥٥) هُمْ وَأَزْوَٰجُهُمْ فِى ظِلَـٰلٍ عَلَى ٱلْأَرَآئِكِ مُتَّكِـُٔونَ (٥٦) لَهُمْ فِيهَا فَـٰكِهَةٌ وَلَهُم مَّا يَدَّعُونَ (٥٧) سَلَـٰمٌ قَوْلًا مِّن رَّبٍّ رَّحِيمٍ (٥٨) وَٱمْتَـٰزُوا ٱلْيَوْمَ أَيُّهَا ٱلْمُجْرِمُونَ (٥٩) ۞ أَلَمْ أَعْهَدْ إِلَيْكُمْ يَـٰبَنِىٓ ءَادَمَ أَن لَّا تَعْبُدُوا ٱلشَّيْطَـٰنَ إِنَّهُ لَكُمْ عَدُوٌّ مُّبِينٌ (٦٠) وَأَنِ ٱعْبُدُونِى هَـٰذَا صِرَٰطٌ مُّسْتَقِيمٌ (٦١) وَلَقَدْ أَضَلَّ مِنكُمْ جِبِلًّا كَثِيرًا أَفَلَمْ تَكُونُوا تَعْقِلُونَ (٦٢) هَـٰذِهِۦ جَهَنَّمُ ٱلَّتِى كُنتُمْ تُوعَدُونَ (٦٣) ٱصْلَوْهَا ٱلْيَوْمَ

بِمَا كُنتُمْ تَكْفُرُونَ (٦٤) ٱلْيَوْمَ نَخْتِمُ عَلَىٰٓ أَفْوَٰهِهِمْ وَتُكَلِّمُنَآ
أَيْدِيهِمْ وَتَشْهَدُ أَرْجُلُهُم بِمَا كَانُواْ يَكْسِبُونَ (٦٥)

*And they say: "When will this promise (i.e.*
*Resurrection) be fulfilled, if you are truthful?" (48) They*
*await only but a single Saihah (shout), which will seize*
*them while they are disputing! (49) Then they will not be*
*able to make bequest, nor they will return to their family.*
*(50) And the Trumpet will be blown (i.e. the second*
*blowing) and behold from the graves they will come out*
*quickly to their Lord. (51) They will say: "Woe to us!*
*Who has raised us up from our place of sleep." (It will be*
*said to them): "This is what the Most Gracious (Allâh)*
*had promised, and the Messengers spoke truth!" (52) It*
*will be but a single Saihah (shout), so behold! They will*
*all be brought up before Us! (53) This Day (Day of*
*Resurrection), none will be wronged in anything, nor*
*will you be requited anything except that which you used*
*to do. (54) Verily, the dwellers of the Paradise, that Day,*
*will be busy with joyful things. (55) They and their wives*
*will be in pleasant shade, reclining on thrones. (56) They*
*will have therein fruits (of all kinds) and all that they ask*
*for. (57) (It will be said to them): Salâm (peace be on*
*you), − a Word from the Lord (Allâh), Most Merciful.*
*(58) (It will be said): "And O you Mujrimûn (criminals,*
*polytheists, sinners, disbelievers in the Islâmic*
*Monotheism, wicked evil ones)! Get you apart this Day*

*(from the believers). (59) Did I not command for you, O Children of Adam, that you should not worship Shaitân (Satan). Verily, he is a plain enemy to you. (60) And that you should worship Me [Alone — Islâmic Monotheism, and set up not rivals, associate-gods with Me]. That is the Straight Path. (61) And indeed he (Satan) did lead astray a great multitude of you. Did you not, then, understand? (62) This is Hell which you were promised! (63) Burn therein this Day, for that you used to disbelieve. (64) This Day, We shall seal up their mouths, and their hands will speak to Us, and their legs will bear witness to what they used to earn. (65)*

## Quran 36:68

وَمَن نُّعَمِّرْهُ نُنَكِّسْهُ فِى ٱلْخَلْقِ ۚ أَفَلَا يَعْقِلُونَ

*And he whom We grant long life, — We reverse him in creation (weakness after strength). Will they not then understand? (68)*

## Quran 36:74-75

وَٱتَّخَذُواْ مِن دُونِ ٱللَّهِ ءَالِهَةً لَّعَلَّهُمْ يُنصَرُونَ (٧٤) لَا يَسْتَطِيعُونَ نَصْرَهُمْ وَهُمْ لَهُمْ جُندٌ مُّحْضَرُونَ (٧٥)

*And they have taken besides Allâh âlihah (gods), hoping that they might be helped (by those so — called gods). (74) They cannot help them, but they will be brought*

forward as a troop against those who worshipped them
(at the time of Reckoning). (75)

## Quran 36:79

قُلْ يُحْيِيهَا ٱلَّذِىٓ أَنشَأَهَآ أَوَّلَ مَرَّةٍ ۖ وَهُوَ بِكُلِّ خَلْقٍ عَلِيمٌ

Say: "He will give life to them Who created them for the
first time! And He is the All-Knower of every creation!"
(79)

## Quran 36:83

فَسُبْحَـٰنَ ٱلَّذِى بِيَدِهِ مَلَكُوتُ كُلِّ شَىْءٍ وَإِلَيْهِ تُرْجَعُونَ

So glorified is He and Exalted above all that they
associate with Him, and in Whose Hands is the dominion
of all things: and to Him you shall be returned. (83)

## Quran 37:6-10

إِنَّا زَيَّنَّا ٱلسَّمَآءَ ٱلدُّنْيَا بِزِينَةٍ ٱلْكَوَاكِبِ (٦) وَحِفْظًا مِّن كُلِّ
شَيْطَـٰنٍ مَّارِدٍ (٧) لَّا يَسَّمَّعُونَ إِلَى ٱلْمَلَإِ ٱلْأَعْلَىٰ وَيُقْذَفُونَ مِن
كُلِّ جَانِبٍ (٨) دُحُورًا ۖ وَلَهُمْ عَذَابٌ وَاصِبٌ (٩) إِلَّا مَنْ
خَطِفَ ٱلْخَطْفَةَ فَأَتْبَعَهُ شِهَابٌ ثَاقِبٌ (١٠)

Verily! We have adorned the near heaven with the stars
(for beauty). (6) And to guard against every rebellious
devil. (7) They cannot listen to the higher group (angels)
for they are pelted from every side. (8) Outcast, and
theirs is a constant (or painful) torment. (9) Except such

as snatch away something by stealing and they are
pursued by a flaming fire of piercing brightness. (10)

## Quran 37:15-34

وَقَالُوٓاْ إِنْ هَٰذَآ إِلَّا سِحْرٌ مُّبِينٌ (١٥) أَءِذَا مِتْنَا وَكُنَّا تُرَابًا
وَعِظَٰمًا أَءِنَّا لَمَبْعُوثُونَ (١٦) أَوَءَابَآؤُنَا ٱلْأَوَّلُونَ (١٧) قُلْ
نَعَمْ وَأَنتُمْ دَٰخِرُونَ (١٨) فَإِنَّمَا هِىَ زَجْرَةٌ وَٰحِدَةٌ فَإِذَا هُمْ
يَنظُرُونَ (١٩) وَقَالُوٓاْ يَٰوَيْلَنَا هَٰذَا يَوْمُ ٱلدِّينِ (٢٠) هَٰذَا يَوْمُ
ٱلْفَصْلِ ٱلَّذِى كُنتُم بِهِۦ تُكَذِّبُونَ (٢١) ۞ ٱحْشُرُواْ ٱلَّذِينَ
ظَلَمُواْ وَأَزْوَٰجَهُمْ وَمَا كَانُواْ يَعْبُدُونَ (٢٢) مِن دُونِ ٱللَّهِ
فَٱهْدُوهُمْ إِلَىٰ صِرَٰطِ ٱلْجَحِيمِ (٢٣) وَقِفُوهُمْ إِنَّهُم مَّسْـُٔولُونَ
(٢٤) مَا لَكُمْ لَا تَنَاصَرُونَ (٢٥) بَلْ هُمُ ٱلْيَوْمَ مُسْتَسْلِمُونَ
(٢٦) وَأَقْبَلَ بَعْضُهُمْ عَلَىٰ بَعْضٍ يَتَسَآءَلُونَ (٢٧) قَالُوٓاْ إِنَّكُمْ
كُنتُمْ تَأْتُونَنَا عَنِ ٱلْيَمِينِ (٢٨) قَالُواْ بَل لَّمْ تَكُونُواْ مُؤْمِنِينَ
(٢٩) وَمَا كَانَ لَنَا عَلَيْكُم مِّن سُلْطَٰنٍ بَلْ كُنتُمْ قَوْمًا طَٰغِينَ
(٣٠) فَحَقَّ عَلَيْنَا قَوْلُ رَبِّنَآ إِنَّا لَذَآئِقُونَ (٣١) فَأَغْوَيْنَٰكُمْ إِنَّا
كُنَّا غَٰوِينَ (٣٢) فَإِنَّهُمْ يَوْمَئِذٍ فِى ٱلْعَذَابِ مُشْتَرِكُونَ
(٣٣) إِنَّا كَذَٰلِكَ نَفْعَلُ بِٱلْمُجْرِمِينَ (٣٤)

And they say: "This is nothing but evident magic!
(15) "When we are dead and have become dust and
bones, shall we (then) verily be resurrected? (16) "And
also our fathers of old?" (17) Say (O Muhammad): "Yes,
and you shall then be humiliated." (18) It will be a single
Zajrah [shout (i.e. the second blowing of the Trumpet)],

and behold, they will be staring! (19) They will say: "Woe to us! This is the Day of Recompense!" (20) (It will be said): "This is the Day of Judgement which you used to deny." (21) It will be said to the angels): "Assemble those who did wrong, together with their companions (from the devils) and what they used to worship (22) "Instead of Allâh, and lead them on to the way of flaming Fire (Hell); (23) "But stop them, verily they are to be questioned. (24) "What is the matter with you? Why do you not help one another (as you used to do in the world)?" (25) Nay, but that Day they shall surrender, (26) And they will turn to one another and question one another. (27) They will say: "It was you who used to come to us from the right side [i.e. from the right side of one of us and beautify for us every evil, enjoin on us polytheism, and stop us from the truth i.e. Islâmic Monotheism and from every good deed]."
(28) They will reply: "Nay, you yourselves were not believers. (29) "And we had no authority over you. Nay! But you were Taghun (transgressing) people (polytheists, and disbelievers). (30) "So now the Word of our Lord has been justified against us, that we shall certainly (have to) taste (the torment). (31) "So we led you astray because we were ourselves astray." (32) Then verily, that Day, they will (all) share in the torment. (33) Certainly, that is how We deal with Al¬Mujrimûn (polytheists, sinners, disbelivers, criminals, the disobedient to Allâh). (34)

إِنَّكُمْ لَذَآئِقُواْ ٱلْعَذَابِ ٱلْأَلِيمِ (٣٨) وَمَا تُجْزَوْنَ إِلَّا مَا كُنتُمْ

تَعْمَلُونَ (٣٩) إِلَّا عِبَادَ ٱللَّهِ ٱلْمُخْلَصِينَ (٤٠) أُوْلَـٰئِكَ لَهُمْ

رِزْقٌ مَّعْلُومٌ (٤١) فَوَاكِهُ وَهُم مُّكْرَمُونَ (٤٢) فِى جَنَّـٰتِ

ٱلنَّعِيمِ (٤٣) عَلَىٰ سُرُرٍ مُّتَقَـٰبِلِينَ (٤٤) يُطَافُ عَلَيْهِم بِكَأْسٍ

مِّن مَّعِينٍ (٤٥) بَيْضَآءَ لَذَّةٍ لِّلشَّـٰرِبِينَ (٤٦) لَا فِيهَا غَوْلٌ وَلَا

هُمْ عَنْهَا يُنزَفُونَ (٤٧) وَعِندَهُمْ قَـٰصِرَٰتُ ٱلطَّرْفِ عِينٌ

(٤٨) كَأَنَّهُنَّ بَيْضٌ مَّكْنُونٌ (٤٩) فَأَقْبَلَ بَعْضُهُمْ عَلَىٰ بَعْضٍ

يَتَسَآءَلُونَ (٥٠) قَالَ قَآئِلٌ مِّنْهُمْ إِنِّى كَانَ لِى قَرِينٌ

(٥١) يَقُولُ أَئِنَّكَ لَمِنَ ٱلْمُصَدِّقِينَ (٥٢) أَءِذَا مِتْنَا وَكُنَّا تُرَابًا

وَعِظَـٰمًا أَءِنَّا لَمَدِينُونَ (٥٣) قَالَ هَلْ أَنتُم مُّطَّلِعُونَ

(٥٤) فَٱطَّلَعَ فَرَءَاهُ فِى سَوَآءِ ٱلْجَحِيمِ (٥٥) قَالَ تَٱللَّهِ إِن

كِدتَّ لَتُرْدِينِ (٥٦) وَلَوْلَا نِعْمَةُ رَبِّى لَكُنتُ مِنَ ٱلْمُحْضَرِينَ

(٥٧) أَفَمَا نَحْنُ بِمَيِّتِينَ (٥٨) إِلَّا مَوْتَتَنَا ٱلْأُولَىٰ وَمَا نَحْنُ

بِمُعَذَّبِينَ (٥٩) إِنَّ هَـٰذَا لَهُوَ ٱلْفَوْزُ ٱلْعَظِيمُ (٦٠) لِمِثْلِ هَـٰذَا

فَلْيَعْمَلِ ٱلْعَـٰمِلُونَ (٦١) أَذَٰلِكَ خَيْرٌ نُّزُلاً أَمْ شَجَرَةُ ٱلزَّقُّومِ

(٦٢) إِنَّا جَعَلْنَـٰهَا فِتْنَةً لِّلظَّـٰلِمِينَ (٦٣) إِنَّهَا شَجَرَةٌ تَخْرُجُ فِى

أَصْلِ ٱلْجَحِيمِ (٦٤) طَلْعُهَا كَأَنَّهُ رُءُوسُ ٱلشَّيَـٰطِينِ

(٦٥) فَإِنَّهُمْ لَأَكِلُونَ مِنْهَا فَمَالِئُونَ مِنْهَا ٱلْبُطُونَ (٦٦) ثُمَّ إِنَّ

لَهُمْ عَلَيْهَا لَشَوْبًا مِّنْ حَمِيمٍ (٦٧) ثُمَّ إِنَّ مَرْجِعَهُمْ لَإِلَى

ٱلْجَحِيمِ (٦٨)

*Verily, you (pagans of Makkah) are going to taste the*
*painful torment; (38) And you will be requited nothing*
*except for what you used to do (evil deeds, sins, and*
*Allâh's disobedience which you used to do in this world);*
*(39) Save the chosen slaves of Allâh (i.e. the true*
*believers of Islâmic Monotheism). (40) For them there*
*will be a known provision (in Paradise), (41) Fruits; and*
*they shall be honoured, (42) In the Gardens of delight*
*(Paradise), (43) Facing one another on thrones,*
*(44) Round them will be passed a cup of pure wine, —*
*(45) White, delicious to the drinkers, (46) Neither will*
*they have Ghoul (any kind of hurt, abdominal pain,*
*headache, a sin) from that, nor will they suffer*
*intoxication therefrom. (47) And beside them will be*
*Qâsirât-at-Tarf [chaste females (wives), restraining their*
*glances (desiring none except their husbands)], with wide*
*and beautiful eyes. (48) (Delicate and pure) as if they*
*were (hidden) eggs (well) preserved. (49) Then they will*
*turn to one another, mutually questioning. (50) A*
*speaker of them will say: "Verily, I had a companion (in*
*the world), (51) Who used to say: "Are you among those*
*who believe (in resurrection after death). (52) "(That)*
*when we die and become dust and bones, shall we indeed*
*(be raised up) to receive reward or punishment*
*(according to our deeds)?" (53) (The speaker) said: "Will*
*you look down?" (54) So he looked down and saw him in*
*the midst of the Fire. (55) He said: "By Allâh! You have*

nearly ruined me. (56) "Had it not been for the Grace of
my Lord, I would certainly have been among those
brought forth (to Hell)." (57) (The dwellers of Paradise
will say): "Are we then not to die (any more)?
(58) "Except our first death, and we shall not be
punished? (after we have entered Paradise)." (59) Truly,
this is the supreme success! (60) For the like of this let
the workers work. (61) Is that (Paradise) better
entertainment or the tree of Zaqqûm (a horrible tree in
Hell)? (62) Truly We have made it (as) a trial for the
Zâlimûn (polytheists, disbelievers, wrong-doers).
(63) Verily, it is a tree that springs out of the bottom of
Hell-fire, (64) The shoots of its fruit-stalks are like the
heads of Shayâtin (devils); (65) Truly, they will eat
thereof and fill their bellies therewith. (66) Then on the
top of that they will be given boiling water to drink so
that it becomes a mixture (of boiling water and Zaqqûm
in their bellies). (67) Then thereafter, verily, their return
is to the flaming fire of Hell. (68)

**Quran 37:110**

كَذَٰلِكَ نَجْزِى ٱلْمُحْسِنِينَ

Thus indeed do We reward the Muhsinûn (good-doers).
(110)

**Quran 37:121**

إِنَّا كَذَٰلِكَ نَجْزِى ٱلْمُحْسِنِينَ

*Verily, thus do We reward the Muhsinûn (good-doers).*
*(121)*

## Quran 37:131

إِنَّا كَذَٰلِكَ نَجْزِى ٱلْمُحْسِنِينَ

*Verily, thus do We reward the Muhsinûn (good-doers,*
*who perform good deeds totally for Allâh's sake only)*
*(131)*

## Quran 37:161-163

فَإِنَّكُمْ وَمَا تَعْبُدُونَ (١٦١) مَآ أَنتُمْ عَلَيْهِ بِفَٰتِنِينَ (١٦٢) إِلَّا مَنْ هُوَ صَالِ ٱلْجَحِيمِ (١٦٣)

*So, verily you (pagans) and those whom you worship*
*(idols) (161) Cannot lead astray [turn away from Him*
*(Allâh) anyone of the believers], (162) Except those who*
*are predestined to burn in Hell! (163)*

## Quran 37:170-179

فَكَفَرُوا۟ بِهِۦ فَسَوْفَ يَعْلَمُونَ (١٧٠) وَلَقَدْ سَبَقَتْ كَلِمَتُنَا لِعِبَادِنَا ٱلْمُرْسَلِينَ (١٧١) إِنَّهُمْ لَهُمُ ٱلْمَنصُورُونَ (١٧٢) وَإِنَّ جُندَنَا لَهُمُ ٱلْغَٰلِبُونَ (١٧٣) فَتَوَلَّ عَنْهُمْ حَتَّىٰ حِينٍ (١٧٤) وَأَبْصِرْهُمْ فَسَوْفَ يُبْصِرُونَ (١٧٥) أَفَبِعَذَابِنَا يَسْتَعْجِلُونَ (١٧٦) فَإِذَا نَزَلَ بِسَاحَتِهِمْ فَسَآءَ صَبَاحُ ٱلْمُنذَرِينَ

(١٧٧) وَتَوَلَّ عَنْهُمْ حَتَّىٰ حِينٍ (١٧٨) وَأَبْصِرْ فَسَوْفَ
يُبْصِرُونَ (١٧٩)

But (now that the Qur'ân has come) they disbelieve
therein (i.e. in the Qur'ân and in Prophet Muhammad,
and all that he brought, the Divine Revelation), so they
will come to know! (170) And, verily, Our Word has
gone forth of old for Our slaves, the Messengers,
(171) That they verily would be made triumphant.
(172) And that Our hosts, they verily would be the
victors. (173) So turn away from them for a while,
(174) And watch them and they shall see! (175) Do they
seek to hasten on Our Torment? (176) Then, when it
descends into their courtyard (i.e. near to them), evil will
be the morning for those who had been warned! (177) So
turn  away from them for a while, (178) And watch and
they shall see! (179)

## Quran 38:11

جُندٌ مَّا هُنَالِكَ مَهْزُومٌ مِّنَ ٱلْأَحْزَابِ

(As they denied Allâh's Message) they will be a defeated
host like the confederates of the old times (who were
defeated). (11)

## Quran 38:15-16

وَمَا يَنظُرُ هَٰٓؤُلَآءِ إِلَّا صَيْحَةً وَٰحِدَةً مَّا لَهَا مِن فَوَاقٍ
(١٥) وَقَالُواْ رَبَّنَا عَجِّل لَّنَا قِطَّنَا قَبْلَ يَوْمِ ٱلْحِسَابِ (١٦)

*And these only wait for a single Saihah [shout (i.e. the blowing of the Trumpet by the angel Isrâfil)] there will be no pause or ending thereto [till everything will perish except Allâh (the only God full of Majesty, Bounty and Honour)]. (15) They say: "Our Lord! Hasten to us Qittana (i.e. our Record of good and bad deeds so that we may see it) before the Day of Reckoning!" (16)*

## Quran 38:26-28

يَٰدَاوُۥدُ إِنَّا جَعَلْنَٰكَ خَلِيفَةً فِى ٱلْأَرْضِ فَٱحْكُم بَيْنَ ٱلنَّاسِ
بِٱلْحَقِّ وَلَا تَتَّبِعِ ٱلْهَوَىٰ فَيُضِلَّكَ عَن سَبِيلِ ٱللَّهِ إِنَّ ٱلَّذِينَ
يَضِلُّونَ عَن سَبِيلِ ٱللَّهِ لَهُمْ عَذَابٌ شَدِيدٌۢ بِمَا نَسُواْ يَوْمَ
ٱلْحِسَابِ (٢٦) وَمَا خَلَقْنَا ٱلسَّمَآءَ وَٱلْأَرْضَ وَمَا بَيْنَهُمَا بَٰطِلًا
ذَٰلِكَ ظَنُّ ٱلَّذِينَ كَفَرُواْ فَوَيْلٌ لِّلَّذِينَ كَفَرُواْ مِنَ ٱلنَّارِ (٢٧) أَمْ
نَجْعَلُ ٱلَّذِينَ ءَامَنُواْ وَعَمِلُواْ ٱلصَّٰلِحَٰتِ كَٱلْمُفْسِدِينَ فِى
ٱلْأَرْضِ أَمْ نَجْعَلُ ٱلْمُتَّقِينَ كَٱلْفُجَّارِ (٢٨)

*O Dâwûd (David)! Verily! We have placed you as a successor on earth, so judge you between men in truth (and justice) and follow not your desire for it will mislead you from the Path of Allâh. Verily! those who wander astray from the Path of Allâh (shall) have a severe torment, because they forgot the Day of Reckoning.*

(26) *And We created not the heaven and the earth and all that is between them without purpose! That is the consideration of those who disbelieve! Then woe to those who disbelieve (in Islâmic Monotheism) from the Fire!* (27) *Shall We treat those who believe (in the Oneness of Allâh — Islâmic Monotheism) and do righteous good deeds, as Mufsidûn (those who associate partners in worship with Allâh and commit crimes) on earth? Or shall We treat the Muttaqûn (pious), as the Fujjâr (criminals, disbelievers, the wicked)?* (28)

## Quran 38:64

هَـٰذَا ذِكْرٌ ۚ وَإِنَّ لِلْمُتَّقِينَ لَحُسْنَ مَـَٔابٍ (٤٩) جَنَّـٰتِ عَدْنٍ مُّفَتَّحَةً لَّهُمُ ٱلْأَبْوَٰبُ (٥٠) مُتَّكِئِينَ فِيهَا يَدْعُونَ فِيهَا بِفَـٰكِهَةٍ كَثِيرَةٍ وَشَرَابٍ (٥١) ۞ وَعِندَهُمْ قَـٰصِرَٰتُ ٱلطَّرْفِ أَتْرَابٌ (٥٢) هَـٰذَا مَا تُوعَدُونَ لِيَوْمِ ٱلْحِسَابِ (٥٣) إِنَّ هَـٰذَا لَرِزْقُنَا مَا لَهُۥ مِن نَّفَادٍ (٥٤) هَـٰذَا ۚ وَإِنَّ لِلطَّـٰغِينَ لَشَرَّ مَـَٔابٍ (٥٥) جَهَنَّمَ يَصْلَوْنَهَا فَبِئْسَ ٱلْمِهَادُ (٥٦) هَـٰذَا فَلْيَذُوقُوهُ حَمِيمٌ وَغَسَّاقٌ (٥٧) وَءَاخَرُ مِن شَكْلِهِۦٓ أَزْوَٰجٌ (٥٨) هَـٰذَا فَوْجٌ مُّقْتَحِمٌ مَّعَكُمْ ۖ لَا مَرْحَبًۢا بِهِمْ ۚ إِنَّهُمْ صَالُواْ ٱلنَّارِ (٥٩) قَالُواْ بَلْ أَنتُمْ لَا مَرْحَبًۢا بِكُمْ ۖ أَنتُمْ قَدَّمْتُمُوهُ لَنَا ۖ فَبِئْسَ ٱلْقَرَارُ (٦٠) قَالُواْ رَبَّنَا مَن قَدَّمَ لَنَا هَـٰذَا فَزِدْهُ عَذَابًا ضِعْفًا فِى ٱلنَّارِ (٦١) وَقَالُواْ مَا لَنَا لَا نَرَىٰ رِجَالًا كُنَّا نَعُدُّهُم مِّنَ ٱلْأَشْرَارِ

أَتَّخَذْنَـٰهُمْ سِخْرِيًّا أَمْ زَاغَتْ عَنْهُمُ ٱلْأَبْصَـٰرُ (٦٣) إِنَّ (٦٢)
ذَٰلِكَ لَحَقٌّ تَخَاصُمُ أَهْلِ ٱلنَّارِ (٦٤)

This is a Reminder, and verily, for the Muttaqûn (pious and righteous persons) is a good final return (Paradise) (49) 'Adn (Edn) Paradise (everlasting Gardens), whose doors will be opened for them. (50) Therein they will recline; therein they will call for fruits in abundance and drinks; (51) And beside them will be Qasirat-at-Tarf chaste females (wives) restraining their glances (desiring none except their husbands)], (and) of equal ages. (52) This it is what you (Al-Muttaqûn - the pious.) are promised for the Day of Reckoning! (53) (It will be said to them)! Verily, this is Our Provision which will never finish; (54) This is so! And for the Tâghûn (transgressors, disobedient to Allâh and His Messenger - disbelievers in the Oneness of Allâh, criminals), will be an evil final return (Fire), (55) Hell! Where they will burn, and worst (indeed) is that place to rest! (56) This is so! Then let them taste it, a boiling fluid and dirty wound discharges. (57) And other (torments) of similar kind — all together! (58) This is a troop entering with you (in Hell), no welcome for them! Verily, they shall burn in the Fire! (59) (The followers of the misleaders will say): "Nay, you (too)! No welcome for you! It is you (misleaders) who brought this upon us (because you

misled us in the world), so evil is this place to stay in!"
(60) They will say: "Our Lord! Whoever brought this
upon us, add to him a double torment in the Fire!"
(61) And they will say: "What is the matter with us that
we see not men whom we used to count among the bad
ones?" (62) Did we take them as an object of mockery, or
have (our) eyes failed to perceive them?" (63) Verily, that
is the very truth, the mutual dispute of the people of the
Fire! (64)

## Quran 38:77-85

قَالَ فَٱخۡرُجۡ مِنۡهَا فَإِنَّكَ رَجِيمٌ (٧٧) وَإِنَّ عَلَيۡكَ لَعۡنَتِىٓ إِلَىٰ يَوۡمِ
ٱلدِّينِ (٧٨) قَالَ رَبِّ فَأَنظِرۡنِىٓ إِلَىٰ يَوۡمِ يُبۡعَثُونَ (٧٩) قَالَ
فَإِنَّكَ مِنَ ٱلۡمُنظَرِينَ (٨٠) إِلَىٰ يَوۡمِ ٱلۡوَقۡتِ ٱلۡمَعۡلُومِ (٨١) قَالَ
فَبِعِزَّتِكَ لَأُغۡوِيَنَّهُمۡ أَجۡمَعِينَ (٨٢) إِلَّا عِبَادَكَ مِنۡهُمُ ٱلۡمُخۡلَصِينَ
(٨٣) قَالَ فَٱلۡحَقُّ وَٱلۡحَقَّ أَقُولُ (٨٤) لَأَمۡلَأَنَّ جَهَنَّمَ مِنكَ
وَمِمَّن تَبِعَكَ مِنۡهُمۡ أَجۡمَعِينَ (٨٥)

(Allâh) said: "Then get out from here, for verily, you are
outcast. (77) "And verily!, My Curse is on you till the
Day of Recompense." (78) [Iblîs (Satan)] said: "My
Lord! Give me then respite till the Day the (dead) are
resurrected." (79) (Allâh) said: "Verily! You are of those
allowed respite (80) "Till the Day of the time appointed."
(81) [Iblîs (Satan)] said: "By Your Might, then I will
surely mislead them all, (82) "Except Your chosen slaves
amongst them (faithful, obedient, true believers of Islâmic

Monotheism)." (83) (Allâh) said: "The Truth is, – and
the Truth I say, – (84) That I will fill Hell with you
[Iblîs (Satan)] and those of them (mankind) that follow
you, together." (85)

## Quran 38:88

وَلَتَعْلَمُنَّ نَبَأَهُۥ بَعْدَ حِينٍ

"And you shall certainly know the truth of it after a
while." (88)

## Quran 39:1

تَنزِيلُ ٱلْكِتَٰبِ مِنَ ٱللَّهِ ٱلْعَزِيزِ ٱلْحَكِيمِ

The revelation of this Book (the Qur'ân) is from Allâh,
the All-Mighty, the All-Wise. (1)

## Quran 39:3

أَلَا لِلَّهِ ٱلدِّينُ ٱلْخَالِصُ وَٱلَّذِينَ ٱتَّخَذُوا مِن دُونِهِۦ أَوْلِيَآءَ مَا
نَعْبُدُهُمْ إِلَّا لِيُقَرِّبُونَآ إِلَى ٱللَّهِ زُلْفَىٰٓ إِنَّ ٱللَّهَ يَحْكُمُ
بَيْنَهُمْ فِى مَا هُمْ فِيهِ يَخْتَلِفُونَ إِنَّ ٱللَّهَ لَا يَهْدِى مَنْ هُوَ
كَٰذِبٌ كَفَّارٌ

Surely, the religion (i.e. the worship and the obedience) is
for Allâh only. And those who take Auliyâ' (protectors,
helpers, lords, gods) besides Him (say): "We worship
them only that they may bring us near to Allâh." Verily,
Allâh will judge between them concerning that wherein

*they differ. Truly, Allâh guides not him who is a liar, and a disbeliever. (3)*

## Quran 39:7-10

إِن تَكْفُرُواْ فَإِنَّ ٱللَّهَ غَنِيٌّ عَنكُمْ وَلَا يَرْضَىٰ لِعِبَادِهِ ٱلْكُفْرَ وَإِن تَشْكُرُواْ يَرْضَهُ لَكُمْ وَلَا تَزِرُ وَازِرَةٌ وِزْرَ أُخْرَىٰ ثُمَّ إِلَىٰ رَبِّكُم مَّرْجِعُكُمْ فَيُنَبِّئُكُم بِمَا كُنتُمْ تَعْمَلُونَ إِنَّهُ عَلِيمٌ بِذَاتِ ٱلصُّدُورِ ﴿٧﴾ وَإِذَا مَسَّ ٱلْإِنسَٰنَ ضُرٌّ دَعَا رَبَّهُ مُنِيبًا إِلَيْهِ ثُمَّ إِذَا خَوَّلَهُ نِعْمَةً مِّنْهُ نَسِىَ مَا كَانَ يَدْعُواْ إِلَيْهِ مِن قَبْلُ وَجَعَلَ لِلَّهِ أَندَادًا لِّيُضِلَّ عَن سَبِيلِهِ قُلْ تَمَتَّعْ بِكُفْرِكَ قَلِيلًا إِنَّكَ مِنْ أَصْحَٰبِ ٱلنَّارِ ﴿٨﴾ أَمَّنْ هُوَ قَٰنِتٌ ءَانَآءَ ٱلَّيْلِ سَاجِدًا وَقَآئِمًا يَحْذَرُ ٱلْأَخِرَةَ وَيَرْجُواْ رَحْمَةَ رَبِّهِ قُلْ هَلْ يَسْتَوِى ٱلَّذِينَ يَعْلَمُونَ وَٱلَّذِينَ لَا يَعْلَمُونَ إِنَّمَا يَتَذَكَّرُ أُوْلُواْ ٱلْأَلْبَٰبِ ﴿٩﴾ قُلْ يَٰعِبَادِ ٱلَّذِينَ ءَامَنُواْ ٱتَّقُواْ رَبَّكُمْ لِلَّذِينَ أَحْسَنُواْ فِى هَٰذِهِ ٱلدُّنْيَا حَسَنَةٌ وَأَرْضُ ٱللَّهِ وَٰسِعَةٌ إِنَّمَا يُوَفَّى ٱلصَّٰبِرُونَ أَجْرَهُم بِغَيْرِ حِسَابٍ ﴿١٠﴾

*If you disbelieve, then verily, Allâh is not in need of you, He likes not disbelief for His slaves. And if you are grateful (by being believers), He is pleased therewith for you. No bearer of burdens shall bear the burden of another. Then to your Lord is your return, and He will inform you what you used to do. Verily, He is the All-Knower of that which is in (men's) breasts. (7) And when some hurt touches man, he cries to his Lord (Allâh*

Alone), turning to Him in repentance, but when He bestows a favour upon him from Himself, he forgets that for which he cried for before, and he sets up rivals to Allâh, in order to mislead others from His Path. Say: "Take pleasure in your disbelief for a while: surely, you are (one) of the dwellers of the Fire!" (8) Is one who is obedient to Allâh, prostrating himself or standing (in prayer) during the hours of the night, fearing the Hereafter and hoping for the Mercy of his Lord (like one who disbelieves)? Say: "Are those who know equal to those who know not?" It is only men of understanding who will remember (i.e. get a lesson from Allâh's Signs and Verses). (9) Say (O Muhammad): "O My slaves who believe (in the Oneness of Allâh Islâmic — Monotheism), be afraid of your Lord (Allâh) and keep your duty to Him. Good is (the reward) for those who do good in this world, and Allâh's earth is spacious (so if you cannot worship Allâh at a place, then go to another)! Only those who are patient shall receive their reward in full, without reckoning." (10)

## Quran 39:13

قُلْ إِنِّىَ أَخَافُ إِنْ عَصَيْتُ رَبِّى عَذَابَ يَوْمٍ عَظِيمٍ

Say (O Muhammad): "Verily, if I disobey my Lord, I am afraid of the torment of a great Day." (13)

## Quran 39:15-18

فَٱعْبُدُوا۟ مَا شِئْتُم مِّن دُونِهِۦ قُلْ إِنَّ ٱلْخَٰسِرِينَ ٱلَّذِينَ خَسِرُوٓا۟ أَنفُسَهُمْ وَأَهْلِيهِمْ يَوْمَ ٱلْقِيَٰمَةِ أَلَا ذَٰلِكَ هُوَ ٱلْخُسْرَانُ ٱلْمُبِينُ (١٥) لَهُم مِّن فَوْقِهِمْ ظُلَلٌ مِّنَ ٱلنَّارِ وَمِن تَحْتِهِمْ ظُلَلٌ ذَٰلِكَ يُخَوِّفُ ٱللَّهُ بِهِۦ عِبَادَهُۥ يَٰعِبَادِ فَٱتَّقُونِ (١٦) وَٱلَّذِينَ ٱجْتَنَبُوا۟ ٱلطَّٰغُوتَ أَن يَعْبُدُوهَا وَأَنَابُوٓا۟ إِلَى ٱللَّهِ لَهُمُ ٱلْبُشْرَىٰ فَبَشِّرْ عِبَادِ (١٧) ٱلَّذِينَ يَسْتَمِعُونَ ٱلْقَوْلَ فَيَتَّبِعُونَ أَحْسَنَهُۥ أُو۟لَٰٓئِكَ ٱلَّذِينَ هَدَىٰهُمُ ٱللَّهُ وَأُو۟لَٰٓئِكَ هُمْ أُو۟لُوا۟ ٱلْأَلْبَٰبِ (١٨)

*So worship what you like besides Him. Say: "The losers are those who will lose themselves and their families on the Day of Resurrection. Verily, that will be a manifest loss!" (15) They shall have coverings of Fire, above them and covering (of Fire) beneath them; with this Allâh does frighten His slaves: "O My slaves, therefore fear Me!" (16) Those who avoid At-Tâghût (false deities) by not worshipping them and turn to Allâh (in repentance), for them are glad tidings; so announce the good news to My slaves, — (17) Those who listen to the Word [good advice Lâ ilâha ill-allâh — (none has the right to be worshipped but Allâh) and Islâmic Monotheism] and follow the best thereof (i.e. worship Allâh Alone, repent to Him and avoid Tâghût) those are (the ones) whom Allâh has guided and those are men of understanding. (18)*

**Quran 39:20**

لَـٰكِنِ ٱلَّذِينَ ٱتَّقَوْا۟ رَبَّهُمْ لَهُمْ غُرَفٌ مِّن فَوْقِهَا غُرَفٌ مَّبْنِيَّةٌ تَجْرِى مِن تَحْتِهَا ٱلْأَنْهَـٰرُ وَعْدَ ٱللَّهِ لَا يُخْلِفُ ٱللَّهُ ٱلْمِيعَادَ (٢٠)

*But those who fear their Lord (Allâh) and keep their duty to Him, for them are built lofty rooms; one above another under which rivers flow (i.e. Paradise). (This is) the Promise of Allâh: and Allâh does not fail in (His) Promise. (20)*

## Quran 39:23-26

ٱللَّهُ نَزَّلَ أَحْسَنَ ٱلْحَدِيثِ كِتَـٰبًا مُّتَشَـٰبِهًا مَّثَانِىَ تَقْشَعِرُّ مِنْهُ جُلُودُ ٱلَّذِينَ يَخْشَوْنَ رَبَّهُمْ ثُمَّ تَلِينُ جُلُودُهُمْ وَقُلُوبُهُمْ إِلَىٰ ذِكْرِ ٱللَّهِ ذَٰلِكَ هُدَى ٱللَّهِ يَهْدِى بِهِ مَن يَشَآءُ وَمَن يُضْلِلِ ٱللَّهُ فَمَا لَهُ مِنْ هَادٍ (٢٣) أَفَمَن يَتَّقِى بِوَجْهِهِ سُوٓءَ ٱلْعَذَابِ يَوْمَ ٱلْقِيَـٰمَةِ وَقِيلَ لِلظَّـٰلِمِينَ ذُوقُوا۟ مَا كُنتُمْ تَكْسِبُونَ (٢٤) كَذَّبَ ٱلَّذِينَ مِن قَبْلِهِمْ فَأَتَـٰهُمُ ٱلْعَذَابُ مِنْ حَيْثُ لَا يَشْعُرُونَ (٢٥) فَأَذَاقَهُمُ ٱللَّهُ ٱلْخِزْىَ فِى ٱلْحَيَوٰةِ ٱلدُّنْيَا وَلَعَذَابُ ٱلْأَخِرَةِ أَكْبَرُ لَوْ كَانُوا۟ يَعْلَمُونَ (٢٦)

*Allâh has sent down the Best statement, a Book (this Qur'ân), its parts resembling each other (in goodness and truth), and oft-repeated. The skins of those who fear their Lord shiver from it (when they recite it or hear it). Then their skin and their heart soften to the remembrance of Allâh. That is the guidance of Allâh. He Guides* therewith whom He wills and whomever Allâh sends astray, for him there is no guide. (23) Is he then, who will confront with his face the awful torment on the Day of Resurrection (as he who enters peacefully in Paradise)? And it will be said to the Zâlimûn (polytheists and wrong-doers): "Taste what you used to earn!" (24) Those before them belied, and so the torment came on them from directions they perceived not. (25) So Allâh made them to taste the disgrace in the present life, but greater is the torment of the Hereafter if they only knew! (26)

## Quran 39:30-37

إِنَّكَ مَيِّتٌ وَإِنَّهُم مَّيِّتُونَ (٣٠) ثُمَّ إِنَّكُمْ يَوْمَ ٱلْقِيَـٰمَةِ عِندَ رَبِّكُمْ تَخْتَصِمُونَ (٣١) ۞ فَمَنْ أَظْلَمُ مِمَّن كَذَبَ عَلَى ٱللَّهِ وَكَذَّبَ بِٱلصِّدْقِ إِذْ جَاءَهُۥٓ أَلَيْسَ فِى جَهَنَّمَ مَثْوًى لِّلْكَـٰفِرِينَ (٣٢) وَٱلَّذِى جَاءَ بِٱلصِّدْقِ وَصَدَّقَ بِهِۦٓ أُوْلَـٰٓئِكَ هُمُ ٱلْمُتَّقُونَ (٣٣) لَهُم مَّا يَشَآءُونَ عِندَ رَبِّهِمْ ذَٰلِكَ جَزَآءُ ٱلْمُحْسِنِينَ (٣٤) لِيُكَفِّرَ ٱللَّهُ عَنْهُمْ أَسْوَأَ ٱلَّذِى عَمِلُوا۟ وَيَجْزِيَهُمْ أَجْرَهُم بِأَحْسَنِ ٱلَّذِى كَانُوا۟ يَعْمَلُونَ (٣٥) أَلَيْسَ ٱللَّهُ بِكَافٍ عَبْدَهُۥ وَيُخَوِّفُونَكَ بِٱلَّذِينَ مِن دُونِهِۦ وَمَن يُضْلِلِ ٱللَّهُ فَمَا لَهُۥ مِنْ هَادٍ (٣٦) وَمَن يَهْدِ ٱللَّهُ فَمَا لَهُۥ مِن مُّضِلٍّ أَلَيْسَ ٱللَّهُ بِعَزِيزٍ ذِى ٱنتِقَامٍ (٣٧)

Verily, you (O Muhammad) will die and verily, they (too) will die. (30) Then, on the Day of Resurrection, you will be disputing before your Lord. (31) Then, who does more wrong than one who utters a lie against Allâh, and denies the truth [this Qur'ân, the Prophet (Muhammad), and the Islâmic Monotheism] when it comes to him! Is there not in Hell an abode for the disbelievers? (32) And he (Muhammad) who has brought the truth (this Qur'ân and Islâmic Monotheism) and (those who) believed therein (i.e. the true believers of Islâmic Monotheism), those are Al- Muttaqûn (the pious and righteous persons) (33) They shall have all that they will desire with their Lord. That is the reward of Muhsinûn (good-doers) (34) So that Allâh may expiate from them the evil of what they did and give them the reward, according to the best of what they used to do (35) Is not Allâh Sufficient for His slave? Yet they try to frighten you with those (whom they worship) besides Him! And whom Allâh sends astray, for him there will be no guide. (36) And whomsoever Allâh guides, for him there will be no misleader. Is not Allâh All-Mighty, Possessor of Retribution? (37)

## Quran 39:39-42

قُلْ يَٰقَوْمِ ٱعْمَلُواْ عَلَىٰ مَكَانَتِكُمْ إِنِّى عَٰمِلٌ فَسَوْفَ تَعْلَمُونَ
(٣٩) مَن يَأْتِيهِ عَذَابٌ يُخْزِيهِ وَيَحِلُّ عَلَيْهِ عَذَابٌ مُّقِيمٌ
(٤٠) إِنَّآ أَنزَلْنَا عَلَيْكَ ٱلْكِتَٰبَ لِلنَّاسِ بِٱلْحَقِّ فَمَنِ ٱهْتَدَىٰ
فَلِنَفْسِهِ وَمَن ضَلَّ فَإِنَّمَا يَضِلُّ عَلَيْهَا وَمَآ أَنتَ عَلَيْهِم بِوَكِيلٍ
(٤١) ٱللَّهُ يَتَوَفَّى ٱلْأَنفُسَ حِينَ مَوْتِهَا وَٱلَّتِى لَمْ تَمُتْ فِى

مَنَامِهَا فَيُمْسِكُ ٱلَّتِى قَضَىٰ عَلَيْهَا ٱلْمَوْتَ وَيُرْسِلُ ٱلْأُخْرَىٰ إِلَىٰٓ أَجَلٍ مُّسَمًّى إِنَّ فِى ذَٰلِكَ لَءَايَٰتٍ لِّقَوْمٍ يَتَفَكَّرُونَ (٤٢)

*Say: (O Muhammad) "O My people! Work according to your way, I am working (according to my way). Then you will come to know, (39) "To whom comes a disgracing torment, and on whom descends an everlasting torment." (40) Verily, We have sent down to you (O Muhammad) the Book (this Qur'ân) for mankind in truth. So whosoever accepts the guidance, it is only for his ownself, and whosoever goes astray, he goes astray only for his (own) loss. And you (O Muhammad) are not a Wakîl (trustee or disposer of affairs, or guardian) over them. (41) It is Allâh Who takes away the souls at the time of their death, and those that die not during their sleep. He keeps those (souls) for which He has ordained death and sends the rest for a term appointed. Verily, in this are signs for a people who think deeply. (42)*

## Quran 39:44-48

قُل لِّلَّهِ ٱلشَّفَٰعَةُ جَمِيعًا لَّهُۥ مُلْكُ ٱلسَّمَٰوَٰتِ وَٱلْأَرْضِ ثُمَّ إِلَيْهِ تُرْجَعُونَ (٤٤) وَإِذَا ذُكِرَ ٱللَّهُ وَحْدَهُ ٱشْمَأَزَّتْ قُلُوبُ ٱلَّذِينَ لَا يُؤْمِنُونَ بِٱلْأَخِرَةِ وَإِذَا ذُكِرَ ٱلَّذِينَ مِن دُونِهِ إِذَا هُمْ يَسْتَبْشِرُونَ (٤٥) قُلِ ٱللَّهُمَّ فَاطِرَ ٱلسَّمَٰوَٰتِ وَٱلْأَرْضِ عَٰلِمَ ٱلْغَيْبِ وَٱلشَّهَٰدَةِ أَنتَ تَحْكُمُ بَيْنَ عِبَادِكَ فِى مَا كَانُواْ فِيهِ يَخْتَلِفُونَ (٤٦) وَلَوْ أَنَّ لِلَّذِينَ ظَلَمُواْ مَا فِى ٱلْأَرْضِ جَمِيعًا وَمِثْلَهُۥ

مَعَهُۥ لَأَفۡتَدَوۡاْ بِهِۦ مِن سُوٓءِ ٱلۡعَذَابِ يَوۡمَ ٱلۡقِيَٰمَةِۚ وَبَدَا لَهُم مِّنَ ٱللَّهِ مَا لَمۡ يَكُونُواْ يَحۡتَسِبُونَ (٤٧) وَبَدَا لَهُمۡ سَيِّـَٔاتُ مَا كَسَبُواْ وَحَاقَ بِهِم مَّا كَانُواْ بِهِۦ يَسۡتَهۡزِءُونَ (٤٨)

Say: "To Allâh belongs all intercession. His is the Sovereignty of the heavens and the earth, Then to Him you shall be brought back." (44) And when Allâh Alone is mentioned, the hearts of those who believe not in the Hereafter are filled with disgust (from the Oneness of Allâh and when those (whom they obey or worship) besides Him [like all false deities other than Allâh, it may be a Messenger, an angel, a pious man, a jinn, or any other creature even idols, graves of religious people, saints, priests, monks and others] are mentioned, behold, they rejoice! (45) Say (O Muhammad): "O Allâh! Creator of the heavens and the earth! All-Knower of the Ghaib (unseen) and the seen. You will judge between your slaves about that wherein they used to differ." (46) And those who did wrong (the polytheists and disbelievers in the Oneness of Allâh), if they had all that is in earth and therewith as much again, they verily, would offer it to ransom themselves therewith on the Day of Resurrection from the evil torment, and there will become apparent to them from Allâh, what they had not been reckoning (47) And the evils of that which they earned will become apparent to them, and they will be encircled by that which they used to mock at! (48)

## Quran 39:51

فَأَصَابَهُمْ سَيِّئَاتُ مَا كَسَبُواْ وَٱلَّذِينَ ظَلَمُواْ مِنْ هَٰؤُلَآءِ سَيُصِيبُهُمْ سَيِّئَاتُ مَا كَسَبُواْ وَمَا هُم بِمُعْجِزِينَ

*So, the evil results of that which they earned overtook them. And those who did wrong of these [people to whom you (Muhammad) have been sent], will also be overtaken by the evil results (torment) for that which they earned, and they will never be able to escape. (51)*

## Quran 39:53-61

۞ قُلْ يَٰعِبَادِىَ ٱلَّذِينَ أَسْرَفُواْ عَلَىٰ أَنفُسِهِمْ لَا تَقْنَطُواْ مِن رَّحْمَةِ ٱللَّهِ إِنَّ ٱللَّهَ يَغْفِرُ ٱلذُّنُوبَ جَمِيعًا إِنَّهُ هُوَ ٱلْغَفُورُ ٱلرَّحِيمُ (٥٣) وَأَنِيبُوٓاْ إِلَىٰ رَبِّكُمْ وَأَسْلِمُواْ لَهُ مِن قَبْلِ أَن يَأْتِيَكُمُ ٱلْعَذَابُ ثُمَّ لَا تُنصَرُونَ (٥٤) وَٱتَّبِعُوٓاْ أَحْسَنَ مَآ أُنزِلَ إِلَيْكُم مِّن رَّبِّكُم مِّن قَبْلِ أَن يَأْتِيَكُمُ ٱلْعَذَابُ بَغْتَةً وَأَنتُمْ لَا تَشْعُرُونَ (٥٥) أَن تَقُولَ نَفْسٌ يَٰحَسْرَتَىٰ عَلَىٰ مَا فَرَّطتُ فِى جَنۢبِ ٱللَّهِ وَإِن كُنتُ لَمِنَ ٱلسَّٰخِرِينَ (٥٦) أَوْ تَقُولَ لَوْ أَنَّ ٱللَّهَ هَدَىٰنِى لَكُنتُ مِنَ ٱلْمُتَّقِينَ (٥٧) أَوْ تَقُولَ حِينَ تَرَى ٱلْعَذَابَ لَوْ أَنَّ لِى كَرَّةً فَأَكُونَ مِنَ ٱلْمُحْسِنِينَ (٥٨) بَلَىٰ قَدْ جَآءَتْكَ ءَايَٰتِى فَكَذَّبْتَ بِهَا وَٱسْتَكْبَرْتَ وَكُنتَ مِنَ ٱلْكَٰفِرِينَ (٥٩) وَيَوْمَ ٱلْقِيَٰمَةِ تَرَى ٱلَّذِينَ كَذَبُواْ عَلَى ٱللَّهِ وُجُوهُهُم مُّسْوَدَّةٌ أَلَيْسَ فِى جَهَنَّمَ مَثْوًى لِّلْمُتَكَبِّرِينَ (٦٠) وَيُنَجِّى ٱللَّهُ ٱلَّذِينَ ٱتَّقَوْاْ بِمَفَازَتِهِمْ لَا يَمَسُّهُمُ ٱلسُّوٓءُ وَلَا هُمْ يَحْزَنُونَ (٦١)

Say: "O 'Ibâdî (My slaves) who have transgressed against themselves (by committing evil deeds and sins)! Despair not of the Mercy of Allâh, verily Allâh forgives all sins. Truly, He is Oft-Forgiving, Most Merciful (53) "And turn in repentance and in obedience with true Faith (Islâmic Monotheism) to your Lord and submit to Him, (in Islâm), before the torment comes upon you, (and) then you will not be helped. (54) "And follow the best of that which is sent down to you from your Lord (i.e. this Qur'ân, do what it orders you to do and keep away from what it forbids), before the torment comes on you suddenly while you perceive not!" (55) Lest a person should say: "Alas, my grief that I was undutiful to Allâh (i.e. I have not done what Allâh has ordered me to do), and I was indeed among those who mocked [at the truth! i.e. Lâ ilâha illallâh (none has the right to be worshipped but Allâh), the Qur'ân, and Muhammad and at the faithful believers] (56) Or (lest) he should say: "If only Allâh had guided me, I should indeed have been among the Muttaqûn (pious and righteous persons - see V.2:2)." (57) Or (lest) he should say when he sees the torment: "If only I had another chance (to return to the world) then I should indeed be among the Muhsinûn (good-doers)." (58) Yes! Verily, there came to you My Ayât (proofs, evidences, verses, lessons, signs, revelations, etc.) and you denied them, and were proud and were among the disbelievers. (59) And on the Day of Resurrection you will see those who lied against Allâh (i.e. attributed to Him sons, partners) — their faces will be black. Is there not in Hell an abode for the arrogant? (60) And Allâh will deliver those who are the Muttaqûn (pious) to their places of success (Paradise). Evil shall touch them not, nor shall they grieve. (61)

## Quran 39:63-65

لَّهُ مَقَالِيدُ ٱلسَّمَـٰوَٰتِ وَٱلْأَرْضِ ۗ وَٱلَّذِينَ كَفَرُواْ بِـَٔايَـٰتِ ٱللَّهِ أُوْلَـٰٓئِكَ هُمُ ٱلْخَـٰسِرُونَ (٦٣) قُلْ أَفَغَيْرَ ٱللَّهِ تَأْمُرُوٓنِّىٓ أَعْبُدُ أَيُّهَا ٱلْجَـٰهِلُونَ (٦٤) وَلَقَدْ أُوحِىَ إِلَيْكَ وَإِلَى ٱلَّذِينَ مِن قَبْلِكَ لَئِنْ أَشْرَكْتَ لَيَحْبَطَنَّ عَمَلُكَ وَلَتَكُونَنَّ مِنَ ٱلْخَـٰسِرِينَ (٦٥)

To Him belong the keys of the heavens and the earth. And those who disbelieve in the Ayât (proofs, evidences, verses, signs, revelations, etc.) of Allâh, such are they who will be the losers. (63) Say (O Muhammad to the polytheists): "Do you order me to worship other than Allâh? O you fools!" (64) And indeed it has been revealed to you (O Muhammad), as it was to those (Allâh's Messengers) before you: "If you join others in worship with Allâh, (then) surely (all) your deeds will be in vain, and you will certainly be among the losers." (65)

## Quran 39:67-75

وَمَا قَدَرُواْ ٱللَّهَ حَقَّ قَدْرِهِۦ وَٱلْأَرْضُ جَمِيعًا قَبْضَتُهُۥ يَوْمَ ٱلْقِيَـٰمَةِ وَٱلسَّمَـٰوَٰتُ مَطْوِيَّـٰتٌ بِيَمِينِهِۦ ۚ سُبْحَـٰنَهُۥ وَتَعَـٰلَىٰ عَمَّا

يُشْرِكُونَ (٦٧) وَنُفِخَ فِى ٱلصُّورِ فَصَعِقَ مَن فِى ٱلسَّمَـٰوَٰتِ وَمَن فِى ٱلْأَرْضِ إِلَّا مَن شَآءَ ٱللَّهُ ثُمَّ نُفِخَ فِيهِ أُخْرَىٰ فَإِذَا هُمْ قِيَامٌ يَنظُرُونَ (٦٨) وَأَشْرَقَتِ ٱلْأَرْضُ بِنُورِ رَبِّهَا وَوُضِعَ ٱلْكِتَـٰبُ وَجِا۟ىٓءَ بِٱلنَّبِيِّـۧنَ وَٱلشُّهَدَآءِ وَقُضِىَ بَيْنَهُم بِٱلْحَقِّ وَهُمْ لَا يُظْلَمُونَ (٦٩) وَوُفِّيَتْ كُلُّ نَفْسٍ مَّا عَمِلَتْ وَهُوَ أَعْلَمُ بِمَا يَفْعَلُونَ (٧٠) وَسِيقَ ٱلَّذِينَ كَفَرُوٓا۟ إِلَىٰ جَهَنَّمَ زُمَرًا حَتَّىٰٓ إِذَا جَآءُوهَا فُتِحَتْ أَبْوَٰبُهَا وَقَالَ لَهُمْ خَزَنَتُهَآ أَلَمْ يَأْتِكُمْ رُسُلٌ مِّنكُمْ يَتْلُونَ عَلَيْكُمْ ءَايَـٰتِ رَبِّكُمْ وَيُنذِرُونَكُمْ لِقَآءَ يَوْمِكُمْ هَـٰذَا قَالُوا۟ بَلَىٰ وَلَـٰكِنْ حَقَّتْ كَلِمَةُ ٱلْعَذَابِ عَلَى ٱلْكَـٰفِرِينَ (٧١) قِيلَ ٱدْخُلُوٓا۟ أَبْوَٰبَ جَهَنَّمَ خَـٰلِدِينَ فِيهَا فَبِئْسَ مَثْوَى ٱلْمُتَكَبِّرِينَ (٧٢) وَسِيقَ ٱلَّذِينَ ٱتَّقَوْا۟ رَبَّهُمْ إِلَى ٱلْجَنَّةِ زُمَرًا حَتَّىٰٓ إِذَا جَآءُوهَا وَفُتِحَتْ أَبْوَٰبُهَا وَقَالَ لَهُمْ خَزَنَتُهَا سَلَـٰمٌ عَلَيْكُمْ طِبْتُمْ فَٱدْخُلُوهَا خَـٰلِدِينَ (٧٣) وَقَالُوا۟ ٱلْحَمْدُ لِلَّهِ ٱلَّذِى صَدَقَنَا وَعْدَهُ وَأَوْرَثَنَا ٱلْأَرْضَ نَتَبَوَّأُ مِنَ ٱلْجَنَّةِ حَيْثُ نَشَآءُ فَنِعْمَ أَجْرُ ٱلْعَـٰمِلِينَ (٧٤) وَتَرَى ٱلْمَلَـٰٓئِكَةَ حَآفِّينَ مِنْ حَوْلِ ٱلْعَرْشِ يُسَبِّحُونَ بِحَمْدِ رَبِّهِمْ وَقُضِىَ بَيْنَهُم بِٱلْحَقِّ وَقِيلَ ٱلْحَمْدُ لِلَّهِ رَبِّ ٱلْعَـٰلَمِينَ (٧٥)

They made not a just estimate of Allâh such as is due to Him. And on the Day of Resurrection the whole of the earth will be grasped by His Hand and the heavens will be rolled up in His Right Hand. Glorified is He, and

*High is He above all that they associate as partners with Him! (67) And the Trumpet will be blown, and all who are in the heavens and all who are on the earth will swoon away, except him whom Allâh wills. Then it will blown a second time and behold, they will be standing, looking on (waiting). (68) And the earth will shine with the light of its Lord (Allâh, when He will come to judge among men) and the Book will be placed (open) and the Prophets and the witnesses will be brought forward, and it will be judged between them with truth, and they will not be wronged. (69) And each person will be paid in full of what he did; and He is Best Aware of what they do. (70) And those who disbelieved will be driven to Hell in groups, till, when they reach it, the gates thereof will be opened (suddenly like a prison at the arrival of the prisoners). And its keepers will say, "Did not the Messengers come to you from yourselves, reciting to you the Verses of your Lord, and warning you of the Meeting of this Day of yours?" They will say: "Yes, but the Word of torment has been justified against the disbelievers!" (71) It will be said (to them): "Enter you the gates of Hell, to abide therein. And (indeed) what an evil abode of the arrogant!" (72) And those who kept their duty to their Lord will be led to Paradise in groups, till, when they reach it, and its gates will be opened (before their arrival for their reception) and its keepers will say: Salâmun 'Alaikum (peace be upon you)! You have done*

well, so enter here to abide therein." (73) And they will say: "All the praises and thanks are to Allâh Who has fulfilled His Promise to us and has made us inherit (this) land. We can dwell in Paradise where we will; how excellent a reward for the (pious good) workers!"
(74) And you will see the angels surrounding the Throne (of Allâh) from all round, glorifying the praises of their Lord (Allâh). And they (all the creatures) will be judged with truth, and it will be said. All the praises and thanks are to Allâh, the Lord of the 'Alamîn (mankind, jinn and all that exists)." (75)

## Quran 40:2-3

تَنزِيلُ ٱلْكِتَـٰبِ مِنَ ٱللَّهِ ٱلْعَزِيزِ ٱلْعَلِيمِ (٢) غَافِرِ ٱلذَّنۢبِ وَقَابِلِ ٱلتَّوۡبِ شَدِيدِ ٱلۡعِقَابِ ذِى ٱلطَّوۡلِ لَآ إِلَـٰهَ إِلَّا هُوَّ إِلَيۡهِ ٱلۡمَصِيرُ (٣)

The revelation of the Book (this Qur'ân) is from Allâh the All-Mighty, the All-Knower. (2) The Forgiver of sin, the Acceptor of repentance, the Severe in punishment, the Bestower (of favours), Lâ ilâha illa Huwa (none has the right to be worshipped but He), to Him is the final return. (3)

## Quran 40:6-12

وَكَذَٰلِكَ حَقَّتۡ كَلِمَتُ رَبِّكَ عَلَى ٱلَّذِينَ كَفَرُوٓاْ أَنَّهُمۡ أَصۡحَـٰبُ ٱلنَّارِ (٦) ٱلَّذِينَ يَحۡمِلُونَ ٱلۡعَرۡشَ وَمَنۡ حَوۡلَهُۥ يُسَبِّحُونَ بِحَمۡدِ

رَبِّهِمْ وَيُؤْمِنُونَ بِهِ وَيَسْتَغْفِرُونَ لِلَّذِينَ ءَامَنُوا رَبَّنَا وَسِعْتَ
كُلَّ شَىْءٍ رَّحْمَةً وَعِلْمًا فَٱغْفِرْ لِلَّذِينَ تَابُوا وَٱتَّبَعُوا سَبِيلَكَ
وَقِهِمْ عَذَابَ ٱلْجَحِيمِ (٧) رَبَّنَا وَأَدْخِلْهُمْ جَنَّٰتِ عَدْنٍ ٱلَّتِى
وَعَدتَّهُمْ وَمَن صَلَحَ مِنْ ءَابَآئِهِمْ وَأَزْوَٰجِهِمْ وَذُرِّيَّٰتِهِمْ إِنَّكَ
أَنتَ ٱلْعَزِيزُ ٱلْحَكِيمُ (٨) وَقِهِمُ ٱلسَّيِّئَاتِ وَمَن تَقِ ٱلسَّيِّئَاتِ
يَوْمَئِذٍ فَقَدْ رَحِمْتَهُ وَذَٰلِكَ هُوَ ٱلْفَوْزُ ٱلْعَظِيمُ (٩) إِنَّ ٱلَّذِينَ
كَفَرُوا يُنَادَوْنَ لَمَقْتُ ٱللَّهِ أَكْبَرُ مِن مَّقْتِكُمْ أَنفُسَكُمْ إِذْ تُدْعَوْنَ
إِلَى ٱلْإِيمَٰنِ فَتَكْفُرُونَ (١٠) قَالُوا رَبَّنَآ أَمَتَّنَا ٱثْنَتَيْنِ وَأَحْيَيْتَنَا
ٱثْنَتَيْنِ فَٱعْتَرَفْنَا بِذُنُوبِنَا فَهَلْ إِلَىٰ خُرُوجٍ مِّن سَبِيلٍ
(١١) ذَٰلِكُم بِأَنَّهُ إِذَا دُعِىَ ٱللَّهُ وَحْدَهُ كَفَرْتُمْ وَإِن يُشْرَكْ بِهِ
تُؤْمِنُوا فَٱلْحُكْمُ لِلَّهِ ٱلْعَلِىِّ ٱلْكَبِيرِ (١٢)

*Thus has the Word of your Lord been justified against those who disbelieved, that they will be the dwellers of the Fire (6) Those (angels) who bear the Throne (of Allâh) and those around it glorify the praises of their Lord, and believe in Him, and ask forgiveness for those who believe (in the Oneness of Allâh) (saying): "Our Lord! You comprehend all things in mercy and knowledge, so forgive those who repent and follow Your Way, and save them from the torment of the blazing Fire! (7) "Our Lord! And make them enter the 'Adn (Eden) Paradise (everlasting Gardens) which you have promised them, — and to the righteous among their fathers, their wives, and their offspring! Verily, You are the All-Mighty, the All-*

Wise. (8) "And save them from (the punishment, for what they did of) the sins, and whomsoever You save from (the punishment for what he did of) the sins (i.e. pardon him) that Day, him verily, You have taken into mercy." And that is the supreme success. (9) Those who disbelieve will be addressed (at the time of entering the Fire): "Allâh's aversion was greater towards you (in the worldly life when you used to reject the Faith) than your aversion towards one another (now in the Fire of Hell, as you are now enemies to one another), when you were called to the Faith but you used to refuse." (10) They will say: "Our Lord! You have made us to die twice (i.e. we were dead in the loins of our fathers and dead after our life in this world), and You have given us life twice (i.e. life when we were born and life when we are Resurrected)! Now we confess our sins, then is there any way to get out (of the Fire)?" (11) (It will be said): "This is because, when Allâh Alone was invoked (in worship) you disbelieved, but when partners were joined to Him, you believed (denied)! So the judgement is only with Allâh, the Most High, the Most Great!" (12)

## Quran 40:15-18

رَفِيعُ ٱلدَّرَجَٰتِ ذُو ٱلۡعَرۡشِ يُلۡقِى ٱلرُّوحَ مِنۡ أَمۡرِهِۦ عَلَىٰ مَن يَشَآءُ مِنۡ عِبَادِهِۦ لِيُنذِرَ يَوۡمَ ٱلتَّلَاقِ (١٥) يَوۡمَ هُم بَٰرِزُونَ لَا يَخۡفَىٰ عَلَى ٱللَّهِ مِنۡهُمۡ شَىۡءٌۚ لِّمَنِ ٱلۡمُلۡكُ ٱلۡيَوۡمَۖ لِلَّهِ ٱلۡوَٰحِدِ

اَلْقَهَّارِ (١٦) اَلْيَوْمَ تُجْزَىٰ كُلُّ نَفْسٍ بِمَا كَسَبَتْ لَا ظُلْمَ اَلْيَوْمَ إِنَّ اَللَّهَ سَرِيعُ اَلْحِسَابِ (١٧) وَأَنذِرْهُمْ يَوْمَ اَلْأَزِفَةِ إِذِ اَلْقُلُوبُ لَدَى اَلْحَنَاجِرِ كَٰظِمِينَ مَا لِلظَّٰلِمِينَ مِنْ حَمِيمٍ وَلَا شَفِيعٍ يُطَاعُ (١٨)

(He is Allâh) Owner of High Ranks and Degrees, the Owner of the Throne. He sends the revelation by His Command to any of His slaves He wills, that he (the person who receives revelation) may warn (men) of the Day of Mutual Meeting (i.e. The Day of Resurrection). (15) The Day when they will (all) come out, nothing of them will be hidden from Allâh. Whose is the kingdom this Day? (Allâh Himself will reply to His Question): It is Allâh's the One, the Irresistible! (16) This Day shall every person be recompensed for what he earned. This day no injustice (shall be done to anybody). Truly, Allâh is Swift in reckoning. (17) And warn them (O Muhammad) of the Day that is drawing near (i.e. the Day of Resurrection), when the hearts will be choking the throats, and they can neither return them (hearts) to their chests nor can they throw them out. There will be no friend, nor an intercessor for the Zâlimûn (polytheists and wrong-doers), who could be given heed to. (18)

**Quran 40:25**

فَلَمَّا جَاءَهُم بِٱلْحَقِّ مِنْ عِندِنَا قَالُوا۟ ٱقْتُلُوٓا۟ أَبْنَآءَ ٱلَّذِينَ ءَامَنُوا۟ مَعَهُۥ وَٱسْتَحْيُوا۟ نِسَآءَهُمْ وَمَا كَيْدُ ٱلْكَٰفِرِينَ إِلَّا فِى ضَلَٰلٍ

*Then, when he brought them the Truth from Us, they said: "Kill the sons of those who believe with him and let their women live", but the plots of disbelievers are nothing but in vain! (25)*

**Quran 40:27-28**

وَقَالَ مُوسَىٰٓ إِنِّى عُذْتُ بِرَبِّى وَرَبِّكُم مِّن كُلِّ مُتَكَبِّرٍ لَّا يُؤْمِنُ بِيَوْمِ ٱلْحِسَابِ (٢٧) وَقَالَ رَجُلٌ مُّؤْمِنٌ مِّنْ ءَالِ فِرْعَوْنَ يَكْتُمُ إِيمَٰنَهُۥٓ أَتَقْتُلُونَ رَجُلًا أَن يَقُولَ رَبِّىَ ٱللَّهُ وَقَدْ جَآءَكُم بِٱلْبَيِّنَٰتِ مِن رَّبِّكُمْ وَإِن يَكُ كَٰذِبًا فَعَلَيْهِ كَذِبُهُۥ وَإِن يَكُ صَادِقًا يُصِبْكُم بَعْضُ ٱلَّذِى يَعِدُكُمْ إِنَّ ٱللَّهَ لَا يَهْدِى مَنْ هُوَ مُسْرِفٌ كَذَّابٌ (٢٨)

*Mûsa (Moses) said: "Verily, I seek refuge in my Lord and your Lord from every arrogant who believes not in the Day of Reckoning!" (27) And a believing man of Fir'aun's (Pharaoh) family, who hid his faith said: "Would you kill a man because he says: My Lord is Allâh, and he has come to you with clear signs (proofs) from your Lord? And if he is a liar, upon him will be (the sin of) his lie; but if he is telling the truth, then some of that (calamity) wherewith he threatens you will befall on* you." *Verily, Allâh guides not one who is a Musrif (a polytheist, or a murderer who shed blood without a right, or those who commit great sins, oppressor, transgressor), a liar! (28)*

## Quran 40:33-35

يَوْمَ تُوَلُّونَ مُدْبِرِينَ مَا لَكُم مِّنَ ٱللَّهِ مِنْ عَاصِمٍ ۗ وَمَن يُضْلِلِ
ٱللَّهُ فَمَا لَهُ مِنْ هَادٍ (٣٣) وَلَقَدْ جَآءَكُمْ يُوسُفُ مِن قَبْلُ
بِٱلْبَيِّنَـٰتِ فَمَا زِلْتُمْ فِى شَكٍّ مِّمَّا جَآءَكُم بِهِۦ ۖ حَتَّىٰٓ إِذَا هَلَكَ قُلْتُمْ
لَن يَبْعَثَ ٱللَّهُ مِنۢ بَعْدِهِۦ رَسُولاً ۚ كَذَٰلِكَ يُضِلُّ ٱللَّهُ مَنْ هُوَ
مُسْرِفٌ مُّرْتَابٌ (٣٤) ٱلَّذِينَ يُجَـٰدِلُونَ فِىٓ ءَايَـٰتِ ٱللَّهِ بِغَيْرِ
سُلْطَـٰنٍ أَتَـٰهُمْ ۖ كَبُرَ مَقْتًا عِندَ ٱللَّهِ وَعِندَ ٱلَّذِينَ ءَامَنُواْ ۚ كَذَٰلِكَ
يَطْبَعُ ٱللَّهُ عَلَىٰ كُلِّ قَلْبِ مُتَكَبِّرٍ جَبَّارٍ (٣٥)

*A Day when you will turn your backs and flee having no protector from Allâh, And whomsoever Allâh sends astray, for him there is no guide. (33) And indeed Yûsuf (Joseph) did come to you, in times gone by, with clear signs, but you ceased not to doubt in that which he did bring to you, till when he died you said: "No Messenger will Allâh send after him." Thus Allâh leaves astray him who is a Musrif (a polytheist, an oppressor, a criminal, sinner who commit great sins) and a Murtâb (one who doubts Allâh's Warning and His Oneness). (34) Those who dispute about the Ayât (proofs, evidences, verses, lessons, signs, revelations, etc.) of Allâh, without any* authority that has come to them, it is greatly hateful and disgusting to Allâh and to those who believe. Thus does Allâh seal up the heart of every arrogant, tyrant. (So they cannot guide themselves to the Right Path). (35)

## Quran 40:39-40

يَـٰقَوْمِ إِنَّمَا هَـٰذِهِ ٱلْحَيَوٰةُ ٱلدُّنْيَا مَتَـٰعٌ وَإِنَّ ٱلْأَخِرَةَ هِيَ دَارُ ٱلْقَرَارِ (٣٩) مَنْ عَمِلَ سَيِّئَةً فَلَا يُجْزَىٰٓ إِلَّا مِثْلَهَا ۖ وَمَنْ عَمِلَ صَـٰلِحًا مِّن ذَكَرٍ أَوْ أُنثَىٰ وَهُوَ مُؤْمِنٌ فَأُوْلَـٰئِكَ يَدْخُلُونَ ٱلْجَنَّةَ يُرْزَقُونَ فِيهَا بِغَيْرِ حِسَابٍ (٤٠)

"O my people! Truly, this life of the world is nothing but a (quick passing) enjoyment, and verily, the Hereafter that is the home that will remain forever."
(39) "Whosoever does an evil deed, will not be requited except the like thereof, and whosoever does a righteous deed, whether male or female and is a true believer (in the Oneness of Allâh), such will enter Paradise, where they will be provided therein (with all things in abundance) without limit. (40)

## Quran 40:43

لَا جَرَمَ أَنَّمَا تَدْعُونَنِىٓ إِلَيْهِ لَيْسَ لَهُ دَعْوَةٌ فِى ٱلدُّنْيَا وَلَا فِى ٱلْأَخِرَةِ وَأَنَّ مَرَدَّنَآ إِلَى ٱللَّهِ وَأَنَّ ٱلْمُسْرِفِينَ هُمْ أَصْحَـٰبُ ٱلنَّارِ

"No doubt you call me to (worship) one who cannot grant (me) my request (or respond to my invocation) in this world or in the Hereafter. And our return will be to Allâh, and Al-Musrifûn (i.e. polytheists and arrogants, those who commit great sins, the transgressors of Allâh's set limits) they shall be the dwellers of the Fire! (43)

## Quran 40:46-52

ٱلنَّارُ يُعْرَضُونَ عَلَيْهَا غُدُوًّا وَعَشِيًّا وَيَوْمَ تَقُومُ ٱلسَّاعَةُ أَدْخِلُوٓا۟ ءَالَ فِرْعَوْنَ أَشَدَّ ٱلْعَذَابِ (٤٦) وَإِذْ يَتَحَآجُّونَ فِى ٱلنَّارِ فَيَقُولُ ٱلضُّعَفَٰٓؤُا۟ لِلَّذِينَ ٱسْتَكْبَرُوٓا۟ إِنَّا كُنَّا لَكُمْ تَبَعًا فَهَلْ أَنتُم مُّغْنُونَ عَنَّا نَصِيبًا مِّنَ ٱلنَّارِ (٤٧) قَالَ ٱلَّذِينَ ٱسْتَكْبَرُوٓا۟ إِنَّا كُلٌّ فِيهَآ إِنَّ ٱللَّهَ قَدْ حَكَمَ بَيْنَ ٱلْعِبَادِ (٤٨) وَقَالَ ٱلَّذِينَ فِى ٱلنَّارِ لِخَزَنَةِ جَهَنَّمَ ٱدْعُوا۟ رَبَّكُمْ يُخَفِّفْ عَنَّا يَوْمًا مِّنَ ٱلْعَذَابِ (٤٩) قَالُوٓا۟ أَوَلَمْ تَكُ تَأْتِيكُمْ رُسُلُكُم بِٱلْبَيِّنَٰتِ قَالُوا۟ بَلَىٰ قَالُوا۟ فَٱدْعُوا۟ وَمَا دُعَٰٓؤُا۟ ٱلْكَٰفِرِينَ إِلَّا فِى ضَلَٰلٍ (٥٠) إِنَّا لَنَنصُرُ رُسُلَنَا وَٱلَّذِينَ ءَامَنُوا۟ فِى ٱلْحَيَوٰةِ ٱلدُّنْيَا وَيَوْمَ يَقُومُ ٱلْأَشْهَٰدُ (٥١) يَوْمَ لَا يَنفَعُ ٱلظَّٰلِمِينَ مَعْذِرَتُهُمْ وَلَهُمُ ٱللَّعْنَةُ وَلَهُمْ سُوٓءُ ٱلدَّارِ (٥٢)

The Fire; they are exposed to it, morning and afternoon, and on the Day when the Hour will be established (it will be said to the angels): "Cause Fir'aun's (Pharaoh) people to enter the severest torment!" (46) And, when they will dispute in the Fire, the weak will say to those who were arrogant;" Verily! We followed you, can you then take from us some portion of the Fire?" (47) Those who were arrogant will say: "We are all (together) in this (Fire)! Verily Allâh has judged between (His) slaves!" (48) And those in the Fire will say to the keepers (angels) of Hell: "Call upon your Lord to lighten for us the torment for a day!" (49) They will say: "Did there not come to you, your Messengers with (clear) evidences (and signs)? They will say: "Yes." They will reply: "Then call (as you like)! And the invocation of the disbelievers is nothing but in vain (as it will not be answered by Allah)!" (50) Verily, We will indeed make victorious Our Messengers and those who believe (in the Oneness of Allâh — Islâmic Monotheism) in this world's life and on the Day when the witnesses will stand forth, (i.e. Day of Resurrection), — (51) The Day when their excuses will be of no profit to Zâlimûn (polytheists, wrong-doers and disbelievers in the Oneness of Allâh). Theirs will be the curse, and theirs will be the evil abode (i.e. painful torment in Hell-fire). (52)

## Quran 40:55

فَاصۡبِرۡ إِنَّ وَعۡدَ ٱللَّهِ حَقٌّ وَٱسۡتَغۡفِرۡ لِذَنۢبِكَ وَسَبِّحۡ بِحَمۡدِ رَبِّكَ بِٱلۡعَشِيِّ وَٱلۡإِبۡكَـٰرِ

So be patient. Verily, the Promise of Allâh is true, and ask forgiveness for your fault, and glorify the praises of your Lord in the Ashi (i.e. the time period after the midnoon till sunset) and in the Ibkâr (i.e. the time period from early morning or sunrise till before midnoon) [it is said that, that means the five compulsory congregational Salât (prayers) or the 'Asr and Fajr prayers]. (55)

## Quran 40:59-60

إِنَّ ٱلسَّاعَةَ لَأَتِيَةٌ لَّا رَيْبَ فِيهَا وَلَٰكِنَّ أَكْثَرَ ٱلنَّاسِ لَا يُؤْمِنُونَ (٥٩) وَقَالَ رَبُّكُمُ ٱدْعُونِىٓ أَسْتَجِبْ لَكُمْ إِنَّ ٱلَّذِينَ يَسْتَكْبِرُونَ عَنْ عِبَادَتِى سَيَدْخُلُونَ جَهَنَّمَ دَاخِرِينَ (٦٠)

Verily, the Hour (Day of Judgement) is surely coming, there is no doubt it, yet most men believe not. (59) And your Lord said: "Invoke Me, [i.e. believe in My Oneness (Islâmic Monotheism)] (and ask Me for anything) I will respond to your (invocation). Verily! Those who scorn My worship [i.e. do not invoke Me, and do not believe in My Oneness, (Islâmic Monotheism)] they will surely enter Hell in humiliation!" (60)

## Quran 40:70-78

ٱلَّذِينَ كَذَّبُواْ بِٱلْكِتَٰبِ وَبِمَآ أَرْسَلْنَا بِهِۦ رُسُلَنَا فَسَوْفَ يَعْلَمُونَ (٧٠) إِذِ ٱلْأَغْلَٰلُ فِىٓ أَعْنَٰقِهِمْ وَٱلسَّلَٰسِلُ يُسْحَبُونَ (٧١) فِى ٱلْحَمِيمِ ثُمَّ فِى ٱلنَّارِ يُسْجَرُونَ (٧٢) ثُمَّ قِيلَ لَهُمْ أَيْنَ مَا كُنتُمْ تُشْرِكُونَ (٧٣) مِن دُونِ ٱللَّهِ قَالُواْ ضَلُّواْ عَنَّا بَل لَّمْ نَكُن نَّدْعُواْ مِن قَبْلُ شَيْـًٔا كَذَٰلِكَ يُضِلُّ ٱللَّهُ ٱلْكَٰفِرِينَ

بِغَيْرِ الْحَقِّ وَبِمَا (٧٤) ذَلِكُم بِمَا كُنتُمْ تَفْرَحُونَ فِى الْأَرْضِ
كُنتُمْ تَمْرَحُونَ (٧٥) ادْخُلُوا أَبْوَابَ جَهَنَّمَ خَالِدِينَ فِيهَا فَبِئْسَ
مَثْوَى الْمُتَكَبِّرِينَ (٧٦) فَاصْبِرْ إِنَّ وَعْدَ اللَّهِ حَقٌّ فَإِمَّا نُرِيَنَّكَ
بَعْضَ الَّذِى نَعِدُهُمْ أَوْ نَتَوَفَّيَنَّكَ فَإِلَيْنَا يُرْجَعُونَ (٧٧) وَلَقَدْ
أَرْسَلْنَا رُسُلاً مِّن قَبْلِكَ مِنْهُم مَّن قَصَصْنَا عَلَيْكَ وَمِنْهُم مَّن لَّمْ
نَقْصُصْ عَلَيْكَ وَمَا كَانَ لِرَسُولٍ أَن يَأْتِىَ بِآيَةٍ إِلَّا بِإِذْنِ اللَّهِ
فَإِذَا جَاءَ أَمْرُ اللَّهِ قُضِىَ بِالْحَقِّ وَخَسِرَ هُنَالِكَ الْمُبْطِلُونَ
(٧٨)

Those who deny the Book (this Qur'ân), and that with
which We sent Our Messengers (i.e. to worship none but
Allâh Alone sincerely, and to reject all false deities and to
confess resurrection after the death for recompense) they
will come to know (when they will be cast into the Fire of
Hell). (70) When iron collars will be rounded over their
necks, and the chains, they shall be dragged along (71) In
the boiling water, then they will be burned in the Fire.
(72) Then it will be said to them: "Where are (all) those
whom you used to join in worship as partners.
(73) "Besides Allâh"? They will say: "They have
vanished from us: Nay, we did not invoke (worship)
anything before." Thus Allâh leads astray the
disbelievers. (74) That was because you had been
exulting in the earth without any right (by worshipping
others instead of Allâh and by committing crimes), and
that you used to rejoice extremely (in your error).

*(75) Enter the gates of Hell to abide therein, and (indeed) what an evil abode of the arrogant! (76) So be patient verily, the Promise of Allâh is true, and whether We show you (O Muhammad) some part of what We have promised them, or We cause you to die, then still it is to Us they all shall be returned. (77) And, indeed We have sent Messengers before you (O Muhammad); of some of them We have related to you their story And of some We have not related to you their story, and it was not given to any Messenger that he should bring a sign except by the Leave of Allâh. But, when comes the Commandment of Allâh, the matter will be decided with truth, and the followers of falsehood will then be lost. (78)*

## Quran 41:8

إِنَّ ٱلَّذِينَ ءَامَنُواْ وَعَمِلُواْ ٱلصَّـٰلِحَـٰتِ لَهُمْ أَجْرٌ غَيْرُ مَمْنُونٍ

*Truly, those who believe (in the Oneness of Allâh and in His Messenger Muhammad – Islâmic Monotheism) and do righteous good deeds, for them will be an endless reward that will never stop (i.e. Paradise). (8)*

## Quran 41:19-25

وَيَوْمَ يُحْشَرُ أَعْدَآءُ ٱللَّهِ إِلَى ٱلنَّارِ فَهُمْ يُوزَعُونَ (١٩) حَتَّىٰ إِذَا مَا جَآءُوهَا شَهِدَ عَلَيْهِمْ سَمْعُهُمْ وَأَبْصَـٰرُهُمْ وَجُلُودُهُم بِمَا كَانُواْ يَعْمَلُونَ (٢٠) وَقَالُواْ لِجُلُودِهِمْ لِمَ شَهِدتُّمْ عَلَيْنَا قَالُوٓاْ أَنطَقَنَا ٱللَّهُ ٱلَّذِىٓ أَنطَقَ كُلَّ شَىْءٍ وَهُوَ خَلَقَكُمْ أَوَّلَ مَرَّةٍ وَإِلَيْهِ

تُرْجَعُونَ (٢١) وَمَا كُنتُمْ تَسْتَتِرُونَ أَن يَشْهَدَ عَلَيْكُمْ سَمْعُكُمْ
وَلَا أَبْصَـٰرُكُمْ وَلَا جُلُودُكُمْ وَلَـٰكِن ظَنَنتُمْ أَنَّ ٱللَّهَ لَا يَعْلَمُ كَثِيرًا
مِّمَّا تَعْمَلُونَ (٢٢) وَذَٰلِكُمْ ظَنُّكُمُ ٱلَّذِى ظَنَنتُم بِرَبِّكُمْ أَرْدَىٰكُمْ
فَأَصْبَحْتُم مِّنَ ٱلْخَـٰسِرِينَ (٢٣) فَإِن يَصْبِرُواْ فَٱلنَّارُ مَثْوًى
لَّهُمْ وَإِن يَسْتَعْتِبُواْ فَمَا هُم مِّنَ ٱلْمُعْتَبِينَ (٢٤) ۞ وَقَيَّضْنَا
لَهُمْ قُرَنَآءَ فَزَيَّنُواْ لَهُم مَّا بَيْنَ أَيْدِيهِمْ وَمَا خَلْفَهُمْ وَحَقَّ عَلَيْهِمُ
ٱلْقَوْلُ فِى أُمَمٍ قَدْ خَلَتْ مِن قَبْلِهِم مِّنَ ٱلْجِنِّ وَٱلْإِنسِ إِنَّهُمْ كَانُواْ
خَـٰسِرِينَ (٢٥)

And (remember) the Day that the enemies of Allâh will
be gathered to the Fire, then they will be driven [(to the
fire), former ones being withheld till their later ones will
join them]. (19) Till, when they reach it (Hell-fire), their
hearing (ears) and their eyes, and their skins will testify
against them as to what they used to do. (20) And they
will say to their skins, "Why do you testify against us?"
They will say: "Allâh has caused us to speak," — He
causes all things to speak, and He created you the first
time, and to Him you are made to return." (21) And you
have not been hiding yourselves (in the world), lest your
ears, and your eyes, and your skins should testify against
you, but you thought that Allâh knew not much of what
you were doing. (22) And that thought of yours which
you thought about your Lord, has brought you to
destruction, and you have become (this Day) of those
utterly lost! (23) Then, if they bear the torment patiently,

then the Fire is the home for them, and if they seek to please Allâh, yet they are not of those who will ever be allowed to please Allâh. (24) And We have assigned them (devils) intimate companions (in this world), who have made fair-seeming to them, what was before them (evil deeds which they were doing in the present worldly life and disbelief in the Reckoning and the Resurrection) and what was behind them (denial of the matters in the coming life of the Hereafter as regards punishment or reward). And the Word (i.e. the torment) is justified against them as it was justified against those who were among the previous generations of jinn and men that had passed away before them. Indeed they (all) were the losers. (25)

## Quran 41:27-32

فَلَنُذِيقَنَّ ٱلَّذِينَ كَفَرُواْ عَذَابًا شَدِيدًا وَلَنَجْزِيَنَّهُمْ أَسْوَأَ ٱلَّذِى كَانُواْ يَعْمَلُونَ (٢٧) ذَٰلِكَ جَزَآءُ أَعْدَآءِ ٱللَّهِ ٱلنَّارُ لَهُمْ فِيهَا دَارُ ٱلْخُلْدِ جَزَآءًۢ بِمَا كَانُواْ بِـَٔايَٰتِنَا يَجْحَدُونَ (٢٨) وَقَالَ ٱلَّذِينَ كَفَرُواْ رَبَّنَآ أَرِنَا ٱلَّذَيْنِ أَضَلَّانَا مِنَ ٱلْجِنِّ وَٱلْإِنسِ نَجْعَلْهُمَا تَحْتَ أَقْدَامِنَا لِيَكُونَا مِنَ ٱلْأَسْفَلِينَ (٢٩) إِنَّ ٱلَّذِينَ قَالُواْ رَبُّنَا ٱللَّهُ ثُمَّ ٱسْتَقَٰمُواْ تَتَنَزَّلُ عَلَيْهِمُ ٱلْمَلَٰٓئِكَةُ أَلَّا تَخَافُواْ وَلَا تَحْزَنُواْ وَأَبْشِرُواْ بِٱلْجَنَّةِ ٱلَّتِى كُنتُمْ تُوعَدُونَ (٣٠) نَحْنُ أَوْلِيَآؤُكُمْ فِى ٱلْحَيَوٰةِ ٱلدُّنْيَا وَفِى ٱلْأَخِرَةِ وَلَكُمْ فِيهَا مَا تَشْتَهِىٓ أَنفُسُكُمْ وَلَكُمْ فِيهَا مَا تَدَّعُونَ (٣١) نُزُلاً مِّنْ غَفُورٍ رَّحِيمٍ (٣٢)

But surely, We shall cause those who disbelieve to taste a severe torment, and certainly, We shall requite them the worst of what they used to do. (27) That is the recompense of the enemies of Allâh: the Fire. Therein will be for them the eternal home, a (deserving) recompense for that they used to deny Our Ayât (proofs, evidences, verses, lessons, signs, revelations, etc.). (28) And those who disbelieve will say: "Our Lord! Show us those among jinn and men who led us astray, that we may crush them under our feet so that they become the lowest." (29) Verily, those who say: "Our Lord is Allâh (Alone)," and then they stand firm, on them the angels will descend (at the time of their death) (saying): "Fear not, nor grieve! But receive the glad tidings of Paradise which you have been promised! (30) "We have been your friends in the life of this world and are (so) in the Hereafter. Therein you shall have (all) that your inner-selves desire, and therein you shall have (all) for which you ask. (31) "An entertainment from (Allâh), the Oft-Forgiving, Most Merciful." (32)

## Quran 41:34-35

وَلَا تَسْتَوِى ٱلْحَسَنَةُ وَلَا ٱلسَّيِّئَةُ ٱدْفَعْ بِٱلَّتِى هِىَ أَحْسَنُ فَإِذَا ٱلَّذِى بَيْنَكَ وَبَيْنَهُۥ عَدَاوَةٌ كَأَنَّهُۥ وَلِىٌّ حَمِيمٌ (٣٤) وَمَا يُلَقَّىٰهَآ إِلَّا ٱلَّذِينَ صَبَرُواْ وَمَا يُلَقَّىٰهَآ إِلَّا ذُو حَظٍّ عَظِيمٍ (٣٥)

*The good deed and the evil deed cannot be equal. Repel (the evil) with one which is better (i.e. Allâh orders the faithful believers to be patient at the time of anger, and to excuse those who treat them badly), then verily! he, between whom and you there was enmity, (will become) as though he was a close friend. (34) But none is granted it (the above quality) except those who are patient - and none is granted it except the owner of the great portion (of happiness in the Hereafter i.e. Paradise and of a high moral character) in this world. (35)*

## Quran 41:39-40

وَمِنْ ءَايَٰتِهِۦٓ أَنَّكَ تَرَى ٱلْأَرْضَ خَٰشِعَةً فَإِذَآ أَنزَلْنَا عَلَيْهَا ٱلْمَآءَ ٱهْتَزَّتْ وَرَبَتْ إِنَّ ٱلَّذِىٓ أَحْيَاهَا لَمُحْىِ ٱلْمَوْتَىٰٓ إِنَّهُۥ عَلَىٰ كُلِّ شَىْءٍ قَدِيرٌ (٣٩) إِنَّ ٱلَّذِينَ يُلْحِدُونَ فِىٓ ءَايَٰتِنَا لَا يَخْفَوْنَ عَلَيْنَآ أَفَمَن يُلْقَىٰ فِى ٱلنَّارِ خَيْرٌ أَم مَّن يَأْتِىٓ ءَامِنًا يَوْمَ ٱلْقِيَٰمَةِ ٱعْمَلُوا۟ مَا شِئْتُمْ إِنَّهُۥ بِمَا تَعْمَلُونَ بَصِيرٌ (٤٠)

*And among His Signs (in this), that you see the earth barren, but when We send down water (rain) to it, it is stirred to life and growth (of vegetations). Verily, He Who gives it life, surely is Able to give life to the dead (on the Day of Resurrection). Indeed! He is Able to do all things. (39) Verily, those who turn away from Our Ayât (proofs, evidences, verses, lessons, signs, revelations, etc. by attacking, distorting and denying them), are not hidden from Us. Is he who is cast into the Fire better or* he who comes secure on the Day of Resurrection? Do what you will. Verily! He is All-Seer of what you do (this is a severe threat to the disbelievers) (40)

Quran 41:42

لَّا يَأْتِيهِ ٱلْبَٰطِلُ مِنۢ بَيْنِ يَدَيْهِ وَلَا مِنْ خَلْفِهِۦ تَنزِيلٌ مِّنْ حَكِيمٍ حَمِيدٍ

Falsehood cannot come to it (the Quran) from before it or behind it (it is) sent down by the All-Wise, Worthy of all praise (Allâh). (42)

**Quran 41:44**

وَلَوْ جَعَلْنَٰهُ قُرْءَانًا أَعْجَمِيًّا لَّقَالُواْ لَوْلَا فُصِّلَتْ ءَايَٰتُهُۥٓ ءَا۬عْجَمِيٌّ وَعَرَبِيٌّ قُلْ هُوَ لِلَّذِينَ ءَامَنُواْ هُدًى وَشِفَآءٌ وَٱلَّذِينَ لَا يُؤْمِنُونَ فِىٓ ءَاذَانِهِمْ وَقْرٌ وَهُوَ عَلَيْهِمْ عَمًى أُوْلَٰٓئِكَ يُنَادَوْنَ مِن مَّكَانٍۭ بَعِيدٍ

And if We had sent this as a Qur'ân in a foreign language (other than Arabic), they would have said: "Why are not its Verses explained in detail (in our language)? What! (A Book) not in Arabic and (the Messenger) an Arab?" Say: "It is for those who believe, a guide and a healing. And as for those who disbelieve, there is heaviness (deafness) in their ears, and it (the Qur'ân) is blindness for them. They are those who are called from a place far away (so they neither listen nor understand). (44)

## Quran 41:46-48

مَّنْ عَمِلَ صَـٰلِحًا فَلِنَفْسِهِۦ وَمَنْ أَسَآءَ فَعَلَيْهَا وَمَا رَبُّكَ بِظَلَّـٰمٍ لِّلْعَبِيدِ (٤٦) ۞ إِلَيْهِ يُرَدُّ عِلْمُ ٱلسَّاعَةِ وَمَا تَخْرُجُ مِن ثَمَرَٰتٍ مِّنْ أَكْمَامِهَا وَمَا تَحْمِلُ مِنْ أُنثَىٰ وَلَا تَضَعُ إِلَّا بِعِلْمِهِۦ وَيَوْمَ يُنَادِيهِمْ أَيْنَ شُرَكَآءِى قَالُوٓاْ ءَاذَنَّـٰكَ مَا مِنَّا مِن شَهِيدٍ (٤٧) وَضَلَّ عَنْهُم مَّا كَانُواْ يَدْعُونَ مِن قَبْلُ وَظَنُّواْ مَا لَهُم مِّن مَّحِيصٍ (٤٨)

Whosoever does righteous good deed it is for (the benefit of) his ownself, and whosoever does evil, it is against his ownself, and your Lord is not at all unjust to (His) slaves. (46) To Him (Alone) is referred the knowledge of the Hour. No fruit comes out of its sheath, nor does a female conceive, nor brings forth (young), except by His Knowledge. And on the Day when He will call unto them (polytheists) (saying): "Where are My (so-called) partners (whom you did invent)?" They will say: "We inform You that none of us bears witness to it (that they are Your partners)!" (47) And those whom they used to invoke before before (in this world) shall disappear from them, and they will perceive that they have no place of refuge (from Allâh's punishment). (48)

## Quran 41:50

وَلَئِنْ أَذَقْنَهُ رَحْمَةً مِّنَّا مِنْ بَعْدِ ضَرَّاءَ مَسَّتْهُ لَيَقُولَنَّ هَٰذَا
لِى وَمَآ أَظُنُّ ٱلسَّاعَةَ قَآئِمَةً وَلَئِن رُّجِعْتُ إِلَىٰ رَبِّىَ إِنَّ لِى
عِندَهُۥ لَلْحُسْنَىٰ فَلَنُنَبِّئَنَّ ٱلَّذِينَ كَفَرُوا۟ بِمَا عَمِلُوا۟ وَلَنُذِيقَنَّهُم
مِّنْ عَذَابٍ غَلِيظٍ

And truly, if We give him a taste of mercy from Us, after
some adversity (severe poverty or disease, etc.) has
touched him, he is sure to say: "This is due to me (merit),
I think not that the Hour will be established. But if I am
brought back to my Lord, surely, there will be for me the
best (wealth) with Him. Then, We verily, will show to
the disbelievers what they have done and We shall make
them taste a severe torment. (50)

## Quran 41:53-54

سَنُرِيهِمْ ءَايَٰتِنَا فِى ٱلْآفَاقِ وَفِىٓ أَنفُسِهِمْ حَتَّىٰ يَتَبَيَّنَ لَهُمْ أَنَّهُ
ٱلْحَقُّ أَوَلَمْ يَكْفِ بِرَبِّكَ أَنَّهُۥ عَلَىٰ كُلِّ شَىْءٍ شَهِيدٌ (٥٣) أَلَآ
إِنَّهُمْ فِى مِرْيَةٍ مِّن لِّقَآءِ رَبِّهِمْ أَلَآ إِنَّهُۥ بِكُلِّ شَىْءٍ مُّحِيطٌ (٥٤)

We will show them Our Signs in the universe, and in
their own selves, until it becomes manifest to them that
this (the Qur'ân) is the truth. Is it not sufficient in
regard to your Lord that He is a Witness over all things?
(53) Verily, they are in doubt concerning the Meeting
with their Lord? (i.e. Resurrection after their death, and
their return to their Lord). Verily! He it is Who is
surrounding all things! (54)

## Quran 42:7-9

وَكَذَٰلِكَ أَوْحَيْنَا إِلَيْكَ قُرْءَانًا عَرَبِيًّا لِّتُنذِرَ أُمَّ ٱلْقُرَىٰ وَمَنْ
حَوْلَهَا وَتُنذِرَ يَوْمَ ٱلْجَمْعِ لَا رَيْبَ فِيهِ فَرِيقٌ فِى ٱلْجَنَّةِ وَفَرِيقٌ
فِى ٱلسَّعِيرِ (٧) وَلَوْ شَآءَ ٱللَّهُ لَجَعَلَهُمْ أُمَّةً وَٰحِدَةً وَلَٰكِن يُدْخِلُ
مَن يَشَآءُ فِى رَحْمَتِهِ وَٱلظَّٰلِمُونَ مَا لَهُم مِّن وَلِىٍّ وَلَا نَصِيرٍ
(٨) أَمِ ٱتَّخَذُوا۟ مِن دُونِهِ أَوْلِيَآءَ فَٱللَّهُ هُوَ ٱلْوَلِىُّ وَهُوَ يُحْىِ
ٱلْمَوْتَىٰ وَهُوَ عَلَىٰ كُلِّ شَىْءٍ قَدِيرٌ (٩)

And thus We have revealed unto you (O Muhammad) a
Qur'ân in Arabic that you may warn the Mother of the
Towns (Makkah) and all around it. and warn (them) of
the Day of Assembling, of which there is no doubt, when
a party will be in Paradise (those who believed in Allâh
and followed what Allâh's Messenger brought them) and
a party in the blazing Fire (Hell) (those who disbelieved
in Allâh and followed not what Allâh's Messenger
brought them). (7) And if Allâh had willed, He could
have made them one nation, but He admits whom He
wills to His Mercy. And the Zâlimûn (polytheists and
wrong-doers) will have neither a Walî (protector, or
guardian) nor a helper. (8) Or have they taken (for
worship) Auliyâ' (guardians, supporters, helpers,
protectors, lords, gods) besides Him? But Allâh, He
Alone is the Walî (Lord, God, Protector). And it is He

*Who gives life to the dead, and He is Able to do all things. (9)*

## Quran 42:15-18

فَلِذَٰلِكَ فَٱدْعُ وَٱسْتَقِمْ كَمَا أُمِرْتَ وَلَا تَتَّبِعْ أَهْوَاءَهُمْ وَقُلْ ءَامَنتُ بِمَا أَنزَلَ ٱللَّهُ مِن كِتَٰبٍ وَأُمِرْتُ لِأَعْدِلَ بَيْنَكُمُ ٱللَّهُ رَبُّنَا وَرَبُّكُمْ لَنَا أَعْمَٰلُنَا وَلَكُمْ أَعْمَٰلُكُمْ لَا حُجَّةَ بَيْنَنَا وَبَيْنَكُمُ ٱللَّهُ يَجْمَعُ بَيْنَنَا وَإِلَيْهِ ٱلْمَصِيرُ (١٥) وَٱلَّذِينَ يُحَاجُّونَ فِى ٱللَّهِ مِنۢ بَعْدِ مَا ٱسْتُجِيبَ لَهُ حُجَّتُهُمْ دَاحِضَةٌ عِندَ رَبِّهِمْ وَعَلَيْهِمْ غَضَبٌ وَلَهُمْ عَذَابٌ شَدِيدٌ (١٦) ٱللَّهُ ٱلَّذِى أَنزَلَ ٱلْكِتَٰبَ بِٱلْحَقِّ وَٱلْمِيزَانَ وَمَا يُدْرِيكَ لَعَلَّ ٱلسَّاعَةَ قَرِيبٌ (١٧) يَسْتَعْجِلُ بِهَا ٱلَّذِينَ لَا يُؤْمِنُونَ بِهَا وَٱلَّذِينَ ءَامَنُوا۟ مُشْفِقُونَ مِنْهَا وَيَعْلَمُونَ أَنَّهَا ٱلْحَقُّ أَلَا إِنَّ ٱلَّذِينَ يُمَارُونَ فِى ٱلسَّاعَةِ لَفِى ضَلَٰلٍ بَعِيدٍ (١٨)

*So unto this (religion of Islâm alone and this Qur'ân) then invite (people) (O Muhammad), and stand firm [on Islâmic Monotheism by performing all that is ordained by Allâh (good deeds), and by abstaining from all that is forbidden by Allâh (sins and evil deeds)], as you are commanded, and follow not their desires but say: "I believe in whatsoever Allâh has sent down of the Book [all the Books, - this Qur'ân and the Books of the old from the Taurât (Torah), the Injeel or the Pages of Ibrâhîm (Abraham)] and I am commanded to do justice among you. Allâh is our Lord and your Lord. For us our deeds* and for you your deeds. There is no dispute between us and you. Allâh will assemble us (all), and to Him is the final return." (15) And those who dispute concerning Allâh (His religion of Islâmic Monotheism, with which Muhammad has been sent), after it has been accepted (by the people), of no use is their dispute before their Lord, and on them is wrath, and for them will be a severe torment.(16) It is Allâh Who has sent down the Book (the Qur'ân) in truth, and the Balance (i.e. to act justly). And what can make you know that perhaps the Hour is close at hand? (17) Those who believe not therein seek to hasten it, while those who believe are fearful of it, and know that it is the very truth. Verily, those who dispute concerning the Hour are certainly in error far away. (18)

## Quran 42:20-26

مَن كَانَ يُرِيدُ حَرْثَ ٱلْأَخِرَةِ نَزِدْ لَهُ فِى حَرْثِهِۦ وَمَن كَانَ
يُرِيدُ حَرْثَ ٱلدُّنْيَا نُؤْتِهِۦ مِنْهَا وَمَا لَهُۥ فِى ٱلْأَخِرَةِ مِن نَّصِيبٍ
(٢٠) أَمْ لَهُمْ شُرَكَـٰٓؤُا۟ شَرَعُوا۟ لَهُم مِّنَ ٱلدِّينِ مَا لَمْ يَأْذَنۢ بِهِ
ٱللَّهُ وَلَوْلَا كَلِمَةُ ٱلْفَصْلِ لَقُضِىَ بَيْنَهُمْ وَإِنَّ ٱلظَّـٰلِمِينَ لَهُمْ
عَذَابٌ أَلِيمٌ (٢١) تَرَى ٱلظَّـٰلِمِينَ مُشْفِقِينَ مِمَّا كَسَبُوا۟ وَهُوَ
وَاقِعٌۢ بِهِمْ وَٱلَّذِينَ ءَامَنُوا۟ وَعَمِلُوا۟ ٱلصَّـٰلِحَـٰتِ فِى رَوْضَاتِ
ٱلْجَنَّاتِ لَهُم مَّا يَشَآءُونَ عِندَ رَبِّهِمْ ذَٰلِكَ هُوَ ٱلْفَضْلُ ٱلْكَبِيرُ
(٢٢) ذَٰلِكَ ٱلَّذِى يُبَشِّرُ ٱللَّهُ عِبَادَهُ ٱلَّذِينَ ءَامَنُوا۟ وَعَمِلُوا۟
ٱلصَّـٰلِحَـٰتِ قُل لَّآ أَسْـَٔلُكُمْ عَلَيْهِ أَجْرًا إِلَّا ٱلْمَوَدَّةَ فِى ٱلْقُرْبَىٰ

وَمَن يَقْتَرِفْ حَسَنَةً نَّزِدْ لَهُ فِيهَا حُسْنًا إِنَّ ٱللَّهَ غَفُورٌ شَكُورٌ
(٢٣) أَمْ يَقُولُونَ ٱفْتَرَىٰ عَلَى ٱللَّهِ كَذِبًا فَإِن يَشَأِ ٱللَّهُ يَخْتِمْ عَلَىٰ
قَلْبِكَ وَيَمْحُ ٱللَّهُ ٱلْبَٰطِلَ وَيُحِقُّ ٱلْحَقَّ بِكَلِمَٰتِهِ إِنَّهُ عَلِيمٌ بِذَاتِ
ٱلصُّدُورِ (٢٤) وَهُوَ ٱلَّذِى يَقْبَلُ ٱلتَّوْبَةَ عَنْ عِبَادِهِ وَيَعْفُوا۟ عَنِ
ٱلسَّيِّئَاتِ وَيَعْلَمُ مَا تَفْعَلُونَ (٢٥) وَيَسْتَجِيبُ ٱلَّذِينَ ءَامَنُوا۟
وَعَمِلُوا۟ ٱلصَّٰلِحَٰتِ وَيَزِيدُهُم مِّن فَضْلِهِ وَٱلْكَٰفِرُونَ لَهُمْ
عَذَابٌ شَدِيدٌ (٢٦)

*Whosoever desires (by his deeds) the reward of the Hereafter, We give him increase in his reward, and whosoever desires the reward of this world (by his deeds), We give him thereof (what is decreed for him), and he has no portion in the Hereafter. (20) Or have they partners with Allâh (false gods), who have instituted for them a religion which Allâh has not ordained? And had it not been for a decisive Word (gone forth already), the matter would have been judged between them. And verily, for the Zâlimûn (polytheists and wrong-doers), there is a painful torment. (21) You will see (on the Day of Resurrection), the Zâlimûn (polytheists and wrong-doers) fearful of that which they have earned, and it (Allâhs Torment) will surely befall them, But those who believe (in the Oneness of Allâh Islâmic Monotheism) and do righteous deeds (will be) in the flowering meadows of the Gardens (Paradise), having what they wish from their Lord. That is the supreme Grace,*

(Paradise). (22) That is (the Paradise) whereof Allâh gives glad tidings to His slaves who believe (in the Oneness of Allâh – Islâmic Monotheism) and do righteous good deeds. Say (O Muhammad): "No reward do I ask of you for this except to be kind to me for my kinship with you." And whoever earns a good righteous deed, We shall give him an increase of good in respect thereof. Verily, Allâh is Oft-Forgiving, Most Ready to appreciate (the deeds of those who are obedient to Him). (23) Or say they: "He has invented a lie against Allâh?" If Allâh willed, He could have sealed up your heart (so that you forget all that you know of the Qur'an). And Allâh wipes out falsehood, and establishes the truth (Islâm) by His Word (this Qur'an). Verily, He knows well what (the secrets) are in the breasts (of mankind). (24) And He it is Who accepts repentance from His slaves, and forgives sins, and He knows what you do. (25) And He answers (the invocation of) those who believe (in the Oneness of Allâh – Islâmic Monotheism) and do righteous good deeds, and gives them increase of His Bounty. And as for the disbelievers, theirs will be a severe torment. (26)

## Quran 42:35-36

وَيَعْلَمَ ٱلَّذِينَ يُجَـٰدِلُونَ فِىٓ ءَايَـٰتِنَا مَا لَهُم مِّن مَّحِيصٍ (٣٥) فَمَآ أُوتِيتُم مِّن شَىْءٍ فَمَتَـٰعُ ٱلْحَيَوٰةِ ٱلدُّنْيَا ۖ وَمَا عِندَ ٱللَّهِ خَيْرٌ وَأَبْقَىٰ لِلَّذِينَ ءَامَنُوا۟ وَعَلَىٰ رَبِّهِمْ يَتَوَكَّلُونَ (٣٦)

And those who dispute (polytheists, with Our Messenger
Muhammad) as regards Our Ayât (proofs, signs, verses,
etc. of Islâmic Monotheism) may know that there is no
place of refuge for them (from Allâh's punishment).
(35) So whatever you have been given is but (a passing)
enjoyment for this worldly life, but that which is with
Allâh (Paradise) is better and more lasting for those who
believe (in the Oneness of Allâh Islâmic Monotheism)
and put their trust in their Lord (concerning all of their
affairs) (36)

## Quran 42:40

وَجَزَٰٓؤُاْ سَيِّئَةٍ سَيِّئَةٌ مِّثْلُهَا فَمَنْ عَفَا وَأَصْلَحَ فَأَجْرُهُۥ عَلَى
ٱللَّهِ إِنَّهُۥ لَا يُحِبُّ ٱلظَّٰلِمِينَ

The recompense for an evil is an evil like thereof, but
whoever forgives and makes reconciliation, his reward is
with Allâh. Verily, He likes not the Zâlimûn (oppressors,
polytheists, and wrong-doers). (40)

## Quran 42:42

إِنَّمَا ٱلسَّبِيلُ عَلَى ٱلَّذِينَ يَظْلِمُونَ ٱلنَّاسَ وَيَبْغُونَ فِى
ٱلْأَرْضِ بِغَيْرِ ٱلْحَقِّ أُوْلَٰٓئِكَ لَهُم عَذَابٌ أَلِيمٌ

The way (of blame) is only against those who oppress
men and rebel in the earth, without justification for such
there will be a painful torment. (42)

# Quran 42:44-47

وَمَن يُضْلِلِ ٱللَّهُ فَمَا لَهُ مِن وَلِيٍّ مِّنۢ بَعْدِهِۦ ۗ وَتَرَى ٱلظَّـٰلِمِينَ لَمَّا رَأَوُاْ ٱلْعَذَابَ يَقُولُونَ هَلْ إِلَىٰ مَرَدٍّ مِّن سَبِيلٍ (٤٤) وَتَرَىٰهُمْ يُعْرَضُونَ عَلَيْهَا خَـٰشِعِينَ مِنَ ٱلذُّلِّ يَنظُرُونَ مِن طَرْفٍ خَفِيٍّ ۗ وَقَالَ ٱلَّذِينَ ءَامَنُوٓاْ إِنَّ ٱلْخَـٰسِرِينَ ٱلَّذِينَ خَسِرُوٓاْ أَنفُسَهُمْ وَأَهْلِيهِمْ يَوْمَ ٱلْقِيَـٰمَةِ ۗ أَلَآ إِنَّ ٱلظَّـٰلِمِينَ فِى عَذَابٍ مُّقِيمٍ (٤٥) وَمَا كَانَ لَهُم مِّنْ أَوْلِيَآءَ يَنصُرُونَهُم مِّن دُونِ ٱللَّهِ ۗ وَمَن يُضْلِلِ ٱللَّهُ فَمَا لَهُ مِن سَبِيلٍ (٤٦) ٱسْتَجِيبُواْ لِرَبِّكُم مِّن قَبْلِ أَن يَأْتِىَ يَوْمٌ لَّا مَرَدَّ لَهُۥ مِنَ ٱللَّهِ ۚ مَا لَكُم مِّن مَّلْجَإٍ يَوْمَئِذٍ وَمَا لَكُم مِّن نَّكِيرٍ (٤٧)

*And whomsoever Allâh sends astray, for him there is no Walî (protector, helper, guardian) after Him. And you will see the Zâlimûn (polytheists, wrong-doers, oppressors) when they behold the torment, they will say: "Is there any way of return (to the world)?" (44) And you will see them brought forward to it (Hell) made humble by disgrace , (and) looking with stealthy glance. And those who believe will say: "Verily, the losers are they who lose themselves and their families on the Day of Resurrection. Verily, the Zâlimûn [i.e. Al-Kâfirûn (disbelievers in Allâh, in His Oneness and in His Messenger, polytheists, wrong-doers)] will be in a lasting torment. (45) And they will have no Auliyâ' (protectors, helper, guardian, lords) to help them other than Allâh.*

*And he whom Allâh sends astray, for him there is no way. (46) Answer the Call of your Lord (i.e. accept the Islâmic Monotheism, O mankind, and jinn) before there comes from Allâh a Day which cannot be averted. (i.e. the Day of Resurrection) You will have no refuge on that Day nor there will be for you any denying (of your crimes as they are all recorded in the Book of your deeds) (47)*

## Quran 42:51-53

﴿۞ وَمَا كَانَ لِبَشَرٍ أَن يُكَلِّمَهُ ٱللَّهُ إِلَّا وَحْيًا أَوْ مِن وَرَآئِ حِجَابٍ أَوْ يُرْسِلَ رَسُولاً فَيُوحِيَ بِإِذْنِهِۦ مَا يَشَآءُ إِنَّهُۥ عَلِىٌّ حَكِيمٌ (٥١) وَكَذَٰلِكَ أَوْحَيْنَآ إِلَيْكَ رُوحًا مِّنْ أَمْرِنَاۚ مَا كُنتَ تَدْرِى مَا ٱلْكِتَـٰبُ وَلَا ٱلْإِيمَـٰنُ وَلَـٰكِن جَعَلْنَـٰهُ نُورًا نَّهْدِى بِهِۦ مَن نَّشَآءُ مِنْ عِبَادِنَاۚ وَإِنَّكَ لَتَهْدِىٓ إِلَىٰ صِرَٰطٍ مُّسْتَقِيمٍ (٥٢) صِرَٰطِ ٱللَّهِ ٱلَّذِى لَهُۥ مَا فِى ٱلسَّمَـٰوَٰتِ وَمَا فِى ٱلْأَرْضِۗ أَلَآ إِلَى ٱللَّهِ تَصِيرُ ٱلْأُمُورُ (٥٣)﴾

*It is not given to any human being that Allâh should speak to him unless (it be) by Revelation, or from behind a veil, or (that) He sends a Messenger to reveal what He wills by His Leave. Verily, He is Most High, Most Wise. (51) And thus We have sent to you (O Muhammad) Ruh (a Revelation, and a Mercy) of Our Command. You knew not what is the Book, nor what is Faith? But We have made it (this Qur'ân) a light wherewith We guide* whosoever of Our slaves We will. And verily, you (O Muhammad) are indeed guiding (mankind) to the Straight Path (i.e. Allâh's Religion of Islâmic Monotheism). (52) The Path of Allâh, to Whom belongs all that is in the heavens and all that is in the earth. Verily, all the matters at the end go to Allâh (for decision). (53)

## Quran 43:19

وَجَعَلُواْ ٱلْمَلَـٰٓئِكَةَ ٱلَّذِينَ هُمْ عِبَـٰدُ ٱلرَّحْمَـٰنِ إِنَـٰثًا أَشَهِدُواْ خَلْقَهُمْ سَتُكْتَبُ شَهَـٰدَتُهُمْ وَيُسْـَٔلُونَ

And they make the angels who themselves are slaves of the Most Gracious (Allâh) females. Did they witness their creation? Their testimony will be recorded, and they will be questioned! (19)

## Quran 43:35-39

وَزُخْرُفًا ۚ وَإِن كُلُّ ذَٰلِكَ لَمَّا مَتَـٰعُ ٱلْحَيَوٰةِ ٱلدُّنْيَا ۚ وَٱلْـَٔاخِرَةُ عِندَ رَبِّكَ لِلْمُتَّقِينَ (٣٥) وَمَن يَعْشُ عَن ذِكْرِ ٱلرَّحْمَـٰنِ نُقَيِّضْ لَهُۥ شَيْطَـٰنًا فَهُوَ لَهُۥ قَرِينٌ (٣٦) وَإِنَّهُمْ لَيَصُدُّونَهُمْ عَنِ ٱلسَّبِيلِ وَيَحْسَبُونَ أَنَّهُم مُّهْتَدُونَ (٣٧) حَتَّىٰٓ إِذَا جَآءَنَا قَالَ يَـٰلَيْتَ بَيْنِى وَبَيْنَكَ بُعْدَ ٱلْمَشْرِقَيْنِ فَبِئْسَ ٱلْقَرِينُ (٣٨) وَلَن يَنفَعَكُمُ ٱلْيَوْمَ إِذ ظَّلَمْتُمْ أَنَّكُمْ فِى ٱلْعَذَابِ مُشْتَرِكُونَ (٣٩)

And adornments of gold. Yet all this (i.e. the roofs, doors, stairs, elevators, thrones of their houses) would have been nothing but an enjoyment of this world. And the Hereafter with your Lord is (only) for the Muttaqûn. (35) And whosoever turns away blindly from the remembrance of the Most Gracious (Allâh) (i.e. this Qur'ân and worship of Allâh), We appoint for him Shaitân (Satan devil) to be a Qarîn (a intimate companion) to him. (36) And verily, they (Satans / devils) hinder them from the Path (of Allâh), but they think that they are guided aright! (37) Till, when (such a one) comes to Us, he says [to his Qarîn (Satan / devil companion)] "Would that between me and you were the distance of the two easts (or the east and west)" a worst (type of) companion (indeed)! (38) It will profit you not this Day (O you who turn away from Allâh's remembrance and His worship) as you did wrong, (and) that you will be sharers (you and your Qarîn) in the punishment. (39)

**Quran 43:41-44**

فَإِمَّا نَذْهَبَنَّ بِكَ فَإِنَّا مِنْهُم مُّنتَقِمُونَ (٤١) أَوْ نُرِيَنَّكَ ٱلَّذِى وَعَدْنَٰهُمْ فَإِنَّا عَلَيْهِم مُّقْتَدِرُونَ (٤٢) فَٱسْتَمْسِكْ بِٱلَّذِىٓ أُوحِىَ إِلَيْكَ ۖ إِنَّكَ عَلَىٰ صِرَٰطٍ مُّسْتَقِيمٍ (٤٣) وَإِنَّهُۥ لَذِكْرٌ لَّكَ وَلِقَوْمِكَ ۖ وَسَوْفَ تُسْـَٔلُونَ (٤٤)

And even if We take you (O Muhammad) away, We shall indeed take vengeance on them. (41) Or (if) We show you that wherewith We threaten them, then verily, We have perfect command over them. (42) So hold you (O Muhammad) fast to that which is revealed to you. Verily you are on the Straight Path. (43) And verily, this (the Qur'ân) is indeed a Reminder for you (O Muhammad) and your people (Quraish people, or your followers), and you will be questioned (about it). (44)

## Quran 43:61-62

وَإِنَّهُۥ لَعِلْمٌ لِّلسَّاعَةِ فَلَا تَمْتَرُنَّ بِهَا وَٱتَّبِعُونِ هَٰذَا صِرَٰطٌ مُّسْتَقِيمٌ (٦١) وَلَا يَصُدَّنَّكُمُ ٱلشَّيْطَٰنُ إِنَّهُۥ لَكُمْ عَدُوٌّ مُّبِينٌ (٦٢)

And he ['Īsā (Jesus), son of Maryam (Mary)] shall be a known sign for (the coming of) the Hour (Day of Resurrection) [i.e. 'Īsā's (Jesus) descent on the earth] . Therefore have no doubt concerning it (i.e. the Day of Resurrection). And follow Me (Allâh) (i.e. be obedient to Allâh and do what He orders you to do, O mankind)! This is the Straight Path (of Islâmic Monotheism, leading to Allâh and to His Paradise). (61) And let not Shaitân (Satan) hinder you (from the right religion, i.e. Islâmic Monotheism), Verily, he (Satan) to you is a plain enemy. (62)

## Quran 43:65-80

فَٱخْتَلَفَ ٱلْأَحْزَابُ مِنۢ بَيْنِهِمْ فَوَيْلٌ لِّلَّذِينَ ظَلَمُواْ مِنْ عَذَابِ يَوْمٍ أَلِيمٍ (٦٥) هَلْ يَنظُرُونَ إِلَّا ٱلسَّاعَةَ أَن تَأْتِيَهُم بَغْتَةً وَهُمْ

لَا يَشْعُرُونَ (٦٦) ٱلْأَخِلَّآءُ يَوْمَئِذٍۭ بَعْضُهُمْ لِبَعْضٍ عَدُوٌّ إِلَّا ٱلْمُتَّقِينَ (٦٧) يَـٰعِبَادِ لَا خَوْفٌ عَلَيْكُمُ ٱلْيَوْمَ وَلَآ أَنتُمْ تَحْزَنُونَ (٦٨) ٱلَّذِينَ ءَامَنُواْ بِـَٔايَـٰتِنَا وَكَانُواْ مُسْلِمِينَ (٦٩) ٱدْخُلُواْ ٱلْجَنَّةَ أَنتُمْ وَأَزْوَٰجُكُمْ تُحْبَرُونَ (٧٠) يُطَافُ عَلَيْهِم بِصِحَافٍ مِّن ذَهَبٍ وَأَكْوَابٍ ۖ وَفِيهَا مَا تَشْتَهِيهِ ٱلْأَنفُسُ وَتَلَذُّ ٱلْأَعْيُنُ ۖ وَأَنتُمْ فِيهَا خَـٰلِدُونَ (٧١) وَتِلْكَ ٱلْجَنَّةُ ٱلَّتِىٓ أُورِثْتُمُوهَا بِمَا كُنتُمْ تَعْمَلُونَ (٧٢) لَكُمْ فِيهَا فَـٰكِهَةٌ كَثِيرَةٌ مِّنْهَا تَأْكُلُونَ (٧٣) إِنَّ ٱلْمُجْرِمِينَ فِى عَذَابِ جَهَنَّمَ خَـٰلِدُونَ (٧٤) لَا يُفَتَّرُ عَنْهُمْ وَهُمْ فِيهِ مُبْلِسُونَ (٧٥) وَمَا ظَلَمْنَـٰهُمْ وَلَـٰكِن كَانُواْ هُمُ ٱلظَّـٰلِمِينَ (٧٦) وَنَادَوْاْ يَـٰمَـٰلِكُ لِيَقْضِ عَلَيْنَا رَبُّكَ ۖ قَالَ إِنَّكُم مَّـٰكِثُونَ (٧٧) لَقَدْ جِئْنَـٰكُم بِٱلْحَقِّ وَلَـٰكِنَّ أَكْثَرَكُمْ لِلْحَقِّ كَـٰرِهُونَ (٧٨) أَمْ أَبْرَمُوٓاْ أَمْرًا فَإِنَّا مُبْرِمُونَ (٧٩) أَمْ يَحْسَبُونَ أَنَّا لَا نَسْمَعُ سِرَّهُمْ وَنَجْوَىٰهُم ۚ بَلَىٰ وَرُسُلُنَا لَدَيْهِمْ يَكْتُبُونَ (٨٠)

But the sects from among themselves differed. So woe to those who do wrong (by ascribing things to 'Īsā (Jesus) that are not true) from the torment of a painful Day (i.e. the Day of Resurrection)! (65) Do they only wait for the Hour that it shall come upon them suddenly, while they perceive not? (66) Friends on that Day will be foes one to another except Al-Muttaqûn (pious) (67) It will be said to the true believers of Islâmic Monotheism): My worshippers! No fear shall be on you this Day, nor shall you grieve, (68) (You) who believed in Our Ayât (proofs, *verses, lessons, signs, revelations, etc.) and were Muslims (i.e. who submit totally to Allâh's Will, and believe in the Oneness of Allâh - Islâmic Monotheism) (69) Enter Paradise, you and your wives, in happiness. (70) Trays of gold and cups will be passed round them, (there will be) therein all that the inner-selves could desire, and all that the eyes could delight in, and you will abide therein forever. (71) This is the Paradise which you have been made to inherit because of your deeds which you used to do (in the life of the world). (72) Therein for you will be fruits in plenty, of which you will eat (as you desire). (73) Verily, the Mujrimûn (criminals, sinners, disbelievers) will be in the torment of Hell to abide therein forever. (74) (The torment) will not be lightened for them, and they will be plunged into destruction with deep regrets, sorrows and in despair therein. (75) We wronged them not, but they were the Zâlimûn (polytheists, wrong-doers). (76) And they will cry: "O Malik (Keeper of Hell)! Let your Lord make an end of us." He will say: "Verily you shall abide forever." (77) Indeed We have brought the truth (Muhammad with the Qur'ân), to you, but most of you have a hatred for the truth. (78) Or have they plotted some plan? Then We too are planning. (79) Or do they think that We hear not their secrets and their private counsel? (Yes We do) and Our Messengers (appointed angels in charge of mankind) are by them, to record. (80)*

## Quran 43:83

فَذَرْهُمْ يَخُوضُواْ وَيَلْعَبُواْ حَتَّىٰ يُلَـٰقُواْ يَوْمَهُمُ ٱلَّذِى يُوعَدُونَ

*So leave them (alone) to speak nonsense and play until they meet the Day of theirs, which they have been promised. (83)*

## Quran 44:16

يَوْمَ نَبْطِشُ ٱلْبَطْشَةَ ٱلْكُبْرَىٰ إِنَّا مُنتَقِمُونَ

*On the Day when We shall seize you with the greatest seizure (punishment). Verily, We will exact retribution. (16)*

## Quran 44:40-57

إِنَّ يَوْمَ ٱلْفَصْلِ مِيقَـٰتُهُمْ أَجْمَعِينَ (٤٠) يَوْمَ لَا يُغْنِى مَوْلًى عَن مَّوْلًى شَيْـًٔا وَلَا هُمْ يُنصَرُونَ (٤١) إِلَّا مَن رَّحِمَ ٱللَّهُ إِنَّهُ هُوَ ٱلْعَزِيزُ ٱلرَّحِيمُ (٤٢) إِنَّ شَجَرَتَ ٱلزَّقُّومِ (٤٣) طَعَامُ ٱلْأَثِيمِ (٤٤) كَٱلْمُهْلِ يَغْلِى فِى ٱلْبُطُونِ (٤٥) كَغَلْىِ ٱلْحَمِيمِ (٤٦) خُذُوهُ فَٱعْتِلُوهُ إِلَىٰ سَوَآءِ ٱلْجَحِيمِ (٤٧) ثُمَّ صُبُّواْ فَوْقَ رَأْسِهِ مِنْ عَذَابِ ٱلْحَمِيمِ (٤٨) ذُقْ إِنَّكَ أَنتَ ٱلْعَزِيزُ ٱلْكَرِيمُ (٤٩) إِنَّ هَـٰذَا مَا كُنتُم بِهِۦ تَمْتَرُونَ (٥٠) إِنَّ ٱلْمُتَّقِينَ فِى مَقَامٍ أَمِينٍ (٥١) فِى جَنَّـٰتٍ وَعُيُونٍ (٥٢) يَلْبَسُونَ مِن سُندُسٍ وَإِسْتَبْرَقٍ مُّتَقَـٰبِلِينَ (٥٣) كَذَٰلِكَ وَزَوَّجْنَـٰهُم بِحُورٍ عِينٍ

يَدْعُونَ فِيهَا بِكُلِّ فَٰكِهَةٍ ءَامِنِينَ (٥٥) لَا يَذُوقُونَ فِيهَا (٥٤)
ٱلْمَوْتَ إِلَّا ٱلْمَوْتَةَ ٱلْأُولَىٰ وَوَقَىٰهُمْ عَذَابَ ٱلْجَحِيمِ (٥٦) فَضْلًا
مِّن رَّبِّكَ ذَٰلِكَ هُوَ ٱلْفَوْزُ ٱلْعَظِيمُ (٥٧)

*Verily, the Day of Judgement (when Allâh will judge*
*between the creatures) is the time appointed for all of*
*them, – (40) The Day when Maula (a near relative)*
*cannot avail Maula (a near relative) in aught, and no*
*help can they receive, (41) Except him on whom Allâh*
*has Mercy. Verily, He is the All-Mighty, the Most*
*Merciful. (42) Verily, the tree of Zaqqûm, (43) Will be*
*the food of the sinners, (44) Like boiling oil, it will boil in*
*the bellies, (45) Like the boiling of scalding water. (46) (It*
*will be said) "Seize him and drag him into the midst of*
*blazing Fire, (47) "Then pour over his head the torment*
*of boiling water, (48) "Taste you (this)! Verily, you were*
*(pretending to be) the mighty, the generous!*
*(49) "Verily, this is that whereof you used to doubt!"*
*(50) Verily! The Muttaqûn (pious - see V.2:2), will be in*
*place of Security (Paradise) (51) Among Gardens and*
*Springs; (52) Dressed in fine silk and (also) in thick silk,*
*facing each other, (53) So (it will be), and We shall marry*
*them to Hur (fair females) with wide, lovely eyes.*
*(54) They will call therein for every kind of fruit in peace*
*and security; (55) They will never taste death therein*
*except the first death (of this world), and He will save*
*them from the torment of the blazing Fire, (56) As a*

Bounty from your Lord! That will be the supreme success! (57)

## Quran 45:7-11

وَيْلٌ لِّكُلِّ أَفَّاكٍ أَثِيمٍ (٧) يَسْمَعُ ءَايَـٰتِ ٱللَّهِ تُتْلَىٰ عَلَيْهِ ثُمَّ يُصِرُّ مُسْتَكْبِرًا كَأَن لَّمْ يَسْمَعْهَا فَبَشِّرْهُ بِعَذَابٍ أَلِيمٍ (٨) وَإِذَا عَلِمَ مِنْ ءَايَـٰتِنَا شَيْئًا ٱتَّخَذَهَا هُزُوًا أُوْلَـٰٓئِكَ لَهُمْ عَذَابٌ مُّهِينٌ (٩) مِّن وَرَآئِهِمْ جَهَنَّمُ وَلَا يُغْنِى عَنْهُم مَّا كَسَبُواْ شَيْئًا وَلَا مَا ٱتَّخَذُواْ مِن دُونِ ٱللَّهِ أَوْلِيَآءَ وَلَهُمْ عَذَابٌ عَظِيمٌ (١٠) هَـٰذَا هُدًى وَٱلَّذِينَ كَفَرُواْ بِـَٔايَـٰتِ رَبِّهِمْ لَهُمْ عَذَابٌ مِّن رِّجْزٍ أَلِيمٌ (١١)

Woe to every sinful liar, (7) Who hears the Verses of Allâh (being) recited to him, yet persists with pride as if he heard them not. So announce to him a painful torment! (8) And when he learns something of Our Verses (this Qur'ân), he makes them a jest. For such there will be a humiliating torment. (9) In front of them there is Hell, and that which they have earned will be of no profit to them, nor (will be of any profit to them) those whom they have taken as Auliyâ' (protectors, helpers) besides Allâh. And theirs will be a great torment. (10) This (Qur'ân) is a guidance. And those who disbelieve in the Ayât (proofs, evidences, verses, lessons, signs, revelations) of their Lord, for them there is a painful torment of Rijz (a severe punishment). (11)

## Quran 45:15-17

مَنْ عَمِلَ صَلِحًا فَلِنَفْسِهِ وَمَنْ أَسَاءَ فَعَلَيْهَا ثُمَّ إِلَىٰ رَبِّكُمْ
تُرْجَعُونَ (١٥) وَلَقَدْ ءَاتَيْنَا بَنِىٓ إِسْرَٰٓءِيلَ ٱلْكِتَٰبَ وَٱلْحُكْمَ
وَٱلنُّبُوَّةَ وَرَزَقْنَٰهُم مِّنَ ٱلطَّيِّبَٰتِ وَفَضَّلْنَٰهُمْ عَلَى ٱلْعَٰلَمِينَ
(١٦) وَءَاتَيْنَٰهُم بَيِّنَٰتٍ مِّنَ ٱلْأَمْرِ فَمَا ٱخْتَلَفُوٓا۟ إِلَّا مِنۢ بَعْدِ مَا
جَآءَهُمُ ٱلْعِلْمُ بَغْيًۢا بَيْنَهُمْ إِنَّ رَبَّكَ يَقْضِى بَيْنَهُمْ يَوْمَ ٱلْقِيَٰمَةِ فِيمَا
كَانُوا۟ فِيهِ يَخْتَلِفُونَ (١٧)

Whosoever does a good deed, it is for his ownself, and
whosoever does evil, it is against (his ownself). Then to
your Lord you will be made to return. (15) And indeed
We gave the Children of Israel the Scripture, and the
understanding of the Scripture and its laws, and the
Prophethood; and provided them with good things, and
preferred them above the 'Alamîn (mankind and jinn of
their time, during that period), (16) And gave them clear
proofs in matters [by revealing to them the Taurât
(Torah)]. And they differed not until after the knowledge
came to them, through envy among themselves. Verily,
Your Lord will judge between them on the Day of
Resurrection about that wherein they used to differ. (17)

## Quran 45:19-22

إِنَّهُمْ لَن يُغْنُوا۟ عَنكَ مِنَ ٱللَّهِ شَيْـًٔا وَإِنَّ ٱلظَّٰلِمِينَ بَعْضُهُمْ أَوْلِيَآءُ
بَعْضٍ وَٱللَّهُ وَلِىُّ ٱلْمُتَّقِينَ (١٩) هَٰذَا بَصَٰٓئِرُ لِلنَّاسِ وَهُدًى
وَرَحْمَةٌ لِّقَوْمٍ يُوقِنُونَ (٢٠) أَمْ حَسِبَ ٱلَّذِينَ ٱجْتَرَحُوا۟
ٱلسَّيِّـَٔاتِ أَن نَّجْعَلَهُمْ كَٱلَّذِينَ ءَامَنُوا۟ وَعَمِلُوا۟ ٱلصَّٰلِحَٰتِ سَوَآءً

مَّحْيَاهُمْ وَمَمَاتُهُمْ سَآءَ مَا يَحْكُمُونَ (٢١) وَخَلَقَ ٱللَّهُ
ٱلسَّمَٰوَٰتِ وَٱلْأَرْضَ بِٱلْحَقِّ وَلِتُجْزَىٰ كُلُّ نَفْسٍ بِمَا كَسَبَتْ
وَهُمْ لَا يُظْلَمُونَ (٢٢)

*Verily, they can avail you nothing against Allâh (if He
wants to punish you). Verily, the Zâlimûn (polytheists,
wrong-doers) are Auliyâ' (protectors, helpers) of one
another, but Allâh is the Walî (Helper, Protector) of the
Muttaqûn (pious). (19) This (Qur'ân) is a clear insight
and evidence for mankind, and a guidance and a mercy
for people who have Faith with certainty. (20) Or do
those who earn evil deeds think that We shall hold them
equal with those who believe (in the Oneness of Allâh —
Islâmic Monotheism) and do righteous good deeds, in
their present life and after their death? Worst is the
judgement that they make. (21) And Allâh has created
the heavens and the earth with truth, in order that each
person may be recompensed what he has earned, and they
will not be wronged. (22)*

## Quran 45:26-35

قُلِ ٱللَّهُ يُحْيِيكُمْ ثُمَّ يُمِيتُكُمْ ثُمَّ يَجْمَعُكُمْ إِلَىٰ يَوْمِ ٱلْقِيَٰمَةِ لَا رَيْبَ
فِيهِ وَلَٰكِنَّ أَكْثَرَ ٱلنَّاسِ لَا يَعْلَمُونَ (٢٦) وَلِلَّهِ مُلْكُ
ٱلسَّمَٰوَٰتِ وَٱلْأَرْضِ وَيَوْمَ تَقُومُ ٱلسَّاعَةُ يَوْمَئِذٍ يَخْسَرُ
ٱلْمُبْطِلُونَ (٢٧) وَتَرَىٰ كُلَّ أُمَّةٍ جَاثِيَةً كُلُّ أُمَّةٍ تُدْعَىٰ إِلَىٰ
كِتَٰبِهَا ٱلْيَوْمَ تُجْزَوْنَ مَا كُنتُمْ تَعْمَلُونَ (٢٨) هَٰذَا كِتَٰبُنَا

يَنطِقُ عَلَيْكُم بِالْحَقِّ إِنَّا كُنَّا نَسْتَنسِخُ مَا كُنتُمْ تَعْمَلُونَ
(٢٩) فَأَمَّا ٱلَّذِينَ ءَامَنُوا۟ وَعَمِلُوا۟ ٱلصَّٰلِحَٰتِ فَيُدْخِلُهُمْ رَبُّهُمْ
فِى رَحْمَتِهِۦ ذَٰلِكَ هُوَ ٱلْفَوْزُ ٱلْمُبِينُ (٣٠) وَأَمَّا ٱلَّذِينَ كَفَرُوا۟
أَفَلَمْ تَكُنْ ءَايَٰتِى تُتْلَىٰ عَلَيْكُمْ فَٱسْتَكْبَرْتُمْ وَكُنتُمْ قَوْمًا مُّجْرِمِينَ
(٣١) وَإِذَا قِيلَ إِنَّ وَعْدَ ٱللَّهِ حَقٌّ وَٱلسَّاعَةُ لَا رَيْبَ فِيهَا قُلْتُم
مَّا نَدْرِى مَا ٱلسَّاعَةُ إِن نَّظُنُّ إِلَّا ظَنًّا وَمَا نَحْنُ بِمُسْتَيْقِنِينَ
(٣٢) وَبَدَا لَهُمْ سَيِّئَاتُ مَا عَمِلُوا۟ وَحَاقَ بِهِم مَّا كَانُوا۟ بِهِۦ
يَسْتَهْزِءُونَ (٣٣) وَقِيلَ ٱلْيَوْمَ نَنسَىٰكُمْ كَمَا نَسِيتُمْ لِقَآءَ يَوْمِكُمْ
هَٰذَا وَمَأْوَىٰكُمُ ٱلنَّارُ وَمَا لَكُم مِّن نَّٰصِرِينَ (٣٤) ذَٰلِكُم بِأَنَّكُمُ
ٱتَّخَذْتُمْ ءَايَٰتِ ٱللَّهِ هُزُوًا وَغَرَّتْكُمُ ٱلْحَيَوٰةُ ٱلدُّنْيَا فَٱلْيَوْمَ لَا
يُخْرَجُونَ مِنْهَا وَلَا هُمْ يُسْتَعْتَبُونَ (٣٥)

Say (to them): "Allâh gives you life, then causes you to die, then He will assemble you on the Day of Resurrection about which there is no doubt. But most of mankind know not." (26) And to Allâh belongs the kingdom of the heavens and the earth. And on the Day that the Hour will be established — on that Day the followers of falsehood (polytheists, disbelievers, worshippers of false deities) shall lose (everything). (27) And you will see each nation humbled to their knees (kneeling), each nation will be called to its Record (of deeds). This Day you shall be recompensed for what you used to do. (28) This Our Record speaks about you with truth. Verily, We were recording what you used to do (i.e. Our angels used to record your deeds). (29) Then, as for those who believed (in the Oneness of Allâh – Islâmic Monotheism) and did righteous good deeds, their Lord will admit them to His Mercy. That will be the evident success. (30) But as for those who disbelieved (it will be said to them): "Were not Our Verses recited to you? But you were proud, and you were a people who were Mujrimûn (polytheists, disbelievers, sinners, criminals)." (31) And when it was said: "Verily! Allâh's Promise is the truth, and there is no doubt about the coming of the Hour," you said;"We know not what is the Hour, we do not think it but as a conjecture, and we have no firm convincing belief (therein)." (32) And the evil of what they did will appear to them, and that which they used to mock at will completely encircle them. (33) And it will be said: "This Day We will forget you as you forgot the Meeting of this Day of yours. And your abode is the Fire, and there is none to help you." (34) This, because you took the revelations of Allâh (this Qur'ân) in mockery, and the life of the world deceived you. So this Day, they shall not be taken out from there (Hell), nor shall they be returned to the worldly life, (so that they repent to Allâh, and beg His Pardon for their sins). (35)

## Quran 46:3

مَا خَلَقْنَا ٱلسَّمَـٰوَٰتِ وَٱلْأَرْضَ وَمَا بَيْنَهُمَآ إِلَّا بِٱلْحَقِّ وَأَجَلٍ مُّسَمًّىۚ وَٱلَّذِينَ كَفَرُواْ عَمَّآ أُنذِرُواْ مُعْرِضُونَ

We created not the heavens and the earth and all that is between them except with truth, and for an appointed term. But those who disbelieve turn away from that whereof they are warned. (3)

## Quran 46:5-6

وَمَنْ أَضَلُّ مِمَّن يَدْعُواْ مِن دُونِ ٱللَّهِ مَن لَّا يَسْتَجِيبُ لَهُ إِلَىٰ يَوْمِ ٱلْقِيَـٰمَةِ وَهُمْ عَن دُعَآئِهِمْ غَـٰفِلُونَ (٥) وَإِذَا حُشِرَ ٱلنَّاسُ كَانُواْ لَهُمْ أَعْدَآءً وَكَانُواْ بِعِبَادَتِهِمْ كَـٰفِرِينَ (٦)

And who is more astray than one who calls on (invokes) besides Allâh, such as will not answer him till the Day of Resurrection, and who are (even) unaware of their calls (invocations) to them? (5) And when mankind are gathered (on the Day of Resurrection), they (false deities) will become their enemies and will deny their worshipping. (6)

## Quran 46:10

قُلْ أَرَءَيْتُمْ إِن كَانَ مِنْ عِندِ ٱللَّهِ وَكَفَرْتُم بِهِۦ وَشَهِدَ شَاهِدٌ مِّنۢ بَنِىٓ إِسْرَآءِيلَ عَلَىٰ مِثْلِهِۦ فَـَٔامَنَ وَٱسْتَكْبَرْتُمْ إِنَّ ٱللَّهَ لَا يَهْدِى ٱلْقَوْمَ ٱلظَّـٰلِمِينَ

Say: "Tell me! If this (Qur'ân) is from Allâh and you deny it, and a witness from among the Children of Israel ('Abdullâh bin Salâm) testifies that [this Qur'ân is from Allâh (like the Taurât (Torah)], and he believed

*(embraced Islâm) while you are too proud (to believe)."*
*Verily, Allâh guides not the people who are Zâlimûn*
*(polytheists, disbelievers and wrong-doers). (10)*

## Quran 46:12-21

وَمِن قَبْلِهِ كِتَـٰبُ مُوسَىٰٓ إِمَامًا وَرَحْمَةً وَهَـٰذَا كِتَـٰبٌ مُّصَدِّقٌ
لِّسَانًا عَرَبِيًّا لِّيُنذِرَ ٱلَّذِينَ ظَلَمُواْ وَبُشْرَىٰ لِلْمُحْسِنِينَ (١٢) إِنَّ
ٱلَّذِينَ قَالُواْ رَبُّنَا ٱللَّهُ ثُمَّ ٱسْتَقَـٰمُواْ فَلَا خَوْفٌ عَلَيْهِمْ وَلَا هُمْ
يَحْزَنُونَ (١٣) أُوْلَـٰٓئِكَ أَصْحَـٰبُ ٱلْجَنَّةِ خَـٰلِدِينَ فِيهَا جَزَآءً بِمَا
كَانُواْ يَعْمَلُونَ (١٤) وَوَصَّيْنَا ٱلْإِنسَـٰنَ بِوَٰلِدَيْهِ إِحْسَـٰنًا حَمَلَتْهُ
أُمُّهُ كُرْهًا وَوَضَعَتْهُ كُرْهًا وَحَمْلُهُ وَفِصَـٰلُهُ ثَلَـٰثُونَ شَهْرًا
حَتَّىٰٓ إِذَا بَلَغَ أَشُدَّهُ وَبَلَغَ أَرْبَعِينَ سَنَةً قَالَ رَبِّ أَوْزِعْنِىٓ أَنْ
أَشْكُرَ نِعْمَتَكَ ٱلَّتِىٓ أَنْعَمْتَ عَلَىَّ وَعَلَىٰ وَٰلِدَىَّ وَأَنْ أَعْمَلَ
صَـٰلِحًا تَرْضَـٰهُ وَأَصْلِحْ لِى فِى ذُرِّيَّتِىٓ إِنِّى تُبْتُ إِلَيْكَ وَإِنِّى
مِنَ ٱلْمُسْلِمِينَ (١٥) أُوْلَـٰٓئِكَ ٱلَّذِينَ نَتَقَبَّلُ عَنْهُمْ أَحْسَنَ مَا
عَمِلُواْ وَنَتَجَاوَزُ عَن سَيِّئَاتِهِمْ فِى أَصْحَـٰبِ ٱلْجَنَّةِ وَعْدَ ٱلصِّدْقِ
ٱلَّذِى كَانُواْ يُوعَدُونَ (١٦) وَٱلَّذِى قَالَ لِوَٰلِدَيْهِ أُفٍّ لَّكُمَآ
أَتَعِدَانِنِىٓ أَنْ أُخْرَجَ وَقَدْ خَلَتِ ٱلْقُرُونُ مِن قَبْلِى وَهُمَا
يَسْتَغِيثَانِ ٱللَّهَ وَيْلَكَ ءَامِنْ إِنَّ وَعْدَ ٱللَّهِ حَقٌّ فَيَقُولُ مَا هَـٰذَآ إِلَّآ
أَسَـٰطِيرُ ٱلْأَوَّلِينَ (١٧) أُوْلَـٰٓئِكَ ٱلَّذِينَ حَقَّ عَلَيْهِمُ ٱلْقَوْلُ فِىٓ
أُمَمٍ قَدْ خَلَتْ مِن قَبْلِهِم مِّنَ ٱلْجِنِّ وَٱلْإِنسِ إِنَّهُمْ كَانُواْ
خَـٰسِرِينَ (١٨) وَلِكُلٍّ دَرَجَـٰتٌ مِّمَّا عَمِلُواْ وَلِيُوَفِّيَهُمْ
أَعْمَـٰلَهُمْ وَهُمْ لَا يُظْلَمُونَ (١٩) وَيَوْمَ يُعْرَضُ ٱلَّذِينَ كَفَرُواْ

عَلَى ٱلنَّارِ أَذْهَبْتُمْ طَيِّبَٰتِكُمْ فِى حَيَاتِكُمُ ٱلدُّنْيَا وَٱسْتَمْتَعْتُم بِهَا فَٱلْيَوْمَ تُجْزَوْنَ عَذَابَ ٱلْهُونِ بِمَا كُنتُمْ تَسْتَكْبِرُونَ فِى ٱلْأَرْضِ بِغَيْرِ ٱلْحَقِّ وَبِمَا كُنتُمْ تَفْسُقُونَ (٢٠) ۞ وَٱذْكُرْ أَخَا عَادٍ إِذْ أَنذَرَ قَوْمَهُ بِٱلْأَحْقَافِ وَقَدْ خَلَتِ ٱلنُّذُرُ مِنْ بَيْنِ يَدَيْهِ وَمِنْ خَلْفِهِ أَلَّا تَعْبُدُوٓا۟ إِلَّا ٱللَّهَ إِنِّىٓ أَخَافُ عَلَيْكُمْ عَذَابَ يَوْمٍ عَظِيمٍ (٢١)

And before this was the Scripture of Mûsâ (Moses) as a guide and a mercy. And this is a confirming Book (the Qur'ân) in the Arabic language, to warn those who do wrong, and as glad tidings to the Muhsinûn (good-doers.). (12) Verily, those who say: "Our Lord is (only) Allâh," and thereafter stand firm (on the Islâmic Faith of Monotheism) on them shall be no fear, nor shall they grieve. (13) Such shall be the dwellers of Paradise, abiding therein (forever) — a reward for what they used to do. (14) And We have enjoined on man to be dutiful and kind to his parents. His mother bears him with hardship And she brings him forth with hardship, and the bearing of him, and the weaning of him is thirty months, till when he attains full strength and reaches forty years, he says: "My Lord! Grant me the power and ability that I may be grateful for Your Favour which You have bestowed upon me and upon my parents, and that I may do righteous good deeds, such as please You, and make my off-spring good. Truly, I have turned to You in repentance, and truly, I am one of the Muslims (submitting to Your Will)." (15) They are those from whom We shall accept the best of their deeds and overlook their evil deeds. (They shall be) among the dwellers of Paradise — a promise of truth, which they have been promised. (16) But he who says to his parents: "Fie upon you both! Do you hold out the promise to me that I shall be raised up (again) when generations before me have passed away (without rising)?" While they (father and mother) invoke Allâh for help (and rebuke their son): "Woe to you! Believe! Verily, the Promise of Allâh is true." But he says: "This is nothing but the tales of the ancient." (17) They are those against whom the Word (of torment) is justified among the previous generations of jinn and mankind that have passed away. Verily, they are ever the losers (18) And for all, there will be degrees according to that which they did, that He (Allâh) may recompense them in full for their deeds. And they will not be wronged. (19) On the Day when those who disbelieve (in the Oneness of Allâh Islâmic Monotheism) will be exposed to the Fire (it will be said): "You received your good things in the life of the world, and you took your pleasure therein. Now this Day you shall be recompensed with a torment of humiliation, because you were arrogant in the land without a right, and because you used to rebel against Allah's Command (disobey Allâh). (20) And remember (Hûd) the brother of 'Ad,

when he warned his people in Al-Ahqâf (the curved sand-
hills in the southern part of Arabian Peninsula). And
surely, there have passed away warners before him and
after him (saying): "Worship none but Allâh; truly, I fear
for you the torment of a mighty Day." (i.e. the Day of
Resurrection)." (21)

## Quran 46:25

تُدَمِّرُ كُلَّ شَىْءٍ بِأَمْرِ رَبِّهَا فَأَصْبَحُوا لَا يُرَىٰ إِلَّا مَسَٰكِنُهُمْ
كَذَٰلِكَ نَجْزِى ٱلْقَوْمَ ٱلْمُجْرِمِينَ

Destroying everything by the Command of its Lord! So
they became such that nothing could be seen except their
dwellings! Thus do We recompense the people who are
Mujrimûn (polytheists, disbelievers, sinners)! (25)

## Quran 46:32-35

وَمَن لَّا يُجِبْ دَاعِىَ ٱللَّهِ فَلَيْسَ بِمُعْجِزٍ فِى ٱلْأَرْضِ وَلَيْسَ لَهُ
مِن دُونِهِ أَوْلِيَاءُ أُوْلَٰئِكَ فِى ضَلَٰلٍ مُّبِينٍ (٣٢) أَوَلَمْ يَرَوْا أَنَّ
ٱللَّهَ ٱلَّذِى خَلَقَ ٱلسَّمَٰوَٰتِ وَٱلْأَرْضَ وَلَمْ يَعْىَ بِخَلْقِهِنَّ بِقَٰدِرٍ
عَلَىٰ أَن يُحْيِىَ ٱلْمَوْتَىٰ بَلَىٰ إِنَّهُ عَلَىٰ كُلِّ شَىْءٍ قَدِيرٌ
(٣٣) وَيَوْمَ يُعْرَضُ ٱلَّذِينَ كَفَرُوا عَلَى ٱلنَّارِ أَلَيْسَ هَٰذَا
بِٱلْحَقِّ قَالُوا بَلَىٰ وَرَبِّنَا قَالَ فَذُوقُوا ٱلْعَذَابَ بِمَا كُنتُمْ
تَكْفُرُونَ (٣٤) فَٱصْبِرْ كَمَا صَبَرَ أُوْلُوا ٱلْعَزْمِ مِنَ ٱلرُّسُلِ
وَلَا تَسْتَعْجِل لَّهُمْ كَأَنَّهُمْ يَوْمَ يَرَوْنَ مَا يُوعَدُونَ لَمْ يَلْبَثُوا إِلَّا
سَاعَةً مِّن نَّهَارٍ بَلَٰغٌ فَهَلْ يُهْلَكُ إِلَّا ٱلْقَوْمُ ٱلْفَٰسِقُونَ (٣٥)

*And whosoever does not respond to Allâh's Caller, he cannot escape on earth, and there will be no Auliyâ' (lord, helpers, supporters, protectors) for him besides Allâh (from Allâh's Punishment). Those are in manifest error. (32) Do they not see that Allâh, Who created the heavens and the earth, and was not wearied by their creation, is Able to give life to the dead? Yes, He surely is Able to do all things. (33) And on the Day when those who disbelieve will be exposed to the Fire (it will be said to them): "Is this not the truth?" They will say: "Yes, By our Lord!" He will say: "Then taste the torment, because you used to disbelieve!" (34) Therefore be patient (O Muhammad) as did the Messengers of strong will and be in no haste about them (disbelievers). On the Day when they will see that (torment) with which they are promised (i.e. threatened, it will be) as if they had not stayed more than an hour in a single day. (O mankind, this Qur'ân is sufficient as) a clear Message (or proclamation to save yourself from destruction). But shall any be destroyed except the people who are Al-Fâsiqûn (the rebellious against Allâh's Command, the disobedient to Allâh)? (35)*

## Quran 47:1-12

ٱلَّذِينَ كَفَرُوا۟ وَصَدُّوا۟ عَن سَبِيلِ ٱللَّهِ أَضَلَّ أَعْمَٰلَهُمْ
(١) وَٱلَّذِينَ ءَامَنُوا۟ وَعَمِلُوا۟ ٱلصَّٰلِحَٰتِ وَءَامَنُوا۟ بِمَا نُزِّلَ
عَلَىٰ مُحَمَّدٍ وَهُوَ ٱلْحَقُّ مِن رَّبِّهِمْ كَفَّرَ عَنْهُمْ سَيِّـَٔاتِهِمْ وَأَصْلَحَ

بَالَهُمْ (٢) ذَٰلِكَ بِأَنَّ ٱلَّذِينَ كَفَرُوا۟ ٱتَّبَعُوا۟ ٱلْبَٰطِلَ وَأَنَّ ٱلَّذِينَ
ءَامَنُوا۟ ٱتَّبَعُوا۟ ٱلْحَقَّ مِن رَّبِّهِمْ كَذَٰلِكَ يَضْرِبُ ٱللَّهُ لِلنَّاسِ
أَمْثَٰلَهُمْ (٣) فَإِذَا لَقِيتُمُ ٱلَّذِينَ كَفَرُوا۟ فَضَرْبَ ٱلرِّقَابِ حَتَّىٰ إِذَآ
أَثْخَنتُمُوهُمْ فَشُدُّوا۟ ٱلْوَثَاقَ فَإِمَّا مَنًّا بَعْدُ وَإِمَّا فِدَآءً حَتَّىٰ تَضَعَ
ٱلْحَرْبُ أَوْزَارَهَآ ذَٰلِكَ وَلَوْ يَشَآءُ ٱللَّهُ لَٱنتَصَرَ مِنْهُمْ وَلَٰكِن
لِّيَبْلُوَا۟ بَعْضَكُم بِبَعْضٍ وَٱلَّذِينَ قُتِلُوا۟ فِى سَبِيلِ ٱللَّهِ فَلَن يُضِلَّ
أَعْمَٰلَهُمْ (٤) سَيَهْدِيهِمْ وَيُصْلِحُ بَالَهُمْ (٥) وَيُدْخِلُهُمُ ٱلْجَنَّةَ
عَرَّفَهَا لَهُمْ (٦) يَٰٓأَيُّهَا ٱلَّذِينَ ءَامَنُوٓا۟ إِن تَنصُرُوا۟ ٱللَّهَ يَنصُرْكُمْ
وَيُثَبِّتْ أَقْدَامَكُمْ (٧) وَٱلَّذِينَ كَفَرُوا۟ فَتَعْسًا لَّهُمْ وَأَضَلَّ أَعْمَٰلَهُمْ
(٨) ذَٰلِكَ بِأَنَّهُمْ كَرِهُوا۟ مَآ أَنزَلَ ٱللَّهُ فَأَحْبَطَ أَعْمَٰلَهُمْ (٩) ۞
أَفَلَمْ يَسِيرُوا۟ فِى ٱلْأَرْضِ فَيَنظُرُوا۟ كَيْفَ كَانَ عَٰقِبَةُ ٱلَّذِينَ مِن
قَبْلِهِمْ دَمَّرَ ٱللَّهُ عَلَيْهِمْ وَلِلْكَٰفِرِينَ أَمْثَٰلُهَا (١٠) ذَٰلِكَ بِأَنَّ ٱللَّهَ
مَوْلَى ٱلَّذِينَ ءَامَنُوا۟ وَأَنَّ ٱلْكَٰفِرِينَ لَا مَوْلَىٰ لَهُمْ (١١) إِنَّ ٱللَّهَ
يُدْخِلُ ٱلَّذِينَ ءَامَنُوا۟ وَعَمِلُوا۟ ٱلصَّٰلِحَٰتِ جَنَّٰتٍ تَجْرِى مِن
تَحْتِهَا ٱلْأَنْهَٰرُ وَٱلَّذِينَ كَفَرُوا۟ يَتَمَتَّعُونَ وَيَأْكُلُونَ كَمَا تَأْكُلُ
ٱلْأَنْعَٰمُ وَٱلنَّارُ مَثْوًى لَّهُمْ (١٢)

Those who disbelieve [in the Oneness of Allâh, and in the
Message of Prophet Muhammad], and hinder (men) from
the Path of Allâh (Islâmic Monotheism), He will render
their deeds vain . (1) But those who believe and do
righteous good deeds, and believe in that which is sent
down to Muhammad — for it is the truth from their
Lord, He will expiate from them their sins, and will make

good their state. (2) That is because those who disbelieve follow falsehood, while those who believe follow the truth from their Lord. Thus does Allâh set forth for mankind their parables. (3) So, when you meet (in fight – Jihâd in Allâh's Cause), those who disbelieve smite (their) necks till when you have killed and wounded many of them, then bind a bond firmly (on them, i.e. take them as captives). Thereafter (is the time) either for generosity (i.e. free them without ransom), or ransom (according to what benefits Islâm), until the war lays down its burden. Thus [you are ordered by Allâh to continue in carrying out Jihâd against the disbelievers till they embrace Islâm and are saved from the punishment in the Hell-fire or at least come under your protection], but if it had been Allâh's Will, He Himself could certainly have punished them (without you). But (He lets you fight), in order to test some of you with others. But those who are killed in the Way of Allâh, He will never let their deeds be lost. (4) He will guide them and set right their state. (5) And admit them to Paradise which He has made known to them (i.e. they will know their places in Paradise better than they used to know their homes in the world). (6) O you who believe! If you help (in the cause of) Allâh, He will help you, and make your foothold firm. (7) But those who disbelieve (in the Oneness of Allâh Islâmic Monotheism), for them is destruction, and (Allâh) will make their deeds vain. (8) That is because they hate that which Allâh has sent down (this Qur'ân and Islâmic laws etc.), so He has made their deeds fruitless. (9) Have they not travelled through the earth, and seen what was the end of those before them? Allâh destroyed them completely and a similar (fate awaits) the disbelievers. (10) That is because Allâh is the Maula (Lord, Master, Helper, Protector, etc.) of those who believe, and the disbelievers have no Maula (lord, master, helper, protector). (11) Certainly! Allâh will admit those who believe (in the Oneness of Allâh Islâmic Monotheism) and do righteous good deeds, to Gardens under which rivers flow (Paradise), while those who disbelieve enjoy themselves and eat as cattle eat, and the Fire will be their abode. (12)

## Quran 47:15

مَّثَلُ ٱلْجَنَّةِ ٱلَّتِى وُعِدَ ٱلْمُتَّقُونَ فِيهَا أَنْهَـٰرٌ مِّن مَّآءٍ غَيْرِ ءَاسِنٍ وَأَنْهَـٰرٌ مِّن لَّبَنٍ لَّمْ يَتَغَيَّرْ طَعْمُهُ وَأَنْهَـٰرٌ مِّنْ خَمْرٍ لَّذَّةٍ لِّلشَّـٰرِبِينَ وَأَنْهَـٰرٌ مِّنْ عَسَلٍ مُّصَفًّى وَلَهُمْ فِيهَا مِن كُلِّ ٱلثَّمَرَٰتِ وَمَغْفِرَةٌ مِّن رَّبِّهِمْ كَمَنْ هُوَ خَـٰلِدٌ فِى ٱلنَّارِ وَسُقُواْ مَآءً حَمِيمًا فَقَطَّعَ أَمْعَآءَهُمْ

The description of Paradise which the Muttaqûn (pious) have been promised (is that) in it are rivers of water the taste and smell of which are not changed, rivers of milk of which the taste never changes, rivers of wine delicious to those who drink; and rivers of clarified honey (clear and

pure) therein for them is every kind of fruit; and
forgiveness from their Lord. (Are these) like those who
shall dwell for ever in the Fire, and be given, to drink,
boiling water, so that it cuts up their bowels? (15)

## Quran 47:17-18

وَٱلَّذِينَ ٱهْتَدَوْاْ زَادَهُمْ هُدًى وَءَاتَىٰهُمْ تَقْوَىٰهُمْ (١٧) فَهَلْ
يَنظُرُونَ إِلَّا ٱلسَّاعَةَ أَن تَأْتِيَهُم بَغْتَةً فَقَدْ جَآءَ أَشْرَاطُهَا فَأَنَّىٰ
لَهُمْ إِذَا جَآءَتْهُمْ ذِكْرَىٰهُمْ (١٨)

While as for those who accept guidance, He increases
their guidance, and bestows on them their piety. (17) Do
they then await (anything) other than the Hour, that it
should come upon them suddenly? But some of its
portents (indications and signs) have already come, and
when it (actually) is on them, how can they benefit then
by their reminder? (18)

## Quran 47:20-21

وَيَقُولُ ٱلَّذِينَ ءَامَنُواْ لَوْلَا نُزِّلَتْ سُورَةٌ فَإِذَآ أُنزِلَتْ سُورَةٌ
مُّحْكَمَةٌ وَذُكِرَ فِيهَا ٱلْقِتَالُ رَأَيْتَ ٱلَّذِينَ فِى قُلُوبِهِم مَّرَضٌ
يَنظُرُونَ إِلَيْكَ نَظَرَ ٱلْمَغْشِىِّ عَلَيْهِ مِنَ ٱلْمَوْتِ فَأَوْلَىٰ لَهُمْ
(٢٠) طَاعَةٌ وَقَوْلٌ مَّعْرُوفٌ فَإِذَا عَزَمَ ٱلْأَمْرُ فَلَوْ صَدَقُواْ ٱللَّهَ
لَكَانَ خَيْرًا لَّهُمْ (٢١)

Those who believe say: "Why is not a Sûrah (chapter of
the Qur'ân) sent down (for us)? But when a decisive

Sûrah (explaining and ordering things) is sent down, and fighting (Jihâd — holy fighting in Allâh's Cause) is mentioned (i.e. ordained) therein, you will see those in whose hearts is a disease (of hypocrisy) looking at you with a look of one fainting to death. But it was better for them (hypocrites, to listen to Allâh and to obey Him). (20) Obedience (to Allâh) and good words (were better for them). And when the matter (preparation for Jihâd) is resolved on, then if they had been true to Allâh, it would have been better for them. (21)

## Quran 47:27-38

فَكَيْفَ إِذَا تَوَفَّتْهُمُ ٱلْمَلَـٰٓئِكَةُ يَضْرِبُونَ وُجُوهَهُمْ وَأَدْبَـٰرَهُمْ (٢٧) ذَٰلِكَ بِأَنَّهُمُ ٱتَّبَعُوا۟ مَآ أَسْخَطَ ٱللَّهَ وَكَرِهُوا۟ رِضْوَٰنَهُۥ فَأَحْبَطَ أَعْمَـٰلَهُمْ (٢٨) أَمْ حَسِبَ ٱلَّذِينَ فِى قُلُوبِهِم مَّرَضٌ أَن لَّن يُخْرِجَ ٱللَّهُ أَضْغَـٰنَهُمْ (٢٩) وَلَوْ نَشَآءُ لَأَرَيْنَـٰكَهُمْ فَلَعَرَفْتَهُم بِسِيمَـٰهُمْ وَلَتَعْرِفَنَّهُمْ فِى لَحْنِ ٱلْقَوْلِ وَٱللَّهُ يَعْلَمُ أَعْمَـٰلَكُمْ (٣٠) وَلَنَبْلُوَنَّكُمْ حَتَّىٰ نَعْلَمَ ٱلْمُجَـٰهِدِينَ مِنكُمْ وَٱلصَّـٰبِرِينَ وَنَبْلُوَا۟ أَخْبَارَكُمْ (٣١) إِنَّ ٱلَّذِينَ كَفَرُوا۟ وَصَدُّوا۟ عَن سَبِيلِ ٱللَّهِ وَشَآقُّوا۟ ٱلرَّسُولَ مِنۢ بَعْدِ مَا تَبَيَّنَ لَهُمُ ٱلْهُدَىٰ لَن يَضُرُّوا۟ ٱللَّهَ شَيْـًٔا وَسَيُحْبِطُ أَعْمَـٰلَهُمْ (٣٢) ۞ يَـٰٓأَيُّهَا ٱلَّذِينَ ءَامَنُوٓا۟ أَطِيعُوا۟ ٱللَّهَ وَأَطِيعُوا۟ ٱلرَّسُولَ وَلَا تُبْطِلُوٓا۟ أَعْمَـٰلَكُمْ (٣٣) إِنَّ ٱلَّذِينَ كَفَرُوا۟ وَصَدُّوا۟ عَن سَبِيلِ ٱللَّهِ ثُمَّ مَاتُوا۟ وَهُمْ كُفَّارٌ فَلَن يَغْفِرَ ٱللَّهُ لَهُمْ (٣٤) فَلَا تَهِنُوا۟ وَتَدْعُوٓا۟ إِلَى ٱلسَّلْمِ وَأَنتُمُ ٱلْأَعْلَوْنَ

وَٱللَّهُ مَعَكُمْ وَلَن يَتِرَكُمْ أَعْمَٰلَكُمْ (٣٥) إِنَّمَا ٱلْحَيَوٰةُ ٱلدُّنْيَا لَعِبٌ
وَلَهْوٌ وَإِن تُؤْمِنُواْ وَتَتَّقُواْ يُؤْتِكُمْ أُجُورَكُمْ وَلَا يَسْـَٔلْكُمْ أَمْوَٰلَكُمْ
(٣٦) إِن يَسْـَٔلْكُمُوهَا فَيُحْفِكُمْ تَبْخَلُواْ وَيُخْرِجْ أَضْغَٰنَكُمْ
(٣٧) هَٰٓأَنتُمْ هَٰٓؤُلَآءِ تُدْعَوْنَ لِتُنفِقُواْ فِى سَبِيلِ ٱللَّهِ فَمِنكُم مَّن
يَبْخَلُ وَمَن يَبْخَلْ فَإِنَّمَا يَبْخَلُ عَن نَّفْسِهِۦ وَٱللَّهُ ٱلْغَنِىُّ وَأَنتُمُ
ٱلْفُقَرَآءُ وَإِن تَتَوَلَّوْاْ يَسْتَبْدِلْ قَوْمًا غَيْرَكُمْ ثُمَّ لَا يَكُونُوٓاْ أَمْثَٰلَكُم
(٣٨)

*Then how (will it be) when the angels will take their souls at death, smiting their faces and their backs? (27) That is because they followed that which angered Allâh, and hated that which pleased Him. So He made their deeds fruitless. (28) Or do those in whose hearts is a disease (of hypocrisy), think that Allâh will not bring to light all their hidden ill-wills? (29) Had We willed, We could have shown them to you, and you should have known them by their marks; but surely, you will know them by the tone of their speech! And Allâh knows (all) your deeds. (30) And surely, We shall try you till We test those who strive hard (for the Cause of Allâh) and As-Sabirun (the patient ones), and We shall test your facts (i.e. the one who is a liar, and the one who is truthful). (31) Verily, those who disbelieve, and hinder (men) from the Path of Allâh (i.e. Islâm), and oppose the Messenger (by standing against him and hurting him), after the guidance has been clearly shown to them, they will not* hurt Allâh in the least, but He will make their deeds fruitless, (32) O you who believe! Obey Allâh, and obey the Messenger (Muhammad) and render not vain your deeds. (33) Verily, those who disbelieve, and hinder (men) from the Path of Allâh (i.e. Islâm); then die while they are disbelievers, - Allâh will not forgive them. (34) So be not weak and ask not for peace (from the enemies of Islâm), while you are having the upper hand. Allâh is with you, and He will never decrease the reward of your good deeds. (35) The life of this world is but play and pastime, but if you believe (in the Oneness of Allâh — Islâmic Monotheism), and fear Allâh, and avoid evil, He will grant you your wages, and will not ask you your wealth. (36) If He were to ask you of it, and press you, you would covetously withhold, and He will bring out all your (secret) ill-wills. (37) Behold! You are those who are called to spend in the Cause of Allâh, yet among you are some who are niggardly. And whoever is niggardly, it is only at the expense of his ownself. But Allâh is Rich (Free of all needs), and you (mankind) are poor. And if you turn away (from Islâm and the obedience to Allâh), He will exchange you for some other people, and they will not be your likes. (38)

## Quran 48:1-8

إِنَّا فَتَحْنَا لَكَ فَتْحًا مُّبِينًا (١) لِّيَغْفِرَ لَكَ ٱللَّهُ مَا تَقَدَّمَ مِن ذَنۢبِكَ وَمَا تَأَخَّرَ وَيُتِمَّ نِعْمَتَهُۥ عَلَيْكَ وَيَهْدِيَكَ صِرَٰطًا مُّسْتَقِيمًا

(٢) وَيَنصُرَكَ ٱللَّهُ نَصْرًا عَزِيزًا (٣) هُوَ ٱلَّذِىٓ أَنزَلَ ٱلسَّكِينَةَ فِى قُلُوبِ ٱلْمُؤْمِنِينَ لِيَزْدَادُوٓاْ إِيمَـٰنًا مَّعَ إِيمَـٰنِهِمْۗ وَلِلَّهِ جُنُودُ ٱلسَّمَـٰوَٰتِ وَٱلْأَرْضِۚ وَكَانَ ٱللَّهُ عَلِيمًا حَكِيمًا (٤) لِّيُدْخِلَ ٱلْمُؤْمِنِينَ وَٱلْمُؤْمِنَـٰتِ جَنَّـٰتٍ تَجْرِى مِن تَحْتِهَا ٱلْأَنْهَـٰرُ خَـٰلِدِينَ فِيهَا وَيُكَفِّرَ عَنْهُمْ سَيِّـَٔاتِهِمْۚ وَكَانَ ذَٰلِكَ عِندَ ٱللَّهِ فَوْزًا عَظِيمًا (٥) وَيُعَذِّبَ ٱلْمُنَـٰفِقِينَ وَٱلْمُنَـٰفِقَـٰتِ وَٱلْمُشْرِكِينَ وَٱلْمُشْرِكَـٰتِ ٱلظَّآنِّينَ بِٱللَّهِ ظَنَّ ٱلسَّوْءِۚ عَلَيْهِمْ دَآئِرَةُ ٱلسَّوْءِۖ وَغَضِبَ ٱللَّهُ عَلَيْهِمْ وَلَعَنَهُمْ وَأَعَدَّ لَهُمْ جَهَنَّمَۖ وَسَآءَتْ مَصِيرًا (٦) وَلِلَّهِ جُنُودُ ٱلسَّمَـٰوَٰتِ وَٱلْأَرْضِۚ وَكَانَ ٱللَّهُ عَزِيزًا حَكِيمًا (٧) إِنَّآ أَرْسَلْنَـٰكَ شَـٰهِدًا وَمُبَشِّرًا وَنَذِيرًا (٨)

*Verily, We have given you (O Muhammad) a manifest victory. (1) That Allâh may forgive you your sins of the past and the future[], and complete His Favour on you, and guide you on the Straight Path; (2) And that Allâh may help you with strong help. (3) He it is Who sent down As-Sakinah (calmness and tranquillity) into the hearts of the believers, that they may grow more in Faith along with their (present) Faith. And to Allâh belong the hosts of the heavens and the earth, and Allâh is Ever All-Knower, All-Wise. (4) That He may admit the believing men and the believing women to Gardens under which rivers flow (i.e. Paradise), to abide therein forever, and He may expiate from them their sins, and that is with Allâh, a supreme success, (5) And that He may punish the Munâfiqûn (hypocrites), men and women, and also* the Mushrikûn men and women, who think evil thoughts about Allâh, for them is a disgraceful torment, And the Anger of Allâh is upon them, and He has cursed them and prepared Hell for them — and worst indeed is that destination. (6) And to Allâh belong the hosts of the heavens and the earth. And Allâh is Ever All-powerful, All-Wise. (7) Verily, We have sent you (O Muhammad) as a witness, as a bearer of glad tidings, and as a warner (8)

## Quran 48:10

إِنَّ ٱلَّذِينَ يُبَايِعُونَكَ إِنَّمَا يُبَايِعُونَ ٱللَّهَ يَدُ ٱللَّهِ فَوْقَ أَيْدِيهِمْ فَمَن نَّكَثَ فَإِنَّمَا يَنكُثُ عَلَىٰ نَفْسِهِۦ وَمَنْ أَوْفَىٰ بِمَا عَٰهَدَ عَلَيْهُ ٱللَّهَ فَسَيُؤْتِيهِ أَجْرًا عَظِيمًا

Verily, those who give Bai'âh (pledge) to you (O Muhammad) they are giving Bai'âh (pledge) to Allâh. The Hand of Allâh is over their hands. Then whosoever breaks his pledge, breaks it only to his own harm, and whosoever fulfils what he has covenanted with Allâh, He will bestow on him a great reward. (10)

## Quran 48:13

وَمَن لَّمْ يُؤْمِنۢ بِٱللَّهِ وَرَسُولِهِۦ فَإِنَّآ أَعْتَدْنَا لِلْكَٰفِرِينَ سَعِيرًا

And whosoever does not believe in Allâh and His Messenger (Muhammad), then verily, We have prepared for the disbelievers a blazing Fire. (13)

قُل لِّلْمُخَلَّفِينَ مِنَ ٱلْأَعْرَابِ سَتُدْعَوْنَ إِلَىٰ قَوْمٍ أُوْلِى بَأْسٍ شَدِيدٍ تُقَٰتِلُونَهُمْ أَوْ يُسْلِمُونَ ۖ فَإِن تُطِيعُواْ يُؤْتِكُمُ ٱللَّهُ أَجْرًا حَسَنًا ۖ وَإِن تَتَوَلَّوْاْ كَمَا تَوَلَّيْتُم مِّن قَبْلُ يُعَذِّبْكُمْ عَذَابًا أَلِيمًا (١٦) لَّيْسَ عَلَى ٱلْأَعْمَىٰ حَرَجٌ وَلَا عَلَى ٱلْأَعْرَجِ حَرَجٌ وَلَا عَلَى ٱلْمَرِيضِ حَرَجٌ ۗ وَمَن يُطِعِ ٱللَّهَ وَرَسُولَهُ يُدْخِلْهُ جَنَّٰتٍ تَجْرِى مِن تَحْتِهَا ٱلْأَنْهَٰرُ ۖ وَمَن يَتَوَلَّ يُعَذِّبْهُ عَذَابًا أَلِيمًا ۞ (١٧) لَّقَدْ رَضِىَ ٱللَّهُ عَنِ ٱلْمُؤْمِنِينَ إِذْ يُبَايِعُونَكَ تَحْتَ ٱلشَّجَرَةِ فَعَلِمَ مَا فِى قُلُوبِهِمْ فَأَنزَلَ ٱلسَّكِينَةَ عَلَيْهِمْ وَأَثَٰبَهُمْ فَتْحًا قَرِيبًا (١٨) وَمَغَانِمَ كَثِيرَةً يَأْخُذُونَهَا ۗ وَكَانَ ٱللَّهُ عَزِيزًا حَكِيمًا (١٩) وَعَدَكُمُ ٱللَّهُ مَغَانِمَ كَثِيرَةً تَأْخُذُونَهَا فَعَجَّلَ لَكُمْ هَٰذِهِ وَكَفَّ أَيْدِىَ ٱلنَّاسِ عَنكُمْ وَلِتَكُونَ ءَايَةً لِّلْمُؤْمِنِينَ وَيَهْدِيَكُمْ صِرَٰطًا مُّسْتَقِيمًا (٢٠) وَأُخْرَىٰ لَمْ تَقْدِرُواْ عَلَيْهَا قَدْ أَحَاطَ ٱللَّهُ بِهَا ۚ وَكَانَ ٱللَّهُ عَلَىٰ كُلِّ شَىْءٍ قَدِيرًا (٢١) وَلَوْ قَٰتَلَكُمُ ٱلَّذِينَ كَفَرُواْ لَوَلَّوُاْ ٱلْأَدْبَٰرَ ثُمَّ لَا يَجِدُونَ وَلِيًّا وَلَا نَصِيرًا (٢٢) سُنَّةَ ٱللَّهِ ٱلَّتِى قَدْ خَلَتْ مِن قَبْلُ ۖ وَلَن تَجِدَ لِسُنَّةِ ٱللَّهِ تَبْدِيلًا (٢٣) وَهُوَ ٱلَّذِى كَفَّ أَيْدِيَهُمْ عَنكُمْ وَأَيْدِيَكُمْ عَنْهُم بِبَطْنِ مَكَّةَ مِنۢ بَعْدِ أَنْ أَظْفَرَكُمْ عَلَيْهِمْ ۚ وَكَانَ ٱللَّهُ بِمَا تَعْمَلُونَ بَصِيرًا (٢٤)

*Say (O Muhammad) to the bedouins who lagged behind:
"You shall be called to fight against a people given to
great warfare, then you shall fight them, or they shall*

surrender. Then if you obey, Allâh will give you a fair reward, but if you turn away as you did turn away before, He will punish you with a painful torment." (16) No blame or sin is there upon the blind, nor is there blame or sin upon the lame, nor is there blame or sin upon the sick (that they go not for fighting). And whosoever obeys Allâh and His Messenger (Muhammad), He will admit him to Gardens beneath which rivers flow (Paradise); and whosoever turns back, He will punish him with a painful torment. (17) Indeed, Allâh was pleased with the believers when they gave the Bai'âh (pledge) to you (O Muhammad) under the tree, He knew what was in their hearts, and He sent down As-Sakinah (calmness and tranquillity) upon them, and He rewarded them with a near victory, (18) And abundant spoils that they will capture. And Allâh is Ever All-Mighty, All-Wise. (19) Allâh has promised you abundant spoils that you will capture, and He has hastened for you this, and He has restrained the hands of men from you, that it may be a sign for the believers, and that He may guide you to a Straight Path. (20) And other (victories and much booty, He promises you) which are not yet within your power, indeed Allâh compasses them, And Allâh is Ever Able to do all things. (21) And if those who disbelieve fight against you, they certainly would have turned their backs, then they would have found neither a Walî (protector, guardian) nor a helper.

*(22) That has been the Way of Allâh already with those who passed away before. And you will not find any change in the Way of Allâh. (23) And He it is Who has withheld their hands from you and your hands from them in the midst of Makkah, after He had made you victors over them. And Allâh is Ever the All-Seer of what you do. (24)*

## Quran 48:27-29

لَّقَدْ صَدَقَ ٱللَّهُ رَسُولَهُ ٱلرُّءْيَا بِٱلْحَقِّ لَتَدْخُلُنَّ ٱلْمَسْجِدَ ٱلْحَرَامَ إِن شَآءَ ٱللَّهُ ءَامِنِينَ مُحَلِّقِينَ رُءُوسَكُمْ وَمُقَصِّرِينَ لَا تَخَافُونَ فَعَلِمَ مَا لَمْ تَعْلَمُوا۟ فَجَعَلَ مِن دُونِ ذَٰلِكَ فَتْحًا قَرِيبًا (٢٧) هُوَ ٱلَّذِىٓ أَرْسَلَ رَسُولَهُۥ بِٱلْهُدَىٰ وَدِينِ ٱلْحَقِّ لِيُظْهِرَهُۥ عَلَى ٱلدِّينِ كُلِّهِۦ وَكَفَىٰ بِٱللَّهِ شَهِيدًا (٢٨) مُّحَمَّدٌ رَّسُولُ ٱللَّهِ وَٱلَّذِينَ مَعَهُۥٓ أَشِدَّآءُ عَلَى ٱلْكُفَّارِ رُحَمَآءُ بَيْنَهُمْ تَرَىٰهُمْ رُكَّعًا سُجَّدًا يَبْتَغُونَ فَضْلًا مِّنَ ٱللَّهِ وَرِضْوَٰنًا سِيمَاهُمْ فِى وُجُوهِهِم مِّنْ أَثَرِ ٱلسُّجُودِ ذَٰلِكَ مَثَلُهُمْ فِى ٱلتَّوْرَىٰةِ وَمَثَلُهُمْ فِى ٱلْإِنجِيلِ كَزَرْعٍ أَخْرَجَ شَطْـَٔهُۥ فَـَٔازَرَهُۥ فَٱسْتَغْلَظَ فَٱسْتَوَىٰ عَلَىٰ سُوقِهِۦ يُعْجِبُ ٱلزُّرَّاعَ لِيَغِيظَ بِهِمُ ٱلْكُفَّارَ وَعَدَ ٱللَّهُ ٱلَّذِينَ ءَامَنُوا۟ وَعَمِلُوا۟ ٱلصَّٰلِحَٰتِ مِنْهُم مَّغْفِرَةً وَأَجْرًا عَظِيمًا (٢٩)

*Indeed Allâh shall fulfil the true vision which He showed to His Messenger [i.e. the Prophet saw a dream that he has entered Makkah along with his companions, having their (head) hair shaved and cut short] in very truth.*

Certainly, you shall enter Al¬Masjid¬al¬Harâm; if Allâh wills, secure, (some) having your heads shaved, and (some) having your head hair cut short, having no fear. He knew what you knew not, and He granted besides that a near victory. (27) He it is Who has sent His Messenger (Muhammad) with guidance and the religion of truth (Islâm), that He may make it (Islâm) superior over all religions. And All-Sufficient is Allâh as a Witness. (28) Muhammad is the Messenger of Allâh, And those who are with him are severe against disbelievers, and merciful among themselves. You see them bowing and falling down prostrate (in prayer), seeking Bounty from Allâh and (His) Good Pleasure. The mark of them (i.e. of their Faith) is on their faces (foreheads) from the traces of prostration (during prayers). This is their description in the Taurât (Torah). But their description in the Injeel is like a (sown) seed which sends forth its shoot, then makes it strong, and becomes thick, and it stands straight on its stem, delighting the sowers that He may enrage the disbelievers with them. Allâh has promised those among them who believe (i.e. all those who follow Islâmic Monotheism, the religion of Prophet Muhammad till the Day of Resurrection) and do righteous good deeds, forgiveness and a mighty reward (i.e. Paradise). (29)

**Quran 49:3**

إِنَّ ٱلَّذِينَ يَغُضُّونَ أَصْوَٰتَهُمْ عِندَ رَسُولِ ٱللَّهِ أُوْلَٰٓئِكَ ٱلَّذِينَ ٱمْتَحَنَ ٱللَّهُ قُلُوبَهُمْ لِلتَّقْوَىٰ لَهُم مَّغْفِرَةٌ وَأَجْرٌ عَظِيمٌ

*Verily, those who lower their voices in the presence of Allâh's Messenger, they are the ones whose hearts Allâh has tested for piety. For them is forgiveness and a great reward. (3)*

## Quran 50:11

رِّزْقًا لِّلْعِبَادِ وَأَحْيَيْنَا بِهِ بَلْدَةً مَّيْتًا كَذَٰلِكَ ٱلْخُرُوجُ

*A provision for (Allâh's) slaves. And We give life therewith to a dead land. Thus will be the resurrection (of the dead). (11)*

## Quran 50:19-35

وَجَآءَتْ سَكْرَةُ ٱلْمَوْتِ بِٱلْحَقِّ ذَٰلِكَ مَا كُنتَ مِنْهُ تَحِيدُ (١٩) وَنُفِخَ فِى ٱلصُّورِ ذَٰلِكَ يَوْمُ ٱلْوَعِيدِ (٢٠) وَجَآءَتْ كُلُّ نَفْسٍ مَّعَهَا سَآئِقٌ وَشَهِيدٌ (٢١) لَّقَدْ كُنتَ فِى غَفْلَةٍ مِّنْ هَٰذَا فَكَشَفْنَا عَنكَ غِطَآءَكَ فَبَصَرُكَ ٱلْيَوْمَ حَدِيدٌ (٢٢) وَقَالَ قَرِينُهُ هَٰذَا مَا لَدَىَّ عَتِيدٌ (٢٣) أَلْقِيَا فِى جَهَنَّمَ كُلَّ كَفَّارٍ عَنِيدٍ (٢٤) مَّنَّاعٍ لِّلْخَيْرِ مُعْتَدٍ مُّرِيبٍ (٢٥) ٱلَّذِى جَعَلَ مَعَ ٱللَّهِ إِلَٰهًا ءَاخَرَ فَأَلْقِيَاهُ فِى ٱلْعَذَابِ ٱلشَّدِيدِ (٢٦) ۞ قَالَ قَرِينُهُ رَبَّنَا مَآ أَطْغَيْتُهُ وَلَٰكِن كَانَ فِى ضَلَٰلٍ بَعِيدٍ (٢٧) قَالَ لَا تَخْتَصِمُوا لَدَىَّ وَقَدْ قَدَّمْتُ إِلَيْكُم بِٱلْوَعِيدِ (٢٨) مَا يُبَدَّلُ ٱلْقَوْلُ لَدَىَّ وَمَآ أَنَا۠ بِظَلَّٰمٍ لِّلْعَبِيدِ (٢٩) يَوْمَ نَقُولُ لِجَهَنَّمَ هَلِ ٱمْتَلَأْتِ

وَتَقُولُ هَلْ مِن مَّزِيدٍ (٣٠) وَأُزْلِفَتِ ٱلْجَنَّةُ لِلْمُتَّقِينَ غَيْرَ بَعِيدٍ (٣١) هَـٰذَا مَا تُوعَدُونَ لِكُلِّ أَوَّابٍ حَفِيظٍ (٣٢) مَّنْ خَشِيَ ٱلرَّحْمَـٰنَ بِٱلْغَيْبِ وَجَآءَ بِقَلْبٍ مُّنِيبٍ (٣٣) ٱدْخُلُوهَا بِسَلَـٰمٍ ذَٰلِكَ يَوْمُ ٱلْخُلُودِ (٣٤) لَهُم مَّا يَشَآءُونَ فِيهَا وَلَدَيْنَا مَزِيدٌ (٣٥)

*And the stupor of death will come in truth: "This is what you have been avoiding!" (19) And the Trumpet will be blown — that will be the Day whereof warning (had been given) (i.e. the Day of Resurrection). (20) And every person will come forth along with an (angel) to drive (him), and an (angel) to bear witness. (21) (It will be said to the sinners): "Indeed you were heedless of this, now We have removed your covering, and sharp is your sight this Day!" (22) And his companion (angel) will say: "Here is (this Record) ready with me!" (23) (Allah will say to the angels): "Both of you throw into Hell, every stubborn disbeliever (in the Oneness of Allâh, in His Messengers) — (24) "Hinderer of good, transgressor, doubter, (25) "Who set up another ilâh (god) with Allâh, Then both of you cast him in the severe torment." (26) His companion (Satan — devil)] will say: "Our Lord! I did not push him to transgression, (in disbelief, oppression, and evil deeds) but he was himself in error far astray." (27) Allâh will say: "Dispute not in front of Me, I had already, in advance, sent you the threat. (28) The Sentence that comes from Me cannot be changed, and I*

am not unjust to the slaves." (29) On the Day when We
will say to Hell: "Are you filled?" It will say: "Are there
any more (to come)?" (30) And Paradise will be brought
near to the Muttaqûn (pious) not far off. (31) (It will be
said): "This is what you were promised, - (it is) for those
oft-returning (to Allâh) in sincere repentance, and those
who preserve their covenant with Allâh (by obeying Him
in all what He has ordered, and worshipping none but
Allâh Alone, i.e. follow Allâh's religion, Islâmic
Monotheism). (32) "Who feared the Most Gracious
(Allâh) in the Ghaib (unseen) and brought a heart turned
in repentance (to Him - and absolutely free from each and
every kind of polytheism). (33) "Enter you therein in
peace and security — this is a Day of eternal life!"
(34) There they will have all that they desire — and We
have more (for them, i.e. a glance at the All-Mighty, All-
Majestic) (35)

## Quran 50:41-44

وَٱسْتَمِعْ يَوْمَ يُنَادِ ٱلْمُنَادِ مِن مَّكَانٍ قَرِيبٍ (٤١) يَوْمَ يَسْمَعُونَ
ٱلصَّيْحَةَ بِٱلْحَقِّ ذَلِكَ يَوْمُ ٱلْخُرُوجِ (٤٢) إِنَّا نَحْنُ نُحْيِ
وَنُمِيتُ وَإِلَيْنَا ٱلْمَصِيرُ (٤٣) يَوْمَ تَشَقَّقُ ٱلْأَرْضُ عَنْهُمْ
سِرَاعًا ذَلِكَ حَشْرٌ عَلَيْنَا يَسِيرٌ (٤٤)

And listen on the Day when the caller will call from a
near place, (41) The Day when they will hear As-Saihah
(shout) in truth, that will be the Day of coming out (from

the graves i.e. the Day of Resurrection). (42) Verily, We
it is Who give life and cause death; and to Us is the final
return, (43) On the Day when the earth shall be cleft,
from off them, (they will come out) hastening forth. That
will be a gathering, quite easy for Us. (44)

## Quran 51:5-6

إِنَّمَا تُوعَدُونَ لَصَادِقٌ (٥) وَإِنَّ ٱلدِّينَ لَوَاقِعٌ (٦)

Verily, that which you are promised is surely true.
(5) And verily, the Recompense is sure to happen. (6)

## Quran 51:13-16

يَوْمَ هُمْ عَلَى ٱلنَّارِ يُفْتَنُونَ (١٣) ذُوقُواْ فِتْنَتَكُمْ هَـٰذَا ٱلَّذِى كُنتُم
بِهِۦ تَسْتَعْجِلُونَ (١٤) إِنَّ ٱلْمُتَّقِينَ فِى جَنَّـٰتٍ وَعُيُونٍ
(١٥) ءَاخِذِينَ مَآ ءَاتَـٰهُمْ رَبُّهُمْ إِنَّهُمْ كَانُواْ قَبْلَ ذَٰلِكَ مُحْسِنِينَ
(١٦)

(It will be) a Day when they will be tried (punished i.e.
burnt) over the Fire! (13) "Taste you your trial
(punishment i.e. burning)! This is what you used to ask
to be hastened!" (14) Verily, the Muttaqûn (pious) will
be in the midst of Gardens and Springs (in the Paradise),
(15) Taking joy in the things which their Lord has given
them. Verily, they were before this Muhsinûn (good-
doers) (16)

## Quran 51:22-23

وَفِى ٱلسَّمَآءِ رِزْقُكُمْ وَمَا تُوعَدُونَ (٢٢) فَوَرَبِّ ٱلسَّمَآءِ
وَٱلْأَرْضِ إِنَّهُ لَحَقٌّ مِّثْلَ مَآ أَنَّكُمْ تَنطِقُونَ (٢٣)

*And in the heaven is your provision, and that which you
are promised. (22) Then, by the Lord of the heaven and
the earth, it is the truth (i.e. what has been promised to
you), just as it is the truth that you can speak. (23)*

## Quran 51:55

وَذَكِّرْ فَإِنَّ ٱلذِّكْرَىٰ تَنفَعُ ٱلْمُؤْمِنِينَ

*And remind for verily, the reminding profits the
believers. (55)*

## Quran 51:59-60

فَإِنَّ لِلَّذِينَ ظَلَمُوا۟ ذَنُوبًا مِّثْلَ ذَنُوبِ أَصْحَـٰبِهِمْ فَلَا يَسْتَعْجِلُونِ
(٥٩) فَوَيْلٌ لِّلَّذِينَ كَفَرُوا۟ مِن يَوْمِهِمُ ٱلَّذِى يُوعَدُونَ (٦٠)

*And verily, for those who do wrong, there is a portion of
torment like to the evil portion of torment (which came
for) their likes (of old), so let them not ask Me to hasten
on! (59) Then, woe to those who disbelieve (in Islâmic
Monotheism) from their Day which they have been
promised (for their punishment). (60)*

## Quran 52:7-28

إِنَّ عَذَابَ رَبِّكَ لَوَٰقِعٌ (٧) مَّا لَهُ مِن دَافِعٍ (٨) يَوْمَ تَمُورُ
ٱلسَّمَآءُ مَوْرًا (٩) وَتَسِيرُ ٱلْجِبَالُ سَيْرًا (١٠) فَوَيْلٌ يَوْمَئِذٍ

لِّلْمُكَذِّبِينَ ﴿١١﴾ ٱلَّذِينَ هُمْ فِى خَوْضٍ يَلْعَبُونَ ﴿١٢﴾ يَوْمَ يُدَعُّونَ إِلَىٰ نَارِ جَهَنَّمَ دَعًّا ﴿١٣﴾ هَٰذِهِ ٱلنَّارُ ٱلَّتِى كُنتُم بِهَا تُكَذِّبُونَ ﴿١٤﴾ أَفَسِحْرٌ هَٰذَآ أَمْ أَنتُمْ لَا تُبْصِرُونَ ﴿١٥﴾ ٱصْلَوْهَا فَٱصْبِرُوٓاْ أَوْ لَا تَصْبِرُواْ سَوَآءٌ عَلَيْكُمْ إِنَّمَا تُجْزَوْنَ مَا كُنتُمْ تَعْمَلُونَ ﴿١٦﴾ إِنَّ ٱلْمُتَّقِينَ فِى جَنَّٰتٍ وَنَعِيمٍ ﴿١٧﴾ فَٰكِهِينَ بِمَآ ءَاتَٰهُمْ رَبُّهُمْ وَوَقَٰهُمْ رَبُّهُمْ عَذَابَ ٱلْجَحِيمِ ﴿١٨﴾ كُلُواْ وَٱشْرَبُواْ هَنِيٓئًا بِمَا كُنتُمْ تَعْمَلُونَ ﴿١٩﴾ مُتَّكِئِينَ عَلَىٰ سُرُرٍ مَّصْفُوفَةٍ وَزَوَّجْنَٰهُم بِحُورٍ عِينٍ ﴿٢٠﴾ وَٱلَّذِينَ ءَامَنُواْ وَٱتَّبَعَتْهُمْ ذُرِّيَّتُهُم بِإِيمَٰنٍ أَلْحَقْنَا بِهِمْ ذُرِّيَّتَهُمْ وَمَآ أَلَتْنَٰهُم مِّنْ عَمَلِهِم مِّن شَىْءٍ كُلُّ ٱمْرِئٍ بِمَا كَسَبَ رَهِينٌ ﴿٢١﴾ وَأَمْدَدْنَٰهُم بِفَٰكِهَةٍ وَلَحْمٍ مِّمَّا يَشْتَهُونَ ﴿٢٢﴾ يَتَنَٰزَعُونَ فِيهَا كَأْسًا لَّا لَغْوٌ فِيهَا وَلَا تَأْثِيمٌ ﴿٢٣﴾ ۞ وَيَطُوفُ عَلَيْهِمْ غِلْمَانٌ لَّهُمْ كَأَنَّهُمْ لُؤْلُؤٌ مَّكْنُونٌ ﴿٢٤﴾ وَأَقْبَلَ بَعْضُهُمْ عَلَىٰ بَعْضٍ يَتَسَآءَلُونَ ﴿٢٥﴾ قَالُوٓاْ إِنَّا كُنَّا قَبْلُ فِىٓ أَهْلِنَا مُشْفِقِينَ ﴿٢٦﴾ فَمَنَّ ٱللَّهُ عَلَيْنَا وَوَقَٰنَا عَذَابَ ٱلسَّمُومِ ﴿٢٧﴾ إِنَّا كُنَّا مِن قَبْلُ نَدْعُوهُ إِنَّهُ هُوَ ٱلْبَرُّ ٱلرَّحِيمُ ﴿٢٨﴾

*Verily, the Torment of your Lord will surely come to pass, (7) There is none that can avert it; (8) On the Day when the heaven will shake with a dreadful shaking, (9) And the mountains will move away with a (horrible) movement. (10) Then woe that Day to the beliers; (11) Who are playing in falsehood. (12) The Day when they will be pushed down by force to the Fire of Hell, with a horrible, forceful pushing. (13) This is the Fire which you used to belie. (14) Is this magic, or do you not see? (15) Taste you therein its heat, and whether you are patient of it or impatient of it, it is all the same. You are only being requited for what you used to do. (16) Verily, the Muttaqûn (pious) will be in Gardens (Paradise), and Delight. (17) Enjoying in that which their Lord has bestowed on them, and (the fact that) their Lord saved them from the torment of the blazing Fire. (18) "Eat and drink with happiness because of what you used to do." (19) They will recline (with ease) on thrones arranged in ranks. And We shall marry them to Hûr (female, fair ones) with wide lovely eyes.(20) And those who believe and whose offspring follow them in Faith, to them shall We join their offspring, and We shall not decrease the reward of their deeds in anything. Every person is a pledge for that which he has earned. (21) And We shall provide them with fruit and meat, such as they desire. (22) There they shall pass from hand to hand a (wine) cup, free from any Laghw (dirty, false, evil vain talk between them), and free from sin (because it will be lawful for them to drink). (23) And there will go round boy-servants of theirs, to serve them as if they were preserved pearls. (24) And some of them draw near to others, questioning. (25) Saying: "Aforetime, we were afraid (of the punishment of Allâh) in the midest of our families. (26) "So Allâh has been gracious to us, and has*

saved us from the torment of the Fire. (27) "Verily, We
used to invoke Him (Alone and none else) before. Verily,
He is Al¬Barr (the Most Subtle, Kind, Courteous, and
Generous), the Most Merciful." (28)

## Quran 52:45-47

فَذَرْهُمْ حَتَّىٰ يُلَٰقُوا۟ يَوْمَهُمُ ٱلَّذِى فِيهِ يُصْعَقُونَ (٤٥) يَوْمَ لَا
يُغْنِى عَنْهُمْ كَيْدُهُمْ شَيْـًٔا وَلَا هُمْ يُنصَرُونَ (٤٦) وَإِنَّ لِلَّذِينَ
ظَلَمُوا۟ عَذَابًا دُونَ ذَٰلِكَ وَلَٰكِنَّ أَكْثَرَهُمْ لَا يَعْلَمُونَ (٤٧)

So leave them alone till they meet their Day, in which
they will sink into a fainting (with horror). (45) The Day
when their plotting shall not avail them at all nor will
they be helped (i.e. they will receive their torment in
Hell). (46) And verily, for those who do wrong, there is
another punishment (i.e. the torment in this world and in
their graves) before this, but most of them know not. (47)

## Quran 53:31

وَلِلَّهِ مَا فِى ٱلسَّمَٰوَٰتِ وَمَا فِى ٱلْأَرْضِ لِيَجْزِىَ ٱلَّذِينَ
أَسَٰٔٓوا۟ بِمَا عَمِلُوا۟ وَيَجْزِىَ ٱلَّذِينَ أَحْسَنُوا۟ بِٱلْحُسْنَى

And to Allâh belongs all that is in the heavens and all
that is in the earth, that He may requite those who do evil
with that which they have done (i.e. punish them in
Hell), and reward those who do good, with what is best
(i.e. Paradise). (31)

## Quran 53:38-44

أَلَّا تَزِرُ وَازِرَةٌ وِزْرَ أُخْرَىٰ (٣٨) وَأَن لَّيْسَ لِلْإِنسَٰنِ إِلَّا مَا
سَعَىٰ (٣٩) وَأَنَّ سَعْيَهُۥ سَوْفَ يُرَىٰ (٤٠) ثُمَّ يُجْزَىٰهُ ٱلْجَزَآءَ
ٱلْأَوْفَىٰ (٤١) وَأَنَّ إِلَىٰ رَبِّكَ ٱلْمُنتَهَىٰ (٤٢) وَأَنَّهُۥ هُوَ
أَضْحَكَ وَأَبْكَىٰ (٤٣) وَأَنَّهُۥ هُوَ أَمَاتَ وَأَحْيَا (٤٤)

*That no burdened person (with sins) shall bear the
burden (sins) of another. (38) And that man can have
nothing but what he does (good or bad), (39) And that
his deeds will be seen, (40) Then he will be recompensed
with a full and the best recompense (41) And that to your
Lord (Allâh) is the End (Return of everything). (42) And
that it is He (Allâh) Who makes (whom He wills) laugh,
and makes (whom He wills) weep. (43) And that it is He
(Allâh) Who causes death and gives life. (44)*

## Quran 53:47

وَأَنَّ عَلَيْهِ ٱلنَّشْأَةَ ٱلْأُخْرَىٰ

*And that upon Him (Allâh) is another bringing forth
(Resurrection). (47)*

## Quran 53:57-58

أَزِفَتِ ٱلْأَزِفَةُ (٥٧) لَيْسَ لَهَا مِن دُونِ ٱللَّهِ كَاشِفَةٌ (٥٨)

*The Day of Resurrection draws near, (57) None besides
Allâh can avert it, (or advance it, or delay it). (58)*

## Quran 54:3-8

وَكَذَّبُواْ وَٱتَّبَعُواْ أَهْوَآءَهُمْ وَكُلُّ أَمْرٍ مُّسْتَقِرٌّ (٣) وَلَقَدْ
جَآءَهُم مِّنَ ٱلْأَنۢبَآءِ مَا فِيهِ مُزْدَجَرٌ (٤) حِكْمَةٌۢ بَٰلِغَةٌۖ فَمَا تُغْنِ
ٱلنُّذُرُ (٥) فَتَوَلَّ عَنْهُمْۘ يَوْمَ يَدْعُ ٱلدَّاعِ إِلَىٰ شَىْءٍ نُّكُرٍ
(٦) خُشَّعًا أَبْصَٰرُهُمْ يَخْرُجُونَ مِنَ ٱلْأَجْدَاثِ كَأَنَّهُمْ جَرَادٌ
مُّنتَشِرٌ (٧) مُّهْطِعِينَ إِلَى ٱلدَّاعِۖ يَقُولُ ٱلْكَٰفِرُونَ هَٰذَا يَوْمٌ
عَسِرٌ (٨)

They belied (the Verses of Allâh, this Qur'ân), and
followed their own lusts. And every matter will be settled
[according to the kind of deeds (good deeds will take their
doers to Paradise, and similarly evil deeds will take their
doers to Hell)]. (3) And indeed there has come to them
news (in this Qur'ân) wherein there is (enough warning)
to check (them from evil), (4) Perfect wisdom (this
Qur'ân), but (the preaching of) warners benefit them not,
(5) So (O Muhammad) withdraw from them. The Day
that the caller will call (them) to a terrible thing. (6) They
will come forth, with humbled eyes from (their) graves as
if they were locusts spread abroad, (7) Hastening towards
The caller, the disbelievers will say: "This is a hard Day."
(8)

## Quran 54:40

وَلَقَدْ يَسَّرْنَا ٱلْقُرْءَانَ لِلذِّكْرِ فَهَلْ مِن مُّدَّكِرٍ

And indeed, We have made the Qur'ân easy to understand and remember, then is there any that will remember (or receive admonition)? (40)

## Quran 54:45-50

سَيُهْزَمُ ٱلْجَمْعُ وَيُوَلُّونَ ٱلدُّبُرَ (٤٥) بَلِ ٱلسَّاعَةُ مَوْعِدُهُمْ وَٱلسَّاعَةُ أَدْهَىٰ وَأَمَرُّ (٤٦) إِنَّ ٱلْمُجْرِمِينَ فِى ضَلَٰلٍ وَسُعُرٍ (٤٧) يَوْمَ يُسْحَبُونَ فِى ٱلنَّارِ عَلَىٰ وُجُوهِهِمْ ذُوقُواْ مَسَّ سَقَرَ (٤٨) إِنَّا كُلَّ شَىْءٍ خَلَقْنَٰهُ بِقَدَرٍ (٤٩) وَمَآ أَمْرُنَآ إِلَّا وَٰحِدَةٌ كَلَمْحِ بِٱلْبَصَرِ (٥٠)

Their multitude will be put to flight, and they will show their backs. (45) Nay, but the Hour is their appointed time (for their full recompense), and the Hour will be more grievous and more bitter. (46) Verily, the Mujrimûn (polytheists, disbelievers, sinners, criminals) are in error (in this world) and will burn (in the Hell-fire in the Hereafter). (47) The Day they will be dragged on their faces into the Fire (it will be said to them): "Taste you the touch of Hell!" (48) Verily, We have created all things with Qadar (Divine Preordainments of all things before their creation, as written in the Book of Decrees Al-Lauh Al-Mahfûz). (49) And Our Commandment is but one, as the twinkling of an eye. (50)

## Quran 54:52-55

وَكُلُّ شَىۡءٍ فَعَلُوهُ فِى ٱلزُّبُرِ (٥٢) وَكُلُّ صَغِيرٍ وَكَبِيرٍ مُّسۡتَطَرٌ (٥٣) إِنَّ ٱلۡمُتَّقِينَ فِى جَنَّٰتٍ وَنَهَرٍ (٥٤) فِى مَقۡعَدِ صِدۡقٍ عِندَ مَلِيكٍ مُّقۡتَدِرٍ (٥٥)

*And everything they have done is noted in (their) Records (of deeds). (52) And everything, small and big, is written down (in Al-Lauh Al-Mahfûz). (53) Verily, The Muttaqûn (the pious - see V.2:2), will be in the midst of Gardens and Rivers (Paradise). (54) In a seat of truth (i.e. Paradise), near the Omnipotent King (Allâh the one, the All-Blessed, the Most High, the Owner of Majesty and Honour). (55)*

## Quran 55:26-27

كُلُّ مَنۡ عَلَيۡهَا فَانٍ (٢٦) وَيَبۡقَىٰ وَجۡهُ رَبِّكَ ذُو ٱلۡجَلَٰلِ وَٱلۡإِكۡرَامِ (٢٧)

*Whatsoever is on it (the earth) will perish. (26) And the Face of your Lord full of Majesty and Honour will remain forever. (27)*

## Quran 55:31-76

سَنَفۡرُغُ لَكُمۡ أَيُّهَ ٱلثَّقَلَانِ (٣١) فَبِأَىِّ ءَالَآءِ رَبِّكُمَا تُكَذِّبَانِ (٣٢) يَٰمَعۡشَرَ ٱلۡجِنِّ وَٱلۡإِنسِ إِنِ ٱسۡتَطَعۡتُمۡ أَن تَنفُذُواْ مِنۡ أَقۡطَارِ ٱلسَّمَٰوَٰتِ وَٱلۡأَرۡضِ فَٱنفُذُواْ لَا تَنفُذُونَ إِلَّا بِسُلۡطَٰنٍ (٣٣) فَبِأَىِّ ءَالَآءِ رَبِّكُمَا تُكَذِّبَانِ (٣٤) يُرۡسَلُ عَلَيۡكُمَا شُوَاظٌ

مِّن نَّارٍ وَنُحَاسٌ فَلَا تَنتَصِرَانِ (٣٥) فَبِأَيِّ ءَالَآءِ رَبِّكُمَا
تُكَذِّبَانِ (٣٦) فَإِذَا ٱنشَقَّتِ ٱلسَّمَآءُ فَكَانَتْ وَرْدَةً كَٱلدِّهَانِ
(٣٧) فَبِأَيِّ ءَالَآءِ رَبِّكُمَا تُكَذِّبَانِ (٣٨) فَيَوْمَئِذٍ لَّا يُسْـَٔلُ عَن
ذَنۢبِهِۦٓ إِنسٌ وَلَا جَآنٌّ (٣٩) فَبِأَيِّ ءَالَآءِ رَبِّكُمَا تُكَذِّبَانِ
(٤٠) يُعْرَفُ ٱلْمُجْرِمُونَ بِسِيمَٰهُمْ فَيُؤْخَذُ بِٱلنَّوَٰصِى وَٱلْأَقْدَامِ
(٤١) فَبِأَيِّ ءَالَآءِ رَبِّكُمَا تُكَذِّبَانِ (٤٢) هَٰذِهِۦ جَهَنَّمُ ٱلَّتِى
يُكَذِّبُ بِهَا ٱلْمُجْرِمُونَ (٤٣) يَطُوفُونَ بَيْنَهَا وَبَيْنَ حَمِيمٍ ءَانٍ
(٤٤) فَبِأَيِّ ءَالَآءِ رَبِّكُمَا تُكَذِّبَانِ (٤٥) وَلِمَنْ خَافَ مَقَامَ رَبِّهِۦ
جَنَّتَانِ (٤٦) فَبِأَيِّ ءَالَآءِ رَبِّكُمَا تُكَذِّبَانِ (٤٧) ذَوَاتَآ أَفْنَانٍ
(٤٨) فَبِأَيِّ ءَالَآءِ رَبِّكُمَا تُكَذِّبَانِ (٤٩) فِيهِمَا عَيْنَانِ تَجْرِيَانِ
(٥٠) فَبِأَيِّ ءَالَآءِ رَبِّكُمَا تُكَذِّبَانِ (٥١) فِيهِمَا مِن كُلِّ فَٰكِهَةٍ
زَوْجَانِ (٥٢) فَبِأَيِّ ءَالَآءِ رَبِّكُمَا تُكَذِّبَانِ (٥٣) مُتَّكِئِينَ عَلَىٰ
فُرُشٍ بَطَآئِنُهَا مِنْ إِسْتَبْرَقٍ وَجَنَى ٱلْجَنَّتَيْنِ دَانٍ (٥٤) فَبِأَيِّ
ءَالَآءِ رَبِّكُمَا تُكَذِّبَانِ (٥٥) فِيهِنَّ قَٰصِرَٰتُ ٱلطَّرْفِ لَمْ
يَطْمِثْهُنَّ إِنسٌ قَبْلَهُمْ وَلَا جَآنٌّ (٥٦) فَبِأَيِّ ءَالَآءِ رَبِّكُمَا تُكَذِّبَانِ
(٥٧) كَأَنَّهُنَّ ٱلْيَاقُوتُ وَٱلْمَرْجَانُ (٥٨) فَبِأَيِّ ءَالَآءِ رَبِّكُمَا
تُكَذِّبَانِ (٥٩) هَلْ جَزَآءُ ٱلْإِحْسَٰنِ إِلَّا ٱلْإِحْسَٰنُ (٦٠) فَبِأَيِّ
ءَالَآءِ رَبِّكُمَا تُكَذِّبَانِ (٦١) وَمِن دُونِهِمَا جَنَّتَانِ (٦٢) فَبِأَيِّ
ءَالَآءِ رَبِّكُمَا تُكَذِّبَانِ (٦٣) مُدْهَآمَّتَانِ (٦٤) فَبِأَيِّ ءَالَآءِ
رَبِّكُمَا تُكَذِّبَانِ (٦٥) فِيهِمَا عَيْنَانِ نَضَّاخَتَانِ (٦٦) فَبِأَيِّ
ءَالَآءِ رَبِّكُمَا تُكَذِّبَانِ (٦٧) فِيهِمَا فَٰكِهَةٌ وَنَخْلٌ وَرُمَّانٌ
(٦٨) فَبِأَيِّ ءَالَآءِ رَبِّكُمَا تُكَذِّبَانِ (٦٩) فِيهِنَّ خَيْرَٰتٌ حِسَانٌ

فَبِأَيِّ ءَالَاءِ رَبِّكُمَا تُكَذِّبَانِ (٧٠) حُورٌ مَّقْصُورَاتٌ فِى
ٱلْخِيَامِ (٧٢) فَبِأَيِّ ءَالَاءِ رَبِّكُمَا تُكَذِّبَانِ (٧٣) لَمْ يَطْمِثْهُنَّ
إِنسٌ قَبْلَهُمْ وَلَا جَآنٌّ (٧٤) فَبِأَيِّ ءَالَاءِ رَبِّكُمَا تُكَذِّبَانِ
(٧٥) مُتَّكِئِينَ عَلَىٰ رَفْرَفٍ خُضْرٍ وَعَبْقَرِيٍّ حِسَانٍ (٧٦)

*We shall attend to you, O you two classes (jinn and men)! (31) Then which of the Blessings of your Lord will you both (jinn and men) deny? (32) O assembly of jinn and men! If you have power to pass beyond the zones of the heavens and the earth, then pass beyond (them)! But you will never be able to pass them, except with authority (from Allâh)! (33) Then which of the Blessings of your Lord will you both (jinn and men) deny? (34) There will be sent against you both, smokeless flames of fire and (molten) brass, and you will not be able to defend yourselves. (35) Then which of the Blessings of your Lord will you both (jinn and men) deny? (36) Then when the heaven is rent asunder, and it becomes rosy or red like red-oil, or red hide (37) Then which of the Blessings of your Lord will you both (jinn and men) deny? (38) So on that Day no question will be asked of man or jinni as to his sin, [because they have already been known from their faces either white (dwellers of Paradise - true believers of Islamic Monotheism) or black (dwellers of Hell - polytheists; disbelievers, criminals)]. (39) Then which of the Blessings of your Lord will you both (jinn and men) deny? (40) The Mujrimûn (polytheists, criminals, sinners) will be known by their marks (black faces), and they will be seized by their forelocks and their feet. (41) Then which of the Blessings of your Lord will you both (jinn and men) deny? (42) This is Hell which the Mujrimûn (polytheists, criminals, sinners) denied. (43) They will go between it (Hell) and the fierce boiling water! (44) Then which of the Blessings of your Lord will you both (jinn and men) deny? (45) But for him who fears the standing before his Lord, there will be two Gardens (i.e. in Paradise). (46) Then which of the Blessings of your Lord will you both (jinn and men) deny? (47) With spreading branches. (48) Then which of the Blessings of your Lord will you both (jinn and men) deny? (49) In them (both) will be two springs flowing (free). (50) Then which of the Blessings of your Lord will you both (jinn and men) deny? (51) In them (both) will be every kind of fruit in pairs. (52) Then which of the Blessings of your Lord will you both (jinn and men) deny? (53) Reclining upon the couches lined with silk brocade, and the fruits of the two Gardens will be near at hand. (54) Then which of the Blessings of your Lord will you both (jinn and men) deny? (55) Wherein both will be Qasirat-ut-Tarf [chaste fmales (wives) restraining their glances, desiring none except their husbands], with whom no man or jinni has had Tamth before them. (56) Then which of the Blessings of your Lord will you both (jinn and men) deny? (57) (In beauty) they are like rubies and coral. (58) Then which of the Blessings of your Lord will you both (jinn and men) deny? (59) Is there any reward for good other than good? (60) Then which of the Blessings of your Lord will you both (jinn and men) deny? (61) And besides these two, there are two other Gardens (i.e. in Paradise). (62) Then which of the Blessings of your Lord will you both (jinn and men) deny? (63) Dark green (in colour). (64) Then which of the Blessings of your Lord will you both (jinn and men) deny? (65) In them (both) will be two springs gushing forth. (66) Then which of the Blessings of your Lord will you both (jinn and men) deny? (67) In them (both) will be fruits, and date- palms and pomegranates. (68) Then which of the Blessings of your Lord will you both (jinn and men) deny? (69) Therein (Gardens) will be Khairâtun-Hisân [fair (wives) good and beautiful]. (70) Then which of the Blessings of your Lord will you both (jinn and men) deny? (71) Hûr (beautiful, fair females) guarded in pavilions; (72) Then which of the Blessings of your Lord will you both (jinn and men) deny? (73) With Whom no man or jinni has had Tameth before them. (74) Then which of the Blessings of your Lord will you both (jinn and men) deny? (75) Reclining on green cushions and rich beautiful mattresses. (76)*

**Quran 56:1-56**

إِذَا وَقَعَتِ ٱلْوَاقِعَةُ (١) لَيْسَ لِوَقْعَتِهَا كَاذِبَةٌ (٢) خَافِضَةٌ رَّافِعَةٌ (٣) إِذَا رُجَّتِ ٱلْأَرْضُ رَجًّا (٤) وَبُسَّتِ ٱلْجِبَالُ بَسًّا (٥) فَكَانَتْ هَبَآءً مُّنبَثًّا (٦) وَكُنتُمْ أَزْوَاجًا ثَلَٰثَةً (٧) فَأَصْحَٰبُ ٱلْمَيْمَنَةِ مَآ أَصْحَٰبُ ٱلْمَيْمَنَةِ (٨) وَأَصْحَٰبُ ٱلْمَشْئَمَةِ مَآ أَصْحَٰبُ ٱلْمَشْئَمَةِ (٩) وَٱلسَّٰبِقُونَ ٱلسَّٰبِقُونَ (١٠) أُو۟لَٰٓئِكَ ٱلْمُقَرَّبُونَ (١١) فِى جَنَّٰتِ ٱلنَّعِيمِ (١٢) ثُلَّةٌ مِّنَ ٱلْأَوَّلِينَ (١٣) وَقَلِيلٌ مِّنَ ٱلْءَاخِرِينَ (١٤) عَلَىٰ سُرُرٍ مَّوْضُونَةٍ (١٥) مُّتَّكِئِينَ عَلَيْهَا مُتَقَٰبِلِينَ (١٦) يَطُوفُ عَلَيْهِمْ وِلْدَٰنٌ مُّخَلَّدُونَ (١٧) بِأَكْوَابٍ وَأَبَارِيقَ وَكَأْسٍ مِّن مَّعِينٍ (١٨) لَّا يُصَدَّعُونَ عَنْهَا وَلَا يُنزِفُونَ (١٩) وَفَٰكِهَةٍ مِّمَّا يَتَخَيَّرُونَ (٢٠) وَلَحْمِ طَيْرٍ مِّمَّا يَشْتَهُونَ (٢١) وَحُورٌ عِينٌ (٢٢) كَأَمْثَٰلِ ٱللُّؤْلُؤِ ٱلْمَكْنُونِ (٢٣) جَزَآءً بِمَا كَانُوا۟ يَعْمَلُونَ (٢٤) لَا يَسْمَعُونَ فِيهَا لَغْوًا وَلَا تَأْثِيمًا (٢٥) إِلَّا قِيلًا سَلَٰمًا سَلَٰمًا (٢٦) وَأَصْحَٰبُ ٱلْيَمِينِ مَآ أَصْحَٰبُ ٱلْيَمِينِ (٢٧) فِى سِدْرٍ مَّخْضُودٍ (٢٨) وَطَلْحٍ مَّنضُودٍ (٢٩) وَظِلٍّ مَّمْدُودٍ (٣٠) وَمَآءٍ مَّسْكُوبٍ (٣١) وَفَٰكِهَةٍ كَثِيرَةٍ (٣٢) لَّا مَقْطُوعَةٍ وَلَا مَمْنُوعَةٍ (٣٣) وَفُرُشٍ مَّرْفُوعَةٍ (٣٤) إِنَّآ أَنشَأْنَٰهُنَّ إِنشَآءً (٣٥) فَجَعَلْنَٰهُنَّ أَبْكَارًا (٣٦) عُرُبًا أَتْرَابًا (٣٧) لِّأَصْحَٰبِ ٱلْيَمِينِ (٣٨) ثُلَّةٌ مِّنَ ٱلْأَوَّلِينَ (٣٩) وَثُلَّةٌ مِّنَ ٱلْءَاخِرِينَ (٤٠) وَأَصْحَٰبُ ٱلشِّمَالِ مَآ أَصْحَٰبُ ٱلشِّمَالِ (٤١) فِى سَمُومٍ وَحَمِيمٍ (٤٢) وَظِلٍّ مِّن يَحْمُومٍ (٤٣) لَّا بَارِدٍ وَلَا كَرِيمٍ (٤٤) إِنَّهُمْ كَانُوا۟ قَبْلَ ذَٰلِكَ مُتْرَفِينَ

(٤٥) وَكَانُواْ يُصِرُّونَ عَلَى ٱلۡحِنثِ ٱلۡعَظِيمِ (٤٦) وَكَانُواْ
يَقُولُونَ أَئِذَا مِتۡنَا وَكُنَّا تُرَابًا وَعِظَٰمًا أَءِنَّا لَمَبۡعُوثُونَ
(٤٧) أَوَءَابَآؤُنَا ٱلۡأَوَّلُونَ (٤٨) قُلۡ إِنَّ ٱلۡأَوَّلِينَ وَٱلۡأَخِرِينَ
(٤٩) لَمَجۡمُوعُونَ إِلَىٰ مِيقَٰتِ يَوۡمٍ مَّعۡلُومٍ (٥٠) ثُمَّ إِنَّكُمۡ أَيُّهَا
ٱلضَّآلُّونَ ٱلۡمُكَذِّبُونَ (٥١) لَأَكِلُونَ مِن شَجَرٍ مِّن زَقُّومٍ
(٥٢) فَمَالِئُونَ مِنۡهَا ٱلۡبُطُونَ (٥٣) فَشَٰرِبُونَ عَلَيۡهِ مِنَ ٱلۡحَمِيمِ
(٥٤) فَشَٰرِبُونَ شُرۡبَ ٱلۡهِيمِ (٥٥) هَٰذَا نُزُلُهُمۡ يَوۡمَ ٱلدِّينِ
(٥٦)

*When the Event (i.e. the Day of Resurrection) befalls.*
*(1) And there can be no denyial of its befalling.*
*(2) Bringing low (some — those who will enter Hell)*
*Exalting (others- those who will enter Paradise).*
*(3) When the earth will be shaken with a terrible shake.*
*(4) And the mountains will be powdered to dust. (5) So*
*that they will become floating dust particles. (6) And you*
*(all) will be in three groups. (7) So those on the Right*
*Hand (i.e. those who will be given their Records in their*
*right hands) — how (fortunate) will be those on the*
*Right Hand! (As a respect for them, because they will*
*enter Paradise). (8) And those on the Left Hand (i.e.*
*those who will be given their Record in their left hands)*
*— how (unfortunate) will be those on the Left Hand? (As*
*a disgrace for them, because they will enter Hell).*
*(9) And those foremost [[in Islâmic Faith of Monotheism*
*and in performing righteous deeds) in the life of this*

*world on the very first call for to embrace Islâm,] will be foremost (in Paradise). (10) These will be those nearest (to Allâh). (11) In the Gardens of Delight (Paradise). (12) A multitude of those (foremost) will be from the first generations (who embraced Islâm). (13) And a few of those (foremost) will be from the later generations. (14) (They will be) on thrones woven with gold and precious stones, (15) Reclining thereon, face to face. (16) Immortal boys will go around them (serving). (17) With cups, and jugs, and a glass of the flowing wine, (18) Wherefrom they will get neither any aching of the head, nor any intoxication. (19) And with fruit, that they may choose. (20) And with the flesh of fowls that they desire. (21) And (there will be) Hur (fair females) with wide, lovely eyes (as wives for the pious), (22) Like unto preserved pearls. (23) A reward for what they used to do. (24) No Laghw (dirty, false, evil vain talk) will they hear therein, nor any sinful speech (like backbiting). (25) But only the saying of: Salâm!, Salâm! (greetings with peace)! (26) And those on the Right Hand- how (fortunate) will be those on the Right Hand? (27) (They will be) among thornless lote-trees, (28) And Among Talh (banana-trees) with fruits piled one above another, (29) In shade long-extended, (30) And by water flowing constantly, (31) And fruit in plenty, (32) Whose supply is not cut off (by change of season) nor are they out of reach. (33) And on couches or thrones, raised high.*

(34) Verily, We have created them (maidens) of special creation. (35) And made them virgins. (36) Loving (their husbands only), (and) of equal age. (37) For those on the Right Hand. (38) A multitude of those (on the Right Hand) will be from the first generation (who embraced Islâm). (39) And a multitude of those (on the Right Hand) will be from the later generations. (40) And those on the Left Hand how (unfortunate) will be those on the Left Hand? (41) In fierce hot wind and boiling water. (42) And shadow of black smoke. (43) (That shadow) neither cool, nor (even) pleasant, (44) Verily, before that, they indulged in luxury, (45) And were persisting in great sin (joining partners in worship along with Allâh, committing murder and other crimes). (46) And they used to say: "When we die and become dust and bones, shall we then indeed be resurrected? (47) "And also our forefathers?" (48) Say (O Muhammad): "(Yes) verily, those of old, and those of later times. (49) "All will surely be gathered together for appointed Meeting of a known Day. (50) "Then moreover, verily, you the erring-ones, the deniers (of Resurrection)! (51) "You verily will eat of the trees of Zaqqûm. (52) "Then you will fill your bellies therewith, (53) "And drink boiling water on top of it. (54) "And you will drink (that) like thirsty camels!" (55) That will be their entertainment on the Day of Recompense! (56)

## Quran 56:60-61

413

نَحْنُ قَدَّرْنَا بَيْنَكُمُ ٱلْمَوْتَ وَمَا نَحْنُ بِمَسْبُوقِينَ (٦٠) عَلَىٰ أَن نُّبَدِّلَ أَمْثَٰلَكُمْ وَنُنشِئَكُمْ فِى مَا لَا تَعْلَمُونَ (٦١)

*We have decreed death to you all, and We are not outstripped, (60) To transfigure you and create you in (forms) that you know not. (61)*

## Quran 56:88-95

فَأَمَّآ إِن كَانَ مِنَ ٱلْمُقَرَّبِينَ (٨٨) فَرَوْحٌ وَرَيْحَانٌ وَجَنَّتُ نَعِيمٍ (٨٩) وَأَمَّآ إِن كَانَ مِنْ أَصْحَٰبِ ٱلْيَمِينِ (٩٠) فَسَلَٰمٌ لَّكَ مِنْ أَصْحَٰبِ ٱلْيَمِينِ (٩١) وَأَمَّآ إِن كَانَ مِنَ ٱلْمُكَذِّبِينَ ٱلضَّآلِّينَ (٩٢) فَنُزُلٌ مِّنْ حَمِيمٍ (٩٣) وَتَصْلِيَةُ جَحِيمٍ (٩٤) إِنَّ هَٰذَا لَهُوَ حَقُّ ٱلْيَقِينِ (٩٥)

*Then, if he (the dying person) be of the Muqarrabûn (those brought near to Allâh), (88) (There is for him) rest and provision, and a Garden of Delights (Paradise). (89) And if he (the dying person) be of those on the Right Hand, (90) Then there is safety and peace (from the Punishment of Allâh) for those on the Right Hand. (91) But if he (the dying person) be of the denying (of the Resurrection), the erring (away from the Right Path of Islâmic Monotheism), (92) Then for him is entertainment with boiling water. (93) And burning in Hell-fire. (94) Verily, this! This is an absolute Truth with certainty. (95)*

## Quran 57:2

لَهُۥ مُلْكُ ٱلسَّمَٰوَٰتِ وَٱلْأَرْضِ ۖ يُحْىِۦ وَيُمِيتُ ۖ وَهُوَ عَلَىٰ كُلِّ شَىْءٍ قَدِيرٌ

*His is the kingdom of the heavens and the earth, It is He Who gives life and causes death; and He is Able to do all things. (2)*

## Quran 57:5

لَّهُۥ مُلْكُ ٱلسَّمَٰوَٰتِ وَٱلْأَرْضِ ۚ وَإِلَى ٱللَّهِ تُرْجَعُ ٱلْأُمُورُ

*His is the kingdom of the heavens and the earth. And to Allâh return all the matters (for decision). (5)*

## Quran 57:7

ءَامِنُوا۟ بِٱللَّهِ وَرَسُولِهِۦ وَأَنفِقُوا۟ مِمَّا جَعَلَكُم مُّسْتَخْلَفِينَ فِيهِ ۖ فَٱلَّذِينَ ءَامَنُوا۟ مِنكُمْ وَأَنفَقُوا۟ لَهُمْ أَجْرٌ كَبِيرٌ

*Believe in Allâh and His Messenger (Muhammad), and spend of that whereof He has made you trustees. And such of you as believe and spend (in Allâh's Way), theirs will be a great reward. (7)*

## Quran 57:10-15

وَمَا لَكُمْ أَلَّا تُنفِقُوا۟ فِى سَبِيلِ ٱللَّهِ وَلِلَّهِ مِيرَٰثُ ٱلسَّمَٰوَٰتِ وَٱلْأَرْضِ ۚ لَا يَسْتَوِى مِنكُم مَّنْ أَنفَقَ مِن قَبْلِ ٱلْفَتْحِ وَقَٰتَلَ ۚ أُو۟لَٰٓئِكَ أَعْظَمُ دَرَجَةً مِّنَ ٱلَّذِينَ أَنفَقُوا۟ مِنۢ بَعْدُ وَقَٰتَلُوا۟ ۚ وَكُلًّا

415

وَعَدَ اللَّهُ الْحُسْنَىٰ ۚ وَاللَّهُ بِمَا تَعْمَلُونَ خَبِيرٌ ﴿١٠﴾ مَّن ذَا الَّذِى يُقْرِضُ اللَّهَ قَرْضًا حَسَنًا فَيُضَاعِفَهُ لَهُ وَلَهُ أَجْرٌ كَرِيمٌ ﴿١١﴾ يَوْمَ تَرَى الْمُؤْمِنِينَ وَالْمُؤْمِنَاتِ يَسْعَىٰ نُورُهُم بَيْنَ أَيْدِيهِمْ وَبِأَيْمَانِهِم بُشْرَاكُمُ الْيَوْمَ جَنَّاتٌ تَجْرِى مِن تَحْتِهَا الْأَنْهَارُ خَالِدِينَ فِيهَا ذَٰلِكَ هُوَ الْفَوْزُ الْعَظِيمُ ﴿١٢﴾ يَوْمَ يَقُولُ الْمُنَافِقُونَ وَالْمُنَافِقَاتُ لِلَّذِينَ آمَنُوا انظُرُونَا نَقْتَبِسْ مِن نُّورِكُمْ قِيلَ ارْجِعُوا وَرَاءَكُمْ فَالْتَمِسُوا نُورًا فَضُرِبَ بَيْنَهُم بِسُورٍ لَّهُ بَابٌ بَاطِنُهُ فِيهِ الرَّحْمَةُ وَظَاهِرُهُ مِن قِبَلِهِ الْعَذَابُ ﴿١٣﴾ يُنَادُونَهُمْ أَلَمْ نَكُن مَّعَكُمْ ۖ قَالُوا بَلَىٰ وَلَٰكِنَّكُمْ فَتَنتُمْ أَنفُسَكُمْ وَتَرَبَّصْتُمْ وَارْتَبْتُمْ وَغَرَّتْكُمُ الْأَمَانِيُّ حَتَّىٰ جَاءَ أَمْرُ اللَّهِ وَغَرَّكُم بِاللَّهِ الْغَرُورُ ﴿١٤﴾ فَالْيَوْمَ لَا يُؤْخَذُ مِنكُمْ فِدْيَةٌ وَلَا مِنَ الَّذِينَ كَفَرُوا ۚ مَأْوَاكُمُ النَّارُ ۖ هِيَ مَوْلَاكُمْ ۖ وَبِئْسَ الْمَصِيرُ ﴿١٥﴾

*And what is the matter with you that you spend not in the Cause of Allâh? And to Allâh belongs the heritage of the heavens and the earth. Not equal among you are those who spent and fought before the conquering (of Makkah with those among you who did so later). Such are higher in degree than those who spent and fought afterwards. But to all, Allâh has promised the best (reward). And Allâh is All-Aware of what you do. (10) Who is he that will lend Allâh a goodly loan, then (Allâh) will increase it manifold to his credit (in repaying), and he will have (besides) a good reward (i.e. Paradise). (11) On the Day* you shall see the believing men and the believing women their light running forward before them and by their right hands. Glad tidings for you this Day! Gardens under which rivers flow (Paradise), to dwell therein forever! Truly, this is the great success! (12) On the Day when the hypocrites men and women will say to the believers: "Wait for us! Let us get something from your light!" It will be said: "Go back to your rear! Then seek a light!" So a wall will be put up between them, with a gate therein. Inside it will be mercy, and outside it will be torment." (13) (The hypocrites) will call the believers: "Were we not with you?" The believers will reply: "Yes! But you led yourselves into temptations, you looked forward for our destruction; you doubted (in Faith); and you were deceived by false desires, till the Command of Allâh came to pass. And the chief deceiver (Satan) deceived you in respect of Allâh." (14) So this Day no ransom shall be taken from you (hypocrites), nor of those who disbelieved, (in the Oneness of Allâh Islâmic Monotheism). Your abode is the Fire, That is your maula (friend — proper place), and worst indeed is that destination. (15)

## Quran 57:18-22

إِنَّ ٱلْمُصَّدِّقِينَ وَٱلْمُصَّدِّقَٰتِ وَأَقْرَضُوا۟ ٱللَّهَ قَرْضًا حَسَنًا يُضَٰعَفُ لَهُمْ وَلَهُمْ أَجْرٌ كَرِيمٌ (١٨) وَٱلَّذِينَ ءَامَنُوا۟ بِٱللَّهِ وَرُسُلِهِ أُو۟لَٰٓئِكَ هُمُ ٱلصِّدِّيقُونَ وَٱلشُّهَدَآءُ عِندَ رَبِّهِمْ لَهُمْ أَجْرُهُمْ

وَنُورُهُمْ ۗ وَٱلَّذِينَ كَفَرُواْ وَكَذَّبُواْ بِـَٔايَٰتِنَآ أُوْلَٰٓئِكَ أَصْحَٰبُ ٱلْجَحِيمِ (١٩) ٱعْلَمُوٓاْ أَنَّمَا ٱلْحَيَوٰةُ ٱلدُّنْيَا لَعِبٌ وَلَهْوٌ وَزِينَةٌ وَتَفَاخُرٌ بَيْنَكُمْ وَتَكَاثُرٌ فِى ٱلْأَمْوَٰلِ وَٱلْأَوْلَٰدِ ۖ كَمَثَلِ غَيْثٍ أَعْجَبَ ٱلْكُفَّارَ نَبَاتُهُۥ ثُمَّ يَهِيجُ فَتَرَىٰهُ مُصْفَرًّا ثُمَّ يَكُونُ حُطَٰمًا ۖ وَفِى ٱلْأَخِرَةِ عَذَابٌ شَدِيدٌ وَمَغْفِرَةٌ مِّنَ ٱللَّهِ وَرِضْوَٰنٌ ۚ وَمَا ٱلْحَيَوٰةُ ٱلدُّنْيَآ إِلَّا مَتَٰعُ ٱلْغُرُورِ (٢٠) سَابِقُوٓاْ إِلَىٰ مَغْفِرَةٍ مِّن رَّبِّكُمْ وَجَنَّةٍ عَرْضُهَا كَعَرْضِ ٱلسَّمَآءِ وَٱلْأَرْضِ أُعِدَّتْ لِلَّذِينَ ءَامَنُواْ بِٱللَّهِ وَرُسُلِهِۦ ۚ ذَٰلِكَ فَضْلُ ٱللَّهِ يُؤْتِيهِ مَن يَشَآءُ ۚ وَٱللَّهُ ذُو ٱلْفَضْلِ ٱلْعَظِيمِ (٢١) مَآ أَصَابَ مِن مُّصِيبَةٍ فِى ٱلْأَرْضِ وَلَا فِىٓ أَنفُسِكُمْ إِلَّا فِى كِتَٰبٍ مِّن قَبْلِ أَن نَّبْرَأَهَآ ۚ إِنَّ ذَٰلِكَ عَلَى ٱللَّهِ يَسِيرٌ (٢٢)

*Verily, those who give Sadaqât (i.e. Zakât and alms, etc.), men and women, and lend Allâh a goodly loan, it shall be increased manifold (to their credit), and theirs shall be an honourable good reward (i.e. Paradise). (18) And those who believe in (the Oneness of) Allâh and His Messengers, they are the Siddiqûn (i.e. those followers of the Prophets who were first and foremost to believe in them), and the martyrs with their Lord, they shall have their reward and their light. But those who disbelieve (in the Oneness of Allâh - Islâmic Monotheism) and deny Our Ayât (proofs, evidences, verses, lessons, signs, revelations, etc.), they shall be the dwellers of the blazing Fire. (19) Know that the life of this world is only play* and amusement, pomp and mutual boasting among you, and rivalry in respect of wealth and children, (it is) as the likeness of vegetation after rain, thereof the growth is pleasing to the tiller; afterwards it dries up and you see it turning yellow; then it becomes straw. But in the Hereafter (there is) a severe torment (for the disbelievers, evil-doers), and (there is) Forgiveness from Allâh and (His) Good Pleasure (for the believers – good-doers), And the life of this world is only a deceiving enjoyment. (20) Race with one another in hastening towards forgiveness from your Lord (Allâh), and Paradise the width whereof is as the width of the heaven and the earth, prepared for those who believe in Allâh and His Messengers. That is the Grace of Allâh which He bestows on whom He is pleased with. And Allâh is the Owner of Great Bounty. (21) No calamity befalls on the earth or in yourselves but is inscribed in the Book of Decrees (Al-Lauh Al-Mahfûz), before We bring it into existence. Verily, that is easy for Allâh. (22)

## Quran 57:28

يَـٰٓأَيُّهَا ٱلَّذِينَ ءَامَنُوا۟ ٱتَّقُوا۟ ٱللَّهَ وَءَامِنُوا۟ بِرَسُولِهِۦ يُؤْتِكُمْ كِفْلَيْنِ مِن رَّحْمَتِهِۦ وَيَجْعَل لَّكُمْ نُورًا تَمْشُونَ بِهِۦ وَيَغْفِرْ لَكُمْ وَٱللَّهُ غَفُورٌ رَّحِيمٌ

O you who believe [in Mûsa (Moses) (i.e. Jews) and 'Îsā (Jesus) (i.e. Christians)]! Fear Allâh, and believe in His

Messenger (Muhammad), He will give you a double portion of His Mercy, and He will give you a light by which you shall walk (straight), and He will forgive you. And Allâh is Oft-Forgiving, Most Merciful. (28)

## Quran 58:4-12

فَمَن لَّمْ يَجِدْ فَصِيَامُ شَهْرَيْنِ مُتَتَابِعَيْنِ مِن قَبْلِ أَن يَتَمَاسَّا فَمَن لَّمْ يَسْتَطِعْ فَإِطْعَامُ سِتِّينَ مِسْكِينًا ذَلِكَ لِتُؤْمِنُواْ بِٱللَّهِ وَرَسُولِهِ وَتِلْكَ حُدُودُ ٱللَّهِ وَلِلْكَفِرِينَ عَذَابٌ أَلِيمٌ (٤) إِنَّ ٱلَّذِينَ يُحَادُّونَ ٱللَّهَ وَرَسُولَهُ كُبِتُواْ كَمَا كُبِتَ ٱلَّذِينَ مِن قَبْلِهِمْ وَقَدْ أَنزَلْنَا ءَايَتٍ بَيِّنَتٍ وَلِلْكَفِرِينَ عَذَابٌ مُّهِينٌ (٥) يَوْمَ يَبْعَثُهُمُ ٱللَّهُ جَمِيعًا فَيُنَبِّئُهُم بِمَا عَمِلُواْ أَحْصَئهُ ٱللَّهُ وَنَسُوهُ وَٱللَّهُ عَلَىٰ كُلِّ شَىْءٍ شَهِيدٌ (٦) أَلَمْ تَرَ أَنَّ ٱللَّهَ يَعْلَمُ مَا فِى ٱلسَّمَوَٰتِ وَمَا فِى ٱلْأَرْضِ مَا يَكُونُ مِن نَّجْوَىٰ ثَلَثَةٍ إِلَّا هُوَ رَابِعُهُمْ وَلَا خَمْسَةٍ إِلَّا هُوَ سَادِسُهُمْ وَلَا أَدْنَىٰ مِن ذَٰلِكَ وَلَا أَكْثَرَ إِلَّا هُوَ مَعَهُمْ أَيْنَ مَا كَانُواْ ثُمَّ يُنَبِّئُهُم بِمَا عَمِلُواْ يَوْمَ ٱلْقِيَمَةِ إِنَّ ٱللَّهَ بِكُلِّ شَىْءٍ عَلِيمٌ (٧) أَلَمْ تَرَ إِلَى ٱلَّذِينَ نُهُواْ عَنِ ٱلنَّجْوَىٰ ثُمَّ يَعُودُونَ لِمَا نُهُواْ عَنْهُ وَيَتَنَٰجَوْنَ بِٱلْإِثْمِ وَٱلْعُدْوَٰنِ وَمَعْصِيَتِ ٱلرَّسُولِ وَإِذَا جَآءُوكَ حَيَّوْكَ بِمَا لَمْ يُحَيِّكَ بِهِ ٱللَّهُ وَيَقُولُونَ فِى أَنفُسِهِمْ لَوْلَا يُعَذِّبُنَا ٱللَّهُ بِمَا نَقُولُ حَسْبُهُمْ جَهَنَّمُ يَصْلَوْنَهَا فَبِئْسَ ٱلْمَصِيرُ (٨) يَأَيُّهَا ٱلَّذِينَ ءَامَنُواْ إِذَا تَنَٰجَيْتُمْ فَلَا تَتَنَٰجَوْاْ بِٱلْإِثْمِ وَٱلْعُدْوَٰنِ وَمَعْصِيَتِ ٱلرَّسُولِ وَتَنَٰجَوْاْ بِٱلْبِرِّ وَٱلتَّقْوَىٰ وَٱتَّقُواْ ٱللَّهَ ٱلَّذِىٓ إِلَيْهِ تُحْشَرُونَ (٩) إِنَّمَا ٱلنَّجْوَىٰ مِنَ ٱلشَّيْطَنِ

لِيَحْزُنَ ٱلَّذِينَ ءَامَنُوا۟ وَلَيْسَ بِضَآرِّهِمْ شَيْـًٔا إِلَّا بِإِذْنِ ٱللَّهِ وَعَلَى ٱللَّهِ فَلْيَتَوَكَّلِ ٱلْمُؤْمِنُونَ (١٠) يَـٰٓأَيُّهَا ٱلَّذِينَ ءَامَنُوٓا۟ إِذَا قِيلَ لَكُمْ تَفَسَّحُوا۟ فِى ٱلْمَجَـٰلِسِ فَٱفْسَحُوا۟ يَفْسَحِ ٱللَّهُ لَكُمْ وَإِذَا قِيلَ ٱنشُزُوا۟ فَٱنشُزُوا۟ يَرْفَعِ ٱللَّهُ ٱلَّذِينَ ءَامَنُوا۟ مِنكُمْ وَٱلَّذِينَ أُوتُوا۟ ٱلْعِلْمَ دَرَجَـٰتٍ وَٱللَّهُ بِمَا تَعْمَلُونَ خَبِيرٌ (١١) يَـٰٓأَيُّهَا ٱلَّذِينَ ءَامَنُوٓا۟ إِذَا نَـٰجَيْتُمُ ٱلرَّسُولَ فَقَدِّمُوا۟ بَيْنَ يَدَىْ نَجْوَىٰكُمْ صَدَقَةً ذَٰلِكَ خَيْرٌ لَّكُمْ وَأَطْهَرُ فَإِن لَّمْ تَجِدُوا۟ فَإِنَّ ٱللَّهَ غَفُورٌ رَّحِيمٌ (١٢)

And he who finds not (the money for freeing a slave) must fast two successive months before they both touch each other. And he who is unable to do so, should feed sixty Miskîns (poor). That is in order that you may have perfect Faith in Allâh and His Messenger. These are the limits set by Allâh. And for disbelievers, there is a painful torment. (4) Verily, those who oppose Allâh and His Messenger (Muhammad) will be disgraced, as those before them (among the past nation), were disgraced. And We have sent down clear Ayât (proofs, evidences, verses, lessons, signs, revelations, etc.). And for the disbelievers is a disgracing torment. (5) On the Day when Allâh will resurrect them all together (i.e. on the Day of Resurrection) and inform them of what they did. Allâh has kept account of it, while they have forgotten it. And Allâh is Witness over all things. (6) Have you not seen that Allâh knows whatsoever is in the heavens and whatsoever is on the earth? There is no Najwa (secret *counsel) of three, but He is their fourth (with His Knowledge, while He Himself is over the Throne, over the seventh heaven), nor of five but He is their sixth (with His Knowledge), not of less than that or more, but He is with them (with His Knowledge) wheresoever they may be; And afterwards on the Day of Resurrection, He will inform them of what they did. Verily, Allâh is the All-Knower of everything. (7) Have you not seen those who were forbidden to hold secret counsels, and afterwards returned to that which they had been forbidden, and conspired together for sin and wrong doing and disobedience to the Messenger (Muhammad). And when they come to you, they greet you with a greeting wherewith Allâh greets you not, and say within themselves: "Why should Allâh punish us not for what we say?" Hell will be sufficient for them, they will burn therein, and worst indeed is that destination! (8) O you who believe! When you hold secret counsel, do it not for sin and wrong-doing, and disobedience towards the Messenger (Muhammad) but do it for Al-Birr (righteousness) and Taqwa (virtues and piety); and fear Allâh unto Whom you shall be gathered. (9) Secret counsels (conspiracies) are only from Shaitân (Satan), in order that he may cause grief to the believers. But he cannot harm them in the least, except as Allâh permits, and in Allâh let the believers put their trust (10) O you who believe! When you are told to make room in the* assemblies, (spread out and) make room. Allâh will give you (ample) room (from His Mercy). And when you are told to rise up [for prayers, Jihâd (fighting in Allâh's Cause), or for any other good deed], rise up. Allâh will exalt in degree those of you who believe, and those who have been granted knowledge. And Allâh is Well-Acquainted with what you do. (11) O you who believe! When you (want to) consult the Messenger (Muhammad) in private, spend something in charity before your private consultation. That will be better and purer for you. But if you find not (the means for it), then verily, Allâh is Oft-Forgiving, Most Merciful. (12)

## Quran 58:15-22

أَعَدَّ ٱللَّهُ لَهُمْ عَذَابًا شَدِيدًا إِنَّهُمْ سَآءَ مَا كَانُوا۟ يَعْمَلُونَ
(١٥) ٱتَّخَذُوٓا۟ أَيْمَٰنَهُمْ جُنَّةً فَصَدُّوا۟ عَن سَبِيلِ ٱللَّهِ فَلَهُمْ عَذَابٌ
مُّهِينٌ (١٦) لَّن تُغْنِىَ عَنْهُمْ أَمْوَٰلُهُمْ وَلَآ أَوْلَٰدُهُم مِّنَ ٱللَّهِ شَيْـًٔا
أُو۟لَٰٓئِكَ أَصْحَٰبُ ٱلنَّارِ هُمْ فِيهَا خَٰلِدُونَ (١٧) يَوْمَ يَبْعَثُهُمُ ٱللَّهُ
جَمِيعًا فَيَحْلِفُونَ لَهُ كَمَا يَحْلِفُونَ لَكُمْ وَيَحْسَبُونَ أَنَّهُمْ عَلَىٰ
شَىْءٍ أَلَآ إِنَّهُمْ هُمُ ٱلْكَٰذِبُونَ (١٨) ٱسْتَحْوَذَ عَلَيْهِمُ ٱلشَّيْطَٰنُ
فَأَنسَىٰهُمْ ذِكْرَ ٱللَّهِ أُو۟لَٰٓئِكَ حِزْبُ ٱلشَّيْطَٰنِ أَلَآ إِنَّ حِزْبَ
ٱلشَّيْطَٰنِ هُمُ ٱلْخَٰسِرُونَ (١٩) إِنَّ ٱلَّذِينَ يُحَآدُّونَ ٱللَّهَ
وَرَسُولَهُ أُو۟لَٰٓئِكَ فِى ٱلْأَذَلِّينَ (٢٠) كَتَبَ ٱللَّهُ لَأَغْلِبَنَّ أَنَا۠
وَرُسُلِىٓ إِنَّ ٱللَّهَ قَوِىٌّ عَزِيزٌ (٢١) لَّا تَجِدُ قَوْمًا يُؤْمِنُونَ بِٱللَّهِ
وَٱلْيَوْمِ ٱلْءَاخِرِ يُوَآدُّونَ مَنْ حَآدَّ ٱللَّهَ وَرَسُولَهُ وَلَوْ كَانُوٓا۟

ءَابَآءَهُمْ أَوْ أَبْنَآءَهُمْ أَوْ إِخْوَٰنَهُمْ أَوْ عَشِيرَتَهُمْ أُوْلَـٰٓئِكَ كَتَبَ
فِى قُلُوبِهِمُ ٱلْإِيمَـٰنَ وَأَيَّدَهُم بِرُوحٍ مِّنْهُ وَيُدْخِلُهُمْ جَنَّـٰتٍ تَجْرِى
مِن تَحْتِهَا ٱلْأَنْهَـٰرُ خَـٰلِدِينَ فِيهَا رَضِىَ ٱللَّهُ عَنْهُمْ وَرَضُوا۟ عَنْهُ
أُوْلَـٰٓئِكَ حِزْبُ ٱللَّهِ أَلَآ إِنَّ حِزْبَ ٱللَّهِ هُمُ ٱلْمُفْلِحُونَ (٢٢)

*Allâh has prepared for them a severe torment. Evil indeed is that which they used to do. (15) They have made their oaths a screen (for their evil actions). Thus they hinder (men) from the Path of Allâh, so they shall have a humiliating torment. (16) Their children and their wealth will avail them nothing against Allâh. They will be the dwellers of the Fire, to dwell therein forever. (17) On the Day when Allâh will resurrect them all together (for their account), then they will swear to Him as they swear to you (O Muslims). And they think that they have something (to stand upon). Verily, they are liars! (18) Shaitân (Satan) has overpowered them. So he has made them forget the remembrance of Allâh. They are the party of Shaitân (Satan). Verily, it is the party of Shaitân (Satan) that will be the losers! (19) Those who oppose Allâh and His Messenger (Muhammad), they will be among the lowest (most humiliated). (20) Allâh has decreed: "Verily! It is I and My Messengers who shall be the victorious." Verily, Allâh is All-Powerful, All-Mighty. (21) You (O Muhammad) will not find any people who believe in Allâh and the Last Day, making friendship with those who oppose Allâh and His*

Messenger (Muhammad), even though they were their fathers or their sons or their brothers or their kindred (people). For such He has written Faith in their hearts, and strengthened them with Rûh (proofs, light and true guidance) from Himself. And He will admit them to Gardens (Paradise) under which rivers flow to dwell therein (forever). Allâh is pleased with them, and they with Him. They are the Party of Allâh. Verily, it is the Party of Allâh that will be the successful. (22)

## Quran 59:3-4

وَلَوْلَا أَن كَتَبَ ٱللَّهُ عَلَيْهِمُ ٱلْجَلَاءَ لَعَذَّبَهُمْ فِى ٱلدُّنْيَا ۖ وَلَهُمْ فِى ٱلْأَخِرَةِ عَذَابُ ٱلنَّارِ (٣) ذَٰلِكَ بِأَنَّهُمْ شَاقُّوا۟ ٱللَّهَ وَرَسُولَهُۥ ۖ وَمَن يُشَاقِّ ٱللَّهَ فَإِنَّ ٱللَّهَ شَدِيدُ ٱلْعِقَابِ (٤)

And had it not been that Allâh had decreed exile for them, He would certainly have punished them in this world, and in the Hereafter theirs shall be the torment of the Fire. (3) That is because they opposed Allâh and His Messenger (Muhammad). And whosoever opposes Allâh, then verily, Allâh is Severe in punishment. (4)

## Quran 59:9

وَٱلَّذِينَ تَبَوَّءُو ٱلدَّارَ وَٱلْإِيمَـٰنَ مِن قَبْلِهِمْ يُحِبُّونَ مَنْ هَاجَرَ إِلَيْهِمْ وَلَا يَجِدُونَ فِى صُدُورِهِمْ حَاجَةً مِّمَّآ أُوتُوا۟

وَيُؤْثِرُونَ عَلَىٰ أَنفُسِهِمْ وَلَوْ كَانَ بِهِمْ خَصَاصَةٌ وَمَن يُوقَ شُحَّ نَفْسِهِ فَأُولَـٰئِكَ هُمُ ٱلْمُفْلِحُونَ ٩ (

*And (it is also for) those who, before them, had homes (in Al-Madinah) and had adopted the Faith, love those who emigrate to them, and have no jealousy in their breasts for that which they have been given (from the booty of Banu An-Nadîr), and give them (emigrants) preference over themselves, even though they were in need of that. And whosoever is saved from his own covetousness, such are they who will be the successful. (9)*

## Quran 59:11-17

۞ أَلَمْ تَرَ إِلَى ٱلَّذِينَ نَافَقُوا۟ يَقُولُونَ لِإِخْوَٰنِهِمُ ٱلَّذِينَ كَفَرُوا۟ مِنْ أَهْلِ ٱلْكِتَـٰبِ لَئِنْ أُخْرِجْتُمْ لَنَخْرُجَنَّ مَعَكُمْ وَلَا نُطِيعُ فِيكُمْ أَحَدًا أَبَدًا وَإِن قُوتِلْتُمْ لَنَنصُرَنَّكُمْ وَٱللَّهُ يَشْهَدُ إِنَّهُمْ لَكَـٰذِبُونَ (١١) لَئِنْ أُخْرِجُوا۟ لَا يَخْرُجُونَ مَعَهُمْ وَلَئِن قُوتِلُوا۟ لَا يَنصُرُونَهُمْ وَلَئِن نَّصَرُوهُمْ لَيُوَلُّنَّ ٱلْأَدْبَـٰرَ ثُمَّ لَا يُنصَرُونَ (١٢) لَأَنتُمْ أَشَدُّ رَهْبَةً فِى صُدُورِهِم مِّنَ ٱللَّهِ ذَٰلِكَ بِأَنَّهُمْ قَوْمٌ لَّا يَفْقَهُونَ (١٣) لَا يُقَـٰتِلُونَكُمْ جَمِيعًا إِلَّا فِى قُرًى مُّحَصَّنَةٍ أَوْ مِن وَرَآءِ جُدُرٍ بَأْسُهُم بَيْنَهُمْ شَدِيدٌ تَحْسَبُهُمْ جَمِيعًا وَقُلُوبُهُمْ شَتَّىٰ ذَٰلِكَ بِأَنَّهُمْ قَوْمٌ لَّا يَعْقِلُونَ (١٤) كَمَثَلِ ٱلَّذِينَ مِن قَبْلِهِمْ قَرِيبًا ذَاقُوا۟ وَبَالَ أَمْرِهِمْ وَلَهُمْ عَذَابٌ أَلِيمٌ (١٥) كَمَثَلِ ٱلشَّيْطَـٰنِ إِذْ قَالَ لِلْإِنسَـٰنِ ٱكْفُرْ فَلَمَّا كَفَرَ قَالَ إِنِّى بَرِىٓءٌ

مِّنكَ إِنِّىٓ أَخَافُ ٱللَّهَ رَبَّ ٱلۡعَٰلَمِينَ (١٦) فَكَانَ عَٰقِبَتَهُمَآ أَنَّهُمَا فِى ٱلنَّارِ خَٰلِدَيۡنِ فِيهَاۚ وَذَٰلِكَ جَزَٰٓؤُاْ ٱلظَّٰلِمِينَ (١٧)

*Have you not observed the hypocrites who say to their friends among the people of the Scripture who disbelieve: "(By Allâh) If you are expelled, we (too) indeed will go out with you, and we shall never obey any one against you, and if you are attacked (in fight), we shall indeed help you." But Allâh is Witness, that they verily, are liars. (11) Surely, if they (the Jews) are expelled, never will they (hypocrites) go out with them, and if they are attacked, they will never help them. And (even) if they do help them, they (hypocrites) will turn their backs, and they will not be victorious. (12) Verily, you (believers in the Oneness of Allâh — Islâmic Monotheism) are more fearful in their breasts than Allâh. That is because they are a people who comprehend not (the Majesty and Power of Allâh). (13) They fight not against you even together, except in fortified townships, or from behind walls. Their enmity among themselves is very great. You would think they were united, but their hearts are divided, That is because they are a people who understand not. (14) They are like their immediate predecessors, they tasted the evil result of their conduct, and (in the Hereafter, there is) for them a painful torment. (15) (Their allies deceived them) like Shaitân (Satan), when he says to man: "Disbelieve in Allâh." But* when (man) disbelieves in Allâh, Shaitân (Satan) says: "I am free of you, I fear Allâh, the Lord of the 'Alamîn (mankind, jinn and all that exists)!" (16) So the end of both will be that they will be in the Fire, abiding therein. Such is the recompense of the Zâlimûn (i.e. polytheists, wrong-doers, disbelievers in Allâh and in His Oneness). (17)

## Quran 59:20

لَا يَسْتَوِىٓ أَصْحَـٰبُ ٱلنَّارِ وَأَصْحَـٰبُ ٱلْجَنَّةِ أَصْحَـٰبُ ٱلْجَنَّةِ هُمُ ٱلْفَآئِزُونَ

Not equal are the dwellers of the Fire and the dwellers of the Paradise. It is the dwellers of Paradise that will be successful. (20)

## Quran 60:1

يَـٰٓأَيُّهَا ٱلَّذِينَ ءَامَنُوا۟ لَا تَتَّخِذُوا۟ عَدُوِّى وَعَدُوَّكُمْ أَوْلِيَآءَ تُلْقُونَ إِلَيْهِم بِٱلْمَوَدَّةِ وَقَدْ كَفَرُوا۟ بِمَا جَآءَكُم مِّنَ ٱلْحَقِّ يُخْرِجُونَ ٱلرَّسُولَ وَإِيَّاكُمْ أَن تُؤْمِنُوا۟ بِٱللَّهِ رَبِّكُمْ إِن كُنتُمْ خَرَجْتُمْ جِهَـٰدًا فِى سَبِيلِى وَٱبْتِغَآءَ مَرْضَاتِى تُسِرُّونَ إِلَيْهِم بِٱلْمَوَدَّةِ وَأَنَا۠ أَعْلَمُ بِمَآ أَخْفَيْتُمْ وَمَآ أَعْلَنتُمْ وَمَن يَفْعَلْهُ مِنكُمْ فَقَدْ ضَلَّ سَوَآءَ ٱلسَّبِيلِ

O you who believe! Take not My enemies and your enemies (i.e. disbelievers and polytheists) as friends, showing affection towards them, while they have disbelieved in what has come to you of the truth (i.e. Islâmic Monotheism, this Qur'ân, and Muhammad), and have driven out the Messenger (Muhammad) and yourselves (from your homeland) because you believe in Allâh your Lord! If you have come forth to strive in My Cause and to seek My Good Pleasure, (then take not these disbelievers and polytheists, as your friends). You show friendship to them in secret, while I am All-Aware of what you conceal and what you reveal. And whosoever of you (Muslims) does that, then indeed he has gone (far) astray, from the Straight Path. (1)

## Quran 60:3

لَن تَنفَعَكُمۡ أَرۡحَامُكُمۡ وَلَآ أَوۡلَٰدُكُمۡ يَوۡمَ ٱلۡقِيَٰمَةِ يَفۡصِلُ بَيۡنَكُمۡ وَٱللَّهُ بِمَا تَعۡمَلُونَ بَصِيرٌ

Neither your relatives nor your children will benefit you on the Day of Resurrection (against Allâh). He will judge between you. And Allâh is the All-Seer of what you do. (3)

## Quran 60:6

لَقَدۡ كَانَ لَكُمۡ فِيهِمۡ أُسۡوَةٌ حَسَنَةٌ لِّمَن كَانَ يَرۡجُواْ ٱللَّهَ وَٱلۡيَوۡمَ ٱلۡأَخِرَۚ وَمَن يَتَوَلَّ فَإِنَّ ٱللَّهَ هُوَ ٱلۡغَنِيُّ ٱلۡحَمِيدُ

Certainly, there has been in them an excellent example for you to follow — for those who look forward to (the Meeting with) Allâh and the Last Day. And whosoever

*turns away, then verily, Allâh is Rich (Free of all needs),*
*Worthy of all Praise. (6)*

## Quran 61:8-14

يُرِيدُونَ لِيُطْفِؤُوا۟ نُورَ ٱللَّهِ بِأَفْوَٰهِهِمْ وَٱللَّهُ مُتِمُّ نُورِهِۦ وَلَوْ كَرِهَ ٱلْكَٰفِرُونَ (٨) هُوَ ٱلَّذِىٓ أَرْسَلَ رَسُولَهُۥ بِٱلْهُدَىٰ وَدِينِ ٱلْحَقِّ لِيُظْهِرَهُۥ عَلَى ٱلدِّينِ كُلِّهِۦ وَلَوْ كَرِهَ ٱلْمُشْرِكُونَ (٩) يَٰٓأَيُّهَا ٱلَّذِينَ ءَامَنُوا۟ هَلْ أَدُلُّكُمْ عَلَىٰ تِجَٰرَةٍ تُنجِيكُم مِّنْ عَذَابٍ أَلِيمٍ (١٠) تُؤْمِنُونَ بِٱللَّهِ وَرَسُولِهِۦ وَتُجَٰهِدُونَ فِى سَبِيلِ ٱللَّهِ بِأَمْوَٰلِكُمْ وَأَنفُسِكُمْ ذَٰلِكُمْ خَيْرٌ لَّكُمْ إِن كُنتُمْ تَعْلَمُونَ (١١) يَغْفِرْ لَكُمْ ذُنُوبَكُمْ وَيُدْخِلْكُمْ جَنَّٰتٍ تَجْرِى مِن تَحْتِهَا ٱلْأَنْهَٰرُ وَمَسَٰكِنَ طَيِّبَةً فِى جَنَّٰتِ عَدْنٍ ذَٰلِكَ ٱلْفَوْزُ ٱلْعَظِيمُ (١٢) وَأُخْرَىٰ تُحِبُّونَهَا نَصْرٌ مِّنَ ٱللَّهِ وَفَتْحٌ قَرِيبٌ وَبَشِّرِ ٱلْمُؤْمِنِينَ (١٣) يَٰٓأَيُّهَا ٱلَّذِينَ ءَامَنُوا۟ كُونُوٓا۟ أَنصَارَ ٱللَّهِ كَمَا قَالَ عِيسَى ٱبْنُ مَرْيَمَ لِلْحَوَارِيِّۦنَ مَنْ أَنصَارِىٓ إِلَى ٱللَّهِ قَالَ ٱلْحَوَارِيُّونَ نَحْنُ أَنصَارُ ٱللَّهِ فَـَٔامَنَت طَّآئِفَةٌ مِّنۢ بَنِىٓ إِسْرَٰٓءِيلَ وَكَفَرَت طَّآئِفَةٌ فَأَيَّدْنَا ٱلَّذِينَ ءَامَنُوا۟ عَلَىٰ عَدُوِّهِمْ فَأَصْبَحُوا۟ ظَٰهِرِينَ (١٤)

*They intend to put out the Light of Allâh (i.e. the*
*Religion of Islâm, this Qur'ân, and the Prophet*
*Muhammad) with their mouths. But Allâh will bring*
*His Light to perfection even though the disbelievers hate*
*(it). (8) He it is Who has sent His Messenger*
*(Muhammad) with guidance and the religion of truth*

*(Islâmic Monotheism) to make it victorious over all (other) religions even though the Mushrikûn (polytheists, pagans, idolaters, and disbelievers in the Oneness of Allâh and in His Messenger Muhammed) hate (it). (9) O You who believe! Shall I guide you to a trade that will save you from a painful torment? (10) That you believe in Allâh and His Messenger (Muhammad), and that you strive hard and fight in the Cause of Allâh with your wealth and your lives, that will be better for you, if you but know! (11) (If you do so) He will forgive you your sins, and admit you into Gardens under which rivers flow, and pleasant dwellings in Adn (Edn) Paradise; that is indeed the great success. (12) And also (He will give you) another (blessing) which you love, help from Allâh (against your enemies) and a near victory. And give glad tidings to the believers. (13) O you who believe! Be you helpers (in the Cause) of Allâh as said 'Īsā (Jesus), son of Maryam (Mary), to the Hawârîyyun (the disciples) : "Who are my helpers (in the Cause) of Allâh?" The Hawârîyyun (the disciples) said: "We are Allâh's helpers" (i.e. we will strive in His Cause!). Then a group of the Children of Israel believed and a group disbelieved. So We gave power to those who believed against their enemies, and they became the victorious (uppermost). (14)*

**Quran 62:8-11**

قُلْ إِنَّ ٱلْمَوْتَ ٱلَّذِى تَفِرُّونَ مِنْهُ فَإِنَّهُ مُلَـٰقِيكُمْ ثُمَّ تُرَدُّونَ إِلَىٰ عَـٰلِمِ ٱلْغَيْبِ وَٱلشَّهَـٰدَةِ فَيُنَبِّئُكُم بِمَا كُنتُمْ تَعْمَلُونَ (٨) يَـٰٓأَيُّهَا ٱلَّذِينَ ءَامَنُوٓاْ إِذَا نُودِىَ لِلصَّلَوٰةِ مِن يَوْمِ ٱلْجُمُعَةِ فَٱسْعَوْاْ إِلَىٰ ذِكْرِ ٱللَّهِ وَذَرُواْ ٱلْبَيْعَ ذَٰلِكُمْ خَيْرٌ لَّكُمْ إِن كُنتُمْ تَعْلَمُونَ (٩) فَإِذَا قُضِيَتِ ٱلصَّلَوٰةُ فَٱنتَشِرُواْ فِى ٱلْأَرْضِ وَٱبْتَغُواْ مِن فَضْلِ ٱللَّهِ وَٱذْكُرُواْ ٱللَّهَ كَثِيرًا لَّعَلَّكُمْ تُفْلِحُونَ (١٠) وَإِذَا رَأَوْاْ تِجَـٰرَةً أَوْ لَهْوًا ٱنفَضُّوٓاْ إِلَيْهَا وَتَرَكُوكَ قَآئِمًا قُلْ مَا عِندَ ٱللَّهِ خَيْرٌ مِّنَ ٱللَّهْوِ وَمِنَ ٱلتِّجَـٰرَةِ وَٱللَّهُ خَيْرُ ٱلرَّٰزِقِينَ (١١)

*Say (to them): "Verily, the death from which you flee will surely meet you, then you will be sent back to (Allâh), the All-Knower of the unseen and the seen, and He will tell you what you used to do." (8) O you who believe (Muslims)! When the call is proclaimed for the Salât (prayer) on Friday (Jumu'ah prayer), come to the remembrance of Allâh [Jumu'ah religious talk (Khutbah) and Salât (prayer)] and leave off business (and every other thing), That is better for you if you did but know! (9) Then when the (Jumu'ah) Salât (prayer) is ended, you may disperse through the land, and seek the Bounty of Allâh (by working, etc.), and remember Allâh much, that you may be successful (10) And when they see some merchandise or some amusement [beating of Tambur (drum) etc.] they disperse headlong to it, and leave you (Muhammad) standing [while delivering Jumu'ah's religious talk (Khutbah)]. Say "That which Allâh has is* better than any amusement or merchandise! And Allâh is the Best of providers." (11)

## Quran 63:8-9

يَقُولُونَ لَبِن رَّجَعْنَا إِلَى ٱلْمَدِينَةِ لَيُخْرِجَنَّ ٱلْأَعَزُّ مِنْهَا ٱلْأَذَلَّ
وَلِلَّهِ ٱلْعِزَّةُ وَلِرَسُولِهِۦ وَلِلْمُؤْمِنِينَ وَلَكِنَّ ٱلْمُنَفِقِينَ لَا يَعْلَمُونَ
(٨) يَأَيُّهَا ٱلَّذِينَ ءَامَنُواْ لَا تُلْهِكُمْ أَمْوَٰلُكُمْ وَلَا أَوْلَٰدُكُمْ عَن
ذِكْرِ ٱللَّهِ وَمَن يَفْعَلْ ذَٰلِكَ فَأُوْلَٰٓئِكَ هُمُ ٱلْخَٰسِرُونَ (٩)

They (hyprocrites) say: "If we return to Al-Madinah, indeed the more honourable ('Abdûllah bin Ubai bin Salul, the chief of hyprocrites at Al¬Madinah) will expel therefrom the meaner (i.e. Allâh's Messenger)." But honour, power and glory belong to Allâh, and to His Messenger (Muhammad), and to the believers, but the hypocrites know not. (8) O you who believe! Let not your properties or your children divert you from the remembrance of Allâh. And whosoever does that, then they are the losers. (9)

## Quran 63:11

وَلَن يُؤَخِّرَ ٱللَّهُ نَفْسًا إِذَا جَآءَ أَجَلُهَآ وَٱللَّهُ خَبِيرٌۢ بِمَا تَعْمَلُونَ

And Allâh grants respite to none when his appointed time (death) comes. And Allâh is All-Aware of what you do. (11)

## Quran 64:5-7

أَلَمْ يَأْتِكُمْ نَبَؤُاْ ٱلَّذِينَ كَفَرُواْ مِن قَبْلُ فَذَاقُواْ وَبَالَ أَمْرِهِمْ وَلَهُمْ
عَذَابٌ أَلِيمٌ (٥) ذَٰلِكَ بِأَنَّهُۥ كَانَت تَّأْتِيهِمْ رُسُلُهُم بِٱلْبَيِّنَٰتِ
فَقَالُوٓاْ أَبَشَرٌ يَهْدُونَنَا فَكَفَرُواْ وَتَوَلَّواْ وَّٱسْتَغْنَى ٱللَّهُ وَٱللَّهُ غَنِىٌّ
حَمِيدٌ (٦) زَعَمَ ٱلَّذِينَ كَفَرُوٓاْ أَن لَّن يُبْعَثُواْ قُلْ بَلَىٰ وَرَبِّى
لَتُبْعَثُنَّ ثُمَّ لَتُنَبَّؤُنَّ بِمَا عَمِلْتُمْ وَذَٰلِكَ عَلَى ٱللَّهِ يَسِيرٌ (٧)

*Has not the news reached you of those who disbelieved
aforetime? And so they tasted the evil result of their
disbelief, and theirs will be a painful torment. (5) That
was because there came to them their Messengers with
clear proofs (signs), but they said: "Shall mere men guide
us?" So they disbelieved and turned away (from the
truth), But Allâh was not in need (of them). And Allâh is
Rich (Free of all needs), Worthy of all praise. (6) The
disbelievers pretend that they will never be resurrected
(for the Account). Say: "Yes! By my Lord, you will
certainly be resurrected, then you will be informed of
(and recompensed for) what you did, and that is easy for
Allâh. (7)*

## Quran 64:9-11

يَوْمَ يَجْمَعُكُمْ لِيَوْمِ ٱلْجَمْعِ ذَٰلِكَ يَوْمُ ٱلتَّغَابُنِ وَمَن يُؤْمِنۢ بِٱللَّهِ
وَيَعْمَلْ صَٰلِحًا يُكَفِّرْ عَنْهُ سَيِّئَاتِهِۦ وَيُدْخِلْهُ جَنَّٰتٍ تَجْرِى مِن
تَحْتِهَا ٱلْأَنْهَٰرُ خَٰلِدِينَ فِيهَآ أَبَدًا ذَٰلِكَ ٱلْفَوْزُ ٱلْعَظِيمُ
(٩) وَٱلَّذِينَ كَفَرُواْ وَكَذَّبُواْ بِـَٔايَٰتِنَآ أُوْلَٰٓئِكَ أَصْحَٰبُ ٱلنَّارِ
خَٰلِدِينَ فِيهَا وَبِئْسَ ٱلْمَصِيرُ (١٠) مَآ أَصَابَ مِن مُّصِيبَةٍ إِلَّا

بِإِذْنِ ٱللَّهِ وَمَن يُؤْمِنۢ بِٱللَّهِ يَهْدِ قَلْبَهُۥ وَٱللَّهُ بِكُلِّ شَىْءٍ عَلِيمٌ (١١)

*(And remember) the Day when He will gather you (all) on the Day of Gathering, that will be the Day of mutual loss and gain (i.e. loss for the disbelievers as they will enter the Hell-fire and gain for the believers as they will enter Paradise). And whosoever believes in Allâh and performs righteous good deeds, He will expiate from him his sins, and will admit him to Gardens under which rivers flow (Paradise) to dwell therein forever, that will be the great success. (9) But those who disbelieved (in the Oneness of Allâh - Islâmic Monotheism) and denied Our Ayât (proofs, evidences, verses, lessons, signs, revelations, etc.), they will be the dwellers of the Fire, to dwell therein forever. And worst indeed is that destination (10) No calamity befalls, but by the Leave [i.e. Decision and Qadar (Divine Preordainments)] of Allâh, and whosoever believes in Allâh, He guides his heart [to the true Faith with certainty, i.e. what has befallen him was already written for him by Allâh from the Qadar (Divine Preordainments)], And Allâh is the All-Knower of everything. (11)*

**Quran 64:14-17**

يَـٰٓأَيُّهَا ٱلَّذِينَ ءَامَنُوٓا۟ إِنَّ مِنْ أَزْوَٰجِكُمْ وَأَوْلَـٰدِكُمْ عَدُوًّا لَّكُمْ فَٱحْذَرُوهُمْ وَإِن تَعْفُوا۟ وَتَصْفَحُوا۟ وَتَغْفِرُوا۟ فَإِنَّ ٱللَّهَ غَفُورٌ

رَّحِيمٌ (١٤) إِنَّمَا أَمْوَالُكُمْ وَأَوْلَادُكُمْ فِتْنَةٌ وَٱللَّهُ عِندَهُ أَجْرٌ
عَظِيمٌ (١٥) فَٱتَّقُوا ٱللَّهَ مَا ٱسْتَطَعْتُمْ وَٱسْمَعُوا وَأَطِيعُوا
وَأَنفِقُوا خَيْرًا لِّأَنفُسِكُمْ وَمَن يُوقَ شُحَّ نَفْسِهِ فَأُوْلَٰئِكَ هُمُ
ٱلْمُفْلِحُونَ (١٦) إِن تُقْرِضُوا ٱللَّهَ قَرْضًا حَسَنًا يُضَاعِفْهُ لَكُمْ
وَيَغْفِرْ لَكُمْ وَٱللَّهُ شَكُورٌ حَلِيمٌ (١٧)

*O you who believe! Verily, among your wives and your children are your enemies (who may stop you from the obedience of Allâh), therefore beware of them! But if you pardon (them) and overlook, and forgive (their faults), then verily, Allâh is Oft-Forgiving, Most Merciful. (14) Your wealth and your children are only a trial, whereas Allâh! With Him is a great reward (Paradise). (15) So keep your duty to Allâh and fear Him as much as you can; listen and obey; and spend in charity, that is better for yourselves. And whosoever is saved from his own covetousness, then they are the successful ones. (16) If you lend Allâh a goodly loan (i.e. spend in Allâh's Cause) He will double it for you, and will forgive you. And Allâh is Most Ready to appreciate and to reward, Most Forbearing, (17)*

## Quran 65:1-5

يَٰٓأَيُّهَا ٱلنَّبِيُّ إِذَا طَلَّقْتُمُ ٱلنِّسَاءَ فَطَلِّقُوهُنَّ لِعِدَّتِهِنَّ وَأَحْصُوا
ٱلْعِدَّةَ وَٱتَّقُوا ٱللَّهَ رَبَّكُمْ لَا تُخْرِجُوهُنَّ مِنۢ بُيُوتِهِنَّ وَلَا
يَخْرُجْنَ إِلَّا أَن يَأْتِينَ بِفَٰحِشَةٍ مُّبَيِّنَةٍ وَتِلْكَ حُدُودُ ٱللَّهِ وَمَن يَتَعَدَّ

حُدُودَ ٱللَّهِ فَقَدْ ظَلَمَ نَفْسَهُ لَا تَدْرِى لَعَلَّ ٱللَّهَ يُحْدِثُ بَعْدَ ذَٰلِكَ أَمْرًا (١) فَإِذَا بَلَغْنَ أَجَلَهُنَّ فَأَمْسِكُوهُنَّ بِمَعْرُوفٍ أَوْ فَارِقُوهُنَّ بِمَعْرُوفٍ وَأَشْهِدُوا ذَوَىْ عَدْلٍ مِّنكُمْ وَأَقِيمُوا ٱلشَّهَٰدَةَ لِلَّهِ ذَٰلِكُمْ يُوعَظُ بِهِ مَن كَانَ يُؤْمِنُ بِٱللَّهِ وَٱلْيَوْمِ ٱلْأَخِرِ وَمَن يَتَّقِ ٱللَّهَ يَجْعَل لَّهُ مَخْرَجًا (٢) وَيَرْزُقْهُ مِنْ حَيْثُ لَا يَحْتَسِبُ وَمَن يَتَوَكَّلْ عَلَى ٱللَّهِ فَهُوَ حَسْبُهُ إِنَّ ٱللَّهَ بَٰلِغُ أَمْرِهِ قَدْ جَعَلَ ٱللَّهُ لِكُلِّ شَىْءٍ قَدْرًا (٣) وَٱلَّٰٓئِى يَئِسْنَ مِنَ ٱلْمَحِيضِ مِن نِّسَآئِكُمْ إِنِ ٱرْتَبْتُمْ فَعِدَّتُهُنَّ ثَلَٰثَةُ أَشْهُرٍ وَٱلَّٰٓئِى لَمْ يَحِضْنَ وَأُوْلَٰتُ ٱلْأَحْمَالِ أَجَلُهُنَّ أَن يَضَعْنَ حَمْلَهُنَّ وَمَن يَتَّقِ ٱللَّهَ يَجْعَل لَّهُ مِنْ أَمْرِهِ يُسْرًا (٤) ذَٰلِكَ أَمْرُ ٱللَّهِ أَنزَلَهُ إِلَيْكُمْ وَمَن يَتَّقِ ٱللَّهَ يُكَفِّرْ عَنْهُ سَيِّـَٔاتِهِ وَيُعْظِمْ لَهُ أَجْرًا (٥)

*O Prophet! When you divorce women, divorce them at their 'Iddah (prescribed periods), and count (accurately) their 'Iddah (periods ). And fear Allâh your Lord (O Muslims), And turn them not out of their (husband's) homes, nor shall they (themselves) leave, except in case they are guilty of some open illegal sexual intercourse. And those are the set limits of Allâh. And whosoever transgresses the set limits of Allâh, then indeed he has wronged himself. You (the one who divorces his wife) know not, it may be that Allâh will afterward bring some new thing to pass (i.e. to return her back to you if that was the first or second divorce). (1) Then when they are about to attain their term appointed, either take them*

back in a good manner or part with them in a good
manner. And take as witness two just persons from
among you (Muslims). And establish the testimony for
Allâh. That will be an admonition given to him who
believes in Allâh and the Last Day. And whosoever fears
Allâh and keeps his duty to Him, He will make a way for
him to get out (from every difficulty). (2) And He will
provide him from (sources) he never could imagine. And
whosoever puts his trust in Allâh, then He will suffice
him. Verily, Allâh will accomplish his purpose. Indeed
Allâh has set a measure for all things. (3) And those of
your women as have passed the age of monthly courses,
for them the 'Iddah (prescribed periods), if you have
doubt (about their period), is three months, and for those
who have no courses [(i.e. they are still immature) their
'Iddah (prescribed period) is three months likewise,
except in case of death] . And for those who are pregnant
(whether they are divorced or their husbands are dead),
their 'Iddah (prescribed period) is until they laydown
their burden, and whosoever fears Allâh and keeps his
duty to Him, He will make his matter easy for him.
(4) That is the Command of Allâh, which He has sent
down to you, and whosoever fears Allâh and keeps his
duty to Him, He will expiate from him his sins, and will
enlarge his reward. (5)

**Quran 65:7-8**

لِيُنفِقْ ذُو سَعَةٍ مِّن سَعَتِهِۦ وَمَن قُدِرَ عَلَيْهِ رِزْقُهُۥ فَلْيُنفِقْ مِمَّآ
ءَاتَىٰهُ ٱللَّهُ لَا يُكَلِّفُ ٱللَّهُ نَفْسًا إِلَّا مَآ ءَاتَىٰهَا سَيَجْعَلُ ٱللَّهُ بَعْدَ
عُسْرٍ يُسْرًا (٧) وَكَأَيِّن مِّن قَرْيَةٍ عَتَتْ عَنْ أَمْرِ رَبِّهَا وَرُسُلِهِۦ
فَحَاسَبْنَٰهَا حِسَابًا شَدِيدًا وَعَذَّبْنَٰهَا عَذَابًا نُّكْرًا (٨)

Let the rich man spend according to his means, and the
man whose resources are restricted, let him spend
according to what Allâh has given him. Allâh puts no
burden on any person beyond what He has given him.
Allâh will grant after hardship, ease. (7) And many a
town (population) revolted against the Command of its
Lord and His Messengers, and We called it to a severe
account (i.e. torment in this worldly life), and we shall
punish it with a horrible torment (in Hell, in the
Hereafter). (8)

## Quran 65:10-11

أَعَدَّ ٱللَّهُ لَهُمْ عَذَابًا شَدِيدًا فَٱتَّقُوا۟ ٱللَّهَ يَٰٓأُو۟لِى ٱلْأَلْبَٰبِ ٱلَّذِينَ
ءَامَنُوا۟ قَدْ أَنزَلَ ٱللَّهُ إِلَيْكُمْ ذِكْرًا (١٠) رَّسُولًا يَتْلُوا۟ عَلَيْكُمْ
ءَايَٰتِ ٱللَّهِ مُبَيِّنَٰتٍ لِّيُخْرِجَ ٱلَّذِينَ ءَامَنُوا۟ وَعَمِلُوا۟ ٱلصَّٰلِحَٰتِ
مِنَ ٱلظُّلُمَٰتِ إِلَى ٱلنُّورِ وَمَن يُؤْمِنۢ بِٱللَّهِ وَيَعْمَلْ صَٰلِحًا يُدْخِلْهُ
جَنَّٰتٍ تَجْرِى مِن تَحْتِهَا ٱلْأَنْهَٰرُ خَٰلِدِينَ فِيهَآ أَبَدًا قَدْ أَحْسَنَ
ٱللَّهُ لَهُۥ رِزْقًا (١١)

Allâh has prepared for them a severe torment. So fear
Allâh and keep your duty to Him, O men of

understanding — who have believed! - Allâh has indeed sent down to you a Reminder (this Qur'ân). (10) (And has also sent to you) a Messenger (Muhammad), who recites to you the Verses of Allâh (the Qur'ân) containing clear explanations, that He may take out, those who believe and do righteous good deeds from the darkness (of polytheism and disbelief) to the light (of Islamic Monotheism). And whosoever believes in Allâh and performs righteous good deeds, He will admit him into Gardens under which rivers flow (Paradise), to dwell therein forever. Allâh has indeed granted for him an excellent provision. (11)

## Quran 66:6-10

يَـٰٓأَيُّهَا ٱلَّذِينَ ءَامَنُوا۟ قُوٓا۟ أَنفُسَكُمْ وَأَهْلِيكُمْ نَارًا وَقُودُهَا ٱلنَّاسُ وَٱلْحِجَارَةُ عَلَيْهَا مَلَـٰٓئِكَةٌ غِلَاظٌ شِدَادٌ لَّا يَعْصُونَ ٱللَّهَ مَآ أَمَرَهُمْ وَيَفْعَلُونَ مَا يُؤْمَرُونَ (٦) يَـٰٓأَيُّهَا ٱلَّذِينَ كَفَرُوا۟ لَا تَعْتَذِرُوا۟ ٱلْيَوْمَ إِنَّمَا تُجْزَوْنَ مَا كُنتُمْ تَعْمَلُونَ (٧) يَـٰٓأَيُّهَا ٱلَّذِينَ ءَامَنُوا۟ تُوبُوٓا۟ إِلَى ٱللَّهِ تَوْبَةً نَّصُوحًا عَسَىٰ رَبُّكُمْ أَن يُكَفِّرَ عَنكُمْ سَيِّـَٔاتِكُمْ وَيُدْخِلَكُمْ جَنَّـٰتٍ تَجْرِى مِن تَحْتِهَا ٱلْأَنْهَـٰرُ يَوْمَ لَا يُخْزِى ٱللَّهُ ٱلنَّبِىَّ وَٱلَّذِينَ ءَامَنُوا۟ مَعَهُ نُورُهُمْ يَسْعَىٰ بَيْنَ أَيْدِيهِمْ وَبِأَيْمَـٰنِهِمْ يَقُولُونَ رَبَّنَآ أَتْمِمْ لَنَا نُورَنَا وَٱغْفِرْ لَنَآ إِنَّكَ عَلَىٰ كُلِّ شَىْءٍ قَدِيرٌ (٨) يَـٰٓأَيُّهَا ٱلنَّبِىُّ جَـٰهِدِ ٱلْكُفَّارَ وَٱلْمُنَـٰفِقِينَ وَٱغْلُظْ عَلَيْهِمْ وَمَأْوَىٰهُمْ جَهَنَّمُ وَبِئْسَ ٱلْمَصِيرُ (٩) ضَرَبَ ٱللَّهُ مَثَلًا لِّلَّذِينَ كَفَرُوا۟ ٱمْرَأَتَ نُوحٍ وَٱمْرَأَتَ لُوطٍ

كَانَتَا تَحْتَ عَبْدَيْنِ مِنْ عِبَادِنَا صَـٰلِحَيْنِ فَخَانَتَاهُمَا فَلَمْ يُغْنِيَا
عَنْهُمَا مِنَ ٱللَّهِ شَيْـًٔا وَقِيلَ ٱدْخُلَا ٱلنَّارَ مَعَ ٱلدَّٰخِلِينَ (١٠)

*O you who believe! Ward off from yourselves and your families against a Fire (Hell) whose fuel is men and stones, over which are (appointed) angels stern (and) severe, who disobey not, (from executing) the Commands they receive from Allâh, but do that which they are commanded. (6) (It will be said in the Hereafter) O you who disbelieve (in the Oneness of Allâh - Islâmic Monotheism)! Make no excuses this Day! You are being requited only for what you used to do. (7) O you who believe! Turn to Allâh with sincere repentance! It may be that your Lord will expiate from you your sins, and admit you into Gardens under which rivers flow (Paradise) the Day that Allâh will not disgrace the Prophet (Muhammad) and those who believe with him, Their Light will run forward before them and (with their Records — Books of deeds) in their right hands They will say: "Our Lord! Keep perfect our Light for us [and do not put it off till we cross over the Sirât (a slippery bridge over the Hell) safely] and grant us forgiveness. Verily, You are Able to do all things ." (8) O Prophet (Muhammad)! Strive hard against the disbelievers and the hypocrites, and be severe against them; their abode will be Hell, and worst indeed is that destination.(9) Allâh sets forth an example for those who* disbelieve, the wife of Nûh (Noah) and the wife of Lut (Lot). They were under two of our righteous slaves, but they both betrayed them (their husbands by rejecting their doctrine) So they [Nûh (Noah) and Lut (Lot)] availed them (their respective wives) not, against Allâh, and it was said: "Enter the Fire along with those who enter!" (10)

## Quran 67:2

ٱلَّذِى خَلَقَ ٱلْمَوْتَ وَٱلْحَيَوٰةَ لِيَبْلُوَكُمْ أَيُّكُمْ أَحْسَنُ عَمَلًا وَهُوَ ٱلْعَزِيزُ ٱلْغَفُورُ

Who has created death and life, that He may test you which of you is best in deed. And He is the All-Mighty, the Oft-Forgiving; (2)

## Quran 67:5-12

وَلَقَدْ زَيَّنَّا ٱلسَّمَآءَ ٱلدُّنْيَا بِمَصَٰبِيحَ وَجَعَلْنَٰهَا رُجُومًا لِّلشَّيَٰطِينِ وَأَعْتَدْنَا لَهُمْ عَذَابَ ٱلسَّعِيرِ (٥) وَلِلَّذِينَ كَفَرُواْ بِرَبِّهِمْ عَذَابُ جَهَنَّمَ وَبِئْسَ ٱلْمَصِيرُ (٦) إِذَآ أُلْقُواْ فِيهَا سَمِعُواْ لَهَا شَهِيقًا وَهِىَ تَفُورُ (٧) تَكَادُ تَمَيَّزُ مِنَ ٱلْغَيْظِ كُلَّمَآ أُلْقِىَ فِيهَا فَوْجٌ سَأَلَهُمْ خَزَنَتُهَآ أَلَمْ يَأْتِكُمْ نَذِيرٌ (٨) قَالُواْ بَلَىٰ قَدْ جَآءَنَا نَذِيرٌ فَكَذَّبْنَا وَقُلْنَا مَا نَزَّلَ ٱللَّهُ مِن شَىْءٍ إِنْ أَنتُمْ إِلَّا فِى ضَلَٰلٍ كَبِيرٍ (٩) وَقَالُواْ لَوْ كُنَّا نَسْمَعُ أَوْ نَعْقِلُ مَا كُنَّا فِىٓ أَصْحَٰبِ ٱلسَّعِيرِ (١٠) فَٱعْتَرَفُواْ بِذَنۢبِهِمْ فَسُحْقًا لِّأَصْحَٰبِ ٱلسَّعِيرِ (١١) إِنَّ ٱلَّذِينَ يَخْشَوْنَ رَبَّهُم بِٱلْغَيْبِ لَهُم مَّغْفِرَةٌ وَأَجْرٌ كَبِيرٌ (١٢)

And indeed We have adorned the nearest heaven with lamps, and We have made such lamps (as) missiles to drive away the Shayâtin (devils), and have prepared for them the torment of the blazing Fire (5) And for those who disbelieve in their Lord (Allâh) is the torment of Hell, and worst indeed is that destination (6) When they are cast therein, they will hear the (terrible) drawing in of its breath as it blazes forth (7) It almost bursts up with fury. Every time a group is cast therein, its keeper will ask: "Did no warner come to you?" (8) They will say: "Yes indeed a warner did come to us, but we belied him and said: 'Allâh never sent down anything (of revelation), you are only in great error.'" (9) And they will say: "Had we but listened or used our intelligence, we would not have been among the dwellers of the blazing Fire!" (10) Then they will confess their sin. So, away with the dwellers of the blazing Fire (11) Verily, those who fear their Lord unseen (i.e. they do not see Him, nor His Punishment in the Hereafter), theirs will be forgiveness and a great reward (i.e. Paradise). (12)

## Quran 67:15

هُوَ ٱلَّذِى جَعَلَ لَكُمُ ٱلْأَرْضَ ذَلُولاً فَٱمْشُواْ فِى مَنَاكِبِهَا وَكُلُواْ مِن رِّزْقِهِۦ ۖ وَإِلَيْهِ ٱلنُّشُورُ

He it is, Who has made the earth subservient to you (i.e. easy for you to walk, to live and to do agriculture on it), so walk in the path thereof and eat of His provision, and to Him will be the Resurrection. (15)

## Quran 67:20

أَمَّنْ هَـٰذَا ٱلَّذِى هُوَ جُندٌ لَّكُمْ يَنصُرُكُم مِّن دُونِ ٱلرَّحْمَـٰنِ إِنِ ٱلْكَـٰفِرُونَ إِلَّا فِى غُرُورٍ

*Who is he besides the Most Gracious that can be an army to you to help you? The disbelievers are in nothing but delusion (20)*

## Quran 67:24-29

قُلْ هُوَ ٱلَّذِى ذَرَأَكُمْ فِى ٱلْأَرْضِ وَإِلَيْهِ تُحْشَرُونَ (٢٤) وَيَقُولُونَ مَتَىٰ هَـٰذَا ٱلْوَعْدُ إِن كُنتُمْ صَـٰدِقِينَ (٢٥) قُلْ إِنَّمَا ٱلْعِلْمُ عِندَ ٱللَّهِ وَإِنَّمَا أَنَا نَذِيرٌ مُّبِينٌ (٢٦) فَلَمَّا رَأَوْهُ زُلْفَةً سِيئَتْ وُجُوهُ ٱلَّذِينَ كَفَرُوا۟ وَقِيلَ هَـٰذَا ٱلَّذِى كُنتُم بِهِ تَدَّعُونَ (٢٧) قُلْ أَرَءَيْتُمْ إِنْ أَهْلَكَنِىَ ٱللَّهُ وَمَن مَّعِىَ أَوْ رَحِمَنَا فَمَن يُجِيرُ ٱلْكَـٰفِرِينَ مِنْ عَذَابٍ أَلِيمٍ (٢٨) قُلْ هُوَ ٱلرَّحْمَـٰنُ ءَامَنَّا بِهِ وَعَلَيْهِ تَوَكَّلْنَا فَسَتَعْلَمُونَ مَنْ هُوَ فِى ضَلَـٰلٍ مُّبِينٍ (٢٩)

*Say: "It is He Who has created you from the earth, and to Him shall you be gathered (in the Hereafter)." (24) They say: "When will this promise (i.e. the Day of Resurrection) come to pass if you are telling the truth?" (25) Say (O Muhammad): "The knowledge (of its exact time) is with Allâh only, and I am only a plain warner." (26) But when they will see it (the torment on the Day of*

Resurrection) approaching, the faces of those who disbelieve will change and turn black with sadness and in grief and it will be said (to them): "This is (the promise) which you were calling for!" (27) Say (O Muhammad): "Tell me! If Allâh destroys me, and those with me, or He bestows His Mercy on us — who can save the disbelievers from a painful torment?" (28) Say: "He is the Most Gracious (Allâh), in Him we believe, and in Him we put our trust. So you will come to know who is it that is in manifest error." (29)

## Quran 68:15-16

إِذَا تُتْلَىٰ عَلَيْهِ ءَايَـٰتُنَا قَالَ أَسَـٰطِيرُ ٱلْأَوَّلِينَ (١٥) سَنَسِمُهُۥ عَلَى ٱلْخُرْطُومِ (١٦)

When Our Verses (of the Qur'ân) are recited to him, he says: "Tales of the men of old!" (15) We shall brand him on the snout (nose)! (16)

## Quran 68:33-45

كَذَٰلِكَ ٱلْعَذَابُ وَلَعَذَابُ ٱلْأَخِرَةِ أَكْبَرُ لَوْ كَانُوا۟ يَعْلَمُونَ (٣٣) إِنَّ لِلْمُتَّقِينَ عِندَ رَبِّهِمْ جَنَّـٰتِ ٱلنَّعِيمِ (٣٤) أَفَنَجْعَلُ ٱلْمُسْلِمِينَ كَٱلْمُجْرِمِينَ (٣٥) مَا لَكُمْ كَيْفَ تَحْكُمُونَ (٣٦) أَمْ لَكُمْ كِتَـٰبٌ فِيهِ تَدْرُسُونَ (٣٧) إِنَّ لَكُمْ فِيهِ لَمَا تَخَيَّرُونَ (٣٨) أَمْ لَكُمْ أَيْمَـٰنٌ عَلَيْنَا بَـٰلِغَةٌ إِلَىٰ يَوْمِ ٱلْقِيَـٰمَةِ إِنَّ لَكُمْ لَمَا تَحْكُمُونَ (٣٩) سَلْهُمْ أَيُّهُم بِذَٰلِكَ زَعِيمٌ (٤٠) أَمْ لَهُمْ

شُرَكَآءُ فَلْيَأْتُواْ بِشُرَكَآبِهِمْ إِن كَانُواْ صَـٰدِقِينَ ﴿٤١﴾ يَوْمَ
يُكْشَفُ عَن سَاقٍ وَيُدْعَوْنَ إِلَى ٱلسُّجُودِ فَلَا يَسْتَطِيعُونَ
﴿٤٢﴾ خَـٰشِعَةً أَبْصَـٰرُهُمْ تَرْهَقُهُمْ ذِلَّةٌۖ وَقَدْ كَانُواْ يُدْعَوْنَ إِلَى
ٱلسُّجُودِ وَهُمْ سَـٰلِمُونَ ﴿٤٣﴾ فَذَرْنِى وَمَن يُكَذِّبُ بِهَـٰذَا
ٱلْحَدِيثِۖ سَنَسْتَدْرِجُهُم مِّنْ حَيْثُ لَا يَعْلَمُونَ ﴿٤٤﴾ وَأُمْلِى لَهُمْ
إِنَّ كَيْدِى مَتِينٌ ﴿٤٥﴾

*Such is the punishment (in this life), but truly, the
punishment of the Hereafter is greater, if they but knew.
(33) Verily, for the Muttaqûn (pious and righteous
persons) are Gardens of delight (Paradise) with their
Lord. (34) Shall We then treat the Muslims (believers of
Islamic Monotheism, doers of righteous deeds) like the
Mujrimûn (criminals, polytheists and disbelievers)?
(35) What is the matter with you? How judge you?
(36) Or have you a Book where in you learn, (37) That
you shall therein have all that you choose? (38) Or have
you oaths from Us, reaching to the Day of Resurrection
that yours will be what you judge? (39) Ask them, which
of them will stand surety for that! (40) Or have they
"partners"? Then let them bring their "partners" if they
are truthful! (41) (Remember) the Day when the Shin
shall be laid bare (i.e. the Day of Resurrection) and they
shall be called to prostrate themselves (to Allâh), but they
(hypocrites) shall not be able to do so. (42) Their eyes will
be cast down and ignominy will cover them; they used to*

be called to prostrate themselves (offer prayers), while they were healthy and good (in the life of the world, but they did not). (43) Then leave Me Alone with such as belie this Qur'ân. We shall punish them gradually from directions they perceive not. (44) And I will grant them a respite. Verily, My Plan is strong. (45)

## Quran 69:1-3

ٱلۡحَآقَّةُ (١) مَا ٱلۡحَآقَّةُ (٢) وَمَآ أَدۡرَىٰكَ مَا ٱلۡحَآقَّةُ (٣)

The Inevitable (i.e. the Day of Resurrection)! (1) What is the Inevitable? (2) And what will make you know what the Inevitable is? (3)

## Quran 69:13-32

فَإِذَا نُفِخَ فِى ٱلصُّورِ نَفۡخَةٌ وَٰحِدَةٌ (١٣) وَحُمِلَتِ ٱلۡأَرۡضُ وَٱلۡجِبَالُ فَدُكَّتَا دَكَّةً وَٰحِدَةً (١٤) فَيَوۡمَئِذٍ وَقَعَتِ ٱلۡوَاقِعَةُ (١٥) وَٱنشَقَّتِ ٱلسَّمَآءُ فَهِىَ يَوۡمَئِذٍ وَاهِيَةٌ (١٦) وَٱلۡمَلَكُ عَلَىٰٓ أَرۡجَآئِهَاۚ وَيَحۡمِلُ عَرۡشَ رَبِّكَ فَوۡقَهُمۡ يَوۡمَئِذٍ ثَمَٰنِيَةٌ (١٧) يَوۡمَئِذٍ تُعۡرَضُونَ لَا تَخۡفَىٰ مِنكُمۡ خَافِيَةٌ (١٨) فَأَمَّا مَنۡ أُوتِىَ كِتَٰبَهُۥ بِيَمِينِهِۦ فَيَقُولُ هَآؤُمُ ٱقۡرَءُواْ كِتَٰبِيَهۡ (١٩) إِنِّى ظَنَنتُ أَنِّى مُلَٰقٍ حِسَابِيَهۡ (٢٠) فَهُوَ فِى عِيشَةٍ رَّاضِيَةٍ (٢١) فِى جَنَّةٍ عَالِيَةٍ (٢٢) قُطُوفُهَا دَانِيَةٌ (٢٣) كُلُواْ وَٱشۡرَبُواْ هَنِيٓـًٔا بِمَآ أَسۡلَفۡتُمۡ فِى ٱلۡأَيَّامِ ٱلۡخَالِيَةِ (٢٤) وَأَمَّا مَنۡ أُوتِىَ كِتَٰبَهُۥ بِشِمَالِهِۦ فَيَقُولُ يَٰلَيۡتَنِى لَمۡ أُوتَ كِتَٰبِيَهۡ (٢٥) وَلَمۡ

أَدْرِ مَا حِسَابِيَهْ (٢٦) يَٰلَيْتَهَا كَانَتِ ٱلْقَاضِيَةَ (٢٧) مَا أَغْنَىٰ
عَنِّى مَالِيَهْ (٢٨) هَلَكَ عَنِّى سُلْطَٰنِيَهْ (٢٩) خُذُوهُ فَغُلُّوهُ
(٣٠) ثُمَّ ٱلْجَحِيمَ صَلُّوهُ (٣١) ثُمَّ فِى سِلْسِلَةٍ ذَرْعُهَا سَبْعُونَ
ذِرَاعًا فَٱسْلُكُوهُ (٣٢)

Then when the Trumpet will be blown with one blowing
(the first one), (13) And the earth and the mountains
shall be removed from their places, and crushed with a
single crushing. (14) Then on that Day shall the (Great)
Event befall. (15) And the heaven will berent asunder, for
that Day it (the heaven) will be frail, and torn up.
(16) And the angels will be on its sides, and eight angels
will, that Day, bear the Throne of your Lord above them.
(17) That Day shall you be brought to Judgement, not a
secret of you will be hidden. (18) Then as for him who
will be given his Record in his right hand will say:
"Here! read my Record! (19) "Surely, I did believe that I
shall meet my Account!" (20) So he shall be in a life,
well-pleasing. (21) In a lofty Paradise, (22) The fruits in
bunches whereof will be low and near at hand. (23) Eat
and drink at ease for that which you have sent on before
you in days past! (24) But as for him who will be given
his Record in his left hand, will say: "I wish that I had
not been given my Record! (25) "And that I had never
known, how my Account is! (26) "Would that it had
been my end (death)! (27) "My wealth has not availed
me; (28) "My power (and arguments to defend myself)

*have gone from me!" (29) (It will be said): "Seize him
and fetter him; (30) Then throw him in the blazing Fire.
(31) "Then fasten him with a chain whereof the length is
seventy cubits!" (32)*

## Quran 69:35-37

فَلَيْسَ لَهُ ٱلْيَوْمَ هَٰهُنَا حَمِيمٌ (٣٥) وَلَا طَعَامٌ إِلَّا مِنْ غِسْلِينٍ
(٣٦) لَّا يَأْكُلُهُ إِلَّا ٱلْخَٰطِئُونَ (٣٧)

*So no friend has he here this Day, (35) Nor any food
except filth from the washing of wounds, (36) None will
eat it except the Khâti'ûn (sinners, disbelievers,
polytheists). (37)*

## Quran 69:48-51

وَإِنَّهُ لَتَذْكِرَةٌ لِّلْمُتَّقِينَ (٤٨) وَإِنَّا لَنَعْلَمُ أَنَّ مِنكُم مُّكَذِّبِينَ
(٤٩) وَإِنَّهُ لَحَسْرَةٌ عَلَى ٱلْكَٰفِرِينَ (٥٠) وَإِنَّهُ لَحَقُّ ٱلْيَقِينِ
(٥١)

*And verily, this (Qur'ân) is a Reminder for the
Muttaqûn (pious) (48) And verily, We know that there
are some among you that belie (this Qur'ân). (49) And
indeed it (this Qur'ân) will be an anguish for the
disbelievers (on the Day of Resurrection). (50) And
Verily, it (this Qur'ân) is an absolute truth with
certainty(51)*

## Quran 70:1-4

سَأَلَ سَائِلٌ بِعَذَابٍ وَاقِعٍ (١) لِّلْكَـٰفِرِينَ لَيْسَ لَهُ دَافِعٌ (٢) مِّنَ اللَّهِ ذِى الْمَعَارِجِ (٣) تَعْرُجُ الْمَلَـٰئِكَةُ وَالرُّوحُ إِلَيْهِ فِى يَوْمٍ كَانَ مِقْدَارُهُ خَمْسِينَ أَلْفَ سَنَةٍ (٤)

*A questioner asked concerning a torment about to befall (1) Upon the disbelievers, which none can avert, (2) From Allâh, the Lord of the ways of ascent. (3) The angels and the Rûh [Jibril (Gabriel)] ascend to Him in a Day the measure whereof is fifty thousand years. (4)*

**Quran 70:6-17**

إِنَّهُمْ يَرَوْنَهُ بَعِيدًا (٦) وَنَرَىٰهُ قَرِيبًا (٧) يَوْمَ تَكُونُ السَّمَاءُ كَالْمُهْلِ (٨) وَتَكُونُ الْجِبَالُ كَالْعِهْنِ (٩) وَلَا يَسْـَٔلُ حَمِيمٌ حَمِيمًا (١٠) يُبَصَّرُونَهُمْ يَوَدُّ الْمُجْرِمُ لَوْ يَفْتَدِى مِنْ عَذَابِ يَوْمِئِذٍ بِبَنِيهِ (١١) وَصَـٰحِبَتِهِ وَأَخِيهِ (١٢) وَفَصِيلَتِهِ الَّتِى تُـٔوِيهِ (١٣) وَمَن فِى الْأَرْضِ جَمِيعًا ثُمَّ يُنجِيهِ (١٤) كَلَّا إِنَّهَا لَظَىٰ (١٥) نَزَّاعَةً لِّلشَّوَىٰ (١٦) تَدْعُواْ مَنْ أَدْبَرَ وَتَوَلَّىٰ (١٧)

*Verily! they see it (the torment) afar off. (6) But We see it (quite) near. (7) The Day that the sky will be like the boiling filth of oil, (or molten copper or silver or lead). (8) And the mountains will be like flakes of wool. (9) And no friend will ask a friend (about his condition), (10) Though they shall be made to see one another [(i.e. on the Day of Resurrection), there will be none but see* his father, children and relatives, but he will neither speak to them nor will ask them for any help]. The Mujrim, (criminal, sinner, disbeliever) would desire to ransom himself from the punishment of that Day by his children. (11) And his wife and his brother, (12) And his kindred who sheltered him, (13) And all that are in the earth, so that it might save him. (14) By no means! Verily, it will be the Fire of Hell! (15) Taking away (burning completely) the head skin! (16) Calling (all) such as turn their backs and turn away their faces (from Faith) (17)

## Quran 70:26-28

وَٱلَّذِينَ يُصَدِّقُونَ بِيَوْمِ ٱلدِّينِ (٢٦) وَٱلَّذِينَ هُم مِّنْ عَذَابِ رَبِّهِم مُّشْفِقُونَ (٢٧) إِنَّ عَذَابَ رَبِّهِمْ غَيْرُ مَأْمُونٍ (٢٨)

And those who believe in the Day of Recompense, (26) And those who fear the torment of their Lord, (27) Verily, the torment of their Lord is that before which none can feel secure − (28)

## Quran 70:35

أُوْلَـٰٓئِكَ فِى جَنَّـٰتٍ مُّكْرَمُونَ

Such shall dwell in the Gardens (i.e. Paradise) honoured. (35)

## Quran 70:38

أَيَطْمَعُ كُلُّ ٱمْرِئٍ مِّنْهُمْ أَن يُدْخَلَ جَنَّةَ نَعِيمٍ

*Does every man of them hope to enter the Paradise of Delight? (38)*

## Quran 70:42-44

فَذَرْهُمْ يَخُوضُوا۟ وَيَلْعَبُوا۟ حَتَّىٰ يُلَٰقُوا۟ يَوْمَهُمُ ٱلَّذِى يُوعَدُونَ (٤٢) يَوْمَ يَخْرُجُونَ مِنَ ٱلْأَجْدَاثِ سِرَاعًا كَأَنَّهُمْ إِلَىٰ نُصُبٍ يُوفِضُونَ (٤٣) خَٰشِعَةً أَبْصَٰرُهُمْ تَرْهَقُهُمْ ذِلَّةٌ ذَٰلِكَ ٱلْيَوْمُ ٱلَّذِى كَانُوا۟ يُوعَدُونَ (٤٤)

*So leave them to plunge in vain talk and play about, until they meet their Day which they are promised — (42) The Day when they will come out of the graves quickly as racing to a goal, (43) With their eyes lowered in fear and humility, ignominy covering them (all over)! That is the Day which they were promised! (44)*

## Quran 71:18

ثُمَّ يُعِيدُكُمْ فِيهَا وَيُخْرِجُكُمْ إِخْرَاجًا

*Afterwards He will return you into it (the earth), and bring you forth (again on the Day of Resurrection)? (18)*

## Quran 72:15-17

وَأَمَّا ٱلْقَٰسِطُونَ فَكَانُوا۟ لِجَهَنَّمَ حَطَبًا ﴿١٥﴾ وَأَلَّوِ ٱسْتَقَٰمُوا۟
عَلَى ٱلطَّرِيقَةِ لَأَسْقَيْنَٰهُم مَّآءً غَدَقًا ﴿١٦﴾ لِّنَفْتِنَهُمْ فِيهِ وَمَن
يُعْرِضْ عَن ذِكْرِ رَبِّهِۦ يَسْلُكْهُ عَذَابًا صَعَدًا ﴿١٧﴾

*And as for the Qâsitûn (disbelievers who deviated from the Right Path), they shall be firewood for Hell, (15) If they (non-Muslims) had believed in Allâh, and went on the Right Way (i.e. Islâm) We would surely have bestowed on them water (rain) in abundance. (16) That We might try them thereby. And whosoever turns away from the Reminder of his Lord (i.e. this Qur'ân — and practise not its laws and orders), He will cause him to enter in a severe torment (i.e. Hell). (17)*

## Quran 72:23-25

إِلَّا بَلَٰغًا مِّنَ ٱللَّهِ وَرِسَٰلَٰتِهِۦ وَمَن يَعْصِ ٱللَّهَ وَرَسُولَهُۥ فَإِنَّ لَهُۥ
نَارَ جَهَنَّمَ خَٰلِدِينَ فِيهَآ أَبَدًا ﴿٢٣﴾ حَتَّىٰ إِذَا رَأَوْا۟ مَا يُوعَدُونَ
فَسَيَعْلَمُونَ مَنْ أَضْعَفُ نَاصِرًا وَأَقَلُّ عَدَدًا ﴿٢٤﴾ قُلْ إِنْ
أَدْرِىٓ أَقَرِيبٌ مَّا تُوعَدُونَ أَمْ يَجْعَلُ لَهُۥ رَبِّىٓ أَمَدًا ﴿٢٥﴾

*"(Mine is) but conveyance (of the truth) from Allâh and His Messages (of Islâmic Monotheism), and whosoever disobeys Allâh and His Messenger, then verily, for him is the Fire of Hell, he shall dwell therein forever." (23) Till, when they see that which they are promised, then they will know who it is that is weaker concerning helpers and less important concerning numbers (24) Say: "I know*

not whether (the punishment) which you are promised is near or whether my Lord will appoint for it a distant term (25)

## Quran 72:27-28

إِلَّا مَنِ ٱرْتَضَىٰ مِن رَّسُولٍ فَإِنَّهُ يَسْلُكُ مِنْ بَيْنِ يَدَيْهِ وَمِنْ خَلْفِهِ رَصَدًا (٢٧) لِّيَعْلَمَ أَن قَدْ أَبْلَغُواْ رِسَٰلَٰتِ رَبِّهِمْ وَأَحَاطَ بِمَا لَدَيْهِمْ وَأَحْصَىٰ كُلَّ شَىْءٍ عَدَدًا (٢٨)

Except to a Messenger (from mankind) whom He has chosen (He informs him of unseen as much as He likes), and then He makes a band of watching guards (angels) to march before him and behind him (27) [He (Allâh) protects them (the Messengers)], till He sees that they (the Messengers) have conveyed the Messages of their Lord (Allâh). And He (Allâh) surrounds all that which is with them, and He (Allâh) keeps count of all things (i.e. He knows the exact number of everything) (28)

## Quran 73:12-14

إِنَّ لَدَيْنَآ أَنكَالاً وَجَحِيمًا (١٢) وَطَعَامًا ذَا غُصَّةٍ وَعَذَابًا أَلِيمًا (١٣) يَوْمَ تَرْجُفُ ٱلْأَرْضُ وَٱلْجِبَالُ وَكَانَتِ ٱلْجِبَالُ كَثِيبًا مَّهِيلاً (١٤)

Verily, with Us are fetters (to bind them), and a raging Fire. (12) And a food that chokes, and a painful torment. (13) On the Day when the earth and the mountains will be in violent shake, and the mountains will be a heap of sand poured out. (14)

## Quran 73:17-18

فَكَيْفَ تَتَّقُونَ إِن كَفَرْتُمْ يَوْمًا يَجْعَلُ ٱلْوِلْدَٰنَ شِيبًا
(١٧) ٱلسَّمَآءُ مُنفَطِرٌ بِهِۦ كَانَ وَعْدُهُۥ مَفْعُولًا (١٨)

*Then how can you avoid the punishment, if you disbelieve, on a Day (i.e. the Day of Resurrection) that will make the children grey-headed? (17) Whereon the heaven will be cleft asunder? His Promise is certainly to be accomplished (18)*

## Quran 73:20

إِنَّ رَبَّكَ يَعْلَمُ أَنَّكَ تَقُومُ أَدْنَىٰ مِن ثُلُثَيِ ٱلَّيْلِ وَنِصْفَهُۥ ۞
وَثُلُثَهُۥ وَطَآئِفَةٌ مِّنَ ٱلَّذِينَ مَعَكَ وَٱللَّهُ يُقَدِّرُ ٱلَّيْلَ
وَٱلنَّهَارَ عَلِمَ أَن لَّن تُحْصُوهُ فَتَابَ عَلَيْكُمْ فَٱقْرَءُواْ مَا
تَيَسَّرَ مِنَ ٱلْقُرْءَانِ عَلِمَ أَن سَيَكُونُ مِنكُم مَّرْضَىٰ
وَءَاخَرُونَ يَضْرِبُونَ فِى ٱلْأَرْضِ يَبْتَغُونَ مِن فَضْلِ ٱللَّهِ
وَءَاخَرُونَ يُقَٰتِلُونَ فِى سَبِيلِ ٱللَّهِ فَٱقْرَءُواْ مَا تَيَسَّرَ مِنْهُ
وَأَقِيمُواْ ٱلصَّلَوٰةَ وَءَاتُواْ ٱلزَّكَوٰةَ وَأَقْرِضُواْ ٱللَّهَ قَرْضًا
حَسَنًا وَمَا تُقَدِّمُواْ لِأَنفُسِكُم مِّنْ خَيْرٍ تَجِدُوهُ عِندَ ٱللَّهِ هُوَ
خَيْرًا وَأَعْظَمَ أَجْرًا وَٱسْتَغْفِرُواْ ٱللَّهَ إِنَّ ٱللَّهَ غَفُورٌ
رَّحِيمٌ

Verily, your Lord knows that you do stand (to pray at (also night) a little less than two-thirds of the night, or half the night, or a third of the night, and a party of those with you, And Allâh measures the night and the day. He knows that you are unable to pray the whole night, so He has turned to you (in mercy). So, recite you of the Qur'ân as much as may be easy for you. He knows that there will be some among you sick, others travelling through the land, seeking of Allâh's Bounty; yet others fighting in Allâh's Cause. So recite as much of the Qur'ân as may be easy (for you), and perform As-Salât (Iqâmat-as-Salât) and give Zakât, and lend to Allâh a goodly loan, And whatever good you send before you for yourselves, (i.e. Nawâfil non-obligatory acts of worship: prayers, charity, fasting, Hajj and 'Umrah), you will certainly find it with Allâh, better and greater in reward. And seek Forgiveness of Allâh. Verily, Allâh is Oft-Forgiving, Most-Merciful (20)

## Quran 74:8-31

فَإِذَا نُقِرَ فِى ٱلنَّاقُورِ (٨) فَذَٰلِكَ يَوْمَئِذٍ يَوْمٌ عَسِيرٌ (٩) عَلَى ٱلْكَـٰفِرِينَ غَيْرُ يَسِيرٍ (١٠) ذَرْنِى وَمَنْ خَلَقْتُ وَحِيدًا (١١) وَجَعَلْتُ لَهُۥ مَالاً مَّمْدُودًا (١٢) وَبَنِينَ شُهُودًا (١٣) وَمَهَّدتُّ لَهُۥ تَمْهِيدًا (١٤) ثُمَّ يَطْمَعُ أَنْ أَزِيدَ (١٥) كَلَّآ إِنَّهُۥ كَانَ لِأَيَـٰتِنَا عَنِيدًا (١٦) سَأُرْهِقُهُۥ صَعُودًا (١٧) إِنَّهُۥ فَكَّرَ وَقَدَّرَ (١٨) فَقُتِلَ كَيْفَ قَدَّرَ (١٩) ثُمَّ قُتِلَ كَيْفَ قَدَّرَ

(٢٠) ثُمَّ نَظَرَ (٢١) ثُمَّ عَبَسَ وَبَسَرَ (٢٢) ثُمَّ أَدْبَرَ
وَٱسْتَكْبَرَ (٢٣) فَقَالَ إِنْ هَـٰذَآ إِلَّا سِحْرٌ يُؤْثَرُ (٢٤) إِنْ
هَـٰذَآ إِلَّا قَوْلُ ٱلْبَشَرِ (٢٥) سَأُصْلِيهِ سَقَرَ (٢٦) وَمَآ أَدْرَىٰكَ
مَا سَقَرُ (٢٧) لَا تُبْقِى وَلَا تَذَرُ (٢٨) لَوَّاحَةٌ لِّلْبَشَرِ
(٢٩) عَلَيْهَا تِسْعَةَ عَشَرَ (٣٠) وَمَا جَعَلْنَآ أَصْحَـٰبَ ٱلنَّارِ إِلَّا
مَلَـٰٓئِكَةً وَمَا جَعَلْنَا عِدَّتَهُمْ إِلَّا فِتْنَةً لِّلَّذِينَ كَفَرُواْ لِيَسْتَيْقِنَ ٱلَّذِينَ
أُوتُواْ ٱلْكِتَـٰبَ وَيَزْدَادَ ٱلَّذِينَ ءَامَنُوٓاْ إِيمَـٰنًا وَلَا يَرْتَابَ ٱلَّذِينَ
أُوتُواْ ٱلْكِتَـٰبَ وَٱلْمُؤْمِنُونَ وَلِيَقُولَ ٱلَّذِينَ فِى قُلُوبِهِم مَّرَضٌ
وَٱلْكَـٰفِرُونَ مَاذَآ أَرَادَ ٱللَّهُ بِهَـٰذَا مَثَلًا كَذَٰلِكَ يُضِلُّ ٱللَّهُ مَن يَشَآءُ
وَيَهْدِى مَن يَشَآءُ وَمَا يَعْلَمُ جُنُودَ رَبِّكَ إِلَّا هُوَ وَمَا هِىَ إِلَّا
ذِكْرَىٰ لِلْبَشَرِ (٣١)

Then, when the Trumpet is sounded (i.e. the second blowing of horn); (8) Truly, that Day will be a Hard Day — (9) Far from easy for the disbelievers. (10) Leave Me Alone (to deal) with whom I created Alone (without any means)! (11) And then granted him resources in abundance. (12) And children to be by his side! (13) And made life smooth and comfortable for him! (14) After all that he desires that I should give more; (15) Nay! Verily, he has been opposing Our Ayât (proofs, evidences, verses, lessons, signs, revelations). (16) I shall oblige him to (climb a slippery mountain in the Hell-fire called As¬Sa'ûd, or) face a severe torment! (17) Verily, he thought and plotted; (18) So let him be cursed! how he *plotted! (19) And once more let him be cursed, how he plotted! (20) Then he thought; (21) Then he frowned and he looked in a bad tempered way; (22) Then he turned back and was proud; (23) Then he said: "This is nothing but magic from that of old; (24) "This is nothing but the word of a human being!" (25) I will cast him into Hellfire (26) And what will make you know (exactly) what Hell-fire is? (27) It spares not (any sinner), nor does it leave (anything unburnt)! (28) Burning and blackening the skins! (29) Over it are nineteen (angels as guardians and keepers of Hell). (30) And We have set none but angels as guardians of the Fire, and We have fixed number (19) only as a trial for the disbelievers, in order that the people of the Scripture (Jews and Christians) may arrive at a certainty [that this Qur'ân is the truth as it agrees with their Books regarding their number (19) which is written in the Taurât (Torah) and the Injeel] and that the believers may increase in Faith (as this Qur'ân is the truth) and that no doubt may be left for the people of the Scripture and the believers, and that those in whose hearts is a disease (of hypocrisy) and the disbelievers may say: "What Allâh intends by this (curious) example ?" Thus Allâh leads astray whom He wills and guides whom He wills. And none can know the hosts of your Lord but He. And this (Hell) is nothing else than a (warning) reminder to mankind. (31)*

**Quran 74:35-48**

إِنَّهَا لَإِحْدَى ٱلْكُبَرِ (٣٥) نَذِيرًا لِّلْبَشَرِ (٣٦) لِمَن شَآءَ مِنكُمْ أَن يَتَقَدَّمَ أَوْ يَتَأَخَّرَ (٣٧) كُلُّ نَفْسٍ بِمَا كَسَبَتْ رَهِينَةٌ (٣٨) إِلَّا أَصْحَـٰبَ ٱلْيَمِينِ (٣٩) فِى جَنَّـٰتٍ يَتَسَآءَلُونَ (٤٠) عَنِ ٱلْمُجْرِمِينَ (٤١) مَا سَلَكَكُمْ فِى سَقَرَ (٤٢) قَالُواْ لَمْ نَكُ مِنَ ٱلْمُصَلِّينَ (٤٣) وَلَمْ نَكُ نُطْعِمُ ٱلْمِسْكِينَ (٤٤) وَكُنَّا نَخُوضُ مَعَ ٱلْخَآئِضِينَ (٤٥) وَكُنَّا نُكَذِّبُ بِيَوْمِ ٱلدِّينِ (٤٦) حَتَّىٰ أَتَٮٰنَا ٱلْيَقِينُ (٤٧) فَمَا تَنفَعُهُمْ شَفَـٰعَةُ ٱلشَّـٰفِعِينَ (٤٨)

Verily, it (Hell, or their denial of the Prophet Muhammad, or the Day of Resurrection) is but one of the greatest (signs). (35) A warning to mankind — (36) To any of you that chooses to go forward (by working righteous deeds), or to remain behind (by committing sins), (37) Every person is a pledge for what he has earned, (38) Except those on the Right, (i.e. the pious true believers of Islâmic Monotheism); (39) In Gardens (Paradise) they will ask one another, (40) About Al-Mujrimûn (polytheists, criminals, disbelievers), (And they will say to them): (41) "What has caused you to enter Hell?" (42) They will say: "We were not of those who used to offer the Salât (prayers) (43) "Nor we used to feed Al-Miskin (the poor); (44) "And we used to talk falsehood (all that which Allâh hated) with vain talkers (45) "And we used to belie the Day of Recompense (46) "Until there came to us (the death) that is certain."

*(47) So no intercession of intercessors will be of any use to them (48)*

## Quran 74:53-54

كَلَّا بَل لَّا يَخَافُونَ ٱلْأَخِرَةَ (٥٣) كَلَّا إِنَّهُ تَذْكِرَةٌ (٥٤)

*Nay! But they fear not the Hereafter (from Allâh's punishment). (53) Nay, verily, this (Qur'ân) is an admonition. (54)*

## Quran 75:1-30

لَا أُقْسِمُ بِيَوْمِ ٱلْقِيَامَةِ (١) وَلَا أُقْسِمُ بِٱلنَّفْسِ ٱللَّوَّامَةِ (٢) أَيَحْسَبُ ٱلْإِنسَانُ أَلَّن نَّجْمَعَ عِظَامَهُ (٣) بَلَىٰ قَادِرِينَ عَلَىٰ أَن نُّسَوِّىَ بَنَانَهُ (٤) بَلْ يُرِيدُ ٱلْإِنسَانُ لِيَفْجُرَ أَمَامَهُ (٥) يَسْئَلُ أَيَّانَ يَوْمُ ٱلْقِيَامَةِ (٦) فَإِذَا بَرِقَ ٱلْبَصَرُ (٧) وَخَسَفَ ٱلْقَمَرُ (٨) وَجُمِعَ ٱلشَّمْسُ وَٱلْقَمَرُ (٩) يَقُولُ ٱلْإِنسَانُ يَوْمَئِذٍ أَيْنَ ٱلْمَفَرُّ (١٠) كَلَّا لَا وَزَرَ (١١) إِلَىٰ رَبِّكَ يَوْمَئِذٍ ٱلْمُسْتَقَرُّ (١٢) يُنَبَّؤُا۟ ٱلْإِنسَانُ يَوْمَئِذٍ بِمَا قَدَّمَ وَأَخَّرَ (١٣) بَلِ ٱلْإِنسَانُ عَلَىٰ نَفْسِهِ بَصِيرَةٌ (١٤) وَلَوْ أَلْقَىٰ مَعَاذِيرَهُ (١٥) لَا تُحَرِّكْ بِهِ لِسَانَكَ لِتَعْجَلَ بِهِ (١٦) إِنَّ عَلَيْنَا جَمْعَهُ وَقُرْءَانَهُ (١٧) فَإِذَا قَرَأْنَاهُ فَٱتَّبِعْ قُرْءَانَهُ (١٨) ثُمَّ إِنَّ عَلَيْنَا بَيَانَهُ (١٩) كَلَّا بَلْ تُحِبُّونَ ٱلْعَاجِلَةَ (٢٠) وَتَذَرُونَ ٱلْأَخِرَةَ (٢١) وُجُوهٌ يَوْمَئِذٍ نَّاضِرَةٌ (٢٢) إِلَىٰ رَبِّهَا نَاظِرَةٌ (٢٣) وَوُجُوهٌ يَوْمَئِذٍ بَاسِرَةٌ (٢٤) تَظُنُّ أَن يُفْعَلَ بِهَا فَاقِرَةٌ (٢٥) كَلَّا إِذَا بَلَغَتِ ٱلتَّرَاقِىَ

(٢٦) وَقِيلَ مَنْ رَاقٍ (٢٧) وَظَنَّ أَنَّهُ ٱلْفِرَاقُ (٢٨) وَٱلْتَفَّتِ ٱلسَّاقُ بِٱلسَّاقِ (٢٩) إِلَىٰ رَبِّكَ يَوْمَئِذٍ ٱلْمَسَاقُ (٣٠)

*I swear by the Day of Resurrection; (1) And I swear by the self-reproaching person (a believer). (2) Does man (a disbeliever) think that We shall not assemble his bones? (3) Yes, We are Able to put together in perfect order the tips of his fingers. (4) Nay! (Man denies Resurrection and Reckoning. So he) desires to continue committing sins. (5) He asks: "When will be this Day of Resurrection?" (6) So, when the sight shall be dazed, (7) And the moon will be eclipsed, (8) And the sun and moon will be joined together (by going one into the other or folded up or deprived of their light).(9) On that Day man will say: "Where (is the refuge) to flee?" (10) No! There is no refuge! (11) Unto your Lord (Alone) will be the place of rest that Day. (12) On that Day man will be informed of what he sent forward (of his evil or good deeds), and what he left behind (of his good or evil traditions). (13) Nay! Man will be a witness against himself [as his body parts (skin, hands, legs, etc.) will speak about his deeds]. (14) Though he may put forth his excuses (to cover his evil deeds). (15) Move not your tongue concerning (the Qur'ân, O Muhammad) to make haste therewith. (16) It is for Us to collect it and to give you (O Muhammad) the ability to recite it (the Qur'ân), (17) And when We have recited it to you [O Muhammad*

through Jibril (Gabriel)], then follow you its (the Qur'ân's) recital. (18) Then it is for Us (Allâh) to make it clear (to you). (19) Not [as you think, that you (mankind) will not be resurrected and recompensed for your deeds], but you (men) love the present life of this world, (20) And neglect the Hereafter. (21) Some faces that Day shall be Nâdirah (shining and radiant).
(22) Looking at their Lord (Allâh); (23) And some faces, that Day, will be Bâsirah (dark, gloomy, frowning, and sad), (24) Thinking that some calamity is about to fall on them; (25) Nay, when (the soul) reaches to the collar bone (i.e. up to the throat in its exit), (26) And it will be said: "Who can cure him (and save him from death)?"
(27) And he (the dying person) will conclude that it was (the time) of parting (death); (28) And one leg will be joined with another leg (shrouded)(29) The drive will be, on that Day, to your Lord (Allâh)! (30)

## Quran 75:40

أَلَيْسَ ذَٰلِكَ بِقَٰدِرٍ عَلَىٰٓ أَن يُحْۦِىَ ٱلْمَوْتَىٰ

Is not He (Allâh Who does that), Able to give life to the dead? (Yes! He is Able to do all things). (40)

## Quran 76:4-7

إِنَّآ أَعْتَدْنَا لِلْكَٰفِرِينَ سَلَٰسِلَا۟ وَأَغْلَٰلاً وَسَعِيرًا (٤) إِنَّ ٱلْأَبْرَارَ يَشْرَبُونَ مِن كَأْسٍ كَانَ مِزَاجُهَا كَافُورًا (٥) عَيْنًا يَشْرَبُ

462

بِهَا عِبَادُ ٱللَّهِ يُفَجِّرُونَهَا تَفْجِيرًا (٦) يُوفُونَ بِٱلنَّذْرِ وَيَخَافُونَ يَوْمًا كَانَ شَرُّهُ مُسْتَطِيرًا (٧)

*Verily, We have prepared for the disbelievers iron chains, iron collars, and a blazing Fire. (4) Verily, the Abrâr (the pious and righteous) shall drink of a cup (of wine) mixed with (water from a spring in Paradise called) Kâfûr. (5) A spring wherefrom the slaves of Allâh will drink, causing it to gush forth abundantly. (6) They (are those who) fulfill (their) vows, and they fear a Day whose evil will be wide-spreading. (7)*

## Quran 76:10-22

إِنَّا نَخَافُ مِن رَّبِّنَا يَوْمًا عَبُوسًا قَمْطَرِيرًا (١٠) فَوَقَىٰهُمُ ٱللَّهُ شَرَّ ذَٰلِكَ ٱلْيَوْمِ وَلَقَّٰهُمْ نَضْرَةً وَسُرُورًا (١١) وَجَزَىٰهُم بِمَا صَبَرُواْ جَنَّةً وَحَرِيرًا (١٢) مُّتَّكِئِينَ فِيهَا عَلَى ٱلْأَرَائِكِ لَا يَرَوْنَ فِيهَا شَمْسًا وَلَا زَمْهَرِيرًا (١٣) وَدَانِيَةً عَلَيْهِمْ ظِلَٰلُهَا وَذُلِّلَتْ قُطُوفُهَا تَذْلِيلاً (١٤) وَيُطَافُ عَلَيْهِم بِآنِيَةٍ مِّن فِضَّةٍ وَأَكْوَابٍ كَانَتْ قَوَارِيرَا۠ (١٥) قَوَارِيرَ مِن فِضَّةٍ قَدَّرُوهَا تَقْدِيرًا (١٦) وَيُسْقَوْنَ فِيهَا كَأْسًا كَانَ مِزَاجُهَا زَنجَبِيلاً (١٧) عَيْنًا فِيهَا تُسَمَّىٰ سَلْسَبِيلاً (١٨) ۞ وَيَطُوفُ عَلَيْهِمْ وِلْدَٰنٌ مُّخَلَّدُونَ إِذَا رَأَيْتَهُمْ حَسِبْتَهُمْ لُؤْلُؤًا مَّنثُورًا (١٩) وَإِذَا رَأَيْتَ ثَمَّ رَأَيْتَ نَعِيمًا وَمُلْكًا كَبِيرًا (٢٠) عَلَيْهِمْ ثِيَابُ سُندُسٍ خُضْرٌ وَإِسْتَبْرَقٌ وَحُلُّواْ أَسَاوِرَ مِن فِضَّةٍ وَسَقَىٰهُمْ رَبُّهُمْ شَرَابًا

طَهُورًا (٢١) إِنَّ هَٰذَا كَانَ لَكُمْ جَزَاءً وَكَانَ سَعْيُكُم مَّشْكُورًا (٢٢)

"Verily, We fear from our Lord a Day, hard and distressful, that will make the faces look horrible (from extreme dislike to it)." (10) So Allâh saved them from the evil of that Day, and gave them Nadhrah (a light of beauty) and joy. (11) And their recompense shall be Paradise, and silken garments, because they were patient. (12) Reclining therein on raised thrones, they will see there neither the excessive heat of the sun, nor the excessive bitter cold, (as in Paradise there is no sun and no moon). (13) And the shade thereof is close upon them, and the bunches of fruit thereof will hang low within their reach. (14) And amongst them will be passed round vessels of silver and cups of crystal — (15) Crystal-clear, made of silver. They will determine the measure thereof (according to their wishes). (16) And they will be given to drink there of a cup (of wine) mixed with Zanjabîl (ginger). (17) A spring there, called Salsabîl. (18) And round about them will (serve) boys of everlasting youth. If you see them, you would think them scattered pearls. (19) And when you look there (in Paradise), you will see a delight (that cannot be imagined), and a great dominion. (20) Their garments will be of fine green silk, and gold embroidery. They will be adorned with bracelets of silver, and their Lord will give them a pure drink.

(21) (And it will be said to them): "Verily, this is a reward for you, and your endeavour has been accepted." (22)

## Quran 76:27

إِنَّ هَـٰٓؤُلَآءِ يُحِبُّونَ ٱلْعَاجِلَةَ وَيَذَرُونَ وَرَآءَهُمْ يَوْمًا ثَقِيلاً

Verily, these (disbelievers) love the present life of this world, and put behind them a heavy Day (that will be hard). (27)

## Quran 76:31

يُدْخِلُ مَن يَشَآءُ فِى رَحْمَتِهِ وَٱلظَّـٰلِمِينَ أَعَدَّ لَهُمْ عَذَابًا أَلِيمًا

He will admit to His Mercy whom He wills and as for the Zâlimûn – (polytheists, wrong-doers) He has prepared a painful torment. (31)

## Quran 77:1-19

وَٱلْمُرْسَلَـٰتِ عُرْفًا (١) فَٱلْعَـٰصِفَـٰتِ عَصْفًا (٢) وَٱلنَّـٰشِرَٰتِ نَشْرًا (٣) فَٱلْفَـٰرِقَـٰتِ فَرْقًا (٤) فَٱلْمُلْقِيَـٰتِ ذِكْرًا (٥) عُذْرًا أَوْ نُذْرًا (٦) إِنَّمَا تُوعَدُونَ لَوَٰقِعٌ (٧) فَإِذَا ٱلنُّجُومُ طُمِسَتْ (٨) وَإِذَا ٱلسَّمَآءُ فُرِجَتْ (٩) وَإِذَا ٱلْجِبَالُ نُسِفَتْ (١٠) وَإِذَا ٱلرُّسُلُ أُقِّتَتْ (١١) لِأَىِّ يَوْمٍ أُجِّلَتْ (١٢) لِيَوْمِ ٱلْفَصْلِ (١٣) وَمَآ أَدْرَىٰكَ مَا يَوْمُ ٱلْفَصْلِ (١٤) وَيْلٌ يَوْمَئِذٍ لِّلْمُكَذِّبِينَ (١٥) أَلَمْ نُهْلِكِ ٱلْأَوَّلِينَ (١٦) ثُمَّ نُتْبِعُهُمُ ٱلْأَخِرِينَ

(١٧) كَذَٰلِكَ نَفْعَلُ بِٱلْمُجْرِمِينَ (١٨) وَيْلٌ يَوْمَئِذٍ لِّلْمُكَذِّبِينَ (١٩)

*By the winds (or angels or the Messengers of Allâh) sent forth one after another. (1) And by the winds that blow violently, (2) And by the winds that scatter clouds and rain; (3) And by the Verses (of the Qur'ân) that separate the right from the wrong. (4) And by the angels that bring the revelations to the Messengers, (5) To cut off all excuses or to warn; (6) Surely, what you are promised must come to pass. (7) Then when the stars lose their lights; (8) And when the heaven is cleft asunder; (9) And when the mountains are blown away; (10) And when the Messengers are gathered to their time appointed; (11) For what Day are these signs postponed? (12) For the Day of sorting out (the men of Paradise from the men destined for Hell). (13) And what will explain to you what is the Day of sorting out? (14) Woe that Day to the deniers (of the Day of Resurrection)! (15) Did We not destroy the ancients? (16) So shall We make later generations to follow them. (17) Thus do We deal with the Mujrimûn (polytheists, disbelievers, sinners, criminals)! (18) Woe that Day to the deniers (of the Day of Resurrection)! (19)*

**Quran 77:29-45**

ٱنطَلِقُوٓاْ إِلَىٰ مَا كُنتُم بِهِۦ تُكَذِّبُونَ (٢٩) ٱنطَلِقُوٓاْ إِلَىٰ ظِلٍّ ذِى ثَلَٰثِ شُعَبٍ (٣٠) لَّا ظَلِيلٍ وَلَا يُغْنِى مِنَ ٱللَّهَبِ (٣١) إِنَّهَا

466

تَرْمِى بِشَرَرٍ كَٱلْقَصْرِ (٣٢) كَأَنَّهُ جِمَٰلَتٌ صُفْرٌ (٣٣) وَيْلٌ
يَوْمَئِذٍ لِّلْمُكَذِّبِينَ (٣٤) هَٰذَا يَوْمُ لَا يَنطِقُونَ (٣٥) وَلَا يُؤْذَنُ
لَهُمْ فَيَعْتَذِرُونَ (٣٦) وَيْلٌ يَوْمَئِذٍ لِّلْمُكَذِّبِينَ (٣٧) هَٰذَا يَوْمُ
ٱلْفَصْلِ جَمَعْنَٰكُمْ وَٱلْأَوَّلِينَ (٣٨) فَإِن كَانَ لَكُمْ كَيْدٌ فَكِيدُونِ
(٣٩) وَيْلٌ يَوْمَئِذٍ لِّلْمُكَذِّبِينَ (٤٠) إِنَّ ٱلْمُتَّقِينَ فِى ظِلَٰلٍ
وَعُيُونٍ (٤١) وَفَوَٰكِهَ مِمَّا يَشْتَهُونَ (٤٢) كُلُواْ وَٱشْرَبُواْ
هَنِيٓئًا بِمَا كُنتُمْ تَعْمَلُونَ (٤٣) إِنَّا كَذَٰلِكَ نَجْزِى ٱلْمُحْسِنِينَ
(٤٤) وَيْلٌ يَوْمَئِذٍ لِّلْمُكَذِّبِينَ (٤٥)

(It will be said to the disbelievers): "Depart you to that
which you used to deny! (29) "Depart you to a shadow
(of Hell-fire smoke ascending) in three columns,
(30) "Neither shady, nor of any use against the fierce
flame of the Fire." (31) Verily, It (Hell) throws sparks
(huge) as Al-Qasr [a fort or a (huge log of wood)],
(32) As if they were yellow camels or bundles of ropes.
(33) Woe that Day to the deniers (of the Day of
Resurrection)! (34) That will be a Day when they shall
not speak (during some part of it), (35) And they will not
be permitted to put forth any excuse. (36) Woe that Day
to the deniers (of the Day of Resurrection)! (37) That will
be a Day of Decision! We have brought you and the men
of old together! (38) So if you have a plot, use it against
Me (Allâh)! (39) Woe that Day to the deniers (of the Day
of Resurrection)! (40) Verily, the Muttaqûn (pious) shall
be amidst shades and springs. (41) And fruits, such as

they desire. (42) "Eat and drink comfortably for that
which you used to do. (43) Verily, thus We reward the
Muhsinûn (good-doers) (44) Woe that Day to the deniers
(of the Day of Resurrection)! (45)

## Quran 78:17-40

إِنَّ يَوْمَ ٱلْفَصْلِ كَانَ مِيقَـٰتًا (١٧) يَوْمَ يُنفَخُ فِى ٱلصُّورِ فَتَأْتُونَ
أَفْوَاجًا (١٨) وَفُتِحَتِ ٱلسَّمَآءُ فَكَانَتْ أَبْوَٰبًا (١٩) وَسُيِّرَتِ
ٱلْجِبَالُ فَكَانَتْ سَرَابًا (٢٠) إِنَّ جَهَنَّمَ كَانَتْ مِرْصَادًا
(٢١) لِّلطَّـٰغِينَ مَـَٔابًا (٢٢) لَّـٰبِثِينَ فِيهَآ أَحْقَابًا (٢٣) لَّا
يَذُوقُونَ فِيهَا بَرْدًا وَلَا شَرَابًا (٢٤) إِلَّا حَمِيمًا وَغَسَّاقًا
(٢٥) جَزَآءً وِفَاقًا (٢٦) إِنَّهُمْ كَانُوا۟ لَا يَرْجُونَ حِسَابًا
(٢٧) وَكَذَّبُوا۟ بِـَٔايَـٰتِنَا كِذَّابًا (٢٨) وَكُلَّ شَىْءٍ أَحْصَيْنَـٰهُ
كِتَـٰبًا (٢٩) فَذُوقُوا۟ فَلَن نَّزِيدَكُمْ إِلَّا عَذَابًا (٣٠) إِنَّ لِلْمُتَّقِينَ
مَفَازًا (٣١) حَدَآئِقَ وَأَعْنَـٰبًا (٣٢) وَكَوَاعِبَ أَتْرَابًا
(٣٣) وَكَأْسًا دِهَاقًا (٣٤) لَّا يَسْمَعُونَ فِيهَا لَغْوًا وَلَا كِذَّٰبًا
(٣٥) جَزَآءً مِّن رَّبِّكَ عَطَآءً حِسَابًا (٣٦) رَّبِّ ٱلسَّمَـٰوَٰتِ
وَٱلْأَرْضِ وَمَا بَيْنَهُمَا ٱلرَّحْمَـٰنِ لَا يَمْلِكُونَ مِنْهُ خِطَابًا
(٣٧) يَوْمَ يَقُومُ ٱلرُّوحُ وَٱلْمَلَـٰئِكَةُ صَفًّا لَّا يَتَكَلَّمُونَ إِلَّا مَنْ
أَذِنَ لَهُ ٱلرَّحْمَـٰنُ وَقَالَ صَوَابًا (٣٨) ذَٰلِكَ ٱلْيَوْمُ ٱلْحَقُّ فَمَن
شَآءَ ٱتَّخَذَ إِلَىٰ رَبِّهِ مَـَٔابًا (٣٩) إِنَّآ أَنذَرْنَـٰكُمْ عَذَابًا قَرِيبًا يَوْمَ
يَنظُرُ ٱلْمَرْءُ مَا قَدَّمَتْ يَدَاهُ وَيَقُولُ ٱلْكَافِرُ يَـٰلَيْتَنِى كُنتُ تُرَٰبًا
(٤٠)

*Verily, the Day of Decision is a fixed time, (17) The Day
when the Trumpet will be blown, and you shall come
forth in crowds (groups after groups). (18) And the
heaven shall be opened, and it will become as gates,
(19) And the mountains shall be moved away from their
places and they will be as if they were a mirage.
(20) Truly, Hell is a place of ambush − (21) A dwelling
place for the Tâghûn (those who transgress the boundry
limits set by Allâh like polytheists, disbelievers in the
Oneness of Allâh, hyprocrites, sinners, criminals),
(22) They will abide therein for ages, (23) Nothing cool
shall they taste therein, nor any drink. (24) Except
boiling water, and dirty wound discharges − (25) An
exact recompense (according to their evil crimes) (26) For
verily, they used not to look for a reckoning. (27) But
they belied Our Ayât (proofs, evidences, verses, lessons,
signs, revelations, and that which Our Prophet brought)
completely. (28) And all things We have recorded in a
Book. (29) So taste you (the results of your evil actions);
No increase shall We give you, except in torment.
(30) Verily, for the Muttaqûn, there will be a success
(Paradise); (31) Gardens and vineyards, (32) And young
full-breasted (mature) maidens of equal age, (33) And a
full cup (of wine). (34) No Laghw (dirty, false, evil talk)
shall they hear therein, nor lying; (35) A reward from
your Lord, an ample calculated gift (according to the best
of their good deeds). (36) (From) the Lord of the heavens*

and the earth, and whatsoever is in between them, the
Most Gracious with whome they dare to speak (on the
Day of Resurrection except by His Leave). (37) The Day
that Ar-Rûh [Jibril (Gabriel) or another angel] and the
angels will stand forth in rows, none they will not speak
except him whom the Most Gracious (Allâh) allows, and
he will speak what is right. (38) That is (without doubt)
the True Day, so, whosoever wills, let him seek a place
with (or a way to) His Lord (by obeying Him in this
worldly life)! (39) Verily, We have warned you of a near
torment — the Day when man will see that (the deeds)
which his hands have sent forth, and the disbeliever will
say: "Woe to me! Would that I were dust!" (40)

## Quran 79:1-14

وَٱلنَّٰزِعَٰتِ غَرْقًا (١) وَٱلنَّٰشِطَٰتِ نَشْطًا (٢) وَٱلسَّٰبِحَٰتِ
سَبْحًا (٣) فَٱلسَّٰبِقَٰتِ سَبْقًا (٤) فَٱلْمُدَبِّرَٰتِ أَمْرًا (٥) يَوْمَ
تَرْجُفُ ٱلرَّاجِفَةُ (٦) تَتْبَعُهَا ٱلرَّادِفَةُ (٧) قُلُوبٌ يَوْمَئِذٍ وَاجِفَةٌ
(٨) أَبْصَٰرُهَا خَٰشِعَةٌ (٩) يَقُولُونَ أَءِنَّا لَمَرْدُودُونَ فِى
ٱلْحَافِرَةِ (١٠) أَءِذَا كُنَّا عِظَٰمًا نَّخِرَةً (١١) قَالُوا تِلْكَ إِذًا
كَرَّةٌ خَاسِرَةٌ (١٢) فَإِنَّمَا هِىَ زَجْرَةٌ وَٰحِدَةٌ (١٣) فَإِذَا هُم
بِٱلسَّاهِرَةِ (١٤)

By those (angels) who pull out (the souls of the
disbelievers and the wicked) with great violence; (1) By
those (angels) who gently take out (the souls of the

believers); (2) *And by those that swim along (i.e. angels or planets in their orbits). (3) And by those that press forward as in a race (i.e. the angels or stars or the horses) (4) And by those angels who arrange to do the Commands of their Lord, (so verily, you disbelievers will be called to account). (5) On the Day (when the first blowing of the Trumpet is blown), the earth and the mountains will shake violently (and everybody will die), (6) The second blowing of the Trumpet follows it (and everybody will be resurrected), (7) (Some) hearts that Day will shake with fear and anxiety. (8) Their eyes will be downcast. (9) They say: "Shall we indeed be returned to (our) former state of life? (10) "Even after we are crumbled bones?" (11) They say: "It would in that case, be a return with loss!" (12) But, it will be only a single Zajrah [shout (i.e., the second blowing of the Trumpet)]. (13) When, behold, they find themselves on the surface of the earth alive after their death, (14)*

## Quran 79:34-46

فَإِذَا جَاءَتِ ٱلطَّآمَّةُ ٱلْكُبْرَىٰ (٣٤) يَوْمَ يَتَذَكَّرُ ٱلْإِنسَـٰنُ مَا سَعَىٰ (٣٥) وَبُرِّزَتِ ٱلْجَحِيمُ لِمَن يَرَىٰ (٣٦) فَأَمَّا مَن طَغَىٰ (٣٧) وَءَاثَرَ ٱلْحَيَوٰةَ ٱلدُّنْيَا (٣٨) فَإِنَّ ٱلْجَحِيمَ هِىَ ٱلْمَأْوَىٰ (٣٩) وَأَمَّا مَنْ خَافَ مَقَامَ رَبِّهِۦ وَنَهَى ٱلنَّفْسَ عَنِ ٱلْهَوَىٰ (٤٠) فَإِنَّ ٱلْجَنَّةَ هِىَ ٱلْمَأْوَىٰ (٤١) يَسْـَٔلُونَكَ عَنِ ٱلسَّاعَةِ أَيَّانَ مُرْسَىٰهَا (٤٢) فِيمَ أَنتَ مِن ذِكْرَىٰهَآ (٤٣) إِلَىٰ رَبِّكَ

مُنتَهَنهَا (٤٤) إِنَّمَآ أَنتَ مُنذِرُ مَن يَخْشَنهَا (٤٥) كَأَنَّهُمْ يَوْمَ
يَرَوْنَهَا لَمْ يَلْبَثُوٓاْ إِلَّا عَشِيَّةً أَوْ ضُحَنهَا (٤٦)

*But when there comes the greatest catastrophe (i.e. the Day of Recompense), (34) The Day when man shall remember what he strove for, (35) And Hell-fire shall be made apparent in full view for (every) one who sees, (36) Then, for him who transgressed all bounds (in disbelief, oppression and evil deeds of disobedience to Allâh). (37) And preferred the life of this world (by following his evil desires and lusts), (38) Verily, his abode will be Hell-fire; (39) But as for him who feared standing before his Lord, and restrained himself from impure evil desires, and lusts. (40) Verily, Paradise will be his abode. (41) They ask you (O Muhammad) about the Hour, - when will be its appointed time? (42) You have no knowledge to say anything about it, (43) To your Lord belongs (the knowledge of) the term thereof? (44) You (O Muhammad ) are only a warner for those who fear it, (45) The Day they see it, (it will be) as if they had not tarried (in this world) except an afternoon or a morning. (46)*

**Quran 80:33-42**

فَإِذَا جَآءَتِ ٱلصَّآخَّةُ (٣٣) يَوْمَ يَفِرُّ ٱلْمَرْءُ مِنْ أَخِيهِ
(٣٤) وَأُمِّهِۦ وَأَبِيهِ (٣٥) وَصَـٰحِبَتِهِۦ وَبَنِيهِ (٣٦) لِكُلِّ ٱمْرِئٍ
مِّنْهُمْ يَوْمَئِذٍ شَأْنٌ يُغْنِيهِ (٣٧) وُجُوهٌ يَوْمَئِذٍ مُّسْفِرَةٌ

(٣٨) ضَاحِكَةٌ مُّسْتَبْشِرَةٌ (٣٩) وَوُجُوهٌ يَوْمَئِذٍ عَلَيْهَا غَبَرَةٌ (٤٠) تَرْهَقُهَا قَتَرَةٌ (٤١) أُوْلَـٰئِكَ هُمُ ٱلْكَفَرَةُ ٱلْفَجَرَةُ (٤٢)

Then, when there comes As-Sâkhkhah (the second blowing of the Trumpet on the Day of Resurrection) — (33) That Day shall a man flee from his brother, (34) And from his mother and his father, (35) And from his wife and his children. (36) Everyman, that Day, will have enough to make him careless of others. (37) Some faces that Day, will be bright (true believers of Islâmic Monotheism). (38) Laughing, rejoicing at good news (of Paradise). (39) And other faces, that Day, will be dust-stained; (40) Darkness will cover them, (41) Such will be the Kafarah (disbelievers in Allâh, in His Oneness, and in His Messenger Muhammad, etc.), the Fajarah (wicked evil doers). (42)

## Quran 81:1-14

إِذَا ٱلشَّمْسُ كُوِّرَتْ (١) وَإِذَا ٱلنُّجُومُ ٱنكَدَرَتْ (٢) وَإِذَا ٱلْجِبَالُ سُيِّرَتْ (٣) وَإِذَا ٱلْعِشَارُ عُطِّلَتْ (٤) وَإِذَا ٱلْوُحُوشُ حُشِرَتْ (٥) وَإِذَا ٱلْبِحَارُ سُجِّرَتْ (٦) وَإِذَا ٱلنُّفُوسُ زُوِّجَتْ (٧) وَإِذَا ٱلْمَوْءُ‌ۥدَةُ سُئِلَتْ (٨) بِأَيِّ ذَنۢبٍ قُتِلَتْ (٩) وَإِذَا ٱلصُّحُفُ نُشِرَتْ (١٠) وَإِذَا ٱلسَّمَآءُ كُشِطَتْ (١١) وَإِذَا ٱلْجَحِيمُ سُعِّرَتْ (١٢) وَإِذَا ٱلْجَنَّةُ أُزْلِفَتْ (١٣) عَلِمَتْ نَفْسٌ مَّآ أَحْضَرَتْ (١٤)

When the sun is wound round and lost its light (is lost and is overthrown). (1) And when the stars fall; (2) And when the mountains are made to pass away; (3) And when the pregnant she-camels are be neglected; (4) And when the wild beasts are gathered together; (5) And when the seas become as blazing Fire or overflow; (6) And when the souls are joined with their bodies (the good with the good and bad with the bad). (7) And when the female (infant) buried alive (as the pagan Arabs used to do) is questioned. (8) For what sin was she killed? (9) And when the (written) pages [of deeds (good and bad) of every person] are laid open; (10) And when the heaven is stripped off and taken away from its place; (11) And when Hell-fire is set ablaze. (12) And when Paradise is brought near, (13) (Then) every person will know what he has brought (of good and evil). (14)

## Quran 82:1-5

إِذَا ٱلسَّمَآءُ ٱنفَطَرَتْ (١) وَإِذَا ٱلْكَوَاكِبُ ٱنتَثَرَتْ (٢) وَإِذَا ٱلْبِحَارُ فُجِّرَتْ (٣) وَإِذَا ٱلْقُبُورُ بُعْثِرَتْ (٤) عَلِمَتْ نَفْسٌ مَّا قَدَّمَتْ وَأَخَّرَتْ (٥)

When the heaven is cleft asunder. (1) And when the stars have fallen and scattered; (2) And when the seas are burst forth; (3) And when the graves are turned upside down (and bring out their contents). (4) (Then) a person

*will know what he has sent forward and (what he has)*
*left behind (of good or bad deeds). (5)*

**Quran 82:9-19**

كَلَّا بَلْ تُكَذِّبُونَ بِٱلدِّينِ (٩) وَإِنَّ عَلَيْكُمْ لَحَٰفِظِينَ
(١٠) كِرَامًا كَٰتِبِينَ (١١) يَعْلَمُونَ مَا تَفْعَلُونَ (١٢) إِنَّ
ٱلْأَبْرَارَ لَفِى نَعِيمٍ (١٣) وَإِنَّ ٱلْفُجَّارَ لَفِى جَحِيمٍ
(١٤) يَصْلَوْنَهَا يَوْمَ ٱلدِّينِ (١٥) وَمَا هُمْ عَنْهَا بِغَآئِبِينَ
(١٦) وَمَآ أَدْرَىٰكَ مَا يَوْمُ ٱلدِّينِ (١٧) ثُمَّ مَآ أَدْرَىٰكَ مَا يَوْمُ
ٱلدِّينِ (١٨) يَوْمَ لَا تَمْلِكُ نَفْسٌ لِّنَفْسٍ شَيْـًٔا ۖ وَٱلْأَمْرُ يَوْمَئِذٍ لِّلَّهِ
(١٩)

*Nay! But you deny the Ad-Din (i.e. the Day of*
*Recompense). (9) But verily, over you (are appointed*
*angels in charge of mankind) to watch you ,*
*(10) Kirâman (Honourable) Kâtibîn writing down (your*
*deeds), (11) They know all that you do. (12) Verily, the*
*Abrâr (pious and righteous) will be in Delight*
*(Paradise); (13) And verily, the Fujjâr (the wicked,*
*disbelievers, polytheists sinners and evil-doers) will be in*
*the blazing Fire (Hell), (14) Therein they will enter, and*
*taste its burning flame on the Day of Recompense,*
*(15) And they (Al-Fujjâr) will not be absent therefrom.*
*(16) And what will make you know what the Day of*
*Recompense is? (17) Again, what will make you know*
*what the Day of Recompense is? (18) (It will be) the Day*

when no person shall have power (to do) anything for another, and the Decision, that Day, will be (wholly) with Allâh. (19)

## Quran 83:4-12

أَلَا يَظُنُّ أُوْلَٰٓئِكَ أَنَّهُم مَّبْعُوثُونَ (٤) لِيَوْمٍ عَظِيمٍ (٥) يَوْمَ يَقُومُ ٱلنَّاسُ لِرَبِّ ٱلْعَٰلَمِينَ (٦) كَلَّا إِنَّ كِتَٰبَ ٱلْفُجَّارِ لَفِى سِجِّينٍ (٧) وَمَآ أَدْرَىٰكَ مَا سِجِّينٌ (٨) كِتَٰبٌ مَّرْقُومٌ (٩) وَيْلٌ يَوْمَئِذٍ لِّلْمُكَذِّبِينَ (١٠) ٱلَّذِينَ يُكَذِّبُونَ بِيَوْمِ ٱلدِّينِ (١١) وَمَا يُكَذِّبُ بِهِۦٓ إِلَّا كُلُّ مُعْتَدٍ أَثِيمٍ (١٢)

Do they not think that they will be resurrected (for reckoning), (4) On a Great Day, (5) The Day when (all) mankind will stand before the Lord of the 'Alamîn (mankind, jinn and all that exists)? (6) Nay! Truly, the Record (writing of the deeds) of the Fujjâr (disbelievers, polytheists sinners, evil-doers and wicked) is (preserved) in Sijjîn. (7) And what will make you know what Sijjîn is? (8) A Register inscribed. (9) Woe, that Day, to those who deny. (10) Those who deny the Day of Recompense. (11) And none can deny it except every transgressor beyond bounds, (in disbelief, oppression and disobedience to Allâh), the sinner! (12)

## Quran 83:15-28

كَلَّا إِنَّهُمْ عَن رَّبِّهِمْ يَوْمَئِذٍ لَّمَحْجُوبُونَ (١٥) ثُمَّ إِنَّهُمْ لَصَالُواْ
ٱلْجَحِيمِ (١٦) ثُمَّ يُقَالُ هَٰذَا ٱلَّذِى كُنتُم بِهِ تُكَذِّبُونَ (١٧) كَلَّا
إِنَّ كِتَٰبَ ٱلْأَبْرَارِ لَفِى عِلِّيِّينَ (١٨) وَمَآ أَدْرَىٰكَ مَا عِلِّيُّونَ
(١٩) كِتَٰبٌ مَّرْقُومٌ (٢٠) يَشْهَدُهُ ٱلْمُقَرَّبُونَ (٢١) إِنَّ
ٱلْأَبْرَارَ لَفِى نَعِيمٍ (٢٢) عَلَى ٱلْأَرَآئِكِ يَنظُرُونَ (٢٣) تَعْرِفُ
فِى وُجُوهِهِمْ نَضْرَةَ ٱلنَّعِيمِ (٢٤) يُسْقَوْنَ مِن رَّحِيقٍ مَّخْتُومٍ
(٢٥) خِتَٰمُهُ مِسْكٌ وَفِى ذَٰلِكَ فَلْيَتَنَافَسِ ٱلْمُتَنَٰفِسُونَ
(٢٦) وَمِزَاجُهُ مِن تَسْنِيمٍ (٢٧) عَيْنًا يَشْرَبُ بِهَا ٱلْمُقَرَّبُونَ
(٢٨)

Nay! Surely, they (evil-doers) will be veiled from seeing
their Lord that Day. (15) Then, verily they will indeed
enter (and taste) the burning flame of Hell. (16) Then, it
will be said to them: "This is what you used to deny!"
(17) Nay! Verily, the Record (writing of the deeds) of Al-
Abrâr (the pious and righteous), is (preserved) in
'Illiyyûn. (18) And what will make you know what
'Illiyyûn is? (19) A Register inscribed. (20) To which
bear witness those nearest (to Allâh, i.e. the angels).
(21) Verily, Al-Abrâr (the pious who fear Allâh and
avoid evil) will be in Delight (Paradise). (22) On thrones,
looking (at all things). (23) You will recognise in their
faces the brightness of delight. (24) They will be given to
drink of pure sealed wine. (25) The last thereof (that
wine) will be the smell of Musk, and for this let (all)
those strive who want to strive (i.e. hasten earnestly to

the obedience of Allâh). (26) It (that wine) will be mixed
with Tasnîm. (27) A spring whereof drink those nearest
to Allâh. (28)

## Quran 83:34-36

فَٱلْيَوْمَ ٱلَّذِينَ ءَامَنُواْ مِنَ ٱلْكُفَّارِ يَضْحَكُونَ (٣٤) عَلَى
ٱلْأَرَآئِكِ يَنظُرُونَ (٣٥) هَلْ ثُوِّبَ ٱلْكُفَّارُ مَا كَانُواْ يَفْعَلُونَ
(٣٦)

But this Day (the Day of Resurrection) those who believe
will laugh at the disbelievers (34) On (high) thrones,
looking (at all things). (35) Are not the disbelievers paid
(fully) for what they used to do? (36)

## Quran 84:1-12

إِذَا ٱلسَّمَآءُ ٱنشَقَّتْ (١) وَأَذِنَتْ لِرَبِّهَا وَحُقَّتْ (٢) وَإِذَا
ٱلْأَرْضُ مُدَّتْ (٣) وَأَلْقَتْ مَا فِيهَا وَتَخَلَّتْ (٤) وَأَذِنَتْ لِرَبِّهَا
وَحُقَّتْ (٥) يَـٰٓأَيُّهَا ٱلْإِنسَـٰنُ إِنَّكَ كَادِحٌ إِلَىٰ رَبِّكَ كَدْحًا
فَمُلَـٰقِيهِ (٦) فَأَمَّا مَنْ أُوتِىَ كِتَـٰبَهُ بِيَمِينِهِۦ (٧) فَسَوْفَ
يُحَاسَبُ حِسَابًا يَسِيرًا (٨) وَيَنقَلِبُ إِلَىٰٓ أَهْلِهِۦ مَسْرُورًا
(٩) وَأَمَّا مَنْ أُوتِىَ كِتَـٰبَهُ وَرَآءَ ظَهْرِهِۦ (١٠) فَسَوْفَ يَدْعُواْ
ثُبُورًا (١١) وَيَصْلَىٰ سَعِيرًا (١٢)

When the heaven is split asunder, (1) And listens to and
obeys its Lord — and it must do so; (2) And when the
earth is stretched forth, (3) And has cast out all that was

in it and become empty, (4) And listens to and obeys its Lord, and it must do so; (5) O man! Verily, you are returning towards your Lord with your deeds and actions (good or bad), a sure returning, and you will meet (i.e. the results of your deeds which you did). (6) Then, as for him who will be given his Record in his right hand, (7) He surely will receive an easy reckoning, (8) And will return to his family in joy! (9) But whosoever is given his Record behind his back, (10) He will invoke (for his) destruction, (11) And he shall enter a blazing Fire, and be made to taste its burning. (12)

## Quran 84:16-19

فَلَا أُقْسِمُ بِٱلشَّفَقِ (١٦) وَٱلَّيْلِ وَمَا وَسَقَ (١٧) وَٱلْقَمَرِ إِذَا ٱتَّسَقَ (١٨) لَتَرْكَبُنَّ طَبَقًا عَن طَبَقٍ (١٩)

So I swear by the afterglow of sunset; (16) And by the night and whatever it gathers in its darkness; (17) And by the moon when it is at the full, (18) You shall certainly travel from stage to stage (in this life and in the Hereafter). (19)

## Quran 84:25

إِلَّا ٱلَّذِينَ ءَامَنُواْ وَعَمِلُواْ ٱلصَّٰلِحَٰتِ لَهُمْ أَجْرٌ غَيْرُ مَمْنُونٍ

Save those who believe and do righteous good deeds, for them is a reward that will never come to an end (i.e. Paradise). (25)

## Quran 85:10-13

إِنَّ ٱلَّذِينَ فَتَنُوا۟ ٱلْمُؤْمِنِينَ وَٱلْمُؤْمِنَـٰتِ ثُمَّ لَمْ يَتُوبُوا۟ فَلَهُمْ عَذَابُ جَهَنَّمَ وَلَهُمْ عَذَابُ ٱلْحَرِيقِ (١٠) إِنَّ ٱلَّذِينَ ءَامَنُوا۟ وَعَمِلُوا۟ ٱلصَّـٰلِحَـٰتِ لَهُمْ جَنَّـٰتٌ تَجْرِى مِن تَحْتِهَا ٱلْأَنْهَـٰرُ ذَٰلِكَ ٱلْفَوْزُ ٱلْكَبِيرُ (١١) إِنَّ بَطْشَ رَبِّكَ لَشَدِيدٌ (١٢) إِنَّهُ هُوَ يُبْدِئُ وَيُعِيدُ (١٣)

*Verily, those who put into trial the believing men and believing women (by torturing them and burning them), and then do not turn in repentance, (to Allâh), then they will have the torment of Hell, and they will have the punishment of the burning Fire. (10) Verily, those who believe and do righteous good deeds, for them will be Gardens under which rivers flow (Paradise). That is the great success. (11) Verily, (O Muhammad ) the Seizure (Punishment) of your Lord is severe and painful. (12) Verily, He it is Who begins (punishment) and repeats (punishment in the Hereafter) (or originates the creation of everything, and then repeats it on the Day of Resurrection). (13)*

## Quran 86:8-16

إِنَّهُ عَلَىٰ رَجْعِهِ لَقَادِرٌ (٨) يَوْمَ تُبْلَى ٱلسَّرَآئِرُ (٩) فَمَا لَهُ مِن قُوَّةٍ وَلَا نَاصِرٍ (١٠) وَٱلسَّمَآءِ ذَاتِ ٱلرَّجْعِ (١١) وَٱلْأَرْضِ ذَاتِ ٱلصَّدْعِ (١٢) إِنَّهُ لَقَوْلٌ فَصْلٌ

(١٣) وَمَا هُوَ بِٱلْهَزْلِ (١٤) إِنَّهُمْ يَكِيدُونَ كَيْدًا (١٥) وَأَكِيدُ كَيْدًا (١٦)

*Verily, (Allâh) is Able to bring him back (to life)! (8) The Day when all the secrets (deeds, prayers, fasting, etc.) will be examined (as to their truth) (9) Then he will have no power, nor any helper. (10) By the sky (having rain clouds) which gives rain, again and again. (11) And the earth which splits (with the growth of trees and plants), (12) Verily, this (the Qur'ân) is the Word that separates (the truth from falsehood, and commands strict laws for mankind to cut the roots of evil). (13) And it is not a thing for amusement. (14) Verily, they are but plotting a plot (against you O Muhammad ). (15) And I (too) am planning a plan. (16)*

## Quran 87:10-15

سَيَذَّكَّرُ مَن يَخْشَىٰ (١٠) وَيَتَجَنَّبُهَا ٱلْأَشْقَى (١١) ٱلَّذِى يَصْلَى ٱلنَّارَ ٱلْكُبْرَىٰ (١٢) ثُمَّ لَا يَمُوتُ فِيهَا وَلَا يَحْيَىٰ (١٣) قَدْ أَفْلَحَ مَن تَزَكَّىٰ (١٤) وَذَكَرَ ٱسْمَ رَبِّهِ فَصَلَّىٰ (١٥)

*The reminder will be received by him who fears (Allâh), (10) But it will be avoided by the wretched, (11) Who will enter the great Fire (and will be made to taste its burning). (12) There he will neither die (to be in rest) nor live (a good living). (13) Indeed whosoever purifies himself (by avoiding polytheism and accepting Islâmic*

Monotheism) shall achieve success, (14) And remembers
(glorifies) the Name of his Lord (worships none but
Allâh), and prays (five compulsory prayers and Nawâfil
— additional prayers). (15)

## Quran 87:17

وَٱلْأَخِرَةُ خَيْرٌ وَأَبْقَىٰٓ

Although the Hereafter is better and more lasting. (17)

## Quran 88:1-16

هَلْ أَتَىٰكَ حَدِيثُ ٱلْغَٰشِيَةِ (١) وُجُوهٌ يَوْمَئِذٍ خَٰشِعَةٌ (٢) عَامِلَةٌ
نَّاصِبَةٌ (٣) تَصْلَىٰ نَارًا حَامِيَةً (٤) تُسْقَىٰ مِنْ عَيْنٍ ءَانِيَةٍ
(٥) لَّيْسَ لَهُمْ طَعَامٌ إِلَّا مِن ضَرِيعٍ (٦) لَّا يُسْمِنُ وَلَا يُغْنِى
مِن جُوعٍ (٧) وُجُوهٌ يَوْمَئِذٍ نَّاعِمَةٌ (٨) لِّسَعْيِهَا رَاضِيَةٌ
(٩) فِى جَنَّةٍ عَالِيَةٍ (١٠) لَّا تَسْمَعُ فِيهَا لَٰغِيَةً (١١) فِيهَا عَيْنٌ
جَارِيَةٌ (١٢) فِيهَا سُرُرٌ مَّرْفُوعَةٌ (١٣) وَأَكْوَابٌ مَّوْضُوعَةٌ
(١٤) وَنَمَارِقُ مَصْفُوفَةٌ (١٥) وَزَرَابِىُّ مَبْثُوثَةٌ (١٦)

Has there come to you the narration of the overwhelming
(i.e. the Day of Resurrection)? (1) Some faces, that Day,
will be humiliated (in the Hell-fire, i.e. the faces of all
disbelievers, Jews and Christians). (2) Labouring (hard in
the worldly life by worshipping others besides Allâh),
weary (in the Hereafter with humility and disgrace).
(3) They will enter in the hot blazing Fire, (4) They will
be given to drink from a boiling spring, (5) No food will

there be for them but a poisonous thorny plant, (6) Which
will neither nourish nor avail against hunger (7) (Other)
faces, that Day, will be joyful, (8) Glad with their
endeavour (for their good deeds which they did in this
world, along with the true Faith of Islâmic Monotheism).
(9) In a lofty Paradise (10) Where they shall neither hear
harmful speech nor falsehood, (11) Therein will be a
running spring, (12) Therein will be thrones raised high,
(13) And cups set at hand (14) And cushions set in rows,
(15) And rich carpets (all) spread out (16)

## Quran 88:24-26

فَيُعَذِّبُهُ ٱللَّهُ ٱلْعَذَابَ ٱلْأَكْبَرَ (٢٤) إِنَّ إِلَيْنَآ إِيَابَهُمْ (٢٥) ثُمَّ إِنَّ
عَلَيْنَا حِسَابَهُم (٢٦)

Then Allâh will punish him with the greatest
punishment. (24) Verily, to Us will be their return;
(25) Then verily, for Us will be their reckoning. (26)

## Quran 89:21-30

كَلَّآ إِذَا دُكَّتِ ٱلْأَرْضُ دَكًّا دَكًّا (٢١) وَجَآءَ رَبُّكَ وَٱلْمَلَكُ صَفًّا
صَفًّا (٢٢) وَجِأْىٓءَ يَوْمَئِذٍۭ بِجَهَنَّمَ يَوْمَئِذٍ يَتَذَكَّرُ ٱلْإِنسَـٰنُ
وَأَنَّىٰ لَهُ ٱلذِّكْرَىٰ (٢٣) يَقُولُ يَـٰلَيْتَنِى قَدَّمْتُ لِحَيَاتِى
(٢٤) فَيَوْمَئِذٍ لَّا يُعَذِّبُ عَذَابَهُۥٓ أَحَدٌ (٢٥) وَلَا يُوثِقُ وَثَاقَهُۥٓ
أَحَدٌ (٢٦) يَـٰٓأَيَّتُهَا ٱلنَّفْسُ ٱلْمُطْمَئِنَّةُ (٢٧) ٱرْجِعِىٓ إِلَىٰ رَبِّكِ

رَاضِيَةً مَّرْضِيَّةً (٢٨) فَٱدْخُلِى فِى عِبَـٰدِى (٢٩) وَٱدْخُلِى جَنَّتِى (٣٠)

*Nay! When the earth is ground to powder, (21) And your Lord comes with the angels in rows, (22) And Hell will be brought near that Day. On that Day will man remember, but how will that remembrance (then) avail him? (23) He will say: "Alas! Would that I had sent forth (good deeds) for (this) my life!" (24) So on that Day, none will punish as He will punish (25) And none will bind (the wicked, disbelievers and polytheists) as He will bind. (26) (It will be said to the pious — believers of Islamic Monotheism): "O (you) the one in (complete) rest and satisfaction! (27) "Come back to your Lord, Well-pleased (yourself) and well-pleasing (unto Him)! (28) "Enter you, then, among My (honoured) slaves, (29) "And enter you My Paradise!" (30)*

**Quran 90:4**

لَقَدْ خَلَقْنَا ٱلْإِنسَـٰنَ فِى كَبَدٍ

*Verily, We have created man in toil. (4)*

**Quran 90:19-20**

وَٱلَّذِينَ كَفَرُوا۟ بِـَٔايَـٰتِنَا هُمْ أَصْحَـٰبُ ٱلْمَشْـَٔمَةِ (١٩) عَلَيْهِمْ نَارٌ مُّؤْصَدَةٌ (٢٠)

But those who disbelieved in Our Ayât (proofs,
evidences, verses, lessons, signs, revelations, etc.), they
are those on the Left Hand (the dwellers of Hell) (19) The
Fire will be shut over them (i.e. they will be enveloped by
the Fire without any opening or window or outlet. (20)

## Quran 91:1-10

وَٱلشَّمْسِ وَضُحَٰهَا (١) وَٱلْقَمَرِ إِذَا تَلَٰهَا (٢) وَٱلنَّهَارِ إِذَا
جَلَّٰهَا (٣) وَٱلَّيْلِ إِذَا يَغْشَٰهَا (٤) وَٱلسَّمَآءِ وَمَا بَنَٰهَا
(٥) وَٱلْأَرْضِ وَمَا طَحَٰهَا (٦) وَنَفْسٍ وَمَا سَوَّٰهَا
(٧) فَأَلْهَمَهَا فُجُورَهَا وَتَقْوَٰهَا (٨) قَدْ أَفْلَحَ مَن زَكَّٰهَا
(٩) وَقَدْ خَابَ مَن دَسَّٰهَا (١٠)

By the sun and its brightness; (1) By the moon as it
follows it (the sun); (2) By the day as it shows up (the
sun's) brightness; (3) By the night as it conceals it (the
sun); (4) By the heaven and Him Who built it; (5) By the
earth and Him Who spread it, (6) And by Nafs (Adam or
a person or a soul), and Him Who perfected him in
proportion; (7) Then He showed him what is wrong for
him and what is right for him; (8) Indeed he succeeds
who purifies his ownself (i.e. obeys and performs all that
Allâh ordered, by following the true Faith of Islâmic
Monotheism and by doing righteous good deeds).
(9) And indeed he fails who corrupts his ownself (i.e.
disobeys what Allâh has ordered by rejecting the true

*Faith of Islâmic Monotheism or by following polytheism or by doing every kind of evil wicked deeds) (10)*

## Quran 92:1-21

وَٱلَّيْلِ إِذَا يَغْشَىٰ (١) وَٱلنَّهَارِ إِذَا تَجَلَّىٰ (٢) وَمَا خَلَقَ ٱلذَّكَرَ وَٱلْأُنثَىٰ (٣) إِنَّ سَعْيَكُمْ لَشَتَّىٰ (٤) فَأَمَّا مَنْ أَعْطَىٰ وَٱتَّقَىٰ (٥) وَصَدَّقَ بِٱلْحُسْنَىٰ (٦) فَسَنُيَسِّرُهُ لِلْيُسْرَىٰ (٧) وَأَمَّا مَنۢ بَخِلَ وَٱسْتَغْنَىٰ (٨) وَكَذَّبَ بِٱلْحُسْنَىٰ (٩) فَسَنُيَسِّرُهُ لِلْعُسْرَىٰ (١٠) وَمَا يُغْنِى عَنْهُ مَالُهُۥ إِذَا تَرَدَّىٰ (١١) إِنَّ عَلَيْنَا لَلْهُدَىٰ (١٢) وَإِنَّ لَنَا لَلْأَخِرَةَ وَٱلْأُولَىٰ (١٣) فَأَنذَرْتُكُمْ نَارًا تَلَظَّىٰ (١٤) لَا يَصْلَىٰهَآ إِلَّا ٱلْأَشْقَى (١٥) ٱلَّذِى كَذَّبَ وَتَوَلَّىٰ (١٦) وَسَيُجَنَّبُهَا ٱلْأَتْقَى (١٧) ٱلَّذِى يُؤْتِى مَالَهُۥ يَتَزَكَّىٰ (١٨) وَمَا لِأَحَدٍ عِندَهُۥ مِن نِّعْمَةٍ تُجْزَىٰٓ (١٩) إِلَّا ٱبْتِغَآءَ وَجْهِ رَبِّهِ ٱلْأَعْلَىٰ (٢٠) وَلَسَوْفَ يَرْضَىٰ (٢١)

*By the night as it envelops; (1) By the day as it appears in brightness; (2) By Him Who created male and female; (3) Certainly, your efforts and deeds are diverse (different in aims and purposes); (4) As for him who gives (in charity) and keeps his duty to Allâh and fears Him, (5) And believes in Al-Husna. (6) We will make smooth for him the path of ease (goodness). (7) But he who is greedy miser and thinks himself self-sufficient. (8) And gives belies Al-Husna; (9) We will make smooth for him the path for evil; (10) And what will his wealth avail him when he goes down (in destruction). (11) Truly! on Us is* (to give) guidance, (12) And truly, unto Us (belong) the last (Hereafter) and the first (this world). (13) Therefore I have warned you of a blazing (Hell); (14) None shall enter it save the most wretched, (15) Who denies and turns away. (16) And Al-Muttaqûn (the pious and righteous) will be far removed from it (Hell). (17) He who spends his wealth for increase in self-purification, (18) And who has (in mind) no favour from anyone, (19) Except to seek the Countenance of his Lord, the Most High; (20) He surely, will be pleased (when he will enters Paradise). (21)

**Quran 93:1-5**

وَٱلضُّحَىٰ (١) وَٱلَّيْلِ إِذَا سَجَىٰ (٢) مَا وَدَّعَكَ رَبُّكَ وَمَا قَلَىٰ (٣) وَلَلْأَخِرَةُ خَيْرٌ لَّكَ مِنَ ٱلْأُولَىٰ (٤) وَلَسَوْفَ يُعْطِيكَ رَبُّكَ فَتَرْضَىٰٓ (٥)

By the forenoon (after); (1) By the night when it darkens (and stands still). (2) Your Lord (O Muhammad) has neither forsaken you nor hates you. (3) And indeed the Hereafter is better for you than the present (life of this world). (4) And verily, your Lord will give you (all good) so that you shall be well-pleased. (5)

**Quran 94:5-6**

فَإِنَّ مَعَ ٱلْعُسْرِ يُسْرًا (٥) إِنَّ مَعَ ٱلْعُسْرِ يُسْرًا (٦)

*Verily, along with every hardship is relief, (5) Verily, along with hardship is relief (i.e. there is one hardship with two reliefs, so one hardship cannot overcome two reliefs) (6)*

## Quran 95:1-6

وَٱلتِّينِ وَٱلزَّيْتُونِ (١) وَطُورِ سِينِينَ (٢) وَهَٰذَا ٱلْبَلَدِ ٱلْأَمِينِ (٣) لَقَدْ خَلَقْنَا ٱلْإِنسَٰنَ فِىٓ أَحْسَنِ تَقْوِيمٍ (٤) ثُمَّ رَدَدْنَٰهُ أَسْفَلَ سَٰفِلِينَ (٥) إِلَّا ٱلَّذِينَ ءَامَنُوا۟ وَعَمِلُوا۟ ٱلصَّٰلِحَٰتِ فَلَهُمْ أَجْرٌ غَيْرُ مَمْنُونٍ (٦)

*By the fig, and the olive, (1) By Mount Sinai, (2) By this city of security (Makkah) , (3) Verily, We created man in the best stature (mould), (4) Then We reduced him to the lowest of the low, (5) Save those who believe (in Islâmic Monotheism) and do righteous deeds, Then they shall have a reward without end (Paradise). (6)*

## Quran 96:15-18

كَلَّا لَئِن لَّمْ يَنتَهِ لَنَسْفَعًۢا بِٱلنَّاصِيَةِ (١٥) نَاصِيَةٍ كَٰذِبَةٍ خَاطِئَةٍ (١٦) فَلْيَدْعُ نَادِيَهُۥ (١٧) سَنَدْعُ ٱلزَّبَانِيَةَ (١٨)

*Nay! If he (Abû Jahl) ceases not, We will catch him by the forelock — (15) A lying, sinful forelock! (16) Then, let him call upon his council (of helpers), (17) We will call the guards of Hell (to deal with him)! (18)*

## Quran 97:1-5

إِنَّا أَنزَلْنَاهُ فِى لَيْلَةِ ٱلْقَدْرِ (١) وَمَآ أَدْرَاكَ مَا لَيْلَةُ ٱلْقَدْرِ
(٢) لَيْلَةُ ٱلْقَدْرِ خَيْرٌ مِّنْ أَلْفِ شَهْرٍ (٣) تَنَزَّلُ ٱلْمَلَـٰئِكَةُ
وَٱلرُّوحُ فِيهَا بِإِذْنِ رَبِّهِم مِّن كُلِّ أَمْرٍ (٤) سَلَـٰمٌ هِىَ حَتَّىٰ
مَطْلَعِ ٱلْفَجْرِ (٥)

*Verily, We have sent it (this Qur'ân) down in the night*
*of Al-Qadr (Decree) (1) And what will make you know*
*what the night of Al-Qadr (Decree) is? (2) The night of*
*Al-Qadr (Decree) is better than a thousand months (i.e.*
*worshipping Allâh in that night is better than*
*worshipping Him a thousand months, i.e. 83 years and 4*
*months) (3) Therein descend the angels and the Rûh*
*[Jibril (Gabriel)] by Allâh's Permission with all Decrees,*
*(4) (All that night), there is Peace (and Goodness from*
*Allâh to His believing slaves) until the appearance of*
*dawn. (5)*

## Quran 98:1

لَمْ يَكُنِ ٱلَّذِينَ كَفَرُواْ مِنْ أَهْلِ ٱلْكِتَـٰبِ وَٱلْمُشْرِكِينَ مُنفَكِّينَ
حَتَّىٰ تَأْتِيَهُمُ ٱلْبَيِّنَةُ

*Those who disbelieve from among the people of the*
*Scripture (Jews and Christians) and Al-Mushrikûn, were*
*not going to leave (their disbelief) until there came to*
*them clear evidence (1)*

## Quran 98:6-8

إِنَّ ٱلَّذِينَ كَفَرُواْ مِنْ أَهْلِ ٱلْكِتَبِ وَٱلْمُشْرِكِينَ فِى نَارِ جَهَنَّمَ خَلِدِينَ فِيهَا أُوْلَٰٓئِكَ هُمْ شَرُّ ٱلْبَرِيَّةِ (٦) إِنَّ ٱلَّذِينَ ءَامَنُواْ وَعَمِلُواْ ٱلصَّلِحَٰتِ أُوْلَٰٓئِكَ هُمْ خَيْرُ ٱلْبَرِيَّةِ (٧) جَزَآؤُهُمْ عِندَ رَبِّهِمْ جَنَّٰتُ عَدْنٍ تَجْرِى مِن تَحْتِهَا ٱلْأَنْهَٰرُ خَلِدِينَ فِيهَا أَبَدًا رَّضِىَ ٱللَّهُ عَنْهُمْ وَرَضُواْ عَنْهُ ذَٰلِكَ لِمَنْ خَشِىَ رَبَّهُ (٨)

*Verily, those who disbelieve (in the religion of Islâm, the Qur'ân and Prophet Muhammad) from among the people of the Scripture (Jews and Christians) and Al-Mushrikûn will abide in the Fire of Hell. They are the worst of creatures. (6) Verily, those who believe [in the Oneness of Allâh, and in His Messenger Muhammad) including all obligations ordered by Islâm] and do righteous good deeds, they are the best of creatures (7) Their reward with their Lord is 'Adn (Eden) Paradise (Gardens of Eternity), underneath which rivers flow, They will abide therein forever, Allâh will be pleased with them, and they with Him. That is for him who fears his Lord. (8)*

## Quran 99:1-8

إِذَا زُلْزِلَتِ ٱلْأَرْضُ زِلْزَالَهَا (١) وَأَخْرَجَتِ ٱلْأَرْضُ أَثْقَالَهَا (٢) وَقَالَ ٱلْإِنسَٰنُ مَا لَهَا (٣) يَوْمَئِذٍ تُحَدِّثُ أَخْبَارَهَا (٤) بِأَنَّ رَبَّكَ أَوْحَىٰ لَهَا (٥) يَوْمَئِذٍ يَصْدُرُ ٱلنَّاسُ أَشْتَاتًا لِّيُرَوْاْ أَعْمَٰلَهُمْ (٦) فَمَن يَعْمَلْ مِثْقَالَ ذَرَّةٍ خَيْرًا يَرَهُ (٧) وَمَن يَعْمَلْ مِثْقَالَ ذَرَّةٍ شَرًّا يَرَهُ (٨)

When the earth is shaken with its (final) earthquake.
(1) And when the earth throws out its burdens, (2) And
man will say: "What is the matter with it?" (3) That
Day it will declare its information (about all that
happened over it of good or evil). (4) Because your Lord
will inspire it. (5) That Day mankind will proceed in
scattered groups that they may be shown their deeds.
(6) So whosoever does good equal to the weight of an
atom (or a small ant), shall see it. (7) And whosoever
does evil equal to the weight of an atom (or a small ant),
shall see it. (8)

## Quran 100:9-11

﴿ أَفَلَا يَعْلَمُ إِذَا بُعْثِرَ مَا فِى ٱلْقُبُورِ (٩) وَحُصِّلَ مَا فِى
ٱلصُّدُورِ (١٠) إِنَّ رَبَّهُم بِهِمْ يَوْمَئِذٍ لَّخَبِيرُ (١١)

Knows he not that when the contents of the graves are
poured forth (all mankind is resurrected)? (9) And that
which is in the breasts (of men) is made known?
(10) Verily, that Day (i.e. the Day of Resurrection) their
Lord will be Well-Acquainted with them (as to their
deeds and will reward them for their deeds). (11)

## Quran 101:1-11

ٱلْقَارِعَةُ (١) مَا ٱلْقَارِعَةُ (٢) وَمَآ أَدْرَىٰكَ مَا ٱلْقَارِعَةُ
(٣) يَوْمَ يَكُونُ ٱلنَّاسُ كَٱلْفَرَاشِ ٱلْمَبْثُوثِ (٤) وَتَكُونُ
ٱلْجِبَالُ كَٱلْعِهْنِ ٱلْمَنفُوشِ (٥) فَأَمَّا مَن ثَقُلَتْ مَوَازِينُهُ

(٦) فَهُوَ فِى عِيشَةٍ رَّاضِيَةٍ (٧) وَأَمَّا مَنْ خَفَّتْ مَوَازِينُهُ (٨) فَأُمُّهُ هَاوِيَةٌ (٩) وَمَآ أَدْرَىٰكَ مَا هِيَهْ (١٠) نَارٌ حَامِيَةٌ (١١)

*Al-Qâri'ah (the striking Hour i.e. the Day of Resurrection), (1) What is the striking (Hour)? (2) And what will make you know what the striking (Hour) is? (3) It is a Day whereon mankind will be like moths scattered about, (4) And the mountains will be like carded wool, (5) Then as for him whose balance (of good deeds) will be heavy,(6) He will live a pleasant life (in Paradise). (7) But as for him whose balance (of good deeds) will be light, (8) He will have his home in Hawiyah (pit, i.e. Hell) (9) And what will make you know what it is? (10) (It is) a fiercey blazing Fire! (11)*

## Quran 102:3-8

كَلَّا سَوْفَ تَعْلَمُونَ (٣) ثُمَّ كَلَّا سَوْفَ تَعْلَمُونَ (٤) كَلَّا لَوْ تَعْلَمُونَ عِلْمَ ٱلْيَقِينِ (٥) لَتَرَوُنَّ ٱلْجَحِيمَ (٦) ثُمَّ لَتَرَوُنَّهَا عَيْنَ ٱلْيَقِينِ (٧) ثُمَّ لَتُسْـَٔلُنَّ يَوْمَئِذٍ عَنِ ٱلنَّعِيمِ (٨)

*Nay! You shall come to know! (3) Again, Nay! You shall come to know! (4) Nay! If you knew with a sure knowledge (the end result of piling up, you would not have been occupied yourselves in worldly things) (5) Verily, You shall see the blazing Fire (Hell)! (6) And again, you shall see it with certainty of sight! (7) Then,* on that Day, you shall be asked about the delights (you indulged in, in this world)! (8)

## Quran 103:1-3

وَٱلْعَصْرِ (١) إِنَّ ٱلْإِنسَٰنَ لَفِى خُسْرٍ (٢) إِلَّا ٱلَّذِينَ ءَامَنُواْ وَعَمِلُواْ ٱلصَّٰلِحَٰتِ وَتَوَاصَوْاْ بِٱلْحَقِّ وَتَوَاصَوْاْ بِٱلصَّبْرِ (٣)

By Al-'Asr (the time). (1) Verily, man is in loss,
(2) Except those who believe (in Islâmic Monotheism)
and do righteous good deeds, and recommend one another
to the truth (i.e. order one another to perform all kinds of
good deeds (Al-Ma'ruf) which Allâh has ordained, and
abstain from all kinds of sins and evil deeds (Al-Munkar)
which Allâh has forbidden), and recommend one another
to patience (for the sufferings, harms, and injuries which
one may encounter in Allâh's Cause during preaching
His religion of Islâmic Monotheism or Jihâd). (3)

## Quran 104:1-9

وَيْلٌ لِّكُلِّ هُمَزَةٍ لُّمَزَةٍ (١) ٱلَّذِى جَمَعَ مَالاً وَعَدَّدَهُ (٢) يَحْسَبُ أَنَّ مَالَهُ أَخْلَدَهُ (٣) كَلَّا لَيُنۢبَذَنَّ فِى ٱلْحُطَمَةِ (٤) وَمَآ أَدْرَٰلكَ مَا ٱلْحُطَمَةُ (٥) نَارُ ٱللَّهِ ٱلْمُوقَدَةُ (٦) ٱلَّتِى تَطَّلِعُ عَلَى ٱلْأَفْـِٔدَةِ (٧) إِنَّهَا عَلَيْهِم مُّؤْصَدَةٌ (٨) فِى عَمَدٍ مُّمَدَّدَةٍۭ (٩)

Woe to every slanderer and backbiter. (1) Who has
gathered wealth and counted it, (2) He thinks that his

wealth will make him last forever! (3) Nay! Verily, he will be thrown into the crushing Fire (4) And what will make you know what the crushing Fire is? (5) The fire of Allâh, kindled, (6) Which leaps up over the hearts, (7) Verily, it shall be closed upon them, (8) In pillars stretched forth (i.e. they will be punished in the Fire with pillars). (9)

## Quran 108:1-3

إِنَّآ أَعْطَيْنَـٰكَ ٱلْكَوْثَرَ (١) فَصَلِّ لِرَبِّكَ وَٱنْحَرْ (٢) إِنَّ شَانِئَكَ هُوَ ٱلْأَبْتَرُ (٣)

Verily, We have granted you (O Muhammad ) Al-Kauthar (a river in Paradise);(1) Therefore turn in prayer to your Lord and sacrifice (to Him only) (2) For he who hates you (O Muhammad), he will be cut off from every posterity (good thing in this world and in the Hereafter). (3)

## Quran 109:1-5

قُلْ يَـٰٓأَيُّهَا ٱلْكَـٰفِرُونَ (١) لَآ أَعْبُدُ مَا تَعْبُدُونَ (٢) وَلَآ أَنتُمْ عَـٰبِدُونَ مَآ أَعْبُدُ (٣) وَلَآ أَنَا۠ عَابِدٌ مَّا عَبَدتُّمْ (٤) وَلَآ أَنتُمْ عَـٰبِدُونَ مَآ أَعْبُدُ (٥)

Say (O Muhammad to these Mushrikûn and Kâfirûn): "O Al-Kâfirûn (disbelievers in Allâh, in His Oneness, in His Angels, in His Books, in His Messengers, in the Day

of Resurrection, and in Al-Qadar)! (1) "I worship not
that which you worship, (2) "Nor will you worship that
which I worship. (3) "And I shall not worship that which
you are worshipping. (4) "Nor will you worship that
which I worship. (5)

## Quran 110:1-3

إِذَا جَاءَ نَصْرُ ٱللَّهِ وَٱلْفَتْحُ (١) وَرَأَيْتَ ٱلنَّاسَ يَدْخُلُونَ فِى دِينِ
ٱللَّهِ أَفْوَاجًا (٢) فَسَبِّحْ بِحَمْدِ رَبِّكَ وَٱسْتَغْفِرْهُ إِنَّهُ كَانَ تَوَّابًا
(٣)

When there comes the Help of Allâh (to you, O
Muhammad against your enemies) and the conquest (of
Makkah), (1) And you see that the people enter Allâh's
religion (Islâm) in crowds, (2) So glorify the Praises of
your Lord, and ask His Forgiveness. Verily, He is the
One Who accepts the repentance and Who forgives. (3)

## Quran 111:1-5

تَبَّتْ يَدَا أَبِى لَهَبٍ وَتَبَّ (١) مَا أَغْنَىٰ عَنْهُ مَالُهُ وَمَا كَسَبَ
(٢) سَيَصْلَىٰ نَارًا ذَاتَ لَهَبٍ (٣) وَٱمْرَأَتُهُ حَمَّالَةَ ٱلْحَطَبِ
(٤) فِى جِيدِهَا حَبْلٌ مِّن مَّسَدٍ (٥)

Perish the two hands of Abû Lahab (an uncle of the
Prophet), and perish he! (1) His wealth and his children
will not benefit him! (2) He will be burnt in a Fire of
blazing flames! (3) And his wife too, who carries wood

(thorns of Sadan which she used to put on the way of the Prophet , or use to slander him). (4) In her neck is a twisted rope of Masad (palm fibre). (5)

**Quran 112:3**

لَمْ يَلِدْ وَلَمْ يُولَدْ

"He begets not, nor was He begotten;